# EARLY
# INTERVENTION
# with MULTI-RISK
# FAMILIES

# EARLY INTERVENTION with MULTI-RISK FAMILIES

## An Integrative Approach

by

**SARAH LANDY, PH.D.**
Hincks-Dellcrest Institute
and University of Toronto
Ontario, Canada

and

**ROSANNE MENNA, PH.D.**
University of Windsor
Ontario, Canada

·P·A·U·L·H·
BROOKES
PUBLISHING CO.®

Baltimore • London • Sydney

**Paul H. Brookes Publishing Co.**
Post Office Box 10624
Baltimore, Maryland 21285-0624

www.brookespublishing.com

Typeset by Integrated Publishing Solutions, Grand Rapids, Michigan.
Manufactured in the United States of America by
Sheridan Books, Inc., Chelsea, Michigan.

The individuals described in this book are composites or fictional accounts
based on the authors' actual experiences. Individuals' names have been
changed and identifying details have been altered to protect confidentiality.

Information on the definition of borderline personality disorder (BPD) in
Chapter 1 is reprinted with permission from the *Diagnostic and Statistical
Manual of Mental Disorders, Fourth Edition, Text Revision* (Copyright 2000).
American Psychiatric Association.

The information provided in this book is in no way meant to substitute
for a medical or mental health practitioner's advice or expert opinion.
Readers should consult a health or mental health professional if they
are interested in more information. This book is sold without warranties
of any kind, express or implied, and the publisher and authors disclaim
any liability, loss, or damage caused by the contents of this book.

Third printing, July 2013.

**Library of Congress Cataloging-in-Publication Data**
Landy, Sarah.
    Early intervention with multi-risk families : an integrative approach /
by Sarah Landy and Rosanne Menna.
       p.    cm.
    Includes bibliographical references and index.
    ISBN-13: 978-1-55766-691-8 (pbk.)
    ISBN-10: 1-55766-691-1 (pbk.)
    1. Family social work. 2. Family psychotherapy. 3. Problem families.
    I. Menna, Rosanne.   II. Title.
    HV697.L36 2006
    362.82'53—dc22                                    2005036338

British Library Cataloguing in Publication data are available from the
British Library.

# Contents

# About the Authors

**Sarah Landy, Ph.D.,** Hincks-Dellcrest Institute; Assistant Professor, Department of Psychiatry, University of Toronto, Ontario, Canada

Dr. Landy is a developmental-clinical psychologist who has worked for more than 25 years in early intervention. She has a doctorate from the University of Saskatchewan and completed training at the Child Development Unit, Harvard University. In addition to her work at the Hincks-Dellcrest Institute, she is Assistant Professor at the University of Toronto and Adjunct Professor at York University, where she currently is teaching students earning a Certificate in Infant Mental Health. She also serves as a consultant for and provides training at a number of programs and organizations including Invest in Kids Foundation, Toronto Department of Public Health, and Parents for Better Beginnings. Her programs have been used in other provinces in Canada and in other countries.

Dr. Landy has worked as a clinician, home visitor, early intervention program developer, clinical and program director, researcher, and teacher. Her research interests include the study of young children with aggression and behavior problems; interventions for very high-risk, traumatized parents; assessment of children with autism spectrum disorder and severe difficulties with emotion regulation; and evaluation of community-based early intervention programs.

Dr. Landy has published extensively on early intervention and multi-risk families, including more than 50 articles and chapters and two books for Paul H. Brookes Publishing Co., titled *Pathways to Competence: Encouraging Healthy Social and Emotional Development in Young Children* (2002) and *Pathways to Competence for Young Children: A Parenting Program* (2006). Dr. Landy has received the Canadian Psychological Foundation award for contribution to knowledge, the YWCA Women of Distinction award for the professions, and the Canadian Psychological Association award for distinguished contribution to the community.

**Rosanne Menna, Ph.D.,** Associate Professor, Department of Psychology, University of Windsor, Ontario, Canada

Dr. Menna is Associate Professor in the Department of Psychology at the University of Windsor in Ontario, Canada. She is a clinical psychologist and is active in the supervision and training of clinicians. She became involved in the area of early intervention and treatment of high-risk families while she was a postdoctoral fellow in developmental psychopathology at the Hincks-Dellcrest Institute. She has published articles and contributed to books on topics concerned with child development, parenting, developmental psychopathology, and the assessment and treatment of children and their families. Her research focuses on the development of competence and coping in children and adolescents and the risk for developmental psychopathology. In her private practice she works with children, adolescents, and families; supervises clinicians; and offers consultation to mental health agencies and child care centers.

# Foreword

Promoting the healthier development of children growing up in the context of multiple family stresses is an extraordinary challenge because service providers must identify and target the problems that demand immediate attention without losing sight of the complex interplay of individual and family influences that support or undermine children's functioning. Practitioners of early intervention often cope with this challenge through systematic reliance on a favored theoretical orientation or a handful of personally compatible clinical strategies as ways of making their work more intellectually and emotionally manageable. This comprehensive new book by Drs. Landy and Menna provides a timely correction to this understandable—but ultimately unhelpful—tendency by emphasizing the crucial importance of adopting an integrative theoretical framework and by modeling the use of such a framework through two specific case examples that are followed from a variety of perspectives throughout the book. In doing so, this book stands both as a model for early intervention and as a much-needed articulation of a social stance that deserves to be widely adopted and implemented.

Ambitious in its scope, the volume examines the needs of children and families enduring the compounded burden of socioeconomic, cultural, developmental, and psychological stress and trauma from a variety of perspectives, always returning to the implications of this analysis for effective intervention and emphasizing the importance of deploying the full range of appropriate clinical strategies for as long as needed in order to prevent or lessen later psychopathology. This is a courageous stance in light of the ever-increasing pressure on practitioners to conduct short-term treatment in an effort to make ever-more-scarce financial and human resources stretch to reach the increasing number of children and families at highest need. The authors make clear that the pressure to curtail services constitutes a false economy because, although the children and families at highest need compose a small percentage of the total population, they constitute the majority of individuals who are most costly to society in terms of physical and mental health problems, unemployment, substance abuse, and criminality. The intergenerational transmission of these problems from parent to child represents an enormous financial and quality-of-life burden for society at large because the behavioral problems and social costs posed by the individual are borne by all.

As a training tool, this book serves a dual purpose because it offers a scholarly review of the literature on child development and early intervention while modeling the use of this information in clinical practice. The reader is skillfully guided through the thorny process of clinical decision making in a way that never shies away from honoring the complexity of the individual and family needs. The painstaking description of the range of intervention strategies available through diverse theoretical orientations is at times nothing short of breathtaking. I found myself inwardly thanking the authors throughout my reading for their patience and thoroughness in compiling and describing the core competencies as well as the sophisticated clinical skills that are deployed by effective clinicians in the course of their work. This comprehensiveness will help the book become a steady companion for the reader rather than a one-time reading experience because there will be new facets to discover and practice as other facets are understood and incorporated as a routine part of the work. The wholehearted commitment of the clinician to the family is a prerequisite to success, and thus, the hypothetical interventionists featured in the book are laudable role models for their generosity with their time and energy and for their ability to surmount the ubiquitous temptation to judge those who do not live up to our standards in their parenting practices. As an additional bonus, the appendices at the end of some chapters offer valuable information about programs and instruments that practitioners can use to guide systematic assessment and to frame intervention.

Drs. Landy and Menna have made an important contribution not only to practitioners of early intervention but also to the service community. The final section of the book articulates how their model approach to intervention can be incorporated and supported within coordinated community systems. By describing strategies for buttressing children's healthy development and mental health through the crucial roles played by key service systems such as child protection, mental health, health care, and child care, they illustrate the viability of placing intervention with high-need children and families as an essential component of the community-wide system of prevention and early intervention for all children. We are indebted to their efforts.

*Alicia F. Lieberman, Ph.D.*
*Professor and Vice Chair for Academic Affairs*
*University of California at San Francisco*

# Acknowledgments

The people who have contributed to the writing of this book are too numerous to mention. We are grateful for the many colleagues who work in various early intervention programs in which we have been involved who always provide respect, understanding, and encouragement for the hundreds of children and families that they support and encourage to grow and to flourish. Many of these ideas were conceived, implemented, and further developed with these caring people who work with families in high-risk areas in Ontario, Canada, and beyond.

Many other people worked on this book and helped make it a reality. In particular, we express our thanks to the wonderful staff at Paul H. Brookes Publishing Co., including Senior Acquisitions Editor Jessica Allan for her patience, understanding, and knowledge as she helped us form the book and made suggestions to make it more understandable and relevant. We are also grateful to Senior Book Production Editor Leslie Eckard, who helped make sure the ideas were coherent for the reader and readily accessible and who took the book through the long and sometimes difficult process of final production. We are very appreciative for their commitment and belief in the importance of a book on working with high-risk families.

We also thank J. Stone for her generosity in giving her permission to use the drawings and quotations on the section pages and for her interest in and dedication to helping children in difficult circumstances. We are grateful to Invest in Kids Foundation for allowing us to use some of their published text in Chapter 5. We acknowledge the guidance that they have provided to parents in supporting the development of children in families and child cares through such initiatives as Growing Together.

Our deep gratitude and respect go to those families who were involved and supported in the many programs on which the book is based. These families were able to teach us much more than any theory or textbook could do. We learned that really listening to their stories, understanding their dreams for their children, and appreciating their strengths was an essential foundation for any intervention approaches that are provided.

We would like to thank our colleagues who share our belief in the importance of the first 6 years of life and of finding ways to work with multi-risk children and families in those early years. These individuals include Susan Bradley; Dana Brynelsen; Claudia Koshinsky Clipsham, who contributed to Chapter 5; Joanne Cooper; Nilofar Liakat; Mirek Lojkasek; Leah Malamet; Freda Martin; Denise Martyn; Jackie Smith; Elizabeth Thompson; and Rhona Wolpert. Rosanne also would like to thank her colleagues Martin Ruck, Daniel Keating, and Dona Matthews, who have contributed to her thinking and practice over the years. We would both like to thank Dara Sikljovan for her assistance with the tables in the appendix to Chapter 2. Our thanks also go to Mary Damianakis, who served as research assistant for this book and *Pathways to Competence* (2002). She was always available, meticulous, and understanding of the writing process. Without her work, support, and friendship, this book would never have been completed. We would also like to thank our families for their support during the writing of this book and the many other projects in which we have been involved.

*To my brother, Dr. Ian Marshall,*
*who deeply understands the need for a book on*
*supporting and enhancing the development of children in multi-risk families,*
*with admiration and immeasurable thanks for his interest and friendship over the years*
*—SL*


*To my parents,*
*whose strength and support have been an inspiration to me*
*—RM*

# Introduction

Nothing determines the course of individuals' lives more than their families. A strong family unit, no matter the size or makeup of the family, with adequate supports and resilient members, can withstand almost anything life can throw its way. Stories abound of young children growing up in abject poverty who succeed despite the odds because they benefited from the support of caring individuals, whether they were parents, extended family members, or service providers who provided help and nurturance early enough to avoid lifelong problems. Most parents want to provide the best for their children, and many seek supports when they know they cannot "go it alone." However, many families facing multiple challenges become lost in a system that they see as threatening and that often fails to provide them with the complex services that they require and instead, looks at their needs in a piecemeal fashion.

The explosion in research and understanding about the developing brain since the late 1980s (Davidson & Fox, 1989; Gunnar, 1998; Schore, 1994; Siegel, 1999) has prompted a growing realization of the importance of the experiences a child receives in the first few years of life for later development. The widely published success of certain early intervention programs such as the Perry Preschool Project (Schweinhart, Montie, Xiang, Barnett, Belfield, & Nores, 2005) and the Prenatal and Early Infancy Project (Olds et al., 1997) has contributed to the belief in the importance of prevention and early intervention programs. Many believe these programs provide a window of opportunity through which to enhance the development of all infants and young children. As a result, funding for certain early intervention initiatives in North America has increased significantly. In spite of this increased support, however, the practice of early intervention may be at a critical crossroads as it becomes evident that although certain approaches have been established as best practices or are evidence based, other, more unidimensional efforts are not serving those families most at risk and have not been able to demonstrate their effectiveness. Without evidence of effectiveness, the promise of early intervention to reduce poor outcomes for children will not be realized. This book establishes the need for an integrative approach to intervention with multi-risk families and outlines numerous strategies for providing interventions to help children during their formative early years. However, the theoretical constructs and multidisciplinary interventions described in this book can work for families with children of any age.

## WHO ARE THESE MULTI-RISK FAMILIES?

Multiple risk is about more than just exposure to risk factors. Multi-risk families are often those with few protective factors, in which the interactions between parents and children are most compromised, intergenerational problems exist and have become entrenched, and children may be at risk for abuse and/or neglect from family members. To make matters worse, families with multiple risks are often more likely to receive services from inexperienced professionals and to be seen as beyond help because adequate services are unavailable. Individuals in these families may be labeled as resistant, chaotic, and uncooperative, and they are given little hope that things can get better. Consequently, these families are often resistant to receiving services and are more likely to drop out of programs or to attend them only sporadically. Files are quickly closed; thus, families and children fail to get the help they need.

The evidence continues to mount that children growing up in families with multiple risk factors, particularly if they experience trauma, are most likely to develop problems (Sameroff, Seifer, Barocas, Zax, & Greenspan, 1987). Although extremely high-risk families may only constitute about 8%–10% of all families, children who are members of these families are thought to compose 70% of all children who have mental health problems and adjustment difficulties. It has been found, for example, that of children who are the victims of maltreatment, 80% have disorganized attachment, which has been linked in adolescence with higher levels of psychopathology including internalizing (e.g., anxiety and depression) and externalizing (e.g., delinquency and aggression) symptoms and disorders. They are also more likely to need special education services and to drop out of school (Cicchetti & Barnett, 1991; Lyons-Ruth, Bronfman, & Atwood, 1999; Schuengel, Bakersmans-Kranenburg, van IJzendoorn, & Blom, 1999). The costs of growing up with multiple risks are great, both to individuals and to society (Keating & Hertzman, 1999). Typically, youth who commit crimes or attempt suicide faced multiple risk factors and traumas growing up in families with significant psychosocial stressors, including poverty, family and neighborhood violence, abuse, and neglect (De Bellis, 2001; Garbarino, 2002). In particular, research has shown that a significant percentage of children, as high as 65% in some studies, who have severe difficulties in the early years and do not receive intervention will continue to have ongoing problems in later years (Barkley, Fischer, Edelbrock, & Smallish, 1990; Campbell, 1995; Fonagy, Target, Cottrell, Phillips, & Kurtz, 2000; Meltzer, Gatward, Corbin, Goodman, & Ford, 2003; Rose, Rose, & Feldman, 1989; Weiss & Hechtman, 1993). As a result, these children and families consume a highly disproportionate percentage of the costs and resources designated for mental health, education services, criminal justice, and welfare services (Greenspan, 1986; Scott, Knapp, Henderson, & Maughan, 2001).

## TERMINOLOGY AND CATEGORIES USED

Throughout this book, the term *prevention* refers to any program or approach that is used to prevent later difficulties and to enhance the cognitive, behavioral, emotional, social, and physical development of young children during the prenatal period through 6 years of age. Prevention programs are often offered to whole communities, especially those communities that are considered to be at high risk due to factors such as poverty and violent neighborhoods. *Early intervention* refers to programs that are provided when a child or parents are identified as showing some type of specific difficulty that is seen as placing the child's development at risk.

Approaches to providing early intervention can be divided into four categories: 1) child focused, 2) parenting programs focused on enhancing the parent–child interaction or relationship, 3) parent focused, and 4) two-generation programs focused on both children and parents (St. Pierre & Layzer, 1998). Although enhancement of child development is the primary goal of most programs, many programs have sought to improve a number of other outcomes, as well. These include improving the birth weight of infants, reducing child maltreatment, enhancing parenting interactions, increasing the number of children with secure attachments, and enhancing parents' sense of personal and parenting competence. Programs are typically provided in various environments such as exclusively in homes, in centers, in both homes and centers, in child care and schools, and in clinicians' offices.

Because certain families face multiple risk factors, multidimensional or complex interventions that integrate a number of approaches adapted to a particular child and family are most likely to benefit the family as a whole in helping them overcome their particular circumstances and difficulties (Fonagy, Target, Cottrell, & Kurtz, 2002; Gold, 1996; Hubble, Duncan, & Miller, 1999; Kazdin & Weisz, 2003). As stated by Wachs, "Given that development is multidetermined . . . the less likely we are to find maximal gains associated with unidimensional intervention" (2000, p. 319). This is particularly true of children in families at highest risk who face multiple challenges. Some early intervention studies and approaches with older children and families have found that multisystemic and comprehensive approaches are the most effective (Conduct Problems Prevention Research Group, 1992; Greenspan, Wieder, Nover, Lieberman, Lourie, & Robinson, 1987; Henggeler, Schoenwald, Rowland, & Cunningham, 2002; Kurtz, 2004).

Nevertheless, it is clear that adequate assessment of parents, children, and parent–child interactions is seldom carried out, and unidimensional approaches are frequently used. In fact, many service providers and agencies use similar approaches with all families according to their training, theoretical perspective, or personal experience. The belief of and adherence to one particular approach has sometimes led to conflict between the advocates of various approaches or an "either/or" approach and the formation of different "camps" of service providers. An atmosphere of divisiveness has often resulted that has allowed little acceptance or integration of various approaches to intervention. For example, clinical approaches are pitted against empowerment philosophies and strategies, individual and/or interactional approaches are criticized by proponents of community development, and cognitive-behavioral techniques are sometimes seen as unacceptable by therapists who use more psychodynamic therapies (see Table I-1 for a summary of some of these differences and more detailed descriptions in Chapter 3). This segregation into camps impedes the overall progress toward a deeper understanding of the process of early intervention and significantly impairs growth toward an integrative theory and practices based on a holistic understanding of child development, parenting, and therapeutic change. Also, the focus on only one approach to intervention does not allow an interventionist to be open to understanding the unique perspective or needs of each child, parent, and family.

**Table I-1.**  Overview of divisions between various intervention approaches

| Psychodynamic approaches | Social support and empowerment approaches |
| --- | --- |
| Emphasize the effect of parents' early history on their interactions with their child | Believe that when parents feel better about themselves and the emphasis is on the positive, parents will do better than when the focus of intervention is on the unconscious |
| Consider the effect of unconscious thoughts and feelings on behavior and examine the deeper meaning of parents' statements | Largely ignore the unconscious and emphasize current beliefs and plans for the future |
| Emphasize consideration of parents' defensive functioning and how it influences their ability to deal with problems | Emphasize strengths rather than risk |
| See the relationship between a service provider and parent(s) as a critical part of the intervention | Focus on the present and not the past |
| | Actively involve the parent in choosing the goals for intervention |
| Perceive social support and empowerment approaches as ignoring the internal world of the individual and how this internal world influences perception and behavior | Link parents to support services in the community |

| Clinical and therapeutic approaches | Community development approaches |
| --- | --- |
| Stress the importance of parents and children receiving interventions that can overcome the particular difficulties that they have | See clinical approaches as pathologizing the child or parent; believe that only individuals' strengths should be identified and worked with |
| Offer interventions that vary according to the particular problems faced by the child and family, and work with them individually or together to overcome the difficulties | Focus on enhancing the community around the family because the family will be better able to function if the community is more supportive |
| See assessment of the child and family as an important precursor to intervention | Having the parent involved in choosing suitable interventions is crucial for successful outcomes |

| Psychoanalytic approaches | Cognitive-behavioral approaches |
| --- | --- |
| Believe that it is crucial to go deeply into memories so that early developmental conflicts can be resolved | Believe that distorted cognitive processes contribute to symptoms such as depression and aggression |
| View the birth of a child as a significant trigger for memories—both conscious and unconscious—that affect a parent's view of his or her child and his or her interaction with the child | Consider emotions to be influenced by cognitions, and so it is not necessary to target them directly in the intervention |
| | Believe that it is not important to delve into the past but that changing current cognitions can alleviate or prevent symptoms from developing |
| | Provide strategies to help parents who have been traumatized to calm down and prevent triggering (e.g., mindfulness-based approaches) |

| Psychoanalytic approaches | Cognitive-behavioral approaches |
|---|---|
| Perceive nondirective approaches as critical for memories to surface<br>View the "transference" or interactions within the relationship between the therapist and client and the emotional content of the sessions as critical | Use directive approaches and give the individual behavioral strategies to change his or her cognitions to more positive and constructive ones |

| Individual risk approaches | Population health and health promotion approaches |
|---|---|
| Look for variables in individuals and families that can place development at risk and try to shift them or overcome them<br>Consider the number and nature of risks and design interventions to improve them or significantly reduce them<br>Emphasize the individual's characteristics, rather than consider community factors (e.g., the family is "living in poverty") | Identify risks on a population health basis and provide large groups of parents with information that can enhance the health and development of their children<br>Consider various aspects of parenting and development and provide information<br>Believe that population-wide strategies that can be applied in order to improve functioning of a large number of families (e.g., improvement of housing; supporting breast feeding) are more cost-effective than individualized approaches targeted at multi-risk families and their children |

As explained in Chapter 3, each of these approaches to early intervention has merits and brings unique and important perspectives to the field. As is stressed throughout this book, however, an integrative approach that uses strengths from various theoretical and intervention approaches and decides on the most appropriate approaches for a particular child and family is the most effective. Boundaries between theories must be dissolved, and knowledge from a variety of theoretical perspectives and approaches needs to be considered. In this way, a number of principles of service provision can be developed to which information about intervention strategies can be linked. More integrative theories, such as a transactional or ecological and contextual approach, are available and have the potential to unite rather than divide, and to incorporate a variety of approaches together.

The danger may be that without programs that meet the needs of these families, little overall effect in improving child outcomes or reduction of problems will be felt in society. As a result, governments may fail to adequately fund or may draw funds away from early intervention programs, which will be accused of not having been able to prevent problems or enhance development in ways that were expected or promised. Only with all levels of the service system working together to support families at the highest risk through integrative approaches will the promise of the early intervention movement be truly fulfilled.

## HOW TO USE THIS BOOK

This book is intended for service providers, including home visitors, health professionals, various kinds of mental health workers, and other professionals, who work in early intervention programs with multi-risk families in which a child is at risk for compromised development. It is divided into four main sections that follow the model of assessment and intervention set out in Chapter 3 (see Figure 3.2). In Section I, the theoretical framework for work with multi-risk families is outlined. The context for early intervention is described, and research and information is provided that should be considered in designing any early intervention strategies. Section I also describes ways for distinguishing the most at-risk families from low-risk or moderate-risk families and identifies the types of risks that cause the most challenges to successful intervention. Various types of risks such as maternal depression are described, and implications for their effects on parenting are given. Last, an integrative approach to early intervention and a model that can be used as a guide to work with children and families are described.

Section II delves into some of the reasons that multi-risk families may be resistant to receiving intervention services as well as provides strategies for engaging and supporting them. Two main case studies are used to illustrate the intervention strategies discussed throughout the book. Strategies are provided that can overcome certain psychological challenges that may make it difficult to work with parents, such as low self-reflectivity and primitive defense mechanisms. Supportive approaches and ways to enhance parents' sense of competence are described.

In Section III, each chapter describes, in detail, intervention strategies for parents and their children when a parent has an identified difficulty that has been linked to poor outcomes for children, such as unresolved loss and trauma; problems with emotion regulation or problem solving; and cognitions or parenting beliefs that are not supportive of positive interactions, including negative attributions of children. These approaches have been used successfully with parents facing particular challenges and can be integrated into a more multidimensional intervention plan. It is clear that many programs will not be able to offer all of the interventions that are described; however, the section provides a range of strategies for which service providers can receive training and can readily integrate into their everyday practice.

Section IV considers ways for choosing and coordinating available services for parents and children that are adapted to the readiness of the family and their availability for being involved in various intervention approaches. The critical importance and challenges of integrating services within teams, in organizations, and across wider service systems are described. Suggestions are made for how organizations and communities can best support service providers who work with multi-risk families and, consequently, significantly affect the lives of infants and young children.

# SECTION 1

# SETTING THE STAGE
# AND THEORETICAL
# FRAMEWORK

© j. stone, inc. 2005

*We must never replace wisdom with information because
information resides in the mind and true wisdom
resides in the soul.*
—J. Stone, 1997

New research and understanding have transformed knowledge about how infants and young children develop and the effects of early experiences on developmental outcomes. This new knowledge has focused on the importance of attachment and a relational view of development; the contribution of both nature (genetics and biology) and nurture (the environment) on the brain and consequently on developmental outcomes; the devastating effects, sometimes chronic, of trauma on functioning; and the impact of social and environmental circumstances on families. Although a number of successful models of prevention and early intervention programs have been developed in North America and in other parts of the world, very few communities have prevention and early intervention programs that have the capacity to meet the complex needs of multi-risk families and to adapt and integrate services to meet the individual needs of children and families for specialized services. Without these complex and integrated systems, the promise of early intervention will not be fulfilled.

This section presents a research and theoretical framework that lays the foundation for a model of intervention with multi-risk families that is designed to assess children and families and then to adapt services and the way in which they are provided to meet the complex needs of these families.

Chapter 1 explores the characteristics of types of multi-risk parents and the evidence of potentially devastating effects on the development of children in these families. The chapter uses a transactional approach, and considers cumulative risk models, as well as contributors, to child resilience. Key points for working with various types of multi-risk families are summarized. The chapter ends with a focus on the proximal variables that contribute to child development in early childhood, and identifies a number of psychological characteristics of parents that dramatically affect their parenting and willingness to be involved in intervention services. These include: defensive functioning, level of self-reflectivity, unresolved loss and trauma, parental attributions, and emotion regulation. An understanding of these characteristics is important in determining the process and type of intervention that will need to be provided in order to help these families cope with or overcome their particular risks and foster protective factors. The chapter closes with a description of a number of assessment instruments that can be used to measure these characteristics.

Chapter 2 summarizes the findings of the evaluation of a variety of types of early intervention programs and short-term interventions for children and families. The chapter opens by acknowledging the challenges of evaluating early intervention programs, particularly those that are community based. The outcomes and effectiveness of a variety of early intervention programs and more clinical interventions are then described. Evidence for the effectiveness of and necessity for multisystem, often longer-term interventions, provided within coordinated systems of agencies to meet the complex needs of multi-risk children and their families, is also discussed. The chapter closes with a list of principles for providing early intervention with multi-risk families.

The final chapter in this section, Chapter 3, provides an integrative theoretical framework for early intervention and reviews a number of theoretical perspectives that contribute to our understanding of intervention. A model for assessment and intervention is presented. This framework is used to organize the sections of the book, and can be used as a model in the prescriptive selection of various intervention strategies.

# Characteristics of Multi-Risk Families

For a long time, people have been divided on their views about the origins of individual differences and disorders in children and adults. The debate, commonly referred to as "nature versus nurture," centers on whether these differences are determined by biology or the environment, and still continues between front line proponents of one or the other (Rutter, 2000a).

In the mid to late 1990s, researchers from the discipline of developmental psychopathology have taken this debate a step further and have begun to explore characteristics within a child and her environment that can enhance competence and enable the child to overcome adversity and risks that adversely affect developmental outcomes (Cicchetti & Rogosch, 1996). Why does Joey, who lives in a foster home, whose mother is in prison for drug abuse, and whose father left his mother before he was born, still do well in school and remain optimistic and friendly when his friend Melanie struggles in every area of her life, even though she appears to have every advantage? Professionals are trying to understand not only how individual characteristics influence development but also the "symphonic causation" or complex interplay of multiple risks and protective factors that leads to a variety of developmental outcomes (Boyce, 2001, Boyce & Ellis, 2005). In other words, development results from very complex systems, and as one researcher noted, "Single causes are unlikely, and interactions and nonlinearities are to be expected" (Pennington, 2002, p. 5). Sroufe (1990, 1997) used the metaphor of a branching tree to illustrate this nonlinearity, with atypical development reflected in branchings that move away from the trunk of the tree. If the distance of the branches from the trunk of the tree is great, this represents substantial deviation. Figure 1.1 shows how different pathways can demonstrate normal adaptation throughout (Pathway B) or maladaptive adaptation continuing from the beginning (Pathway A). Others may show deviation at first, then adaptation (Pathway C), or early, typical development followed by subsequent negative changes toward psychopathology (Pathway D).

A related and even more challenging dilemma involves the mind–brain relationship and how the mind or psychological factors can affect the development of the brain, and vice versa. In other words, psychopathology has to be understood in terms of how both genetic or biological *and* psychological factors influence brain function (Pennington, 2002). This relationship is explored in more detail in a later section of this chapter as a way to understand the influence of various parental risk factors on child development and the implications of this model for intervention.

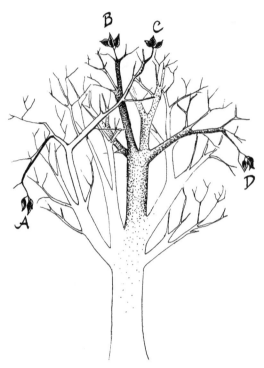

**Figure 1.1.** Pathways of development as a branching tree. Pathways can demonstrate normal adaptation throughout (Pathway B) or maladaptive adaptation continuing from the beginning (Pathway A). Others may show deviation at first, then adaptation (Pathway C), or early typical development followed by subsequent negative changes toward psychopathology (Pathway D). (From Sroufe, L.A. Psychopathology as an outcome of development. *Development and Psychopathology, 9,* 251–268 ©1997; reprinted with the permission of Cambridge University Press.)

The study of risk and protective factors attempts to understand the role that they play in the development of children, and descriptions of these factors can be used to help design interventions for children and families. In this context, risk factors refer to variables that are associated with an increased probability of compromised and problematic development (Coie et al., 1993). Conversely, protective factors are strengths that improve and enhance child functioning under conditions that would otherwise result in compromised development (Coie et al., 1993; Rutter, 1990). Resilience is defined as a "dynamic process encompassing positive adaptation within the context of significant adversity" (Luthar, Cicchetti, & Becker, 2000, p. 543).

The research literature that is concerned with risk and protective factors in child development includes a number of studies utilizing different methodologies. Longitudinal studies allow for the study of the effect of risk and protective factors on a child over time and consideration of the effect of the timing of exposure on their impact. Other methodologies include cross-sectional studies of different children at various ages with the same risk factors (e.g., children of depressed mothers, parents with psychosis), large-scale epidemiological studies of the prevalence of certain disorders in children, and small sample investigations of children considered to be at risk (e.g., premature infants). The smaller samples have allowed for in-depth assessment of variables, such as parent–child interactions, which are difficult to consider in large-scale investigations. Outcomes considered are most commonly the child's intellectual, social, and academic functioning and the presence or absence of behavioral and emotional problems and psychopathology. Risk and protective factors that have been considered in these studies include biological and genetic factors within the child and environmental factors. Environmental factors include more proximal variables that are closest to the child such as interactional and parenting variables, family dysfunction, and parental history and current functioning; and more distal variables such as sociodemographic factors including low socioeconomic status, overcrowding, and single-parent status. Although these distal variables do not have as much of a direct influence on the child, they have an influence through their effect on the parent–child interactions (Garmezy, 1985; O'Connor & Rutter, 1996).

## OVERVIEW OF RISK AND PROTECTIVE FACTORS

This chapter begins with a brief review of research that has considered the impact of risk and protective factors on child outcome, and then points out the significance of this understanding for designing early intervention strategies for children and families.

## Findings from Various Studies of Risk and Resilience

Several studies using different approaches have considered the types of variables that affect development. They have also explored how a variety of risk factors may together dramatically affect a child's development, even reducing IQ score and increasing the incidence of behavioral, emotional, and social problems.

*The Effect of Risk Status on Development*     The Kauai Study, one of the first longitudinal studies to examine the effect of risk and protective factors on child development, followed all of the children born on one Hawaiian island into adulthood (Werner, 1989, 1995; Werner & Smith, 1977, 1982, 1992). In the study, children defined as high risk had been exposed to four or more of the following risk factors:

- Moderate to severe perinatal stress

- Poverty

- Low levels of maternal education

- Family discord, desertion, or divorce

- Parental alcoholism

- Parental mental illness

Two thirds of the children considered to be high risk developed serious learning or behavior problems by 18 years of age.

In another study, Project Competence, researchers followed a community sample of 200 children and their families. Data were collected on various aspects of family functioning such as mother–child relationships, consistency of family rules and discipline practices, and stability (i.e., few changes in marital status and moves). Children exposed to lower ratings of family functioning or cohesion and less stability were more likely to have social competence problems and to have lower levels of cognitive functioning than were other children who had more positive experiences (Garmezy, 1985, 1987; Garmezy, Masten, & Tellegen, 1984; Masten, Morrison, Pellegrini, & Tellegen, 1990).

One of the most impressive studies was the Rochester Longitudinal Study (Sameroff, Seifer, Baldwin, & Baldwin, 1993; Seifer, Sameroff, Baldwin, & Baldwin, 1992), which resulted in the transactional theory of development that has significantly influenced our understanding of child development and early intervention. The researchers followed a clinical sample of families at risk due to maternal mental illness and a community-matched comparison group without psychiatric illness within the family. Again, the study found that children in the high-risk group had poorer cognitive and mental health outcomes than did children in the comparison sample without the same risk factors.

Similar results were found in a number of other studies. In the early to mid 1990s, The National Institute of Mental Health (NIMH) study, for example, found that 69% of children in a low-risk group at 9 years of age were functioning well compared with only 33% of the high-risk children in families in which the mother or both parents were depressed (Radke-Yarrow, McCann, DeMulder, Belmont, Martinez, & Richardson, 1995; Radke-Yarrow & Sherman, 1990). In two studies of children with mentally ill parents, it was found that the incidence of behavior problems was increased in children when the psychiatric condition of the parents was related to poor parenting or a negative parent–child relationship (Stiffman, Jung, & Feldman, 1986; Teti & Gelfand, 1991). In epidemiological studies that have assessed the prevalence of psychiatric disorder and correlated this with a number of selected variables, similar relationships between risk factors and disorder have been found. These studies include Britain's Isle of Wight and inner-city London study (Rutter, 1987; Rutter, Tizard, & Yule, 1976) and the Ontario Child Health Study (OCHS), conducted in Canada (Boyle et al., 1987; Offord et al., 1992; Rae-Grant, Thomas, Offord, & Boyle, 1989). Both studies found that parental problems, poor family functioning or marital distress, and a number of demographic variables were associated with psychological disorders in children. Neither study, however, assessed more proximal variables such as parent–child interactions or other parenting variables.

***The Significance of the Number of Risk Factors or Cumulative Risk Models***   A number of studies have emphasized the importance of the effect of the *number* of risk factors on child outcome. As Sameroff and Fiese stated about the findings of the Rochester Longitudinal Studies, for example,

> Although there were statistically significant effects for a single risk factor at the population level, most children with a single risk factor did not have a major developmental problem. However, when we created a multiple risk score that was the total number of risks for each individual family, major differences were found on mental health and intelligence measures between those with few risks and many risks at each of our assessment ages. (2000a, p. 6)

Rutter (1989) also reported that very few individual risk factors have a major effect on development but that the number of risk factors a child faced increased the risk for disorder in a multiplicative fashion. Children with one risk factor were no more likely than children with no risk factors to have a psychiatric disturbance; however, the risk for children with any two factors was four times higher than it was for those who were exposed to no risk factors. In other words, the combined effects of risk factors are more devastating than the sum of their individual effects. Appleyard, Egeland, van Dulmen, and Sroufe (2005) provided further evidence for the relevance of a cumulative effect in a longitudinal study of at-risk urban children. In addition to establishing the importance of the number of risk factors, the researchers also studied the significance of the timing of the risk factors and how it can influence "the pathways to adaptation or maladaptation" (Appleyard et al., 2005, p. 236). Using data collected from participants in early childhood, middle childhood, and adolescence, they concluded that the number of risks in early childhood can predict behavior problems in adolescence. Consequently, the researchers emphasized the critical importance of early experience and advocate for services that can reduce these risks as early as possible (Appleyard et al., 2005).

The model of the effect of cumulative risks was studied by Belsky and Isabella (1988) in predicting attachment security. They found that no single risk variable was as predictive as cumulative effects. Infants with zero, one, two, and three risk factors had a 92%, 83%, 38%, and 17% probability respectively of being securely attached. In general, studies have found that children who are exposed to four or more risk factors, especially if these risk factors are more significant ones, are likely to have their development compromised.

## Types of Risk and Protective Factors that Can Affect the Development of the Child

Determining the relative importance of various types of risk factors and answering questions about the relative contribution of proximal and distal risk variables and biological and environmental factors to child outcome has been difficult. In some studies, such variables as the psychological functioning of parents, parent–child interaction, family functioning, or parenting characteristics were not measured in any depth and, therefore, were not considered.

In a study on development that considered data from a sample of Canadian children, the National Longitudinal Survey of Children and Youth (NLSCY), Landy and Tam (1997) found that for children who lived in low-income areas, positive parenting practices were protective of child functioning. In fact, children living in high-risk situations who received positive parenting had higher scores on developmental measures than did children living in more favorable and higher socio-economic circumstances who were exposed to negative parenting. These findings suggested that proximal parenting variables such as high criticism and punitive discipline, as opposed to distal variables such as poverty or other community factors, may be particularly influential in determining outcomes for young children.

When children at extreme biological risk are followed longitudinally, relationships are frequently found between the biological risk and negative developmental outcomes. When these biological risks are less severe (such as for premature infants without additional complications), it has generally been found that environmental risks have more influence on outcomes (Blair & Ramey, 1997; Weisglas-Kuperus, Baerts, Smirkovsky, & Sauer, 1993). An interesting longitudinal study of children with developmental delays who were exposed to medical risk in childhood found that by the time these children reached 10–12 years of age, overall maternal stress, teaching style, unresolved grief, and personality structure contributed more than medical history to these children's competence and school adaptation (Mantini-Atkinson, 1993; Marcovitch, Goldberg, & MacGregor, 1992). Although little is known about it yet, the weighting or balance of particular sets of risk factors may determine the discrete or particular outcomes of certain children.

Several risk and protective factors have been found to affect child development. These can be categorized somewhat into child characteristics, interactional or parenting variables, parental history, and current functioning,

***Child Characteristics***    One of the most significant risks for infants is extremely low birth weight (LBW) or extreme prematurity. The lower the birth weight, the greater the risk that the child will have ongoing health and developmental problems, especially if there are other neurological complications (Allen, Donohue, & Dusman, 1993; Downie, Jakobson, Frisk, & Ushycky, 2003; Hack, Taylor, & Klein, 1994). Other biological and/or genetic conditions also pose significant risks in terms of cognitive and other developmental areas. Chronic medical conditions, frequent hospitalizations, and repeated illnesses can be difficult for families to manage, and can be related to later psychosocial and academic difficulties when the child enters school (Offord, Boyle, Fleming, & Blum, 1989; Schultz-Jøgensen, Kyng, Maar, Rasmussen, & Højlund, 1987). Difficult temperament characteristics, such as a high response to various stimuli or irritability, can lead to persistent arousal of the child's sympathetic nervous system, resulting in anxiety, irritability, intensity of response, and other reactions (Coll, Kagan, & Resnick, 1984; Thomas, Chess, & Birch, 1968). These characteristics of the "difficult" child have been found to be very challenging for parents and children, and were related to more acting-out and other emotional problems in later childhood and adolescence (Lee & Bates, 1985; Thomas & Chess, 1985).

***Interactional and Parenting Variables***    Because they are proximal variables, interactional and parenting variables are some of the most important to consider in predicting child outcomes. Some interactional variables that are considered risk factors include lack of sensitivity and responsiveness, misattunement to an infant's cues, inconsistency, and negative emotionality. These factors, when extreme, can significantly influence the quality of the child's attachment and can lead to the development of later emotional and social difficulties. For some parents, lack of knowledge about development and appropriate parenting strategies can lead to difficulties with discipline and lack of encouragement of language and other aspects of development. Abuse and neglect of children and removal into foster care have been found to result in a significant prevalence of psychiatric disorders in adolescents (67% of adolescents in such homes compared with 15% of adolescents living in their own families who have not been abused) (Dimigen, Del Priore, Butler, Evans, Ferguson, & Swan, 1999; McCann, James, Wilson, & Dunn, 1996). In addition, when one or both parents have a psychiatric condition, a child's development may be compromised. However, the outcome will depend on such factors as the nature and severity of the illness, whether a parent is frequently hospitalized, and if there is another caregiver in the home to buffer a child from the effects of the parent's illness (Anthony, 1982; Bell & Pearl, 1982; Phares & Compas, 1993; Wieder, Jasnow, Greenspan, & Strauss, 1983). A known risk factor is a significant level of depression in a parent, particularly the mother. This has been shown to increase the child's vulnerability to developing anxiety and behavioral disorders (Beardslee, Bemporad, Keller, & Klerman, 1983; Carro, Grant, Gotlib, & Compas, 1993; Pape, Byrne, & Ivask, 1996). The effect of parental psychopathology on child rearing is described in more detail in this chapter in a later section.

A number of other factors can place a child's development at risk, including parental drug and alcohol abuse (Reich, Earls, Frankel, & Shayka, 1993), parents having less than average intelligence (Luthar & Zigler, 1992), and criminality of either parent (Fisher, 1995; Gobel & Shindledecker, 1993). Researchers have also found that some less obvious or latent variables, such as parents' own experience of being parented (especially if it was traumatic and included abuse, neglect, or significant loss and is unresolved) can dramatically affect their ability to parent and the attachment security of their children (Benoit & Parker, 1994; Main & Goldwyn, 1984).

***Family Sociodemographic and Societal Factors***    Sociodemographic variables that relate to the family environment, such as academic difficulties and emotional and behavioral disorders, can also significantly increase children's risk for later problems. Low socioeconomic status, particularly if the family is living below the poverty line, has frequently been shown to be a significant risk factor (Offord & Lipman, 1996; Zyblock, 1996). When a family lives in poverty, it means the parents must constantly struggle to provide children with their basic needs for food, shelter, and clothing. Poverty can also mean living in substandard housing and in violent neighborhoods. Exposure to violence has been found in some studies to be an important predictor of later child psychopathology (Dubrow & Garbarino, 1989; Fitzpatrick, 1997; Miller, Wasserman, Neugebauer, Gorman-Smith, & Kamboukos, 1999; Offord et al., 1989). Children from homeless families have a particularly high incidence of dysfunction (Dail, 1990; Schteingart, Molnar, Klein, & Lowe, 1995). Parents living in poverty find it challenging to meet their children's basic needs; they often find it difficult to talk to, spend time with, and read to their children. Nurturing interactions may be difficult to provide because parents may be depleted of energy and have feelings of hopelessness and depression (McLoyd & Wilson, 1991). Adolescent parenting increases children's risk for having both physical and emotional complications (Luthar & Zigler, 1992; Weinman, Robinson, Simmons, Schreiber, & Stafford, 1989). When other risk factors—such as poverty, depression, and drug and alcohol abuse—are also present, the risk rises substantially (Hechtman, 1989). Other significant risks include severe family dysfunction, especially if it includes spousal abuse (Fergusson, Horwood, & Lynskey, 1992; Grych, Jouriles, Swank, McDonald, & Norwood, 2000; Pedersen, 1994). Marital problems have been related to the presence of behavior problems in toddlers and preschool children (Jouriles, Pfiffner, & O'Leary, 1988; Webster-Stratton & Hammond, 1999). Isolation and lack of social supports can also result from such situations and can contribute to their ongoing maintenance (Allen, Bruin, & Finlay, 1992; Moroney, 1992). In addition, chronic family adversity, stresses, or "hassles" have been found to correlate with infant attachment problems, insecurity, and disorganization, although researchers found variables related to parent psychological risk variables to be the most powerful predictors of disorganized attachment (Dubow, Edwards, & Ippolito, 1997; Shaw & Vondra, 1993). Even family size and birth order have been associated with behavior problems, with middle children in large families more at risk (Kazdin, 1995).

In summary, a variety of variables have been found to be associated with poor outcomes in children, but multiple pathways and processes determine the ultimate patterns of adaptation or maladaptation (Cicchetti & Rogosch, 1996; Zeanah, Boris, & Larrieau, 1997) (See Table 1.1 for a summary of possible risk factors).

**Table 1.1.**   Types of risk factors that contribute to poor outcomes in children

| Variables within the child | Interactional or parenting variables | Parental history and current functioning | Family functioning, sociodemographic, community, and societal factors |
|---|---|---|---|
| Genetic predispositions | Lack of sensitivity or attunement to infant's cries or signals | Parental mental illness, character disorder, or depression | Chronic unemployment |
| Various chromosomal and other disorders | Negative affect toward child | Serious medical condition | Inadequate income/housing |
| Central nervous system abnormalities | Lack of vocalization to child | Parent is incoherent, confused, or dissociated | Frequent moves/no telephone |
| Very low birth weight/prematurity | Little eye-to-eye contact | History of developmental delay | Education of less than completion of 10th grade |
| Failure-to-thrive/feeding difficulties | Negative attributions toward child | History of criminal or young offender's record | Single teenage parent |
| Developmental delays | Lack of parenting knowledge | Older child is or has been in foster care | Violence reported in the family |
| Congenital abnormalities/illnesses | Neglect of child's physical, medical, and emotional needs | Mother experienced loss of previous child | Severe family dysfunction and/or instability |
| Very difficult temperament/extreme crying and irritability | Very punitive discipline | Alcohol and drug abuse | Lack of support/isolation |
| Very lethargic/nonresponsive | Lack of encouragement for child's development | Background of severe abuse, neglect, or loss in childhood that is unresolved | Recent life stresses (death, job loss, immigration) |
| Low or high muscle tone | Physical, emotional, and sexual abuse | Other loss or trauma | Neighborhood problems and community violence |
| Resists holding/hypersensitive to touch | Removal into foster care | | Stressful life events and daily "hassles" |
| | | | Violent television and video games available for child |
| | | | Size of family and birth order |

## Protective Factors and Mechanisms that Can Affect the Development of Children

Some professionals in the field of early childhood intervention have described protective factors or strengths as the opposite of risk variables; however, they are not simply the *absence* of risk factors but rather, the opposite end of a spectrum. For example, isolation would be seen as a risk factor, whereas the opposite, having a supportive family network or support system within the community, could act as a protective factor. Lack of sensitivity or intrusiveness in mother–infant interactions would be risk factors, whereas sensitivity to the infant's cues and attunement to the emotions of the infant would be significant protective factors.

These protective factors can, therefore, be seen as falling into similar categories as those discussed previously: 1) personal characteristics within the child; 2) relationship variables that can provide the child with a secure relationship with a warm, empathetic adult, either within the family or the community; 3) personal characteristics of parents that can contribute to positive parenting practices and to their being strong identification figures for the child; and 4) a social environment or community that reinforces or supports positive efforts made by the child.

*Protective Mechanisms*   Rutter (1990) has also identified four protective mechanisms or processes that can be set in place and that account for individual variation in outcomes (See Table 1.2 for examples of protective mechanisms).

1.  Reducing the impact of a difficult situation

2.  Promoting the child's self-esteem

3.  Providing support in the environment for the child

4.  Providing supports for a child who is facing a very difficult situation

**Table 1.2.**   Protective mechanisms or processes that account for individual variation in outcomes and strategies for enhancing them

| Protective mechanism | Examples |
| --- | --- |
| Reduction of risk impact | Providing other supports for a child whose mother is mentally ill, particularly if the mother has to be hospitalized frequently |
| Promotion of self-esteem and self-efficacy | Encouraging an interest or talent such as music or sport and noticing positive behaviors and efforts in the home |
| Opening up of opportunities for getting help and meeting people | Provision of tutoring or a special person in the community to whom the child can relate |
| Reduction of negative chain reaction after risk exposure | Supporting a child who is often hospitalized by being at the hospital or providing play therapy |

**Table 1.3.**   Sources and characteristics of resilient children and adolescents

| Source | Characteristics |
|---|---|
| Individual | Appealing, sociable, outgoing, easygoing disposition or temperament |
| | Above average intelligence and problem-solving ability |
| | Certain talent or positive interest |
| Primary relationships | Close relationship to caring parent figure |
| | Authoritative parenting: warmth, structure, high expectations |
| Secondary relationships | Connections to extended supportive network |
| | Bonds to prosocial adults outside the family |
| | Connections to prosocial organization |
| | Attending effective schools |

*Resiliency*   In all of the studies that have examined the effect of various risk factors on child outcomes, although a significant percentage of children are adversely affected by various risk factors, a smaller percentage do not show any obvious negative outcomes. These children, previously referred to as "invulnerable" and more recently as "resilient," have a number of factors that seem to protect them from the negative outcomes that develop for less-fortunate children. Masten and Coatsworth (1998) described these resilient children as being protected by one or more of the following aspects of influence: personal characteristics of the child such as being sociable and outgoing, supportive relationships of the child with parents or other caregiving figures, and effective connections with adults outside the family and with schools and positive agencies (see Table 1.3).

## THEORETICAL APPROACHES TO UNDERSTANDING THE CONTRIBUTION OF RISK AND PROTECTIVE FACTORS

Perhaps the most well-known and important theories that consider the contribution of risk and protective factors are the ecological and transactional models.

## Ecological Approaches

*Ecological approaches* consider the social contexts within which development occurs and how they affect human development (Bronfenbrenner, 1979). Children are significantly affected by parent–child interactions, which are, in turn, significantly affected by families, social networks, neighborhoods, communities, and culture. The quality of the links between the family and these wider environments influences development. Good links support development and provide a sense of continuity with the outside world for the child. As well, the goodness of fit between processes at successive levels of influence in the child's environment exerts a considerable effect on the child's developmental outcome (Lerner, Walsh, & Howard, 1998). For instance, if the values that are operating within a child's family, school setting, and the larger culture are at odds, the child is at greater risk for poor out-

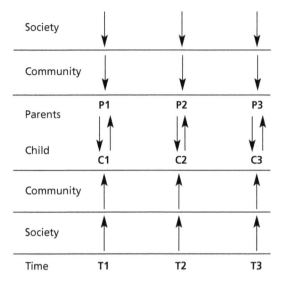

**Figure 1.2.** A diagram of the transactional model approach. The model emphasizes that child development results from a transactional process between child and caregiver across time within the context in which the child is developing (*Key:* P = Parent; C = Child; T = Time).

come, even though none of the value systems by themselves are necessarily detrimental. Furthermore, the goodness of fit between the child's own characteristics and the demands placed on him in a given social context play a critical role in determining the extent to which he is able to adapt successfully to that context. Another example that influences a child's outcome is the importance of the goodness of fit between the child's temperamental characteristics and the parent's interactive style. Ecological theory emphasizes interventions that focus on enhancement of the social environment, family support systems, and use of community services. Interventions, according to this theory, need to take into account the cultural context of the family if they are to be successful and meaningful (Barrera & Corso, 2003; Hanson & Lynch, 2003).

## Transactional Model

The *transactional model* (Sameroff, 1983, 1993; Sameroff & Chandler, 1975; Sameroff et al., 1993) considers child outcomes as a combination of the individual's characteristics and her environment. The model emphasizes the dynamic interplay among genetic and environmental variables, and child development is viewed as resulting from a transactional process involving a child and caregiver within the social context in which the child is developing. The child's behavior at any time is a product of transactions between child characteristics, family characteristics, and the social context. Internal changes within the infant or child and the parent result as the two interact with one another, and both then show behavioral and emotional responses as a result of those internal changes or adaptations to the environment (see Figure 1.2). For example, a child who is more temperamentally intense and sensitive may get upset frequently, setting up a high level of frustra-

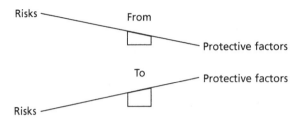

**Figure 1.3.** This model shows that when the number of risk factors is high and protective factors are low, the goal is to change the balance to move toward a lower number of risk factors and a higher number of protective factors.

tion and tension in the parent, who then begins to react by yelling at the child or pushing him away and making the child increasingly upset. At each developmental phase (e.g., when the child starts to walk) the family system strives for homeostasis, and if one developmental phase is distorted or omitted, all subsequent phases can be altered. For example, if an insecure attachment is developed, it can negatively affect later developmental stages (Sameroff & Fiese, 2000 a, b).

In this model, the more risk factors, the greater the likelihood of negative transactional processes becoming established and the greater will be the child's or family's inability to self-correct. Specific risk can result in many different types of negative outcomes depending on the individuality of the transactional processes in each family. Analysis of risk and protective factors is helpful both in terms of identifying infants at risk and determining which aspects of the system can best be considered as the focus for intervention. Also, in treatment or intervention, protective factors need to be enhanced and protective mechanisms put in place so as to build competencies or resilience in children and to reduce developmental disorders and psychopathology (Bloomquist & Schnell, 2002; Cummings, Davies, & Campbell, 2000; Reid, 1993; Yoshikawa, 1994) (see Figure 1.3).

## HOW PARENTING RISKS AFFECT CHILD DEVELOPMENT

A full discussion of the research on the effects on children of various types of parenting difficulties is beyond the scope of this book. As described in the next sections, however, research has shown that many of these difficulties or problems in parents can result in developmental delays in certain areas of development or psychopathology in their children. A number of situations can put a child at risk for compromised development. These can refer to one or both parents and can be summarized under the following categories:

1.  Child is at risk due to a genetic or biological condition

2.  Parent suffers from a psychiatric disorder, addiction, or a significant developmental disability

3.  Parent is coping with an overwhelming number of sociological or environmental challenges, such as extreme poverty and lack of adequate housing, which compromises her ability to provide a safe and secure environment for the child

4.  Parent is unable to provide adequate nurturing and responsive interactions with a child and may use harsh and angry interactions or even abusive discipline or withdraws from or neglects the child.

Of course, in some families, two or more of these conditions may co-exist, making the level of risk to the child extreme. In multi-risk families, a child's development can be compromised as a result of contributions from the child's genetic and biological predisposition, the parent–child interaction, and/or the neighborhood and other sociological conditions in which the child lives. These varying influences interact to affect brain development, which in turn results in different symptoms, behaviors, and developmental outcomes (Cummings & Cicchetti, 1990; Pennington, 2002). These behavioral and social responses can then lead to a secondary neurological disturbance because it sets up an ongoing negative feedback system and limits the positive social stimulation that the child might experience. For example, one of the major symptoms of autism spectrum disorders in children is the failure to develop adequate joint attention skills with others, which leads a child to withdraw and play on his own and hinders his ability to share pleasure with caregivers and other children. This can result in a negative feedback system and can limit the social stimulation that the child receives, thus contributing to secondary neurological disturbance.

By contrast, if a child with no obvious genetic or biological contributors is frequently exposed to harsh and angry parenting, abuse, or inconsistent responsiveness from caregivers, his development is also likely to be compromised. This kind of parenting can result in the child developing very withdrawn or aggressive behavioral patterns that can, in turn, result in increasingly negative parenting and reactions from caregivers. Again, the cyclical nature of such parenting can limit the positive stimulation and reponses that the child receives and negatively influence neurological development. This transactional approach to understanding developmental outcomes is described in more detail in the next section. (See also Figure 1.4).

Considering how various types of risks and resulting difficulties are transmitted to children is important. Contributing variables can be summarized under the following categories: genetic transmission, parenting interactions, and brain develpment and neuroendocrinology.

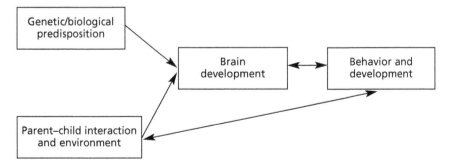

**Figure 1.4.**  A transactional model for the development of child difficulties. Genetic/biological predispositions and parent–child interactions and the environment influence brain development, which then influences behavior and development, which has a two-way relationship with parent–child interaction.

## Genetic Transmission

Research has demonstrated that there is an increased risk for some disorders in certain families. For various psychopathologies such as depression, schizophrenia, and borderline personality disorder (BPD), children of parents with these disorders are genetically predisposed to develop similar difficulties. For example, identical twins of mothers with depression experience depression more frequently than do fraternal twins, even when they are adopted separately and grow up in different households (60% compared with 30%) (Kendler et al., 1995). The association between parent and offspring depression has been found to be particularly high with bipolar disorder, even when the child's first serious episode occurs in adolescence (Thapar & McGuffin, 1996). As well, the children of mothers with schizophrenia are at more risk for developing the disorder than are children of mothers without schizophrenia (Beiser, 1998). These children may also present challenges because they experience sensory and mobility difficulties and have medical needs associated with these tendencies (Walker & Emory, 1983). Other children with this predisposition may be socially unresponsive or temperamentally difficult and easily hyperaroused, which leads to excessive crying, irritability, and difficulty with soothing. As well, some children of mothers with schizophrenia have lower scores on intelligence tests.

## Parenting Interactions

The quality of a parent's interactions and relationships with a child may affect the child's development and influence the development of his brain. On the one hand, very responsive, warm, and attuned interactions can enhance neurological structure and biochemistry and contribute to positive developmental outcomes. On the other hand, when parenting interactions are harsh and/or more subtle types of parenting difficulties are present, such as lack of emotional availability or unresponsiveness, development can be compromised. Failure to soothe a distressed infant can lead to chronic states of hyperarousal or stress in the child. When parental interactions are intrusive and/or insensitive to the child's cues, various disorganized behaviors are often displayed by the child that are indicative of early signs of psychopathology.

## Brain Development and Neuroendrocrinology

Chronic failure to soothe a distressed baby, neglect, or various harsh parenting behaviors—especially those that involve abuse—can lead to a state of hyperarousal and chronic stress that contribute to neurological and biochemical changes. These may affect the functioning of the hypothalamic-pituitary-adrenal (HPA) axis and lead to associated deficits in brain development (Perry, 2001; Yehuda, 1998). Research has identified evidence of changes in patterns and responsiveness of neural pathways, which become more readily activated as a result of maltreatment (Glaser, 2000; Mohr & Fantuzzo, 2000; Rossman & Ho, 2000). Children with insecure attachment to their mothers have higher cortisol production in response to stress (Gunnar, Brodersen, Nachmias, Buss, & Rigatuso, 1996; Spangler & Schieche,

1998). Changes in the hippocampus can follow dysregulation of the HPA axis and result in deficits in short-term memory. These changes can be linked to an increased incidence of depression and anxiety later in life. Children of mothers with depression have also been shown to have actual changes in their biochemistry and have higher heart rates, lower vagal tone and lower levels of serotonin, as well as higher cortisol and norepinephrine levels than children of nondepressed mothers (Abrams, Field, Scafidi, & Prodromidis, 1995; Field, 1998b; Field et al., 1988). They also may mirror the right hemispheric activity of their mothers in interactions. (See a later section on mothers with depression for more information of these neurological effects.)

Child abuse and other trauma can have detrimental effects on brain development, resulting in the actual deterioration of synapses and reduction in the size of particular areas of the brain such as Broca's area, which is responsible for language.

## TYPES OF MULTI-RISK FAMILIES

Individuals at multiple risk cannot be classified easily, nor should they be. All individuals and families have their own circumstances that they are dealing with. However, research has been able to identify particular types of challenges of many types of at-risk parents.

## Teenage Parents

Teenagers who become parents are a population characterized by multiple risks. Perhaps the most challenging dimension for teenage parents is that a number of developmental tasks that should be worked on and resolved during adolescence often get short circuited, and there is not time or opportunity to work them through. These tasks include developing self-identity, becoming independent, and finding peer acceptance.

For the teenage parent, these maturational steps are often put on hold, at least temporarily. Girls must cope with pregnancy, and both the young mother and father must face the stressors inherent in the challenging role of being a parent. Teenagers also have a tendency to be very present-oriented and impulsive, sometimes placing themselves at risk and making parenting more challenging (Cassidy, Zoccolillo, & Hughes, 1996; Crockenberg, 1987). They often experience mood changes and unpredictable reactions as a result of hormonal changes. Teenage parenthood is often associated with high school drop-out, and the normal insecurity and uncertainty of adolescence is compounded if family members reject the young parents and their babies. Teenagers may also feel isolated from peer supports and envious of the things their nonpregnant or nonparenting peers are able to do.

A number of other factors also influence a young person's ability to parent. These include their age (individuals vary greatly between 12 and 19 years of age), the amount of support the mother receives from the father of the baby, and the amount and type of support available from the young parents' families. As well, the meaning of the child to the parents and the temperament and characteristics of the child can make a difference. The young people's ability to get an education, to find suitable employment, and the availability of support programs in the community also play a role.

Taken as a group, teenage parents generally have less optimal interactions and child-rearing patterns with their infants and young children. Teenage mothers tend to be less sensitive, responsive, and emotionally positive with their infants and young children (Landy, Montgomery, Schubert, Cleland, & Clark, 1983; Osofsky, & Eberhart-Wright, 1992; Zeanah, Keener, Anders, & Vieira-Baker, 1987). As noted by Lester (1992), teenage mothers may misread their infants' cues, often misinterpreting their infants' cries, and, as a consequence, this leads to poor caregiving. They are also less verbally responsive and stimulating (Landy, Clark, Schubert, & Jillings, 1983; Osofsky & Eberhart-Wright, 1988). As noted by Osofsky, Hann, & Peebles (1993),

> When observing interactions between adolescent mothers and their infants, one is frequently struck with the quietness of the interaction. Many mothers talk very little to their infants and young children, and, as might be expected, the children verbalize little. (p. 110)

Related to these behaviors, compared with adult mothers, teenage mothers have been found to lack knowledge of developmental milestones and to have less realistic expectations for their children. They may underestimate infant abilities in some areas, and in others, expect their children to reach milestones too early (Fodi, Grolnick, Bridges, & Berko, 1990; Osofsky et al., 1993). Teenage mothers are also more likely to perceive their infants' temperament as difficult, which may well contribute to more negative interactions (Field, Widmayer, Stringer, & Ignatoff, 1980; Frodi, 1983). During toddlerhood, teenage mothers frequently find parenting particularly challenging—often perceiving their child's increasing independence as rejecting of them (Crockenberg, 1987). Perhaps most concerning, various researchers have described teenage mothers as more likely to display dysregulated patterns of affective interactions, with negative emotions and anger predominant, and as mentioned previously, they have a tendency to misread their children's emotional cues (Leadbeater & Linares, 1992). During infancy, children of teenage mothers are less likely to experience empathetic responsiveness and nurturing when upset and distressed (Leadbeater, Bishop, & Raver, 1996). In some studies the parenting of teenage fathers has been described as similar to that of teenage mothers. Some studies have found that, similar to fathers of any age, teenage fathers are more apt to engage in physical rather than verbal exhanges with their infants and young children. They tend to play more with their children and are engaged in less caretaking interactions. They have also been found to be quite punitive at times (Lamb & Elster, 1986). Research has also shown that teenage fathers' involvement in routine caretaking and their emotional investment in their male infants is related to the infants' attachment to them. The quality and quantity of father–infant interactions have also been found to be related to a child's outcomes; put simply, the better quality and the more time spent with a child, the better are the child's cognitive development, behavior, trust in others, and self-esteem (Park, Power, & Fisher, 1980).

In general, children of adolescent mothers have poorer outcomes than do children of older mothers. These differences, which include cognitive functioning and psychosocial problems, first occur in the preschool years and continue into the elementary school years. By adolescence, school achievement is lower and misbehavior and other school problems are markedly higher (Moore, Morrison, & Green, 1997). Children of teenage parents are also more likely to become teenage parents themselves (Hardy, Shapiro, Astone, Brooks-Gunn, Miller, & Hilton, 1997).

## Parents with Significant Psychopathology

Interest in parents with psychopathology has emphasized understanding how various mental health problems can affect the nature and quality of parent–child interactions and influence short- and long-term child outcomes (Zahn-Waxler, Duggal, & Gruber, 2002).

*Mothers with Depression*    A significant body of literature has found significant adverse effects of parental depression on the outcomes of children (Cummings et al., 2000; Goodman & Gotlib, 1999). Some negative outcomes that have been found include lower mental and motor development, difficulties with emotion regulation, and lack of social competence. Because most of the literature on parent depression is on the effects of maternal depression and the close link with postpartum depression (PPD), this section discusses the depression of mothers rather than both mothers and fathers, and begins with a discussion of PPD and how it may affect the infant and other children in the family. Whereas for some mothers, PPD is an isolated, brief event that remits early in the postpartum period, others continue to experience PPD up to a year later and some may also experience another episode before the child reaches age 3 (Phillips & O'Hara, 1991). In one study of PPD, the lower the maternal feelings of self-efficacy, the greater was the maternal depression, and the more likely the mother was to report depression 6 months later (Gross, Conrad, Fogg, & Wothke, 1994). When PPD is more chronic, it is more likely to have adverse effects on children (Campbell, Cohn, & Meyers, 1995; Jacobsen, 1999). PPD varies from mild to very severe and it may be unipolar (i.e., depression only) or bipolar (i.e., swings from depression to elation). Not surprisingly, the more severe the depression, the greater the effect on children (Murray & Cooper, 1992). Bipolar depression in mothers typically is more problematic for children than mild or moderate unipolar depression because the mood swings can make interactions more unpredictable and less sensitive to the child's needs. Postpartum psychosis, not to be mistaken for typical PPD, is a very serious condition that has been linked with the high-profile cases of infanticide reported by the press. Some women with severe depression may also have anxiety disorders and other disorders such as character disorder, creating more symptomatology.

Because, following an episode of PPD, some women have another episode later or the depression becomes more chronic, this section discusses the effect of various types of depression on mothers' interactions with their infants and young children. First, it is important to note that not all mothers with depression have poor interactions with their infants (Campbell et al., 1995). The extent to which interactions are affected depends on the severity of the depression and the supports available to the mother. However, some research has found that depressed mothers show more negative facial expressions in interactions with their infants and that their infants are less attentive, vocalize less, and are less playful than infants of nondepressed mothers (Cohn, Matias, Tronick, Connell, & Lyons-Ruth, 1986; Field, 1984; 1998b). As well, a depressed mother's interactions with her infant are often dramatically dysynchronous and tend to be one of two kinds: 1) disengaged, self-absorbed, psychologically unavailable, lacking in pleasure and interest; and 2) irritable and overintrusive. These two responses may alternate, but depressed mothers often match far more negative than positive emotions of their infants, and the infant tends to mirror the mothers' behavior (Jameson, Gelfand, Kalcsar, & Teti, 1997). Errors in attunement to infants' cues and temporary disengagement between the two occur in all typical parent–infant interactions. Depressed mothers, unlike typical mothers, however, tend not to repair their errors (Campbell, et al., 1995). Mothers who are depressed tend to be less responsive and more helpless, hostile, critical, and disorganized as a result of their feelings of lack of self-efficacy (Cutrona & Troutman, 1986b; DeMulder & Radke-Yarrow, 1991; Teti, Gelfand, Messinger, & Isabella, 1995).

As mentioned in a previous section, research has shown that interactions of depressed mothers with their children affect the neurological systems underlying their behaviors (Dawson, Frey, Self, et al., 1999). As early as the first month, infants of mothers with depression show a similar brain wave pattern to their mothers during face-to-face interactions with them (Field, 1998b). Specifically, on an EEG (electroencephalogram), they tend to show reduced left frontal lobe activity compared with right frontal lobe activity. It has been shown that the left and right frontal lobes show expression of specific emotions (Dawson, Grofer Klinger, Panagiotides, Hill, & Spieker, 1992). The left frontal lobe is activated during approach emotions such as joy and interest as well as anger, and the right frontal lobe is activated during negative emotions related to withdrawal such as sadness, anxiety, disgust, and distress. More right hemisphere activation occurs, for example, when a child is upset during a separation. The reduced left frontal lobe activity in children of mothers who are depressed becomes more permanent by the age of 32 months. At that age, even when interacting with a positive, animated caregiver, the child's right hemisphere remains activated while the left lobe is typically less active (Field, Fox, Pickens, & Nawrocki, 1995). By this age the hemispheric preference is seen to be an acquired trait and not just a current state difference. A similar difference between right and left lobe activity is found in depressed mothers themselves (Dawson, Frey, Panogiotides, et al., 1999).

***Parents with Schizophrenia***    Although schizophrenia affects only 1% of the population, it is a significant mental health problem and can adversely affect parenting capacity and child outcomes (Göpfert, Webster, & Seeman, 1996; Rutter, 1996). With advances in medication, more women suffering from psychotic illness are becoming parents. Surveys published in the 1990s have found that approximately 50% of women with schizophrenia are mothers. Out of this population, only one third remain involved with their children to some degree, few have sole custody, and most are not living with their children's fathers (Joseph, Joshi, Lewin, & Abrams, 1999; Miller & Finnerty, 1996; Ritsher, Coursey, & Farrell, 1997). In general, recent studies have found greater deficits in interactions of women with schizophrenia with their children than in women with other disorders (Zahn-Waxler et al., 2002).

Nevertheless, as with other types of high-risk parents, research has shown that child outcome depends on a variety of things including the severity and duration of the illness, the parent's willingness to stay on medication, the parent's ability to parent when she is with the child, the number and length of hospitalizations, and the supports available to the parents and the child that can protect against the risk factors. In one study, several of the symptoms of postpartum psychosis correlated with the quality of mother–infant interactions (Snellen, Mack, & Trauer, 1999). Also, it is likely that child outcomes result from a combination of genetic vulnerability and environmental stress, including the parenting the child receives and family functioning.

Aspects of a mother's personality and psychopathology affect the manner in which she interacts with her children, which in turn affects the child's later psychological adjustment. Although findings have differed somewhat, in general, studies have found that parenting by women with schizophrenia tends to be less reciprocal, responsive, and involved (Göpfert et al., 1996). They also touch and play less with their infants and provide little sensory and motor stimulation (Cohler, Gallant, Grunebaum, Weiss, & Gamer, 1980; Cohler, Stott, & Musick, 1987; Goodman & Brumley, 1990; Nellen, Mack, & Traver, 1999; Riordan, Appleby, & Faragher, 1999; Snellen et al., 1999). Schizophrenia often reduces the parent's ability to recognize the nonverbal cues, affects, and facial expressions of their infants and young children. As a result, they often misinterpret infants' cues (Appleby & Faragher, 1999). Mothers with psychosis also have difficulty distinguishing their own needs from those of their children, and deny concerns about their ability to provide care for their children (Cohler et al., 1980). They may also project their own impulses onto their children, causing them confusion (Klehr, Cohler, & Musick, 1983). In one study, mothers with schizophrenia were found to provide a child-rearing environment of lower quality, with less variety in terms of stimulation, than did mothers without mental illness. The researchers concluded that mothers with schizophrenia were more withdrawn and less emotionally involved with their children than were typical mothers who were not depressed or who had no mental illnesses. These types of interactions correlated with the children's mental development in the study (Goodman & Brumley, 1990).

This emotional withdrawal may have an effect on attachment. Studies have shown that children of mothers with schizophrenia were more likely to be anxiously attached than children in typical control groups, indicating that parenting interactions had been less sensitive and responsive (D'Angelo, 1986; Naslund, Persson-Blennow, McNeil, Kaij, & Malmquist-Larsson, 1984). Women with mental disorders experience a tremendous range in parenting difficulty, however, and it is important to examine the quality of parenting in each family (Goodman & Brumley, 1990).

A large body of literature has documented the adverse impact that parenting by schizophrenic parents has on their children's development (although these findings have not been supported by all studies). The deficits identified have included social, cognitive, emotional, and physical domains (D'Angelo, 1986; Goodman & Brumley, 1990; Naslund et al., 1984).

***Parents with Borderline Personality Disorder***    Borderline personality disorder (BPD) is one of the personality disorders that are characterized by the *Diagnostic and Statistical Manual of Mental Disorders, Fourth Edition, Text Revision* as an "enduring pattern of inner experience and behavior that deviates markedly from the expectations of the individual's culture" (American Psychiatric Association,

2000, p. 685). Some of the other common personality or character disorders include paranoid personality disorder, narcissistic personality disorder, and obsessive-compulsive personality disorder. Whether there is one entity of BPD or there are actually several different syndromes or phenomenological experiences under one umbrella term has been a subject of controversy among therapists for a considerable period of time. As a diagnostic label, BPD is also controversial because of the negative connotations that are often attached to it. As discussed by Tutek and Linehan (1993), it includes a mishmash of behavioral, physiological, and emotional characteristics beyond the diagnostic criteria listed next that make its diagnosis and clinical treatment complicated. Also, using the clinical label often obscures the unique subjective experience of each individual and can be detrimental to clinical work.

People with BPD are characterized by patterns of instability in interpersonal relationships, self-image, and emotions, and they show significant impulsivity. Another significant characteristic is that individuals with BPD are terrified by real or imagined abandonments and will use extreme measures to overcome them. As indicated in the DSM-IV-TR, a diagnosis of BPD is based on an individual demonstrating at least five of the following characteristics:

- Frantic efforts to avoid real or imagined abandonment

- A pattern of unstable and intense interpersonal relationships, characterized by alternating between extremes of idealization and devaluation

- Identity disturbance, markedly and persistently unstable self-image or sense of self

- Impulsivity in at least two areas that are potentially self-damaging

- Recurrent suicidal behavior, gestures, or threats; or self-mutilating behavior

- Affective instability due to a marked reactivity of mood

- Chronic feelings of emptiness

- Inappropriate, intense anger and difficulty controlling anger

- Transient, stress-related paranoid ideation or severe dissociative symptoms (American Psychiatric Association, 2000, p. 710)

A high percentage of people with BPD report very difficult experiences during childhood, including physical or sexual abuse or neglect and prolonged separations from their caregivers. Furthermore, in a study conducted by Paris and associates, it was found that higher ratings on an index of problems with parents—especially the mother—during childhood, resulted in poorer overall outcome (Paris, 1990; Paris, Zweig-Frank, & Guzder, 1993).

At both the representational and behavioral level, parenting is the most difficult role for an individual with BPD. A mother's terror of being abandoned by the child and her tendency to experience any of the child's independence as rejection lock the mother with BPD and her child into a constant struggle against the child's individuation. The parent's inconsistency, unpredictability, and uncontained rage result in the child feeling total uncertainty about whether he will experience an affectionate response or a verbal or physical slap. Consequently, love and hate are frequently mixed and cause the child intense confusion. This feeling is often exaggerated by the pattern of abnormal thought processes and explanations that characterize conversations with the parent with BPD. Threats of abandonment or actual abandonment are common, even though the parent punishes or discourages the child's independence at other times. The borderline parent expects to be taken care of but frequently criticizes any attempts at helping that the child offers. The parent is extremely jealous of any successes the child may have, and often demeans these successes as insignificant (Lawson, 2002). Thus, the child may become a target of the parent's projections and blamed for any difficulties in the parent's life situation (Feldman & Guttman, 1984). Discipline is either inconsistent or very rigid and extremely punitive.

Not all parents with BPD act in these ways with their children and may instead turn their hostility on themselves with suicidal gestures and threats and self-mutilating behaviors. In any case, they do not provide the nurturing, stimulation, consistency, and warm structure that infants and young children require.

## Parents with Unresolved Loss and Trauma

Millions of children and adults across the world are exposed to traumatic experiences that affect their psychological, biological, and social equilibrium, and a significant proportion of individuals who have been exposed to these traumas develop symptoms such as flashbacks and nightmares about the traumatic event(s) they were exposed to. In some instances these symptoms do not remit, and the person is diagnosed with posttraumatic stress disorder (PTSD). Frequently, individuals who are being discussed in this section, such as substance abusers, child abusers, those with severe depression or bipolar disorder, and very high-risk teenage parents, have been exposed to loss and trauma that continue to affect their functioning. Some studies have suggested that 55%–90% of individuals with BPD have histories of childhood trauma (Gunderson & Sabo, 1993; van der Kolk et al., 1994). As pointed out by Sabo (1997), population studies show that a significant percentage of women are exposed to childhood sexual abuse (20%–33%), whereas only 2% of the population meet criteria for BPD (Allen, 2001; Herman, 1981). However, it is likely that a very significant percentage of people who have been sexually abused experience some of the symptoms of BPD but do not meet the criteria fully. Because of the significance of the influence of unresolved loss and trauma on parenting, Chapter 9 in Section III of this book discusses its effects on parenting, and a variety of interventions for parents with it are described in some detail.

## Parents Who Abuse Substances

In contrast to the stereotypes, female substance abusers who become pregnant are a diverse group, with various risk factors and strengths (Lester, Boukydis, & Twomey, 2000). Many women who use drugs during pregnancy and after their infants are born are suffering from other psychiatric disorders such as depression, anxiety, and personality disorders that produce a complex set of problems that need to be addressed in intervention (Beckwith, Howard, Espinosa, & Tyler, 1999;

Lester et al., 2000). They also are often dealing with the after-effects of difficult life histories including trauma, loss, abuse, and parental substance abuse (Brooks, Zuckerman, Bamforth, Cole, & Kaplan-Sanoff, 1994). Many parents with substance abuse problems became addicted as a way to overcome feelings of very low self-esteem and a negative self-image, and thus they have great difficulties with affect control and self-regulation (Brooks et al., 1994). These difficulties may manifest themselves in behaviors such as excessive anxiety, phobias, and paranoid ideation about the world and the people in it. Of course, effects vary depending on the types of substances used. Parents who abuse substances may use a variety of drugs and/or alcohol or combinations thereof that differ significantly in terms of the effect they can have prenatally on the fetus, as well throughout a child's life on the parents' ability to parent. Many individuals who are addicted to these drugs become subsumed by the need to get money to buy them, and consequently, they live in environments characterized by chaos, violence, and poverty.

Fortunately, some protective factors that can be present have been identified. Research has found that 1) low use of illegal drugs by the father may offset high drug use by the mother (Brooks, Tseng, & Cohen, 1996), and 2) improving goodness of fit between parental caregiving behavior and the infant's regulatory needs contributes to more sensitive parent–infant interactions (Brooks et al., 1994).

As mentioned previously, substance abuse by mothers has unique applications to parenthood, including the possible effects of such abuse on the developing fetus during pregnancy and ongoing effects in the postpartum period as a result of the drug's effect on the infant and mother's interactions with him (Freir, 1994; Weston, Ivins, Zuckerman, Jones, & Lopez, 1989). Perhaps the best-known and most understood effects of substance use during pregnancy has been the effects of alcohol use. An affected child may be identified with fetal alcohol syndrome (FAS), alcohol-related birth defects (ARBD), or alcohol-related neurodevelopmental disorder (ARND). In the United States and Canada, 1 to 3 children in 1,000 have fetal alcohol related abnormalities. In some native communities and inner-city populations, as many as 10%–20% of the children may be affected (Astley & Clarren, 1997; Cordero, Floyd, Martin, Davis, & Hymbaugh, 1994; Stratton, Howe, & Battaglia, 1996).

Infants who have been exposed to drugs in utero are often more difficult to settle and to relate to. Consequently, they may present parents who abuse substances with significant challenges. If parents are still using drugs postnatally, the effects of the drugs themselves may limit the extent to which they can respond sensitively to their children's cues, or even to be able to meet their basic needs. As well, with the co-occurrence for these parents of psychiatric disorders and symptoms of unresolved loss and trauma, their lack of self-reflectivity and empathy for their children may make the parenting role excruciatingly difficult. Thus, when an infant or young child who has compromised capacities to self-regulate to begin with due to drug exposure during pregnancy is parented by someone who also has difficulty with self-regulation, the outcome for the infant is likely to be compromised.

In addition, alcohol and drug abuse has been consistently related to child abuse and neglect of various kinds. It is especially high for those who are using illegal drugs because those users are more likely to have antisocial personalities and poor ego and superego development. Often, if parents are using drugs they may be engaging in antisocial and dangerous activities to raise money to buy the drugs, placing their children at significant risk. There may also be periods in which they are living in poverty, without adequate housing or the basic necessities needed by infants and young children.

The literature that has examined the effects of substance abuse on parenting and child outcome has suffered from a number of methodological problems, making it difficult to associate specific parenting deficits with negative child outcomes. In general, studies have shown that parenting deficits pose significant risks for children's development, particularly for poor impulse control, conduct problems, and poorer overall adjustment (Bornstein, Mayes, & Park, 1998).

## Families Experiencing Violence

Many types of violence may occur within families, including wife or husband abuse, child abuse or neglect, sibling abuse, abuse of older adults, caregiver abuse, and adolescent abuse of parents. Each has a serious impact on the sense of security and safety felt within the family. Especially vulnerable to the effects of such violence are the young children in the family, who experience it either as targets or as witnesses. Therefore, in any early intervention/prevention program, any such violence must be addressed in order to promote the security of the children and other family members.

For the present discussion, the battering of women and child maltreatment are considered more fully because they are so common. These kinds of abuse are estimated to occur in as many as 37% of families, or with 20 million people in the United States (The Commonwealth Fund, 1993). A considerable amount of overlap exists between various types of abuse in a family. In studies of child abuse, approximately 50% of cases also involve the abuse of the child's mother (Sudermann & Jaffe, 1999). In studies of homes in which domestic violence occurs, in 26%–70% of cases, the children are also being abused (Bowker, Arbitell, & McFerron, 1988; Straus & Gelles, 1990; Suh & Abel, 1990). This high degree of overlap suggests that when one type of abuse is identified, particular care should be exercised to determine if other types of abuse are also occurring in the family.

***Spousal Abuse***    It is estimated that 2–4 million women in the United States and 1 million in Canada are victims of domestic violence (Witwer & Crawford, 1995). The number of children exposed to this type of violence is significantly higher. It is estimated that at least 40% and perhaps as many as 80% of children witness these domestic violence attacks (Jaffe, Sudermann, & Reitzel, 1992). This means that as many as 3.3 million children in the United States witness violence each year (Carlson, 1984). The effects of family violence on children can be both direct and indirect. The direct effects occur if children are in the middle of the abuse and see and hear it. They may try and get between parents to stop it and may get hurt. Sometimes they experience direct effects because they are removed from the family in order to be kept safe, or they move with their mothers into a shelter. They may experience indirect effects because of the effects of the violence on their mother's physical—and even more likely—emotional availability. They may also experience harsh discipline from one or both parents and, at times, may be blamed for the fights (Cummings & Zahn-Waxler, 1992).

Couple violence typically leaves each parent less emotionally and physically available to a child and less effective as a caretaker (Erel & Burman, 1995). The parenting of both the abuser and the victim is often marginal for different reasons. The abuser presents children with inconsistency and a model of lack of ability to contain aggression and negative emotions and to resolve conflicts. Marital conflict may cause breakdowns in discipline and reduce the sensitivity and responsivity of both parents to their children's needs.

Men who are violent seem to see fatherhood in terms of having "rights" with children, and they are more concerned about maintaining control over their children than with nurturing them and showing empathy for them. They may demonstrate this feeling of entitlement by showing favoritism and conditional "love," and by undermining of the mother (Cummings & O'Reilly, 1997). Children are particularly affected when parents' quarrels are about them, such as when parents argue about discipline and child rearing (Jenkins & Smith, 1991; Jouriles, Murphy, Farris, Smith, Richters, & Waters, 1991). Parents in aggressive, violent marriages often enact two styles of child discipline that may change quickly and dramatically. In other words, inconsistent, lax discipline may alternate with a coercive, power-assertive, authoritarian style when the parent feels angry, ineffectual, and dominated by the child (Cummings & Davies, 1994a).

***Child Maltreatment***    Child maltreatment includes abuse and neglect. Abuse can be physical, sexual, and/or emotional. Emotional abuse has been the most difficult to define. It is generally described as acts that can damage a child's behavioral, cognitive, affective, or physical functioning. Neglect of a child can include physical neglect (e.g., not providing food, physical care, medical treatment, shelter, hygiene, safety, education) or emotional neglect (e.g., consistently failing to comfort an upset or anxious child, chronically ignoring the requests of a child for attention, consistently not showing affection to the child). Although these divisions are useful, many children suffer from several kinds of abuse or neglect.

The problem of abuse and neglect is massive, although few statistics are available on the incidence of neglect and emotional abuse (MacMillan, 2000). Also, the incidence reported depends entirely on how it is defined and how extensively it is investigated. In the United States, 2 million reports of child abuse and neglect are made annually. In Canada, an estimated 135,573 child maltreatment reports were investigated in 1998 (Trocmé & Wolfe, 2001). This corresponds to an estimated incidence rate of 252 investigations per 1,000 children. Of these, 45% were confirmed, and 22% remained suspicious but could not be proven. These statistics could be based on an over-reporting of false cases (about 50%), but under-reporting of unknown cases also occurs, so these two trends probably balance each other out. In other words, it is important to consider that it is likely that as many cases were occurring that were not reported (Trocmé & Wolfe, 2001). It is also important to remember that the effects of abuse and neglect do not go away, but continue to reverberate for years, sometimes for a lifetime, and so the numbers of children at any time suffering from its effects are enormous (Cicchetti & Olsen, 1990; Trocmé & Caunce, 1995).

Parents who abuse their children have very low frustration tolerance and have been shown to have greater psychophysiological reaction to their childrens's behavior, which they find to be particularly stressful and frustrating (Dishbrow, Doerr, & Caulfield, 1977; Frodi & Lamb, 1980; Mash, Johnston, & Kovitz, 1983; Susman, Trickett, Iannotti, Hollenbeck, & Zahn-Waxler, 1985; Wolfe, Fairbank, Kelly, & Bradlyn, 1983). Researchers have also found that these parents are not as able to stop small problem behaviors in their children from escalating (Reid, Taplin, & Lorber, 1981). They often have unrealistic expectations of their children and see themselves as inadequate or incompetent in the parenting role. Daphne Bugental and colleagues (2000) found that many abusive parents perceived a significant power discrepancy, typically seeing the child as powerful and controlling and intentionally annoying them and themselves as ineffectual (see Section III, Chapter 12 for a further discussion of this type of imbalance). Abusive parents seem to process social information differently and have been assessed as making more negative evaluations and attributions of their children's behavior (Milner, 1993). Along with this kind of attribution, parents who abuse their children fail to understand each individual child's needs, abilities, who the child "is," and perhaps most important, how the child thinks and feels. In other words, the parent wants the child to meet his needs, but lacks empathy to see the child as a separate being with unique needs and capacities of her own.

Significant differences also were found in parenting style and the discipline strategies used by neglectful and abusive parents (Crittenden, 1981). Using the categories proposed by Baumrind (1971, 1973), neglectful parents have a distinct kind of permissive parenting in which they show hostility and little caring and love, whereas abusive parents are often authoritarian and low in responsiveness to their child's needs (Lamborn, Mounts, Steinberg, & Dornbusch, 1991). Abusive, authoritarian parents tend to have very strict and rigid views of discipline. Many of these parents believe that corporal punishment is effective, for example. The immediate antecedent of child abuse frequently involves parental discipline attempts. For example, Gil (1970) reported that 63% of abusive incidents developed out of disciplinary action taken by caregivers. It has also been found that abusive parents not only use more punitive discipline but also they use fewer requests and reasoning techniques with their children (Trickett & Kuczynski, 1986).

Other characteristics that are associated with abuse and neglect include parent substance abuse, sociopathic or violent tendencies, moderate to severe intellectual limitations, and physical illness (Ayoub & Jacewitz, 1982). Although many abused individuals do not show a repetition of the abusive behaviors, many do. Also, some abusive parents can react relatively sensitively with their children in less-stressful parenting interactions such as when playing; however, these same parents may be triggered to become abusive in certain situations that they find particularly stressful. Certainly, the work of Bugental and others (2000) has demonstrated how negative attributions that may arise out of early experiences influence parenting interactions. It should also be pointed out that unresolved loss and trauma and in extreme cases, PTSD and dissociation and the episodic memories that remain inaccessible to conscious memory may be retriggered in stressful situations that "remind" the parent, or are similar in certain aspects, to his own experience of abuse. This retriggering, which is not something the parent is aware of, may lead to abuse or extreme withdrawal, even dissociation, without rational control and must be considered in evaluating parenting capacity and risk potential. In other words, when a child shouts "no" and has a tantrum it may trigger the parent's memories of being a small child himself and hearing his own parents shouting negative comments or showing rage reactions to such behavior (Crittenden, Lang, Claussen, & Partridge, 2000).

Table 1.4 summarizes the key points of working with various types of high-risk families.

**Table 1.4.**    Summary of key points of working with various types of multi-risk families

- On the one hand, each special population has unique characteristics that are important to consider in designing interventions for it. On the other hand, these diverse groups share a number of similarities in terms of needs for support and intervention.
- For most of the groups, intervention to improve the parent–child interactions and relationship is necessary, but approaches for the parents that can enhance feelings of self-confidence may also be crucial.
- In each group, individuals fall within a range of competence and adjustment that differentiates the types and intensity of intervention required, as well as the prognosis.
- The first step in providing intervention must be a comprehensive and detailed assessment of the child, parents, parent–child interactions, and of other aspects of the environment. This information is then used to decide on the most suitable intervention to provide.
- For many groups, studies have shown that the type of emotion regulation provided by the parents can be an issue and can result in the child having difficulties in dealing with negative emotions. Consequently, the type of emotion regulation often needs to be a focus of the interventions.
- With some of the populations described, support for the parents *and* child care for the child may be essential if the child is to have positive outcomes.
- For parents in most of the categories discussed, those with greatest dysfunction—almost without exception—have experienced very rejecting or abusive experiences during early childhood that are unresolved. The resulting memories then have a significant effect on these parents' ability to parent their own children. Providing appropriate interventions that can help parents deal with these memories and reintegrate them into conscious memories may be crucial.
- With many multi-risk populations, establishing a trusting relationship may be the most difficult as well as one of the most crucial aspects of the treatment.
- In extreme cases in which parents are experiencing mental illness or family violence, or when drugs and alcohol are being used to such an extent that parenting is significantly impaired or the child is at risk for abuse, it may be necessary to report the situation to Child Protective Services and remove the child until the situation can be stabilized.
- For some parents (e.g., teenage mothers, substance users), group approaches may be particularly helpful.
- For many children, it is critically important to stabilize family situations by enhancing support systems, if they are lacking.

## UNDERSTANDING AND
## ASSESSING MULTI-RISK FAMILIES

Although various factors in the environment are indications of risk, they do not necessarily describe the process by which risk is transmitted. For this we need to understand the nature of the impact of the immediate or proximal variables on the development of the child.

In the transactional/ecological/contextual model, the interactions of the child and parent are situated at the center of the inner circle of influences on the development of the child. As discussed, various other variables influence the behavior of the parent and child as they meet in interactions. The infant is inextricably connected with the actions of adult caregivers, most often his parents. For example, in the earliest stages, his caregivers regulate his bodily functions until the external patterning they provide gradually becomes internalized and synchronized with the child's own biological rhythms, at which point the child is capable of a greater degree of biological self-regulation.

The patterning of the interaction between the parent/caregiver and the child becomes increasingly influential on the child's development over time. It affects the child's view of himself, of others, and of the world that is carried with him as new situations are experienced and new relationships determine how he behaves and ultimately how competently he develops.

Detailed consideration of the factors that are most proximal to a child is necessary in order to understand how the child's development is most immediately influenced by them. Figure 1.5 is a magnified view of the inner circles of influence around the child. Other factors outside this inner circle, such as the community in which the family lives and the service system that is available to them, are not dis-

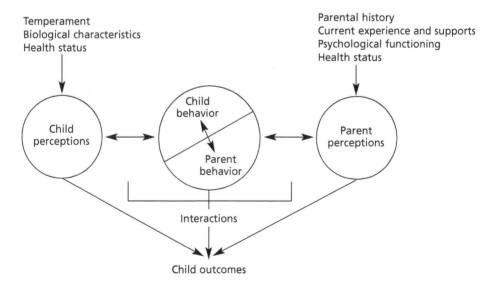

**Figure 1.5.** A diagram depicting how the interactions of the child and parent are at the center of inner circles of proximal, or close, variables that have a direct effect on the development of the child. An understanding of the impact of proximal variables is key to understanding child development.

cussed here because they are usually not central in the intervention, although they may indirectly influence the parents' interactions with the child.

## Proximal Variables

This section describes the important aspects of proximal variables and provides suggestions for their assessment (Landy, 2004).

*Child Characteristics*    A child's interaction is strongly influenced by her biological characteristics and/or any genetic conditions. As well, the child's temperament will significantly influence how she deals with the world and particularly how she interacts with parents. Other aspects of the child that are important include her level of responsiveness and whether she sends clear cues or signals to her parents about the need for interaction.

One of the most important characteristics that develops out of the early interactions with caregivers is the child's quality of attachment. When attachment is secure rather than insecure, the child has an internal sense of being safe and the caregiver's availability provides the infant with a secure base from which she can explore the environment. The child's quality of attachment to her parents and other caregivers influences how she interacts with her caregivers and her developmental outcomes. Four qualitatively different patterns of behavioral organization related to attachment are discussed in greater detail in Section III, Chapter 10.

*Psychological Functioning of the Parents*    Proximal variables such as parent psychological functioning and the parent–infant/child interaction also have great impact on the development of infants and young children. Therefore, it is critical to consider them in determining the level of family risk. A number of researchers, theorists, and clinicians from a variety of fields have written about the effects of an individual's psychological characteristics on their functioning in various areas of their lives. Some of these psychological factors have their greatest impact on parenting styles and parent–infant/child interactions, whereas others have their greatest effect on the process of intervention. It is also important to note that many influence the parents' capacity to deal with adverse aspects of the family and community environment. All ultimately affect the development of the infant/child and the success of the intervention, and need therefore to be a focus of assessment and intervention with multi-risk families. The characteristics are listed in Table 1.5 and are described briefly in the next section, which also includes some ways to assess them. Other assessment instruments that can be used are listed in the Appendix to this chapter.

The following aspects of psychological functioning significantly affect parenting and the intervention:

*Defensive Functioning*    Defensive functioning relates to how an individual deals with anxiety and other negative emotions. It is related to coping style, but it is more concerned with unconscious processes than coping style, which reflects both unconscious and conscious processes. On the one hand, some people have good coping skills and a realistic understanding of themselves and others. Some of the more productive defenses that are likely to be used by this kind of person are intellectualisation and sublimation. Parents who have more difficulty with parenting or who have psychological problems, on the other hand, are more likely to

**Table 1.5.** Psychological and interactional characteristics affecting parenting and the choice of intervention

- Defensive functioning
- Self-reflectivity and empathy for the child
- Sense of competence
- Unresolved loss and trauma
- Sensitivity and responsiveness to the child
- Emotion regulation
- Parenting knowledge and attributions of the child
- Planning and problem solving

use more primitive defenses such as splitting, projection, and impulsive acting out. A person's defensive functioning can be indicative of the kind of intervention that will work best for them.

Although personality measures can be used, defensive functioning can also be assessed by listening to parents talk about how they cope with difficult situations and stress. How much does a parent internalize anger and anxiety and how often does self-blame occur? Or does the person externalize, use more primitive defenses, and blame others—projecting anger on others, or acting out on him- or herself? These factors are meaningful when tendencies are extreme and the individual experiences a great deal of anxiety about being able to parent, or anger and frustration toward the child and other family members. The parent's defensive style will also affect how she relates to the service provider, how she responds to being approached about services, and how comfortable she feels during subsequent sessions.

*Capacity for Self-Reflectivity and Empathy for the Child*     Fonagy, Steele, Steele, Moran, and Higgitt (1991) defined the reflective self as the "internal observer of mental life" and noted that "the reflective self knows that the self feels, perceives, reacts, and so on" (p. 202). As the writers described it, people with a reflective self not only feel angry or rejected but also know that they have the feeling and reflect on why and how they have it.

Linked to self-reflectivity is the ability for perspective taking, which implies that the individual can take into account not only their own mental states but also the mental states of others and why they behave in certain ways. This capability is also known as *theory of mind.* Obviously, a link exists between the understanding of self and other, as we can only understand ourselves as a result of our observations of the mental activities of others. This capacity for having a reflective self develops in the infant–caregiver relationship, although in individuals with pervasive developmental disorder (PDD) or autism spectrum disorders, the failure to develop a theory of mind is related to genetic factors and neurological impairment. A poorly established capacity to reflect on mental functioning in oneself and other is also present in BPD. In both cases the individual may show an apparent lack of caring about other people and even cruelty toward them, and may experience a constant fear of abandonment and of disintegration or fragmentation.

A parent's capacity to be empathetic to her child will be obvious in two main areas: 1) sensitivity and attunement to her infant's cues and emotions, and 2) attributions of the child's behavior. Observation of the parent–infant/child interaction can be important in determining the parent's level of empathy for her child. This will include how consistently the parent responds to the child when the child is upset, ill, crying, or physically hurt. Another important observation will include how responsive and sensitive the parent is to the child's other cues without being overly intrusive (e.g., not continuing to wave a rattle in the child's face when he is obviouisly overwhelmed, tickling a child who is begging for it to stop). The parent's interest and involvement with the child will also be an important indicator of her ability to be empathetic toward her child.

In addition to observing interactions, it is important to listen to a parent's conversations about the child and how accurate she is in talking about the child's feelings and point of view of an event. For example, when the child seems tired and whiny, is the parent able to see that the child may be feeling isolated, sad, or ill? Or can the parent only see the situation from her own point of view? Is the child perceived as a burden or as spoiled? Empathy for others and understanding another's point of view can also be assessed from parents' descriptions of other adults in their lives.

*Unresolved Loss and Trauma*    When memories of trauma or loss remain unprocessed, they often become dissociated and remain at an unconscious level, available to be triggered by even subtle reminders of the traumatizing event. The memory of the event or events is initially stored as sensory fragments, and the individual has no verbal memory or complete story of what actually happened. Although the person may be able to recite the facts of the traumatic event(s), there is no detailed narrative of what happened or what they experienced or felt, or any way of making sense of it or coming to terms with it.

When unconscious memories of the event are triggered, the individual re-experiences the frightening feelings and perceptions belonging to the past. After interpersonal violence, such as domestic violence or rape, even emotional and physical intimacy can be a reminder of the horror and fear of what happened to the person. At times, even after a narrative of the event has been formed, memories may resurface as flashbacks, visual images, or somatic sensations. Research suggests that the younger the person at the time of the trauma and the more prolonged the trauma was, the greater the likelihood of re-experiencing it (Briere & Conte, 1993; Herman & Shatzow, 1987; van der Kolk & van der Hart, 1991).

Resolution of loss or trauma can be judged by listening to parents' descriptions of their early experience. For example,

- Is it difficult to understand the person's thoughts about the trauma? Incoherence suggests unresolved trauma.

- Does the parent acknowledge the effect of the past on current functioning and parenting? If not, it usually indicates that trauma has not been resolved.

- Do descriptions of how the person's parents behaved fit with the adjectives she used to describe her relationship with them? For example, if a parent describes her relationship with her own parent as "loving," can she describe some experiences that match the descriptor, such as "My father, although he worked hard, always read me a story when he was home or tried to call me if he was away"? Or do the examples given not fit with the description of "loving" (e.g., "My mother made sure our clothes were clean")?

- Does the individual show signs of dissociation, of "going away in her head," or staring into space when certain situations are described?

- Are there signs that the parent shows—perhaps by becoming obviously distressed or flushed—that thoughts or intense feelings from the past are being triggered, or does the parent talk about such experiences as if they are happening in the present?

- Does the parent talk about a difficult early experience of being parented but appear to have come to some acceptance or resolution of it? If the parent is excessively preoccupied about the past or the influence of the difficult experience is totally denied, it is likely to be unresolved.

*Sense of Competence*    Having a sense of parental competence or self-confidence, or the perception that one is able to care for and understand one's children, is an important capacity that has been found to relate to more general measures of self-esteem. Low self-confidence is associated with poor mother–infant interactions (Bohlin & Hagekull, 1987; MacPhee, Fritz, & Miller-Heyl, 1996; Teti & Gelfand, 1991). Some researchers have suggested that the relationship between maternal self-confidence and parenting ability may be complex and curvilinear, such that excessively high maternal self-confidence may not allow for acknowledging the complexity of parenting choices, whereas very low maternal self-confidence may make the parent unsure and anxious in her parenting interactions.

Parenting competence is also related to the degree to which individuals believe they have some control over what happens (i.e., *internal locus of control*) and how much they see fate as controlling everything (i.e., *external locus of control*). Locus of control is also linked with parenting; for example, parents with a sense of having little power may believe they have little ability to influence their children.

A parent's sense of competence will be obvious in how he disciplines and manages his child's behavior and care. The parent with little sense of his own competence is unable to manage the child and presents with uncertainty, indicating in subtle ways to the child that he is frightened or feels unable to manage the child's behavior. Communications with the child are often unclear and responses are extremely reactive to difficult child behaviors (Bugental, Matyla, & Lewis, 1989). This lack of belief in one's own competence may also be demonstrated in a seeming inability to manage any challenges and in being unable to problem solve or to cope with stressful situations.

*Sensitivity and Responsiveness to the Child*    Parent interactions with their children are important influences on their child's development. Moreover, a number of approaches to working with multi-risk families emphasize the importance of using strategies and methods to intervene in order to enhance these interactions. Some parenting characteristics that are typically fostered include sensitivity to the child's cues, positive emotionality, acceptance of the child, and responsivity. A parent's capacity to be sensitive, emotionally available, and responsive to her child is influenced by a number of the psychological characteristics discussed previously, so it is important to assess these characteristics in order to better target interventions for improving interactional behavior if it is problematic.

These parenting characteristics can be observed in interactions in which the parent is playing with or feeding her child. Observations of how the parent responds when the child is upset, frustrated, or hurt are particularly important. Those parents who fail to respond to the child at these times are particularly concerning. Alternatively, a variety of interactional measures rather than informal observations can be used to assess the interaction and the level of the various parent interactional variables mentioned previously. The effects of parents exhibiting frightening or frightened (fr) behaviors when they are interacting with their children are discussed in detail in Section III, Chapter 9.

*Emotion Regulation*    *Emotion regulation* refers to the process by which people control and self-regulate their internal response to emotions as well as their outward expression. The importance of emotion regulation to adult functioning and parenting cannot be emphasized enough. Emotion regulation is a significant influence on parenting, especially in the child's early years. When parents have emotion regulation difficulties, children may be deprived of the opportunity to have emotions accepted and to learn how to modulate them. If parents have extreme difficulties with emotion regulation it can compromise their children's development, particularly the child's capacity to manage their own emotional reactions.

Assessing emotion regulation will probably have to happen over time, although some instances of difficulties may be obvious immediately. For example if a mother is depressed or very anxious it may be observed in early sessions. It is unlikely, however that the parent will openly express anger early, but she may talk about these problems within a few sessions or home visits. In order to assess a mother's depression, it is important to ask questions about her sleeping and eating patterns, energy level, feelings of hopelessness and despair, and any suicide ideation. It is also critical to check for any psychotic symptoms such as delusions and hallucinations and, if present, how they may relate to the child. This kind of evaluation will need to be carried out by a psychiatrist or other qualified health professional. The mother's ability to regulate her infant's emotional upsets can be assessed by observing if she consistently responds to her child when he is crying or frustrated by talking, picking up, or calming him.

*Parenting Belief Systems and Attributions of the Child*    The beliefs parents have about child development and parenting are related to their parenting and to their children's developmental outcomes. These beliefs can be influenced by their own beliefs about the child, cultural beliefs, their own experiences growing up, and how they see their parenting roles.

*Attributions* are a parent's beliefs about her child and about her subjective experience of him (Zeanah & Barton, 1989). According to attribution theorists, attribution processes are subject to errors or biases, and these biases are important for understanding dysfunctional parent–child relations (Hewstone, 1989). Dix and Grusec (1985) talked about misattributions in which a child's behavior is interpreted as directed against the parent, especially when the behavior is negative. Such biases encourage negative emotional states in the parent and may lead to extreme punitiveness (Dix & Grusec, 1985). In a more positive situation, the child's desirable behaviors are attributed to internal causes (personality traits), and undesirable behaviors to external causes. These attributions serve to increase the child's feelings of personal worth and the parent's feeling of competence, and to reinforce a positive view of the child, thus strengthening the parent–child relationship (Dix & Grusec, 1985). In attachment literature, parents' working models of their child have been found to be related to the child's quality of attachment to the parents, and this may occur across generations (Benoit & Parker, 1994).

In conflictual parent–child relationships, however, parents' attributions appear to reverse, and the child's misbehaviors are attributed to internal, stable, and controllable causes within the child. The child is then blamed for negative behavior, and no credit is given for positive behavior. Such biased attributions also function to preserve parents' self-esteem by removing the need to consider their own contribution or responsibility for the development and maintenance of child misbehavior. Studies of parental attribution of delinquent children show that parents of those children who were delinquent and also described as highly disturbed use dispositional factors to explain their children's negative behavior (Alexander, Waldron, Barton & Mas, 1989; Sagatum, 1991). Similar attributions have been found to be used by abusive parents (Bradley & DeV. Peters, 1991; Crittenden, 1985; Lahey, Conger, Atkinson, & Treiber, 1984; Mash et al., 1983; Reid, Kavanagh, & Baldwin, 1987; Susman et al., 1985).

Assessment of parents' attributions of their children can usually occur by listening to how a parent describes his child and observing how the parent interacts with and disciplines his child. The following types of questions may elicit interesting information from a parent and suggestions about how he views the child:

- How would you describe your baby when she was first born?

- What kind of temperament or personality does your child have now?

- Who does your child remind you of?

- What do you think your child will be like when he is a teenager?

- How did you choose your baby's name?

- How easy is your child to manage?

*Capacity for Planning and Problem Solving*    In order to maintain adequate structure in day-to-day life and to successfully carry out the tasks of parenting, it is essential to have the ability to consider an action, its course, and its consequences, before embarking on the activity (e.g., getting a job, preparing a child for child care, cooking a meal). This need for planning and problem solving often requires the ability to control immediate impulses that would be detrimental to one's self and the child. This type of adaptation includes how persistent and flexible the individual is in her approach to problem solving, particularly during times of crisis when difficulties or conflict occur. Planning and problem solving also requires a certain level of cognitive functioning that parents with developmental delays may lack, and as a consequence, they are likely to have significant difficulty with planning and problem solving in many areas of their lives as well as in providing their children with the necessary level of stimulation and nurturance.

In-depth intellectual assessment is usually not carried out unless it is believed to be necessary in order to determine the need for special services for the parent, however. In general, cognitive capacity will be assessed from the parent's conversation and ability to cope with problems and crises that arise. If a parent is constantly having crises and not resolving them satisfactorily, this may be some indication of difficulty with problem solving and planning. Education level and employability will also be important clues to an individual's abilty to problem solve. As well, parents' ways of handling conflict with each other and with their child can indicate their ability to deal with difficult issues.

***Other Influences on the Parent*** A number of external variables influence how a parent interacts with his child. Of these, the level of family functioning is crucial. Key factors are whether the parents have adaptive ways to solve problems and conflict and how supportive they are of one another. Since the 1990s, there has been a growing interest in considering the triadic dynamic between the child and his parents (i.e., the mother–father–infant triad) and beyond the triad to include the siblings and how all the family members interact with one another (Fivaz-Depeursinger, & Corboz-Warnery, 1999; McHale, 2003; McHale & Fivaz-Depeursinger, 1999). Co-parenting dynamics are believed to relate to various developmental outcomes for the child. They have been evaluated through such means as interaction videos that reveal such variables as cooperation, family warmth, and antagonism (competitiveness) (McHale, 2003). In some situations, it may be necessary for a service provider to work with the whole family if the child's development is being negatively affected by the parents' difficult relationship or the family dynamics. Of course, if there is family violence in the home, it is especially important for a service provider to intervene because the child may be at risk.

Table 1.6 identifies the differences between risk factors in low-, moderate-, and high-risk families and shows the type and intensity of risk factors that each deals with.

**Table 1.6.** Characteristics/variables of parent(s)* and child used for determining level of risk

| Characteristic or variable | Level of risk | | |
|---|---|---|---|
| | Low risk | Moderate risk | High risk |
| Risk factors | Less than four risk factors | Between four and eight risk factors | More than eight risk factors |
| Protective factors | Several protective factors | Few protective factors to balance risk factors | Protective factors are rare and do not detract from risk factors |
| Child-responsiveness | Child is responsive, content, and appears to be attached to the parent(s) | Child is sometimes responsive, content some of the time | Child may be unresponsive and withdrawn and is obviously unhappy a great deal of the time |
| Child's perception of being cared for | Child seems to have expectation that he or she will be cared for | Child sometimes seems to expect to be cared for | Child seems to distrust mother and may withdraw or act out for attention |
| Parent's/family's openness to intervention | Parent is willing to use the services and to try out suggestions. Parent is open to interventionist | Parent is somewhat ambivalent about using the services and about the interventionist | Family rejects services and may be suspicious of interventionist |

| | | | |
|---|---|---|---|
| Use of coping strategies/ defense mechanisms | Parent uses coping strategies rather than defensive responses most of the time | Parent uses higher order defenses such as repression and sublimation | Parent uses primitive defenses such as splitting and projection |
| Self-reflectivity | Parent can be self-reflective | Parent exhibits some self-reflectivity except in certain areas of functioning | Parent lacks capacity for self-reflectivity |
| Capacity for empathy | Parent has good capacity for empathy for the child | Parent is only able to be empathetic toward the child in certain situations | Parent shows no empathy for the child when he or she is upset and sad |
| Locus of control | Parent has internal locus of control and strong sense of self-efficacy | Parent has mixed locus of control and has some sense of self-efficacy in certain situations | Parent has an external locus of control, and sense of self-efficacy is very low |
| Parental self-confidence | Parent exhibits realistic self-confidence about parenting | Parent tends to be anxious and to judge him- or herself to be a bad parent | Parent's self-confidence about parenting is very low or extremely high and parent demonstrates unrealistic confidence about parenting |
| Past history of being parented | Parent's history of being parented was positive or parent has resolved any trauma | Some issues from past history impeding parent's ability to respond to child at times | Parent has a history of unresolved loss and trauma that is significantly impeding his or her ability to respond to child |
| Parent–child interactions | Parent–child interactions are warm, sensitive, and responsive | Interaction is sometimes sensitive and responsive but can be rejecting | Interactions are insensitive, ignoring of the child's cues, and hostile |
| Family relationships | Family interactions seem to be warm and caring; family members have ways to deal with conflict | Family interactions are questionable but are manageable | Very conflictual, even violent, family relationships and no ways to deal with problems |
| Emotion regulation | Parent has good emotion regulation | Parent has some difficulty with emotion regulation | Parent frequently loses control of his emotions or is very depressed, anxious, or angry |

*(continued)*

**Table 1.6.**   *(continued)*

| Characteristic or variable | Level of risk | | |
| --- | --- | --- | --- |
| | Low risk | Moderate risk | High risk |
| Attributions of the child and beliefs about child development | Parent has positive attributions of the child and adequate knowledge of child development | Parent's attributions of the child and beliefs about child development tend to be distorted but are not totally negative | Parent's attributions of the child and beliefs about child development are distorted and very negative and hostile |
| Parental intelligence | Parent has average to above average intelligence | Parent may have some cognitive limitations | Parent has significant cognitive limitations and thinks very concretely |
| Problem-solving ability | Parent has good problem-solving skills and ability to plan and organize around issues | Parent has some problem-solving skills and ability to plan but can be impulsive at times | Parent is very impulsive. Does not think things through and may place child and self at risk as a consequence |
| Cultural beliefs | Cultural beliefs and practices are protective of child | Some distortions about the child occur because of cultural beliefs, but are not destructive | Cultural beliefs about the child could lead to harm (e.g., parent hold beliefs about the need for harsh corporal punishment to bring a child under control) |

*Note: Most of these characteristics/variables may refer to just one or both parents

## CONCLUSION

In this chapter, a number of types of risks and possible protective factors are described as well as how they can affect developmental outcomes for children. Studies are also included that have helped to elucidate the process by which various risks can lead to developmental difficulties and various emotional, social, and behavioral problems in the children. These include the effect of the number and type of risks that the child is exposed to. The last sections of the chapter describe a number of psychological characteristics of parents that can affect parent–child interactions and various characteristics of the family that, as proximal factors, can dramatically affect the development of children. These characteristics are described in more detail in Sections II and III of this book, and strategies and interventions are discussed that can be used by service providers to improve them when they are placing a child's development at risk. A list of measures assessing parent–child interactions and psychological functioning is described in Appendix A.1.

# Selected Assessment Instruments

## ASSESSING INTERACTIONS AND THE PSYCHOLOGICAL FUNCTIONING OF PARENTS

In addition to the suggestions made for assessing parent–infant/child interaction and the psychological functioning of parents in this chapter, it may sometimes be necessary for clinical reasons to explore them in more depth because a great deal of concern arises about a particular area. This concern could, for example, be about postpartum depression or about a parent's external locus-of-control that seems to be getting in the way of her trying to improve her parenting behavior or to discipline her child.

Most of the tests listed in Table A.1 are parent-report measures and a few are based on the observation of parent–infant/child interactions. These measures typically have adequate to good psychometric properties that would enable them to be used for evaluation of interventions or programs.

**Table A.1.** Selected measures of parent–child interactions and the psychological functioning of parents

| Tool/instrument | Age range | Items/administration time | General description | Psychometric properties |
|---|---|---|---|---|
| **Defensive Functioning** | | | | |
| Ego Function Assessment Scale (EFA) (Bellak, Hurvich, & Gediman, 1973) | Adults | 10 questions scored on a scale from 1 (*poor*) to 7 (*excellent*) or, alternatively, on a scale from 1 (*poor*) to 13 (*excellent*)<br><br>Individual administration<br><br>The manual reports that this instrument is not easily learned and is cumbersome to use. Administration time not reported but is expected to be about 10 minutes per scale | Designed to assess 12 ego functions that were thought to be necessary and sufficient to describe the personality of the individual. Assesses functioning in areas of 1) reality testing, 2) judgment, 3) sense of reality, 4) regulation of affect and impulses, 5) object relations, 6) thought processes, 7) adaptive regression in the service of the ego, 8) defensive functioning, 9) stimulus barrier, 10) autonomous functioning, 11) synthetic integrative functioning, and 12) mastery/competence. | Although the manual includes no information about its reliability, the authors state that the EFA is a reliable and valid quantitative technique. The minimal evidence that does exist regarding the EFA's reliability and validity suggests that they are modest.<br><br>The authors suggest various uses of the EFA in areas such as Professional Standards Review Organizations and third-party funding, forensic psychiatry and legal responsibility, the monitoring of psychotherapeutic drugs, research and planning in psychotherapy, and psychological testing. |
| Sentence Completion Test of Ego Development (SCT) (Loevinger, 1979; 1985) | Adults | 36 question stems to complete | Assesses ego development based on nine stages ranging from "impulsive" to "integrated" | Inter-rater reliability 72%<br><br>Internal consistency is approximately .85. The median item validity for women is approximately .50; for men it is approximately .45. The difference in item validity is completely accounted for by the difference in variability. Correcting for the difference in variability brings the median validity for men to .52, or alternatively, takes the median validity for women down to .44.<br><br>The SCT has substantial correlation with tests of related concepts. |

## Self-Reflectivity and Empathy for the Child

| | | | | |
|---|---|---|---|---|
| Caregiver's Mind-Mindedness (MM) (Meins, Fernyhough, Fradley, & Tuckey, 2001; Meins et al., 2003). | Parents of any age with young children | 10-minute videotaped infant-mother interaction scored on five dimensions | Assesses five categories of maternal responsiveness or mind-mindedness: 1) maternal responsiveness to infant's direction of gaze, 2) maternal responsiveness to infant's object-directed action, 3) imitation, 4) encouragement of autonomy, and 5) mind-related comments | Construct and predictive validity has been well demonstrated. Caregiver's Mind-Mindedness (MM) has been found to be related to children's theory-of-mind scores or mentalizing abilities. |
| The Parent Development Interview (Aber, Slade, Berger, Bresgi, & Kaplan, 1985; Slade, Bernbach, Grienenberger, Wohlgemuth Levy, & Locker, 2001) | Parent of any age with an infant or young child | 45 items, semi-structured interview The interview takes between 1½–2 hours to administer. | The Parent Development Interview examines parents' representations of their children, themselves as parents, and their relationships with their children. Part of the interview asks parents to describe their children's internal experience, or how their child feels during situations such as separation. | Reliability coefficients range from .80–.95, with a mean of .87. Preliminary studies indicate that a mother's capacity to understand her own or her child's behavior in terms of mental states is significantly related to her own attachment status and her child's attachment status, and to disrupted affective communication in the dyad. Even more important, maternal self-reflectivity appears to mediate the relation between adult and child attachment; thus, a mother's capacity to reflect on and understand her child's internal experience accounts for the relation between attachment status and her child's sense of security and safety. |
| Reflective Self-Function Scale (Fonagy, Steele, Steele, Moran, & Higgitt, 1991; Fonagy, Target, Steele, & Steele, 1998) | Adults | The scale was developed to be used with the Adult Attachment Interview (AAI), which takes about 1–1½ hours to administer. | The Reflective Self-Function Scale assesses "the parents' quality of understanding of another's intentionality." The scale has nine levels ranging from No Reflective Self-Function to Complete Reflective Self-Function, with each level clearly defined in the scale. It cannot be used without training by the scale originators. However, the understanding of the levels of self-reflectivity can be useful clinically. | Comparison of ratings on the Reflective Self-Function Scale and infant attachment have shown that ratings were significantly related to parents' interactions with their infants. Parents with low reflective self-functioning have difficulty being sensitive to and showing understanding and empathy for their infants. |

*(continued)*

**Table A.1.** *(continued)*

| Tool/instrument | Age range | Items/administration time | General description | Psychometric properties |
|---|---|---|---|---|
| Sense of competence | | | | |
| | | | **Sense of Competence and Maternal Self-Confidence** | |
| Internal/External Locus of Control Scale (Rotter, 1966) | Adults | 29 items, 10 minutes | Designed to assess the individual's perception of events as caused by factors inside one's self or by external forces beyond one's control. Two independent factors have been found: General Control and Political Control. | Test–retest correlations are high. Concurrent validity with other scales measuring similar constructs has been found. |
| Pearlin Sense of Mastery Scale (Pearlin & Schooler, 1978) | Adolescents and adults | 7 items, 5 minutes | The Pearlin Sense of Mastery Scale is a brief measure that can assess the extent to which an individual feels in control of life as opposed to feeling ruled by fate. There are 7 items with a 4-point rating from Strongly Agree to Strongly Disagree. Scores are additive, and higher scores indicate greater control. | Cronbach alpha coefficients range from .73 to .80 for each item. Test–retest reliabilities of .66 have been reported. Stressful events such as job loss have been shown to reduce sense of personal efficacy. |
| Rosenberg Self-Esteem Scale (RSES) Rosenberg, 1965, 1979) | Adolescents grade levels 9–12 and adults. Has recently been used with grade-school children | 10- and 7-item versions available; 5 minutes | The RSES is a multidimensional measure of self-esteem that assesses an individual's sense of acceptance and self-worth. Subjects are asked to rate items on a 5-point scale. Possible scores on self-acceptance and self-worth range from 1 (*low self-esteem*) to 5 (*high self-esteem*). High self-esteem signifies that the individual respects him or herself as worthy; low self-esteem reflects both lack of self-respect and feelings of inadequacy.<br><br>The RSES has been widely used in psychological research. | The RSES was standardized on a sample of 5,024 high school students. Internal consistency of .77 for the total score has been reported. Concurrent validity has been established by a demonstrated high relationship between self-concept and depressed affect. Test–retest reliability of .61 over 7 months has been reported. The RSES is a strong predictor of delinquency, unwed pregnancy, drug use, and so forth. |

| Measure | Population | Description | Reliability/Validity |
|---|---|---|---|
| Tennessee Self-Concept Scale–2nd Edition (TSCS-2) (Fitts & Warren, 1996) | Ages 7–90 | 82 items on Adult form and 76 items on Child form; self-administered either in a group or individual settings for 10–20 minutes. Can be scored by hand in 10 minutes and includes a profile sheet to graph results. Provides excellent interpretative resources. Service available for computerized scoring and test interpretation | The TSCS-2 is designed as a multi-dimensional self-concept assessment instrument. Changes from the previous version include dropping some scales (e.g., Psychopathology, General Maladjustment), reducing the number of items (100 to 80), including a Child version (7–14 years) and an Adult version (13–90 years), renorming using 1,944 adults and 1,396 children, and providing substantially improved guidance for interpreting the scores. It is claimed that there are no sex, ethnic, education, or socioeconomic differences in the means, although the scores increase with age (with a marked change occurring at age 18; hence the Adult and Child versions). | Reliability has been estimated using Cronbach's alpha, with internal consistencies ranging from a low of .73 on the Social Self-Concept scale to a high of .93 on Total Self-Concept. Test-retest reliability (over a period of 1 to 2 weeks) for both the Adult and Child Forms is slightly lower, with scores ranging from .47 to .82 for the Adult form and .55 to .83 on the Child form. An extensive section of the manual provides adequate evidence of the construct validity in the form of principal components analysis. Concurrent validity information shows acceptable levels of correlations of the TSCS with other psychological measures. |

**Maternal self-confidence**

| Measure | Population | Description | Reliability/Validity |
|---|---|---|---|
| Maternal Self-Report Inventory (MSI) (Shea & Tronick, 1988) | Any mother with a newborn | Long form: 100 items Short form: 26 items; 10 minutes for short version | The MSI measures dimensions of perceived areas of competence including Caretaking Ability, General Ability and Preparedness for Mothering Role, Acceptance of Baby, Expected Relationship with Baby, Parental Acceptance, Image and Health, and Feelings Concerning Pregnancy, Labor, and Delivery. | The measure was validated with a sample of 30 mothers of healthy newborns, 1 month after delivery. Concurrent validity was demonstrated with correlations of the total MSI scale with another self-esteem measure of .75. Mothers of healthier infants had higher scores on the scale. |
| Parenting Sense of Competence Scale (PSOC) (Johnston & Mash, 1989) | Any parent regardless of age with infants or children of any age | 17 items; 5 minutes | The PSOC has parents rate themselves on a 6-point scale on items designed to measure parents' ability to meet the demands of parenting situations. The scale taps two aspects of parenting: 1) satisfaction with parenting, including frustration and anxiety; and 2) efficacy, reflecting competence, problem-solving ability, and capability in the parenting role. It can be used with parents with infants and children of all ages. | Cronbach alpha coefficients for reliability range from .82 to .87 for the two scales. The measure has been found to correlate positively with two factors on a maternal attitude scale and negatively with infant difficulty. |

*(continued)*

**Table A.1.** (*continued*)

| Tool/instrument | Age range | Items/administration time | General description | Psychometric properties |
|---|---|---|---|---|
| | | **Sense of Competence and Maternal Self-Confidence** (*continued*) | | |
| *Maternal self-confidence (continued)* | | | | |
| Toddler Care Questionnaire (TCQ) (Gross & Rocissano, 1988; Gross, Fogg, Webster-Stratton, Garvey, Julion, & Grady, 2003) | Any mother regardless of age with a toddler | 38 items; 5 minutes | The TCQ measures "maternal confidence," which is defined as the mother's perception of her effectiveness in managing a series of tasks or situations relevant to raising her toddler. Mothers rate their confidence in their ability to perform parenting tasks specific to their children. Ratings range on a 5-point scale from *Very little confidence* to *Quite a lot of confidence*. The items are summed to get a total score. Higher scores indicate greater maternal confidence. | Researchers have reported internal consistency, with Cronbach's alpha reliability estimated from .91 to .95 and test–retest reliability of .87 over a 4-week interval.<br><br>A positive correlation has been found between maternal confidence and the mother's knowledge of child development and parenting. Negative relationships between TCQ scores and the Beck Depression Inventory and dimensions of difficult toddler temperament have been found.<br><br>Validity of the TCQ has been supported in clinical trials showing improvements in TCQ scores following parent training interventions that were maintained up to 1-year post-intervention. |

Social Support

| | | | | |
|---|---|---|---|---|
| Perceived Social Support from Friends (PSS-FR) and Family (PSS-FA) Scales (Procidano & Heller, 1983) | Adults | The original instrument includes two scales: a 20-item Friends scale and a 20-item Family scale. | Assesses perceived support given by friends and family. Participants answer each question "yes," "no," or "don't know." | High correlation with a number of other family assessment tests. Further psychometric analyses were conducted to identify a reduced measurement that would adequately assess general support from family and friends. The results of these analyses produced two 7-item measures. The internal consistency for the Family scale (.84) and for the Friends scale (.81) is acceptable. Test–retest reliability is also good for both the Family ($r = .94$) and the Friends ($r = .88$) scales. |
| Social Provisions Scale (SPS) (Cutrona & Russell, 1989) | Adults | 6-item version available, which asks one question about each component. Participants are asked to rate the degree that each of the components is provided.<br><br>5 minutes | Multidimensional self-report instrument that offers the possibility of discriminating between six distinct types of social support and assesses global support. Two questions for each component rated on 7-point scale covers 6 components or "provisions" of social support: 1) attachment, 2) social integration, 3) opportunity for nurturance, 4) reassurance of worth, 5) reliable alliance, and 6) guidance. Each provision is assessed by four items, two that describe the presence and two that describe the absence of the provision. | Reliability for the total support score was .92, with reliabilities of the four-item subscales ranging from .76 to .84. Confirmatory factor analysis supports the six-factor structure of the measure, and consistent differences in patterns of association with various outcome variables have been found for the six provisions.<br><br>Chronbach's alpha is .65, with concurrent correlations ranging from .3 to .6. The discriminant validity of the scale has been demonstrated against measures of mood (e.g., depression), personality (e.g., introversion–extraversion, neuroticism), and social desirability. Validity studies show the scale to be related to life satisfaction, stress, and loneliness measures. Several studies provide evidence for the validity of the Social Provisions Scale among adolescent mothers, older adults, public school teachers, and hospital nurses. |

*(continued)*

45

**Table A.1.** (*continued*)

| Tool/instrument | Age range | Items/administration time | General description | Psychometric properties |
|---|---|---|---|---|
| | | **Unresolved Loss and Trauma** | | |
| Atypical Maternal Behavior Instrument for Assessment and Classification (AMBIANCE) (Bronfman, Parsons, & Lyons-Ruth, 2000) | Parents with their 12- to 24-month-old infants | Coding system used for scoring 10–20 minutes of parent–child interaction.<br><br>20 minutes to score | The instrument scores five dimensions of parent behaviors that indicate a disruption in ability to respond in a manner that provides the infant with an effective strategy for eliciting care: 1) affective communication errors; 2) role-reversal/boundary confusion; 3) fearful, dissociated, disoriented, or disorganized behavior; 4) intrusiveness/negativity; and 5) withdrawal from the child.<br><br>In addition, the AMBIANCE provides a) a summary score obtained by adding scores for each of the five dimensions; b) a qualitative 7-point scale for level of disrupted communication; and c) a bivariate classification for disrupted or not-disrupted communication.<br><br>The interaction is scored for "fr" behaviors (i.e., those that are frightened or frightening). Two types of disrupted communication are identified: 1) Intrusive/Self-Referential (frightening) or 2) Helpless/Fearful (frightened). | "Fr" behaviors are correlated with infant disorganization, which is related to psychopathology in longitudinal studies. |

| Measure | Population | Description | Psychometrics |
|---|---|---|---|
| Childhood Trauma Questionnaire (CTQ) Bernstein & Fink (1998) | Adults | Designed to assess the frequency and severity (0 = never true, 5 = very often true) of different types of abuse and neglect that took place when the client was growing up. A total score measures the extent of maltreatment and 5 empirically derived factor scores measure emotional and physical abuse, sexual abuse, emotional neglect, and physical neglect. | Internal consistencies range from .79 to .95. Test–retest reliabilities range between .80 and .88. Good convergent validity with measures of disturbance |
| Impact of Event Scale (IES) (Horowitz, 1986) | Adults | Widely used questionnaire measuring trauma-related intrusion and avoidance. Individuals rate the frequency of each symptom within the past 7 days on a four-point scale ranging from 0 (not at all experienced) to 3 (often experienced) | Split-half reliability of .86, test–retest reliability of .87 and alphas for the subscales of .78 and .80 have been reported |
| The Adult Attachment Interview (AAI) (Main & Goldwyn, 1994) | Adults, but has been used with adolescents and with children as young as 10 years of age | 21 questions for parents, 18 questions for non-parents<br><br>1–2 hours depending on responses<br><br>The AAI is intended to assess the individual's state of mind with respect to attachment and to elicit unconscious material. Individuals are asked about discipline, whether they experienced abuse, loss and other trauma. Individuals can be classified as Autonomous, Dismissive, or Preoccupied. They can also be identified as Unresolved/Disorganized or may show no evidence of this. | The AAI classifications have been found to show a similar distribution to infants' and toddlers' quality of attachment. This distribution varies according to setting (i.e., whether the sample is clinical or nonclinical), level of risk, and socioeconomic status. Significant stability from 2–3 months apart have been found ranging from 78%–95%. The AAI is predictive of caregiving behavior of the adult, and somewhat less predictive, but still significantly, of the infant's behavior in the Strange Situation. The overall correspondence between coherence versus incoherence in a parent's interview and secure versus insecure Strange Situation response of the infant to that parent is very strong, yielding an effect size of 1.06. |

(continued)

**Table A.1.** *(continued)*

| Tool/instrument | Age range | Items/administration time | General description | Psychometric properties |
|---|---|---|---|---|
| **Parent–Infant–Child Interactions (see also Parent–Child Interaction measures under Emotion Regulation)** | | | | |
| Home Observation of the Environment (HOME) (Caldwell & Bradley, 1984) | Adults of any age with young children. Two versions—one regarding children from birth to 3 years and the other, children from 3 to 6 years | 45–55 items usually completed during a home visit lasting about one hour. Information needed to score the inventory is obtained through observation and interview done in the home with the child and the child's primary caregiver. | Designed to assess the quality of stimulation and support available to a child in the home environment. Measures constructs such as maternal responsiveness, involvement and acceptance of the child, organization of the child's physical environment, and opportunity for a variety of stimulation. Used with a variety of cultural groups and uses observation and interview | Interrater reliabilities range from .75 to .95 and HOME scores correlate substantially with children's scores on cognitive tests. For example, the HOME correlated at age 3 years with the Stanford-Binet test of Intelligence (.59) and with the Illinois Test of Psycholinguistic Abilities Scale .57 for African American children and .74 for Caucasian children. |
| Nursing Child Assessment Feeding and Teaching Scales (NCAFS and NCATS) (Barnard, 1979) | Adults with children from birth to 3 years. Two versions—one to assess feeding interaction, the other to assess teaching interaction | 6 specific categories including four for the parent and two for the child. 10 minutes for interaction and time for scoring; requires training to administer and score | Categories assessed: For parents: 1) sensitivity to the child's cues, 2) ability to alleviate the infant's distress, and 3) ability to mediate the environment in ways that foster cognitive development, and 4) ability to mediate the environment in ways that foster social/ emotional development. For infant: 1) ability to produce clear cues for the caregiver and 2) ability to respond to the caregiver | Reliability has been found to be .83 for the total parent score. In some studies the scale has distinguished between pre-term, failure-to-thrive, and full-term infants' IQs at 2 years. Both scales have demonstrated strong internal consistency and test–retest reliability for the caregiver and child total scores and for most sub-scales. |

| Measure | Population | Description | Reliability/Validity |
|---|---|---|---|
| Parent–Caregiver Involvement Scale (PCIS) (Farran, Kasari, Comfort, & Jay, 1986) | Caregivers of any age; infants and young children from 3–36 months | Eleven items coded for 10 minutes of interaction, sampled either in a laboratory or at home, live or videotaped<br><br>Equally appropriate for mothers of infants with disabilities | The PCIS gives a comprehensive description of caregiver interaction with infants with and without disabilities. Measures 11 aspects of parenting related to the construct of sensitivity. Each is rated for amount, quality, and appropriateness in the context of the dyadic interaction. Each of the behaviors is rated on a 5-point scale for Physical Involvement, Verbal Involvement, Responsiveness to Child, Play Interaction, Control of Activities, Directives and Demands, Relationship Among Activities, Positive Statements, Negative Statements, and Goal Setting. Can be used clinically and for research. | Test–retest reliabilities ranged from .79 to .85 and have been found for aggregate scores obtained 6 weeks apart. |
| Parent–Child Relationship Inventory (PCRI) (Gerard, 1994) | Parents of any age with young children | Scores are obtained for seven content scales: 1) Parental Support, 2) Satisfaction with Parenting, 3) Involvement, 4) Communication, 5) Limit Setting, 6) Autonomy, and 7) Role Orientation; and two validity scales: 1) Social Desirability and 2) Inconsistency<br><br>The PCRI is normative and standardized. The PCRI has an interpretive manual and scoring system. | The PCRI is a self-report inventory that yields a quantified description of the parent–child relationship while giving an overall picture of the subjective quality of relationship. | Alpha coefficients for the PCRI scales range from .70 to .88. Test–retest reliability and construct validity have been demonstrated. |
| Parenting Practices Scale (Strayhorn & Weidman, 1988) | Parents of any age with preschool children | 34 items; 15 minutes | The Parenting Practices scale, a self-report instrument, assesses the favorability of parenting practices with preschool children. The 34 items relate to cognitions of practices of parenting that were selected as affecting the quality of the parent–child relationship. Items are scored from 0–6. The scale has been used for clinical and/or research purposes. | The scale has excellent reliability as well as good internal consistency and 6-month stability. Concurrent validity has been established by demonstration of the scale's ability to distinguish between children with and without behavior problems. |

*(continued)*

**Table A.1.** (continued)

| Tool/instrument | Age range | Items/administration time | General description | Psychometric properties |
|---|---|---|---|---|
| **Emotion Regulation** | | | | |
| Beck Depression Inventory (BDI) (Beck, 1973) | 13 years and up | 21 items with four options per item. Takes 4–10 minutes to complete. | The BDI is the most widely used clinical self-report test of depression. Typically, only the total score is used with guidelines to distinguish between a range from normal to extremely severe depression. Items assess cognitive-affective and somatic-performance aspects of depression. Unfortunately, the test is subject to faking through social desirability. | Test–retest reliability has been found to range from .60 to .83 for nonpsychiatric samples. Strong discriminant validity has been found in a number of studies. Concurrent and construct validity have been reported in a number of studies, with the test correlating highly with other tests of depression and clinical ratings. |
| Coping with Children's Negative Emotions Scales (CCNES) (Eisenberg & Fabes, 1994; Fabes, Eisenberg, Karbon, & Bernzweig, 1994) | Parents with young children ages up to 6 years of age | 12 distressing situations described, 20 minutes | The CCNES assesses the degree to which parents perceive themselves as reactive to young children's negative affect in situations. Parents are presented with 12 situations in which children are expected to express distress and negative affect (e.g., being teased and having an injection). Parents are asked to assess on a 7-point scale for each of the situations how they would deal with it (e.g., encourage expression of affect, punitive minimization, problem-focused socialization reaction). Six subscales are derived that reflect the specific types of coping response parents tend to use in these situations. | Measurement of reliability and validity of the CCNES and its subscales are found to be well within the acceptable ranges and test–retest analyses revealed little difference in the mean scores over a 4-month period of time. The CCNES is internally reliable and has sound test–retest reliability. The CCNES is generally a valid instrument that relates to theoretically similar constructs. Concurrent validity analyses revealed that the subscales of the CCNES are generally related in logical ways to other measures with similar or the same constructs. |
| Edinburgh Postnatal Depression Scale (EPDS)(Cox, Holden, & Sagovsky, 1987) | Adolescents and women following childbirth | 10 items with 4 options ranging in degrees; 5 minutes The EPDS is best administered during the second or third month postpartum; | The EPDS is a 10-question self-administered screening tool for postpartum depression. Possible EPDS scores range from 0 to 30. A cut-off score of 14 or above indicates that the mother is depressed and requires further assessment. | Validation studies have shown that mothers who score 14 or more on the EPDS are suffering from a depressive illness of varying severity, and non-depressed mothers do not score above the cut-off score. Reported sensitivity of 86% and specificity of 78% when |

| Measure | Population | Method/Scoring | Description | Reliability/Validity |
|---|---|---|---|---|
| Emotional Availability Scales (EAS) (Biringen, Robinson, & Emde, 1988/1993) | Mothers with children from birth to 6 years of age | 5 dimensions scored on 10 minutes of free play interaction | The EAS assess maternal sensitivity and other interactional characteristics. The Scales focus on behavioral style rather than discrete behaviors. The EAS examines five relationship dimensions: maternal sensitivity, maternal structuring/intrusiveness, maternal overt and covert hostility, and child involvement with the mother. | Interrater reliabilities for various samples have ranged from Cohen's Kappas beginning at .75 for relatively short interactional segments to over .9 for interactions which were longer than 15 minutes. Test–retest reliabilities over several months approach .66–.90. Concurrent validity has been demonstrated with patterns of emotional availability on the scales related to both maternal and infant attachment. Further validation of the EAS has linked emotional availability of scores with peer social interactions and coping strategies in 18 month and 3-year-old children. |
| Parent–Child Early Relational Assessment (ERA) (Clark, 1986) | Parents with children ages 2 months to 5 years | Videotaped interactions of 4–10 minute episodes. Global rating instrument with 6-point Likert scale. Each of six points are behaviorally anchored. 65 items of child and parent interactions scored. Scoring extensive and time consuming. Duration, frequency, and intensity taken into account in each item. | The Parent–Child ERA was developed as a measure of both affective and behavioral aspects of the early parent–child relationship. The measure is intended to measure maternal affect as a regulatory or organizing function for the infant.<br><br>Dyads can be observed during free play, a structured teaching task, a feeding, and a separation and a reunion. Parents are rated on their tone of voice, overall mood, expressed affect, attitude toward the child, affective and behavioral involvement, and parental style. The child is rated on expressed affect and overall mood, behavior and adaptive abilities, activity level, and communication. There are also variables to rate dyadic variables such as synchrony. | Interrater reliability has been reported as ranging from correlations of .59 to .96 for individual items, with a mean interrater correlation across items of .81. With respect to discriminant validity, the maternal affective, involvement, and responsiveness scale of the ERA have been found to differentiate the interactions of mentally ill and well mother–child dyads in two independent studies. ERA scales have also been found to discriminate interactions of schizophrenic and depressed mothers with toddlers with sleep problems and those without. For predictive validity, significant correlations were found between the quality of interactions on the ERA and the child's competence and coping abilities. Other studies have found links with the ERA and child empathy, IQ, and infant attachment security. |

used in the postnatal context. It is a useful screening instrument as long as further assessment takes place when issues are identified.

*(continued)*

**Table A.1.** (continued)

| Tool/instrument | Age range | Items/administration time | General description | Psychometric properties |
|---|---|---|---|---|
| | | **Emotion Regulation (continued)** | | |
| The Center for Epidemiological Studies Depression Scale (CES-D) (Myers & Weissman, 1980) | Adolescents and adults | 20 questions, 5 minutes | The CES-D is a self-report depression symptom scale. The questions are responded to on a 4-point scale and assess the frequency and intensity of symptoms in the last week. The CES-D has been used extensively as a screening instrument for depression in primary care and community based settings. Excellent screen for use in epidemiological studies. | Early validation studies indicated that the CES-D had high internal consistency and good construct validity in both clinical and community samples. Test–retest correlations vary from .48 to .50 after 3 months. The CES-D correlates between .8 and .3 with other depression scales. |
| | | **Parent Cognitions (Knowledge, Beliefs, and Attributions)** | | |
| High Scope Knowledge Scale (Epstein, 1979; 1980a,b). | Parents during pregnancy or with children from birth to 6 years of age | 73 items; 20 minutes. Assessment uses card-sorting technique. Parents sort items of the developmental milestones into piles by age. Can be administered orally by examiner. Choices are then transferred to a scoring sheet. The scores indicate correct, early, or late expectations and can be computed according to various areas of development. | The High Scope Knowledge Scale has been used to assess parents' knowledge of the age of emergence of infant abilities and behaviors. | Correct expectations correlate with supportive mother–child interactions in the first year of life. Early expectations correlate with demanding or controlling style of interactions and late expectations are related to lack of stimulation by young parents. The scale has found that teenage mothers tend to underestimate what infants can do. |

| Measure | Population | Format | Description | Psychometric properties |
|---|---|---|---|---|
| Knowledge of Infant/Child Development Inventories (KIDI) (MacPhee, 1981) | Parents with children from birth to 6 years | Two versions, birth to 3 and 3–6 years; 75 items; 20 minutes | The KIDI was developed to assess parents' knowledge of child development and parenting practices. Sub-scores are obtained for norms and milestones, principles, parental health, and safety. Parents are asked if they agree with or disagree with or are not sure about each of the 48 statements. | A test–retest reliability of .92 for the total score over a 2-week interval has been reported. Reasonable internal consistency has been found, with a coefficient alpha value of .85 for 226 mothers who completed the scale. Evidence for the scale's validity was provided by the finding that mothers scored higher than college students, and in a study in which a correlation of .65 was found between scores on the KIDI and ratings of the quality of mother–infant interaction. |
| Parent Attachment Interview (PAI) (Biringen & Bretherton, 1998) | Parents of young children | Questions with optional probes; 45–90 minutes | The PAI taps parental representations, or internal working models of aspects of the parent–child relationship. Among the topics covered by the PAI are the mother's thoughts and feelings at the time of the baby's birth; the baby's personality during the first 2 months and in the present; separation experiences such as at bedtime and night-time; autonomy-related negotiations; emotion communications between mother and child; intergenerational similarities; and differences in parenting styles, such as similarities and differences in how the mother versus the father handled parenting, whether the mother saw herself in her child, and what she envisioned for the child's adolescent and adult years. Participants are rated on a 9-point sensitivity/insight scale concerning their relationship to their children. | Questionnaire results have been found to be related to findings on temperament questionnaires and also to mothers' descriptions of their children's attention span and sociability. Correlations with self-report measures of maternal personality and emotional state were also found. |

*(continued)*

**Table A.1.** (*continued*)

| Tool/instrument | Age range | Items/administration time | General description | Psychometric properties |
|---|---|---|---|---|
| | | **Parent Cognitions (Knowledge, Beliefs, and Attributions)** (*continued*) | | |
| Parent Attribution Test (PAT) (Bugental, Blue, & Cruzcosa, 1989) | Parents of any age with children up to adolescence | 26 items rated on a 7-point scale; 20 minutes | The PAT assesses the perceived balance of power or control between parents and children. That is, it is concerned with parents' subjective causal analysis of caregiving outcomes. This self-report measure asks parents to rate the importance of potential causes of caregiving outcome on a 7-point rating scale ranging from "not at all important" to "very Important." Questions are framed within a hypothetical interaction (baby-sitting), allowing the instrument to be used with nonparents as well as parents. Items included on the PAT were originally provided by parents (as potential causes of caregiving success or failure) and were grouped into scales on the basis of parental judgments of item similarity: 1) "self" causes that are easily controlled, 2) "self" causes that are not easily controlled, 3) "child" causes that are easily controlled by child and 4) "child" causes that are not easily controlled by child. Gives measure of parents' sense of power of self between themselves and child. | Test–retest stability coefficients have been found of .63 for the measure. Construct validity has been found with PAT scores associated with negative reactivity and increases in the use of force, and negative affect. The scores are also predictive of child abuse. |
| Working Model of the Child Interview (WMCI) (Zeanah & Benoit, 1995) | Any parent regardless of age who is pregnant or has an infant or young child | 16 interview questions; 1–2 hours. Scoring is complex and training is required. | The WMCI is a semi-structured, open-ended interview used to access parents' internal representations or working models of their relationship to a particular child. The interview is scored for 6 scales of parents' representations of their child: 1) richness of detail, 2) openness to change, 3) intensity of involvement, 4) coherence, 5) caregiver sensitivity, and 6) acceptance. Parents are rated as Balanced, Distorted, or Disengaged. | The scales have been shown to predict parental behaviors with their infants similar to the Adult Attachment Interview (AAI). |

**Parent Planning and Problem Solving**

| | | | |
|---|---|---|---|
| Parent Means-End Problem-Solving Instrument (PMPSI) (Wasik, Bryant, & Fishbein, 1980) | Adults with children of any age | 10 items; 30 minutes | In the PMPSI, parents are read the beginning and the end of a story/situation that is commonly faced by parents of young children. Following each reading, the parent is asked to make up the "middle" of the story. The stories are scored on 5 dimensions: 1) total number of items in which relevant solutions were given; 2) total number of relevant solutions; 3) total number of items on which elaboration occurred; 4) total number of solutions on which elaboration did not occur; and 5) total number of content areas in all of the stories. | Inter-rater reliability reported by the authors has ranged from .86 to .93. The 4-week test–retest reliability was shown to be adequate on the dimension of relevant solutions ($r = .65$). The PMPSI has shown discriminant validity on the mean number of relevant solutions between mothers in a low income SES group, mothers from a general community sample, and a heterogeneous group of mothers from a day care center. |

## CHAPTER 2

# Evaluation of the Effectiveness of Various Early Intervention Approaches

## *Implications for Practice*

As discussed in Chapter 1, children living in multi-risk families are at risk for developing a variety of cognitive, behavioral, emotional, and social difficulties. These difficulties are often striking, and may first appear in infants who were born healthy and are not biologically at risk or may occur during children's first year of life. The stresses faced by many parents such as living in poverty and in violent neighborhoods, being unemployed, and having few supports make providing consistent nurturing to their children challenging. Often, parents in multi-risk families have experienced recent trauma and loss as well as abuse and neglect as they were growing up. Some may also be struggling with mental health challenges such as anxiety or depression or have character disorders of various kinds. These families, in order to meet the needs of their children, require complex, multi-dimensional approaches to prevention and early intervention that are selected on the basis of the specific problems they face. These strategies must be integrated at a theoretical and systems level so as to optimize their effectiveness. In general, on the one hand, early childhood *prevention* programs are designed to increase the probability of children having a typical developmental trajectory and to prevent the development of disorders. Early *intervention* programs, on the other hand, have typically been designed to provide services to families and children when there are clear indications that a child is already showing atypical development or emotional or social difficulties or there are significant issues within the family that indicate that a child is significantly at risk for developing difficulties. As a consequence of both approaches working to serve very young children, the differences between the two can at times be blurred. This chapter reviews some of the approaches that have been used to meet the needs of multi-risk families and describes some conclusions that can be made from the results of various early intervention evaluation studies.

Governments and agencies involved in providing prevention and early intervention, in order to enhance outcomes for children, want to ensure that programs provide services that are empirically supported approaches or "best practices." They also want to ensure that funding dollars are spent in the best way possible or on interventions that are most likely to improve outcomes for children. A number of barriers hinder the search for finding simple answers to determining the best or most effective ways to improve outcomes for children who are exposed to multiple risks, however. These difficulties include the complexity of programs, the challenge of determining the aspects of the program that made a difference if improvements are found, and the lack of methodologically sound evaluation of many of the programs. For many service providers, there is a great deal of confusion about how to organize programs, what intervention strategies to use with individual families, and how old a child should be for optimum intervention effectiveness. Uncertainty also surrounds the efficacy of short-term interventions compared with those that are longer term.

The next sections of this chapter discuss evidence on the efficacy of various approaches to prevention and early intervention, and based on that information, outline some principles of successful early intervention. Because this book focuses on interventions with a more clinical emphasis that are suitable for working with families contending with multiple risks, these types of interventions are described in the most detail.

## THE GOALS AND COMPONENTS OF EARLY INTERVENTION PROGRAMS

Although the ultimate goal of prevention and early intervention approaches is to enhance the development of children, they are typically focused on enhancing one or more aspects of the parent–child system (see Chapter 1, Figure 1.5). These are 1) the child, 2) the parent 3) the parent–child interaction or relationship, or 4) aspects of both parent and child functioning.

In addition to the different focus or goals of early intervention programs, they also vary in terms of a number of other features and program components:

- *Population:* Whereas some programs are provided as universal interventions or are open to all families with infants and young children living in a particular geographic area, others are provided only for certain populations such as for low birth weight infants (LBWs), parents with drug addictions, or disadvantaged families on welfare.

- *Outcomes:* Although different parts of the parent–child system are targeted, the outcomes that the program is focusing on, and therefore, evaluating, vary significantly; for instance, the program may be focusing on such variables as the incidence of child abuse, the number of parents on welfare, interactions of parents with their children, and various child development outcomes.

- *Location:* Differences are also found in terms of the location or where the intervention takes place; for example, some programs are provided in homes, some in child-care centers, and some in early intervention centers.

- *Professional background:* The qualifications, discipline, training, and other characteristics of those conducting the intervention also vary significantly, with some interventions provided by community representatives, paraprofessionals, public health nurses, early childhood educators, mental health professionals, or professionals from other disciplines.

- *Timing, duration, and intensity:* Programs also vary according to the timing, duration, and intensity of the program. Some programs are provided only during a mother's pregnancy, whereas others are available for infants, toddlers or preschoolers and are of different duration. Programs can be limited to a certain number of sessions, and also vary as to whether the intervention is provided weekly or less frequently.

- *Theoretical perspectives and assumptions:* The agency, affiliation, and the program's theoretical perspectives and assumptions can also be very different. Some may emphasize social support, community development, early childhood education, health promotion, or more psychodynamic approaches.

- *Type of intervention:* Although it is often the least well articulated, the type of intervention provided is critical. Some common types include specialized childcare, health promotion, parent support, parenting groups, parent education, or mental-health interventions.

- *Number of interventions used, or program complexity or flexibility:* Some programs use only one approach such as childcare or a certain clinical intervention for all families, whereas others are multidimensional or include several types of interventions in the one program, or are varied according to the needs of the particular child and family. This last component has often not been well-articulated; some programs use a highly structured and predetermined curriculum whereas others prefer to remain nondirective and to move flexibly between various intervention modalities. In the more flexible programs, interventionists design the content of the intervention according to an assessment of the needs of the child and family at that particular time and reassess and adapt the intervention periodically. The next section discusses some challenges of evaluating early intervention programs and follows this with a brief review of the findings of various evaluation studies.

## CHALLENGES OF EVALUATION

Early intervention programs have been researched extensively, but are very difficult to evaluate scientifically for a number of reasons. Table 2.1 presents a summary of these challenges. Some of these challenges of evaluating early intervention programs are described next.

Historically, randomized controlled trials (RCT) have been considered the optimal or the gold standard experimental design for evaluating prevention and early intervention programs. In RCT, individuals are randomly assigned to different types of intervention programs or to a nonintervention control group. Proponents of RCT do not accept observational studies as methodologically sound. This has created an insurmountable barrier for some programs because, for many universal programs that make strategies of intervention available to all families, it has not been possible to use this kind of research design because it requires a nonintervention group. Even if it were possible to include a group that would not receive intervention, many feel that not intervening with some families creates an impossible ethical dilemma. In addition, for the many programs that use multiple types of interventions, it would be impossible for these programs to have a large

**Table 2.1.**  Challenges of evaluating early intervention programs

| Challenge | Effect on findings |
| --- | --- |
| Difficulty with using randomized control trials (RCT) leads to more quasi-experimental designs | Unclear if the results are due to the effects of the program or other variables |
| Difficulty finding suitable matched comparison groups | May be comparing the effects of a program in one area to effects of a different program in another area |
| Problem finding large-enough sample sizes | May have minimal sample sizes, making the consideration of the effect on outcomes of a number of variables difficult to measure |
| Problem finding appropriate tests and the tendency to use paper and pencil measures completed by parents | Tests may not have adequate validity or reliability or may not be measuring the variable the researchers intend to measure |
| The service providers collecting data know the experimental group the parent and child are assigned to | Results are invalid because of the possibility of unintentional skewing of results by service providers collecting the data |
| Staff in many community-based programs are resistant to evaluation | May only accept "nonthreatening" measures that do not evaluate the critical variables |
| Failure to assess appropriate outcome variables | Cannot make conclusions about effects that are not measured. May miss critical data |
| Problems differentiating the effects of various program components | May not be able to say which program component led to a positive or negative outcome, so does not contribute to program planning |
| Attrition rates and the number of sessions attended are often not reported | May not be meaningful results if, for example, all multi-risk families dropped out or attended only a few of the sessions and only less at-risk families were retained |
| Problems with assessing long-term effects of programs | Often, results that are positive initially drop away later or some improvements may not be evident until later, so erroneous conclusions about program effectiveness may be made |
| Few studies of long-term effects are available | This makes it difficult to assess possible "sleeper" effects of the program |

enough sample of families participating in each type of intervention to meet the stringent requirements of this method.

Another well-accepted research design uses comparison groups living in the same area or in areas with similar sociodemographics rather than control groups. This approach also presents challenges, however. If the comparison group is composed of families who did not want to be involved in the intervention or who moved into the area after the intervention commenced, they may not be comparable with families in the intervention group on a variety of variables. For comparison groups in other areas, it is seldom possible to ensure that families are not receiving intervention from other agencies or individuals. If they are receiving other interventions, the research is really comparing various types of interventions rather than the success of the intervention versus no intervention or the effect of using regular community resources alone. Adding to these challenges, populations in many community programs are extremely heterogeneous. As well, the lack of large sample sizes often does not allow for stratification of subjects in order to examine the differential effects of the program according to such diverse variables as age, race, gender, education of parents, and the economic condition of the families receiving the services. Because of this, it has often been difficult to take into account the diversity of families that receive services from one program and the differences in program effects related to various characteristics of the families. Other evaluations have suffered from a lack of adequate measures that are useful with multicultural populations, that are acceptable to families, and that can document change.

Often, subjectivity versus objectivity is an issue. Evaluators may use questionnaires that are to be completed by parents, and yet it cannot be assumed that parents' perceptions will accurately reflect a child's behavior, symptoms, or intellectual capacity. In addition, measures are often administered by program staff who are aware of the group assignments of the subjects, and thus their objectivity may be compromised. In many community-based programs, program staff are resistant to evaluation because they see the measures and process as too intrusive for families.

As was discussed earlier in this chapter, programs vary in terms of what they are targeting for intervention. Thus, another major flaw in evaluating some programs has been that during the program's outset, only certain outcome variables were selected for examination; thus, valuable data that would indicate success in other areas are lost and the number of potentially improved variables are reduced. Many evaluations have not been able to differentiate the effects of various program components from those of others and often ignore the number, content, and quality of each component as significant variables.

Another very important flaw in the reporting of findings is that many programs that are designed for multi-risk families have difficulty involving some families, or once families are involved, they leave, which causes very high attrition rates. This makes it very difficult to evaluate the overall effectiveness of these programs (Arcia, Keyes, Gallagher, & Herrick, 1993; Hauser-Cram, Warfield, Upshur, & Weisner, 2000; Sontag & Schacht, 1993). Other parents may begin an intervention but only attend sporadically so that the percentage of available program components attended is low or there are limited dose effects (Erikson, 1991). This has made it very difficult to measure and evaluate the effect of these differences on outcomes (Brinker, 1997). Most of the published studies that report positive findings do not report these attrition rates, any lack of improvement, or possible negative or detrimental effects on families. Similarly, the size of program effects is seldom considered in reporting results. This is important because although outcomes may be in a positive direction, the program effects are often quite small, indicating that the program produced a positive trend but not necessarily a significant effect. Few pro-

grams have followed participants for more than 3 years after intervention terminated. Long-term results are particularly important in order to evaluate a program's success in reducing risks and increasing children's resilience to psychosocial
stressors. Also, only a handful of studies have replicated a program and evaluated
the program effects with various populations and in different communities.

Although evaluation research has been able to look at success primarily in
terms of outcomes, it has been very difficult to study the effectiveness of interventions that are more prescriptive and vary according to the particular needs of
families because the intervention cannot be readily codified in manuals. Also,
many interventions are provided by untrained therapists, who may not understand the criteria or follow a required frame of reference (Westen, Novotny, &
Thompson-Brenner, 2004).

Focusing on techniques of intervention has often also ignored therapist characteristics, qualities of the setting, quality of the parent–interventionist relationship, and level of family dysfunction, all of which may be critically important in
determining the success of intervention (Barnard, 1998; Pharis & Levin, 1991).
Because of limitations on the conclusions that can be drawn from single studies,
the use of meta-analytic methods that consider a large number of outcome measures drawn from across a number of studies is increasing. Although this strategy
may be a useful method, it means the loss of information on the effectiveness of
particular program approaches, and it is difficult at times to discern study differences in terms of important conditions of intervention such as setting, interventionist characteristics and training, and adherence to the intervention approach
(Fonagy, Target, Coltrell, Phillips, & Kurtz, 2002; Kazdin, 2000a).

## EARLY INTERVENTION
## PROGRAMS AND THEIR EFFECTIVENESS

As has been pointed out, early intervention programs vary significantly in terms
of their intervention goals and the types of interventions used. During the 1960s,
the focus of the majority of early intervention tended to be on improving a child's
IQ scores or developmental level. More recently, multidimensional approaches
and two-generational programs have grown in popularity that consider the whole
family and focus on improving broader child and parent outcomes. This has resulted in some highly visible and successful programs and agreement that the
early years are an important focus for intervention. They also provide a unique
opportunity for improving child development outcomes. From these studies a
number of principles and values have emerged that are beginning to give some direction for providing for the needs of multi-risk families and for developing programs to meet them.

Early intervention programs fall under several categories or types. In some
programs, the exclusive or primary intervention used is provided at a center or in
the home (e.g., Olds, Chamberlain, & Tatelbaum, 1986), whereas in others, home
visiting is not used or is combined with other center-based strategies such as parenting groups, competence-building initiatives for parents, more clinical initiatives, and community development approaches. Information on various types of

early intervention programs and more short-term focused and multidimensional approaches and their effectiveness is outlined next.

## Child-Focused Center-Based Programs

Child-focused programs work directly with young children to improve their chances for positive developmental outcomes and success in school. Some of the programs may also include initiatives for parents such as parenting groups or home visiting to enhance their interactions with their children. These types of programs have provided enriched preschool services for children at risk for compromised development. Enrichment has included special emphasis on providing activities to enhance cognitive, fine and gross motor, language, and social adaptive skills (see Table A.2.1 for a description of these programs and the findings of the evaluations). The research finding of these center-based programs for children are summarized in this section and the program on which the finding is based is also identified and any further relevant references listed.

In a review of 27 intervention programs, more improvements in cognitive development—both short term and long term—were found for children who attended center-based programs than for those who were only provided with home-based interventions (Benasich, Brooks-Gunn, & Clewell, 1992). In general, high-quality early childhood programs that were provided in therapeutic preschools or child cares have consistently shown significant short-term effects on children's cognitive development. However, although early gains of 10 IQ points were typically found, these gains often faded during the elementary school years for graduates of many of these programs (e.g., Carolina Abecedarian Project; Early Training Project; Experimental Variation of Head Start; Infant Health and Development Program; Yale Child Welfare Research Project) (Farran, 2000a).

Nevertheless, longer term effects have often been found in such domains as school achievement, school progress, and educational outcomes. Improvements in the behavioral and socio-emotional functioning of children have also been found for some programs (e.g., Syracuse University Family Development Program). Some follow-up studies of the children into adolescence and adulthood have revealed that program participants had, for example, less criminal involvement and arrests (e.g., Perry Preschool Program). When it has been possible to determine the populations of children who are most likely to benefit from these interventions, it has been found that in groups of children with disabilities, those who have the most severe disabilities typically show the least developmental gains. Children who are at risk due to socioeconomic disadvantage are most responsive to intervention (Brinker, 1992).

When studies have considered the effects of different interventions on outcomes, it has been found that children who begin programs earlier, such as during infancy or their preschool years, and who receive more years of intervention, tend to have better outcomes (e.g., Carolina Abecedarian Project). Only a handful of studies have explored the effectiveness of different curriculum approaches, and those that did had different conclusions (e.g., Center-Based Home Visiting Comparison Study; Curriculum Comparison Study; Even Start Family Literacy Program; Louisville Comparison of Three Preschool Curricula) (see Appendix Table A2.4). In some studies the effects were similar for different curricula, but in the

Louisville Comparison of Three Preschool Curriculum study it was found that a very directive approach was not as successful as a more nondirective intervention, and the children who received the intervention had twice as many delinquent acts and poorer relationships with others than did children who received the other interventions (Schweinhart, Weikart, & Larner, 1986). Although most believe that it is beneficial for parents to be involved in their children's programs, in some studies, parent participation did not appear to improve child outcomes over and above direct intervention with the child (e.g., Optimal Growth Project, see Appendix Table A2.3). Project Care, a second-generation of the Carolina Abecedarian project, found that adding a family education home visiting component to the program did not improve outcomes and when it was provided on its own, the children actually had lower scores on outcome measures than did the control group (Vernon-Feagans, 1996).

## Child- and Parent-Focused Home Visiting Programs

Home visiting is not an intervention in itself; rather, the term *home visiting* refers to a place in which the intervention occurs. Consequently, before an opinion on the efficacy of home visiting can be made, it is crucial to understand what a home visiting intervention entails. Early intervention through home visiting is provided to improve the outcomes of infants with both biological and nonbiological risk factors. Infant conditions of risk have typically included clearly identified conditions at birth such as prematurity; Down syndrome and other chromosomal disorders; and physical disabilities such as cerebral palsy, spina bifida, blindness, or deafness. These programs often provide support to families; carry out and demonstrate physiotherapy, occupational therapy, or speech therapy in the home; and teach parents about medical interventions that may be necessary for their children. Other home visiting programs emphasize working with families in which a child has no identified biological risk but is seen as being developmentally at risk because of a number of parent, family, or sociodemographic factors that are known to compromise a child's development.

The focus of home visiting programs for children with biological risk factors has changed dramatically since the 1980s. Rather than only focusing intervention on the child, a much more family-focused approach is typically used in which the emphasis is on the needs identified by the family and on helping and supporting parents to become the primary interventionists for their infants and young children. Similarly, when service providers are working with families with psychosocial risk factors, the parents are usually involved in selecting goals for the intervention and as partners in supporting their children. Information on some of the best known and well researched home visiting programs is provided in Appendix Table A2.2, and some of the programs are identified in this section to discuss the findings of these programs.

Although it has been difficult to identify clear conclusions about home visiting programs, and disentangling determinants of their effectiveness can be a complex process, some conclusions about their effectiveness and the components that contribute to their success have been identified. Home visiting programs generally have some impact on parent education, employment, and self-sufficiency. Some programs also have a positive effect on parent–child interactions and relationships, with children showing a greater likelihood of developing secure attachments (e.g., Elmira Prenatal and Early Infancy Program; Menninger Infant Project) (Brookes-Gunn, Berlin, & Fuligni, 2000). In general, an inverted U-shaped association has been found between the level of risk and effectiveness of intervention. (See Table 1.5 for an explanation of these levels of risk.) In other words, those least at risk or at low risk and at high risk benefit least from home visiting programs, and those at moderate risk usually show the best outcomes. Home visiting is most effective when it is carried out by professionals, particularly with families who have multiple risks or when parents have been exposed to trauma and loss that has not been resolved or have mental health problems or other challenges (Olds, Henderson, Kitzman, Eckenrode, Cole, & Tatelbaum, 1998; Olds, Robinson, Luckey, O'Brien, Korfmacher, Hiatt, et al., 1999). The services of paraprofessionals may be essential in reaching families from different cultures and ethnic groups, however. Given this, a "blended" model in which professionals and paraprofessionals such as community home visitors work together to share expertise is often most effective (Korfmacher, O'Brien, Hiatt, & Olds, 2000; Wasik & Roberts, 1994). When successful programs are replicated with different populations or in different communities, service providers may have less education than in the original study or the quality of relationships between the staff and participants may not be as positive and, as a consequence, the programs may not produce the same improved outcomes (Olds et al., 1999).

As is the case with programs for children provided in child care and preschools, the more intense, more frequent, and the longer the period of time that home visits are provided, the better the outcomes. Also, mothers who receive both prenatal and postnatal home visits have been shown to benefit more than do those who receive only postnatal visits (e.g., Montreal Home Visitation Program). Longevity of intervention is not an easy goal to reach; as discussed earlier, families at multiple risk tend to drop out of intervention in general, and the same holds true for home visitation. Research has shown that as many as 30%–70% of parents who are at high risk drop out in the first year of intervention, when only about half of the proposed visits have been completed. This indicates that as much effort needs to be put into increasing parents' interest in and motivation to be involved in services as in the content of the interventions. This applies particularly to the initial stages of intervention. In order to affect specific outcomes such as the sensitivity of parent–child interactions and security of attachment, interventions that focus on or target improvement in these outcomes are most successful. In other words, what happens during home visits is essential and needs to be adapted to the identified needs of the child and family. Home visiting alone, without direct intervention with the child, often does not improve child outcomes because it is not focused intensely enough on the child's problem area (e.g., University of California Preterm Infant Study) (Farran, 2000).

## Combination Programs Including Home Visiting and In-Center Programs for Parents

A number of programs have provided a combination of home visiting and various in-center programs focused on enhancing parenting. The additional approaches have included, for example, medical checkups, a telephone service that provides parenting information or support, drop-in centers, video feedback, and parent education groups. (See Appendix Table A2.3 for information on a number of these programs and their evaluations.) The findings from these programs are very similar to those of home visiting only programs, and in general these programs found an increase in continuing education and lower rates of childbearing (e.g., Infant Health and Development Program, Appendix Table A2.1; Yale Child Welfare Project). Also, most projects indicated improved parent–child interactions (Brooks-Gunn et al., 2000). In general, some of the best outcomes are obtained when home visiting is not the only strategy and is augmented by other center-based services (Gomby, Larson, Lewit, & Behrman, 1993). Parents in multi-risk families have been found to need intensive, multidimensional, and specialized approaches to get them involved as well as intensive programs delivered by highly trained professionals to be effective in producing relevant outcomes (e.g., Better Beginnings, Better Futures Project; Menninger Infant Project; Relationship-Based Intervention with At-Risk Mothers) (Olds & Kitzman, 1993). Findings of the Steps Towards Effective Enjoyable Parenting (STEEP) suggest that if the cognitive and emotional status of parents is more impaired, the programs may not be effective without specialized interventions adapted to their needs.

## Two-Generation Programs

Two-generation programs (also known as parent- and child-focused programs) were developed as a way to target the multigenerational, multidimensional, and complex issues of high-risk families. These approaches seek to help families overcome multiple risks by enhancing not only children's current lives but also parents' skills and competencies in order that they may learn to give and continue to provide young children with the best possible start in life. They are also intended to increase parents' sense of self-efficacy and to support them to become economically self-sufficient. These two-generation programs typically include 1) a developmentally appropriate early childhood program; 2) parenting education; and 3) an adult education, literacy, or job skills and training component. Not every program can provide all of these various program components on site, so families may be referred outside the program for child care and/or other services such as job skills and literacy training, making it difficult to monitor their quality and evaluate them. (See Appendix Table A2.4 for information on some of these programs.)

A number of conclusions can be made about these types of programs. Unfortunately, the evidence for the success of two-generation programs is mixed, and no long-term effects have yet been documented, although sleeper effects may be found later. These mixed results are disappointing because the concept makes sense, the programs are well received by families, and participation rates are generally high. As with other programs, the more intensive two-generation programs have produced the best results, suggesting that the programs may need to be matched to the number of risk factors families face and to become more intensive as risks increase (e.g., Child and Family Resource Program; Comprehensive Child Development Program). One of these programs' biggest challenges has been that parents often did not follow through on referrals to outside agencies for certain aspects of the intervention such as literacy and job training. Also, the quality and type of approach may not have been effective in some outside agencies. This may have significantly contributed to the poor outcomes of some studies. Most programs do not improve child outcomes, and any positive trends toward improvement were usually for parents (e.g., Center-Based Home Visiting Comparison Study; Curriculum Comparison Study; Even Start Family Literacy Program).

## Short-Term, Focused Interventions

A number of studies of the effectiveness of more short-term interventions have been carried out. In some evaluations, when two such approaches are compared, researchers have examined the question of which approach works best for whom and with what outcomes. These interventions are sometimes provided in the home or center and in the types of early intervention and prevention programs discussed previously. Others are provided as short-term approaches in community agencies or in more clinical settings when delays, or behavioral, social, or emotional issues in infants and young children have been identified and are being treated. These interventions are described briefly in this chapter, and the results related to their evaluations are summarized in Appendix Table A2.5. Some of the interventions are also described in more detail in Sections II and III of this book.

*Interventions for Improving Parent–Child Interactions and Attachment Relationships*    A number of short-term approaches to enhancing the parent–child interaction and relationship have been used, and are described next.

*Watch, Wait, and Wonder*    Watch, Wait, and Wonder (WWW) is an intervention that takes place over 8–18 sessions. Each session begins with 20 minutes of parent–child play, during which the parent is asked to watch her child, not to intrude, and to follow his lead. The therapist then discusses with the parent what she observed about her child's experience and how she felt during the session. The approach has been compared with a more psychodynamic and family approach and was found to reduce child symptoms such as eating or sleeping problems, to enhance attachment and interactions, to reduce the number of children with disorganized attachment, to enhance infant developmental functioning, and to reduce parental stress (Cohen et al., 1999; Cohen, Lojkasek, Muir, Muir, & Parker, 2002).

*Floor Time*    Floor time is an intervention in which the therapist actively guides the mother or other caregiver in ways to interact with her infant in a sensitive and responsive manner (Hanna & Wilford, 1990). In one study, the approach was compared with a directive sensory integration approach in which infants were trained directly to acquire specific skills such as focusing on an object and self-calming, and parents were helped to cope with the children's symptoms of inattention and irritability (DeGangi & Greenspan, 1997). Floor time was found to be more effective than the directive sensory integration approach in reducing child symptoms.

*Soft Baby Carriers*    One study examined the use of soft baby carriers (e.g., Snugglis) in which the baby was supported close to the mother compared with the use of a hard infant seat in which the baby was placed away from the mother (Anisfeld, Casper, Nozyce, & Cunningham, 1990). Mothers were given the products in the hospital and were asked to use them every day. At 12 months, infants who were carried in the soft baby carriers were more likely to be securely attached.

*Videotape Viewing*    The use of *videotape viewing* is an intervention that focuses on enhancing the parent–infant/child interaction. In one study (McDonough, 1993b, 1995), parents and the therapist watched a videotaped interaction between the parent and infant or child and discussed the interaction. In another study, the intervention was effective in reducing child symptoms, and maternal sensitivity to the children was enhanced. This approach was compared with a more psychodynamic approach and was found to be as effective (Robert-Tissot et al., 1996).

In a very different intervention, mothers in the postpartum period were shown one of two videotapes. The first provided information about infant development and affectionate handling of the newborn, and the second showed basic caregiving skills. Mothers discussed the content of the videos with a nurse. Mothers who saw the video on affectionate handling of their infants became more sensitive to their infants than those who saw the video on basic caregiving skills (Wendland-Carro, Piccinini, & Millar, 1999).

A *videotaped mother–infant interaction* with discussion was also used with a sample of mothers with insecure (dismissive or preoccupied) attachment classifications (Bakermans-Kranenburg, Juffer, & van IJzendoorn, 1998). In addition to viewing the videotape, some of the mothers also received written information about sensitive parenting, whereas another group had an additional discussion about the mother's personal experience of being parented herself. Mothers in both groups were found to be more sensitive toward their infants when they reached 13 months. However, dismissive mothers benefited most from receiving additional written information, whereas preoccupied mothers improved more from additional discussion about their experiences of being parented.

*Direct Coaching of the Interaction*    More *direct coaching of the interaction* has also been used. Van den Boom (1994, 1995) intervened with mothers of infants identified as temperamentally difficult. The intervention focused on enhancing the sensitivity or maternal responsiveness to their infants by helping mothers adjust their behavior to their infants' unique cues by guiding them through various stages of the response process. They were coached to read their infants' cues, to imitate them, and to soothe them when they were upset. The intervention had more success with mothers of temperamentally difficult infants than with adoptive middle-class mothers with infants not identified as irritable (Juffer, Hoksbergen, Riksen-Walraven, & Kohnstamm, 1997) and with mothers from a lower socioeconomic class with non-irritable infants (Meij, 1992). For the mothers with infants who were not irritable, no differences were found for those who received the intervention compared with those who did not, suggesting that mothers with infants who did not have regulatory difficulties were able to respond to their infants sensitively without the direction provided by the intervention (Meij, 1992).

In an intervention that used *coaching the interaction*, the interventionist offered suggestions to the mother via an earpiece microphone from behind a one-way-mirror. Mothers were coached to respond when the infant attended, and to decrease responses when the infant was not attending (Parker-Loewen & Lytton, 1987). The intervention was compared with another in which mothers were given toys for their infants, and no difference in maternal sensitivity between the two approaches was found.

*Interventions Focused on Enhancing Parents' Attributions of Their Children*    Because parental negative attributions of their children are often associated with poor outcomes for children, a number of interventions have been developed to improve parental attributions.

*Cognitive Appraisal Approach*    In one study, a *cognitive appraisal approach* was used that focused on changing parents' negative attributions or their internal working models of their children (Bugental, 1999; Duggan et al., 1999). In an area with a high incidence of abuse, mothers were randomly assigned to one of two intervention approaches or to a control group who only received services available in the community. In one intervention group, mothers received supportive home visiting only. In the other they received home visiting as well as the cognitive appraisal approach. In the latter group, each mother was asked about a problem she was having with her child. She was then encouraged to problem solve about possible reasons for why the problem was happening until she came up with one that did not imply blaming of the child. The mother was then supported to identify a strategy she could use with her child to overcome the problem. Results indicated that the incidence of abuse in the nonintervention control group was 36%, in the standard home visiting only group 20%, while in the group who received home visiting and the attributional augmentation the incidence was only 4%.

*The Brazelton Neonatal Behavioral Assessment*    The *Brazelton Neonatal Behavioral Assessment* (BNBAS) (Nugent & Brazelton, 2000) has been used to enhance parents' attitudes toward their babies and, ultimately, child outcomes. In general, including mothers as active participants in the interaction by teaching them how to elicit their infant's responses is particularly helpful in enhancing their interactions with their infants (Gomes-Pedro, Patricio, Carvalho, Goldschmidt, Torgal-Garcia, & Monteiro, 1995). This approach has been least successful with mothers at greater psychological risk and with those who have less social support and general life satisfaction, however (Beeghly, Brazelton, Flannery, Nugent, Barrett, & Tronick, 1995; Worobey & Belsky, 1986).

*Interventions Focused on Improving Children's Developmental Outcomes*    A number of short-term interventions have focused on improving children's developmental outcomes. Some of these are provided for children with no major developmental disabilities, whereas others have been found to be successful with children who have developmental disorders such as an autism spectrum disorder, behavior problems such as conduct disorder, or emotional disorders such as anxiety or depression.

One intervention or strategy that has been used in a number of different cultures and with a variety of groups of multi-risk infants is *infant massage* (Field, 1998b, 2000). Parents have been shown how to do the massage, and in some studies with infants at multiple risk who have regulatory disorders, prematurity, and exposure to HIV, the infants showed greater weight gain and became less irritable and slept better than infants who were not massaged (Field, 2000; Field & Hernandez-Reif, 2001; Ottenbacher, Muller, Brandt, Heintzelman, Hojem, & Sharpe, 1987). It has also been found that when depressed mothers massage their infants, their face-to-face interactions with their infants improve. When fathers massage their infants, the infants greet their fathers with more eye contact, smiling, vocalizing and reaching behavior (Scholz & Samuels, 1992). Results have been very encouraging, but the challenge has been to identify the underlying physiological changes that contribute to the identified improvements. It is believed that massage stimulates growth because it "leads to a release of gastro-intestinal food absorption hormones, probably stimulated by vagal activity" (Field, 1995, p. 10).

Interventions used to *enhance language development* often rely on the mother or other primary caregiver to implement a program to facilitate children's language development. In some approaches, positive effects have primarily been found in parents' improved ability to facilitate their children's language, but not in overcoming children's language delays (Dale, Crain-Thoreson, Notari-Syverson, & Cole, 1996: Levenstein, Levenstein, Shiminski, & Stolzberg, 1998; Manolson, Ward, & Dodington, 1995; Whitehurst, Falco, Lonigan, Fischel, Valdez-Menchaca, & Caulfield, 1988). In another study, however, parents were found to be nearly as effective as speech pathologists in helping their children to enhance their language (Fey, Cleave, Long, & Hughes, 1993).

In a study aimed at enhancing the outcomes of low-birth-weight (LBW) infants, Barrerra, Doucet, and Kitching (1990) used two different approaches to enhance the infants' development. The first approach emphasized enhancing infant development in five domains, and the second approach emphasized enhancing the mother–infant interaction. Both groups did better than a no-intervention control group, but different effects were found when the infants were 16 months old for the two interventions. The infants in Group 1 showed improvements in social competence, and in Group 2, parent–infant interactions were improved (Barrera, Rosenbaum, & Cunningham, 1986).

For young children with *conduct disorders and aggressive behavior,* cognitive therapy is usually not suitable because children may be too young to be trained to use cognitive strategies. A number of parenting programs have been used to improve parenting skills and reduce child conduct problems that may bring a child's functioning back into the typical range (Kazdin, 2000b, Yoshikawa, 1995). Some of these programs are more behaviorally oriented, whereas others emphasize the caregiver–child relationship or a combined approach. In general, programs that incorporate both behavioral methods and relationship-based strategies are most effective (e.g., The Incredible Years) (Kazdin, 1997, 2000b; Webster-Stratton, Kolpacoff, & Hollinsworth, 1988; Webster-Stratton & Hammond, 1997).

Although there is no known cure for *autism,* some interventions are being used that have been shown to yield dramatic improvements in behavior and symptoms, especially for children who are more high functioning and who have milder symptoms. The best-researched methods are behavioral interventions such as *applied behavior analysis* (ABA), which has been researched by Lovass and colleagues (McEachin, Smith, & Lovass, 1993). Dawson and Osterling (1997) reviewed eight different early intervention programs for children with autism spectrum disorders that used these behavioral approaches usually involving more than twenty hours per week, and found an average IQ score gain of 20 points from an initial IQ in the mid 50s. Half of the children who participated in these interventions were successfully integrated into school programs. The parents are typically involved in a co-therapist role and extend the intervention into the home. Other researchers such as Greenspan and Gutstein are currently evaluating the effect of play-based intervention and of focusing on enhancing the interpersonal relationships of the children and providing special activities to foster pragmatic language and symbolic thinking rather than only intervening to change behavior. Unfortunately, no control groups have been included in the evaluations, and children have not been followed up for very long. However, these interventions show great promise and their use is increasing (Farran, 2000).

Children with emotional disorders such as separation anxiety disorders and depression and other anxiety disorders are less likely to be referred for treatment unless the symptoms are extreme because such disorders often go unnoticed. Again, cognitive behavioral interventions are typically not appropriate for young children, and individual psychodynamic play therapy, family interventions, and parent–child interaction interventions are most frequently used (Target & Fonagy, 1994 a, b).

**Clinical Interventions with a Variety of Multi-Risk Parents**     Interventions may vary according to the challenges experienced by the family members involved and the factors identified as placing the child at risk. Various kinds of interventions are used with mothers with postpartum depression, including: *Nondirective counseling*, which gives mothers the opportunity to talk about any current concerns, including any concerns regarding the pregnancy and their infants, and *cognitive behavior therapy* (CBT), which helps mothers work through any anxieties they may have about caring for their infants. In *psychodynamic therapy*, the mothers' own attachment histories are explored. One study using all three types of intervention revealed that mothers' depressed mood remitted more quickly when they were receiving any of the interventions than when they were only receiving routine care (Cooper & Murray, 1997). In another study, women with postpartum depression were provided with 8 weeks of home visitation that focused on listening, social support, and counseling. The outcomes were compared with those of women with postpartum depression who did not receive the home visitation intervention. At the end of the 8 weeks, postpartum depression remitted in 69% of the intervention group compared with 38% of the control group.

Lieberman, Weston, and Pawl (1991) studied the effects of *infant–parent psychotherapy* with high-risk mothers and their toddlers who were insecurely attached. Mothers and infants or toddlers participated in sessions together with an interventionist in the home or an office playroom according to the preference of the mother. In the intervention, a more psychodynamic approach was used and no formal instruction on parenting skills was provided, but the home visitors responded to the affective experience of mother and child and only gave information when it was requested. The information given was designed to be clinically attuned to the child's temperament and individual style. During the intervention, developmental guidance was provided at appropriate times; the parents' perceptions, attributions, feelings, and reactions to the child were explored; distortions were corrected; and the parent–child relationship was enhanced. After the intervention, mothers in the intervention group were found to be more sensitive and responsive with their infants and the infants were found to more likely be securely attached than in the non-intervention group.

Another study compared two very different approaches aimed at supporting and intervening with multi-risk mothers during home visits (Barnard, Magyary, Sumner, Booth, Mitchell, & Spieker, 1988). The interventions were 1) an *Infor-*

*mation and Resource (IR model)*, a didactic approach that promoted the physical health of the mother and child, provided information, and taught desirable practices in a very straightforward manner; and 2) *Mental Health (MH) model,* described as a process-oriented, less directive, therapeutic approach in which the parent was an active participant rather than a passive trainee. In examining with which families each of the approaches was most successful, the MH model proved to be more effective than the IR with very problematic multi-risk families and they were more likely to continue their involvement with the program and to have more significant gains (Barnard et al., 1988).

Another study compared three types of interventions—family centered, parent-centered, or advocacy—that were used with economically disadvantaged families with infants with *failure to thrive* (FTT). In this multi-risk group of infants, 51% of the infants became securely attached as a result of the interventions with no differences between the approaches reported (Brinich, Drotar, & Brinich, 1989).

Another program, called the *Infant Stimulation Mother Training* (Badger, 1977, 1979), compared home visiting with a group intervention for teenage mothers 16 years old and younger and their newborn infants. The group intervention was found to be more successful and the teenagers who were in it were more likely to become employed and less likely to have subsequent pregnancies than those who had home visits only. Few changes were found for the home visiting only group.

***Trends about the Effects of Short-Term Interventions***    Many types of short-term, focused interventions have been shown to be very successful in improving various types of targeted outcomes. Although the methods and approaches used in these interventions vary significantly, some general conclusions can be made about their efficacy: It is clear that some relatively brief interventions that focused on enhancing the mother–child interaction were successful in enhancing mothers' sensitivity in interactions and in increasing the percentage of securely attached and reducing the number of disorganized children (Bakermans-Kranenburg, van IJzendoorn, & Juffer, 2003). When two approaches were used to enhance interactions, they were usually both successful, but differed in the aspects of the parent–child dyad they improve. Although research on the efficacy of interventions with different populations is limited, interventions based on various theoretical perspectives that inform the approach have been found to work well with some populations, and some approaches are more successful in improving certain outcomes than others (e.g., Improving the Outcomes of Low Birth Weight Infants; Evaluating 3 Types of Intervention for Mothers with Post Partum Depression). Also, for parents with more serious psychological problems and with many risk factors, a "mental health approach," in which the parent is encouraged to talk and is listened to, has been most successful in keeping the parents engaged and in affecting positive changes (Barnard et al., 1988).

## Multisystem Interventions with Very High-Risk Families

The challenges of evaluating early intervention programs that are community-based and that are provided for multi-risk families has prompted the need for considering findings from other populations that may have been written about in a different literature. Namely, approaches have been studied that have been found to be effective with older populations such as adolescents and for young children and their families in more clinical settings such as children's mental health centers or in hospitals. A number of studies have been conducted with very high risk and multi-risk populations parents of older children, including parents who abuse their children, families in which a child has severe behavioral or emotional problems, or parents who have a psychiatric problem. A meta-analysis that included the results of 56 programs designed to promote family wellness and prevent child maltreatment found that the least successful programs (i.e., those that had the lowest effect sizes) were those in which 12 or fewer visits were conducted in 6 months or less. The most successful programs used intensive family preservation approaches, empowerment, and strength-based approaches, as well as a component of social support. The effect sizes for these programs suggested that positive outcomes for parents in the interventions exceeded 66% of those in control groups. This study suggests that only with intense, multi-component programs can multi-risk families change their patterns of parenting and child abuse be reduced (MacLeod & Wilson, 2000).

The *National Clinical Evaluation Study* (NCES) evaluated the efficacy of 19 separate projects for young children funded by the National Center on Child Abuse and Neglect (Daro, 1993). The duration of the intervention was found to have had a significant effect on outcome, with programs of at least 13–18 months being the most effective. It was also concluded that eclectic therapies, such as those that help families to meet their material needs, behavior-based programs, and psychodynamic and family system perspectives, were necessary. Results also suggested that for greatest effectiveness, the combination and order of these approaches should be adapted to the needs of the family. For example, when poverty and housing were issues, approaches that focused on helping the parents find housing and employment preceded interventions focused on enhancing parenting skills. Daro (1993) suggested that those parents who have not improved after this length of time may need to be referred to another program, or if absolutely necessary, have their parental rights revoked for as long as needed.

Although it has rarely been used specifically in early intervention programs, a multisystemic (MST) approach developed by Henggeler and associates (2002) may be the type of model needed with multi-risk families and young children (Henggeler, Schoenwald, Rowland, & Cunningham, 2002). The approach is very well-researched and has been used with children in very high-risk families that have complex, intergenerational problems and multiple needs. As Henggeler and colleagues (2002) noted, "If a problem is multidetermined (or complex), logic suggests that to optimize the probability of favorable outcomes interventions should have the capacity to address the multiple risk factors contributing to the problem" (Henggeler et al., 2002, p.5). MST or multimodal intervention uses a variety of interventions including family therapy, parent training, supportive therapy, social skills training, case management, and advocacy. The intervention emphasizes the need for the various components of intervention to be highly individualized and sufficiently integrated. The interventions are highly flexible and emphasize reducing barriers to services and using effective intervention approaches and contacts that emphasize the positives and use strengths to encourage change. They are also developmentally appropriate for the child. Although most of the research on this kind of intervention approach has been with adolescents, the principles of MST are very pertinent for working with the multi-risk families who are the focus of this book. In fact, preliminary results on using MST approaches with young children and their families are promising (Pickrel, 1997). The approaches used included family-based intervention, concrete assistance, intervention of the child and the parent–child relationship, and other approaches described in this chapter.

The Clinical Infant Development Program (Greenspan, 1986; Greenspan & Wieder, 1987; Greenspan, Wieder, Nover, Lieberman, Lourie, et al., 1987), a program for very high-risk families at risk for abuse, provided services for 49 families with 200 children. The multidimensional program provided multiple services by highly trained professionals, including specialized child care for children and intensive in-home and in-center clinical services for parents. Although it was difficult to evaluate the differential effect of the multiple program components, highly successful effects were found for the children, parents, and parent–child interactions. The program demonstrated that it is possible to enhance the resilience of children facing circumstances that placed them at extreme psychosocial risk. (See Appendix Table A2.6 for information on these programs.)

A number of conclusions can be made about multisystemic approaches, including evidence that an eclectic approach that integrates a variety of approaches and is individualized or prescribed for a particular family is crucial for high-risk and/or multi-risk parents. Also, the length, intensity, type of intervention components, and style of intervention need to be matched to the participants' level of risk, motivation, abilities, the age of the child(ren), and the issues that are being addressed. Effective interventions go through various stages, as well, including the initial building of relationships and meeting the family's practical needs, followed by targeting approaches to the specific needs of the family and then building on the parents' strengths with various kinds of parent training.

## CONCLUSIONS FROM EVALUATION RESEARCH AND IMPLICATIONS FOR EARLY INTERVENTION

The question of whether early intervention is successful in enhancing the outcomes of infants and young children and in preventing developmental delays and emotional, social, and behavioral problems cannot be answered simply or definitively. In fact, what we still need to learn about the effects of early intervention programs, especially the more multi-dimensional ones, may far outweigh what we do know. The fact that we cannot speak unequivocally about their success or failure is due in part to the complexity and diversity of the programs, the challenges of evaluation, and the differences in the populations they serve. Moreover, it is unlikely that we will be able to be more definitive and give a clearer determination in the near future. As pointed out by Karoly and colleagues, all one can make are "inferences as to what some programs *can* do, depending on the characteristics of the program and the families it serves" (1998, p. xiii).

Many of the programs mentioned in this chapter adhered to one or two theoretical orientations and approaches. For greater success, early childhood professionals need to apply knowledge from many theoretical perspectives and from research on the multiple variables that contribute to risk and resilience in children in order to make a variety of strategies available to them and their families (Leventhal, Brooks-Gunn, & Kamerman, 1997). A "second-generation" of programs that can provide information about what works, with whom, and at what stage of a child's development is also needed (Guralnick, 1997). This will ensure that successful interventions can be replicated with integrity for other, similar situations. It is increasingly clear that early childhood intervention professionals need to be able to delineate situations, ages, and types of populations for which the intervention is helpful, and more important, for whom it is not suitable. Without this critical information, useful interventions will be misused and cast away as ineffective. They must also have a clear idea of goals. Some conclusions regarding early intervention according to goals are given in Table 2.2.

A set of general principles for early intervention that can inform practitioners about what is needed in order to provide quality services to the most at-risk families are outlined next:

- *Home visiting may be an essential component* of programs for the most high-risk families: These families are unlikely to have access to programs or to attend them in most agencies without outreach. It may also be necessary to continue to adopt strategies to keep parents involved in interventions and to reduce dropouts. With immigrant populations having home visitors from the same cultural background and able to speak the language used by the parents may be crucial.

- *There is a need to distinguish between prevention and early intervention and between less and more at-risk families:* It is important to distinguish between prevention and early intervention approaches and what ensures success for both. Many programs have been successful in showing improvements in various factors for less at-risk families; however, when families are at very high risk the same strategies may not be as successful, and thus, more focused and intensive services are required.

- *Starting early in a child's life is important:* Research indicates that in some situations, programs that begin earlier in a child's life, either during the prenatal period or at birth, have been shown to be more likely to be successful than programs that begin after the child is 1 or 2 years of age. Early plasticity of the brain allows opportunity to optimize brain structure and biochemistry. Interventions provided early can also avoid negative interactional patterns and attributions between parent and child becoming firmly entrenched. For example, the persistent effects of the Carolina Abecedarian Project have been attributed to the fact that children began the program in early infancy and continued over the first 5 years of life. In some studies, beginning in the prenatal period has enhanced the health and safety of the child, whereas in others this has not been proven. This indicates that it cannot be concluded that programs initiated after this early period can have no positive effects.

- *Intensity and duration of the intervention counts:* Some investigators have challenged the idea that more intense and longer interventions are more effective. This is primarily because these are variables that are rarely studied. An exception to this is the Infant Health and Development Program that found a positive association between intensity of participation and child cognitive gains

**Table 2.2.**   Conclusions on early interventions according to goals

| Goal | Conclusions |
|---|---|
| Changing child outcomes | Research suggests that when children already have developmental delays or other special needs or disorders, have been abused or neglected, or are at extreme psychosocial risk, child outcomes are best enhanced by interventions that work directly with the children, such as educational center-based child care, therapeutic nurseries, or specialized child interventions. This is likely to be because of the greater intensity that direct child intervention can provide for the children. Also, if play therapy is used, it needs to be adapted to the needs of the child and their specific problem areas.

Although children's development is best enhanced by direct intervention, supporting parents whose children are showing difficulties and providing them with appropriate strategies to work with their children has been shown to enhance parent-child relationships. It has also resulted in greater maternal self-confidence and satisfaction, improved educational attainment and labor force participation for the parents, reduction in welfare, and criminal involvement. Therefore, it is important, if parent–child interactions are compromised, that approaches to enhance parents' sensitivity to their child's cues should be focused on as well. |
| Changing parent–infant interactions | Increasing mothers' sensitivity to their infants' cues can be achieved with a variety of short-term approaches, such as viewing videotaped examples of the parent–child interactions and the Watch, Wait, and Wonder approach.

Changing parents' negative attributions or views of their infants can also be critical and can occur by providing information on their infant's unique characteristics and individuality and by helping parents problem solve in order to come up with effective strategies to overcome difficulties their children may be having. This improved understanding of their children can enhance the parent–child interaction and relationship and improve outcomes for children. |
| Helping very high-risk parents | With very high-risk families, especially those at risk for abuse and neglect, comprehensive, multisystemic, intense, and high-quality programs are essential. A range of intervention strategies that are provided frequently and long term needs to be available to meet the multiple needs of these families. These include support, feedback on interactions, and discussion and other approaches to improve child and parent representations. These can best be provided within one program or, if this is not possible, through a well-established system of linkages with other community services or networks to which referrals can be made.

Multi-risk families need a range of services from provision of concrete needs, crisis intervention, supportive services, shorter term interventions, and longer term interventions that can deal with the effects of unresolved loss and trauma. For very high-risk families, basic survival needs such as finding adequate food and housing must be met first.

In general, with multi-risk families, when parents have a history of trauma or loss, programs need to provide interventions of high intensity and over a long period of time in which the development of a parent-interventionist relationship is key. Brief, focused interventions have been shown to be effective in bringing about |

change in a particular aspect of functioning, however, or to provide parents with understanding and strategies to change the parent–child interaction and attachment and certain behavioral patterns. Nonetheless, these need to be embedded within a framework of the long-term availability of service providers. In fact, families do not necessarily have to be seen at the same intensity throughout the intervention and can leave the program for a period of time or be seen less frequently, with the understanding that they can come back if they are concerned about their child or if circumstances change for the family.

Families at highest risk may need a mental health approach that is less didactic and that follows the parent's lead and considers the parent's goals for the intervention. This kind of approach puts the parent as an active participant in the intervention and avoids parents' perception of being in a hierarchical relationship in which they feel a sense of powerlessness. Providing a sense of partnership between parents and interventionist needs to be a focus of the intervention. This is particularly important when the parents have experienced loss and trauma.

Families at highest risk need to have interventions provided by professionals or highly trained, well-supported paraprofessionals. Nurses may be particularly important during pregnancy and immediately postpartum because of the health questions and breast-feeding issues frequently raised by parents at these times. When parents have psychological issues or psychiatric difficulties, mental health professionals may be critical.

(Brooks-Gunn et al., 1994). In two studies of home visiting in Jamaica, weekly visits were associated with higher child development scores than biweekly visits, and those who had biweekly visits did better than those who received monthly visits (Powell & Grantham-McGregor, 1989). These intensity effects have also been found for children with autism (McEachin et al., 1993). However, it should also be noted that there is evidence that short-term interventions targeted at specific areas of concern can often contribute to significant improvements in the areas that are targeted (e.g., Watch, Wait, and Wonder, Interactional Guidance, interventions that focus on enhancing an aspect of child development such as speech and language or emotion regulation).

- *Initial and ongoing assessment and monitoring is critical:* Because research has shown that interventions tailored to particular areas of concern are the most successful, the first stage of intervention should include an assessment of risk, protective factors, and identified needs of the children and family in order to choose the most suitable interventions. Ongoing monitoring and assessment is also necessary to see if adjustments need to occur in the intervention. When changes occur and some risks or difficulties are overcome or new patterns of need arise, the intervention will need to be adjusted to meet the new needs of the family.

- *Tailor approaches to particular at-risk parent groups:* When an outcome is being targeted for a particular parent population, interventions that have been shown to be effective with that population need to be used (e.g., group approaches for teenage mothers or mental health approaches of very high-risk parents).

- Services are usually most effective with families at moderate-risk as opposed to low-risk or very high-risk. Families who are low risk and can help themselves usually show few benefits from prevention and home visiting programs. Families at moderate risk will suffer more without services, so they are more likely to show improvements compared with those who did not receive services. The children in families at high risk whose development is most in jeopardy have the greatest need for services and are most likely to have negative outcomes without appropriate intervention, however. Research has shown that for families at highest risk, their needs go far beyond information provision and support and require specialized services in a comprehensive framework that addresses the complex needs of the family (Shonkoff & Phillips, 2000). In many communities, however, personnel are not adequately trained to deal with these high-risk parents or children and there is an urgent need for *coordinated services* in different agencies to be developed to meet their needs.

- *Service providers should be well trained:* Service providers are most effective when they have a considerable level of professional expertise and the ability to engage the parents and to keep them interested and feeling supported. For example, the mothers and children receiving the Infant Health and Development Program stayed in the program because emphasis was given to making them feel comfortable and adapting the program to meeting their expressed needs.

- *Use a variety of approaches:* A variety of individual and group interventions can be effective in improving parenting skills, and in certain situations can reduce emotional, social, and behavioral problems of children.

Although we have much to learn about what works best, with whom, and when, early intervention research to date teaches us about the effectiveness of certain approaches with multi-risk families and the lack of success of others. Because it is clear that certain approaches can work well if they are appropriate for a particular family, children and families need to be assessed in order to choose the best strategies and approaches available. We need to abandon the idea that one approach can be used with everyone. Instead, we need integrative approaches to early intervention in which a number of theoretical orientations and interventions based on them are combined in order to provide intervention that can best meet the needs of a particular child and family (Shonkoff & Meisels, 2000). As stated by Egeland, Weinfield, Bosquet, and Cgebg:

> The indiscriminate implementation of an intervention program for high risk parents is doomed to failure unless the program identifies the unique needs and circumstances of each family as part of the intervention program. (2000, p. 73)

# Selected Early
# Intervention Programs

## ASSESSING EARLY
## INTERVENTION PROGRAMS
## BY TYPE, OBJECTIVES, OUTCOME
## VARIABLES, RESULTS, AND OTHER FACTORS

As Chapter 2 has pointed out, early intervention programs vary significantly in terms of their intervention goals and types of interventions used. In the last several decades, programs focusing solely on improving children's IQ scores and or developmental skills have been replaced by more multi-dimensional programs that look at the child in context of a family and community system and at the family's needs as a whole, among other goals.

Tables A2.1–A2.6 show the huge range of programs that have been or are available to families at multiple risk. As is shown by the results column of each, these programs have been implemented with varying degrees of success. However, the information provided on these programs does provide valuable testament to the need for an integrated approach to looking at families at multiple risk.

**Table A2.1.** Center-based programs for children, with or without other initiatives for parents

| Program | Program objectives and description | Description of participants | Research design | Outcome variables | Results |
|---|---|---|---|---|---|
| Carolina Abecedarian Project (Campbell, Helms, Sparling & Ramey,1998; Campbell & Ramey, 1994; Ramey, Bryant, Campbell, Sparling, & Wasik, 1990, Vernon-Feagans, 1996) | Four groups: 1) Pre-school intervention (infants through age 5) as well as 3 years of primary school education up to age 8 2) preschool treatment only (infancy to age 5) 3) primary school treatment only 4) untreated control group | African American families, high risk on socioeconomic index Full-term infants | Random assignment to intervention (I) group (n = 57) and control (C) group (n = 54). Follow-up at 15 years; I (n = 48), C (n = 44) Children in both the intervention and control groups received social services and nutritional supplements. | • Intelligence (preschool IQ scores; Stanford-Binet [4th ed.]; Thorndike, Hagen, & Satler [1986]; and Wechsler Intelligence Scale for Children–Revised [WISC-R] Weschler [1974]) • School achievement (i.e, reading, math, written language, and knowledge on Woodcock-Johnson; Woodcock & Johnson [1989]) • School progress (e.g., special education, grade retention, school record) | Positive effects for preschool treatment groups. School-age intervention alone not effective IQ score: I = 93.7 > C = 88.4 School achievement tests: I > C, positive trend Special education: I = 25% < C = 48% Grade retention: I = 39% < C = 59% |
| Chicago Child–Parent Center (CPC) (Fuerst & Fuerst, 1993; Reynolds, 1994, 1997; Reynolds, Temple, Robertson, & Mann, 2001) | A large-scale, comprehensive intervention; preschool and kindergarten program and school-age services up to 3rd grade. Support services and workshops on a variety of topics for parents | African American 3- and 4-year old children from low-income families living in the inner city; received up to 6 years of services | Children were assigned to one of three groups: Intervention (I) group (N = 989) completed preschool and kindergarten program and had services up to 3rd grade. Two matched comparison groups: C (1): Did not attend CPC preschool C (2): Living in neighborhoods similar to those of the children in the intervention group; also did not receive CPC services | • Educational attainment • Grade retention • Special education services • Juvenile arrests | At 20 years of age: School completion: I (49.75) > C (1) and (2) (38.5%) School dropout: I (46.7%) < C (1) and (2) (55%) Grade retention: I (21.9%) < C (1) and (2) (32.3%) Special education services: I (10%) < C (1) and (2) (15%) Juvenile arrests: I (16.9%) < C (1) and (2) (25.1%) |

(continued)

**Table A2.1.** (continued)

| Program | Program objectives and description | Description of participants | Research design | Outcome variables | Results |
|---|---|---|---|---|---|
| Comparison of three preschool curricula (Schweinhart, Weikart, & Larner, 1986) | Three preschool curricula: 1) High/Scope teacher and child both plan and initiate projects and work together 2) Distar with teacher initiating and child following 3) Nursery School tradition with child initiated and teacher followed. Intervention was given for 2½ hours, 5 days a week; once every 2 weeks parent and child present | 3- and 4-year-old children in families of low socioeconomic status and at risk for school failure according to test scores | Children (N = 68) randomly assigned to one of three programs or no intervention controls. Followed up at 15 years (N = 54); a retention rate of 79% was found | • Intelligence<br>• School achievement<br>• Delinquency<br>• Social behavior | Mean IQ score of children in all programs rose 27 points in first year of program, and when children were age 10, mean score was 94. IQ score and school achievement similar for all three groups. Children in the Distar program engaged in twice as many delinquent acts, had poorer relations with families, and reached out to others less. Did not do worse than children who did not attend the program. |
| Early Training Project (Gray, Ramsey, & Klaus, 1983) | Home visits bimonthly Summer part-day preschool program, 1 year or 2 years, to enhance children's development and instill achievement orientation | Children from low-income, low education, public housing, un-skilled or semi-skilled parents 3½–4½ years old | Randomized assignment to intervention (I) group (n = 44) or control (C) group (n = 21) Followed up after 17 years | • IQ score<br>• Achievement tests<br>• Special education<br>• Grade retention<br>• High school graduation | After 17 years, positive effects were found for girls only. Fewer children were enrolled in special education classes I = 5% < C = 29%. No other effects |
| Experimental variation of Head Start (Karnes, Schwedel, & Williams, 1983) | Part-time preschool program enhanced higher level thinking skills of children utilizing a manualized program. Special program for parents of potentially gifted children | Children in Head Start programs, some identified as potentially gifted. Ages ranged from 4–5 years old | Experimental (I) classroom (n = 116) and control (C) classroom, who which did not receive enriched program (n = 24). Not randomized, high attrition, followed up post high school | • Intelligence<br>• School achievement<br>• School progress<br>• Teacher attitude to classes | IQ score at age 13: I = 85 < C = 91 Achievement tests: No significant differences were found Grade retention: I = 10% < C = 16% Teacher attitude: Teachers had more positive attitude toward their classes. I > C |

| Program (Reference) | Intervention | Sample | Design | Measures | Results |
|---|---|---|---|---|---|
| Houston Parent–Child Development Center (Andrews, Blumenthal, Johnson, Malone, & Wallace, 1982; Johnson, 1988; Johnson & Walker, 1991) | In year 1, professional educator provided home visits (25 visits) emphasizing developing mothering skills. In year 2, mother and child attended center 4 mornings a week. Children attended preschool, mothers attended class in child health and development and English. Fathers took part in weekend educational sessions. | Mexican Americans who were impoverished Children 1 or 3 years of age in program for 2 years | Random assignment with high attrition Intervention (I) group ($n = 97$), Control (C) group ($n = 119$) Followed up at grades 2 to 5 | • School achievement and progress<br>• Bilingual education<br>• Behavior problems in children<br>• Children's IQ scores<br>• Interactive skills of mothers<br>• Home environment | Achievement tests: I = 58% > C = 46% Bilingual education: I = 16% < C = 36% Classroom hostility: I < C, fewer behavior problems Parenting skills: Mothers in intervention group had better interactive skills with their children and provided a more educationally stimulating environment |
| Infant Health and Development Program (Brooks-Gunn, McCormack, Shapiro, Benasich, & Black, 1994; Infant Health and Development Program, 1990; McCarton et al., 1997) | Intervention from 12 months to 3 years. Home visits to age 3; center-based schooling from 12 months to 3 years, pediatric surveillance. Parents received developmental education, problem-solving curriculum, and group meetings. | Infants weighing 2500 grams or less, 37 weeks gestation or less. English-speaking mothers without drug abuse or psychiatric hospitalization | Random assignment stratified by birth weight > 2001–2500 grams (heavy) < 2000 (light) Intervention (I) group ($n = 377$); Control (C) group received pediatric surveillance ($n = 608$) | • IQ score and vocabulary at age 3 and 5 years<br>• Behavior and health measures<br>• Use of services<br>• Mothers' employment | IQ score and vocabulary measures: At 5 years, intervention group children showed no differences on IQ score and vocabulary measures: I = C (For heavy infants there were differences: I = 97 > C = 92) I mothers were employed for more months and returned to the work force earlier than C group mothers. Use of health care was higher in intervention group: I > C. |

*(continued)*

**Table A2.1.** *(continued)*

| Program | Program objectives and description | Description of participants | Research design | Outcome variables | Results |
|---|---|---|---|---|---|
| Louisville Curriculum Comparison Study (Miller & Bizzell, 1983, 1984) | 1-year-old children in one of four pre-kindergarten groups | African American 4-year-olds | Random assignment with comparison group from original pool and same neighborhood. I ($n$ = 214), C ($n$ = 34) Age at outcome 15–18 years | • Intelligence<br>• School achievement<br>• School progress | No differences between outcomes for different curricula overall:<br>IQ score (15 years): I = C<br>School achievement: I = C<br>Special education: (18 years) I = 32% < C = 63%<br>Grade retention at 18 years: I = 26% < C = 58%<br>High school graduation: I = 67% > C = 53% |
| Perry Preschool Program (Berrueta-Clement, Schweinhart, Barnett, Epstein, & Weikart, 1984; Schweinhart, Montie, Xiang, Barnett, Belfield, & Nores, 2005; Schweinhart & Weikart, 1997) | Program objective to improve cognitive and social outcomes in the short and long-term. Children entered program at 3 or 4 years of age until age 5. Children received 2½ hours of center-based program and 90-minute teacher home visits per week for 8 months of the year. Teachers had bachelor of arts degrees and certification in education. | African American children with IQ scores of less than 85 at program entry | Random assignment to intervention (I) group ($n$ = 58) and control (C) group ($n$ = 65). Latest follow-up at 40 years of age | • Intelligence (Stanford-Binet or WISC-R)<br>• School achievement (California Achievement Tests)<br>• School progress (i.e., special education, grade retention, graduation)<br>• Employment rate and welfare participation<br>• Monthly earnings<br>• Criminal records<br>• Teen pregnancy | IQ score: (14 yrs) I = 81 = C = 81<br>Achievement tests (at age 14): I > C<br>Grade point average (at age 19): I > C<br>Special education (at 19): I = 37% < C = 50%<br>Grade retention (grade 12): I = 15% < C = 20%<br>High school graduation: I = 67% > C = 47%<br>At 40 years:<br>Arrested 5+ times I = 36% < C = 55%<br>Earning $20k: I = 60% > C = 40%<br>Employed: I = 76% > C = 62%<br>Ever sentenced: I = 19% < C = 43% |

| Program | Description | Population | Study design | Outcomes | Results |
|---|---|---|---|---|---|
| Philadelphia Project (Beller, 1983; Furstenberg, Cook, Eccles, Elder, & Sameroff, 1999) | To improve the developmental outcomes for children. Early intervention program and home visits for up to 3 years. Home visits and part-time preschool program. Four days on creativity and discovery. One day home visit by teacher. | Economically disadvantaged preschoolers from urban high poverty areas | Three groups of children compared by participation. I (1): pre-k and kindergarten I (2): kindergarten only I (3): no school experience until grade 1 No random assignment, matched comparison group (C) from same kindergarten class Followed up at 18 years I (n = 60), C (n = 53) | • Intelligence<br>• School achievement<br>• School progress | IQ (10 years): I = 98 > C = 91 Achievement: I = C, positive trend Special education: (grade 12) I = 5% = C = 6% Grade retention: I = 38% < C = 53% positive trend |
| Project Care (Wasik, Ramey, Bryant, & Sparling, 1990) | Center-based program designed to address cognitive and social domains of development. Well-trained teachers. Home-based program; weekly home visits were provided for 3 years. Control group received free formula and diapers. Crisis intervention was provided. | Parents who were considered disadvantaged due to educational and social circumstances | Two intervention groups, N = 64: I (1): home-based visits and child care (n = 16) I (2): home-based visits only (n = 25) C (n = 23) Children tested several times between 6 and 54 months of age | • Cognitive development of children | I (1) > I (2) and (C) on cognitive test results |

(continued)

**Table A2.1.** *(continued)*

| Program | Program objectives and description | Description of participants | Research design | Outcome variables | Results |
|---|---|---|---|---|---|
| Syracuse University Family Development Program (Lally, Mangione, & Honig, 1988) | Full-time child care Home visits, health/nutrition, and service resources | African American families Children from 6 months to 5 years old | No random assignment (matched comparison groups selected at 36 months) Initial sample size: I (n = 108); C (n = 74) Last follow-up at age 15 Intervention group (I = 82) Comparison group (C = 72) | • Intelligence • Teachers' ratings of child behavior • School progress (e.g., grades, attendance, failures) • Rate of criminal activities • Future plans | For most outcomes, girls showed differences, boys did not: IQ score: I = C School grades (girls only): I > C School attendance (girls only): I > C Teacher ratings on self-esteem and impulsivity (girls only): I > C Positive future plans (boys and girls): I > C Delinquency (boys and girls): I = 6% < C = 22% |
| Yale Child Welfare Research Project (Seitz & Apfel, 1994; Seitz, Rosenbaum, & Apfel, 1985) | Program provided to mothers from pregnancy to 30 months postpartum. Mothers provided a coordinated set of medical and social services. Child care, 28 home visits by social worker, house calls by pediatrician, and well-baby visits. Developmental examinations | Families residing in depressed inner-city area with incomes below federal poverty level | Quasi-experimental with 2 comparison groups recruited 2 years later. Followed up 5 and 10 years later. At 10 years: I (n = 16), C (n = 16). | • Mother's education, income, welfare • Children's school attendance, special school, services, IQ scores (Peabody Individual Achievement Test; [PIAT] [Dunn & Markwardt, 1970]; WISC-R) | After 10 years, mothers showed more Self-supporting behaviors: I > C Higher levels of education: I > C Smaller family sizes: I < C Children's school attendance: I > C Special education: I = 25% < C = 50% IQ score: I = C |

**Table A2.2.** Child- and parent-focused home visiting programs

| Program | Program objectives and description | Description of participants | Research design | Outcome variables | Results |
|---------|-----------------------------------|---------------------------|----------------|-------------------|---------|
| Child Parent Enrichment Program (CPEP) (Barth, Hacking, & Ash, 1986) | To reduce incidence of abuse and neglect CPEP services involved 6 months of home visits by paraprofessionals and linkage to other community resources. Home visits by paraprofessionals from approximately end of mother's pregnancy until about 6 months postpartum, two visits per month | Women referred to the CPEP during or just after pregnancy if identified as at risk for engaging in child abuse | Experimental research design: intervention (I) group (n = 97) and control (C) group (n = 94). Control group received traditional community services. | • Pregnancy problems and adjustment to baby<br>• Birth weight, well baby care, and emergency room visits<br>• Incidence of abuse and neglect | Analysis showed an advantage for the CPEP group in prenatal care, birth outcomes, better reports of child temperament, and better indicators of child welfare. CPEP mothers also tended to report better well-being.<br>No difference between groups: I = C in incidence of abuse and neglect<br>Well baby care and emergency room visits: I < C<br>Pregnancy problems and adjustment to baby: I = C |

*(continued)*

**Table A2.2.** *(continued)*

| Program | Program objectives and description | Description of participants | Research design | Outcome variables | Results |
|---|---|---|---|---|---|
| Elmira Prenatal and Early Infancy Program (Kitzman, Olds, & Henderson, 1997; Olds, 1997; Olds et al., 1998; Olds, Hill, Robinson, Song, & Little, 2000) | Reduction of various problems in both parents and children (see outcome variables) Home visits provided by trained nurses. Families received an average of 31 home visits | First-time mothers who were young, single, and from low socioeconomic groups Pregnant women were recruited if they were at less than 26 weeks of gestation, had no previous live births, no specific chronic illnesses thought to contribute to fetal growth retardation or preterm delivery, and at least two of the following risk conditions: 1) were unmarried, 2) had less than 12 years of education, 3) were unemployed. | (*N* = 400) Random assignment to Intervention (I) group (*n* = 216 or to Control (C) group (*n* = 184). Groups differed according to when the intervention began and how long it lasted (i.e., only during pregnancy or until child was age 2 years). Followed to 15 years of age (*N* = 324). | I) Parents: • Number of arrests and conviction • Incidence of child abuse II) Children: • Incidences of running away • Arrests and convictions • Sex partners • Cigarettes and alcohol consumption | I) Parents: By 15 years: Arrests: I = .24 < C = .53. Convictions: I = .13 = C = .18 Incidence of child abuse: I = 29% < C = 54%. II) Children: Fewer incidents of running away: I = 0.24 < C = 0.60 Fewer arrests: I = 0.20 < C = 0.45 Fewer convictions: I = 0.09 < C = 0.47 Fewer lifetime sex partners: I = 0.92 < C = 2.48 Fewer cigarettes smoked per day: I = 1.50 < C = 2.50 Fewer days of alcohol use in past 6 months: I = 1.09 < 2.49 Concluded the beneficial effects of the program were greater for families at greater risk (for low-income or unmarried women, and those who smoked during pregnancy). |

| Program | Purpose/Description | Sample | Design | Measures | Results |
|---|---|---|---|---|---|
| Florida Parent Education Infant and Toddler Program (Gordon & Jester, 1977; Jester & Guinagh, 1983) | To contribute to breaking the poverty cycle by enhancing children's development and increasing mothers' levels of self-esteem and internal control Trained paraprofessionals provided weekly home visits from 3 months to 3 years of age | Low-income families (N = 285) with children (infant to age 5) with no major complications. Several participants were teenage single mothers. | Complex research design with low retention rates. Three waves of children, each randomly assigned to intervention (I) or control (C) group. Intervention (29) Controls (23) at last follow up at age 3. Treatment groups received treatment for 1, 2 or 3 years. | • IQ, school achievement, school dropout<br>• Classroom behavior and children's self-concept | I had higher IQ scores, school achievement: I > C and lower school dropout: I < C Classroom behavior: I = C |
| Home Intervention for Children with Failure to Thrive (Black, Dubowitz, Hutcheson, Berenson-Howard, & Starr, 1995) | A community-based agency provided weekly home visits from trained lay home visitors, supervised by a community health nurse. The intervention provided maternal support and promoted parenting, child development, use of informal and formal resources, and parent advocacy. Focused on parent–child relationships and feeding. For one year children received nutrition intervention. | Children (N = 130) younger than 25 months, weight below 5th percentile. Mothers mostly African American, single, with limited education | Randomly assigned to two groups: (I) clinic services plus home intervention (n = 64), or (C) clinic services only (n = 66). | • Children's growth (weight and height), receptive language (Receptive-Expressive Emergent Language Scale [REEL]; Bzoch & League, 1971), and home environment (Home Observation for Measurement of the Environment; HOME: Caldwell, & Bradley, 1984)<br>• Cognitive and motor development of children (Bayley Scales of Infant Development; Bayley, 1969) | Children's weight and height improved in both groups I = C. Children in intervention group had better receptive language and more child-oriented home environments that controls I > C. Younger children had higher cognitive development. There were no changes in motor development associated with intervention status. Concluded that early home intervention can promote a nurturing home environment effectively and can reduce the developmental delays often experienced by low-income children with failure to thrive. |

*(continued)*

**Table A2.2.** *(continued)*

| Program | Program objectives and description | Description of participants | Research design | Outcome variables | Results |
|---|---|---|---|---|---|
| Jamaican Study of Deprived Urban Children (Powell & Granthan-McGregor, 1989) | To provide health and nutritional advice and psychosocial stimulation; to improve the development of deprived urban children in Jamaica. Home visits by paraprofessionals were supervised by nurses for 1 year beginning when the child was 6–30 months old | Predominantly mothers who were African American and from low-income families | Random assignment to Intervention group (I), visited weekly ($n = 29$), or Control group (C), which received no visits ($n = 29$). Followed to end of the program | • Griffith Mental Scale (Griffith, 1954) | Scores on Griffith Mental Scale at end of program I = 110 > C = 99. I IQ scores were increased 8.9 points in the year |
| Montreal Home Visitation Program (Larson, 1980) | To reduce incidence of child abuse and to improve parenting interactions. Paraprofessionals visited from 6 weeks to 15 months (10 visits) | Working class income with no more than high school education, no significant illness during pregnancy or history of psychiatric illness | Random assignment to three groups: Intervention group I (1) ($n = 36$), visited pre- and postnatally; I (2), visited only postnatally; and (C) ($n = 44$). Followed to 15 months old | • Number of well baby visits and accidents rates <br> • Home environment and maternal behaviors | Group I (1) had higher scores on home environment and maternal behaviors than the other two groups; also had fewer reports of injuries |

| Study | Description | Population | Design | Outcomes | Results |
|---|---|---|---|---|---|
| University of California Preterm Infant Study (Beckwith, 1988) | Supportive home visiting. Mediated between family and community resources, provided concrete help, and developed parents' observational skills of their infants. | Parents with low incomes who have preterm infants with health problems | Random assignment to intervention (I) group (n = 37), or control (C) group (n = 55). Data from 70 families were obtained 1 year later. | • Parents' interactions with their infants<br>• Infant performance on the Bayley Scales of Infant Development | Intervention group had increased involvement and reciprocal interactions with their infants in first year of life: I > C<br>Only modest differences found in the infants as measured on the Bayley Scales of Infant Development |
| Vermont Intervention Program for Mothers of Low Birth Weight Infants (Achenbach, Phares, Howell, Rauh, & Nurcombe, 1990; Nurcombe, Howell, Rauh, Teti, Ruoff, & Brennan, 1984) | Aimed to increase self confidence and skills of mothers in caring for infants<br>7 daily sessions during week prior to discharge and 4 home visits at 3, 14, 30, and 90 days post discharge by neonatal intensive care nurse | Infants weighing less than 2,250 grams who have no congenital anomalies or severe neurological defects | Intervention (I) group (n = 24) and Control (C) group (n = 32) and additional comparison group with infants > 2,800 grams, > 37 weeks gestation (n = 37) | • Cognitive scores of children at 7 years on Kaufman Intelligence Scale<br>• Mother's ratings of their self-confidence in mothering, role satisfaction, and perception of their child's temperament | Cognitive mean scores higher in I = 107 > C = 96 and very similar to scores of normal birth weight children = 106<br>Significant effects of the intervention found on mother's ratings of role satisfaction and perception of child's temperament but not on self-confidence. |
| Verbal Interaction Project (Levenstein, O'Hara, & Madden, 1983; Madden, O'Hara, & Levenstein, 1984) | Home visits by paraprofessionals emphasizing enhancement of language<br>Visits conducted from when child is 21–35 months for 2 years | Families (88% African American) in low-income housing, who have less than a year of education, semi-skilled jobs | 6 groups with 3 matched comparison groups<br>Intervention (I) group (n = 111) compared with 3 matched comparison (C) groups (n = 51)<br>Not randomized; followed up to Grade 7 | • IQ scores<br>• Grade retention<br>• Special education incidence in Grade 7 | IQ score: I = 101.9 > C = 93.6<br>Grade retention: I = 13% < C = 19% positive trend<br>Special education: I = 14% < C = 30% |

**Table A2.3.** Combination programs including home visiting and in-center programs for parents

| Program | Program objectives and description | Description of participants | Research design | Outcome variables | Results |
|---|---|---|---|---|---|
| Better Beginnings, Better Futures Project (Peters et al., 2000; Peters, et al., 2004) | To prevent problems and promote child development in social, emotional, behavioral, physical, and cognitive domains. Eight sites that developed programs tailored to local communities. All provided home visiting and various in-center programs such as parenting groups, drop-in centers, community development.<br><br>A comprehensive community-based childhood development project as the result of collaboration among three Ontario, Canada ministries: Community, Family and Children's Services; Education; and Health and Long Term Care. | Eight low-income communities<br><br>Children from birth to 4 years, or 4–8 years | Comparison data from children and families living in similar communities to where sites are. Baseline focal design with baseline data before program began. Longitudinal comparison site design. Various sample sizes in each site. | I) Child outcomes<br>• Ratings of child emotional problems<br>• School readiness<br>Special Education<br>• Child development | Emotional problems: 27% decrease in child emotional problems at the two younger child sites and a 7% decrease in three sites that provided services for older children<br><br>Special education: Number of students requiring special education services decreased in two of the three sites that provided services for older children.<br><br>Child development: No consistent cross-site improvement in child development<br><br>Concluded that changes were strongest for programs that were intensive, continual, and focused. Sites that provided intensive, center-based educational programs were only ones to improve child outcomes |

| Program | Intervention | Design/Sample | Measures | Results |
|---|---|---|---|---|
| Child Health Supervision Project (Gutelius, Kirsch, MacDonald, Brooks, & McErlean, 1977) | Routine health care and counseling from a nurse beginning in 7th month of pregnancy. After birth, mother received complete well baby care until child was 3 years of age. Provided home visits and group meetings on child rearing and personal issues | Unmarried mothers between the ages of 15–18 years in low income areas who were having their first infants and who were identified by 7th month of pregnancy. Randomly assigned to Intervention (I) group ($n = 47$) or Control (C) group ($n = 48$) | Parents:<br>• Diet and feeding habits<br>• Sleeping patterns<br>• Child rearing<br>Children:<br>• Development<br>• Intelligence<br>• Behavior problems | Cognitive ability at 3 years<br>I > C (decreased later)<br>Behavior problems: I = C<br>Parenting: I > C<br>Mothers' staying in school, fathers' job stability: I > C |
| Home Instruction Program for Preschool Youngsters (HIPPY) (Baker, 1996; Baker & Piotrkowski, 1995; Baker, Piotrkowski, & Brooks-Gunn, 1998) | Aims to help parents prepare their 4- to 5-year-old children for school by enhancing children's home learning environments.<br>Bi-monthly home visits and group meetings on alternate weeks. Emphasis on using story books and educational activities for 15 minutes each day. Used role playing to demonstrate use of materials (books and activity sheets). Home visitors trained paraprofessionals.<br>Two-year program. Group meetings less well attended by mothers | Parents with limited formal education; children 4–5 years of age.<br>Two sites: Two cohorts of children followed from beginning of program until one year after program completion. Site 1: random assignment to Intervention (I) group, ($n = 122$) and Control (C) group ($n = 125$). Site 2 families compared with matched families in the community. Two cohorts at each site. Attrition varied from 35% to 50% | • Children's cognitive skills<br>• School achievement<br>• Adjustment to classroom | Children's cognitive skills were greater:<br>I = 52 > C = 49<br>For cohort 1 in both sites, children scored higher on school achievement: I > C<br>Children had more successful entry into school: I > C<br>Positive outcomes not found for cohort 2, suggesting difficulty with replication |

*(continued)*

93

| Program | Program objectives and description | Description of participants | Research design | Outcome variables | Results |
|---|---|---|---|---|---|
| Infant Stimulation Mother Training Program (Badger, 1977, 1979) | To improve mothers' sense of competence and satisfaction with parenting role. Either received infant stimulation curriculum with home visits or training program in-center, with similar information services provided by nurses or social workers to reduce infant developmental morbidity | Mother–infant pairs: a) young mothers, 16 years and under b) older mothers, 18 years and older First-born infants who were gestationally mature and who had 5-minute Apgar scores over 7. | 48 families randomly assigned to two Intervention (I) groups: (1) home visits only (*n* = 24) or (2) in-center training groups only (*n* = 24) Two subgroups of younger and older mother-infant pairs (*n* = 12) within each group | Infant development: Scores on Bayley Scales of Infant Development (Bayley, 1969) • Mother's employment • Subsequent pregnancies | Infants of young mothers in home visited group obtained significantly lower mean mental score (79) than those of young mothers in center training group (99): I(2) > I(1) Families in-center group program I (2) did better than those in I (1) home visited only: Mothers more likely to be employed I(2) > I(1) Less subsequent pregnancies I(2) < I(1) |
| Infants at Social Risk Program (Lyons-Ruth, Connell, Grunebaum, & Botein, 1990) | Weekly home visits by experienced staff member and lay visitors on family health and social service needs. Weekly group meetings. Modeled and reinforced positive interactions with their children. Participants spent 13 months in the program. | Subjects referred from health, educational, and social services agencies serving low-income families due to concerns about quality of caregiving environment. Infants between birth and 9 months at study entry. Poverty and maternal depression prevalent 4–18 months approx. | Intervention (I) group (*n* = 31) compared to comparison (C) group (*n* = 10) identified at 18 months by clinical referral (2) Matched comparison group in same neighborhood not identified by social services matched on a number variables (*n* = 35). Independent analysis of depressed mothers. | • Infant mental development • Attachment to mothers • Maternal behavior • Maternal involvement with infants • Disorganization in children | No difference on infant development: I = C No differences on maternal behavior ratings: I = C Home visited infants of depressed mothers outperformed nonvisited infants by 10 points on Bayley Mental Scale. Twice as likely to be securely attached Fewer infants disorganized in intervention group: I = 53% < C = 70% Increased number of securely attached children in intervention group |

| Program | Description | Sample | Design | Outcome measures | Results |
|---|---|---|---|---|---|
| Kansas Healthy Start Home Visitor Program (Barquest & Martin, 1984) | To reduce incidence of child abuse. Home visits to encourage use of appropriate services<br><br>Provided phone line and drop-in center one morning a week | Newborns to 18 months postpartum; urban pregnant teenagers | Intervention (I) group (n = 54) and control (C) group (n = 130) | • Home environment<br>• Mental and motor development<br>• Use of services | No differences on development I = C<br>No differences on home environment: I = C<br>Significant increases in visits to health departments, family planning clinics, and immunizations: I > C |
| Menninger Infant Project (Osofsky, Culp, Eberhart-Wright, Ware, & Hann, 1988) | To improve the developmental outcomes of infants of teenage mothers<br><br>Community home visitors provided home visits once a week for 4 weeks, then once a month; crisis line; and drop-in center | Teenage mothers from low-income groups | Random assignment to intervention (I) group (n = 130) or comparison (C) group (n = 54) | • Mothers' interactions with infants<br>• Infant development | No significant difference found, although infants of mothers who had been involved in the intervention did better than those who did not accept intervention: I = C<br>Mothers involved in home visiting (I) had more positive scores in both feeding and play interactions with their infants: I = C |

*(continued)*

**Table A2.3.** *(continued)*

| Program | Program objectives and description | Description of participants | Research design | Outcome variables | Results |
|---|---|---|---|---|---|
| Mother–Infant Communication Program (Klein & Briggs, 1987) | To facilitate positive and effective interaction strategies between caregivers and their infants<br><br>Home visits and center-based programs (e.g., support groups), for 3 years; nondirective, videotape feedback | Infants in NICU and parents at risk for poor parenting skills | 45 families not randomly assigned. Intervention group I-1: home visits only (*n* = 15); Intervention group I-2: home visits and center-based groups (*n* = 22); Intervention group I-3: small local group sessions only (*n* = 8), and matched comparison (C) group (*n* = 18) | • Home Observation for Measurement of the Environment; HOME: (Caldwell, & Bradley, 1984)<br>• Infant language development | Home visit only group had better outcomes on HOME Inventory: I > C, but not statistically significant.<br>I(2) Home visits and groups showed better outcomes on Home Inventory and infant language development: I(2) > I(1) and C |
| Optimal Growth Project (Caruso, 1989) | To reduce the incidence of abuse and neglect<br>Group meetings, home visits, and counseling and educational components. Infant stimulation tasks provided to parents from pregnancy to 5 years postnatal. Weekly visits by paraprofessionals during pregnancy, then biweekly. | African American, unmarried mothers with low incomes | Intervention (I) group (*n* = 171) or comparison (C) group (*n* = 91) | • Child development<br>• Incidence of abuse and neglect | No difference on child variables: I = C<br>Complete absence of abuse in intervention group I (no abuse) < C = 14% |

| Program | Goals/Intervention | Sample | Design/Methods | Measures | Results |
|---|---|---|---|---|---|
| Parents as Teachers Program (PAT) (Wagner & Clayton, 1999; Wagner & McElroy, 1992) | To increase parents' knowledge of child development, to prepare children for success in school, and to inform parents about good parenting<br><br>Monthly home visits by trained parent educator and group meetings, and "drop-in and play." Child screening and referral to appropriate services. Received average of 20 visits over 3 years | Mothers from the majority of families were Latina, many of whom spoke Spanish predominantly; approximately 50% were single mothers; and one in five received welfare benefits. | 2000 sites, served more than 500,000. Northern California Demonstration Program.<br><br>Families randomly assigned to Intervention (I) group (n = 298), Control (C) group (n = 199).<br><br>43% of parents in the program dropped out. Used multivariate analysis controlling for a variety of variables such as receiving welfare. | • Parenting knowledge, attitudes, and behavior<br>• Child development and health<br>• Home environment assessed at first, second, and third birthdays | In Salinas Valley PAT no differences found for parenting knowledge attitudes, and behavior I = C<br><br>Children's self-help skills were improved: I > C<br><br>Positive trend for social development<br><br>No difference in children's health: I = C<br><br>Multivariate analysis suggested small positive effects not seen in original analysis for children's cognitive and social development and self-help skills. Latina mothers and their children benefited more than did mothers who were not Latina. Variations in attendance affected outcomes for children. |
| Relationship-Based Intervention with At-Risk Mothers (Heinicke, Fineman, Ruth, Recchia, Guthrie, & Rodning, 1999) | To increase positive relationships between mothers and children in terms of sensitivity, respect, and attachment<br><br>Intervention started during pregnancy and first year post-partum. Home visits and group session (17 group sessions and 36 home visits on average). Home visits by mental health professionals | Mothers at risk because of poverty and lack of support | Random assignment to intervention (I) group (n = 31) or control (C) group (n = 33). | • Maternal sensitivity<br>• Mother's respect for child's autonomy<br>• Attachment (A, B, C and disorganization) | I > C on all variables<br><br>I < C for disorganization: I = 4 (13%) < C = 9 (27%) |

*(continued)*

97

**Table A2.3.** *(continued)*

| Program | Program objectives and description | Description of participants | Research design | Outcome variables | Results |
|---|---|---|---|---|---|
| Steps Towards Effective, Enjoyable Parenting (STEEP) (Egeland & Erickson, 2004) | To bring support and learning to new mother–infant pairs and to enhance the parent–child relationship and prevent social and emotional problems among children born to first-time parents who are challenged by risk factors such as poverty, youth, limited education, social isolation, and stressful life circumstances. Home visits, parenting groups, and "Seeing is Believing" videotaping strategy. Practical support and advice. Parents were helped to discuss their own childhood experiences. Interventionists, mothers with some experience with working with mothers from low-income groups. Received program until child was 12 months of age (30 sessions on average). Fathers and other family members were included in the home-based activities and periodic family events. | First-time mothers recruited during pregnancy or after birth from various agencies (*N* = 154). Were either on welfare, poor, and uninsured. Education level no more than high school | Random assignment to Intervention (I) group (*n* = 74) or Control (C) group (*n* = 80) | • Attachment classification of child<br>• Expectations about child development and parenting<br>• Social support<br>• Home environment<br>• Sensitivity to child | When compared with control group, intervention performed better than control group (I > C). Specifically, I showed<br><br>• More realistic expectations about child development and parenting<br>• Decreased social isolation<br>• Improved quality of home environment<br><br>However,<br><br>• Infants not more likely to be securely attached and did not reduce disorganized attachment, rather, increased it.<br><br>Control subjects showed a tendency to move toward more secure attachment by 19 months, whereas that was not true for the intervention group.<br><br>Concluded that to understand the limitations of the program's effectiveness it is important to consider the cognitive and emotional status of the participants (the program participants were considered to have more psychological impairments than was typical) |

**Table A2.4.** Two-generation programs

| Program | Program objectives and description | Description of participants | Research design | Outcome variables | Results |
|---------|-----------------------------------|----------------------------|-----------------|-------------------|---------|
| Avance Family Support and Education Program (Johnson & Walker, 1991) | To teach parents to teach their children and to meet the parents' needs for education and job training Annually, about 2,500 families living in low socioeconomic status (SES) area participated in Avance programs; mothers attended 3-hour classes once per week for first year of program. Monthly home visits were conducted by staff. Second-year adult literacy and basic education for families who complete parenting program. Educational child care for 3 hours a week. | Mothers with children age birth through two at entry into program; families living in low SES area | Random assignment to intervention group (I) and control group (C). Sample sizes varied in different settings. Across all settings (n = 2500) | • Cognitive levels<br>• Iowa Tests of Basic Skills (Hoover, Dunbar, & Frisbie, 2001)<br>• Child behavior<br>• Parenting attitudes<br>• Home environment<br>• Use of community resources<br>• Participation in general education development (GED) or English as a second language | Cognitive levels: I = C<br>Iowa Tests of Basic Skills: I > C<br>Child behavior: I = C<br>Parenting attitudes/efficacy: I > C<br>Home learning environment: I > C<br>Use of community resources: I > C<br>Participation in GED or English as a second language: I = 67% > C = 33%<br><br>Mothers who were married and who had more education had more positive education and parenting outcomes.<br><br>The intervention group did better on all measures except parenting attitudes, which was the same as for the control group. |

*(continued)*

**Table A2.4.** (continued)

| Program | Program objectives and description | Description of participants | Research design | Outcome variables | Results |
|---|---|---|---|---|---|
| Center-Based Home Visiting Comparison Study (Field, Widmayer, Greenberg, & Stoller, 1982) | To evaluate the effectiveness of two parent training modalities with teenage mothers and their infants<br><br>Two intervention groups: One received Comprehensive Employment Training, paid teacher's aid in nursery, parent training, job training; and one received parent training through 6 months of biweekly home visits by psychology student | Teenage, low-income, African American mothers trained during their infants' first 6 months | Two intervention groups:<br>1 (I) nursery group (n = 40) and 1 (2) home visited group (n = 40) and a control group (C) (n = 40), which received neither of the two interventions<br><br>Outcomes at 2 years | Infants:<br>• Weight<br>• Development on Bayley Mental and Motor Scales (Bayley, 1969)<br><br>Mothers:<br>• Return to work or school<br>• Pregnancy rate | Positive outcomes:<br>Infants of both groups weighed more than controls: I > C<br><br>Infants in nursery group performed better than home visited group: I (1) > I (2)<br><br>Mothers in nursery group had greater rate of return to work and fewer repeat pregnancies: I (1) > I (2) |
| Child and Family Resource Program (CFRP) (Travers, Nauta, & Irwin, 1982) | To support families and to help parents to become more effective caregivers and educators in order to promote their children's growth and development<br><br>Monthly home visits and twice-per quarter center-based sessions. Comprehensive social and educational services provided by 11 projects to more than 1,000 families per year; funded from 1973–1983 | Parents with children birth to age 5 in low SES families | Randomly assigned to program (I) or no services (C)<br><br>Attendance at center activities very sporadic | • Child cognitive levels<br>• Child health<br>• Child behavior<br>• Parenting attitudes<br>• Parent–child interaction<br>• Employment and training<br>• Locus of control<br>• Use of public assistance | Cognitive: I = C<br>Child health: I = C<br>Child behavior: I = C<br>Positive changes:<br>Participation in Head Start: I = 62% > C = 32%<br>Parenting attitudes: I > C<br>Locus of control: I > C<br>Parent–child interactions: I > C<br>Employment and training: I = 74% > C = 68%<br><br>Use of public assistance: I > C<br><br>Stronger results for active participants and for those mothers who saw themselves as able to cope with life problems |

| Comprehensive Child Development Program (CCDP) (Goodson, Layzer, St. Pierre, Bernstein, & Lopez, 2000; St. Pierre, Layzer, 1998; St. Pierre, Layzer, Goodson, & Bernstein, 1997) | To enhance the physical, social, emotional, and intellectual development of children in low-income families from birth to age five; provide support to their parents and other family members; and assist families in becoming economically self-sufficient. Home visits used as the primary means of delivering both to do case management and early childhood education. Services began in child's first year of life and continued until child entered school. Two visits from paraprofessionals a month, each 1 hour long. Individual goals set for each family | Children and families from low-income groups; one-third were teenage mothers. The total evaluation sample across the 21 projects consisted of 4,410 families. 24 sites, 21 evaluated | Intervention (I) group ($n = 2,213$); Control group (C), ($n = 2,197$). Attrition: 20% dropout in first year; 40% by 2.5 years. Assumptions underlying the design were that all low-income families have a complicated set of needs and that CCDP programs should ensure that all of those needs are met. | Children: <br>• Cognitive <br>• Cooperative behavior <br>• Physical growth <br>• Health behavior <br>• Participation in child care <br><br>Parents: <br>• Attitudes <br>• Expectations for the child <br>• Home learning environment <br>• Parent–child interaction <br>• Time with child <br>• Participation in parenting classes <br>• Participation in academic and vocational training <br>• Welfare | Five years after the program began, CCDP had no significant effects on parents or children compared with controls. However, there were some positive trends in parents. |

(continued)

**Table A2.4.** *(continued)*

| Program | Program objectives and description | Description of participants | Research design | Outcome variables | Results |
|---|---|---|---|---|---|
| Even Start Family Literacy Program (St. Pierre, Swartz, Gamse, Murray, Ceck, & Nickel, 1995) | Family-focused intervention program designed to break the intergenerational cycle of poverty and low literacy. Parents had to be eligible to participate in an adult education program under the Adult Education Act. Even Start has three goals: 1) to help parents improve (family) literacy or basic education skills, 2) to help parents become full-time partners in educating their children, and 3) to assist children in reaching their full potential as learners. The program has three core components that addressed its goals: 1) Families took part in early childhood education, parenting education, and adult education, as mandatory requirements. Intensity and duration varied across sites. 2) The number of Even Start programs across the United States increased over time from 76 sites in the 1989 to 770 sites in the 2004, serving approximately one million parents and children. 3) The average site served approximately 54 families. The average length of participation was 7 months. Used existing (e.g., Head Start) services to avoid duplication. | Parents and children up to age 8 from low-income families. Child at entry birth to 8 years | Randomized controlled field trial included 463 families from 18 sites willing to participate. About two-thirds of the sample (*n* = 309) was randomly assigned to an intervention group (I) and one-third (*n* = 154) to a control group (C). Participants in the intervention group began the Even Start program immediately, whereas participants in the control group were not allowed to begin the Even Start program for one year. Data were collected at pre-intervention, post-intervention 1 year later, and in a one-year follow-up. Pretest data on child and adult literacy skills were collected in the fall; posttest data were collected in the spring/summer, and follow-up data were collected in the following spring. | • Child development<br>• Language development<br>• Participation in early childhood programs<br>• Parents' expectations for children<br>• Home learning environment<br>• Participation in parenting programs<br><br>Measures: a) children (Peabody Picture Vocabulary Test-Revised [Dunn & Dunn, 1981], Woodcock-Johnson Battery, Story & Print Concepts [Woodcock & Johnson, 1989a]); b) parents (Woodcock-Johnson Battery); c) teacher report on children (Social Skills Rating System) (SSRS) (Gresham & Elliot, 1990), d) parent reports on economic and educational status, child literacy-related skills, home literacy environment and activities; e) parent assessment of children (Vineland Adaptive Behavior Scale/Communication Domain; Sparrow, Balla, & Cicchetti, 1984), and f) school records | The two groups did not significantly differ 1 year after the Even Start intervention on parenting measures.<br><br>Positive results: Participation in early childhood program and parenting programs: I = 95% > C = 8%<br><br>Parents' attainment of General Education Development (GED) certificate: I = 22% > C = 6%.<br><br>Positive relationship between amount of instruction and child cognitive development and vocabulary and attainment of general education development (GED) certificate<br><br>No program impacts found at post-test.<br><br>The only significant difference between the control and intervention groups was in teacher ratings of behavior problems using the SSRS. Teachers rated elementary school-age intervention group children as having fewer behavior problems than control group children.<br><br>Results of the 1-year follow-up: Children and parents made gains on a variety of measures, but they did not gain more than children and parents in the control group. |

| Head Start Family Service Centers (Swartz, Bernstein, & Levin, 2000; Swartz, Smith, Berghauer, Bernstein, & Gardine, 1994) | Head Start Services for 4-year-olds, case management, needs assessment, referral to services, and support services<br><br>Adult literacy and employment training provided through partnerships with local service agencies | Children 4 years of age from low SES<br><br>Families with the additional program components provided by Family Service Centers (FSC) were compared with those who received Head Start only. | Parental measures:<br>• Amount of participation in literacy and employment services<br>• Reading at home<br>• Literacy test<br>• Depression<br>• Drug/alcohol consumption<br>• Health rating | Meeting with case manager or social worker:<br>FSC families > Head Start only families<br>Engaging in educational and employment activities:<br>FSC families > than Head Start only families<br>Working toward a degree:<br>FSC families = 48% > Head Start only families = 34%<br>Improved literacy, employment, and substance abuse: FSC families = Head Start only families |

*(continued)*

**Table A2.4.** *(continued)*

| Program | Program objectives and description | Description of participants | Research design | Outcome variables | Results |
|---|---|---|---|---|---|
| New Chance Program (Quint, Bos, & Polit, 1997) | To determine whether New Chance Program had any impact on child development, educational attainment, family life, emotional and physical health, employment and earnings, and welfare status. Also, to determine the costs of implementing the program<br><br>Free child care in high quality centers. In addition<br><br>Phase 1: Full-week program for mothers: life skills, parenting education, pediatric health education<br><br>Phase 2: Vocational training, internships, and job placement<br><br>Average participation: 6 months | 2,322 mothers; child younger than 2 years; low SES families. | Mothers were randomly assigned to intervention (I) group (*n* = 1,553) or to a control (C) group (*n* = 769). At the 42-month follow-up, data were collected from 1,401 participants and 678 control group members. The sample was selected from 16 sites from 10 different states across the United States. | • Child development<br>• Language development<br>• Participation in early childhood programs<br>• Home learning environment and reading materials<br>• Employment and income<br>• Psychological outcomes<br>• Participation in adult education | In most areas, participants did not show greater gains than those in the control group.<br><br>Child outcomes were not improved, although there were some differences between the two groups for parents.<br><br>Positive results:<br><br>GED attainment: I = 43% > C = 30%<br><br>College credit: I > C<br><br>Parenting attitudes: I > C<br><br>Emotional support of children: I > C<br><br>Use of child care: I = 63% > C = 33%<br><br>Participation in parenting program: I = 67% > C = 21%<br><br>Participation in health education: I = 49% > C = 11%<br><br>Participation in skill-building program: I = 33% > C = 22%<br><br>Participation in education programs: I = 85% > C = 60%<br><br>Participation in family planning: I = 52% > C = 12% |

**Table A2.5.** Studies of various short-term early intervention approaches

*Interventions that focused on improving parent–child interactions and relationships*

| Program | Program objectives and description | Description of participants | Research design | Outcome variables | Results |
|---|---|---|---|---|---|
| Adopted Children Study (Juffer, Bakermans-Kranenburg, & van IJzendoorn, 2005) | To increase mothers' sensitivity in responding to their children and to increase secure attachment in children. Two interventions: Mothers were either provided with 1) a personal book focused on sensitive parenting only, or 2) a personal book and home visits with personal video feedback. Sessions were conducted for 6 to 9 months by female psychologists. | Adoptive families with children adopted before 6 months of age. Middle-upper middle class families (N = 130). | Randomized intervention study. Two intervention groups and one control group: I (1) mothers received personal book only (n = 30), I (2) mothers received the same personal book and three home-based sessions of video feedback (n = 49); the third group (C) did not receive intervention (received a booklet on adoption issues) | • Maternal responsiveness<br>• Attachment (ABC)<br>• Disorganized attachment | The intervention with video feedback and the personal book resulted in enhanced maternal sensitive responsiveness. I (2) > I (1), C Children of mothers who received this intervention were less likely to be classified with disorganized attachment at the age of 12 months, and received lower scores on the rating scale for disorganization than did children in the control group. I (2) < C Concluded that nurturing processes or environmental factors may influence attachment disorganization and disorganization in infants can be changed through parenting interventions |

*(continued)*

**Table A2.5.** (*continued*)

Interventions that focused on improving parent–child interactions and relationships

| Program | Program objectives and description | Description of participants | Research design | Outcome variables | Results |
|---------|-----------------------------------|----------------------------|-----------------|-------------------|---------|
| Coaching the Interaction (van den Boom, 1994, 1995) | To study effects of enhancing maternal sensitive responsiveness on quality of mother–infant interaction, infant exploration, and attachment<br><br>The intervention focused on enhancing maternal sensitivity to infants' cues. Mothers were coached to read their infants' cues, to imitate them, and to soothe their infants when they were upset. Between 6–9 months received intervention sessions with a female psychologist. | 100 mothers and infants. Selected on the basis of irritability on the BNABS at 15 days postpartum. | Randomly assigned to the intervention (I) group (*n* = 50) and control (C) group (*n* = 50). A factorial design was created to enable assessment of pre-intervention differences between the two groups as well as the assessment of the interaction of preintervention testing with the intervention; each group consisted of two subgroups of mother-infant pairs (*n* = 25). | • Maternal interactional variables<br>• Infant interactional variables<br>• Infant exploratory behavior<br>• Attachment classification of the infants<br>• Disorganization in child | In the intervention group with temperamentally difficult infants, the following behaviors were more positive:<br><br>Maternal responsiveness, stimulation<br><br>Visual attentiveness and control<br><br>Infant sociability, ability to soothe self, and more exploratory behavior<br><br>Attachment:<br><br>I = 62% securely attached > C = 22%<br><br>At 12 months of age, significantly more intervention group dyads than control group dyads were securely attached than control group dyads.<br><br>Evidence of sustained effects of the first year intervention program was still seen in the third year |

| | | | | | |
|---|---|---|---|---|---|
| Comparing an intervention that focused on improving the sensitivity of interactions with one that gave information (Wendland-Carro, Piccinini, & Millar, 1999) | To examine efficacy of a brief intervention designed to influence mothers' sensitive responsiveness toward their infants. Provided two interventions: 1) Mothers were shown video of the administration of the BNBAS and other clips of sensitive handling of an infant, 2) mothers were shown video of basic caregiving and given information on such topics as skin rashes and immunization | 36 mothers and their infants shortly after birth, with a follow-up at 1 month | Mothers and their infants, 2 or 3 days following delivery, randomly assigned to either: Intervention (I) that received a program designed to enhance mother–infant interaction ($n = 17$); or a control group (C) that was presented with an intervention emphasizing basic caregiving skills ($n = 19$). Assessed 1 month later during free play and bathing | • Sensitivity of interactions | Mothers in intervention group showed more improvements than mothers in control group: ($I > C$) and<br>• Were more synchronized with their infants<br>• Vocalized more to their infants<br>• Provided more stimulation, and smiling to their infants<br>• Soothed their infants more<br><br>Concluded that even a modest videotaped early intervention can enhance mothers' sensitive responsiveness to the infant |
| Floor time or directed interactional guidance (DeGangi & Greenspan, 1997) | Floor time or child-centered infant therapy approach compared with structured developmental parent guidance about training infants in special skills and giving parents parenting tips<br>6 weeks of intervention for each intervention group | Infants between ages of 14 and 30 months who had difficulties with regulation such as high irritability, inattention, and sensory integration difficulties | Randomly assigned to one of three groups:<br>I (1): Floor time ($n = 8$)<br>I (2): Sensory integration approach ($n = 8$)<br>C: No intervention ($n = 8$) | • Infant symptoms of inattention and irritability | Infant symptoms reduced:<br>I (1) = 75% > I (2) = 37.5% and C = 0% |

(continued)

107

**Table A2.5.** *(continued)*

*Interventions that focused on improving parent–child interactions and relationships*

| Program | Program objectives and description | Description of participants | Research design | Outcome variables | Results |
|---|---|---|---|---|---|
| Occupational therapy intervention (Sajaniemi, Mäkelä, Salokorpi, von Wendt, Hämäläinen, & Hakeamies-Blomqvist, 2001) | To assess the effects of an early occupational therapy intervention on the cognitive and attachment developmental patterns and coordination in extremely low birth weight (ELBW) infants; aimed at supporting parent–child interactions and enhancing motor control and coordination in ELBW infants.<br><br>Weekly home visits between 6–12 months of age in which mothers were taught to adapt the environment to the infant's needs. Implemented by occupational therapists in weekly sessions. | Extremely low birth weight infants (ELBW) (N = 100) | 100 ELBW infants matched in pairs in accordance to their pre-perinatal risk scores and randomly assigned to intervention (I) or non-intervention (C) groups. Assessed again at 2 and 4 years of age: I (n = 49); C (n = 51) | • Parents' sensitivity to infants' cues<br>• Attachment at age 4 years (assessed with the Preschool Assessment of Attachment)<br>• Cognitive development (assessed with the Bayley Scales at age 2 and with the Wechsler Preschool and Primary Scale of Intelligence (WPPSI-R; Wechsler, 1989) at age 4) | More likely to<br>Be securely attached: I > C<br><br>Less likely to have atypical attachment pattern: I = 7 (30%) < C = 14 (56%)<br><br>Cognitive performance was within age norms in both groups at both ages. The intervention did not show any effect on cognitive performance at the age of 2 years. At the age of 4 years, cognitive level was higher overall, and most notably for verbal performance, I > C.<br><br>Concluded that 1) cumulative positive effects may take a long time to show, and 2) focusing the intervention on parenting skills may in the long run give the broadest developmental benefit. |

| | | | | | |
|---|---|---|---|---|---|
| Short-term interactional coaching with mothers of preterm infants (Parker-Loewen & Lytton, 1987) | To examine the effects of short-term interactional coaching on mother–infant interaction patterns of mother–preterm infant dyads<br><br>Interventions:<br><br>1) Interaction was coached via an ear-piece microphone from behind a one-way mirror. Twelve sessions.<br><br>2) Mothers were offered toys for their babies that were delivered to their homes. | Mothers with infants (N = 35) less than 37 weeks gestational age weighing 1000–2000 grams. | Random assignment to intervention and a control group. Mothers in the intervention I (I) group received a 40-minute interactional session in a room equipped with toys over 12 weeks (n = 35).<br><br>Mothers in the control group were offered toys for their babies and the toys were delivered to their homes (n = 35). | • Mother–infant interactions<br>• Mothers asked about their awareness of their infants' cues | No difference in maternal sensitivity after the intervention: I = C<br><br>Mothers in group I (I) thought that their relationship with their infants had been positively affected by the intervention.<br><br>Mothers in control group expressed excitement at being given the toys and in the showing of interest in them.<br><br>Marginally significant difference between the groups that emerged was in having greater knowledge of parenting their children |
| Use of soft baby carriers (Anisfeld, Casper, Nozyce, & Cunningham, 1990) | Mothers given soft baby carrier to use everyday or a hard infant seat after going home from the hospital. | 47 low-income mothers | Randomly assigned to experimental group I (I) use of soft baby carrier (n = 23), or control group (C) use of infant seat (n = 24).<br><br>Follow-up at 13 months. | • Interaction, maternal sensitivity and responsiveness<br>• Attachment classification | Assessments at 3½ months:<br><br>Mothers in the intervention groups were more sensitive and contingently responsive to their infants: I > C<br><br>Assessment at 13 months:<br><br>More I than C infants were securely attached to their mothers: I > C<br><br>Concluded that there may be a causal relationship between increased physical contact, achieved through early carrying in a soft baby carrier, and subsequent security of attachment between infant and mother |

(continued)

**Table A2.5.** *(continued)*

Interventions that focused on improving parent–child interactions and relationships

| Program | Program objectives and description | Description of participants | Research design | Outcome variables | Results |
|---|---|---|---|---|---|
| Use of videotape viewing or interactional guidance (Robert-Tissot et al., 1996) | Videotape viewing was compared with a psychodynamic approach Mother and child were both present in the sessions in both types of intervention. The actual number of sessions attended ranged from 1 to 12 weeks, with the average number being 6–9 weeks | Children under 30 months with sleep, feeding, and behavior disorders and separation and attachment problems | 75 children randomly assigned to: I (1): Videotape viewing (n = 32) or I (2) Psychodynamic therapy (n = 42); no control group Followed up 1 week after therapy and 6 months after therapy ended | • Child symptoms<br>• Maternal sensitivity<br>• Maternal self-esteem | Both interventions successful in treating symptoms at follow-up, at 6 months behavior problems not improved Maternal sensitivity and self-esteem improved Videotape viewing increased sensitivity more, whereas the psychodynamic intervention enhanced self-esteem more Improvements lasted at least several months, with some positive improvement detected at the 6-month follow-up. |
| Video feedback and attachment discussions (Bakermans-Kranenburg, Juffer, & van IJzendoorn, 1998) | Two interventions were compared: 1) Participants were provided written information and watched a video (behavioral level) 2) Parents were provided with written information, watched a video, and discussed mother's experience of being parented (representational level). | 30 mothers with insecure attachment classifications as assessed by Adult Attachment Interview (AAI) (George, Kaplan, & Main, 1985) | 30 mothers randomly assigned to I (1) video only group: (n = 15), I (2) video + discussion of early experiences group (n = 15), or C: a nonintervention control group | • Sensitivity in interactions<br>• Attachment classification | Maternal sensitivity:<br>• Mothers in both groups were more sensitive to their infants at 13 months of age<br>Secure attachment:<br>• No difference in security of attachment. Did not reduce disorganized attachment Dismissive mothers benefited most from |

| | | | | | |
|---|---|---|---|---|---|
| | Implemented during four home visits 7 to 10 months after baby's birth, with personal video feedback. Interventionists had master's or doctorate degrees. | | | | intervention I (1), and preoccupied mothers from I (2) |
| Watch, Wait, and Wonder (WWW) (Cohen et al., 1999; Cohen, Lojkasek, Muir, Muir, & Parker, 2002) | To test the effects of WWW with 12- to 30-month-old clinic infants<br><br>A child-led interaction (WWW) followed by discussion between therapist and parent was compared with a more psychodynamic and family approach. Eight to 18 sessions were provided | 67 12- to 30-month olds with feeding, sleeping, and behavior regulation problems or difficulties with bonding | Randomly assigned to I (1) WWW (n = 34) or I (2) Psychodynamic therapy (n = 33); no control group.<br>Pre- and post-testing. Six-month follow-up: I (1) WWW, (n = 26); I (2) Psychodynamic therapy, (n = 31). | • Symptom reduction<br>• Parenting stress<br>• Parenting competence<br>• Attachment classifications<br>• Bayley Scales of Infant Development<br>• Interactions<br>• Emotion regulation | Both groups improved on all variables<br>Improvements stronger for WWW<br>Infants in WWW group more likely to be securely attached. Disorganization was more reduced in WWW group<br>At 6-month follow-up, positive effects observed from the beginning to the end of intervention in both intervention groups were maintained or improved further, but the change emerged at a different pace. An advantage persisted in the WWW group in relation to mothers' comfort with dealing with infant behaviors and their ratings of parenting stress. |

*(continued)*

111

**Table A2.5.** *(continued)*

*Interventions that focused on enhancing parents' attributions of their children*

| Program | Program objectives and description | Description of participants | Research design | Outcome variables | Results |
|---|---|---|---|---|---|
| Use of a cognitive approach to child abuse prevention (Bugental, 1999; Bugental et al., 2000; Bugental, Ellerson, Lin, Rainey, Kokotovic, O'Hara, 2002) | To test the incremental utility of cognitive retraining as a component within a program designed to prevent child maltreatment<br><br>Compared interventions both unenhanced and enhanced with home visitations consistent with Healthy Start Program. One intervention group added a cognitive appraisal component; interventions were compared with a control group who received only information on services | 96 mothers at risk for child abuse identified in late pregnancy or soon after the baby was born; 73 families completed the program | Randomly assigned to one of the three groups with intervention continuing for 1 year<br><br>Parents in the *unenhanced home visitation:* I (1) condition received home visitation consistent with the Healthy Start program, supplemented with information regarding existing services available in the community (*n* = 34).<br><br>Parents in the *enhanced home visitation:* I (2) condition received information about existing community services, combined with methods used in the Healthy Start program and a brief attributionally based problem-solving discussion at the start of each visit (causal appraisal followed by problem-focused appraisal) (*n* = 35).<br><br>Parents in the *control condition* (C) received no direct services but were provided with information regarding existing services available in the community (*n* = 27). | • Incidence of abuse<br>• Incidence of hostile parenting<br>• Level of depression<br>• Parent attributions of their children | Incidence of abuse: I (2) = 4% < I (1) = 20% < C = 36<br><br>Child health was most improved in I (2)<br><br>Maternal depression was most reduced in I (2) and seemed to mediate outcomes |

| Intervention (citation) | Purpose/Description | Population | Research design/Follow-up | Variables considered | Results |
|---|---|---|---|---|---|
| Use of the administration of the Brazelton Neonatal Behavioral Assessment Scale (BNBAS) to enhance interactions (Nugent & Brazelton, 2000) | Used the administration of the BNBAS with an infant in the neonatal period to enhance parents' understanding of their infant and their sensitivity in interactions | A variety of high-risk parents and infants and more representative populations of newborns | Varied between studies, but parents and infants have typically been followed up during the infant's first year | Typical variables considered include:<br>• Parent–infant interactions<br>• Maternal attitudes toward the infant<br>• Infant outcomes | Results have varied but have been best when<br>• Infants are at risk<br>• Parents are involved in the administration of the assessment items<br>• Parents are not at very high risk |
| *Interventions that focused on improving the child's developmental outcome* | | | | | |
| Applied Behavioral Analysis (ABA) (Dawson & Osterling, 1997; McEachin, Smith, & Lovass, 1993) | To reduce the symptoms and increase various developmental capacities in children with autism | Children with autism | Various studies with different sample sizes | • Development including IQ score<br>• Integration into school programs<br>• Symptoms of autism | IQ gain of 23 points<br>50% successfully integrated into school programs |
| Effectiveness of infant massage (Field, 1998b, 2000; Field & Hernandez-Reif, 2001; Field, Hernandez-Reif, Diego, Feijo, Vera, & Gil, 2004) | To assess the effects of massage on the growth and development of young infants. Individualized massage with the infant has been carried out using a firm touch and making sure that the infant is not hypersensitive to touch. | High-risk mothers and infants as well as infants who are considered typically developing and parents not at risk | Research designs have varied by populations | Variables assessed have included:<br>• Infant state organization<br>• Weight gain<br>• Developmental level<br>• Days of hospitalization | In general, positive effects have been found for all the noted variables<br>It is believed that the massage enhances food absorption hormones leading to stimulation of growth |

(continued)

**Table A2.5.** *(continued)*

*Interventions that focused on improving the child's developmental outcome*

| Program | Program objectives and description | Description of participants | Research design | Outcome variables | Results |
|---|---|---|---|---|---|
| Evaluation of a variety of interventions used to enhance language development through training of parents (see next column for details) | Various interventions have been used to train parents to enhance the language of their children:<br><br>Whitehurst Dialogue Training Program (WDRTP) (Whitehurst et al., 1988); Conversational Language Training program (CLTP) (Dale et al., 1996); Mother Child Home Program (MCHP); and Hanen Early Language Program. (Fey, Cleave, Long, & Hughes, 1993); Manolson, Ward, & Dodington, 1995; Fey et al., 1993).<br><br>The MCHP used toys in the home for several in the home sessions over 7 months of 2 years (Levenstein, Levenstein, Shiminski, & Stolzberg, 1998). | Typically, parents of children with language delays or at risk for having language delays | Research has used delayed intervention groups and assignments to various kinds of interventions. Typically, post-intervention assessment has been used.<br><br>One study using the MCHP with at-risk toddlers followed the children to 17 and 22 years of age. | • Children's development and language skills<br><br>• Parent–child interactional measures | Success has been found most frequently in parent's ability to interact in ways to facilitate the development of their children's language.<br><br>Studies of children with language delays have not usually shown improvements in the children's language development.<br><br>In the MCHP study with at-risk toddlers at follow-up at 17 and 22 years, the children had lower rates of school dropout and higher rates of school graduation. |

114

| Study/Topic | Objectives | Sample | Design/Intervention | Measures | Findings |
|---|---|---|---|---|---|
| Improving the outcome of low-birth-weight infants (Barrera, Doucet, & Kitching, 1990; Barrera, Rosenbaum, & Cunningham, 1986) | To assess the differences between two interventions and two control groups. One group received an intervention that emphasized enhancing the parent–child interaction and the other focused on enhancing the infants' development. Home visits were provided for the first year of the child's life. | Preterm infants (birth weight less than 2,000 grams at less than 37 weeks) and 24 full-term infants (BW of more than 2,500 grams and age at more than 37 weeks) in the first year of life | Random assignment to either a developmental intervention: I (1) group (n = 16), a parent–infant intervention: I (2) group (n = 22), or a no-intervention control group: C (n = 21). A full-term no-intervention control group of infants (gestational period > 37 wks and birth weight (t > 2,500 g) (n = 24) was also used. Outcome measures were obtained at 4, 8, 12, and 16 months. | • Home Observation for Measurement of the Environment (HOME; Caldwell & Bradley, 1984)<br>• Bayley Scales of Infant Development<br>• Vineland Social Maturity Scale (Doll, 1965)<br>• Flint Infant Security Scale<br>• Parent–child interaction using behavioral coding<br>Infants were assessed at 4, 8, 12, and 16 months of age, corrected for prematurity. | Overall the parent–infant intervention group did better than the developmental intervention group: I (2) > I (1)<br>The intervention groups had different effects at 1 year: In general, intervention group I (2) did better on measures of attachment and interaction<br>On Vineland Social Maturity Scale, I (1) > I (2) on social adaptation and competence<br>Both I (1) and I (2) groups did better than the preterm control (C) group.<br>The pre-term no-intervention control group did worse than all groups on all measures. |
| Interventions for children with separation anxiety and other anxiety disorders and depression (Target & Fonagy, 1994 a, b) | To examine the way in which the age of a child at the time of intervention in psychoanalytic psychotherapy related to the outcome of that intervention<br>To reduce symptoms of anxiety and depression | Children with anxiety disorders and depression | Play therapy, parent–child and family interventions | Diagnostic change. Change in overall adaptation (as measured by the Children's Global Assessment Scale [CGAS]) | Younger children were more likely to show significant improvement—further highlighting the importance of a developmental perspective to intervention. |

(continued)

115

**Table A2.5.** *(continued)*

*Interventions that focused on improving the child's developmental outcome*

| Program | Program objectives and description | Description of participants | Research design | Outcome variables | Results |
|---|---|---|---|---|---|
| The Incredible Years (Webster-Stratton, Kolpacoff, & Hollinsworth, 1988; Webster-Stratton & Hammond, 1997) | To reduce child behavior problems and to enhance parents' interactions with their children<br><br>Parent groups and child groups | Parents of children with behavior problems | Various | • Child symptoms<br>• Parent–child interactions<br>• Child ability to problem solve<br>• Parent attitudes | Reduction of child symptoms<br><br>Children increased ability to problem solve<br><br>Improved parent–child interactions and parent attitudes |
| *Clinical intervention with high-risk parents* | | | | | |
| Comparing a Mental Health Model to an Information/Resource Model (Barnard, Magyary, Sumner, Booth, Mitchell, & Spieker, 1988; Booth, Mitchell, Barnard, & Spieker, 1989) | To examine two interventions for parents who did not have the supportive mechanisms that cultures generally provide:<br><br>1) Mental Health model of intervention focused on listening and developing a supportive relationship<br><br>2) Information/resource model, a supportive and health promotion model<br><br>Nurses provided home visits to participants from pregnancy to 1 year postpartum. | Women pregnant 22 weeks or less with low social support (*N* = 147) | Subjects randomly assigned to one of three groups:<br><br>1) I (1) Mental Health model (*n* = 68)<br><br>2) I (2) Information resource model (*n* = 79)<br><br>3) C: no intervention<br><br>Assessed when infants were 12 months and 3 years | • Parental sensitivity on Nursing Child Assessment Teaching Scale (NCATS)<br>• Infant assessment at 1 year | Mothers in intervention groups were more sensitive and competent on NCATS.<br><br>Mothers in the Mental Health approach were more satisfied with the program and were less likely to drop out. This was particularly true of very high risk mothers.<br><br>Mental Health approach was more effective in enhancing maternal self-esteem and confidence in parenting.<br><br>No differences were found between groups on attachment security and neither group was more securely attached than the control group. |

| Evaluating 3 types of intervention for mothers with postpartum depression (Cooper, & Murray, 1997; Cooper, Murray, Wilson & Romaniuk, 2003a, b) | To evaluate the long-term effect on maternal mood of three psychological interventions in relation to routine primary care. Women were followed up on four occasions until 5 years postpartum.<br><br>The therapies were conducted in the mothers' homes on a weekly basis from 8 to 18 weeks postpartum:<br><br>1) Nondirective counseling; 2) Cognitive Behavioral therapy (CBT); 3) Psychodynamic therapy; 4) Routine care usually provided by the health care system. | 193 mothers with postpartum depression<br><br>Three women refused to participate in the study after being informed of their therapy group (one assigned to CBT and two to psychodynamic therapy). Nineteen women dropped out of intervention early (i.e., they had four or fewer sessions) or moved away from the study area.<br><br>Of the women identified as being eligible for the study, 171 (83%) completed therapy. | Random assignment to one of the four conditions:<br><br>I (1) Nondirective counseling (n = 42), I (2) Cognitive Behavioral therapy (CBT) (n = 41), I(3) Psychodynamic therapy (n = 40), and (C) Routine primary care control (n = 48) | • Level of depression<br>• Mother–infant interaction measures<br>• Infant cognitive and emotional development<br>• Secure attachment<br>• Maternal sensitivity<br><br>Mothers were assessed immediately after the intervention phase (at 4.5 months) and at 9, 18, and 60 months postpartum. | Mothers' depression in all the intervention groups remitted more quickly.<br><br>Compared with the control, all three interventions had a significant impact at 4.5 months on maternal mood (as measured by the Edinburgh Postnatal Depression Scale, EPDS).<br><br>Only psychodynamic therapy produced a rate of reduction significantly superior to that of the control group in depression (as measured by the Structured Clinical Interview for DSM-III-R). (I (3) > C).<br><br>The benefit of intervention was no longer apparent by 9 months postpartum. Intervention did not reduce subsequent episodes of postpartum depression.<br><br>None of the other variables were different in the intervention groups.<br><br>None of the interventions increased number of securely attached children or reduced disorganization. |

*(continued)*

**Table A2.5.** *(continued)*

| | | | *Clinical intervention with high-risk parents* | | |
|---|---|---|---|---|---|
| Program | Program objectives and description | Description of participants | Research design | Outcome variables | Results |
| Helping mothers fight depression (Gelfand, Teti, Seiner, & Jameson, 1996) | To enhance parenting skills and counteract the effects of the mothers' depressed affect. Home visits were conducted at 1- to 3-week intervals. Six experienced public health nurses planned individualized programs for the mothers. Twenty-nine home visits were provided. | Clinically depressed mothers with infants 3–13 months old (*N* = 73). | Controlled trial without randomization. Intervention group I (*n* = 37), Control group, usual care C (*n* = 36). Demographically matched to 38 mothers who were not depressed | • Sensitivity to infants<br>• Attachment<br>• Disorganized attachment | Sensitivity: I = C<br>Attachment: I = C<br>Disorganization: I = 10 (32%) disorganized < C = 12 (40%) disorganized |
| Infant–parent psychotherapy (Lieberman, Weston, & Pawl, 1991) | To increase maternal sensitivity and responsiveness of mothers and security of attachment of children. Nondirective, psychodynamic intervention with mother and child present in which the interventionist responded to emotional experience of mother. Intervention lasted 1 year and ended when the child was 24 months. | Parents of infants with insecure attachments at 12 months. Another group of securely attached infants was also followed. | Anxiously attached 12-month-olds and their mothers (as assessed in the Strange Situation) were randomly assigned to an intervention (I) (*n* = 34) and control group C (1) (*n* = 25). Control group C (2) securely attached dyads (*n* = 37). Reassessed at 2 years of age | • Interactional assessment<br>• Q-Sort measure of attachment | Mothers in the intervention group were more sensitive and responsive with their infants: I > C<br>Infants in intervention group more likely to be securely attached but difference was not significant: I > C<br>Decreased child avoidance and resistance and anger were found in the intervention group. Within the intervention group, level of therapeutic process was positively correlated with adaptive scores in child and mother outcome measures. |

| Intervention (Citation) | Purpose | Sample | Design | Outcome measures | Results |
|---|---|---|---|---|---|
| Intervening with infants with nonorganic failure-to-thrive (Brinich, Drotar, & Brinich, 1989) | To improve interactions of parents with their infants and to improve weight gain in infants who appear to have nonorganic failure to thrive (i.e., appears to be caused by feeding problem or parental disorder). Interventions were either 1) family-centered 2) parent-centered, and 3) advocacy oriented. Provided from 5 to 14 months | Infants exhibiting nonorganic failure to thrive (FTT), 5 months of age, from economically disadvantaged families ($N = 59$). | 69 families randomly assigned to one of three interventions: I (1) Family centered ($n = 23$) I (2) Parent centered ($n = 23$) I (3) Advocacy ($n = 23$). No control group for ethical reasons | • Security of attachment | There were no differences on the outcome measures between the intervention and the secure control groups. The groups did not differ in maternal child-rearing attitudes: I = C (2). 51% of total sample was securely attached, with no differences between the groups. I (1) = I (2) = I (3) |
| Listening, social support, and counseling for mothers with postpartum depression (Holden, Sagovsky, Cox, 1989) | To reduce postpartum depression in mothers using listening, social support, and counseling. Provided during 8 weeks of home visiting. Professional interventionists | Women identified as depressed by screening at 6 weeks postpartum and by psychiatric interview at about 13 weeks postpartum ($N = 50$) | Randomly assigned to intervention (I) group ($n = 26$) or control (C) group ($n = 24$) | • Level of depression (as measured by a 10-point self-report scale and psychiatric interviews before and after intervention) | Depression recovery: I = 69% > C = 38% recovering from the postpartum depression after 3 months. Concludes that counseling by health visitors is valuable in managing nonpsychotic postnatal depression |

*(continued)*

**Table A2.6.** Multisystem interventions

| Program | Program objectives and description | Description of participants | Research design | Outcome variables | Results |
|---|---|---|---|---|---|
| Clinical Infant Development Program (Greenspan, 1986; Greenspan & Wieder, 1987; Greenspan, Wieder, Nover, Lieberman, Lourie, et al., 1987; Pharis & Levin, 1991) | To increase the developmental outcomes for infants in high-risk families and to reduce the incidence of abuse in the families. Provided comprehensive intervention services including evaluation, home visiting, and center-based services. Infant center provided individualized therapeutic programs for infant and caregiver. Various groups and training programs. Supported parents in meeting basic needs of food and housing. Professionals and paraprofessionals provided the services. Intervention provided from birth to 6 years | 49 multi-risk families with 200 children at-risk for abuse. Outreached to social service agencies, courts, and service providers for referrals. Recruited families with older child with social and emotional difficulties. Parents with personality impairments | No control or comparison group. Case study method used. Families and the children followed over 5 years. | • Child development<br>• Abuse<br>• Mother–child interaction<br>• Parent mental health status<br>Pre- and post-test outcomes | Highly successful outcomes found for the children, mother–infant interactions with abuse reduced, and parents' interactions with their children dramatically improved |

| Multisystemic (MST) or multimodal intervention (Hengeler, Schoenwald, Rowland, & Cunningham, 2002; Henggeler & Lee, 2003) | To decrease rates of antisocial behavior, improve functioning, and reduce use of out-of-home placements. Uses a variety of intervention strategies including family therapy, parent training, supportive therapy, social skills training, and case management and advocacy | Adolescents presenting serious clinical problems including chronic and violent juvenile offenders, juvenile offenders who abused substances, adolescent sexual offenders, youth in psychiatric crisis (e.g., homicidal, suicidal, psychotic), and maltreating families | Compared intervention groups with groups receiving more standard interventions in multiple sites and studies | • Family relationships<br>• Behavior problems<br>• Criminal offending<br>• Psychiatric symptoms<br>• School attendance<br>• Drug use and alcohol use<br>• Out-of-home placement<br>• Hospitalization | Positive outcomes have been found for all of the outcome measures. Utilizing an ecological conceptualization of youth problems, individualized assessment and intervention planning, and integration of evidence-based techniques, multisystemic therapy addresses risk and protective factors comprehensively, using strong quality-assurance mechanisms. |

## CHAPTER 3

# An Integrative Theoretical Framework for Early Intervention with Multi-Risk Families

In the past, despite being based on what were considered at the time to be sound principles, a number of theoretical approaches to early intervention have been divisive when applied rigidly without taking into consideration various factors such as family variation and the need for the intervention strategies to be adapted to the realities of the family's circumstances. Certain approaches to intervention have been used with all types of families and have been so strictly adhered to that other approaches have been seen not only as ineffective but even as deleterious. Two examples of this kind of rigid adherence to various theoretical views are described that illustrate how destructive a strict adherence to any one theoretical approach can be.

Molly is a social worker at a local family services center who strictly adheres to systematic family therapy. She had instructed Leanne, a mother of four children, to bring her husband and all of the children for a family therapy appointment. Although Leanne wanted to cooperate with the social worker's request, as the time of her appointment approached her husband had not shown up from work, one of her older children refused to go, and another child insisted on staying after school to catch up on homework. When Leanne arrived, tired and exhausted, with only two children and without her husband, the social worker sent them home because "no meaningful work could take place without everyone in the family present." Leanne left, obviously devastated, forlorn and defeated, and never returned to the center.

Ana and Emilio had hoped to get some help for their son, Diego, who was struggling with academics and was acting out in school. They were not sure if he had a learning disability or if other problems could be causing the symptoms. Ana and Emilio were required to complete a number of questionnaires before coming to the center and then were instructed to bring Diego in at a particular time and be interviewed behind a one-way mirror in front of a group of clinicians. When the family did not return after the first interview, which they regarded as intrusive, they were seen as resistant. Little consideration was given to the reasons for their failure to come back or to finding ways to reach out to the family and to provide meaningful services to them.

Such rigidity and inflexibility sometimes arises because of necessary agency policies, but this can be intimidating to multi-risk families. Today, some proponents of social support theory fail to acknowledge that some parents and children have severe problems and that children can be at significant risk for developing delays and behavioral and psychiatric problems as a result. Conversely, more clinical approaches often label children without adequately considering the history and current social situation of each child and family and reasons for a child's symptoms. It seems that interventionists frequently only accept the effectiveness of one type of intervention and, as a consequence, argue against others.

It is critical to begin to use the best of a variety of approaches and to choose them according to their appropriateness for a particular family. In other words, the service provider's favorite theory and approaches and strategies must not direct the intervention direction. Also, for many multi-risk families with complex needs, intervention will need to be comprehensive, multidimensional, and long term. The intervention approaches used must be prescriptive, matched to the needs of the child and family, and focused on alleviating particular risks that have been identified in the assessment.

## VARIOUS THEORETICAL APPROACHES TO EARLY INTERVENTION

A number of theoretical approaches to understanding how development unfolds can inform assessment and early intervention practice. Each of these theories has made a significant contribution to our understanding of child development and has proposed various modes of intervention. Service providers are not expected to have an in-depth understanding of all of these approaches, but they should have at least enough familiarity and flexibility to consider their significance in a particular situation. Often, early intervention programs choose from among all of the possible theories and focus on a few that they believe are basic to their program. These theoretical approaches are described next.

### Developmental Theory and Brain Development

Developmental theory and recent research on the brain shows that children pass through a series of stages during which they resolve a number of developmental issues in order for optimal functioning to occur. Some of these stages include establishing a secure attachment, gaining positive self-esteem, achieving capacity for emotion regulation, and learning to communicate (Greenspan, 1997; Landy, 2002b; Pine, 1985). It is also important to consider aspects of brain development that can either impede or enhance development. As discussed in Chapter 1, a number of influences can create resilience or risk for psychopathology. Some of these are within the child and may be influencing the parent–child interaction—for example, temperament and developmental disorders such as autism spectrum disorders, attention-deficit/hyperactivity disorder (ADHD), and various types of learning disabilities. Others are in the more proximal and distal environment in which the child lives. Assessment of children and families needs to consider how well a child is meeting expected developmental milestones and the reasons for any difficulties. A formal developmental assessment may be necessary in some situations.

Typically, when a child is identified as having a disorder and/or significant delays, a variety of approaches may be used, including providing parents with developmental or pediatric guidance and information about their child's development and how to enhance it. Sometimes programs support parents to find suitable placement for their infant or young child in a specialized child care setting, with the additional support of a home visitor to help parents engage in activities with their child that can encourage their child's development.

## Transactional/Contextual Theory

From this theoretical perspective, children's development is seen as being affected by a variety of factors both within them and the environment around them (Bronfenbrenner, 1979; Lerner, Walsh, & Howard, 1998; Sameroff, 1993). These factors influence the child depending on how proximal (i.e., close) or distal (i.e., distant) they are. Some of these factors place the child's development at risk, whereas others are more protective of it. These factors form concentric circles around the child and include the parent–child interaction, parent characteristics, family atmosphere and context, and factors in the immediate neighborhood and in society (see Figure 3.1).

Both the number of risk factors and their intensity can negatively affect a child's development over time. Strengths and protective factors can enhance development, offset various significant risks, and create resilience in the child, however. In this theory, intervention can initiate and support processes to enhance resilience. In order to assess the child and family, risk and protective factors are considered in all aspects of the developmental context using a variety of assessment strategies (see Chapter 1). This kind of formulation or assessment attempts to ensure that all aspects of the child and her environment are considered and their contribution assessed. Intervention often occurs at different levels and can occur at the individual, interactional, parent, family, or community level. Intervention can identify and enhance potential strengths, including those within the child herself, and external strengths such as people who interact positively with the child. In this way, a positive process of change can be put into place. For all families it is very important to identify the risks and strengths within the child, parent–child interaction, parents, extended family, sociodemographic variables and neighborhood, and to a certain extent—within society.

## Object Relations/Attachment Theory

Object relations theory has had an important and unique point of view in the infant mental health field and has contributed significantly to an understanding of the importance of infants' early experiences to later development. The term *object*

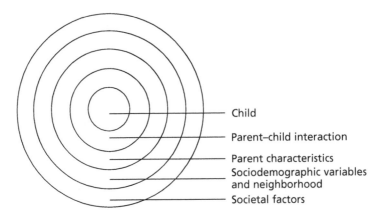

Child
Parent–child interaction
Parent characteristics
Sociodemographic variables and neighborhood
Societal factors

**Figure 3.1.** A contextual approach to intervention with multi-risk families. A child is influenced by various factors ranging from those closest (proximal) to most distant (distal).

*relations* refers to a person's internalized experiences of relationships or interactions with other human beings. Object relations are seen as real or as internal and fantasized. It is difficult to describe one object relations theory because various proponents have tended to focus on different aspects of the theory. Some of the earlier theorists such as Fairbairn (1954) and Klein (1975) emphasized the importance of the early mother–child relationship and saw it as being internalized and forming the basis of an individual's personality. Margaret Mahler emphasized the separation–individuation phase (6–34 months) during which the child becomes more independent and how it is resolved between mother and child as particularly crucial to later development (Mahler, Pine, & Bergman, 1975). Later theorists such as Kohut (1971, 1977) and Kernberg (1976) developed their theories out of their work with patients with severe pathology such as borderline personality disorder. Both see the origins of pathology in distorted or damaged object relations that are formed early and internalized. Kernberg (1975) emphasized defensive splitting, or failure to integrate good and bad images of self and other, which can lead to chaotic and unpredictable relationships with others. Kohut (1977) emphasized how failure to receive empathetic mirroring during early childhood can lead to fixation at a primitive or narcissistic level of functioning in relationships that may be dominated by craving for satisfaction of these needs for acceptance. Each of these theorists has developed a unique approach to intervention; however, they generally agree that the therapist–client relationship itself can lead to change and that issues such as splitting can be dealt with within that context.

*Attachment theory,* a type of object relations theory, originated with John Bowlby (1958, 1965) and has had an enormous influence on early intervention services since that time. With its roots in both ethology and psychoanalysis, attachment and other object relations theories stress the critical importance of children's relationships with their parents—particularly early relationships, for creating a sense of self and beliefs about other people (Cassidy & Shaver, 1999). These *working models of attachment,* once formed, influence how a child sees the world, how he acts or behaves, and even what he remembers about certain incidents and events. Attachment theory has helped focus understanding and assessment of the interaction and the relationship between parent and child. As well, it suggests a number of parent–child interactional variables that need to be considered in any assessment. For example, some of these are parental sensitivity, acceptance of the child, responsiveness to the child's cues, cooperation with the needs of the child, empathy and understanding of the child's thoughts and feelings, and positive emotionality with the child. Interventions that are based on an attachment perspective use approaches that can enhance both the behavioral interactions between parent and child, and they also endeavor to change parental negative attributions of the child to more positive ones.

When an infant is first born, it is difficult to predict what her quality of attachment or relationship with her parents will be when she is 12 months old, when attachment becomes more possible to measure. Some predictions can be made from observing the early interactions between the parent and infant, however. Also, if it is known, the mother's own attachment classification can often predict her baby's attachment classification; in fact, in 80% of the cases, the two are likely to be the same. Of course, once attachment is established, it will continue to influence the child's development, so it is important to monitor the interaction so that the intervention can focus on the attachment and interventions provided to enhance it if problems are identified. Not only is it important to "coach" the interaction but also it is crucial to help the parents overcome some of the issues that may be preoccupying them and thus, affecting the child's attachment. Chapter 10 in Section III discusses more strategies to enhance the interaction.

## Psychoanalytic and Psychodynamic Theories

Early psychoanalytic and psychodynamic theories emphasized the importance of the effect of the unconscious on the way individuals function. Later, the emphasis shifted to drive theory, which focused on the development of personality structure and the balance between the id, ego, and superego and the resulting adaptation to the world (Hollender & Ford, 1990; Horowitz, 1988). These theories of early intervention and parenting emphasize that pregnancy and childbirth can be powerful triggers for "remembering" or being affected by issues from childhood that may be brought to consciousness. These resurfaced memories can dramatically influence the meaning of the transition to parenthood and how a parent cares for a baby (Cohler & Paul, 2002). An infant can become confused or associated with people and events from the past. As a result, earlier traumatic experiences or losses may be brought to consciousness, and these memories may cause a parent to become depressed or angry or even hurtful toward their infant.

These theories also consider how an individual's defensive functioning or how a person copes with anxiety, frustration, and sadness affects her personality structure, adaptation, and behavior. From a psychoanalytic or psychodynamic perspective, then, it is important to assess parents' past history and their understanding of it. It is also helpful to gradually identify any repeating or defeating patterns in these individuals' functioning that may need to become foci of intervention. Both defensive functioning and current adaptive behaviors and relationships need to be considered, and intervention should help to integrate and make sense of any resurfaced memories so that the parent can begin to understand how they may be affecting her patterns of behavior in the present, particularly those that are affecting her child.

Psychodynamic therapists also try and help parents to experience events from the emotional and not just from a more behavioral or a concrete perspective. What happens in the intervention relationship on the transference may also be used to provide insights about how a parent may perceive and relate to other people.

## Trauma Theory

Since the 1990s, the devastating effect of trauma on many aspects of functioning—biochemical, neurological, and psychological—has become increasingly understood (Rothschild, 2000; van der Kolk, McFarlane, & Weisaeth, 1996). The effect of trauma on emotion regulation, memory, and emotionality is particularly important, especially in terms of how, if unresolved, it can trigger negative interactional behavior with one's child. Early trauma can affect development and influence perceptions, impair the symbolic function, and affect behavior on an ongoing basis. When the effects are extreme, trauma can contribute to a number of disorders that are very difficult to overcome and treat. Understanding a person's history is crucial, but it is clear that trauma may not be remembered or may be denied. It also is important to realize that trauma is not only about abuse or loss but also can include parental neglect or lack of nurturance, which can be just as damaging when it is extreme or if a child is particularly vulnerable to its impact.

If an individual has been identified as having a history of trauma, he or she may be vulnerable to such difficulties and disorders as dissociation, post-traumatic stress disorder (PTSD), and depression. Interventions directed toward integrating memories of loss and trauma, particularly when they negatively affect parenting, are extremely complex, and many require service providers with specialized training to provide them. Of course, interventions will vary according to the extremity of symptoms, the timing of the trauma or loss, and the lack of control that the individual felt during the original experience. His or her sense of control during later experiences and also the level of support that was available to the individual are also important considerations.

## Ecological and Social Support Theories

Ecological and social support theories emphasize how the social context within which children live and develop affects how parents interact with their children and, consequently, how children develop. Social support theory emphasizes the strengths of parents, the need for them to be involved in designing interventions, and the effectiveness of empowering parents in order to enhance children's development (Dunst, Trivette, & Thompson, 1991; Weissbourd, 1993). Parents' support networks—often composed of family, friends, or organizations—are important. From this theoretical perspective, assessment of a child and family considers the level and type of supports that are available in the immediate and extended family and community and the need for further supports and possible referral to various agencies. These support networks also advocate the importance of understanding any cultural issues that may be influencing parenting practices. Consequently, instrumental support as well as crisis intervention may be provided as necessary. The service provider, in fact, is seen as part of the support system, and thus behaves in a supportive way. Referrals to appropriate agencies such as drop-in centers and parenting groups are seen as crucial. Frequently, individuals are encouraged to join groups that can build competence, such as those that teach computer skills, English to non–English speakers or English-language learners, budgeting, and so forth.

## Self-Psychology Theory

Self-psychology theory emphasizes the central importance of positive acknowledgment and warm acceptance by parents and others to a child's healthy development and sense of competence. Advocates of this theory also believe that it is crucial to provide a positive, empathetically informed mirror for the child by being accepting of the child's various characteristics and emotions (Fairbairn, 1954; Kohut, 1971, 1977; Mahler, 1968). If a child fails to develop adequate self-esteem, he may continually seek affirmation yet not expect to receive it, which often sets up a cycle of continual rejection that reaffirms his negative sense of self. Parents' self-esteem can significantly affect how they feel toward and relate to others—including their children and the service provider.

Formal assessments make it is possible to examine parents' sense of competence and self-esteem. Actual examples of how a parent behaves in a variety of situations will also give excellent information about how the individual feels about him- or herself. For example, does a mother show grandiosity or unreal expectations? Does she believe that she cannot do anything about a difficult situation? Can she problem solve? Does she have a level of realistic belief that she can manage the situation? An interventionist practicing self-psychology provides *unconditional positive regard* until the parent can gradually be able to see herself more positively. Noticing positive characteristics and affirming positive efforts are important aspects of this kind of intervention.

## Cognitive-Behavioral Theory

In cognitive-behavioral theory, cognition and thought processes are seen as playing a key role in maintaining symptoms and disorders such as depression. In other words, it is not the situations themselves that cause the emotions but our perceptions, expectations, and interpretations of them. Negative cognitions underlie many disorders or difficulties, and, consequently, proponents of this theory believe that it is possible to eliminate the problems by changing the cognitions. Cognitive-behavior therapy (CBT) helps clients acquire a new understanding of situations and teaches ways to establish behavioral control over them. Emotional experience is not ignored, but efforts to influence it take place through cognitive modification. A variety of skills are taught such as using self-talk, relaxation, desensitization, modeling, and building social skills. These strategies are used with children and adults (Beck, 1976; Hayes, Follette, & Follette, 1995; Wolpe, 1969). The use of cognitive-behavioral therapy can be extremely useful for working with parents and children in early intervention. Helping parents change their beliefs about their child, and providing parents with ways to reduce their anxiety through changing their cognitions of themselves as parents, could be beneficial. Cognitive-behavioral strategies can also be taught to parents to help them manage their children's behavior better. As well, mindfulness-based approaches have been found to be particularly effective when parents have unresolved loss and trauma by providing them with strategies to reduce their stress and tendency to be triggered in difficult situations.

## Systems Theory

Theoretically, a system is a "complex of interacting elements" (von Bertalanffy, 1968, p. 55). Systems theory examines the effect on an individual of the social system in which he lives. In fact, the theory maintains that individuals can only be understood within this social system, as part of a whole (von Bertalanffy, 1968). Wachs (2000) has explained that there are two different systems theories that have relevance for understanding child development: 1) dynamic systems theory (or chaos theory) is used to describe more unexpected and unpredictable outcomes, and 2) general systems theory is used to explain the development of more universal behaviors such as sitting up and smiling. Concepts of general systems theory have been used in the study of risk and protective factors. A systems perspective has also been applied in family therapy, in which the child's symptoms are seen as the result of underlying patterns within the family. It has also been applied to conceptualize the community systems that surround a family. Assessment seeks to understand how the child is a part of and affected by the family system and social system around them. Intergenerational patterns and history—as well as reciprocal influences between the child and parents—are also assessed. Intervenors working within this framework will often work with whole families, sometimes including extended family members, and may try to affect various systems outside the family so that they can become more supportive of the child's growth and development.

## Health Promotion and Population Health Theories

Health promotion or population health approaches focus on strategies for the whole population as most efficient and cost effective. In early intervention, this means promoting healthy lifestyles, including reducing smoking and receiving medical care during pregnancy, encouraging breast feeding, and increasing the number of children who receive inoculations. In general, service providers who work in population health consider working with the most at-risk families as too expensive, so the focus is on the middle of the normal curve, or on those families at moderate risk. Epidemiologists may survey several neighborhoods in order to identify the level of risk and to locate areas for intervention. Particular client groups are also considered as at-risk, such as teenage parents, homeless parents, and families living in shelters, and appropriate interventions are provided for them. Early intervention is carried out primarily through providing information individually or in groups on issues such as typical child development, pregnancy, and parenting. Interventionists listen and observe the functioning and interaction of parents and children and provide information that they believe is useful in order to improve aspects of parenting and child development.

## The Need for a Broad, Integrated View

Significant differences can be found among many of these theories, but there are also a number of overlaps or similarities (see Table 3.1 for a summary of these theories). For example, in both attachment theory and self-psychology, an individual's view of self is considered to be crucially important in determining how he behaves

**Table 3.1.** Various theoretical approaches to early intervention with multi-risk families and suggested therapeutic/intervention techniques

| Type of theory | General beliefs/ constructs/considerations | Assessment consideration | Therapeutic relationship/ therapy techniques/interventions |
|---|---|---|---|
| Developmental theory/ brain development theory | A number of developmental issues need to be resolved (e.g., secure attachment, emotion regulation, self-esteem, language and communication). These should occur in sequence, with some forming a foundation for later ones.<br><br>Other considerations:<br><br>• Effects of brain development or impairment on functioning<br><br>• Any learning difficulties that are impeding functioning and may influence the choice of intervention<br><br>• Other variables such as temperament, including sensitivities, intensity, and so forth<br><br>• In what areas the child or adult is currently functioning or has become "stuck" (e.g., at stage of omnipotence) | Some children may need a full assessment of their developmental level and capacities in a number of learning and brain development areas:<br><br>• Functioning level of parent(s) in the areas of cognitive and emotional/social development<br><br>• Any brain impairment that could be evident<br><br>• A variety of disorders (e.g., autism, attention-deficit/hyperactivity disorder)<br><br>• Temperament factors such as hypersensitivity and emotion dysregulation<br><br>• Developmental history | Provide developmental/pediatric guidance.<br><br>Provide infant stimulation or specialized classrooms and therapeutic nurseries or preschools.<br><br>Adapt therapy or intervention to functioning level of the child and parent.<br><br>Monitor development of the child during the intervention.<br><br>When working with parents, consider any brain impairment or temperament characteristics of the child. |
| Transactional/contextual theory | A child's development is the product of factors within the child and the environment.<br><br>Development is influenced by the strengths and risks encountered.<br><br>Parent–child interaction is the most critical in infancy; as child gets older she becomes more influenced by variables in the outside world.<br><br>The number of risk factors has been shown to significantly affect the development of the child over time.<br><br>Intervention can be considered as putting in motion processes to enhance resilience and overcome risks. | Use risk assessments and monitor strengths.<br><br>Identify aspects that require intervention.<br><br>Look at aspects in the child, interaction, parent, family, and larger context.<br><br>Use a variety of assessments strategies in order to assess variables in each area of influence.<br><br>This type of formulation ensures that all aspects that may be important are considered. | Intervention may need to occur at different levels of the system, such as the individual, parent, family, and/or community levels.<br><br>Utilize identified strengths in order to enhance and put into effect various processes that can enhance resilience, which may include identifying people in the "system" who can act as mentors for the child or finding supports for the individual within his environment. |

*(continued)*

**Table 3.1.** *(continued)*

| Type of theory | General beliefs/ constructs/considerations | Assessment consideration | Therapeutic relationship/ therapy techniques/interventions |
|---|---|---|---|
| Object relations/attachment theory | Relationships are key in creating the sense of self and other. | Assess the interactions of infant/child with parent(s) and adult with family and friends. | Interventions may focus on or address the following: |
| | Attachment relationships and interaction, especially in the early years, are key in forming expectations of the world and the people in it. | Projective tests may be helpful in order to assess object relations and capacity for relatedness: | • Improving interaction and enhancing sensitivity, responsiveness, and so forth |
| | Working models of attachment are formed that influence perceptions, actions, and memories of incidences and can create cycles of a sense of competence or of rejection. | • Assessment of attachment classification using The Adult Attachment Interview (AAI) (Kaplan & Main, 1985) | • Parents' behavior and also representations of the child that may be contributing to the interaction |
| | Certain attachment classifications are internalized that are adaptive in the environment initially and may continue to influence ongoing interactions with others in a positive or negative way. | • Q-sort methods of assessing attachment, or short questionnaires | • Enhancing interactions, and as a consequence, attachment; suggestions include Watch, Wait, and Wonder, interactional coaching, and Floor Time |
| | The category of attachment disorganization is one that has a great deal of influence and relationship to psychopathology. | • Observation of the child with others in school or child care | • Reviewing mother's own history to begin to address her difficulties in interacting with her child |
| | | • History of experiences with others, especially with regard to any losses of significant others | |
| | | Observe for signs of role reversal, harshness of discipline, and the parents' involvement with child. | |
| | | Consider the level of sensitivity, responsiveness, intrusiveness, and positive emotionality in interactions. | |

| Psychoanalytic and psychodynamic theories | The following are important considerations for service providers:<br><br>• An understanding of the effect of unconscious motivation and fantasies on current functioning<br><br>• How defensive functioning affects personality and other areas of functioning<br><br>• Impact of early experiences and repressed memories on current functioning<br><br>• Transference and counter-transference in the therapeutic/ intervention relationship | Assess past history and client's interpretation of it as key to current functioning.<br><br>Identify any repeating and defeating patterns in the individual's functioning.<br><br>Assess level of defensive functioning or how the individual deals with anxiety.<br><br>Consider current adaptation, relationships, and perceptions. | Bring unconscious to consciousness so the individual can begin to see and deal with repeating and defeating patterns.<br><br>Help individual adopt a more adaptive level of defensive functioning.<br><br>Encourage the individual to go beyond seeing events in very concrete terms. Enable the individual to experience the emotions and consider the reasons behind the actions.<br><br>Use the transference in the therapeutic relationship to bring insight.<br><br>Use play therapy for children who have unresolved issues and defeating patterns of functioning. |
|---|---|---|---|
| Trauma theory | Trauma has a deleterious effect on biochemical, neurological, and psychological aspects of functioning.<br><br>Trauma theory considers the effects of unresolved trauma on emotionality, emotion regulation, memory, and so forth and how anger can be triggered, leading to abuse.<br><br>Trauma often contributes to the development of a number of disorders and difficulty in a variety of areas of functioning.<br><br>Unresolved trauma can have a powerful influence on how an individual perceives other people and power structures. | Determine if individual had past or more recent history of abuse or other trauma, remembering that, particularly for more vulnerable children, this abuse or trauma may include lack of containment and certain levels of neglect.<br><br>Look for symptoms of dissociation.<br><br>Assess for symptoms of post-traumatic stress disorder (PTSD).<br><br>Assess for alexythymia and consequent difficulties in containing and dealing with emotions.<br><br>Physiological difficulties with levels of arousal and triggers need to be assessed.<br><br>Consider the effect of trauma on self-efficacy, sexuality, and power issues.<br><br>Consider various diagnoses that may be present such as borderline personality disorder, bipolar disorder, depression, etc. | Initially, it may be important to ensure the safety of the child and parent.<br><br>Remember that it will be crucial to not bring memories to the surface too early because this may retraumatize and even fragment the person.<br><br>It is important to build ego functioning before the past is reviewed.<br><br>Enhancing the individual's capacity for emotion regulation is important. This can be done individually or in groups.<br><br>Provide new experiences of nurturance and caring.<br><br>Clearly set boundaries and expectations of how the therapy will proceed.<br><br>Expect that therapy is likely to be long-term and will require a number of modalities. |

(continued)

**Table 3.1.** (continued)

| Type of theory | General beliefs/constructs/considerations | Assessment consideration | Therapeutic relationship/therapy techniques/interventions |
|---|---|---|---|
| Ecological and social support theories | The effect of the social context within which the child develops is crucial. The context significantly affects a child's interactions with the parents and vice versa. Support networks are crucial. Parents need various kinds of support and support systems. Enhancement and empowerment of strengths is emphasized. The "pathologizing" of individuals and the "medical model" is opposed. | Assess level of support available to the family in the extended family, through friends, and the service system. Look at the need for referral to various other agencies. Consider the level of practical support that may be available. Consider the parents' sense of parenting and personal competence as a key determinant of how they interact with their child. Consider cultural issues in assessing parenting and parenting philosophy. | Provide social support by providing instrumental help, crisis intervention, and so forth. Listen to parents and respond to their needs and requests for intervention. Refer individuals to appropriate agencies such as drop-in centers and parenting groups, which are important to enhance a sense of support. Ensure that service providers become part of the support system and act in a supportive way. Provide competence-building groups such as improving computer skills. |
| Self-psychology theory | Positive acknowledgement has a strong impact on development, and the effects of not receiving it can be great. Mirroring of the emotions is key to developing a positive sense of self. Unless this is received at an adequate level, the child and adult will constantly be seeking affirmation but will not expect to receive it, thus setting up situations of constant rejection. Sense of self may be compromised by very early and later experiences with parents and others. | Assess how the individual views himself and his life and how it measures up to his expectations. Assess how he responds in a number of situations. Use measures of self-esteem and self-efficacy if indicated. Consider if the individual has a grandiose sense of self, making it very difficult not to be disappointed by a number of experiences. Consider the individual's sense of locus-of-control and whether the person believes that she can control her life or whether she believes it is all determined by fate. Assess parents' sense of parenting competence. | Provide mirroring for child or adult so that the individual can see herself differently. Affirm the individual's efforts, which is very important in improving sense of agency and self-esteem. Unconditional positive regard may be a necessary but not sufficient condition of therapy. Affirm positive aspects of parenting through use of videotapes of interactions. Notice efforts and do not expect massive changes immediately. Enhance sense of parenting competence by acknowledging strengths. |

| | | | |
|---|---|---|---|
| Cognitive-behavioral theory | Cognition or thought processes are seen as playing a key role in maintenance of symptoms and disorders.<br><br>Cognitions can lead to misinterpretations of the world and experiences that are distorted.<br><br>Symptoms are seen as occurring as a result of these cognitions and, consequently, as being eliminated by changing them.<br><br>Cognitions are seen as underlying a number of disorders, including depression and anxiety disorders.<br><br>Parent cognitions or attributions of their children significantly affect the way they interact with them. | Assess the cognitions that may be leading to symptoms and other difficulties.<br><br>May use questionnaires to understand and assess attributions that may be leading, for example, to depression.<br><br>Assess selective recall of events and how the person may see rejection and impending disaster when it may not be there.<br><br>Use questionnaires and interviews to understand the attributions that parents have of their children. | Experiential aspects of change process can provide means to eradicate symptoms.<br><br>Cognitive-behavior therapy (CBT) uses ways to help client acquire behavioral control and better cognitive understandings of themselves and situations.<br><br>Build new way of viewing the world and interactions with others.<br><br>Use with children or adults.<br><br>Use techniques such as encouraging self-talk, relaxation, desensitization, modeling, and building of social skills.<br><br>Employ various strategies to change parents' negative attributions of their children to more positive ones. |
| Systems theory | Problems reside not in the individual but in the systems around the person.<br><br>Symptoms are the result of underlying patterns within the system, and changing those will eliminate the symptoms.<br><br>The individual is seen as only one part of a total system and is influenced by it.<br><br>Various parts of the system work together to influence the individual. | Assess the family and other systems and how they are affecting the individual within it.<br><br>Assess for violence in the family and between partners.<br><br>Assess reciprocal influences of child and parents.<br><br>Understand life patterns and history, which influence and create the unique patterns of a particular family.<br><br>Consider the influence of the larger system around the family. | Help family members work out difficulties with one another in family sessions where members are present.<br><br>Try to work with the whole family, which may sometimes include extended family members.<br><br>Provide homework that encourages a family to try out new patterns of relating to each other.<br><br>Provide the family with ways to deal with conflict and to cope with problems that arise.<br><br>Work with the larger system around the family when necessary. |

(continued)

**Table 3.1.** *(continued)*

| Type of theory | General beliefs/ constructs/considerations | Assessment consideration | Therapeutic relationship/ therapy techniques/interventions |
|---|---|---|---|
| Health promotion/ population health theories | Strategies aimed at the whole population are more efficient and cost effective.<br><br>It is important to identify health risks and to develop strategies to overcome them (e.g., smoking cessation, pregnancy care, disease prevention through inoculations).<br><br>Promotion of healthy lifestyles is emphasized.<br><br>Enhancing child development through improving parenting skills is crucial.<br><br>Working with the most at-risk families may be perceived as too expensive, so families at the middle of the normal curve may be targeted. | Assess the health and risks in whole neighborhoods and particular client groups, such as teenage mothers.<br><br>Create epidemiological assessments of whole neighborhoods in order to identify risks and locate areas for intervention.<br><br>Assess the level of knowledge in parenting groups before beginning a group. | In early intervention, provide a number of parenting groups targeted at the whole population and not to the most at risk.<br><br>Provide interventions to individual children and families if they need information to improve interactions.<br><br>Provide information on development, pregnancy, and parenting.<br><br>Listen and answer questions and may refer to other agencies that can be helpful.<br><br>Provide population-based information campaigns (e.g., to increase breast-feeding, reduce the incidence of sudden infant death syndrome [SIDS]). |

and his expectation of how other people will behave toward him. In social support theory, ecological theory, and systems theory, parents and consequently, their children, are believed to be significantly affected by the context in which they live, and positive changes in the context can significantly enhance child outcomes. In spite of these overlaps, each of these theories and perspectives offer something significant and unique to a common understanding of early childhood development, and together they can inform service provider's assessment of children and families as well as their approach to intervention.

## INTEGRATIVE APPROACHES TO INTERVENTION

The field of psychotherapy is composed of at least 400 different types of therapy, with many of them showing positive intervention outcome effects (Bruschweiler-Stern et al., 1998; Norcross & Arkowitz, 1992). Because of the increasing antagonism and criticism that has often arisen between adherents to one or other of these theories, a small but increasing number of theorists and clinicians are beginning to integrate ideas from a number of theories in order to create new constructs, theories, and methods of intervention. Norcross and Arkowitz observed "a growing consensus that no one clinical approach is adequate for all problems, patients and situations" (1992, p. 3). Different approaches to integration have been proposed and developed including technical eclecticism, a common factor approach, and theoretical integration (Gold, 1996). Each is described next.

### Technical Eclectism

*Technical eclectism* uses different strategies from a variety of theoretical approaches or schools to best meet the needs of a particular child and family (Norcross et al., 1993; Norcross & Newman, 1992). The choice of strategies is usually based on a very comprehensive assessment and is prescriptive depending on the findings about the child and family (Beutler & Clarkin, 1990; Dryden, 1992; Lazarus, 1997). In other words, the interventionist considers this question: "What intervention, by whom, is most effective for this individual with that specific set of circumstances, and how does it come about?" (Paul, 1969, p. 44).

### Common Factor Approach

With the *common factor* approach, similar and successful strategies are identified in various therapeutic approaches, and there is a realization that no one intervention can work for all families. Some interventions have been found to be successful with certain disorders; for example, cognitive-behavioral strategies have been effective in treating anxiety disorders, depression, and obsessive-compulsive disorder, and longer, staged interventions have been found to be helpful for parents who have complex posttraumatic stress disorder. In addition to cognitive-behavioral approaches, longer term, psychodynamically oriented intervention may be needed for some people with depression for whom a more strict manualized approach cannot provide the extreme attunement to their individual histories and current needs that they require to stay in the intervention.

Research has also looked for common factors across various types of therapeutic interventions and has found a number of similarities that contribute to their effectiveness (Garfield, 2003). Clients respond well when they feel that their concerns have been heard, understood, validated, and accepted, for example. For service providers, the following characteristics of effective therapeutic interventions were identified:

- Emotional availability and the ability to accept, tolerate, and help contain the parent's negative emotions including anger and sadness

- Warmth, unconditional positive regard, and empathetic understanding of the parents' situations and the difficulties they have experienced

- Authenticity and sincerity, or the ability to be perceived as real and approachable

- Hope and positive expectancies that things can be better or the problem can be overcome

- Adequate experience, maturity, and training

- Good communication and interpersonal skills

## Theoretical Integration Approaches

With *theoretical integration* approaches, two or more theoretical schools are combined into a new blending of the approaches at the level of a conceptual explanation and understanding of what is happening. Assessment of the client takes place based on the conceptualization of the way personality as well as psychopathology are formed.

A number of new approaches or theoretical integrative methods have been developed, including interpersonal psychoanalysis (combining object relations and psychoanalytic theories), process-experiential (combining cognitive and Gestalt therapies), and interpersonal-cognitive-experiential (combining self psychology, cognitive, and Gestalt theories) (Norcross & Goldfried, 1992; Wachtel, 1997). Although these new approaches are seen as significant advances or efforts toward integrating various types of therapy, some people are concerned that the result of creating these new therapies will simply be an increasing number and generation of multiple new approaches, which, in some ways, will be as divisive as the theory and methods from which they came. It should be pointed out, however, that many of these integrative approaches including the three just mentioned not only emphasize strategies but also consider the underlying theoretical concepts that they are based on. As a result, they are able to integrate the viewpoints of various distinct and different theoretical considerations.

In spite of concerns, the pursuit of integrative approaches to intervention has assumed a great deal of importance, as demonstrated by the introduction of a number of journals publishing articles on the topic and the significant work of the Society for the Exploration of Psychotherapy Integration (SEPI) (Wachtel, 1997). Unfortunately, a number of obstacles have obscured the total acceptance of integrative approaches in the field of early intervention. One reason is that some service providers are only willing to invest in one approach such as psychoanalytic, cognitive-behavioral, or social support. Another is a lack of commitment to or availability of training in more than one or two approaches. Barriers to adequate evaluation are described in Chapter 2, and as discussed, it is clear that not all approaches or strategies have been evaluated, nor have other types of intervention been considered, such as those used with older children and adults. Consequently, relying only on approaches that have been evaluated or are evidence-based or are considered best practices can be restrictive. In general, the choice of intervention strategies cannot rely on rigid, manualized approaches and needs to be flexible, innovative, and adapted to the characteristics of the parents and children receiving the intervention (Westen, Novotny, & Thompson-Brenner, 2004).

Paul's (1969) statement, quoted earlier, sounds very much like the dilemma facing the field of prevention and early intervention, with this added question: *When* in the child's life should the intervention be provided? In his book on the effectiveness of early intervention, Guralnick (1997) stated

> A major task for second-generation research is to identify those specific (program) features that are associated with optimal outcomes for children and families. It is this issue of specificity that ultimately informs practice, improves the cost-effectiveness of services, minimizes false expectations, provides a research framework for evaluating innovative approaches, and may even be of value in helping us understand the mechanisms through which interventions operate. (Guralnick, 1997, p. 13)

The schools of prescriptive eclecticism and integrative approaches to intervention have much to offer the field of early intervention. *Prescriptive eclecticism* emphasizes the importance of specificity, or of matching a strategy to the needs of the person (Lazarus, 1997), and the importance of therapist characteristics that enable the individual to do this (Beutler & Clarkin, 1990). Some emphasis has also been given to considering not only a person's diagnosis but also focusing on what is causing the symptoms and that individual's particular psychological characteristics in choosing interventions. Integration proponents have also emphasized the critical importance of having a common and broad theoretical understanding of the influences on the development of personality and competence and the strategies that can be effective in enhancing personality, and those strategies that can contribute to positive change in intervention.

This book proposes an integrative approach to early intervention that considers the most important and complementary aspects of the best theories and therapeutic approaches. A number of principles for assessing children and families and choosing an intervention are outlined that need to be considered in deciding on the intervention plan and the approaches that are the best for a particular child, family, and situation. Other principles related to the actual process and techniques of therapy are also provided in Sections II and III of the book.

## Putting the Integrative Approach with Multi-Risk Families into Practice

In this book, an integrative approach to early intervention is explained and operationalized. This approach of the integration of various intervention strategies is essential for work with multi-risk families because, as pointed out in Chapter 1, very high-risk families have multiple risks and needs, and thus, multi-system approaches adapted to those needs are crucial.

In this integrative approach to early intervention with multi-risk families, the principal objective is to enhance the optimal match between families and intervention. This is the approach that an increasing number of evaluation studies are showing to be the most effective, whereas other research has demonstrated that approaches that are not adapted to the needs of multi-risk families are often not successful (see Chapter 2 for a review of these findings). A prescriptive approach to assessing and choosing of approaches that are suitable for a particular family is crucial because one curriculum, technique, or approach cannot possibly be suitable for the unique needs of each family requiring services, and may even be deleterious for some. The prescriptive or eclectic approach, as explained in this chapter, entails use of multiple interventions that may be associated with diverse approaches to therapy.

The approach that is described in this book is integrative in the following ways:

- *Theoretical approach (1):* The theoretical approach uses a variety of theories in order to understand the major issues, risks, and strengths of a family. Service providers use this integrated theoretical position to conduct an assessment to choose and provide appropriate intervention for the child and family, and to facilitate supervision based on a common understanding of these theories.

- *Engaging and supporting families (2):* Similar to the common factor approach, the model emphasizes the need to determine the willingness and the readiness of the family to be involved in various types of interventions. As well, it adapts the intervention approach to the psychological characteristics of the parents so that they are more willing, able, and interested in being involved in intervention. It also chooses goals for intervention with the involvement of parents and adapts them to any issues identified by the parents about her child or themselves that they would like to work on.

- *Intervening to meet the needs of multi-risk families (3):* The approach is prescriptive and chooses the most appropriate available strategies in order to meet the needs of the child and family. In other words, it does not rely on using the same approach for every family but chooses strategies that integrate important approaches into a prescriptive and integrated approach for the family. Often, short-term, focused approaches that have been shown to be effective for overcoming particular problems, such as insensitive parent–child interactions, may be provided within a longer term supportive approach.

- *Coordinating available services (4):* The approach integrates the knowledge of a multidisciplinary team of professionals, home visitors, and other paraprofessionals who work in the same and different agencies. Case management allows the various intervention strategies available in a network of agencies to be integrated into a seamless system so that a coherent intervention plan can be developed that is then clearly communicated to the family and within the intervention team. Support, including reflective supervision, is also provided to the service providers so as to reduce burnout and support these professionals to provide the best service possible.

Each of these four variables is described in more detail next.

The first step before providing any early childhood intervention is to conduct a comprehensive assessment of a family's needs. Some of the important things to consider when assessing a child and family are discussed in this section. When choosing and providing intervention strategies, it is essential to consider the four different types of variables shown in Figure 3.2.

*Theoretical Perspectives*    As outlined at the beginning of the chapter, one of four areas that needs to be considered and discussed is the possible reasons for any symptoms in the child or problems with the interaction and parental functioning. In order to do this, various theoretical perspectives need to be considered. Many agencies have a theoretical framework that is used in order to inform what is done in the program, and it is extremely useful to review the needs of families with this framework in mind. Doing so can help a service provider avoid missing important information that the family provides and assure that a range of possible approaches to intervention are considered.

For example, if the interaction between a parent and child is obviously very negative, it will be important to consider the contribution of the attachment style of the parent and the attributions the parent has of the child. From a psychodynamic perspective, clues may come from parents' defensive functioning or their own past history, which could be affecting their interactions with their child. It is also important to look for any signs of unresolved loss or trauma in the child or parent (even of PTSD). An understanding of parents' sense of self and of their own competence as well as the supports available to them is also critical. Consideration of how the family system and the community around them are influencing the situation with the family and the child is important. For example, if a family is living in an area with a lot of violence in the community or an individual is bringing up children as a single parent, these situations may significantly affect parenting

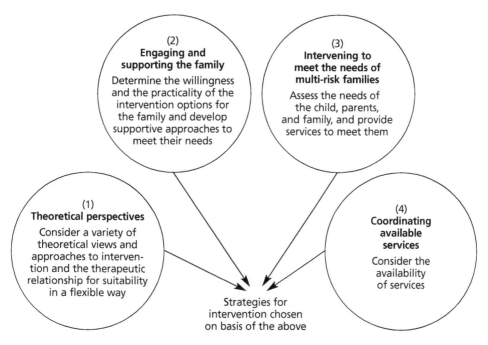

**Figure 3.2.**    Diagram showing the four main areas from which intervention should be chosen. Intervention strategies should be chosen on the basis of these four main areas.

and thus child development. Sometimes a health promotion approach could be important, in which case a parent may then need information on breastfeeding, parenting strategies, or other lifestyle issues. Discussion also needs to consider the child's development and how it is influenced by the complex patterns of possible influences. This process of consideration of all possible contributors usually occurs without a conscious decision process, particularly when a clear theoretical framework is in place in the agency. This theoretical framework also provides a common understanding for the service provider and supervisor to use during reflective supervision.

***Engaging and Supporting the Family by Providing Suitable and Available Intervention Options***     It is imperative to recognize that service professionals can only provide the type and intensity of intervention that parents are ready for and willing and able to be involved in (Prochaska, 1999). Parents need to feel that they are partners with the service provider or interventionist in order for a collaborative and trusting relationship to develop, even though this may limit the interventions that can be provided. In order to keep parents involved, supportive approaches that can accommodate individuals' particular challenging characteristics such as poor self-reflectivity and primitive defense mechanisms need to be considered before interventions are suggested. Interventionists also need to consider issues that the parents are identifying as a concern and to let them know that these will be a focus of the intervention.

The intervention suggestions can then be discussed, with the family integrating their initial request for intervention and any other goals that they may have identified. This is the appropriate time to establish when, how often, and where the interventions will take place. Progress should then reviewed at regular intervals and new strategies suggested when necessary (see Figure 3.3).

***Providing Appropriate Interventions Based on Assessment of the Needs and Strengths of the Child and Family***     When a child and family enter a prevention or early intervention program, it is important to consider and assess how the child is developing, the quality of the parent–child interactions, parents' psychological functioning, family patterns and relationships, and the family's support systems.

A screening instrument may be used to determine if the child's development is delayed or typical, and may be followed up with a more in-depth assessment if delays are identified. The first step in conducting a developmental assessment is to obtain a developmental history of the child from the mother's pregnancy up to the present time. This will be helpful in order to identify any problems the child may have or any indicators or possible reasons for any delays or other presenting problems. If a more detailed assessment is required, a multidisciplinary team should examine various developmental areas when possible. These include fine and gross motor skills; auditory and visual processing and memory; receptive and expressive language; cognitive, social, and emotional development; and self-help skills. Sometimes hearing and vision tests, genetic testing, and neurological examinations may be critical. At times during this process assessments may reveal an underlying condition, disorder, or syndrome.

In addition to assessing the infant or child, other aspects of the environment that influence the child are also considered, including the interactional behavior of the parents and their child. These behaviors are influenced in turn by the parental

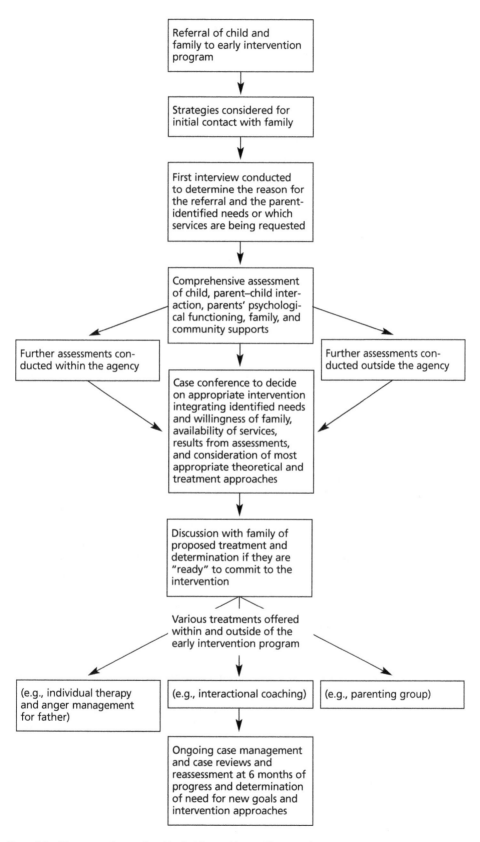

**Figure 3.3.** The process from referral to decision making and intervention.

attributions or views of the child and other beliefs about parenting. These beliefs and views of the child influence how the parent(s) perceives and interacts with the child, and can have a powerful influence on how parents feel about themselves and their circumstances and how they behave in response to various stressful events in their lives. Typically, these attributions are assessed by observing the interactions and considering variables such as parental sensitivity, acceptance, responsiveness, and cooperation with the child. Parental attributions of the child often are apparent during communications between the parents and child, and also surface when parents are asked to describe their child's personality or the reasons for any symptoms that they describe. Beliefs about child development and parenting may also become apparent during these discussions.

As discussed in the previous section, from the different theoretical perspectives a number of aspects of functioning of a particular family need to be identified, but it is also essential to understand the unique patterns and variables that are important in a particular child and family situation. Any extreme risks also need to be identified such as abuse, neglect, or family violence, which—if their presence is verified, will have to be reported to Child Protection Services. Parents should also be interviewed about their experience of being parented. Their feelings about their current situation, employment, and living situation provide clues about their actual lifestyle and any emotional difficulties that they may be experiencing. Information on defensive functioning and coping strategies should be collected as well as relevant details about the parents' support systems both within the family and the community. Family functioning is also an important variable to be considered.

In summary, the child and various aspects of the environment surrounding the child—particularly the proximal variables of the parents, and the parent–child interaction—are assessed to identify strengths and any risks that need intervention strategies. If symptoms are identified in the child it is likely that they are multidetermined or are not the result of one risk factor, and the same symptoms (e.g., delayed language, anxiety, sleeping problems, aggression) result from very different risk factors depending on the child and family interactions. This process of assessing the needs, risks, and strengths of a child and family will take place over time before any absolute conclusions are made. Sometimes new information about a situation may come to light that can clarify what is occurring, and at times, parents may be able to make positive changes quite rapidly after they receive certain information or engage in a intervention.

***Coordination of Available Services***    Understanding the availability of various types of services within the agency and in the wider service system is of critical importance, as well. Only interventions that are available and supported by the organization and the larger service system can be provided, and these realities need to be considered in deciding on any intervention. For example, organizations may delineate the length of intervention that is acceptable and the number of modalities that can be provided. Also, it is very unlikely that any early intervention agency will have professionals trained to provide the range of interventions that would be most appropriate for infants, young children, and their parents. It is, therefore, critically important that staff are aware of approaches that would be most suitable for particular problems, and also where they are available in the

**Table 3.2.** Intervention principles and the process of change

**Principle 1:   Conducting an assessment of the child, parents' psychological functioning and family** is essential in order to gather information to be able to choose optimal strategies for intervention. Interventions must also take into account differences in family structure, roles, and patterns of relating that are due to cultural, racial, and ethnic differences.

**Principle 2:**   Understanding the problems of the child and family must come from a **variety of theoretical perspectives** and disciplines that are integrated into a **prescriptive and eclectic approach.**

**Principle 3:**   The risks to children's development can be very subtle and may not be immediately obvious. Also, because changes in circumstances as a result of intervention are common, **consistent review of cases** and reconsideration of appropriate intervention strategies are necessary.

**Principle 4:**   For children and families with multiple risk factors **and complex needs,** one brief intervention is seldom sufficient; intervention is likely to need to be **multidimensional and longer term.** Change in one part of the parent–child system that occurs through a short-term intervention may affect other parts, however.

**Principle 5:**   The **therapeutic relationship,** or how well the parent(s) feel accepted, validated, understood, and listened to, will influence the success of intervention. Building trust and attuning the intervention to the parent's willingness to be involved is crucial.

**Principle 6:**   The **"process of change"** can occur in a variety of situations and in a number of ways (e.g., following a crisis, in an individual session, during a group experience, as a parent gradually grows in a sense of competence).

**Principle 7:   Parents' willingness or readiness to engage in intervention** is a critical consideration in choosing interventions. Also, making sure that parents' goals are integrated into the intervention is important.

**Principle 8:**   It is critical to acknowledge **parents' strengths,** to integrate them into an intervention plan, and to work consistently to help them find their own strengths and resources within themselves and their families or communities. In this way, families will have continued support when their involvement with a program or service provider ends.

**Principle 9:**   Because interventions are often slow and arduous and changes may be inconsistent (regressions may even occur), **availability of support for staff and reflective supervision is crucial.**

**Principle 10:**   Because interventions are often multidimensional and provided by a number of agencies and service providers, **case conferences and case management** by one of the service providers is important to avoid fragmentation and splitting, as when parents pit one service provider against the other.

community, in order to make appropriate referrals. For example, eye movement desensitization and reprocessing (EMDR), an approach to treating trauma-related reactions, may not be available within most early intervention programs. However, having some understanding of what it does and the type of clients it could help, as well as where it is available in the community, would be very helpful in order to facilitate an appropriate referral. When parents are involved in a number of services, coordination between service providers is critical. Support to service providers is essential because intervention with multi-risk families can be very challenging and progress can at times be very slow.

Figure 3.3 explains the steps of formulation and how it takes place from referral by the parents or a service provider to decision-making and intervention.

The process involves receiving the referral; setting up the initial assessment session with the family; comprehensively assessing the child, parents, and parent–child interaction; and determining any community supports the family has. These needs are considered within the theoretical framework of the agency along with information on the willingness and availability of the family to be involved in services and the interventions that are available in the agency or in other community programs. Decisions are made about the intervention plan to be offered and then discussed with the family. Ideally, the efficacy of the intervention and any changes within the family are then discussed at regular intervals and the intervention adjusted accordingly.

A number of intervention principles that are essential for providing intervention to high risk and complex families are outlined in Table 3.2 and discussed and illustrated in Chapter 4 by describing the process of assessment and intervention in two very different types of multi-risk families.

# ENGAGING
# AND SUPPORTING
# MULTI-RISK FAMILIES

© j. stone, inc. 2005

*Every relationship we have is a journey*
*toward healing and transforming the soul.*
—J. Stone

Intervention can be nothing short of life-saving to multi-risk families—if they participate in it. Although programs and service providers acknowledge it, a significant number of multi-risk parents refuse to attend programs, or they attend individual or group programs for one or two sessions and then drop out. Little attention has been given to adapting services to meet the varying needs of these families, who may be labeled as *resistant* or *hard-to-reach*. Instead, such families are often expected to adapt to the program guidelines rather than the program or intervention adapting to the needs (both pragmatic and psychological) of these children and parents.

This section provides suggestions for ways to adapt programs and interventions to the needs of multi-risk families. It also addresses the psychological characteristics of parents that lead them to perceive that services are not meeting their needs and to reject the intervention. Ways to adapt sessions to families' needs so as to enhance their satisfaction with the services are included. The chapters in this section also describe the nature of various types of supportive interventions that can enable parents to interact in more nurturing ways with their children and that will contribute to their satisfaction with the services.

Chapter 4 presents two illustrative case studies that are then used throughout the book to describe various intervention techniques and approaches. Both case examples illustrate the very complex needs of multi-risk children and their families and some differences in terms of these individuals' intervention needs and willingness and openness to being involved. The cases also illustrate how considering all four types of variables in this integrative model described in Chapter 3—1) theoretical perspectives, 2) suitability and supportiveness of available intervention options, 3) assessment of the needs and strengths of the child and family and provision of appropriate interventions, and 4) availability and coordination of services—is important in assessing families and then in choosing the most appropriate interventions to meet their needs.

Chapter 5 discusses factors that contribute to the perception of families as being hard to reach, and describes ways to adapt services in order to engage them. Because it is clear that the relationship between interventionist and parents is crucial, both to keep the parents involved and to facilitate the process of change, strategies to do this are described.

Chapter 6 examines various types of defense mechanisms and their effect on intervention. The chapter also discusses how these defense mechanisms affect parenting. Ways to adapt the intervention to both accommodate and improve the parents' level of defensiveness are described.

Chapter 7 describes the effects of having very little capacity for self-reflectivity or empathy on parents' ability to interact sensitively and responsively with their child. Evidence is provided for how the lack of these qualities affects a child's attachment relationship with her parent. The chapter also describes the effect of self-reflectivity on the intervention relationship and the parents' willingness to be involved. Strategies to enhance the self-reflectivity of those parents who have very few resources available to them are included.

Chapter 8 describes a variety of approaches to providing supportive interventions in ways that can enhance parents' sense of competence, in their parental role and in other areas of their lives.

## CHAPTER 4

# Illustrative Case Studies

As described in Chapter 3, assessment and intervention to help families exposed to multiple risks can and should take many different forms depending on the families' particular needs. This chapter presents two case studies that describe how assessment and various approaches to intervention are applied and how the individuals within these families respond over time to these interventions. Characteristics of the case-study families have been changed in order to protect their confidentiality. Later chapters in this section and Section III expand on the description of various aspects of these interventions. Although, in many early intervention programs, providing the level of service described in these case studies will not be possible, the families are typical of many families who can benefit from services in the first 6 years of their children's lives. Therefore, it is important that agencies and organizations be aware of the types of interventions that are needed so that aspects of the approaches can be provided within coordinated systems of various agencies available within a certain geographical area.

## CASE STUDY 1

### Mark, a Child with Attention-Deficit/Hyperactivity Disorder, and His Family

***Reason for Referral and Request for Service***   Joan and Michael were the parents of three adopted children, including middle child Mark, 4 years old. Mark had begun having extreme difficulties adjusting to preschool. Since starting school he had been displaying problems with acting aggressively toward other children, not following through with directions, and being very disruptive. Mark's parents were most concerned about what they believed to be a sudden and significant deterioration in his behavior and a drop in his self-esteem, which was leaving him so lacking in confidence that he could not even choose clothes in the morning. He was continually sad and withdrawn and had frequent "meltdowns," or episodes when he was described by both his parents and teacher as completely "losing it." During these times he would become intensely angry and would distance himself from others, becoming inconsolable and refusing to talk about what was upsetting him. These meltdowns happened at least once or twice a week.

Mark often told his mother that other children were saying that she could not be his real mother because he was black and she was white. Mark had become very upset over this and had been seen trying to wash the "black" off of himself, even though his parents had frequently encouraged him to value himself as he was. Because Mark's parents were so concerned about him, they temporarily withdrew him from school and child care. Their pediatrician referred them to a children's mental health center, where they requested that he be assessed, and they sought suggestions for how best to parent him and any interventions that could be provided for him. Mark's parents indicated that they were willing to be involved in intervention 6 times a month, if necessary.

### Initial Assessment

*Child: Mark*    In the initial intake assessment at the center, which was conducted over several sessions, the following information was obtained by interviewing Mark's parents and observing them and their family at the mental health center and in their home:

Mark was adopted at birth from another country and came to live with his parents on discharge from the hospital. His biological mother spoke three languages and was in college at the time that she became pregnant. She experienced a normal pregnancy and was not believed to have abused drugs or alcohol during that time. Mark was born full-term with no complications. Joan and Michael, Mark's adoptive parents, described him as an easy baby who was happy and cuddly and could amuse himself for up to 20 minutes with toys he could grab and kick at. Mark began walking at 11 months, said his first words at 1 year old, and was toilet trained at 4 years old. He had few temper tantrums as a toddler but had started recently to have more frequent and very intense outbursts, described at the time of referral.

Mark began attending child care—both group care and private home care—at 7 months old when Joan returned to work. Before he started school, Mark's parents described him as a happy child. He enjoyed his older brother and younger sister and played well with them. Mark liked to be outside and could concentrate when he was interested in an activity. He liked to tell imaginary stories and to act them out and could amuse himself for up to an hour. His child care teacher and his parents noted that Mark needed structure and firm boundaries, however. At child care, he often forgot to remain with the group and wandered off. His teachers also noticed that Mark had trouble lining up with the other children at the start of the school day. His child care teacher described him as not being interested in new activities, and said that he had difficulty changing activities and making other transitions. He also found it difficult to focus at circle time. Mark's parents described him as a "perfectionist" because he often refused to try an activity or task until he could perform it up to his standards. Consequently, he refused to practice new behaviors or tasks, believing that he should be able to do them without making any effort. This had influenced his ability to attempt and to learn such things as toileting, riding a tricycle, drawing, painting, and printing his name.

Physically, Mark had been a reasonably healthy newborn. Beginning at 7 months, however, Mark had had a number of ear infections and had tubes put in his ear after his first birthday. He had a hearing test at approximately 3 years of age that suggested auditory processing difficulties with his left ear. Mark's parents noticed that at times he seemed to "zone out"; his eyes would glaze over and he would become nonresponsive. At night he was very difficult to wake up and he sometimes slept with his eyes partially open. Mark also had memory lapses, forgetting the names of people and things he had known previously. He had symptoms of exaggerated blinking and other tics. An electroencephalogram (EEG) showed an irregular pattern, so a neurologist was monitoring and observing him regularly because Mark's symptoms indicated the possibility of Tourette syndrome.

On the Wechsler Preschool and Primary Scale of Intelligence (WPPSI-R; Wechsler, 1989), Mark received scores in the average range for his age group (50th percentile). His performance was significantly higher on verbal reasoning tasks (75th percentile) than on nonverbal reasoning tasks (25th percentile). Mark performed best on tests of verbal comprehension and had the most difficulty with tests requiring short-term memory, planning ability, visual-motor coordination, and visual sequencing. This discrepancy was seen as likely to be causing Mark a great deal of frustration because—although he understood what was required of him for printing, copying, and following instructions—he had difficulty completing these kinds of tasks.

Mark was diagnosed as having a nonverbal learning disability (NLD) that was seen as contributing to many of his symptoms and problems. Also, attention-deficit/hyperactivity disorder (ADHD) was raised as an additional possible diagnosis because of his difficulties with executive functions, such as short-term memory and concentration and planning, on the test as well as at school and home.

Observations were carried out at the child care center, at home, and at school as part of the assessment process. At home with his parents, Mark seemed to be more relaxed than in other environments; however, he constantly pushed the boundaries until he got his way. It was also clear that his mother was quite dismissive of any emotions he displayed except for happiness. Her unresponsiveness seemed to be contributing to the somewhat frenetic pace that Mark kept up. Mark appeared to have difficulty settling down between transitions and following routines such as going to bed. He also failed to listen to instructions at home and elsewhere and to follow through with them. At one point at school, Mark became very frustrated with trying to copy shapes and letters and got upset with himself, saying that he was "dumb."

At the child care center, which Mark had attended after school for 2 years, his child care provider described him during an interview as quite disruptive and defiant, particularly at rest times and during transitions. He could also be very rude and aggressive with staff. She noted that consequences did not seem to work well as a discipline strategy for Mark and that he was very difficult to calm down when he got upset. He also found it very difficult to stay on task. Mark shifted his moods suddenly and seemingly without reason; conversely, he could be affectionate and loving at times. In the observational session he seemed to have no difficulty joining in games with the other children and playing cooperatively. In his play, however, he switched rapidly from pretending to be a baby to running around all over the place and wanting to play rough games. He seemed to experience any refusal from the other children to play with him as rejection and acted out as a result. He was also observed to struggle quite a bit with taking turns with the other children.

An observation of a play session between Mark and his mother showed that Mark had the capacity for pretend play and, as would be expected given his age, enjoyed play in which "good guys" and "bad guys" engaged in fights and, in general, good triumphed over evil. He showed the ability to distinguish between reality and fantasy and frequently noted that his play was "just pretend." In puppet play he enjoyed using the puppets to bite and attack each other. Although he was capable of maintaining play themes, they tended not to be very rich, imaginative, or well-developed, but rather to be somewhat aggressive and repetitive.

On projective tests Mark's drawings were quite immature and showed Mark's aggressive feelings and tendency to act out. His drawings and stories also suggested that Mark perceived his mother as uncaring. The stories he told about the pictures on the Children's Apperception Test (CAT) (Bellak & Bellak, 1974) included repeated themes of feeling lonely, lost, and frightened. Mark obviously had issues surrounding being able to trust others, feeling safe and secure, and being able to contain his own "badness." These assessment findings suggested that Mark had not internalized a secure sense of himself and other people that could hold him together when he experienced frustration and other kinds of upset.

*Parent–Child Interactions and Parenting*    Both of Mark's parents showed a number of positive qualities in their interactions with their son. On the one hand, Joan showed a great deal of acceptance of him and obviously cared deeply for him. When she described how Mark had "lost his self-confidence," she was moved to tears thinking of how upset he must feel. On the other hand, in Joan's interactions with Mark, it was obvious that any sadness that he showed was very difficult for her and that she could not help him to manage these feelings. Instead, she had to immediately try to change his mood back to one that was more positive. This often resulted in her dismissing or ignoring his sadness and laughing in a way that seemed heartless and inappropriate. When Mark showed other emotions such as anger and frustration, she seemed to be more able to cope with them and to be appropriately sensitive, responsive, and containing of them. She also enjoyed playing with him and was available to help him with anything he was trying to learn, such as reciting his letters and numbers or completing a puzzle. Her discipline, as observed in the home, was very inconsistent, however, and she frequently failed to follow through after setting a limit. For example, when Mark waved a stick around in a way that was endangering himself and others, she took it away and put it on a shelf. Mark immediately climbed up to retrieve it and continued to wave it around while his mother ignored him, laughing inappropriately.

Michael, Mark's father, tried to be somewhat more consistently firm with Mark. He was concerned that too much structure and too many rules might take away Mark's spirit, however. He often remarked that his wife was too harsh with Mark. Michael believed that she ignored Mark when he was sad. He also cared deeply about Mark and was eager to spend a great deal of time with him. Because his father was stricter, however, Mark sometimes refused to go to him, going to his mother instead to get his own way.

Both parents had positive and relatively realistic attributions and appraisals of Mark and his strengths and difficulties. It appeared from observations made by the assessment team about their interactions with Mark that he had a somewhat avoidant attachment to his mother, as seen when he would not go to her for containment when he was upset. Mark's attachment to his father seemed to be more resistant/ambivalent; although he received more consistent discipline from him, Mark also had some uncertainty in terms of how his father would react to him.

This lack of a clear structure was often exaggerated because Mark's mother would sometimes undermine the firm rules that his father was trying to enforce.

The following specific issues were determined as having a significant impact on Joan and Michael's parenting:

**Mother: Joan's Psychological Functioning**    Joan had a background of *unresolved trauma* as a result of being raised by a depressed mother who was emotionally unavailable to her, especially during her early childhood. This meant that Joan had not experienced responsiveness when she became upset and as a consequence, she found it overwhelming and difficult to deal with sadness or pain in others. Joan also had several miscarriages before the decision was made to adopt their children, and she had not had a chance to discuss or adequately resolve these more recent losses. Although Joan functioned well in most areas of her life, was highly educated, and was employed in a very responsible administrative position, she had developed some *defense mechanisms* that caused her difficulties in close relationships with her husband and children. Her complete denial of her own sadness and inability to acknowledge sadness in members of her family made closeness and nurturing of others very difficult for her. As a consequence, she often used humor inappropriately with Mark, as well as repressing negative emotions such as anger and anxiety in order to manage them.

Her own *attachment* to her mother was obviously insecure, which contributed to Joan's habit of dismissing her own and others' sad emotions. Because she could not respond with nurturing to Mark when he was hurt, ill, or sad, he had developed an avoidant attachment pattern. Joan's capacity for *self-reflectivity* about her behavior with Mark and how she understood him was initially extremely limited, and she rarely considered Mark's understanding and thoughts about what was going on. For example, she was unable to understand the possible impact on Mark of being in four different child care arrangements by the time he was 18 months old because she believed that "they were all good babysitters."

Joan's *attributions* of Mark were generally positive, although it did seem that, at times, she saw him as being controlling and herself as unable to manage his behavior and to provide for his emotional needs. Joan's sense of self-confidence as an employee was high; however, as a parent Joan lacked a *sense of competence*. This was exacerbated by the many miscarriages she had suffered before adopting their three children and her feelings of failure because of Mark's difficulties—most noteworthy, his own lost sense of self-efficacy. This clearly was triggering her feelings of inadequacy as a parent.

Joan had adequate *emotion regulation* in some areas and was able to manage her own and Mark's anger and aggression relatively well. She was unable to calm him or to be nurturing when he was sad, frustrated, or depressed, however, and as she did with her own sadness, she denied, avoided, or laughed off these feelings. This left Mark with a perception of being rejected and misunderstood as well as hyperaroused and overwhelmed.

Joan's capacity for *planning and problem-solving* in most areas of her life was excellent; however, at times it was difficult for her to consider Mark's emotional needs in her planning to the same degree as she planned for his educational ones.

In summary, Joan functioned well and was very capable in many areas of her life. However, patterns laid down in her childhood of having her feelings dismissed and coping with them on her own now made it very difficult for her to be nurturing with Mark and understanding of his need for responsiveness and nurturing when he was upset, hurt, or ill, and at his most vulnerable.

*Father: Michael's Psychological Functioning*    Michael came from a family of four and had a twin brother with whom he was very close. In fact, he and his brother often got together with their families, and his brother and sister-in-law were very supportive of Michael, Joan, and their children. Michael was the only member of his family who had gone to college, and this had given him an air of being special in the family. He sometimes felt that perhaps too much emphasis had been placed on the cognitive and academic part of his development and functioning at the expense of the somewhat uncertain and sensitive aspects of his personality. Nevertheless, he was able to go to his parents for support if he was unhappy or concerned about things, and generally, although not consistently, he received their understanding.

Michael was drawn to Joan as soon as he met her because of her competence in her career and her ability to laugh off upsetting situations. These traits, of course, became less appealing when the children arrived and his and Joan's very different parenting styles became evident.

Michael's psychological functioning showed some difficulties in the following areas. Although he had not been traumatized by his upbringing, Michael seemed to have experienced some *inconsistent nurturing and containment* of his emotional needs. His twin had been very small at birth and had required extra care, which may have affected how emotionally available Michael's mother was to him during his early months. As mentioned previously, Michael perceived a disproportionate emphasis on the development of his intellectual and academic functioning as he was growing up, which, although stimulating for Michael, placed him under some stress, and he often felt the pressure of his parents' expectations. This had resulted in Michael having a somewhat *preoccupied attachment* to his parents in which he continually sought reassurance of their approval. Michael's level of self-reflectivity and empathy for Mark was quite high; however, at times, he was unable to set firm limits because of his concern that Mark would become upset and unhappy. He also wanted to make sure that Mark's emotional needs were met in a different way from how his had been addressed while he was growing up. He was not overwhelmed with this but it did imply that he was not always able to be firm and to provide the structure that Mark needed.

Michael lacked *self-confidence* at work after a new promotion and did not see himself as a competent parent. He often became quite upset and talked about what he saw as his failure as a parent to make Mark happy. Although Michael was able to manage his own emotion regulation, he had far more difficulty with helping Mark to contain his; for example, if Mark became upset he would feel guilty. Although it was clear that Michael understood what was needed to discipline Mark and did try to follow through with it even when Mark complained or seemed upset, without the support of his wife he often backed off and gave in to him. Michael seemed very unsure about how to manage Mark and how to help him with his learning and emotional issues. He seemed unable to *problem solve around parenting issues*, although in other areas he did well.

## FORMULATING THE INTERVENTION

Although the family had many strengths, Mark's difficulties were beginning to affect the family system, leading to *family conflict*. The couple's disagreements over discipline and Michael's increasing frustration with Joan's lack of empathy and "toughness" toward Mark were sources of some concern. Also, the couple tended not to talk about any disagreement because Joan was not interested in talking about her feelings or their relationship, whereas Michael tended to be far more preoccupied with feelings.

Set out next is a summary of the difficulties and risks as well as the strengths that were identified in this family, and some of the intervention strategies that were used during the intervention. Professionals working with Mark used an integrative approach (as presented in Chapter 3) in formulating intervention for the family. First, a variety of theoretical approaches to intervention were reviewed for suitability. Second, the parents' willingness to be involved in and availability for intervention was considered. Third, the unique needs and difficulties of the child and family were assessed in order to choose the appropriate approaches. Fourth and last, the availability of services within the clinic and community was determined so that the best possible intervention could be provided.

## 1) Theoretical Approaches

In the discussion of this case study, a number of theoretical perspectives and ideas for intervention from a variety of disciplines were considered. These are described here:

*Developmental Theory and Brain Development*    The assessment clearly indicated that Mark had a learning disability and many symptoms of ADHD, which made it difficult for him to concentrate and focus, contain his impulses, and plan activities. Intervention was needed to help Mark's parents and teachers learn to interact in ways that were conducive to promoting Mark's developmental needs. It was also important that he have individual intervention as well. The individual in charge of the family's case made the suggestion that Mark receive follow-up evaluations by a neurologist who could continue to monitor Mark's irregular EEG patterns for signs of Tourette syndrome and other conditions. The neurologist would then be considered as part of the family's extended team of professionals.

*Transactional Theory*    Clearly, Mark had a significant number of challenges that placed his development at risk in spite of a variety of protective factors. These difficulties manifested themselves differently as he developed and were affecting his parents' view of him and their interactions with him, which, in turn, affected his developing view of himself. Intervention had to consider all of the areas of need or risk and to provide multiple approaches.

*Object Relations/Attachment Theory*    Mark's relationship with his parents was key to understanding his current functioning. Their interactions with him had contributed to Mark's developing an insecure attachment to each of them. In his mother's case, this insecure attachment went back for generations. In order to overcome this history of poor attachment, interventions that were offered included developmental guidance, parenting information, and psychodynamic therapy for Joan.

***Psychodynamic Theory***    Both Mark's mother and father had adopted different defense mechanisms, which resulted in them tending to ignore certain reactions in Mark and to emphasize others. Their early experiences and unconscious memories were unwittingly affecting their interactions with their children. Both parents attended sessions related to their marriage, and Joan participated in psychodynamic therapy in order to foster better relationships with their children.

***Trauma Theory***    Because in early childhood Joan had never experienced appropriate calming and nurturing of her own sadness, she had learned to withdraw from certain emotions in other people that could be triggered in herself in certain situations. She also had not resolved the trauma and loss of several miscarriages and of not being able to have her own children. Joan was gradually helped to understand and acknowledge her past and more recent traumas and to adopt strategies to calm herself.

***Ecological/Social Support Theory***    Mark and his family had a number of supports in their extended family, lived in a good neighborhood, and were involved in the school the children attended and in other community activities. They had adequate income to be able to provide a good education for Mark and his siblings and for extracurricular activities to encourage any talents and interests they had. These activities were encouraged during intervention.

***Self-Psychology Theory***    Both parents and Mark had not experienced mirroring of emotions, and although they had a positive view of themselves in many areas, they had poor self-image in others. Mark had been identified as having very poor self-esteem and had difficulty in trying new activities because he was afraid of failure. At times, he was extremely grandiose, and as a consequence, was often disappointed when he was unable to meet his own expectations immediately of being able to do things without practicing, such as riding a bicycle and writing his name.

Joan had a very low sense of parenting competence as did Michael, who found it difficult to communicate with his son and to discipline him consistently. Efforts were directed at helping Joan to use self-psychology (i.e., to examine her own background and motivations) to begin to understand and provide nurturance to Mark when he was upset in a way she had not experienced when she was a child.

***Cognitive-Behavior Theory***    Mark appeared to have beliefs about his adoption and his learning difficulties that were dramatically affecting his functioning. Although Joan had a number of positive attributions of Mark, she also often attributed Mark's behavior to characteristics within him, which may have been because she had little belief in her ability to discipline him effectively. Both Michael and Joan were supported to problem-solve about how to support and discipline Mark. Play therapy was suggested to help Mark to change his negative attributions of himself and to deal with other conflicts and concerns.

***Systems Theory***    This was certainly a parenting system under a great deal of stress, particularly regarding differences in how to discipline. Also, Michael often felt his needs were not met, and at times felt that Mark and Joan pushed him out of the family. Although the wider system surrounding them was supportive, the family system itself appeared to be becoming less able to deal with and to problem solve in times of conflict and stress. Marital sessions were held to help Joan and Michael to understand each other's needs and to work together to provide for their children's emotional needs, as well as for their own.

*Health Promotion/Population Health*    Although Mark's family had a relatively high income and lived in a low-risk area of the city, the parents lacked knowledge of parenting strategies and of child development, which made it difficult for them to understand their child. They were very capable of using information, however, and thus were amenable to suggestions on how to work with their child on such health promotion areas as sleeping and discipline in new ways. The following factors are very important influences on the ultimate success of health promotion intervention.

## 2) The Stage of or Willingness to Be Involved in the Intervention

Mark's parents were very willing to meet in the evenings and to bring him for intervention sessions. A number of intervention possibilities were available for Mark and his family in the children's mental health clinic and the community in which the family lived that matched the families' availability.

## 3) The Risks, Strengths, and Needs of the Family

The risks, strengths, and needs of the family are outlined in the referral information in the assessment section. It is clear that this is a family with many strengths, but it is also important to recognize that Mark, with his needs, presented both parents with a number of challenges that they found very difficult to deal with. For Joan in particular, Mark's needs also raised a great deal of previously unconscious issues around her own experience of being parented and the past and more current traumas that she had faced. Michael found that being a father for his challenging son made him feel incompetent in a way that—up to that time—had been quite unfamiliar to him. This was unsettling and difficult to consolidate with his previous sense of himself. Also, Mark was at high risk for ongoing developmental and behavioral problems without intervention.

The strengths and risks that Mark and his family faced are summarized in Table 4.1.

## 4) Intervention Strategies Available

The completion of this assessment revealed the therapeutic approaches and strategies that could be utilized effectively with Mark and his family. Intervention was planned and took place over 1 year, during which time Mark's diagnosis of ADHD was clarified. Medication was prescribed for the ADHD that significantly improved Mark's ability to focus and concentrate and reduced some of his negative behaviors. The intervention was relatively short but multidimensional, and was carried out by a psychologist who provided the mother's individual therapy and parent sessions and a child and youth service provider who conducted the play therapy and parenting information sessions with supervision by the psychologist.

Table 4.1.    Assessment of strengths and risks and suggested interventions for Mark and his family

| Subject/area of intervention | Strengths or protective factors | Difficulties/risks | Suggested interventions |
|---|---|---|---|
| The child: Mark | Mark has an average intellectual capacity. He is able to reach out to his parents and other adults with whom he comes into contact. He is very well coordinated, and is interested in various sports. Mark's two siblings are doing well. | Mark has learning disabilities, particularly in the area of nonverbal learning. He has difficulty focusing and concentrating on learning tasks. Mark tends to be impulsive and does not typically plan and think ahead about things. He has problems with emotion regulation and with containing his frustration. Mark can be noncompliant, rude, and defiant at times. He has difficulty in relating to other children and in taking their perspective and showing empathy and concern to them consistently. Mark tends toward splitting, which makes him capable of sudden switches of moods and changes in perceptions of self and other. | Consult with child care providers and school staff about Mark's needs in the classroom. Initiate play therapy for Mark to help him to cope with his issues around the adoption and to encourage him to deal with his anxiety over his lack of emotional containment. Work with parents and provide them with strategies to manage and nurture Mark and to understand his learning disabilities. |
| Parent–child interactions | Both parents have deep concern and love for Mark and let him know this in many ways. | Mark's mother (Joan) has a great deal of difficulty with dealing with Mark's frustration and sadness, and instead of nurturing him, Joan laughs at him in an effort to bring | Provide parent education and problem solving about finding appropriate strategies to use to discipline Mark. |

| Subject/area of intervention | Strengths or protective factors | Difficulties/risks | Suggested interventions |
|---|---|---|---|
| | Both parents (particularly the father) enjoy playing with Mark and having good times with him.<br><br>Both parents show encouragement and appropriate structuring of his learning. | his mood back to a positive one.<br><br>Both parents have difficulty with providing structure and limits, so there is a great deal of inconsistency.<br><br>Because of not wanting to "break his spirit," the father (Michael) sometimes hesitates to stop Mark's behavior at times when it would be appropriate to do so.<br><br>As a consequence of these interactions, Mark has an insecure attachment to both parents. | Provide developmental guidance to explain Mark's needs for limits and how they can help to get him beyond his current grandiosity and ego-centricity.<br><br>Support parents to enhance their attachment to Mark by helping him feel safe with them. |
| Parents' psychological functioning | Both parents have strong ego functioning, are well educated, and employed.<br><br>Neither parent uses very primitive defensive functioning, although Joan uses denial and repression extensively.<br><br>Michael's capacity for self-reflectivity and empathy for the child is very good.<br><br>Both parents are able to manage their own emotional expression, although the strategies are not appropriate on the mother's part. | Joan has a great deal of difficulty with dealing with her own and Marks' sadness.<br><br>Joan has very little capacity for self-reflectivity and for understanding and interpreting Mark's mind and feelings.<br><br>Joan seems to have some unresolved loss and trauma from her early experiences and recent miscarriages.<br><br>Michael has very little sense of parenting competence, and this affects his ability to provide firm discipline. | Arrange for individual, psychodynamically oriented counseling for Joan to help her integrate her painful past and improve her capacity for self-reflectivity.<br><br>Counsel Joan to help her identify signs that she is getting upset with Mark and to learn to calm down. |

*(continued)*

Table 4.1.    (continued)

| Subject/area of intervention | Strengths or protective factors | Difficulties/risks | Suggested interventions |
|---|---|---|---|
| | Both parents have the capacity for planning and problem solving in many situations. | Michael also has some difficulty problem solving about parenting issues that relate to Mark. | |
| Family functioning and support systems | Both parents have satisfactory careers that place them in a middle income level.<br><br>The family lives in a pleasant neighborhood.<br><br>Support is provided from both extended families, especially from Michael's.<br><br>The family has enough income to send Mark to a private school where he is able to have some extra attention.<br><br>The parents are committed to each other and their marriage. | Parents' different styles of discipline lead to significant conflict at times between the couple.<br><br>Michael is upset by Joan's apparent lack of empathy for Mark, and her dismissing of sadness or unhappiness.<br><br>The parents do not have a support system of other families bringing up children adopted from Mark's native country.<br><br>Job pressures sometimes make it difficult for the parents to find time for the children. | Arrange for parent sessions to provide parenting information and to deal with the developing conflict between the parents. |

## THE COURSE OF INTERVENTION

Mark and his parents participated in the following types of interventions.

*Individual Therapy for Joan*   Joan agreed to participate in psychodynamically oriented individual therapy, during which she explored her own relationships with her parents—particularly with her mother—that were affecting her ability to parent Mark. Joan was able to understand that although she was trying very hard to be different from her own mother, inadvertently, her overcompensation for her mother's depression was not allowing her to accept Mark's negative feelings and, in a sense, she had been repeating her mother's lack of understanding and nurturance. She also explored how her desperation to have a child, her guilt over her feeling that she had "taken" Mark from his natural mother, and the joy at having a child may have been making it difficult for her to set adequate limits and to discipline Mark.

Joan's ability for self-reflectivity and empathetic consideration of Mark and his problems expanded over the first few months of intervention. She became clearer about why she responded in the way she did, and hence she was more understanding of Mark's needs and could adjust her parenting accordingly.

Perhaps the most powerful moment in the therapy came after Mark's mother described her reaction after Mark had become very upset when a child had mentioned that Mark and his mother couldn't be related because they were of different races. Joan recounted how she had dismissed what must have been a very painful incident to Mark as a stupid remark and had laughed about it, as she typically did. The interventionist noticed that Joan's eyes were welling up with tears, however. The interventionist drew attention to this and asked about any other reactions that she was having. She was then able to concentrate on the bodily signs of anxiety she was feeling such as elevated heartbeat, sweaty palms, and other feelings of panic. With this awareness of her body's reactions, she realized that she was actually dismissing the pain that she and Mark must have felt in the situation. By encouraging Joan to explore her need to deal with upsetting material in this way, rather than allowing herself to acknowledge the pain, she was able to gradually identify this defensive way of reacting and to begin, at last, to be more understanding with Mark. In this way, she could acknowledge his sadness and frustration rather than cut off the emotion immediately. She was also able to eventually talk about the pain she had felt about her own mother's lack of emotional availability for her.

***Additional Parenting Meetings***   Because of the parents' strong need and desire for information about parenting, and particularly about helping Mark to manage his challenges, Joan and Michael attended monthly meetings in which information was provided and suggestions were made for issues that frequently arose with Mark's behavior.

Although many strategies for working with Mark were suggested and a number were used, Joan and Michael still had difficulty with being consistent and firm. For example, as part of the assessment, Mark and his parents were observed during dinner at their home. During the meal Mark kept getting up on a ledge and jumping down in a dangerous way. His parents repeatedly told him not to do it, but he continued until he eventually tired of the game. Later, during a counseling session, it became clear that both Mark's mother and father were finding it difficult to do what they called "breaking his spirit," which, in reality, meant setting limits. By discussing their concerns that discipline would not let Mark be himself and their need for Mark to feel contained, Joan and Michael were able to at last be firmer and more consistent in their discipline. Also helpful were sessions that encouraged both parents to problem-solve together in order to come up with and follow through on appropriate discipline strategies.

***Parent Counseling***   Mark's parents also attended parent counseling sessions during which they were asked to describe to each other their feelings about what was happening with Mark and with each other. They were also instructed to ask each other what each needed from the other. Joan was surprised to hear how left out and unsupported Michael felt, and Michael was not aware that Joan was feeling very upset about what she believed was her inability to make Mark happy. This led to a discussion of the feelings that Joan often hid by her tendency to react to her son's sadness by laughing or trying to turn things back to being happy. The interventionist also encouraged them to talk about their experiences growing up and related them to their parenting. These discussions were revealing for both Joan and Michael and allowed them to be more communicative and understanding of each other and more open to trying new parenting techniques together.

***Play Therapy*** Mark's intervention began with a nondirective approach to play therapy in which the interventionist encouraged him to expand his play themes and to include richer characters in stories that he acted out. He was supported to use play activities to resolve some of his conflicts and concerns, such as issues over his adoption, fear that his adoptive parents might leave him, and anxiety that he could not contain his angry, negative feelings and that he would become overwhelmed and could hurt others. After about 6 months of this nondirective intervention, a more cognitive-based approach was used in which Mark was introduced to problem-solving strategies to use in various learning and social situations. These approaches were also modeled for his parents and teacher so that they could use them in their interactions with Mark.

***Consultation with the School*** The psychologist and child and youth service provider consulted regularly with Mark's classroom teacher and other teachers in the school setting in which he was placed. These interventionists informed teachers about some of the reasons for the difficulties that Mark was having and suggested classroom strategies that could be used to work with him.

Mark's teacher expressed a great deal of concern about his lack of empathy for other children. The interventionists provided a careful explanation of the developmental process of gaining empathy and drew the teacher's attention to the gains that Mark had already made through her very appropriate interventions with him. This helped the teacher to see that Mark was indeed making progress. By acknowledging the teachers' excellent work with Mark and providing her with further strategies, the interventionists were instrumental in the school's decision to allow Mark to remain in his original school placement. In fact, by the end of the year, the teacher had this to say on Mark's report card:

*"Mark is a well-organized student. He is always quick to begin his work and does so in a neat, well-organized manner. Mark works quietly and usually finishes within his time frame. He has a very good attitude toward school and responds very well to any reminders of appropriate behaviors in school. He gets on well with his peers and joins into groups well. Mark is a highly motivated student and a pleasure to have in the classroom."*

## CASE STUDY 2

### Nina, a Mother with Unresolved Loss and Trauma and Borderline Symptoms

***Reason for Referral and Request for Service*** Child Protective Services (CPS) referred 26-year-old Nina to a social services agency because her four children had just been returned home after a few weeks in foster care, their third placement in the last year. Services were requested by CPS to improve Nina's parenting and to eliminate the possibility of any physical abuse so that the family could stay together.

On her first contact with the agency, Nina came with all of her children and, for the most part, expressed willingness to be involved in the program. During the first interview she indicated that this would be a way to understand herself and that she hoped it would be a new beginning for herself and her new baby. After this, there were times when she appeared totally uninterested in getting help, and she pointed out that she only came because she had to in order to keep her children. Nina's degree of self-motivation to attend sessions was obviously tenuous, and she experienced a great deal of ambivalence about being involved. When asked what she thought would be most helpful to her, she indicated that she wanted to understand why she did certain things and why her relationships did not last. She also indicated that two of her children, Derrick and Meg, needed help. Derrick tended to get out of control, and the school had been telephoning about his behavior. CPS was concerned about Derrick's behavior and Nina's demeanor with Meg, who seemed to bother her. Nina expressed no interest in improving her parenting ability or acknowledging that she herself had any problems with parenting.

***Initial Assessment***    Much of the necessary information was gathered during early counseling sessions with Nina, and it was determined that the family's complex needs would necessitate that the assessment extend over several sessions.

*The Children*    When Nina joined the program, she had four children: Aaron, 8 years old; Derrick, 5 years old; Meg, 3 years old; and baby Paul, who was 6 weeks old. Intellectual assessment of the three older children showed no significant delays, although their verbal or language development tended to be less advanced than their nonverbal learning. The older children all showed emotional, social, and behavioral difficulties.

The older children were able to engage in play for significant periods of time. During the assessment, they very quickly began to play out the chaos of their existence, with people coming and going and the police arriving to take their mother away to jail. Aaron, the oldest boy, was extremely parentified, which could be observed in his tendency to take care of his mother and look after his siblings at times. Although he did well at school, he was obviously an unhappy and angry child who occasionally lost control and attacked one of his siblings or a child at school. Derrick, the second boy, was totally out of control and continually placed himself at risk, such as by jumping from furniture and climbing on the stove. His recent behaviors had included jumping off a roof, running on the road, and even setting a fire. School personnel were talking about putting him in a special classroom to keep him and the other children in the classroom safe. He was also defiant and aggressive with his siblings and other children, at times. Meg appeared to be the most emotionally abused and neglected. She presented as a sad, whiny little girl who was constantly demanding attention, but she frequently ran away or cowered if it was offered. Paul, the baby, was doing well because Nina was at her most responsive when the children were infants.

*Mother–Child Interactions and Parenting*    Although Nina proclaimed a great deal of caring for her children, this did not match the behavior observed in these first assessment sessions. She showed few attempts to respond to her children, with the exception of the baby, Paul, who appeared well cared for and to whom she at least responded when he was hungry. She showed little interest in interacting with him at other times, however. She seemed to be removed from the other children unless they came to her, asked for something, or acted out by hitting each other or trying to break something. At these times she responded inconsistently: Sometimes she laughed at them, sometimes she appeared frightened, and other times she was frightening and became quite angry and threatening toward them. It was obvious that often she could not tolerate Meg's attempts to get her attention, which often involved whining, clinging, stamping, and asking for things. In marked contrast, she became more animated and sometimes laughed when Derrick acted out aggressively or when Meg's frustration gave way to a temper tantrum.

Perhaps the most poignant moment was when Meg fell down the stairs and lay there, crying plaintively. Nina made no effort to go to her and laughed at her daughter's pain as if she found it amusing. The chilling scene became more meaningful when Nina later talked about the level of deprivation and abuse she had experienced in her own childhood.

*Nina's Psychological Functioning*    Nina's early life history included significant *trauma and abuse*. She was the second of five children. Her parents were both severely alcoholic and her father had been physically violent with his wife and abusive with the children. She also reported being physically abused and sexually molested by her mother between the ages of 2 and 10. Her mother would abuse Nina by fondling and kissing her while telling her that men were no good and that it would be better to find a good woman to be with. It was only when Nina reached puberty that this stopped. Nina noted that her father was particularly violent and abusive with her older brother, whom he beat unmercifully. Some of Nina's memories included huddling under the bed with her younger sisters during her parents' fights, trying to keep the girls quiet so that they would not get hurt. She described that during these times she sometimes felt aroused, but at other times she would think about other things or "go places in her head" as if it were not happening. She shared another powerful memory that illustrated how her mother was totally unavailable and did "nothing to keep her safe." When she was 3 years old, she fell down the stairs, but her mother only laughed. Although she told her mother that her arm hurt, nothing was done until she cried endlessly and could not move it. Two days later the arm was found to be broken. Nina described knowing from that age on that she was on her own and that she could never expect anything or trust anyone.

This information improved the interventionist's understanding of the initial session when Meg fell down the stairs and Nina laughed at her daughter rather than comforting her. Few other details were described. It was as if, as much as possible, she had erased the past in order to survive in the present. Still, it was revealed during the assessment that her background was chaotic, with multiple moves and schools, and that there was no one whom she could identify as supportive. As is outlined in Chapter 9, Nina showed many symptoms indicating that her trauma was unresolved. These included a powerful pull to repeat the trauma, which in turn, constantly retraumatized her. For example, when she was 16 years old, Nina married a 45-year-old man who she said "treated her like a daughter" and wanted her totally under his control. She described the relationship as "weird, freaky, and abusive." Nina's husband kept her totally isolated in the house, never allowing her outside except when accompanied by him. The first two children,

Aaron and Derrick, were from this first relationship. By the time Derrick was 1, the abuse Nina was receiving at the hands of her husband had escalated, and she ran away with her children to a shelter. After leaving the shelter, however, she soon moved in with another abusive man, who left as soon as he discovered she was pregnant with Meg. Another abusive relationship followed in which Paul was conceived, but she left that man during the pregnancy. At the time of the referral, Nina was not living with anyone, but during the intervention she lived with other men. Interestingly, at one point she met a man who came from a stable background, had meaningful employment, and really cared for her children. However, she rejected him, choosing instead another abusive man because, she said, she found the more stable man boring.

This reflects a common symptom of people who have been abused and traumatized like Nina—the need to *repeat the trauma* and to live "on the edge," going through frequent crises to overcome the underlying fear or experience of emptiness, nothingness, abandonment, and betrayal. This became clearer as the intervention progressed. Nina also had a need to detach and little capacity to experience any small emotions, whether pleasure in simple things, or alerting to signs of fear or anger so that she could do things to check out their reality and take steps to calm down. Instead, she would avoid or fail to recognize those signs until something would trigger a rage reaction or extreme fear, during which she reported that she "blacked out" and did not know what she was doing. These "attacks" as she called them appeared to be linked to the *dissociation* she used to withdraw from re-experiencing physiological reactions that had been triggered by the previous abuse.

Nina also escaped the pain or feelings of emptiness by *using drugs and alcohol.* She frequently picked up men and had multiple sex partners and unprotected sex. She also made frantic efforts to avoid real or imagined aloneness or abandonment. Nina's interactions with all of her children suggested unresolved loss and trauma, as well. As described previously, these interactions were characterized by role reversals with Aaron; an inability to provide any nurturance when the children were hurt, ill, or upset; and frightened and frightening behavior toward the children. At times, dissociated and in her own world, Nina totally ignored the reactions of the children. At other times, memories of her trauma were triggered and she would become extremely punitive or abusive with them.

Nina had several symptoms of borderline personality disorder (BPD) and her *defensive functioning* was at a very primitive level. In her initial assessment session, Nina was articulate and did not show evidence of a psychotic thought disorder. However, she dealt with anxiety using extreme denial, splitting, projective identification, and acting out. She also showed some evidence of magical thinking and talked about needing to "exorcise the devil" from Derrick so he would stop misbehaving. She depicted the children and other people as sometimes "good" and at other times as "bad," which indicated that she was engaging in splitting and had an inability to retain positive memories in bad moments and to remember less positive aspects when experiences were good. Unfortunately, Nina also used projective identification and projected the bad parts of herself onto the children—particularly on Derrick and Meg. When they acted in ways that reminded her of herself, Nina punished them for showing the feelings she could not tolerate in herself. In Meg's case, Nina punished the little girl's whiny and needy behavior, for example. As pointed out, Nina often used acting out to create a crisis or to avoid feelings of emptiness and abandonment.

Given that Nina had experienced extreme neglect of her emotional needs and abuse, and later retraumatizations and a lack of either a new nurturing experience or a therapeutic relationship, she met criteria for both a *dismissive attachment* and as having *unresolved loss and trauma.* This type of attachment was played out in her relationships with others and in interactions with her children. Nina had very little insight or *self-reflectivity* about the effect of her past experiences on her current behavior. Her denial of her emotional experiences and rejection of closeness in her current relationships made it difficult for her to identify reasons for her acting out or to see her own role in what happened to her. In fact, her ability to consider her feelings, thoughts, and behavior was minimal at the beginning of the intervention. Because it was so difficult for her to explore what was going on in her own mind, it was not possible for her to understand her children's minds, either, and to acknowledge and empathize with their thoughts and feelings. In fact, very negative motivations were ascribed to them and she had very little capacity to understand or to empathize with their pain or unhappiness.

Nina's *attributions of her children* were not realistic or complex, and particularly for Derrick and Meg, they were mostly negative. More important, she ascribed the cause of any of the children's difficult behaviors to factors within them and she believed that she had no control over them herself. This meant that, not only were the attributions negative but also she felt powerless to do anything about the children's behavior, blaming it all on them, or in Derrick's case, on the devil, without any consideration of the trauma they had experienced. Aaron, who met her needs through role reversal, and Paul, who, at first satisfied her needs for having someone who loved her, were only seen negatively when they no longer played out the roles to which they were assigned.

Given Nina's lack of a sense of control (i.e., *learned helplessness*) as she was growing up, she viewed most events as controlled by fate or negative factors that she could not change or influence in any way. This also led to feelings of being unable to influence the children, or a lack of *parenting competence.* In other words, she believed that Derrick's behavior was a result of the devil ruling him, and that Meg was a weak child who used her whining and crying to bother and control her. Nina saw many situations as hopeless and herself as helpless and unable to do much about them. This also led to feelings of being unable to influence the children and of having a lack of parenting competence.

As mentioned, Nina frequently reacted angrily or abusively to her children, which seemed to occur without warning. She was also unable to deal with her children's need for *emotion regulation,* particularly around sadness and neediness, and she could not provide the nurturing, understanding, or containment the children needed at these times.

Nina did not have the capacity for *planning or problem solving* in any areas of her life, and particularly not in relation to parenting her children. Decisions were made impulsively and without consideration for the possible results of her actions.

The level of *family functioning* was generally chaotic because of the frequent crises that they experienced. Nina's male partners, who came and went, and the family's inability to use adequate strategies to solve conflicts, contributed to this chaos. In spite of this, the children at times supported one another and provided some sense of security for each other. Nina's tendency to become easily frustrated and to shift rapidly between seeing people as good and bad meant that she had virtually no supportive people she could trust in her life. She had no contact with members of her family, except with her brother with schizophrenia whom she tried to look after for a brief period. In the family system, the children tended to play out a variety of roles that allowed them to be noticed, and in some ways they held the family together.

Service providers used the integrated model presented in Chapter 3 in formulating and selecting interventions for this family, and the same four components suggested previously were considered. A summary is discussed next.

## FORMULATING THE INTERVENTION

### 1) Theoretical Approaches

Discussion of this case drew on a number of theoretical perspectives and ideas from a variety of disciplines. These included the following:

***Developmental Theory and Brain Development***    Developmental theory was helpful in understanding the emotional, social, and behavioral challenges faced by Nina's children. It was important to understand that some of the developmental failures occurred because of Nina's difficulties in providing them with nurturing interactions, but also with consistent structure and discipline to help them control their emotions and behavior. The children all struggled with emotion regulation and with managing their behavior. Their insecure attachments also affected their self-esteem and ability to problem solve. The team determined that interventions were needed to support Nina to provide nurturing parenting so that she could help the children to gain these developmental capacities. Given the extreme difficulties they experienced, direct intervention with the children was crucial, however.

***Transactional Theory***    This family was experiencing a number of risks that placed all of the children's development at risk. These risks were ongoing and, thus, were likely to continue to affect the children's development, placing them at risk for having academic and learning difficulties, for developing psychopathology, and certainly for having an insecure and disorganized attachment that would affect their relationships with others. It was clear that with these complex needs, longer term, multidimensional interventions were necessary.

***Object Relations/Attachment Theory***    All of Nina's children had insecure relationships with her, and this insecurity was key to understanding the children's behavior with their mother and with others. Unfortunately, the cross-generational transmission of the effects of unresolved loss and trauma was apparent, causing abusive behavior to be passed from her parents to Nina and from Nina to her children. Consequently, it was important to provide interventions that could improve Nina's interactional behavior, such as interactional guidance and modeling of interactions.

***Psychodynamic Theory***　Nina's defensive functioning resulted in her employing self-defeating ways of dealing with her anxiety. Also, she was constantly triggered by unconscious memories when her children behaved in certain ways, which led to her acting in ways reminiscent of her own mother and to inadvertently lead the children to repeat her own childhood experiences. It was important to encourage Nina to use more adaptive defense mechanisms by providing her with alternative ways to alleviate her anxiety. This took place in supportive therapy and in various group settings. Although it was inappropriate to push Nina to remember her past trauma too early in her intervention, before she had developed adequate ego functioning, it was important to empathize with her traumatic early experiences and to gradually help her to be more aware of their impact on her.

***Trauma Theory***　Obviously, significant and unresolved loss and trauma affected Nina's functioning in multiple areas of her life, as well as in her parenting behavior. A number of strategies were used to help her to overcome the effects of her trauma, including giving her calming strategies such as meditation and relaxation and ongoing support to find ways to deal with the triggering, which could lead her to abuse her children. Medication was suggested, but Nina refused to take it. The children were also dealing with reactions to abuse and neglect and Nina's failure to nurture and calm them when they were hurt, upset, or frustrated.

***Ecological/Social Support Theory***　Nina had no reliable supports from friends or family, partly because she did not want to be around other people, and partly because of the continuing rejection by her family. This isolation added to her difficulties in trying to parent four children. Although she managed her money well, it was difficult to find enough money to pay for some of her children's needs. By being involved in a number of groups at the agency, Nina was gradually able to form some supportive friendships. Also, she began to find a new sense of competence as she took on new roles in the groups.

***Self-Psychology***　Nina and her children had little sense of self-efficacy because they all lacked mirroring and responsiveness in the early stages of development and were constantly seeking affirmation and acknowledgment in negative or self-defeating ways. Nina also had little sense of confidence in her parenting ability. By improving Nina's interactions with the children, the children began to feel more supported. Nina also began to gain a sense of greater competence in her parenting role, and her self-esteem was improved as she became involved in programs at the early intervention center and returned to school.

***Cognitive-Behavioral Theory***　All of the members of Nina's family tended to have negative views of themselves and others. These negative views, of course, arose out of the responses and interactions Nina and her siblings received from their parents and other people, especially when they were infants and young children. Nina's negative attributions of herself, other people, and her children largely affected how she disciplined her children and her tendency to become abusive in certain situations.

***Systems Theory***　Nina's behavior was significantly influenced by the family system in which she grew up and by the alcoholism and drug addiction inherent in the lifestyle that formed a system around her. In the family system made up of Nina and the children, each child adopted a certain role that influenced his or her behavior and continued to keep the family system in place.

Interventions were needed that would help Nina understand the reasons for her children's behavior in a new way and to problem solve about coping with them and changing her negative attributions of them. Family play sessions were used to help the children and Nina to interact in new ways together.

**_Health Promotion/Population Health_**    Because they were living in a violent, high-risk neighborhood and because of the history of neglect, abuse, and violence that was being perpetuated from generation to generation, this was a family who was at the extreme high-risk end of a continuum. The provision of information individually or in groups was not going to be sufficient for Nina to be able to change her parenting interactions in order to prevent her children from developing a number of ongoing problems. As research has shown, information provision has not been successful for parents with mental health issues, and rather than a health promotion approach, a more nondirective and listening style of counselling was necessary both to encourage Nina to agree to intervention and to stay involved in it. As mentioned previously in Case Study 1, the following factors are very important influences on the ultimate success of any intervention.

## 2) The Stage or Willingness to Be Involved in the Intervention

Nina was quite ambivalent about receiving services and very sensitive to any perceived rejection or feelings of lack of control that might be triggered by the intervention. Consequently, it was important to allow her to feel a sense of control in the intervention and to work at her pace in getting her involved in various intervention modalities. This is described in the next sections of this chapter and also in Chapter 5.

## 3) The Risks, Strengths, and Needs of the Family

The risks, strengths, and needs of Nina's family are outlined in Table 4.2. However, it is clear that the risks and needs of the family were complex and multidimensional and that all members of the family needed support if they were to stay together. In spite of the degree of risk and the number of problems, the family had a number of strengths, one of which was Nina's wish to keep her children with her rather than having them removed by CPS. This gave the intervention a goal that was understandable to Nina, that she had requested, and that was very much desired by the children. It did mean that in order to meet her needs, a multisystem and multidimensional approach provided by a team of a social worker, students, a home visitor, and a psychologist, was crucial to meet her needs and those of the children, however, and that progress was slow and regressions frequent before some degree of stability was achieved.

## 4) Intervention Strategies Available

Most of the intervention approaches were provided within the early intervention center that Nina attended; however, for other interventions, such as treatment for her alcohol and drug addiction, Nina was referred to other agencies in the community. CPS also continued to be involved with the family. The intervention then

**Table 4.2.**    Assessment of strengths and risks and formulation of intervention for Nina and her family

| Subject/area of intervention | Strengths or protective factors | Difficulties/risks | Suggested interventions |
|---|---|---|---|
| The children: Aaron, Derrick, Meg, and Paul | All of the children have average intellectual functioning, although they perform less well on tests of verbal intelligence.<br><br>The children are all very likable and continue to reach out to others in an effort to get their needs met.<br><br>The older children have the capacity to use play and other creative activities to express their feelings and to understand their conflicts. | Each of the older children has emotional, social, and behavioral difficulties.<br><br>The children have not developed emotion regulation or behavioral control and sometimes act out aggressively when triggered.<br><br>They have little capacity for empathy for others because they have received very little themselves.<br><br>They have possibly suffered from the effects of trauma and loss from their experiences during Nina's drinking episodes and interactions with her male partners.<br><br>Aaron has been extremely parentified and has little sense of being cared for himself. | Provide play therapy for Aaron and Meg.<br><br>Provide consultation with the children's schools on the family situation and each child's needs.<br><br>Seek a nurturing child care program for Meg.<br><br>Work with Nina to help her find strategies to help Derrick manage his behavior.<br><br>Look into social skills groups in the school for Derrick and sessions to teach him ways to calm down and control his acting-out behavior. |
| Parent–child interactions | Nina's interactions with baby Paul are the most appropriate; she responds by feeding and holding him when he is hungry.<br><br>In some rare moments, Nina is able to enjoy her children and respond to them appropriately (e.g., when Meg played out some of her concerns about her mother being taken away by the police). | At times Nina's interactions with her children are insensitive, unresponsive, intrusive, and rejecting.<br><br>Nina shows many signs of unresolved loss and trauma such as frightened and frightening behavior, teasing, and failure to respond to her children's needs. | Provide interactional guidance to strengthen parent-child relationship between Nina and Meg.<br><br>Model nurturing interactions when appropriate.<br><br>Arrange for Nina to attend parenting groups on development and parenting strategies. |

| Subject/area of intervention | Strengths or protective factors | Difficulties/risks | Suggested interventions |
|---|---|---|---|
| | Nina is committed to keeping her children together and with her, and she spoke about this to them. | The children all have an insecure-ambivalent/resistant attachment and show signs of disorganized attachment as well. | Work with Nina on understanding the causes of her children's behavior and problem-solving around parenting problems. |
| Parent's psychological functioning | Nina has above-average intelligence.<br><br>She is motivated to improve her situation at least part of the time.<br><br>Nina has controlled her finances and has geographic stability (i.e., she has not moved frequently).<br><br>She attends therapy sessions consistently and is interested in understanding herself and her relationships at a deeper level. | Nina's unresolved loss and trauma results in frequent triggering that lead her to dole out harsh discipline or abuse to her children.<br><br>Her lack of self-reflectivity means that she has very little insight into her own actions or empathy for her children.<br><br>Nina uses primitive defenses, which often lead her to blame the children, fail in other relationships, and act out in dangerous ways.<br><br>Nina tends toward making negative attributions of her children and blaming them for their negative behaviors.<br><br>She doubts her own ability to control things and has little sense of parenting competence.<br><br>She has difficulty controlling her own emotions or behaviors, often acting compulsively and drinking frequently. | Provide long-term psychodynamic therapy for Nina.<br><br>Encourage her attendance at a number of groups focusing on such issues as alcohol abuse, anger management, and relaxation and meditation.<br><br>Provide crisis intervention and follow-up discussions of the situations and Nina's reactions to them.<br><br>Encourage Nina to make positive efforts toward getting an education and attending drug and alcohol counseling.<br><br>Empower Nina by encouraging her interests and abilities and her involvement in programs such as a Mother's Club, bead-making, and cooking.<br><br>Later, support her in her decision to go to a university. |

*(continued)*

**Table 4.2.**  *(continued)*

| Subject/area of intervention | Strengths or protective factors | Difficulties/risks | Suggested interventions |
|---|---|---|---|
| | | Nina makes decisions impulsively without any planning or problem solving. | |
| | | She has a history of being involved with a variety of men who had significant difficulties and were often in trouble with the law, which endangered herself and the children. | |
| Family functioning and support systems | Nina is committed to keeping her family together. The children can, at times, be supportive of one another. | Family members have little communication with each other and few strategies to resolve conflicts. Children are placed in roles that influence the way they are expected to behave. All family members are extremely needy, have learned to manage their sadness and pain on their own, and have difficulty providing comfort to each other. No supports outside of the family are in place. | Encourage Nina to be involved in a number of programs at the agency so she can find more positive support systems. Initiate family play sessions followed by discussion of what has occurred. |

included the need for coordinating the services, and a number of case conferences with the services providers responsible for various aspects of the intervention strategies were held.

## THE COURSE OF INTERVENTION

Because the case-study of Nina and her family provides a good example of intervention that was long and complex and involved a variety of therapeutic approaches, only this intervention with Nina will be described. Times that changes occurred are highlighted, and the course of intervention is described in three stages:

- *Stage one:* Establishing the therapeutic alliance and boundaries of intervention
- *Stage two:* Dealing with past trauma and memories
- *Stage three:* Stabilizing and consolidating gains made during the therapy

For very multi-risk clients, this gradual approach, rather than a premature move to accessing memories or early confrontation and interpretation, is crucial in order to lay a foundation of trust and to strengthen ego functioning so that the client can gradually begin to understand the impact of the past on her current functioning patterns. A number of other interventions were provided, as discussed previously.

## Stage One: "Establishing a Therapeutic Relationship" (Duration: 4 months)

In this stage, it was necessary to establish a sense of trust, stability in attendance, and some level of mutuality and collaboration. A top-down, distant, or authoritarian stance could lead to a resurfacing of Nina's anger about the abusive and sadistic nature of her early experiences. At the beginning and throughout her intervention, Nina was encouraged to talk about her goals, giving her a sense of control over what would take place.

Efforts were also made to set boundaries in order to begin to bring Nina's self-destructive and dysfunctional behaviors under control. Unfortunately, Nina had a strong tendency to continue being involved in the patterns of abuse she had suffered long after she left her parents' home. She had been involved in three abusive relationships and had been raped at least three times, following evenings in the bar.

It was also crucial to let her know that any abuse or neglect of the children—whether perpetrated by Nina or one of her boyfriends—was not acceptable and would result in her being reported to CPS. Although the person in charge of her therapy did not make efforts to have Nina remember her early trauma during this stage of intervention, she was helped to begin to realize its role in her present difficulties. It was also important to let Nina know that what had happened to her was unacceptable and to let her experience empathy for the pain of her past. Use of some expressive therapies turned out to be an important way for Nina to find words for previously unspeakable feelings. These included writing poetry, keeping a diary, and creating artwork.

Despite all of the positive effects of therapy, at various times Nina had experiences with her therapist that she perceived to be re-enactments of previous relationships. For example, there were several times when Nina perceived that her therapist, whom she had initially idealized, was letting her down. The first came when a bus that was supposed to pick her up for her art group failed to arrive. It took many discussions before Nina was able to understand and accept that there had been a mistake by the receptionist rather than any intended rejection by the therapist. The next instance was when she called in a "crisis" because the washing machine that she was trying to move would not go down the stairs. The therapist made it clear that this was not really a crisis, although she would have come if it had been. At other times, Nina was upset when the therapist confronted her about driving without a license and about having multiple sex partners. Even with reassurances that the therapist wanted to keep her safe, on each occasion it led to Nina accusing the therapist of being like everyone else in her life—unreliable and critical.

At these times, the therapist would, in turn, feel violated and wonder if the relationship could be sustained.

These experiences needed to be interpreted in order for her intervention to proceed effectively. This process of interpretation can ultimately provide a corrective emotional experience and, in Nina's case, was critical for setting the stage for some resolution of her past.

For several sessions, Nina had talked about her desire to take in her older brother, whom she acknowledged might be violent. She had dreams of them being a family and helping to support each other as a family should. She believed that she could get him straightened out and that he could help by babysitting the children. Her therapist talked about how he might place Nina and her children in danger. One evening, Nina called to tell the therapist that her brother had a knife and was threatening her and her children. On being told that the police were on the way, the therapist went over to the house and found the police taking her brother away. Nina was hysterical, blaming everyone and swearing endlessly. After she calmed down, she was able to describe in detail for the first time the beatings that her brother had received and to express the rage she felt toward her father for these acts. Even more, she expressed her rage toward her mother for ignoring the situation and for not keeping them safe. The therapist did not push for more memories but supported Nina's understanding of the effects of the past on her brother and herself.

This incident gave Nina an opportunity to think about her abuse and to begin to understand its effects in a more powerful way as she talked about her brother's difficulties. This was only a very tentative beginning of a long journey in which Nina began to explore her abuse, however. During this stage of therapy, Nina made little mention of any emotions about events she described and just stated the facts with no consideration as to what may have led to them.

## Stage Two: "Exploring the Abuse" (Duration: 18 months)

In this stage of the intervention, it seemed unclear for a long time whether Nina would be able to progress much further in her ability to nurture her children. She was unable yet to make use of the therapist's suggestions for caring for them. When there was an audience she was able to respond more appropriately, at times, but it was clear that when she was alone with her children she had little caring to give. It was very difficult at this time for Nina to share her therapist with her children. Any attempts to focus on her children met with withdrawal, and she could not tolerate any comments that attempted to interpret her interactions in light of her own needs. It become clear that although she was able to move forward in some areas of her life, she had only made very tentative strides toward being able to achieve resolution of her traumatic beginnings.

At this time another person joined the therapeutic team, a student who would work with Nina on her reactions with Meg using videotape viewing and interactional guidance. Meg continued to present the greatest difficulty for Nina. When Meg cried, it seemed that Nina was constantly reminded of herself, the little girl who lacked nurturance for so long; her unresolved conflicts about being a woman; and her fears about her own sexuality in relation to her daughter. Nina's relationship with Paul remained warm, and she seemed a little more aware of Derrick's needs but was still unable to set consistent limits.

Throughout this period the option of foster care was considered frequently as a way to sustain the children's development. As things began to stabilize, however, it was unlikely that the children would be permanently removed, and her team believed that the separation involved in temporary removal would only compound the difficulty of facilitating Nina's attachment toward her children and of them to her.

During her own therapy, it became evident that Nina was now preoccupied with a new man whom she saw as perfect—as someone who would be able to make everything all right. Efforts to help her to consider any difficulties were unacceptable and she began to slowly withdraw until she could again see the therapist as being supportive.

Her interaction with Paul continued to be nurturing until he began to walk and to show signs of individuation. So it was at this time that the next crisis call came, which again provided powerful material to bring some insight.

The call came quite late, and Nina's voice was barely audible as she began to tell the therapist that she had a strong desire to "end it all." The therapist made inquiries and determined that Nina was in no immediate danger of committing suicide, but was having terrifying feelings of abandonment and aloneness. She assured the therapist that her new man was still in her life but that something had changed that she did not understand. Given her great distress, the therapist agreed to come to her house, unclear as to what may have triggered her intense feelings of sadness. She was relieved that Nina had not turned to alcohol. When the therapist arrived she found Nina sitting in a rocking chair hugging a doll. She was almost in a dissociative state and was talking about how she missed her baby. At that moment, Paul woke up. When Nina picked him up, he struggled to the ground and walked across the floor and, as Nina put it, "walked right away from me." The therapist explored Nina's feelings about this, and suggested that Nina was experiencing a few different feelings simultaneously. One part of her felt extreme sadness while another part felt rage that someone else was "leaving" her to manage on his own.

This incident allowed Nina and her therapist to review a variety of issues extensively, such as her extreme ambivalence about her children. It also gave them the opportunity to explore Nina's need to tell the therapist only about times when she showed caring for her children, in case the therapist rejected her. As she rocked the doll, she suddenly became aware that she had not been using birth control pills, and that she was in danger of becoming pregnant again. Rapidly, she fluctuated between wanting to be free and able to do what she wanted without a baby and wishing she could be pregnant again to fill the void she was feeling as Paul was growing into a toddler. As she talked about both feelings, some reparation of her splitting mechanism became possible. She also began to express her feelings of abandonment by her mother in her own childhood. She then started talking about her feelings toward Meg, and described how she sometimes heard herself speaking to her "just like my mother spoke to me." Gradually, Nina began to struggle with her desires to overcome her past and the strong concerns she shared that she would not be able to do this.

Soon after this, Nina decided to move in with Brad, the new man in her life. At first, she continued to talk about how caring and wonderful he was to her and to her children. Again, Nina rejected efforts to help her to modify her idealization of Brad and what her relationship with him could mean to the family. Unfortunately, it took a crisis before Nina began to have some insight and to make changes.

Nina called early one day to say that Brad had beaten her up again and had left. She sounded out of control with rage and kept talking about how he was like "all men." By the time the therapist arrived, Nina had started to drink and began accusing her of not telling her it would end this way. The therapist interpreted this to Nina as anger caused by the therapist not trying hard enough to keep Nina safe from this violent man, just as her mother had failed her many times before. The interventionist began to review with her what it was that had attracted her to this man. She then revealed that a man, Bob, was "after her" who could offer her more. He was employed, had a stable home, and had showed her real concern over the last 6 months. The therapist suggested that in some way, Brad may be providing her with the excitement that she craved and needed so as not to feel empty, and that Bob did not. Nina began to talk about the same feelings she sometimes had toward her therapist and how she sometimes saw her as a naïve person who did nothing to stop her acting-out behaviors. She then began to reveal some of her risk-taking behaviors that she had kept secret from her therapist. These included escalated drinking and promiscuity. She described needing these outlets because she was now experiencing "weird" feelings that she did not understand. It became clear that she was experiencing flashbacks that had become too powerful to tolerate.

At this point, the therapist again suggested that she needed intervention for her drinking. She refused this but did agree to attend a mothers' group, a relaxation and meditation class, and an anger-management group. These groups became a highly effective medium for Nina, both in terms of the practical skills she learned and because they increased her contact with the outside world and other people. This contact allowed her to become increasingly more grounded in current reality and showed her that controlling her anger and overcoming the dissociative processes she experienced was possible. The groups also taught her the use of new soothing techniques to use when she was hyperaroused, which can be crucial strategies for traumatized individuals to use.

In spite of these positive interventions, Nina still remained full of rage and began to project this rage onto the therapist more frequently. Her extreme psychological pain as she remembered her past caused her to become even more self-absorbed and less available to nurture her children. The idea of placing the children elsewhere was considered again; however, Nina was obviously making efforts in many directions, so the intervention team began to concentrate on finding extra resources for her children. These included after-school programs and therapeutic groups for the boys and excellent all-day child care for Meg. Meg was also accepted for play therapy because her sadness and frequent angry outbursts were becoming more worrisome.

Unexpectedly, Nina continued all of her interventions and asked to increase her therapy to three times a week. This additional support helped her to cope with her traumatic memories and allowed for reviewing of her intense need for excitement and risk-taking behavior. Gradually, Nina began to be able to review her feelings toward her therapist for failing to save her from her pain and for allowing her to be abused again.

At the end of this 9-month period, perhaps the most traumatic crisis occurred when the therapist received a call late at night from a very intoxicated Nina, incoherently shouting that the police were going to take her and the children away. Because it was very difficult to understand what was going on, the therapist told her to hang on and that she would be coming over.

When the therapist arrived, she was confronted by two police officers informing her that Nina had driven intoxicated and had been involved in an accident. They were determined to put her in jail and to place the children in foster care. After much persuading and assurance that Nina would appear in court the next day, the therapist was able to convince them not to incarcerate her immediately. The next day, the therapist arrived early, pulled Nina out of bed, and made her tell the truth about what she had been doing, assuring her that she would remain no matter what. Nina then revealed drunken parties and her risk-taking behavior with men and driving without a license. The therapist assured her of her concern for her and her children's welfare, sobered her up, and insisted that she telephone an alcohol treatment center and make arrangements to enter it. Reluctantly, she capitulated, and with a date set for her treatment, the court agreed on this as an alternative to going to jail. Unfortunately, during the 4-month period that she was in treatment, the children had to be placed in foster care. Nina was allowed to visit them frequently, however, and they were happy to know that their mother was going to be "getting better."

Although this was a turning point for Nina, it took another 9 months of therapy and ongoing support before intervention could be terminated. Nina at last began to understand her repeating patterns of risk-taking behavior, and it was possible to intensify efforts to help her to see the connections between her early experiences and current behavior. During Stage Two of the therapy, Nina became much more able to talk about feelings and make links with the past.

## Stage Three: "Consolidation of Gains" (Duration: 3 months)

During this time, efforts were made to consolidate gains that Nina had made. It was a long, arduous path to begin to help Nina to integrate her frightening memories into a new self—one who perceived herself as worthy of engaging in a "new" external world. At this time, the members of the program saw extraordinary growth in Nina's sense of empowerment; she became the president of the Mothers' Club and began to organize some events and political action against child abuse. She completed her alcohol treatment, joined Alcoholics Anonymous, and took pride in her activities in this organization. Gradually, she risked going back to school, and finally moved away to attend a program that would allow her to work for the justice system. As beliefs in her own abilities expanded, she no longer saw Meg as a weak, helpless child and began to see her as the competent little girl she had become. Paul remained outgoing and loving. Aaron and Derrick continued to have difficulties that were characteristic of their early problems. Nevertheless, the children were succeeding in school and excited about a new beginning.

The therapist received a holiday card 4 years after the beginning of treatment. The note was brief and encouraging.

*I miss you all, but can't afford to come there this Christmas. I hoped to be able to surprise you at the Christmas party where we began. . . . You'd never recognize the children—they're so grown up—and speaking of grown-up, that's the way I feel . . . most of the time anyway . . . at last.*

In both of these cases, intervention was long and multidimensional in order to meet the complex needs of these families. It is clear that one parenting group or a brief intervention, although useful, is not capable of meeting the myriad needs and concerns of children and families facing multiple risks. Although the intervention can sometimes be slow and difficult, the alternative of placing children in foster or permanent care is less likely to meet the needs of children in the long term and can have a devastating impact on families. How much better it is to work with a family's strengths and desires to make its members self-sufficient and fulfilled to the benefit of all.

# Reaching and Engaging
# Hard-to-Reach Families

*With Claudia Koshinsky Clipsham*

As discussed in Chapters 1 and 2, because of the large body of knowledge about the effect of parenting on the developing brain and the success of some interventions in the early years, optimism continues to grow in the human services field about the effectiveness of prevention and early intervention programs, even though their success with multi-risk families is actually far less clear.

Why is evidence of success with these families so difficult to document? For one thing, these populations often do not stay with interventions long enough for changes to be documented. Research has shown that only a small percentage of families with children with behavioral and emotional problems actually attend mental health or early intervention programs (Bird et al., 1988; Fergusson, Horwood, Shannon, & Lawton, 1989; Meltzer, Gatward, Corbin, Goodman, & Ford, 2003; Offord et al., 1992). Moreover, a significant number (at least half) of families who initially attend, drop out prematurely (Wierzbicki & Pekarik, 1993). These findings suggest that both recruitment and retention of families needs to be a major emphasis of providing early intervention services to high-risk families. In many prevention and early intervention programs, a home visiting component breaks down some of the barriers to coming to an intervention facility. The family's lack of psychological readiness or resistance to being involved can still present significant challenges, however.

The phrase *hard to reach* can be used to describe a wide range of families. In general, families approach participating in support programs with varying degrees of motivation. These different types of families range from those whose participation is mandated by child protection agencies to those who have actively sought help because of their own concerns about their parenting, their relationship with their child, or their child's behavior and development. As Prochaska (1999) pointed out, people go through a number of stages during the change process, which unfolds gradually over time. He claimed that any services provided need to be adapted to the family's stage of readiness for change. The stages are: 1) precontemplation (i.e., the individual is not intending to take action in the immediate future); 2) contemplation (i.e., the individual intends to take action toward change

---

Parts of this chapter were originally published in Invest in Kids (2004). *A Guide to Professional Home Visiting: A Strategy for Intervention with High-Risk Families* (Chapter 8: Understanding and Engaging Hard-to-Reach Families), Toronto, ON. It is adapted here by permission.

Claudia Koshinsky Clipsham, Ph.D. (cand.), is a clinician at the Circle for Children and Youth in Care in Toronto, Ontario, Canada. She is also an instructor in the Certificate Program in Infant Mental Health, Division of Continuing Education, Atkinson Faculty of Liberal and Professional Studies, York University, in Toronto.

in the next 6 months); 3) preparation (i.e., the individual intends to take action immediately); 4) action (i.e., the individual has made active changes); 5) maintenance (i.e., the individual is working to prevent relapse); and 6) termination (i.e., the individual is confident about being able to maintain changes). Prochaska, DiClemente, and Norcross (1992) pointed out that intervention has to be matched to the parents' or other caregivers' stage of readiness. For example, for individuals at stage 1 or 2, who have no intention or desire to participate in interventions immediately, approaches that give them information about their children's needs and are experienced as supportive and caring are most likely to be successful in encouraging them to get involved in more in-depth interventions at a later time.

Few people are believed to reach stage 6 or termination, in which they feel confident enough to stop intervention completely. Instead, most individuals or families remain in stage 5, maintenance, for several years or return for support at times when difficult events arise in their lives or when a child reaches a challenging developmental stage.

In order to work effectively or to provide meaningful interventions for families, service providers must first identify the level and source of a family's motivation and the type of services they are willing to use (Lieberman & Pawl, 1993). The process of engaging a family begins by clarifying the avenues through which the family is accessible, as well as the specific factors that make it difficult for them to establish an effective working relationship. Once these factors have been identified and the family's willingness to be involved is determined, intervention strategies can be adapted to meet the specific needs and wishes of the family.

In a sense, working effectively with families who might be labeled "hard to reach" involves a shift from perceiving the *family* as being hard to reach, to thinking about what makes the *service* that is being offered hard to accept for a particular family. This shift puts the emphasis on the interventionist's role in reaching out and adapting the service to the needs of the family, rather than vice versa. It is a shift from providing information only to listening to the struggles a parent is having with a parenting issue or with knowing how to respond to her child when he behaves in a certain way. When a service provider responds to this struggle by helping her to clarify her issues and supporting her to find a more comfortable and adaptive way of interacting with her child, this can be very meaningful to a parent. Adapting the delivery of the service in this way makes it possible for the family to gain access to the services more easily (de la Cuesta, 1994a). Such an approach demands considerable flexibility, conceptual clarity, and maturity on the part of service providers. When intervention is organized by considered formulations of each family's strengths and needs, rather than by therapeutic formulae that are rigidly and uniformly implemented with all clients, the capacity to adapt and apply basic therapeutic principles and considerations across differing circumstances and modalities is necessary (Greenspan et al., 1987; Lieberman, 1985). Developing the expertise to work in this way takes time and effort, both in the initial training stages and in continuing reflection, individually and with colleagues, as the service provider continues to work with families. It also requires the support of the organizations within which the clinician works (Wieder & Greenspan, 1987). These commitments are rewarded when families who would typically not remain engaged with traditional services are served effectively.

The following section discusses some of the factors that contribute to the sense that a family is hard to reach. These factors include pragmatic difficulties that affect the logistics of establishing and maintaining contact with families, and attitudinal factors that may make parents reluctant to agree to initial and ongoing contact. The importance of establishing an effective working relationship with parents of infants and young children are emphasized, as are the impact of cultural differences on the development of working alliances with families. Following this, general principles related to the development of enduring working alliances with families are discussed. Next, the importance of clinicians' recognition and utilization of their own emotional responses to their clients are addressed. Finally, the process of engagement with the two families introduced in Chapter 4 is described in order to illustrate how an interventionist's appraisal of the particular constellation of factors operating within a given family affects the approaches and the strategies she selects.

## FACTORS CONTRIBUTING TO THE PERCEPTION THAT SOME FAMILIES ARE HARD TO REACH

Two types of factors come into play in engaging multi-risk families: 1) pragmatic factors, and 2) attitudinal factors.

## Pragmatic Factors

The following are examples of pragmatic factors that may affect the ease of engaging multi-risk families:

- *The difficulty of contacting the family to invite them to take advantage of services and to arrange a visit:* Not all families or parents have access to a telephone. Other families are difficult to contact because of language barriers; individuals might not speak or understand the language of the person calling them.

- *The impracticability of providing the family with printed materials describing the program:* Individuals from multi-risk families are not always literate, and so they cannot read printed materials. Again, language barriers might also come into play.

- *The difficulty of visiting the family at their home:* In some cases, the interventionist may be required to travel extensively to visit clients at home. This may be inconvenient and time consuming.

- *The possibility of unacceptable levels of safety risk to the home visitor or a family member:* Particular conditions that exist in the family or community may be disturbing and unpredictable for interventionists. For example, if a parent has responded violently to the presence of outside visitors in the past, a worker could be jeopardizing her own safety as well as that of other family members by attempting to meet the family in their home.

- *The lack of access to transportation:* Attending meetings or appointments outside the home may be difficult for a family because of poor access to transportation.

- *The difficulty of juggling schedules:* Scheduling meetings with a family may be difficult because of the working hours of family members.

## Attitudinal Factors

In addition to pragmatic factors, certain attitudes common to families at multiple risk may serve as barriers to intervention:

- *Reluctance to tell family "business" outside the family circle:* For some families, talking about family issues outside the family circle, particularly when admitting that there may be a "problem," is considered disloyal. Members of the family may feel a responsibility to work things out or to smooth things over without outside intervention, and they may view asking for help as an indication that family members are not able to "take care of their own."

- *Belief that seeking help for emotional issues signifies inadequacy or weakness:* Some people regard seeking help for physical health problems to be "normal" and acceptable, but feel that asking a professional for assistance with emotional or relationship issues means that they are "abnormal," "sick," or "crazy." Even acknowledging to themselves that they are experiencing emotional difficulties that are serious enough to warrant seeking help may threaten their images of themselves or provoke profound feelings of shame or humiliation.

- *Belief that service professionals are interfering individuals who do not and cannot understand the real needs of the family (Luker & Chalmers, 1990):* This belief may stem from earlier experiences with professionals, or it may reflect a more generally perceived disparity between the life circumstances of the family and those of professionals, especially if the parents have experienced financial or emotional poverty. If either parent's life history has involved ongoing experiences with unempathic, remote, or intrusive "helpers," he or she will have little reason to expect that a professional could be otherwise (Seligman & Pawl, 1984).

- *Fear of disclosing violent, illegal, or other such negative activity within the family:* In some families, interactions between members are violent or abusive. Furthermore, some family members may be engaging in other types of activities that are illegal (e.g., selling drugs) or that might jeopardize the family's access to services such as social assistance or housing. If illegal immigrants are discovered and reported, they could be deported. Parents who are in these types of situations often hesitate to use community services. Many families at multiple risk, whether they have had a history of dealings with social service agencies or have been referred for the first time, appear to demonstrate a general attitude of protective secrecy. This attitude may have developed in order to survive in conditions in which the disclosure of alleged rule infractions can have a devastating effect on the stability of the family's circumstances. For example, if a mother is being beaten by her partner, he may be threatening to harm her more if she permits or seeks any outside involvement. Or children may be instructed by their mother not to talk about their home life if their father has not completed the legally prescribed immigration process into North America. In another scenario, a mother who is receiving occasional monetary gifts from a boyfriend may fear that a service provider will find out and report her to the authorities, jeopardizing her social assistance income. This would make her very reluctant to seek outside intervention for helping her with childrearing.

- *Fear of disclosure of medical status or prior diagnosis*: Parents may be reluctant to become involved with support services because they fear disclosure of private information regarding their health status, such as having been identified as HIV-positive or diagnosed as having schizophrenia. Parents may have concerns about possible social stigmatization that may result if such information becomes known in the immediate community.

- *Fear of involvement with child protective services:* Parents are frequently hesitant to seek support in helping them cope with their children because they fear that child protective services will become involved. Many people fear that if this happens, they will be at risk of losing their children or of being told by child protective workers how they must parent. These fears can be exacerbated when an individual has had negatively perceived past experiences, either as a parent or as a child, with these organizations. Negative associations can also be fueled when friends or relatives have reported negative experiences. Such past experiences can be potent even for parents who feel fairly confident about their parenting.

- *Hesitation to attend center-based services:* For many families, the office-like, professional atmosphere of a health center feels impersonal and intimidating. Discussing issues about which family members may be feeling uneasy, especially in a situation in which these individuals are not on their "home turf," may heighten their sense of vulnerability. The relatively more bureaucratic and "official" atmosphere may maximize feelings of distrust and disconnection that already exist.

- *Reluctance to admit a service provider into one's home:* Having a visitor come to visit may feel intrusive. Parents may feel that they have less control over what they disclose about themselves in the home setting, and less ability to initiate or terminate the interaction on their own terms. If they feel self-conscious about a lack of material resources or difficulties in maintaining an orderly home with small children to care for, they may feel vulnerable to criticism.

- *Chaotic functioning that prevents engagement in consistent and predictable ways:* The number and intensity of stressors impinging on a family may compromise a parent's capacity to maintain a sense of order and regularity in his life. This sense of chaos may reflect situational, external stresses experienced in adulthood, especially when poverty and isolation erode the sense of predictability and order that is necessary to feel organized. However, an adult's sense of chaos may also reflect a pattern of functioning developed as a result of chaotic and disorganizing experiences affecting him in childhood. For such an adult, making regular, consistent appointments and keeping them may feel almost impossible, because he feels unable to predict what will happen next. And indeed, external life events often do mirror the internal chaos that has characterized an individual's life experience, making it more difficult for the person to maintain a consistent connection with a worker.

- *Fear of losing control:* Some parents may be hesitant to even explore the possibility of seeking supportive services because they fear that once the door is opened, they will relinquish the opportunity to make their own decisions based on their own perceptions and values. They may worry that once they have consented to having some connection with an agency, they will not be able to decide for themselves when and how to make that connection or whether to continue the connection. This fear may be based on past experiences with agencies in which the family perceived a loss of control as a result of their involvement, or it may be rooted more deeply in their early relationships. Because of early experiences with insensitively intrusive and controlling adults and/or of abuse and other trauma, children may develop working models of relationships that predict that involvement will result in loss of control. If these models are carried into adult functioning, parents may still avoid connections as the only way they know to preserve their own sense of appropriate boundaries and autonomy and to avoid being triggered or overwhelmed with memories of the past.

- *Expectation of rejection or criticism:* One of the major factors underlying parents' reluctance to use support services is the sense of vulnerability they feel as parents and the worry that they will be rejected or criticized. To a certain extent, this worry is part of being a new parent. Every mother wants to do the best she can for her child, and meeting the needs of a helpless infant can be overwhelming at times, even for the most confident parent. Parents who are isolated, without a strong familial or other social support structure, are even more vulnerable to such feelings. Parents who have been criticized for their previous parenting of older children may be more prone to expect criticism. The issue is especially problematic for a parent who was consistently criticized and rejected as a child. She may feel that others will reject her and that she will never be "good enough" in the eyes of others (or in her own). When a parent feels extremely vulnerable to what she perceives as probable rejection, she is very unlikely to welcome connections with professionals. Even if she permits some contact to occur, she will likely experience a heightened sensitivity to any perceived criticism or rejection of themselves or their child.

- *Feeling hopeless and beyond help:* Physiological factors alone can make new parents vulnerable to feelings of depression and helplessness, both of which are exacerbated with additional risks such as social isolation, lack of economic and other resources, and so forth. Patterns from the past may also contribute. If a mother received largely unresponsive or ineffective parenting when she was a child, she may have internalized a working model of herself as ineffective in being able to elicit, receive, or give support. The reactivation of these feelings when she becomes a parent may adversely affect her capacity to respond to her child's cues, and it may also have a negative impact on her ability to seek out support and to accept help that is offered.

- *Resistance to talking about issues:* Some parents may be reluctant to ask for professionals' help because of the likelihood that they will be asked personal questions about their past experiences. For some, these kinds of discussions are viewed as irrelevant or as inappropriate intrusions into private matters. For others, additional factors may be operating. If parents have painful and unresolved memories involving trauma and loss, they may be resistant to talking about them because they are not ready to do so. To force a parent to face the memories without sufficient preparation and support may compromise her capacity to remain focused on the immediate task at hand, providing care and protection to her infant. In such a situation, the parent's reluctance may be adaptive and appropriate, at least in the short run.

- *Being at a stage when one is not ready to engage in intervention:* As noted earlier, it may take people a period of time before they acknowledge that they have a problem and are ready to take action to do anything about it. In other words, individuals could be at a pre-contemplation, contemplation, or preparation stage and need different types of outreach approaches (Prochaska, 1999).

- *Not perceiving the services offered as being relevant to their needs:* Parents typically have a certain agenda in mind when they seek help. If a service provider gives a parent information about something she never considered to be relevant, she is likely to feel rejected and misunderstood because it appears that the service provider is not listening to her concerns. For example, if a home visitor insists on talking about activities to use with the new baby when a mother's pressing issue is anxiety about an older child who is becoming angry and difficult, she may find the visit useless and even intrusive.

Although pragmatic factors can present substantial obstacles to successful connection with families, these factors are relatively more amenable to practical problem-solving approaches. Once a mode of operating can be established to overcome these practical hurdles, through what Byrd (1997) called the "selling and scheduling" phase of home visiting, the process can be allowed to proceed to the level of establishing a working alliance with the parent. In contrast, attitudinal factors are usually not resolved definitively by one practical solution. Instead, they are more likely to be addressed gradually, and they involve *who* the interventionist is, *how* she allows herself to be available and present with her client, and her patterns of *responding* and *acting* over time. In other words, the empathic containment that occurs repeatedly during a home visit or clinic session is more important than any one specific practical action or maneuver (Chalmers & Luker, 1991). In a study of the elements of the working alliance between mothers and home visitors, various aspects were found to be related to enhanced parenting, including the mother's perception of the interventionist's empathy for her and the interventionist's perception of the emotional engagement in the session. It was also found that when the approach was adapted to the interests and style of the mother, the intervention was more effective (Korfmacher, 1998).

Parental attitudes vary with respect to the extent to which they represent beliefs or patterns that are deeply engrained or more changeable. If attitudes have not been internalized as the result of early experiences and have emerged more as a result of recent actual events that have been experienced, the beliefs are easier to work with. More recently developed attitudes may make it hard to "get in the door," but once some connection between parent and service provider has been made, the attitudes acknowledged, the relationship clarified, and fears about the intervention allayed, the working alliance can be built with relatively little difficulty. If the beliefs are deeply rooted, long-standing, and central aspects of a parent's sense of self, they will be much more difficult to reframe or change, however. Moreover, they will probably continue to re-emerge; indeed, they may well become the focus of intervention.

## WORKING WITH NEW PARENTS

The profound effects of some of these attitudes on the process of developing a working alliance with parents can be difficult to overcome. The patterns of thinking, feeling, and responding that make it difficult for a parent to form a trusting relationship with an interventionist may be some of the same patterns that make it difficult for him to respond to some of the needs of his child. When these patterns arise in the relationship between parent and home visitor, they provide the home visitor with an opportunity to experience, understand, contain, and respond to them. Sometimes, the clinician may choose to verbally reflect them back to the parent, providing him with the empathy and support that may make it possible for him to become more aware of—and potentially change the destructive aspects of—the old patterns. Alternatively discussing their meaning with the parent may help her relate them to her past experience or to current people or events in her life. Sometimes this may help her see they are not useful patterns to adopt with her child and she may then be motivated to want to change them. At other times, the interventionist may choose not to discuss them at all, but to enact a new pattern in her behavior and response to the parent. In so doing, she may provide the parent with an opportunity to revise the old patterns based on a new experience (Lieberman, 1985, 1991; Lieberman & Pawl, 1993; Seligman & Pawl, 1984).

A person may live her whole life, utilizing and accommodating the patterns that are rooted in her early experience to guide her perceptions and interactions in new relationships. But no experience will force her to draw on those models so intensively as the experience of becoming a parent. The primary tasks that a new mother (or father) faces (everything from keeping the baby alive to relating to the baby), as well as those needed to secure support systems and to transform a sense of self in order to be able to fulfill these tasks, necessitate new patterns of adaptation (Stern, 1995). All of the old half-remembered or even unconscious memories and patterns from early experiences may become reactivated. To the extent that these memories promote a sense of competence and security, they are reassuring, but to the extent that they involve uncertainty, ambivalence, isolation, or fear, they may heighten anxiety. A woman's heightened emotional experience as she is trying to adapt to motherhood may promote her motivation and openness to examining and adapting the old patterns, or it may force her into a more rigid and defensive use of the old ways. Therefore, becoming a parent and the accompanying feelings of vulnerability that attend it may encourage a parent to be relatively more receptive to input—or the converse—to be more resistant to it.

This double-edged aspect of the adaptation to parenthood is especially important to consider when a service provider attempts to build a working alliance with a mother whose attitudes make her hard to reach. Daniel Stern described the most helpful therapeutic approach in these circumstances as one that meets the mother's "desire to be valued, supported, aided, taught, and appreciated by a maternal figure" (1995, p. 186). For a mother whose own upbringing has involved highly conflicted relationships, however, she may crave this closeness and deeply fear it. Much of the behavior that causes her to be perceived as hard to reach may arise from this conflict. Two major tasks emerge for the interventionist. The first involves searching for a domain in which the mother is relatively more available to input. If she is requesting help for a particular aspect of her situation or of her relationship with her child, starting work with her in that area gives her the opportunity to gradually form a relationship with a supportive service provider and to begin to experience the possibility of change (Chalmers & Luker, 1991; de la Cuesta, 1994b). The second task, which builds on the first, involves interacting with the mother in a way that allows her to gradually form a less-conflicted experience of relationships. Another task, based on the initial assessment, is to identify areas of difficulty that the parent has not identified and to gradually help her to become aware of some of the ways in which she behaves with her child that are causing difficulties for the child or with the parent–child relationship.

## Cultural Issues in Forming Working Alliances with Families

Culture refers to the belief system shared by a group of people. These shared values and meanings allow individuals to interpret and understand the behavior and customs of the situation in which they live. Cultural meanings do not exist in isolation, however. Rather, they are constantly being discovered, created, and negotiated by individuals and hence, they are always evolving. Furthermore, an individual is socialized within a number of groups (e.g., racial, ethnic, religious, national, family, school, and community) that share meanings; thus, cultural influences on any individual arise from a transactional relationship between *several* shared meaning contexts and levels of influence, no *one* of which can be considered in isolation (Harwood, Miller, & Irizarry, 1995). Assumptions cannot be made about the particular values and meanings any individual ascribes based on his or her membership in any specific group. Considerable variability can exist between individuals within a given group, based on the transactional relationships between the values of that group, the values of other groups to which they relate, and their personal life experiences and situations.

Among immigrant groups, one factor that produces considerable variability in attitudes between individuals from the same group is the degree of acculturation to the adopted country's culture. This factor may interact with other family dynamics to heighten conflicts between generations within a family. As an example of this, Szapocnik, Kurtines, and Santisteban (1994) discussed Hispanic immigrant families in which the parents are less acculturated than their adolescent children. The children embrace the American emphasis on individualism, whereas their parents continue to place a higher premium on their traditional values of family cohesion and the authority of parents. This interaction between cultural and generational factors heightens the level of conflict between adolescents and their parents, increasing the level of alienation each feels with the other at the time that the child and parents are attempting to negotiate the developmental issues of adolescence.

This dynamic of clashing generations may also play out in situations in which a mother who is an immigrant lives with her extended family, including members of the older generation. Although she herself may be motivated to seek support from outside agencies, if the attitudes of the elders regard such input as inappropriate, it may be very difficult to form a working alliance with the mother.

***Challenges Presented by Cultural Differences Between Interventionists and Families***    Working with families from different cultures can present unique challenges, particularly when the interventionist is from a cultural and ethnic background that differs from the individuals receiving the intervention. Some of these difficulties are discussed next.

- *Language difficulties in making the initial telephone contact to invite individuals to use program services:* Early prevention/intervention programs are often difficult to explain clearly because these programs often work very differently from traditional mental health services, which are more familiar to most people. In fact, these programs can be difficult to explain even to people who speak the same language as the interventionist. Also, for a parent who comes from a country in which answering questions posed by authority figures may have profound and drastic consequences for themselves or their loved ones, being called by a stranger who has information about them may feel threatening. Interpreting what a parent means by her response may also be problematic, if one is not familiar with the polite forms of communication in a particular culture. For instance, if a cultural value is to be nonconfrontational, parents may not say no when they mean no. Instead, they may give an excuse about why they cannot see anyone that day and agree to be called again, when in actuality, they do not have any intention of ever saying yes or any interest in being involved in the program. They may even say yes to a visit because they do not believe that they can say no, and then just not be at home or answer the door when the home visitor arrives (Barrera & Corso, 2003; Lieberman, 1990; Lynch & Hanson, 2004).

- *Ongoing language and communication difficulties:* When parents and interventionists speak different languages, even with the services of interpreters, it may be difficult to express the subtleties and nuances of meaning that allow a rich mutual understanding to develop. Discussion may remain on a relatively superficial level, or it may be distorted if the interpreter inaccurately or incompletely conveys the message. Cultures also vary in the way that subject matter is approached, and the ways in which continuity and change of topic are introduced. Thus, even if the words are understood, the surrounding meaning frame may not be transmitted. It is difficult for a clinician to convey empathy and attunement in a refined way when she has only a limited idea of what the parent is trying to express about her experience. Showing her interest and concern for the parent nonverbally is also complicated when she may not understand all of the pragmatics of nonverbal communication in the client's culture. These limitations may severely constrain the depth of working alliance that the interventionist and parent are able to develop together (Barrera & Corso, 2003).

- *Difficulties in sharing meaning at a deeper level:* Even when parents and interventionists speak the same language, if different systems of shared meaning influence their views of themselves, the world, relationships, parenting, child development, and so forth, then communication between them may be constrained by lack of mutual comprehension. In a way, these gaps in mutual understanding are often more subtle and implicit. In a therapeutic context in which the focus is on the parent's attributions and beliefs about her child, herself, and the relationship, this issue is especially important. Parents' understanding of their children and the meaning of their behavior are influenced by the larger system of meanings shared by members of their same cultural group. The cultural belief systems of parents affect how parents attend to their children's behavior, how they interpret it, the goals they hold for their children, and how they behave in relation to their children (Harkness & Super, 1996; Harwood et al., 1995). If interventionists and families do not find some way of transcending or communicating about their differences in these areas, the potential for productive therapeutic reflection on the parent–child relationship will be very constricted.

- *Differences in perceptions of appropriate dress and behavior of the interventionist:* Families may have particular cultural or religious beliefs about the appropriateness of styles of dress, forms of greeting, body language, topics of discussion, and behavior in interaction. Without some awareness of these issues, an interventionist may be offending a family or family member without even knowing it.

- *Lack of awareness of family dynamics and roles as they relate to interaction with an outsider:* Without understanding the values that operate within a culture and within a particular family, a service provider may fail to include members of the family who expect to be included in the interaction. For instance, if the family culture dictates that the elders of the extended family must assess and approve of the interventionist before the interventionist may establish a relationship with a younger mother, failing to include the elders in the first meeting may bode negatively for the establishment of a working alliance with the family at all.

- *History of oppression of a cultural group:* Many American Indian and First Nations Canadian parents, for example, have either directly or vicariously experienced traumatic separations from their families and communities of origin through placement of children by child welfare agencies in boarding schools or foster care facilities. Many of these parents were further traumatized by abuse experiences while they were in those settings (Horejsi, Craig, & Pablo, 1992). Such a confluence of personal and cultural history, involving traumatic and disruptive associations with child welfare authorities, predisposes many individuals to be extremely mistrustful of contact with agencies. Other cultural groups may have experienced a history of oppression and disparity in power that becomes engraved within the collective memory, constraining the willingness of individuals to open themselves to relationships with outsiders. Collective experiences of violent disturbances of cultural patterns, through experiences such as ethnic cleansing or slavery, may profoundly influence the perceptions of parents about what is necessary for their children to have in order to adapt and survive. These perceptions influence the approaches taken by parents toward raising the next generation (Lieberman, 1990).

• *Conflict between the values of the interventionist and the values of the family:* The values that are prized and promoted by an interventionist attempting to implement a particular clinical modality may conflict with the values held by the client family as a whole or by some members of it. For instance, if a cultural value is for the family to solve problems as a unit, guided by the parental authority figures within it, individual therapy directed at the facilitation of separation–individuation processes in one of the children may be experienced as conflictual rather than supportive. This lack of goodness of fit between levels of influence on the child's development does not enhance the probability of a positive outcome (Hanson & Lynch, 2003).

> ***Adapting Services to Be More Culturally Sensitive***    Different strategies can be used for making intervention more culturally sensitive for other cultural groups (Barrera & Corso, 2003; Rogler, Malgady, Costantino, & Blumenthal, 1987). Lieberman described *cultural sensitivity* as a "special case of general interpersonal sensitivity" that requires "a conscious temporary putting aside of our own values and preconceptions in the service of inquiring about the values and preconceptions of others" (1989, p.197). In order to be culturally sensitive to a parent, interventionists need to maintain an awareness of some possible differences that may exist between her values and theirs that could arise from differing cultural perspectives. One must continually be sensitive to what the parent's culture means to her in particular, in her own particular place and time, with her own unique personal history and family context, however. As Barrera and Corso described the process, it is critical to keep "an open mind and to have extended relationships with families" before the family's experiential context with regard to her cultural beliefs can be understood (2003, p. 58).

The following are some concrete ways for interventionists to make initial contact with families successfully in order to communicate an interest in understanding what is meaningful to the families, whether their cultural backgrounds are similar to or different from the interventionists'.

## Making the Initial Contact with the Family

When making the initial telephone call or connection with the family, the following strategies are useful.

In the first telephone call, it is important to be clear and direct and to tell the parent how you got her name, who you are, and what agency you work with. Also, let the parent know what services you can offer. Sometimes offering immediate help with practical matters is really useful. If you are finding that it is hard for the parent to understand you, offer the possibility of having someone who speaks their first language call them instead.

Ask if the person would like to have more information. If they agree to hearing more, ask if it is an appropriate time to talk or if she would prefer that you call back at a more convenient time. If she says no to a home visit, ask if you can send some information about the program by mail. Suggest that you could call back in the future at a better time (e.g., "I can give you another call when you are not so busy with the new baby").

Ask if there are any immediate services needed and if the person has any questions about services. Engage in conversation, but do not ask a set of questions or fill in an information form. Let the client discuss the information in her own way and in her own time.

Be open to hear what individuals want to tell you. Some parents may want to terminate the conversation immediately, whereas others feel very anxious and in need of reassurance. Use active listening techniques, such as paraphrasing what the person has just said in a way that invites her to expand on it. Ask questions that naturally follow what the individual has already talked about or that is in tune with what is happening at the time. Rather than suddenly asking about her background growing up, ask her these types of personal questions when you are admiring her baby or child. You may want to ask her how having a baby reminds her of how it was for her growing up, for example. This allows her to respond at a level at which she is comfortable and does not push for memories that would be inappropriate at this time. The information-gathering phase of working with clients is interwoven with relationship-building. At this stage, as at every other, sympathetic listening to the concerns of parents and collaborating with them to develop a better understanding of themselves and their children supports the development of a strong working alliance (Seligman, 2000).

Acknowledge the presence of other family members and friends, and follow the clients' lead regarding the extent to which these others are to be involved in the discussion (Seligman & Pawl, 1984). For instance, if the family elders need to approve of you before the mother will be permitted to engage with you, the signals may or may not be clear. If the signals are clear, however, following their lead is very important. Similarly, if the mother and father are both present, the ways they choose to relate to you as individuals and as a couple will show a great deal about the roles they each take and the distribution of responsibilities and concerns in the family.

Throughout the first call, be brief—the person you are talking to may be struggling with a wiggling baby at the same time! Be friendly and inviting, without being overly familiar. Make it clear that the parents are in control from the beginning; you will not contact them again without their express permission to do so. But be clear that you would like to call again if permitted. Offer alternatives regarding a time, language, type of information you can provide, and home or office contact, and let them know that the first contact does not necessarily require an ongoing commitment.

For families who do not have telephones, it may be useful to leave cards or notes in their doors to introduce yourself and to offer a visit. It is important to make it clear that you are just dropping off the information, that you are not assuming that they will receive you without prior notice, and you are willing to return at a time that is mutually agreeable. Otherwise, some individuals may worry that you are there to see if they measure up as parents, so your dropping in may feel like a spot-check. Make it clear that they are still in control. If no one is home, leave the note anyway with an invitation to call you back.

## Making the Initial Home Visit

In the first visit, the information-gathering phase of working with the parent is interwoven with relationship building. At this stage, as at every other, sympathetic listening and collaborating with parents to help them to develop a better understanding of themselves and their children supports a strong working relationship (Seligman, 2000). Other strategies are listed next.

It is critically important to continue to let the parents know that they are in control and the interventionist can show this in a variety of ways. For example, wait to be invited to sit and ask or watch for any messages about what kind of involvement with their children is acceptable for you to engage in.

Ask general questions so that parents can choose what to talk about. Listen to the parents so as to begin to understand their unique interests and capacities. Listen to their stories as they want to tell them and be aware of what they may have chosen to leave out. Engage in conversation but do not ask a set of questions and fill in an information form.

Use active listening techniques; for example, ask questions that naturally follow what the parents have already talked about or that are in tune with what is happening at the time. Following a parent's lead about whether to focus on her own needs or those of her infant is important.

One of the most natural forms of contact with new mothers is through their children. For a mother who is able to positively identify with her child, being able to share her sense of joy in the child's presence, his beauty and gestures, and her concern about his welfare, is a way to establish a connection. In a certain sense, to express delight in a new mother's child is to express delight in her. When a mother is able to sense a worker's sincere interest and concern for her child, this affirmation itself can overcome much resistance. For a mother who has difficulty identifying with her child, this may not be the case. When a mother feels depleted and displaced by her child, and fears that there is not enough support to satisfy her own needs as well as those of her child, a visitor's obvious focus on and delight in the child may be experienced by the mother as rejection or neglect of her own needs. Furthermore, any comment about her parenting might activate her own anxiety about her competence as a parent, and thus be taken as criticism (Lieberman & Pawl, 1993). By following the mother's lead, attuning to her wish to focus on her baby or herself, the visiting worker can begin to develop the relationship.

Although some models of professional involvement require workers to avoid revealing information about themselves as individuals to clients, this is often detrimental to the formation of a working relationship with parents. When visiting parents in their homes, workers are often asked questions about their personal experiences or circumstances. Being prepared to allow families to see who you are as an individual allows a mutual connection to develop more naturally (Jack, 1999). Home visitors may want to share information such as, "I remember this stage with my children; it can be very challenging at times." At the same time, it is important to be clear about appropriate boundaries, which allows families to feel reassured that the worker will remain focused on the parents' needs rather than her own.

It is important to convey interest, empathy, and a desire to be helpful to the client by giving her and her family undivided attention.

Use every opportunity to validate and normalize the family's experience (Chalmers, 1993). For example, if a new mother is feeling overwhelmed, empathize with how tiring having a new baby is, particularly in the first few weeks.

As pointed out by Prochaska (1999), it is critically important to begin to determine the stage that the parent has reached in terms of wanting to learn appropriate ways to interact with her baby. If the parent is at the precontemplation or contemplation stage, it will be important to provide her with information about the positive effects of playing with, soothing, and cuddling her baby. Letting parents know about any groups or information packages and videos that provide this kind of information can also be helpful. Building on her emotional connection to her baby and her desire to be the very best parent she can be can also help prepare her to take action, or to begin to try some activities with her baby.

Helping parents discuss what dreams they have for their baby in the future, especially the kind of person they hope he will be, can often motivate them to work with the child in certain ways. For example, if a father hopes that his child will be courageous and loving, hearing about parenting strategies that can be helpful for the child to develop those characteristics can help him imagine something positive that he can look forward to in the future. Sometimes attending a group with other parents can provide a similar motivation for change.

Describe any services that parents seem interested in and let them choose the type and frequency of involvement they want. It is important during the first and next few visits to identify these areas in which parents may want support, as well as factors that operate to make it difficult for the family to make use of support systems (Luker & Chalmers, 1990). By starting with the focus on what the family wants—not what the interventionists believes they want—the family's immediate needs can be addressed while building a relationship that can carry over into the future (Chalmers & Luker, 1991).

## BUILDING THE RELATIONSHIP AND FACILITATING THE PROCESS OF CHANGE

After the first contact has been made and the family has indicated a willingness to be involved in the intervention, it is then necessary to continue to develop a trusting parent–interventionist relationship so that the parents find their interactions with the interventionist to be helpful. It is important to respect that the family is doing the best they can do at the time. This conveys acceptance of where parents are in the present while maintaining the sense that they are capable of continuing to grow and expand their repertoire of feelings and ways of being with their children (McDonough, 2000).

Enhancing the competence of parents is important, and empowering them to be agents of change in the life of their families is critical. Start by focusing on positive aspects of parent–child interactions and following the parents' lead to move to consider more problematic areas, which allows the parents to work from a position of strength. This will enhance the positive aspects of parents' experiences, bring them to bear on the more difficult areas of their experience, and problem-solve constructively (McDonough, 1993b, 1995, 2000).

Remember that the family has the ultimate control over the direction of the intervention (Luker & Chalmers, 1990). As Lieberman and Pawl (1993) expressed it, "The therapist must genuinely conceptualize the effort as doing something *with* someone and not *to* someone" (p. 430). By working with the parents as partners and respecting their wishes and needs, their sense of efficacy and competence as parents can be facilitated. This experience of mutual respect in the relationship supports their capacity to engage in a similarly respectful relationship with their children based on mutual negotiation and fulfillment rather than on competition and power struggles (Lieberman & Pawl, 1993).

Listening, understanding, acknowledging, and empathizing with the parents' positive and negative experiences is extremely helpful (Chalmers, 1992, 1994; Jack, 1999). Supporting a parent to feel understood, empathizing with her experience, and confirming her reality are all essential in creating a safe and accepting atmosphere. Under these conditions, the parent can afford to reflect on her experiences and her actions and how they might affect her child; thus, she can potentially expand her capacity for self-reflection and empathy. In conditions in which she feels criticized or threatened, she is likely to become more defensive and less able to consider how her child feels. When an interventionist relates empathically to a parent, she is facilitating the parent's capacity to relate empathically to her children (Lieberman, 1991).

Be clear about the boundaries of the clinical work. Explaining client confidentiality and the principle that no information can be shared without the clients' written consent is important. At the same time, it is necessary to acknowledge any exceptional circumstances that apply; for instance, if a family's participation in a program is legally mandated by the child protection system, some information may be required to be shared with child protection workers. Clarifying exactly what types of information have to be shared, as well as what types will not be shared, can be reassuring to the parent. Such a straightforward and open discussion of the issues involved can help to facilitate trust.

## Creating a Trusting Relationship with Parents

Building trust is the most central task in developing an ongoing working relationship with parents. Obstacles or disruptions in the development of trust are likely to reflect patterns developed from the past, and change may only be able to take place from experience with a worker who enacts new patterns of relationships. Some of these new patterns include responding consistently, predictably, and reliably to the parent's communication. It may be essential to be emotionally available when the parents' moods and needs shift, and not to retaliate or judge negative feelings that the parent may express. It is important not to be overwhelmed by the family but to accept and empathize with them whenever possible. Trying to remain open, warm, and available in times of crisis is very important (Berlin, O'Neal, & Brooks-Gunn, 1998; Korfmacher, 1998).

Sometimes practical and concrete help in particular areas, such as securing housing, food, resources, day care, or other services, strengthens the client's sense that someone can respond to her expressed needs in an appropriate, timely, and sensitive way (Pawl, 1993). This may be a starting point for the parent to feel a real connection with the interventionist (Lieberman, 1991).

## Maintaining a Sense of Balance

Following the parents' needs and lead can be extremely difficult for some service providers and may evoke feelings of anxiety and helplessness. Workers may over-identify with the parent or the child and lose a more balanced, neutral perspec-tive. A number of emotions can be stirred up, including feeling rejected by the par-ent, anger toward the parent, joy at progress on a child's part, and disgust if parents place their infants or children at risk (Wright, 1992). These feelings are very com-mon and require reflection and reflective supervision. The necessity for this sup-port and ways that it can be provided by the service agency and within the service system are explained in detail in Section IV of this book.

## ESTABLISHING INITIAL CONTACTS AND
## ONGOING INTERVENTION: CASE-STUDY FAMILIES

The two families described in Chapter 4 presented very different challenges in terms of establishing and maintaining an appropriate and helpful relationship that supported their sense of being understood, and also opened the way for the possibility of change. Although, in many ways, working with Mark's family was less challenging than work-ing with Nina's family, it was necessary to listen to what the parents wanted, to assess the main issues, and to be as sensitive as possible in adapting the services to their needs and availability. In both situations, the families were facing crises that brought into question the efficacy of the services and, at times, a great deal of support was needed to enable the parents to continue. These processes are described next to illustrate the use of some of the suggestions in this chapter for engaging and maintaining families in intervention programs.

### Mark's Family

At the beginning of the intervention with Joan and Michael, they were in the midst of a crisis due to having to remove Mark from school and were genuinely concerned about the difficulties he was experiencing. At first they wanted an easy and rapid so-lution and for Mark to be "fixed," so they felt some resistance to any strategies other than direct "treatment" for Mark. As educated, middle-class parents, they also wanted up-to-date, research-based information, and were proactive in interviewing the service provider to identify whether they felt she and the suggestions for intervention were the best fit for their family.

Although she was definitely ready to try to change and to commit to an interven-tion, Joan was somewhat resistant at first to the idea that some of her own issues and particularly her memories of her own experience of being parented were affecting her parenting with Mark. At first, she seemed to feel that this was a form of mother-blaming, so in early sessions it was crucial to engage primarily in listening and affirming without pushing for memories. After the sessions were under way and she experienced a chance to really talk about her difficult relationship with her own mother, however, the effects of her early experience on her parenting of Mark became much more meaningful.

Joan and Michael were also initially hesitant about agreeing to participate in parent sessions because they believed that their relationship was generally a close and warm one. It was therefore important to point out the disagreements about discipline and to suggest that talking about these would be the focus of the discussion. At that point, Joan and Michael were able to be more accepting of the sessions, and they found the discipline issues and ideas about how to deal with Mark's emotional upsets to be very helpful and an important part of the intervention. It was important, however, to continually monitor their level of comfort with the interventions so that adaptations could be made if necessary. It was also critical to be able to provide Joan and Michael with reassurance that all aspects of Mark's development were being considered and to help them access appropriate medical services and occupational therapy assessment and intervention services as soon as possible.

A crisis occurred at one point because the school that Mark was attending was questioning some of his behavior and their own capability in managing him. Providing consultation to the school and attending the meeting with the parents at this time was crucial for the interventionist's credibility, for the parents' sense of being supported, and most of all, to ensure Mark's continuation at the school. This allowed the intervention to continue and enhanced its effectiveness.

## Nina's Family

Establishing regularity in meeting with Nina was a long and difficult process at first. Sometimes Nina cancelled because one of her children was sick, but more often it was related to her extreme sensitivity to rejection and her chaotic lifestyle. On one occasion, the center's van failed to pick her up because of some confusion with the schedule. On the one hand, this threatened the developing relationship between Nina and her home visitor; on the other hand, the incident provided useful material that could be used to discuss some of her feelings toward the service provider and the intervention program. In the early stages, it was essential to be nonjudgmental and to build on her sense of competence and to emphasize her sense of being understood and "heard," which were very new experiences for her. It was also critical to be available as much as possible to Nina while at the same time establishing some boundaries to reduce the risk of her acting-out by hurting her children, drinking, or using drugs.

Some of the strategies that were most effective with Nina included the following:

- Responding to crises whenever possible, being there when Nina was experiencing moments of despair and affective arousal, and demonstrating acceptance and containment of her extreme feelings was essential.

- Using the circumstances surrounding these crises as discussion points when they were vivid in Nina's memory and talking about the feelings she experienced enabled some of the action of therapy to take place at an emotional level of understanding rather than at a level at which only the events and Nina's behavior were described and understood.

- Encouraging her to take the initiative in selecting groups and other interventions gave her a sense of control over the intervention and prevented her from feeling that intervention was given in a top-down manner.

- Waiting to interpret Nina's actions or comments about them helped the interventionist to listen actively and follow her lead in discussion.

- Giving Nina adequate time to deal with her own issues was something she needed, although it was critically important for the interventionists to attend to the needs of Nina's children. Without this time, Nina tended to perceive a lack of empathy for her own pain, and that she was being left out in favor of the needs of her children.

- Providing practical help, such as food and toys over the holidays, was very helpful.

Although Nina was intelligent, she was extremely naïve about some aspects of her life, such as choosing her partners and relationships and the impact of any abuse and family violence on her children. Moments of change and growth in the therapeutic relationship often occurred during crises and subsequent discussion of the events. They also occurred when Nina could be encouraged to experience admiration for her children's gains and achievements and, when it was appropriate, for positive shifts in her own parenting. For example, when she was able to respond more empathetically to her daughter's pain and understand some possible reasons for her boys' acting out behaviors. These gains were noted by her therapist. These opportunities to connect to Nina around her achievements and growth in parenting capacity were moments that Nina remembered throughout the intervention, and she often referred back to them as times she felt particularly encouraged and supported.

## CHAPTER 6

# Improving Parents'
# Defensive Functioning

ach of us encounters emotion-provoking situations and develops strategies for dealing with them. We also develop and exhibit characteristic ways of coping with the feelings that stressful situations elicit (Lazarus, 1991; Lazarus & Folkman, 1983). *Defense mechanisms* are ways in which people protect themselves from the feelings and thoughts they cannot deal with immediately. These mechanisms allow individuals to keep difficult emotions within manageable limits, to reduce tension, and to restore a sense of balance in their emotional experience. As explained by Fosha, "defense mechanisms are designed to prevent psychic disruption and restore the experience of safety" (2000, p. 115). Unfortunately, long-term reliance on defense mechanisms can lead to self-deception about situations and true feelings. It can seriously restrict learning and growth, and it can prevent change during intervention. For example, a mother who practices the defense mechanism of isolation keeps her family from taking advantage of opportunities to develop new social skills, and it also hinders her involvement with possible supports (Fosha, 2000).

Sigmund Freud (1894) was the first person to write about defense mechanisms. He first identified the defense mechanism of repression and described hysteria as one consequence of the repression of traumatic memories. He later added denial, displacement, rationalization, and depersonalization (Freud, 1906, 1955). His daughter, Anna Freud (1936–1946), subdivided the concept of defense and introduced a number of defenses not proposed by her father including projection, isolation, and turning against self. She suggested a classification system of defenses according to the source of anxiety that gives rise to them (e.g., a child defends against the reality of her small size and slight power). Hartmann (1956, 1958) expanded the concept of defense mechanisms by pointing out that they can be adaptive and are necessary for psychological survival and for dealing with the reality of one's environment and the people in it. These initial descriptions of a number of defense mechanisms have since been expanded and elaborated on by other writers and researchers (e.g., Bellak, 1989; Bond, Gardner, Christian, & Sigal, 1983; DSM-IV-TR, 2000; Haan, 1977, 1993; Horowitz, Znoj, & Stinson, 1996; Perry and Cooper, 1986; Vaillant, 1977, 1992; Vaillant & Drake, 1985).

Contemporary theories of defense mechanisms have expanded the definition of defenses and explain them as part of a set of relational or cognitive patterns that develop in the context of close relationships with others (e.g., Blackman, 2004; Horowitz et al., 1996). For example, attachment theorists have emphasized that the way a parent responds to a child's distressed emotions contributes to the child's quality of attachment or the way the child copes later with emotion-provoking situation. On the one hand, when parents are dismissive of the child's needs for comforting, she learns to defend against them by shutting these needs off. This strategy is then used to manage all close relationships. On the other hand, the child whose mother is constantly overwhelmed with emotions may try to take care of his mother or cling to her to reassure himself of her availability. For a child with parents with unresolved loss or trauma, typically, fear is elicited on a continual basis by parents who demonstrate either frightening and hostile behavior or frightened and helpless behavior (Lyons-Ruth, Yellin, Melnick, & Atwood (in press). This can result in states of mind in which representations of self and other are put into separate compartments that are unintegrated. These representations may get triggered independent of other stored memories. Trauma theorists have extended our understanding of many of the more primitive defenses described in a later section of the chapter by explaining that people who have experienced trauma may have a series of distorted memories and schemas about the world that are stored in different parts of the brain and are not available to voluntary conscious recall. In its extreme, this inability to integrate past and new experiences into a life narrative can contribute to a number of primitive defenses such as splitting and dissociation. These defenses can dramatically impede the parent–interventionist relationship and the process of change for the parent. This failure to recall key memories can disrupt the ability to interpret reality accurately leading to increasing defensive withdrawal (van der Kolk & van der Hart, 1991). This type of memory failure is explained in more detail in Chapter 9. In this chapter, we describe the defenses that are often used by parents in multi-risk families, how they relate to parenting characteristics, and strategies to use during interventions, particularly when parents use more primitive defenses.

## DEFENSIVE FUNCTIONING: AN OVERVIEW

Defensive functioning is used to control painful emotions, ideas, and thoughts such as shame, self-criticism, anxiety, sadness, anger, or loss of self-esteem that may arise in certain situations and could overwhelm and fragment the person. Defenses are also used to avoid experiencing or accepting others' hostility, disapproval, and withdrawal of love. In other words, defenses are used to reduce and eliminate the effects of any experience that is liable to threaten the integrity and stability of an individual's sense of self (Laplanche & Pontalis, 1973/1988). They occur on an unconscious level and often distort reality in a way that makes it easier for the person to deal with it. Individuals typically use the same set of defenses repeatedly (Schneider et al., 2002). The defenses an individual employs frequently arise as the result of a complex interaction of

- Temperament and biological predispositions

- The nature of the stresses and relationships with caregivers that the individual experienced in early childhood

- The defenses modeled by parents and other significant figures in his life

- The consequences of using certain defenses

Defenses are similar to coping strategies, except that defenses are unconscious and coping strategies are conscious attempts to deal with difficult situations and the emotions elicited by them. Coping strategies are flexible and oriented to the reality of the present and to the possibilities of the future, making problem solving possible. Consequently, they are more adaptive than defensive functioning.

Although defenses make it easier for individuals to cope with difficult situations and to restore mental balance, they become problematic when they prevent us from seeing the reality of our difficulties, our own contribution to them, and possible solutions. Defenses are also problematic if they are ineffective in helping an individual to maintain a sense of mental balance. Defenses can also be counterproductive when they are rigid and become overgeneralized to situations in which they are not appropriate and when they supplant other coping mechanisms. Also, when they set the person up for rejection or isolation by others, they can lead to cycles of increasing withdrawal and anger against others.

## Different Levels of Defenses

Everyone uses defenses at certain times in their lives, especially in times of stress, and the type of defenses used and their effect on an individual's ability to maintain contact with reality can determine how well the person is able to adapt to and cope with difficulties in their lives. Personality theorists suggest that, although everyone falls back on defenses under extreme stress, well-functioning individuals are able to manage without defensive distortions, denial of reality, or negative attributions of self and other. In other words, although they may use certain defenses at times, they have a realistic perception of what is going on in the situation, are aware of their own thoughts and feelings, and try to understand those of others. Although they may temporarily use lower level defenses such as denial and avoidance, later they will be able to return to adaptive coping strategies such as thinking about a solution and seeking the support of people in their lives.

Nilofar was devastated when her pediatrician told her that her preschooler may have leukemia. She immediately denied the possibility, citing a variety of other reasons for her son's tiredness and the bruises on his legs. She refused to take him for blood tests and demanded to see another doctor. On arriving home, she did not talk about her fear to her husband and withdrew to bed very early, sleeping very little that night. In the morning, she called the doctor immediately to book the tests and to speak to him about what such a diagnosis might mean for her son. She also met her husband for lunch to tell him about the situation so that he could be with her during any further medical procedures. So initially, Nilofar used the defenses of repression, denial, withdrawal, and devaluing the doctor's opinion, but by morning she had returned to her characteristic and adaptive way of coping with traumatic situations—those of problem solving and seeking the support of people close to her.

## Primitive and Higher Order Defenses

Defenses are sometimes described as *primitive* or *higher order,* and they are typically more likely to be found with certain disorders (e.g., Blackman, 2004; McWilliams, 1994; Paris, 1996; Vaillant & McCullough, 1998). Those that are considered more primitive (e.g., denial, projection) involve putting up a boundary between one's self and the real world in order to keep unpleasant or unacceptable stresses, impulses, and emotions out of awareness. Such defenses pose a problem if they are persistently used to the exclusion of others. Primitive defenses have been described as similar to the simple ways in which infants naturally perceive the world.

As long as they are not used all of the time, the higher order or *mature* defenses (e.g., sublimation and humor) can be adaptive in that they help an individual handle the daily stress of life and can then allow the person to continue to maintain conscious, realistic awareness of the situation and of people's thoughts and feelings—her own and others. They can become problematic, however, if they are used all of the time to avoid confronting problems and making necessary changes in their situation.

Personality theorists suggest that more neurotic, borderline or personality disordered, and psychotic personality structures favor certain defenses (e.g., Bellak, Hurvich, & Gediman, 1973; McWilliams, 1994; Paris, 1996; Vaillant, 1992; Vaillant & Drake, 1985). People with personalities described as being at a more neurotic level deal with anxiety about themselves and external situations by relying on higher order defenses such as repression and sublimation. Individuals with various personality disorders including borderline personality disorder (BPD) usually use more primitive defenses such as denial, splitting, and projective identification and have far less access to the reality of situations and more difficulty finding appropriate ways to deal with them (American Psychiatric Association, 2000). Individuals whose personality structure is described as psychotic (e.g., those with schizophrenia) are withdrawn from reality; have distortions in thought processes such as delusions; and are more likely to use psychotic projection or paranoid ideation, dissociation, and delusional ideation. Some of the main defenses are described next. They are grouped into the three main types of defenses, which each fall in a range of degree of severity: 1) adaptive/neurotic defenses, 2) primitive defenses, and 3) psychotic defenses (see Table 6.1).

## Adaptive/Neurotic Defenses

Most defenses fall along a continuum depending on their nature or severity. The following defenses can be considered normal or adaptive when used to manage a traumatic situation for a short time until the person is able to cope with it. Neurotic defenses are chronic, typically, and can lead to rigidity and failure to deal with the reality of situations.

*Repression*    *Repression* occurs when an individual deals with emotional conflict or stress by forgetting, blocking out, or ignoring unacceptable impulses, thoughts, and feelings and removing them from conscious awareness (American Psychiatric Association, DSM-IV-TR, 2000). These thoughts, impulses, or feelings are consigned to the unconscious because they are upsetting or confusing. Repression may apply to a total experience, such as a traumatic event, a difficult social relationship, or to the affect connected with an experience (e.g., "I don't know why I feel so hot and bothered"). Defensive repression may be used as Nilofar did in order to recover after traumatic news before returning to an adaptive level of functioning. Other adaptive approaches would be avoiding a person or situation,

**Table 6.1.**   Some defense mechanisms categorized by type

| Adaptive/neurotic defenses | Primitive and borderline defenses | Psychotic defenses |
|---|---|---|
| Repression | Denial | Paranoid ideation |
| Defensive humor | Projection | Delusional projection |
| Sublimation | Projective identification | Psychotic denial |
| Intellectualization | Withdrawal | Psychotic distortion |
| Rationalization | Reaction formation | Extensive dissociation or dissociative identity disorder |
| Displacement | Idealization | |
| | Devaluation | |
| | Splitting | |
| | Defensive acting out | |
| | Dissociation | |
| *Additional adaptive/ neurotic defenses\*:* | *Additional primitive defenses\*:* | |
| Undoing | Isolation | |
| Turning against self and others | Omnipotent control | |
| Somatization | Regression | |
| Suppression | Displacement | |

*See Table 6.2 for a description of these additional defenses.

engaging in thought-stopping, or turning one's attention away from a problem that cannot be changed. Defensive repression becomes problematic when it gets in the way of other means of coping or experiencing positive aspects of living, or when it fails to keep disturbing ideas out of consciousness.

**Defensive Humor**   *Defensive humor* allows the individual to focus on the amusing or ironic aspects of the conflict or stress. This can often defuse a stressful situation and reverse overwhelming feelings of sadness or anger. By using humor, an individual is able to relieve tension around the conflict and avoid the expression of feelings without experiencing personal discomfort or becoming immobilized (DSM-IV-TR, 2000). Defensive humor can be problematic when it is used to totally dismiss negative emotions and when it does not allow the person to deal with his own pain or empathize with the feelings of others (see the story of Joan that follows).

**Sublimation**   *Sublimation* is when an individual replaces unacceptable impulses and emotional conflicts with socially acceptable behavior. Defensive sublimation replaces an unacceptable wish, feeling, or thought with a course of action that does not conflict with a person's value system. Sublimation is usually seen as an adaptive and healthy defense because it can be a useful and productive way of channeling emotional conflicts and problematic impulses (DSM-IV-TR, 2000). One could sublimate, for example, by becoming involved in helping others or by concentrating on exercise, hobbies, study, or work.

**Intellectualization**   *Intellectualization* is when the individual deals with emotional conflicts or stressors by excessively engaging in using abstract thinking or making generalizations to control or minimize disturbing feelings (DSM-IV-TR,

2000). The individual talks about feelings in a seemingly emotionless way and avoids the emotional implications of events by talking about them at a purely ideational level. As an adaptive approach, it could involve getting as much information as possible before making a decision or acting on it.

> When Enrique became a father, he made every effort to spend time with his family because he had found his father's distant way of being with him extremely difficult. His father had never been open to discussing any of Enrique's concerns with him and always talked about his decisions in a purely factual way without acknowledging that anything Enrique may have been experiencing was upsetting. One of Enrique's particularly painful memories was when he tried to talk to his father about his intention to get engaged, at which point his father immediately started to talk about the financial advantages and disadvantages of such a decision instead of asking Enrique about the girl he wanted to marry and his feelings about her.

**Rationalization**    *Rationalization* is when an individual makes up logical reasons to account for actions actually performed for other reasons, usually to avoid stress or self-blame. Rationalizations conceal the individual's true motivations for her thoughts, actions, or feelings through the elaboration of reassuring or self-serving but incorrect explanations (DSM-IV-TR, 2000). Rationalization allows the individual to make the best of a difficult situation with minimal resentment and to prove that her actions or those of another person "made sense" or were justified. Defensive rationalization is maladaptive when *everything* is rationalized, however (e.g., when a parent hits her child and insists that she is "doing it for the child's own good").

**Displacement**    *Displacement* is a way of avoiding anxiety or an unacceptable idea by displacing an interest, concern, or emotional reaction onto someone else who is not really responsible. It includes feeling one way toward a person but shifting that feeling onto another person or situation. An overwhelming sense of loss or anger about a loved one's illness could be displaced onto the hospital staff or doctor by blaming them for inadequate care and failing to cure the person, for example. A person who felt unloved by his mother may displace that need onto his wife and consider her to be rejecting and unloving.

## Primitive and Borderline Defenses

Primitive defenses are strong, deep-seated reactions to stressful situations. The more primitive defenses are often alternated, and an individual may use two or more to deal with the same person. For example, a person may use idealization or devaluation with the same person at different times (described later in this chapter). Some people may withdraw and isolate themselves at times, whereas at others they may use defensive acting-out. These are the defenses that are often used by parents who have experienced trauma and who have unintegrated memories of self and others that can be triggered at different times and are not balanced by other stored and conscious memories. Some of the most common primitive defenses are described below.

***Denial***   *Denial* occurs when the individual actively denies that a feeling, behavioral response, or intention is or was present (Freud, 1949). The hallmark of this defense is ignoring an unpleasant reality or realistic interpretation of a potentially threatening event by replacing it with a distorted view that is less threatening. People expressing denial may respond with "I don't care," or "It doesn't matter" to unpleasant situations. With denial, there is avoidance of pain, no anticipation of pain, no danger, and no conflict (Haan, 1977; 1993; Vaillant 1992). Denial can be adaptive initially when used to slow down the response to bad news or extreme trauma. It is maladaptive if it interferes with rational action, however. People who have been traumatized may use denial. In this case, they may accept the facts of the trauma but deny the implications of the traumatic event for their parenting or other functioning (Linehan, 1993). An alcoholic father who insists that he has no drinking problem and a wife who denies that her abusive husband is hurting herself and her children are both practicing maladaptive denial.

***Projection***   *Projection* is the process of ascribing personal feelings, impulses, thoughts, and faults to others or to something outside one's self (Laplanche & Pontalis, 1973/1988; Vaillant, 1992). This happens when what is inside a person is misunderstood as coming from an external source. Projection keeps individuals from acknowledging their own feelings of anger or self-hatred that might be too overwhelming for them to cope with. In its adaptive form, projection is the basis of empathy. Projection can be maladaptive, however, because it can seriously distort one's understanding of other people or events, and if used frequently, may seriously harm relationships with others. Other people may resent being misperceived and may retaliate when treated as judgmental, envious, or persecutory.

When Julie was first married to Robert, he often came home late from work. Although Julie assured Robert of her love for him and was as loving as possible, Robert often accused Julie of rejecting him and being angry with him, and she could not seem to persuade him to believe differently. This mistrust soon began to erode their relationship.

***Projective Identification***   *Projective identification* is similar to projection in that unacceptable feelings, impulses, or thoughts are transferred onto another person. It differs from projection in that a person is able to acknowledge her feelings but disavows ownership or any responsibility for them and sees them as being a justified response to the other person (DSM-IV-TR, 2000; Spillius, 1992). This type of defense occurs when an individual acts in a way that elicits a distorted response from another. An aspect of the self that the person does not wish to acknowledge is induced in another to whom the self is closely related. This is accomplished when an individual acts in such a way that the other person takes on the characteristics projected onto them. For example, an individual may accuse another person of being angry and aggressive and then provoke that person to behave aggressively. In the client–interventionist relationship, this can happen when the client views the interventionist in a distorted way that is determined by the client's view of himself. The client places pressure on the interventionist to experience her in the same way that she experiences herself—as useless, and then accuses the interventionist of being like everyone else in rejecting her. If Julie's husband Robert continues in this blaming way, for example, and begins to point to ways she acts when he comes home late without calling, Julie may begin to feel the way he accuses her of feeling and to act in the rejecting and angry way he accuses her of.

**Withdrawal**    *Withdrawal* is used when an individual is overstimulated or distressed. The individual resists engaging on a feeling level and retreats from the situation, substituting the stimulation of her internal world for the stresses of relating to others. A propensity to use alcohol or drugs to alter one's consciousness is considered a kind of withdrawal. Withdrawal removes the individual from actively participating in interpersonal problem solving and involves a form of psychological escape from reality, although it does not necessarily distort reality (DSM-IV-TR, 2000; Laplanche & Pontalis, 1973/1988; Perry, 1996). It is common with individuals who suffered severe loss or trauma or posttraumatic stress disorder (PTSD).

**Reaction formation**    *Reaction formation* happens when a thought, feeling, or behavior is replaced by an unconsciously derived but consciously felt emphasis on its opposite. The individual turns something into its polar opposite in order to render it less threatening (e.g., an individual transforms hatred for another into love; a parent who was abused avoids disciplining her child at all in order to show her love to her child). Frequently, such efforts to parent in a way that is the opposite of the way one was parented can result in an extreme strain being put on the parent–child relationship (Haan, 1977; 1993; Vaillant, 1986).

**Idealization**    *Idealization* occurs when someone handles emotional conflicts and stress by attributing positive qualities to one's self and others (DSM-IV-TR, 2000). Idealization can be adaptive; for example, when a young child encounters overwhelming fear, she finds comfort in believing that her all-powerful Mommy or Daddy can protect her. As children develop, they de-idealize caregivers so that the normal process of separation and individuation can occur. However, in some people, the need to idealize seems unchanged from childhood. In an effort to manage fear and anxiety, an individual may become attached to someone that she believes is omnipotent, and as a result, she feels that she is safe. In some cases, idealization is used to cope with imperfections in the self. The more dependent one is, the greater the temptation to idealize (McWilliams, 1994). In certain cases, however, an individual with primitive defenses who idealizes her service provider and sees her as "the rescuer" may suddenly flip this idea so that she perceives herself as being rejected, or that she is the "victim" or may become "the attacker" herself (Liotti, 2004).

**Devaluation**    *Devaluation* is the opposite of idealization in that a person deals with emotions, conflicts, or stress by attributing exaggerated negative qualities to the self and others (DSM-IV-TR, 2000). For example, during the course of intervention, a client may at first idealize the therapist and then, when progress is slower than the client expected, he will deny that the therapist can be of any help to him or his children. These kinds of intervention relationships can be extremely difficult and may require the interventionist to focus on empathetic containment and understanding.

**Splitting**    *Splitting* has been defined by Kernberg (1975, 1984) and others as a form of defense characterized by an individual's inability to tolerate mixed feelings, or a failure to integrate good and bad images of self and others. A person using splitting deals with emotional conflicts or stress by seeing himself or others as all good or all bad and is not able to integrate the two into cohesive, meaningful images. Often, the individual will alternately idealize and devalue the same person (e.g., nurturing–rejecting; kind–worthless) (DSM-IV-TR, 2000; Gergely, 2000; Vaillant, 1992). On the one hand, splitting can be anxiety reducing, and when an individual sees herself as all good, it can maintain the individual's self-esteem. On the other hand, a person who has been abused may see herself and the abuser as "bad" and herself as unworthy, and thus be unable to hold onto anything positive. The client's resulting feelings of hostility and desperation will eventually be expressed toward a number of people including the interventionist.

**Defensive Acting Out**    *Defensive acting out* occurs when a person deals with anxiety through action rather than reflection. The behavior is driven by the unconscious need to master the anxiety associated with forbidden feelings and wishes, and with upsetting fears, fantasies, and memories. Acting-out behavior may be self-destructive and/or growth enhancing. It includes any behavior representing feelings that the client does not yet feel safe enough to bring into intervention in the form of words (DSM-IV-TR, 2000). It can range from compulsive running that goes beyond keeping fit, to driving too fast, to engaging in dangerous, impulsive acts such as getting into fights with others, or even committing robbery.

**Dissociation**    *Dissociation* occurs when a person deals with emotional conflicts or internal or external stress by experiencing a temporary alteration or breakdown in the usually integrated functions of consciousness, memory, perception of self or the environment, or sensorimotor behavior (Perry, 1996; Vaillant, 1992). A traumatic event may overwhelm a person's coping capacity and, as a result, dissociation can occur. Symptoms may include losing conscious awareness of what is going on, feeling "spaced out" or as if in a dream, or reliving the trauma through intrusive thoughts or images. Dissociation can lead to amnesia or rapid shifting between different states of mind. Anyone at any age is capable of dissociating under traumatic conditions, especially if she experiences unbearable pain or terror. For instance, a young child may be unable to fight or flee but may escape a trauma by "going away in her head," or dissociating. As discussed in Chapter 9, however, dissociation can also occur long after the original trauma when the person becomes triggered by something similar to the original trauma. For example, a fear reaction may have originated as the result of a rape, but dissociation may be triggered in the victim by a man who stands close to her in a queue or in the subway.

Additional defenses are listed in Table 6.2.

## Psychotic Defenses

*Psychotic defenses* include *paranoid ideation, delusional projection, psychotic denial,* and *distortion.* These more extreme defenses occur during a psychotic break when a person has lost contact with reality, is suffering from a thought disorder, and has extreme restrictions in the range and intensity of his emotional responses. Paranoid and grandiose *delusions* are common psychotic defenses in which the person believes himself to be superior or that another person or other people are persecuting him and have malicious thoughts in general or malicious thoughts about

**Table 6.2.** Additional defenses

| Type of defense | Defense | Description |
|---|---|---|
| Neurotic | Undoing | Expressing a negative impulse and immediately following it by its opposite (e.g., a husband who yells at his wife all of the time apologizes but makes no effort to change) |
| | Turning against self | Dealing with internal or external stress by redirecting negative thoughts and attitudes that were directed outward on the self (e.g., turning anger against self) |
| | Somatization | Reacting to conflict by getting sick or complaining about pain, and sometimes withdrawing from people as a result |
| | Suppression | Dealing with emotional conflict and stress by intentionally avoiding thinking about the disturbing feelings, thoughts, and experiences |
| Borderline | Isolation | Dealing with anxiety and pain by isolating feelings from knowing or ideas (e.g., talking about a stressful event in a matter-of-fact tone) |
| | Omnipotent control | Feeling or reacting as if one has special powers or abilities and is superior to others |
| | Regression | Dealing with internal or external stress by unconsciously returning to earlier modes of acting in the world, such as becoming child-like and depending on others |
| | Displacement | Transferring feelings, thoughts, and behaviors from the initial person (i.e., the source of the emotion) to another (e.g., a young man who is angry with his mother turns his anger on a female supervisor) |

him in particular. This can include believing that one's thoughts are being controlled in order to get one to do certain things. When projection is delusional, the person may believe that they actually see people or hear voices telling them to do something. Often there is an extreme distortion of reality and the person may believe that stories in the newspaper are about him or that his organs have been replaced by those of someone else.

If dissociation occurs, it may be extensive and may result in immobility and—in extremely rare cases—in associative identity disorder (previously called *multiple personality disorder*) (DSM-IV-TR, 2000).

## ASSESSMENT OF DEFENSIVE FUNCTIONING

Clearly, differentiating between the defenses used at various levels of personality organization is difficult. This is because under extreme stress, people can temporarily adopt more primitive or less adaptive defenses than they would use under less difficult circumstances. For example, the person who usually uses more neurotic defenses may temporally use denial or withdrawal to deal with a loss, whereas under the same type of stress, the borderline person may use more defenses at a psychotic level.

Defenses are of great diagnostic value because their frequency, intensity, and quality reveal how people think and manage and what is important to them in any particular context. It is important to identify adaptive and maladaptive defenses and to examine defenses in detail as part of any assessment process. Identifying defenses is useful in planning interventions and in understanding transference reactions and the nature of the working alliance. Some ways to assess defensive functioning are described in the appendix to Chapter 2 and include the Ego Functioning Scale (Bellak, 1989), which can be used to determine an individual's level of defensive functioning. Of course, what happens in initial home visits or clinic sessions will often give the interventionist some idea about the types of defenses the parent uses.

Some questions for the interventionist to consider include the following:

- Does the parent talk about her feelings and thoughts about an event, or only about the facts surrounding the event? In other words, are the emotional reactions consistently denied or unavailable?

- How does the parent describe the thoughts and feelings of other people in her world, such as her children, her partner, or her parents?

- How capable does she seem to be of retaining relationships throughout her history?

- Does the parent appear to act out or to turn against herself in stressful situations?

- Does the parent use splitting or describe her children or other people close to her in very black-and-white or all-or-none terms and ignore the "grays"?

- How does she relate to the interventionist; does she seem to be excessively distant or extremely needy and to want to tell her everything about her history?

- Does her story or responses to the first session seem to be inconsistent, incoherent, and difficult to understand? Do pieces of her story of her life not fit together? Is the story told with genuineness and does it make sense?

- What expressed emotion predominates; anger, sadness, anxiety, or shame?

- Does the parent seem to turn to other people or to helping professionals when under stress?

- Does she have the ability to understand the reality of her situation and to problem-solve about it?

- What appear to be the major defenses being used in normal situations and when the person is under stress? At what level do they appear to be (i.e., neurotic, primitive, or psychotic)?

- Does the person appear to be in contact with reality? If not, how out of touch with reality does she appear to be? Are there delusions and hallucinations being talked about and, if so, do they seem to include the child in a way that could be dangerous (e.g., "The child can fly, so being near the edge of the stairs is not dangerous")?

- Does she at times seem to dissociate or to have brief disruptions in speech and appear to have "gone away in her head"?

If the interventionist suspects that the parent is using primitive or psychotic defenses an assessment by a psychiatrist may be necessary.

## Parenting and the Development of Defensive Functioning

Defenses develop in early childhood and are influenced by early caregiver–child interactions and relationships. Children are dependent on their parents for their physical needs, sense of connection and well-being, and for the structure and support required for the promotion of further growth and development. Every child, at least to some degree, will adapt to meet the requirements of her environment. Defenses are ways of coping that the child develops in order to function.

Over the course of optimal development, children develop a sense of competency—an inner confidence that they can cope successfully by learning new skills, mastering challenges, and interacting with adults and peers (Landy, 2002b). This develops through supportive, positive, and helpful interactions with caregivers. Children experience great joy in the mastery of new skills, but they also experience frustration and anxiety during the process of trying to do new things. This frustration and anxiety can be alleviated through supportive contact with a trusted and empathetic caregiver. As the child explores his environments, he at times retreats to a caregiver for support and at the same time is developing an internal subjective sense of competence. Over time, the child experiences a gradual increase in his ability to tolerate greater uncertainty, overcome larger obstacles, and explore unfamiliar things and events. As a child ages he also becomes better at soothing and comforting himself when frustrated or anxious.

Not only do children advance in their ability to comprehend and problem solve but also they experience a growing expectation of receiving help from others when their own efforts are not enough. Through the development of a secure attachment with a caregiving adult, a child develops the ability to make affectionate attachments with other adults and other children. Children also develop the ability to tolerate mixed feelings and to integrate good and bad aspects of people and things. Similarly, a theory of mind (i.e., the understanding of the perspective of others and their thoughts and feelings) develops, which gives the child the capacity for self-reflectivity and empathy. These emotional developments form a foundation for the capacity to establish intimate, loving relationships, which leads to greater self-affirmation over the child's life course and marked resiliency to stress. A person with this foundation will have less of a need to use primitive defenses and will be more able to respond to situations and emotions in a realistic and mature way.

A child's developing sense of competency can be stifled or blocked by the defenses he develops to deal with his environment. For example, in certain circumstances, rather than developing a sense of competence, children may develop defensive ways of dealing with their interactions with their parents and other events in their environments. These circumstances may include, but are not limited to, parental psychopathology; early neglect; abandonment; and emotional, physical, and sexual abuse. Other, less-dramatic characteristic behaviors of the parent–child interaction and relationship can also lead to the development of defensive mechanisms in the child that can become chronic. These behaviors may include mixed communications that confuse the child, failure to provide calming and comforting to the child when he's upset, actions that are frightened or frightening, and role reversal so the child is left to take care of the parent. Even discipline that is harsh and punitive and continual expression of negative attributions can destroy a child's sense of self-efficacy and lead to the development of primitive defenses.

Parents' levels of defensive functioning are related to how they were parented and, in turn, to how they parent. For example, if a child's characteristics cause a parent excessive anxiety, she may project onto the child her fearful and constricting view of him through the interactions she has with him. Splitting and devaluation may occur and the child may be perceived and talked about as a bad child who has totally negative characteristics. Conversely, a child may be perceived as a special child who is destined for great things. Children in either of these circumstances may distort aspects of themselves to fit with these perceptions.

Chronic traumatization tends to create rigid defenses. A child who has been subjected to chronic trauma may learn to respond to and act in an all-or-nothing fashion, demonstrating behaviors such as acts of aggression, frantic attempts at escape, or intense psychological withdrawal and affective constriction. Dissociative and numbing defenses are particularly likely to develop in response to chronic abuse, although the child may also become enraged and aggressive when he feels under threat (Liotti, 1999; Perry, 1999; Prior, 1996; Pynoos, Steinberg, & Goenjian, 1996; Terr, 1991). These defensive behaviors become established, organized strategies and begin to function below the level of thought. Defensive behavior becomes automatic in situations that evoke memories of the original trauma. Affective constriction may become so generalized that the child's opportunities for cognitive and affective development are compromised (Lyons-Ruth & Jacobvitz, 1999; Terr, 1991).

Chronic traumatization may interfere with the development of a child's ability to test reality, to symbolize, and to use language (Cicchetti & Beeghly, 1987). Studies of young children who have been abused indicate that these children, similar to traumatized adults, have difficulty expressing specific and differentiated emotions. These deficits have been held responsible for the impaired impulse control and acting out seen in many of these youngsters. They have difficulty putting their feelings into words and instead, act out without the ability to resort to intervening symbolic representations that would allow for flexible response strategies (van der Kolk & Fisler, 1994).

Suventini was very upset when she became pregnant because her husband was unhappy about it. He threatened to leave and actually moved out during her third trimester. Early on in the pregnancy, when Suventini found out she was expecting twins, she denied it totally and kept reporting that because one of the twins was not moving, he "could not be there." When the twin boys were born she immediately labeled one twin, Devon, as like herself—"calm and gentle"—and the other, Tyler, as "like their father, angry and vicious." From that time on the splitting and the projections of the "good" and "bad" twin continued—a situation made more intense because both twins were difficult infants whose development was significantly delayed. Suventini with-

drew from friends and isolated herself and the twins. At times she appeared to dissociate during home visits, staring into space and failing to respond at all to the twins as
they pulled at her clothes and screamed to get her attention. At other times her anger
toward the "bad" twin would erupt, and she would berate Tyler by saying he was like
"a snake slithering along the ground" or that he was "abusive just like his father."
When his teeth came through she called him "a monster with fangs." At times, she re-
coiled from him in terror as if he were going to hit her. These alternatively hostile and
helpless interactions caused disorganized behavior in both twins, but more so in Tyler
(the "bad" twin) than in Devon (the "good" twin). Whereas Devon's development continued to improve slowly, Tyler's became increasingly delayed. He seldom tried to master new skills, and even when he finally learned to walk, he showed no elation about
his newfound ability and listlessly sat near his mother as if hoping for the positive attention that he never received. However, he soon stopped looking to his mother when
he was tired or upset and instead cried quietly, rocking back and forth to comfort himself. When Devon and Tyler went to child care when they were 2½ years of age, Tyler
appeared withdrawn from the children and would not respond to the attempts of child
care providers to join in any of the group activities. Along with this withdrawal, Tyler
would, at times, hit out at children if they approached him or the toys he was playing
with or withdrew into a corner of the room. He had little language and seldom played
imaginatively other than to pretend to eat the plastic food in the doll house.

## WORKING WITH PARENTS TO
## ENHANCE DEFENSIVE FUNCTIONING

Parents' defensive functioning obviously affects the way they relate to home visitors or other service providers. Parents may deny any problems that they are having or difficulties or delays in their children for a long period of time before they
are able to seek help for them. Those parents who have experienced abuse may
project onto the service provider, seeing her as persecutory, and thus may distort
the reason for her being in their home as an attempt to take their children away.
Anything an interventionist recommends may be devalued and ignored as useless
or something that was tried before and did not work. After one or two visits, as a
parent's anxiety builds, she may withdraw and refuse to answer the phone or
avoid being home when the service provider comes.

Occasionally, a parent may switch from seeing the service provider as threatening and bad to idealizing her as someone who will be all powerful and who will
help to "cure" a situation or child. These ways of reacting can be extremely frustrating and traumatizing for the service provider, who may withdraw herself.
These are the kinds of defenses used by Nina, introduced in Chapter 4, who took
a significant period of time to let go of her strong defenses and replace them with
more adaptive ways of relating.

### Approaches to Working with Defensive Functioning

Establishing a supportive alliance is of critical importance in working with a parent's maladaptive defenses. One of the therapeutic elements consistently related
to intervention outcome is the therapeutic alliance (Krupnick et al., 1996). As noted

in Chapter 5, a positive alliance is one in which the interventionist is able to connect to the healthier and more reality-oriented qualities of the parent in order to understand her more defended and conflicted parts. A supportive relationship helps the parent to examine her defenses and to contemplate making intentional changes. A healthy alliance also allows the parent to self-reflect and to gain a better understanding of the link between his feelings and behaviors. Guidelines and strategies for developing a supportive therapeutic relationship are presented in Chapters 5 and 7. Sometimes creating a bond with the parent to team up to explore her fears and frustrations about what is going on in her life that is difficult can reduce her anxiety and be helpful. When a parent is using defenses to avoid accepting her own negative feelings, it is crucial for the interventionist to let the parent know that she understands and accepts her negative feelings about her situation. Attending to her fear or anger about having a home visitor or acknowledging how taking care of a difficult child can make her feel anxious and angry can be very helpful and can begin to establish some sense of security in the relationship. It is important during this early phase not to be too intrusive and to push for information but to assure the parent of your availability. On the other hand, reflecting a sense of empathy and acceptance of the emotions displayed and a sense of concern and interest about what is going on with the parent (e.g., "I wonder if some scary feelings are being stirred up right now?") can be helpful.

Several behavioral indicators that the interventionist can use to determine when a healthy alliance has been achieved and defensive functioning reduced are outlined next. When a trusting therapeutic relationship has been established, clients are more likely to

- Discuss their feelings with the interventionist without becoming overly defensive or overwhelmed

- Reflect a willingness to wonder about particular acts or feelings

- Show openness and curiosity toward the interventionist's interpretations regarding their motivation, instead of withdrawing or denying or attempting to rationalize the behavior in question. This may be conveyed through statements such as "I don't know why I did that," or "I think I understand why I felt that way."

- Be more open to discussing their thoughts and feelings instead of feeling frightened and then threatening to act them out. For example, a parent might say, "I don't understand it, but I'm feeling very upset right now about what you just said," instead of saying, "I'm not coming back here, I quit."

- Be able and willing to discuss feelings of loss of control without the previous degree of grandiosity or self-hatred

- Tolerate setbacks, observe them more rationally, avoid catastrophizing, and perceive them in a way that is not so devastating or threatening

- Recognize and discuss emotions during a session instead of denying feelings or confusing emotions (e.g., mistaking anger for pain)

- Show better ability to cope with and to identify mixed feelings and explore them (e.g., simultaneous anger and sadness)

- Acknowledge both sides of a discussion or situation or the "grays" instead of seeing the world and peoples' motivations in black-and-white terms

## Maintaining the Working Alliance

Interventionists should keep in mind that it is important for parents to experience the therapeutic alliance as supportive on an ongoing basis. A parent must feel understood and listened to. Efforts to maintain this must be undertaken throughout the intervention and will need to be the emphasis if the parent uses defenses such as splitting, withdrawal, or devaluation to avoid the interventionist. Be prepared to encounter all sorts of behavior as parents desperately attempt to hold on to their defenses or perceptions about the world. It is important to have patience and to recognize that anxiety may lie behind resistance. Make comments in a way that alleviates some of this anxiety and avoids the power struggles that such behavior often evokes, such as "I know it is hard sometimes to have someone coming here to see you." Make sure that the parent does not perceive you or another interventionist as an omnipotent figure who could invite defiance on the part of the parent. The interventionist can address the parent's free will and autonomy and not impose his or her will on the parent. Ask, "What do you think would be the best way to encourage your daughter to cooperate?"

Defenses are automatically activated as means of protecting individuals from perceived stress and are often activated during intervention. It is important to identify these defenses in parents, to understand the degree to which the defenses protect against anxiety or stress, and to recognize how they could influence intervention planning and the choice of intervention strategies. It is also important to recognize that most defenses arise from previous experiences with interactions and relationships with others. As a consequence, they are most likely to be reactivated during experiences that lead to feelings of lack of control, rejection, or unworthiness, or during times when they experience abandonment and a resulting sense of aloneness or "nothingness."

It is important for the interventionist over time to help the parent become aware of her defenses and how they operate. In an empathetic way, the defenses the parent uses are explored without judging and labeled in terms of the words and behaviors being used. Sometimes the parent can be helped to understand some of the costs of using the defense (e.g., isolating herself and her child) while explaining the benefits of an approach that would be less defended (e.g., finding someone supportive she could share experiences with). Providing this information can empower the parent to feel more in control of possible change mechanisms. Empathy for how difficult change can be while at the same time acknowledging and supporting any positive gains may be crucial. An awareness of defenses allows the parent to gain a measure of control over them. The strategies used to help the parent become aware of her defenses are guided by the defense. For example, for a parent who uses projection, it is important for the interventionist to encourage empathy through strategies such as helping the parent see a situation through another's eyes, imagining how others feel, and using role-playing. With a parent who uses displacement, the interventionist may want to encourage the parent to release negative emotions through socially acceptable channels. These could include exercise, sports, art, and music. With a parent who uses self-blame, the interventionist may encourage her to attribute painful thoughts and feelings appropriately to the environment or other people and to only attribute them to herself when justified.

### *Supporting Parents to Experience, Understand, and Tolerate Feelings*

One of the primary goals in working with parents with more primitive defensive structures is to support their ability to allow and to tolerate a wider range of emotions. This may involve a parent's emotions about past history or about his possible frustration with things in the present, particularly parenting. Letting the parent know that some of these feelings are normal and helping him identify specific behaviors that elicit them can open the way for negative feelings to be more readily tolerated. Some other strategies are given here:

- Encourage the parent to tolerate feelings of frustration and to connect thoughts, feelings and behaviors. Help her feel safe enough so she can draw on the positive coping strategies that she has already developed to deal with distressing emotions. It is important to provide the parent with many opportunities to use words to express feelings that may never have been acknowledged, expressed, communicated, or understood before.

- Provide opportunities to relax anxiety by acknowledging it and help to identify what she is anxious about and problem-solving ways to overcome the situation.

- Tactfully talk about her feelings, frustrations, wishes, and fears as they appear. Sometimes directing attention to thoughts and feelings and to a particular experience alters the flow of her associations and reactions.

- Encourage parents to keep a diary, write poetry, and do art activities as ways to find words or other symbolic ways to express feelings.

- Be aware that individuals who use intellectualization and isolation are often good at reporting concerns or issues verbally. These verbal reports tend to be affectless and not well integrated with their thoughts about their desires or fantasies. It is important to encourage the expression and the act of experiencing the feelings associated with these thoughts by saying how difficult it must be for the individual to think about that problem and that it must make her sad at times.

- Mention any observed changes in body posture as they occur or physiological changes the person talks about and relate them to emotions.

- Indicate interest in the parent's thoughts and feelings, which may encourage the individual to be more willing and able to focus on them than she otherwise might be. Questions and comments also indicate that the interventionist is not afraid to look at and hear about things that make the parent afraid or anxious.

- Have the parent or parents expand on their feelings around an event in their lives such as leaving their country to emigrate or separating from a good relationship.

- Help the parent sort out his mixed feelings if he seems to feel confused about them and let him know that each feeling is meaningful. Also expand on what a described feeling really is. For example, if a parent describes being depressed, is it about feeling empty, abandoned, worthless, exhausted, or something else?

- Give the parent ways to calm herself down if she is becoming overwhelmed or extremely emotional.

- Use examples or metaphors to help parents describe their situations (e.g., "Does it feel like a storm is coming, or how would you describe it?").

- Label the emotions that the parent seems to be feeling and check them out with her. Ask her how intense the feeling is on a scale of 1 to 10, and check with her later if it has been reduced at all.

- Identify stimuli that trigger emotions or other reactions to them. Ask her what she thinks triggers feelings of helplessness or anger toward her child.

Encouraging parents' realistic thoughts and understanding about situations that are going on in the parent's life is an important responsibility of the interventionist. The interventionist may gain the parent's attention about certain cognitions she appears to be having, point out characteristic ways of thinking that the individual engages in such as exaggerating or catastrophizing, and try to interject different thoughts and perspectives in the sequence of the parent's associations. Raising questions about ways of thinking and calling attention to them makes the parent more self-conscious about them, and the defenses become a little less automatic. The parent may then be able to experience some exposure to feelings such as anxiety or fear that they were trying to ward off. Here are some other ways to encourage realistic thoughts and feelings:

- If what the parent is talking about seems not to make sense, search for the kernel of truth in it and acknowledge this piece of the reality.

- Use artistic and literary sources of imagery, metaphors, and stories to communicate understanding of the parent's thoughts, feelings, and concerns.

- If a parent talks about what she believes is going on in a situation or a relationship and yet seems uncertain about it, ask her to tell you about what she knows to be true about the situation. This will often validate her thoughts and feelings and make it possible to get to the reality of the situation. The interventionist will then validate this explanation as understandable.

- Challenge a parent's negative attributions about the self, others, or the world. It is important for the interventionist to not be pulled into the parent's negative view of the world because it would only reinforce the client's beliefs. For example, parents who have had children taken into foster care by child protective agencies may continually criticize their worker and the system. It is important to explain the need for such a system and that sometimes children do need protection, similar to what she had when she was a child, perhaps.

***Using Gentle Interpretations***    Caution should be taken in the timing and presentation of interpretations. In the early phases of therapy, interpretations should be avoided because some parents may not be able to tolerate them at the beginning of an intervention. Interpretation of defenses, make the parent more conscious of her defensive activities and can disrupt the ways in which the parent prevents herself from making contact with experiences she fears and from the possibility of learning that they are not as dangerous as she thinks. Some ways to use interpretation to reduce or eliminate the negative use of defensive functioning are described here:

- Interpret relationship patterns in order to help the parent to gain a better understanding of her behavior. For example, say to the mother who is discussing her new boyfriend, Angelo, "It must be so difficult for you to trust Angelo after other people have left you before. What is scary about it?" Help parents understand how their behavior may be preventing them from getting what they want. One way to do this in the context of a parent's complaints and criticisms about others is to ask, "Did you let them know what you needed?" This provides the interventionist with the opportunity to re-educate the parent about human interdependence.

- Ask the parent if he has seen any recurring patterns in how things seem to turn out for him. If he does not make some suggestions, suggest some and see if they make sense to him.

- Use the way the parent relates to the interventionist and how he feels about her to understand relational patterns and cultivate more adaptive interpersonal skills within the therapeutic relationship.

## Working with Some of the Most Common Primitive Defenses

Many of the difficulties that occur as a result of primitive defenses that are used in other relationships can also affect how much a parent can support and nurture her child. Helping a parent to articulate more clearly about her frustration, anxiety, or confusion in parenting a child and linking it to certain behaviors in the child and situations can help her give more specific words to describe what is so difficult. Within the accepting relationship, supporting the mother to set appropriate limits and to respond to her child's needs for nurturance can enable the mother to escape from feeling resentful and from being overwhelmed, and to find a balance between meeting her child's needs and her own. Next, techniques for working with specific defenses are discussed.

*Working with Splitting*    Splitting is a defense that is often seen in clients with borderline personality disorder. For a parent who engages in splitting, it is important to help her to understand her emotional states and to recreate a situation in which the self is recognized as intentional and real by the interventionist and clearly perceived by the parent. To do so, the interventionist can help the parent to understand and label emotional states by interpreting moment-to-moment changes in them and by focusing the parent's attention on the interventionist's experience. To foster change with these parents, it is best to offer brief and specific comments. It is also important for the interventionist to acknowledge parent's affect in the here-and-now while conveying in words, tone, and posture, that she is able to cope with the parent's emotional state. Talking with the parent about feelings and the reasons behind certain behavior encourages self-reflectivity. This can include naming the emotions experienced by the parent and others and making sure that feelings are included in discussions of events. Strategies for fostering self-reflectivity are presented in Chapter 7 (see Table 7.2). With parents at multiple risk, encouraging self-reflectivity enables them to understand the reasons for their behavior and discourages the use of defenses such as projection and acting-out. This projection was seen in the beliefs that Nina, from Chapter 4, held about herself and projected onto her daughter Meg.

As mentioned previously, individuals who engage in splitting tend to experience people as all good or all bad, rather than being able to integrate positive and negative aspects. Individuals who offer help may be idealized and then immediately cast off as uncaring after a seemingly small failure in empathy. An interventionist can help the parent to gradually integrate the positive and negative aspects of her service provider into a more realistic representation by tolerating the parent's rage when her view shifts from good to bad. It is important that the interventionist not retaliate, but rather, encourages an understanding of what prompted the shift. In addition, helping a parent to integrate her perceptions of her child into a more balanced view rather than projecting all good or all bad perceptions of the child at different times, or making one child in the family "the good one" and another "the bad one," can help the parent to gradually become more evenly sensitive to her child's or children's attributes.

---

**Parent Exercises: Seeing the Grays**

An exercise called *Seeing the Grays* can be used with parents who tend to use splitting indiscriminately. This can be done when helping them modify extreme feelings and can be used individually and in groups. Sometimes people get upset, angry, or elated because they react to a situation without really examining or understanding it. Often, when one is emotionally aroused by negative aspects of people and situations, it is difficult to retain an understanding that people are a mixture of strengths and weaknesses and to remember and focus on the positive.

To do the exercise, write words on a blackboard or flipchart in a continuum, with a word at either end representing the extremes of a concept (e.g., *bad, good; unkind, kind*). Ask parents to name examples of things or people that fall at either end and at various points in-between. This process will help parents to better understand the "grays" or "in-between" of situations, people, their behavior, and their emotional reactions.

---

***Working with Devaluation and Projection***    When working with a parent's defenses, an interventionist typically encounters negative cognitions that the parent has about herself and others (e.g., devaluation, projection). Pointing out to a parent that certain beliefs or understandings about herself, others, or situations may in fact be errors in perception can be effective if at the same time the parent's understanding is accepted and what is offered is given as a possible alternative explanation. Helping the parent to restructure the way she thinks about herself by substituting more objective, rational thoughts for illogical, harsh, self-criticisms that automatically flood into her mind when a negative event occurs can be useful. For example, she may respond well if she is encouraged to substitute comments like "I never do anything right" with "I do a lot of things right." Cognitive restructuring can also be used to alter negative cognitions. This technique is presented in more detail in Chapter 12.

It is also important to be supportive of even the slightest learning in a more positive direction. Noting how the parent has succeeded in changing her approach even a little bit will make it more likely that the parent would eventually be able to hear what the interventionist has to say about the patterns that have not yet changed (Wachtel, 1993). Over the course of the intervention with Nina, for example, the service provider noticed changes in Nina's attributions about her children. The following illustrates how the interventionist focused on noticing the small steps Nina made in the right direction toward responding and understanding her daughter's needs.

> **Nina:** "Meg cried so much yesterday. I think she was scared I might go away for alcohol and drug treatment again. She clung to me; I didn't know what to do . . . it upsets me and I feel all vulnerable again . . . yet I know now I must help her. It all feels too much—but now at least I understand what she needs."
>
> **Interventionist:** "That makes it easier?"
>
> **Nina:** "Yes; and I notice, like you said, if I pay attention to her and let her know I understand, she calms down more quickly."
>
> **Interventionist:** "That is so great that you can do that and see the difference. It must make Meg feel so good when you can be gentle and understanding with her . . . the way you are doing."

***Working with Denial and Withdrawal***   One way to help a parent who is engaging in denial is to increase the parent's capacity for self-observation. In order to do this, the interventionist can turn her attention to breaks or sudden shifts of the emotional content or silence that occur during the session. The breaks in a parent's associations are indicative of various forms of resistance, denial, and withdrawal from the service provider. Repeated attempts to draw the parent's attention to these shifts can lead to a greater capacity for sustaining affective experience and self-observation (Gray, 1973; Kris, 1982). These attempts illuminate the parent's defensive patterns during intervention. Attention can also be drawn to these patterns that the parent discusses in individual and group sessions. This implies that this strategy will help the parent to develop a flexible, less-rigid reliance on these defenses.

During sessions, Carol frequently started to talk about something very meaningful and would then deny the reality of the event and clearly withdraw, sitting motionless and looking out the window. When the therapist would speak quietly yet clearly to her and note that Carol seemed to find it hard to talk about the feelings, this would usually bring her back. When the therapist also mentioned that it could be helpful for Carol to talk about her feelings and that she was there to support her to do that, it would usually enable Carol to go further into them and to understand them better as a result.

***Working with Dissociation***   If moments of dissociation are noticed it can be helpful to point them out to parents and to let them know that although this defense mechanism helps children and adults to survive traumatic events, it is not adaptive later. Once the parent has reached a point that she wants to overcome her tendency to dissociate, she can then begin to recognize the triggers that lead to it and learn some ways to ground herself to prevent it from occurring. Interventionists can encourage parents to identify their own triggers and suggest others that they have noticed that also seem to contribute to moments of dissociation. They can also observe and then suggest other ways the clients seem to find helpful in avoiding dissociation and provide other strategies such as engaging in enjoyable activities, distracting with other thoughts, and learning to self-soothe.

## WORKING WITH PARENT DEFENSES: CASE-STUDY FAMILIES

### Joan

Joan, Mark's mother (described first in Chapter 4), used denial and humor to distance herself from her own sadness and that of her children. Denial was adaptive in that it allowed her to ignore painful feelings and thoughts. It was maladaptive, however, in that it hurt her capacity for closeness and intimacy with her children and husband and made it difficult for her to care emotionally for her children.

Joan's defensive functioning developed in her childhood as the result of being raised by a depressed mother who was emotionally unavailable to her. As a child, Joan had not experienced emotional containment and no one attended to her feelings of sadness. This led her to deny these sad feelings and to use humor to redirect her own and other people's feelings away from the sadness.

Joan entered counseling with a supportive person who helped her to acknowledge her sadness and fears about these feelings. Joan's unconscious fear was that if she allowed herself to experience sadness, she would become so overwhelmed that she would become clinically depressed like her mother. During the course of therapy the interventionist helped Joan to become aware of her sadness by drawing her attention to her immediate tendency to laugh it off or joke about it, and at other times alerting her to her tendency to become agitated, to talk more quickly, and to develop a blushing or rash on her neck when she was talking about a sad event. By examining her sadness and her mother's style of responding to her, Joan was better able to understand her tendency to deny negative feelings and was able to acknowledge sadness in her children and to comfort them. The interventionist also drew Joan's attention to the bodily sensations of anxiety such as sweaty palms and elevated heartbeat that she would experience while describing painful events and dismissing feelings about them. Doing this allowed the interventionist to explore her buried feelings with her and her need to cut them off from her awareness. This exploration allowed Joan to begin to understand and acknowledge her defensive way of dealing with them.

## Nina

Nina relied on more primitive defenses such as splitting, projection, projective identification, and acting-out to deal with her anxiety, anger, and intense fear. She continually projected the bad parts of herself onto her children. When they played them out, she punished the behavior for the feelings they elicited in her that she could not tolerate. She often used acting out to create a crisis or to avoid feelings of emptiness and abandonment. She saw her children, herself, and her interventionist sometimes as good and at other times as bad, evidence of splitting and the inability to retain positive memories in bad moments and to remember less positive aspects when experiences were good.

Through a supportive therapeutic relationship, the interventionist was able to empathize with Nina's traumatic early experiences and to gradually help her to become more aware of their impact on her. The interventionist used crises in Nina's life and the real material generated by them to illustrate some of the defenses that Nina used. For example, her denial of her brother's propensity to violence became very clear when he became out of control and had to be removed from the home. This in turn enabled a number of issues that Nina had previously denied and dissociated to be discussed and dealt with. Over the course of intervention, Nina no longer projected negative views of herself onto her children, especially Meg. She could then appreciate her children as separate feeling, thinking human beings and took great pride in their progress and accomplishments as well as her own.

## CONCLUSION

In both of these cases, the interventionist–client relationship and the supportive style of working led to positive change. Both Joan and Nina used defenses to deal with feelings of sadness, fear, anxiety, and anger. In both cases it was important to first assess the client's past and to understand the function that the individual's defenses served and how they affected her relationships with her children and her children's overall development. It was also critical to identify the type of defenses being used and to be able to utilize the knowledge in order to understand how they affected the therapeutic relationship and the parent–child relationships. The length of intervention was different, with Joan's therapy being relatively short compared with the more complex intervention required by Nina and her family. Through techniques such as interpretation, the unconscious was made conscious so that the clients could begin to understand and deal with their defenses and, in turn, their defeating patterns of behavior. The parents' defensive functioning was then less destructive to their relationships with their children and as a result, to their children's overall development.

# CHAPTER 7

# Enhancing Parents' Self-Reflectivity and Empathy for the Child

Self-reflectivity has been defined as "thinking about thinking" (Main, 1991) or about one's own and other people's minds and motivations for behavior. Several other terms have been used to describe this capacity, including *psychological mindedness, mentalization, insight, introspection, self-awareness, metacognition,* and the *capacity for self-observation* (McCallum & Piper, 1997). Self-reflectivity contributes to a number of areas of functioning, including staying in therapy and having a successful outcome from it, sustaining relationships, and containing intense emotions in one's self and helping one's children to contain them. Self-reflectivity has also been linked to the ability to provide sensitive parenting, which in turn contributes to the development of a secure attachment in a child and influences a number of developmental capacities. Slade described self-reflectivity in parents as "the capacity to keep the baby in mind" (2002, p. 10). It allows a parent to interpret the intentions and feelings that underlie her child's behavior and to act appropriately in response.

Meins and colleagues considered the importance of what they described as *maternal mind-mindedness (MM),* or the ability to treat "one's infant as an individual with a mind" and its contribution to the child's security of attachment and later theory of mind (2003, p. 1199). Some behaviors considered to be associated with MM include responsiveness to changes in the infant's gaze and to the infant's play objects, imitation, and mind-related comments (e.g., "You're really interested in that block. I guess you'd like to hold it"). The practice of suggesting how the child is feeling is also associated with MM (e.g., "I'll bet you're feeling bored and lonely and would like to be held"). The method for assessment of MM is described briefly in Chapter 2.

Self-reflectivity allows parents to ascribe more realistic and positive attributions and less negative and blaming intentions to their children and, consequently, to respond in a more nurturing and sensitive way. For example, a mother with very low self-reflectivity may respond to a crying baby by becoming angry and blaming the baby for being bad because she perceives the baby as intentionally difficult. As a result, she may fail to respond sensitively to the baby and instead, may put the baby to bed, where he continues his crying. Conversely, a parent with high self-reflectivity is likely to respond to the crying baby by trying to understand what he may be feeling or thinking about. The parent may decide that, because the baby has just been fed and changed, he is probably feeling lonely or overwhelmed. The self-reflective parent would be likely to pick the baby up and quietly talk to him and calm him down so that he can fall asleep. This kind of experience will allow the baby to feel secure and to begin to believe that he can make things happen and that his caregiver can be counted on to respond to him. These very different responses, repeated multiple times, can have a significant influence on how the baby thinks and feels about himself and other people in his world and can encourage a sense of self-agency or self-efficacy and self-acceptance.

## SELF-REFLECTIVITY IN EARLY INTERVENTION

Mary Main (1991) was one of the first attachment theorists to emphasize the importance of self-reflectivity. She called it *metacognitive monitoring,* or as mentioned earlier, the ability to "think about one's thinking." A parent may be practicing self-reflectivity when she is thinking about her own parenting and why she acts the way she does; she may also be remembering how her mother and father parented her and how her own parenting style may be related to theirs.

## Self-Reflectivity and Attachment

Main and Goldwyn (1994) developed the Adult Attachment Interview (AAI) to help assess various types of attachment. On the AAI, providing two or more examples of metacognitive thinking is seen as strongly related to autonomous (or secure) attachment. These researchers also designated a coherence of the interview scale on the AAI, not only as a measure of the person's coherence of mind, but also as indicative of the degree of self-reflectivity. A person would be demonstrating coherence of mind, for example, when she is able to use an adjective to describe her relationship with a parent and come up with an example that would fit the descriptor (e.g., "Distant. . . . My father never touched or hugged me or talked to me about how I felt").

The concept of reflectivity was expanded by several researchers to include not only the intersubjective (i.e., thinking about oneself in relation to others) but also interpersonal relating (i.e., thinking about one's behavior and how it affects others) (Fonagy, Gergely, Jurist, & Target, 2002; Fonagy, Leigh, et al., 1995; Fonagy, Steele, Steele, Higgitt, & Target, 1994; Fonagy, Steele, Steele, Moran, & Higgitt, 1991; Fonagy & Target, 1997, 1998; Grienenberger, Kelly, & Slade, 2001; Slade, 2002; Slade, Belsky, Aber, & Phelps, 1999; Slade & Cohen, 1996; Slade, Grienenberger, Bernbach, Levy, & Locker, 2001). *Reflectivity* or *mentalization* defined in this way refers to an adult's capacity to understand his own or another's behavior in terms of the underlying emotions and mental states that contribute to it. Thus, *high reflectivity* refers to the ability to understand behavior and personality in terms of the changing, and sometimes confusing, aspects of emotional experience in oneself and in others. These researchers believe that this knowledge is central for understanding and containing otherwise overwhelming emotions. When emotions are understood, even when they are complex and confusing, they are no longer experienced as frightening or overwhelming, and this ability to mentalize emotions is as important in managing them as it is in expressing them (Fonagy, Gergely, et al., 2002).

The capacity for understanding the thoughts and feelings of oneself and others also enables the differentiation of self from other people.

A number of studies have been carried out to verify the importance of the parents' level of self-reflectivity on attachment security and other aspects of development. These studies have used a scale developed by Fonagy (1994). This Self-Reflective Scale assesses the capacity for self-reflectivity on a 7-point scale (see Chapter 2 for a description). As well, in order to evaluate parents' representations of their children and themselves as parents, Aber, Slade, Berger, Bresgi, and Kaplan (1985) developed the Parent Development Interview (PDI) (see Chapter 2 for a description), a 45-item, semi-structured clinical interview that asks parents about their relationship with their children. Fonagy's scale was then adapted for use with the PDI in order to evaluate parents' capacity for self-reflectivity.

Many studies have demonstrated that a significant concordance varying from 75% to 80% exists between parents' quality of attachment to their own parents and their children's attachment classifications in relation to them (Benoit & Parker, 1994; Benoit, Parker, & Zeanah, 1997; Fonagy, Steele, & Steele, 1991; Zeanah, Benoit, Hirshberg, Barton, & Regan, 1994). These relationships have also been found across three generations, from grandmother to mother and from mother to child. The major characteristics that were thought to explain this similarity between the attachment classifications were behavioral indices such as the sensitivity and responsiveness of the parent to the child's cues. However, a number of studies have focused on self-reflectivity and related it to the quality of attachment between parents and their children as an important mechanism whereby this intergenerational transmission occurs. In a meta-analysis of studies conducted to evaluate the contribution of various factors to attachment security, De Wolff and van IJzendoorn (1995) found a combined effect size of .24 for a parent's sensitivity to her infant in interactions and concluded that other dimensions of parenting are equally important. In a more recent study using the PDI and Fonagy's Self-Reflective Scale to assess parental self-reflectivity, Slade, Grienenberger, and colleagues (2001) found an effect size of .41 between child attachment security and parents' reflective function.

Fonagy and colleagues also found that mothers who exhibited autonomous or secure attachment had significantly higher reflective functioning scores than those who presented with an insecure attachment or unresolved loss and trauma. These researchers concluded, therefore, that the ability to attribute mental states to self and others may be a critical vehicle in the intergenerational transmission of attachment quality.

In other studies, Fonagy and colleagues have demonstrated that lack of reflectivity was a core deficit underlying a great deal of the symptomatology of borderline pathology (Fonagy, Gergely, et al., 2002; Fonagy, Leigh, et al., 1995). The characteristic of having little capacity for self-reflectivity or mentalization is related particularly to an individual's inability to contain his affect and the extraordinary rage reactions that characterize borderline personality disorder (BPD). Lack of self-reflectivity also affects the types of relationships some people have that are characterized by a lack of empathy for the thoughts and feelings of others, as well as an excruciating sensitivity or alertness to any real or perceived rejection by them.

Just as the capacity for self-reflectivity significantly influences a parent's ability to parent her child, it may also significantly influence her willingness to be involved in interventions. Thus, a parent's level of self-reflectivity is an important consideration in deciding on the type of intervention that can best be provided.

## Other Approaches to Understanding Self-Reflectivity

As mentioned in the beginning of this chapter, attachment researchers have had the most to say about the importance of self-reflectivity for parenting interactions and in the transmission of the quality of attachment across generations. A number of other researchers have considered the importance of self-reflectivity for predicting the best type of therapy to be used with people, however, as well as its ultimate success. *Psychological mindedness* (PM) has been defined by cognitive theorists as the capacity to achieve psychological understanding of the thoughts, feelings, and motives of self and others (Hatcher, Hatcher, Berlin, Okla, & Richards, 1990). McCallum and Piper considered the importance of psychological mindedness in therapy and defined it as the "ability to see relationships among thoughts, feelings, and actions, with the goal of learning the meanings and causes of his experiences and behavior" (1997, p. 36). This ability can provide some insight into the parent's defenses and how emotions are being dealt with (see Chapter 6 for further discussions of this).

McCallum and Piper also described how people with *alexithymia,* a disorder characterized by limited ability to be aware of different emotions and to create fantasies, have very little capacity for psychological mindedness. As a consequence, they have an emotionless way of relating to others and a tendency to employ action in an effort to relieve unpleasant emotional tension (Sivik, 1993; Taylor, Bagby, & Parker, 1997). They may also show a tendency to somatize, develop eating disorders, abuse substances, and engage in self-mutilation. These tendencies seem to be used primarily to relieve unbearable tension and arousal. McCallum and Piper (1997), using a measure of psychological mindedness (PM) that they developed, found that the measure predicted dropout in group therapy as well as the amount of time an individual spent working on her issues in the group. Only 14% of those with high PM were group therapy dropouts, whereas 53% of those with low PM dropped out. Success and retention in the group was also related to the severity of the psychiatric disturbance of the participant (Piper, McCallum, & Hassan, 1992).

Most cognitive therapists also consider the capacity for and the type of monitoring of clients' own cognitions and how they relate to psychological functioning. Wells (2000) considered the metacognitive knowledge that a person has about his own cognitions as well as the strategies used to monitor and control them. These include executive functions such as attending, monitoring, and planning. As Wells pointed out, not only are negative self-beliefs destructive but also some strategies such as worrying, ruminating, and self-recrimination may be problematic because they do not allow flexibility in shifting between various executive functions (Wells, 2000). These types of thinking, or a heightened level of self-focus, are seen as related to proneness to anxiety and depression, pathological worry, and obsessive-compulsive symptomatology.

The development of self-reflectivity is briefly described next as well as the characteristics of parenting or support needed to develop it. This developmental approach is then used to discuss ways to engage a parent who has very little self-reflectivity and strategies that can be used in sessions to enhance it.

## THE DEVELOPMENT OF SELF-REFLECTIVITY

Self-reflectivity is a capacity that develops in early childhood. Although it is neurologically and genetically derived, it also unfolds and is influenced by early caregiver–child interactions. The capacity for self-reflectivity typically develops gradually over a child's first 5 or 6 years of life, although clearly it can only unfold within the containment of sensitive understanding and attunement of caregivers. Although originating in early childhood, self-reflectivity continues to develop and to show increasing flexibility over the life span.

The first level of development occurs with the *differentiation of the infant from his primary caregiver.* It has been accepted for some time that at birth, an infant is equipped with amazing perceptual abilities for understanding and learning about the world. Infants prefer people over other stimuli and enjoy contingent face-to-face interactions in which they experience early differentiation of self. Although infants show some capacity for self-regulation of emotional states through thumb-sucking, focusing their eyes on an object, or turning away, they need caregivers to attune to them and to help them modulate their emotional states. Fonagy and colleagues (1991) explained that the development of self-reflectivity begins in the early months with the attunement of the caregiver to the infant's internal world, emotions, and psychological experience. From this understanding the parent adapts interactions and the external world to fit the child, and helps to contain the child's overwhelming emotions. This allows the child to develop *trust in the availability of the parent* and to feel safe in the world.

Toward the end of the first year, infants show the emergence of *social referencing* when they use their parent's facial emotional displays in order to make sense of frightening or ambiguous situations and to decide how to respond (Campos & Stenberg, 1981; Klinnert, Campos, Sorce, Emde, & Svejda, 1983). Starting at about 9 to 15 months old, new communicative behaviors emerge during which infants begin to show *joint attention* as they follow their caregiver's gaze and attend to objects or situations (Carpenter, Nagell, & Tomasello, 1998; Tomasello, 1995). They also begin to use gestures such as pointing out or showing objects to others. According to Tomasello (1999), infants at this stage assume that others are thinking about and understanding things in the same way as they do.

Other signs of emerging self-reflectivity occur around 2 years of age, when young children begin to be able to *differentiate between their own desires and the desires or preferences of another,* or in other words, when they begin to understand that other people's minds and beliefs are different from their own (Repachol & Gopnik, 1997). A child begins to understand that while he likes broccoli, his father much prefers peas, for example. At about the same time, the child may show emotional resonance with or reflect the emotions of another person. For instance, the young child may be upset by her parents' or another child's sadness and may try to comfort that person, primarily in an effort to alleviate her own distress (Hoffman, 2000; Zahn-

Waxler & Radke-Yarrow, 1990). At about the same time, the child develops greater understanding of herself and shows *self-recognition* in the mirror (Lewis & Brooks-Gunn, 1979). She also acquires a more secure ability for object constancy, which enables her to hold onto an image of her caregivers when they are away. This usually goes with an increase in the use of "I" and "you" and a much clearer understanding of the differentiation between the two. Also, if all has gone well, the child has a sound sense of self-agency that occurs from the continuous social contingencies that are experienced within sensitive and attuned parenting interactions.

The development of the capacity for *pretend play,* which includes *taking on different roles, talking about stories, and imagining* provides a child with another means to learn about the perspective of others and to understand and deal with emotions symbolically. During play, the process of switching roles enables the child to reflect on his own thoughts and feelings as well as those of others. While engaging in play or other symbolic activities such as drawing, the child's internal feelings are externalized and experienced as "out there," making them feel more manageable. Children learn to distinguish between pretend and reality and, gradually, between appearance and reality, opening the way to having a theory of mind (Dockett & Smith, 1995; Riblatt, 1995).

During the third year of life, a child develops *a theory of mind,* or an understanding that the thoughts and feelings of another person may be different from her own. Typically, it is not until the child is approximately 4 years old that she establishes a capacity for having a true theory of mind or the ability to think about a second or third person's thoughts as well (Astington, Harris, & Olson, 1988; Hughes & Dunn, 1998). In other words, the child can think about his two friends and how one is thinking about the other (e.g., "I think that you think that Johnny is upset and he doesn't like you, but he is not upset at all and he really likes you"). The development of a theory of mind can be short circuited if the child experiences trauma such as abuse or extreme neglect. In addition, it can be compromised if the caregiver cannot contain the child's overwhelming emotions or anticipate the child's psychological and physical needs, or in other words, when a parent does not have sufficient self-reflectivity herself. When there is a breakdown in the development of this capacity, the child develops defensive strategies that deny her own and other people's affective states, which result in the child having a very rigid way of relating to others and lacking the capacity for empathic interactions with others. When these experiences are traumatic, the child develops a disorganized attachment and loses the capacity for self-reflectivity (Cassidy & Mahr, 2001). Table 7.1 lists strategies parents can use to help children develop self-reflectivity at each developmental level and intervention strategies that can help parents who lack self-reflectivity to gradually acquire the capacity for mentalization and having empathy for the child.

## Parenting and the Development of Self-Reflectivity

In order for self-reflectivity to develop in children, parents need to provide them with a variety of experiences that change as the child develops. These include

- *Providing a secure base.* This encourages the child to explore and try out her own ideas and then to come back for reassurance and understanding.

- *Mirroring or reflecting the child's emotional display.* Typically, mirroring the child's emotional expression by imitating the facial expression can give the baby a sense of synchrony and of being understood. Keep in mind, however, that when a child is very upset, mirroring is not helpful because the child will be more overwhelmed by it. Instead, the parent needs to calm the child and help him to modulate the intensity of the feelings.

- *Getting involved in young children's play,* which can help foster understanding of mental states and containment of emotions. Role playing with young children can be helpful. Also, the parents may adopt a child's mental state and re-present it to him. This kind of scaffolding during play may promote a pretend/real distinction that can be a prelude to the child's developing a theory of mind or an understanding about appearance and reality (Hughes & Dunn, 1998).

- *Talking with the child about feelings and the reasons behind behavior,* which leads to self-reflectivity. This can include naming the emotions of self and others and making sure that feelings are included in discussions of events that have occurred. Effective conversations in which both partners fully participate provide a mechanism to share ideas and to correct misconceptions. During these exchanges parents, peers, or siblings may be able to expand the children's discussions of feelings and provide feedback about their own thoughts and feelings.

- Understanding that the child has *feelings, thoughts, and intentions of his own.* This can enable the parent to link the child's behavior to his feelings or mental state and the parent is then emotionally available to respond to the child based on this understanding. The understanding is then communicated to the child by the parent's actions and her comments to the child (e.g., "I guess you are sad because you can't go outside," "I understand you're frustrated because Susan went to school, and you can't go outside because we're not ready yet."). This process, repeated frequently through words and actions, allows the child's feelings and thoughts to be understood and accepted and encourages the subsequent development of mentalization or self-reflectivity.

Unfortunately, parents without self-reflectivity themselves may be oblivious to their child's thoughts and feelings. A parent with little self-reflectivity will have difficulty containing her own intense feelings and may, as a result, ignore and deny her child's thoughts and feelings. She will also not have the understanding or capacity to engage in the somewhat complex responses described above.

## Encouraging Self-Reflectivity in Parents

Parents who lack the capacity for self-reflectivity often feel inadequate, helpless, and as if they are losing control in their parenting role. As a result, they do not respond well to a number of therapeutic approaches. For this reason, competence-based and supportive approaches are most useful, at least in the early stages of intervention, to help establish a therapeutic alliance, to diminish resistance to intervention, and to build some sense of optimism. The approach also helps parents begin to understand how they can learn to respond appropriately with their children and to enhance their interactions with them (Process of Change Study Group, 1998).

**Table 7.1.**  Strategies for working with parents to develop and/or enhance capacity for self-reflectivity (based on developmental levels)

| Developmental level | Typical age range during which self-reflective developmental steps occur (in years) | Child's developmental level | Adult self-reflection capabilities according to level of self-reflectivity | Interventions strategies appropriate for this developmental level |
|---|---|---|---|---|
| Level 1 | Birth to 1 year | The beginning of differentiation of self occurs. | Differentiation of self and other. | Set clear goals between parent and interventionist. Establish any necessary boundaries. Provide reminders of the interventionist. |
| Level 2 | Birth to 1 year | The infant develops a sense of trust in the world. | Building trust and the therapeutic relationship | Provide an experience of interest in parent's thoughts and feelings. Show understanding, concern, and consistency. Mirror the parent's affect and acknowledge the pain of past or current loss or trauma. Provide a unique experience of being listened to, heard, understood, and accepted. |
| Level 3 | 2–3 | The child is able to understand and react to the feelings of others as a result of responsive caregiving. | Encouraging feelings and understanding them | Encourage expression of feelings when situations are talked about. Support parent to identify, label, and verbalize feelings. Point out any behavioral signs of emotions. Teach ways to deal with overwhelming emotions. Identify any triggers that seem to contribute to the parent becoming overwhelmed by emotions. Provide a "holding" environment that contains the intense emotions of the parent. |

| Level | Age | Developmental capacity | Focus | Interventions |
|---|---|---|---|---|
| Level 4 | 2–3 | The capacity for pretend play and imagination develops and is used to understand the perspective of others. | Encouraging a capacity for symbolization and fantasy | Have the parent replay in their head past events or situations. Have parents work on interpreting their dreams if they discuss them. Have a parent begin to join their child in pretend play. |
| Level 5 | 3–4 | The child develops a rudimentary capacity for theory of mind. | Being able to understand the point of view of other people, including one's child | Encourage a parent to daydream and write down anything she can imagine in the future for her and her child. Show understanding of the thoughts and feelings of the parent. Ask the parent to think about what might be going on in someone's head if an event is being discussed. Encourage the parent to imagine how her child thinks and feels. |
| Level 6 | 4–5 | The capacity for theory of mind expands and the child begins to develop executive functioning, including focusing and problem solving. | Cognitive restructuring, being able to understand situations differently | Help parents begin to see events in less negative and frightening ways. Teach the parent to problem-solve a solution for a difficulty with his child or in another situation he is dealing with. Substitute positive self-talk for negative or catastrophic thinking. |

## Supportive Psychotherapy

Werman defined *supportive psychotherapy* as a form of treatment whose principal concern and focus is to "strengthen mental functions that are acutely or chronically inadequate to cope with the demands of the external world and the patient's inner psychological world" (1984, p.5). He pointed out that supportive psychotherapy is used rather than insight-oriented psychotherapy with a client "whose basic psychological "equipment" is more or less severely underdeveloped" (p.5). The goal is to strengthen the client's psychological capacities and to help them locate supports within their environment. In other words, change is encouraged through experiences that happen within the relationship experience with the interventionist rather than by the use of interpretation by the interventionist. The stage can be set for a "corrective therapeutic experience in which the client first experiences an attunement or understanding before any other strategies or interpretations are offered" (Lieberman & Zeanah, 2000, p. 270). The parent must believe that the therapist really understands how he is feeling. Another characteristic of supportive therapy is that the interventionist works with the parent to help her understand the possibilities of her situation or to problem-solve around various alternate ways of understanding and coping with it (Lieberman, Silverman, & Pawl, 2000). Table 7.2 provides a summary of characteristics of supportive therapy.

## A Developmental Perspective to Enhancing Parental Self-Reflectivity

Lack of self-reflectivity implies either that the individual failed to acquire the capacity or, if it had been acquired at one time, has regressed because of crisis or trauma. Intervention needs to begin at a stage where the impairment occurred. Consequently, as outlined previously, providing an experience that can be seen as one of mirroring by the interventionist can provide a developmental experience that can be reparative.

   *Differentiation of Self and Other*    During the early stage of intervention, it is important to provide a comfortable interchange in which differentiation of the parent and interventionist is clearly established. This may first occur when a parent clearly articulates her wishes and desires as to what can happen in the sessions, and the interventionist clarifies how that can take place and what his role will be. During early sessions it may be important to set boundaries, letting the parent know

**Table 7.2.**   Characteristics of supportive therapy that encourage participation and improve self-reflectivity

**Supportive therapy**
- Builds a sense of optimism
- Helps the client find supports in the environment
- Provides client with an experience of being listened to, understood, and accepted
- Teaches ways to deal with overwhelming emotions
- Encourages any new areas of psychological functioning (e.g., control of anger), or problem solving around a crisis or a parenting issue
- Acknowledges any gains and shows approval

that the intervention will not occur unless the parent cooperates in certain ways, which may include taking medication, attending Alcoholics Anonymous (AA) meetings, agreeing not to attempt suicide, and stopping violence. Sometimes, because the client may have difficulty holding the image of the interventionist in her mind (or lacks object constancy) it may be important to provide her with some kind of reminder of the interventionist (e.g., a card, or written reminder of the next appointment).

*Containing and Understanding Feelings*   Throughout the beginning stages of intervention, showing empathy for the parent's suffering is important. This understanding and concern provides a "holding environment" that can contain the intense emotions of the parent.

It is important to encourage the parent not only to talk about events that are concerning her but also to begin to identify, label, and verbalize feelings that accompany the events. Focusing on the identified emotions is a crucial part of the therapy because clients may not even be able to identify their emotions, or at least will not be able to contain them, and can easily be overwhelmed by them. Helping the parent to see that feelings can be dealt with, that they can be overcome, and can pass relatively quickly with support, can be extremely helpful. These practices form an important basis for therapeutic interventions:

- Showing empathy for the difficulties that the parent is struggling with

- Reflecting the parent's feeling back to indicate that he is heard and understood

- Providing a "holding environment" or a "secure base" so that the parent can begin to risk feeling some of the more difficult emotions

The process of actually beginning to "observe" one's own emotional states in order to understand and label them can also be helpful. Sometimes, when parents find it difficult to identify emotions, pointing out any behavioral expression of them such as sighs, gestures, bodily movements, or signs of body tension can also clarify their feelings. When parents continue to become overwhelmed by their emotional states, whether they are of anxiety, depression, anger, or even rage, it is important to suggest ways to cope with them such as relaxing, journaling, or thinking about something more pleasant. These methods can be used in order to overcome the intense feelings before and after they happen.

Because parents who lack self-reflectivity are often excruciatingly sensitive to any hint of negativity or rejection by the interventionist, it is very important to continue to show acceptance, praise, and pleasure in any gains the parent makes. If the parent does feel rejected, discussing these feelings and reestablishing a sense of acceptance is important.

*Encouraging Symbolization and Fantasy Experiences*   Another capacity that may be missing in parents who lack self-reflectivity is the capacity for representing their situations in a different way and for having fantasy experiences. Here are some ways to help a parent to increase this capacity:

- Encouraging the parent to imagine certain relaxing situations or events that can be replayed in her head can help her to envision the type of outcome for which she yearns.

- Journaling between sessions has been found to be helpful for some parents, particularly if they are encouraged to include feelings and thoughts about events that happen rather than only the event itself.

- Having parents join their child in pretend play and take the part of characters in that play can enhance the child's capacity for pretend play and begin to encourage the parents' own capacity for symbolization and imagination.

- Encouraging the parent to daydream about possible upcoming events and discuss what she can imagine in the future for herself and her child can also move the parent from immediate concrete events into desires, beliefs, and wishes for herself and her child.

### Directly Enhancing Self and Other Representations

As the parent experiences acceptance and understanding from the therapist, she is likely to begin to understand that the therapist may have ideas, beliefs, and desires that are different from her own. A number of strategies can be helpful to develop this ability. The interventionist might ask how something is for the parent and suggest that he has wondered how the situation has been working out. It may also be pointed out by saying "I think at the moment you may be confused or anxious about. . . ." Sometimes asking a parent what he believes the therapist may be thinking can persuade him to think about the thoughts of others. Also, discussion of events and consideration of the thoughts and feelings that the parent had in relation to them can be very helpful. For example, at the beginning of therapy the parent may report a situation that she really dislikes, such as going to her in-laws for dinner with her new baby. At first she may only be able to identify that the outing always ends up with her feeling sad and abandoned. A further step in exploring this situation can include having the parent think about what her in-laws do and what she thinks they are thinking about that may explain their behavior. She may decide that her in-laws are so thrilled with their new grandson that he is all they are thinking about. The interventionist may help her to realize that not paying attention to her does not mean that her in-laws do not care about her anymore. Sometimes it may be important to suggest a variety of alternative ways that the person in the incident may be thinking. Sometimes people with little self-reflectivity feel that all people reject them and cannot be trusted and are out to cheat or hurt them. Helping them find a more realistic view of the beliefs and feelings of other people can be helpful.

### Cognitive Restructuring

When a client appears to have the ability to think about her own cognitions but identifies these thoughts as upsetting and disruptive because they consist of negative, unwanted, or distressing beliefs, the intervention may have a different emphasis. Cognitive techniques can be used to substitute or to replace the negative views of self that can lead to depression. Rather than constantly going back to negative beliefs and attributions, clients can be encouraged to use problem-solving strategies in order to transcend these beliefs. This involves thinking about the situation or task by focusing on it and substituting positive self-talk rather than negative or catastrophic thoughts about it.

Other cognitive theorists also consider clients' ability to monitor their own cognitions and how it is related to psychological functioning. As discussed at the beginning of the chapter, Wells, in discussing metacognitive knowledge, pointed out that not only are negative self-beliefs destructive but also, as noted previously, some strategies such as worrying, ruminating, and self-recrimination can get the person "stuck" and do not allow flexibility in shifting between various views of the situation. These types of thinking or heightened self-focus relate to anxiety, pathological worry, and obsessive-compulsive symptomatology. On the basis of these difficulties, Wells developed "metacognitive focused therapy" (2000, p. 90), which trains people with anxiety and obsessive-compulsive disorders in developing alternative attention, beliefs, and coping strategies that can restructure maladaptive self-beliefs. Some of the strategies include

- Helping the person overcome the tendency to "catastrophize" by learning that stressful situations can be overcome

- Encouraging relaxation in the face of stressful situations

- Encouraging control over attention to negative beliefs or thought stopping when they do occur

- Refocusing attention from negative beliefs to new information that disconfirms the negative belief and replaces it with something more supportive

- Identifying the thoughts, bodily sensations, and external stresses that preceded anxiety, depression, or an obsessive behavior

- Using problem-solving and external focusing on the situation in order to acquire new knowledge about it

- Encouraging focusing on the present and watching one's thoughts and feelings as if they are on a movie screen

These strategies can be useful in sessions in which parents seem to be constantly overwhelmed with worry about situations that are, in fact, solvable, such as the mother who has irrational fears about her pregnancy, or the father who is convinced that his son will become a delinquent. The mother may be supported to get excellent prenatal care and the father to find optimal ways to discipline his child. They can also be encouraged to think about more positive outcomes for the situations they are so concerned about.

## ENCOURAGING PARENT SELF-REFLECTIVITY: CASE-STUDY FAMILIES

In the case studies that were discussed in Chapter 4, both Joan and Nina had difficulty with self-reflectivity and with empathizing with their children. On the one hand, with Nina this difficulty was pervasive and affected all areas of her functioning, particularly her ability to parent and to understand the perspectives and feelings of her children. Joan, on the other hand, was capable of self-reflectivity in many areas of her life and around some parenting issues. Because she found it so difficult to tolerate sadness in herself and others, however, she was not able to accept it in Mark and completely failed to acknowledge, mirror, or contain it for him. As a consequence it meant Mark was cut off from a significant part of his emotionality contributing in part to his aggressive and acting-out behavior.

## Joan

Joan's therapy consisted of helping her to become aware of her own underlying pain and sadness and finding ways of containing it as it was uncovered. Sometimes this involved drawing her attention to her immediate tendency to laugh it off or joke about it, and at other times, alerting her to her tendency to become agitated and to blush or develop a rash on her neck when she was talking about a sad event. As she became able to talk about her mother's depression and how she felt and thought about it as a child, these reactions diminished. It was also extremely helpful when she realized that as a child she had felt completely responsible for her mother's mood. She also felt guilty because, try as she might to cheer her mother up, she was never able to. The relief of acknowledging that she was in fact not responsible as a small child for her mother helped significantly in allowing her to feel sadness and to realize that she could do this without being totally overwhelmed by it as her mother had. Joan was also able to think about how her mother felt as a young woman and to gain some more understanding for why her mother acted the way she did. It turned out her mother had lost a baby before Joan was born, and she had also suffered from postpartum depression following both pregnancies. Joan realized there was very little treatment available for her mother at that time and it was viewed as unacceptable by her extended family to have feelings of depression. Consequently, she just managed as best she could. This understanding made it easier for Joan to relate to her mother's actions and eventually to forgive her for the past. It also opened up the opportunity for Joan to enhance her current relationship with her mother.

After these discussions it was much clearer to Joan why she had found it so difficult to understand, mirror, and contain Mark's sadness. She began to think about why he might feel sad and to explore what he might be thinking about when he became aggressive. Talking about Mark's thoughts and feelings with him allowed Mark to talk about the range of feelings he had repressed. Although he continued to have some difficulty with self-esteem, he did become able to explain his thoughts and feelings to his parents and as a consequence to contain them more successfully.

## Nina

Nina's intervention was provided in three stages in order to accommodate her unresolved loss and trauma. Examples of how her understanding of her own and her children's thoughts and feelings expanded during these stages are provided below.

### Example of Therapy in Stage One

**Therapist:** "How have you been doing this week?"

**Nina:** "We've been doing fine. . . . Derrick got into trouble at school this week, he was sent home for hitting another kid."

**Therapist:** "That must have been very difficult for you."

| | |
|---|---|
| **Nina:** | "Oh it's O.K. I just sent him to his room for it. He's just got to get straightened up or there will be trouble." |
| **Therapist:** | "Do you think he is upset about something?" |
| **Nina:** | "He's just a brat. The teacher says so, too." |
| **Therapist:** | "He must get frustrated sometimes as the children tease him at times." |
| **Nina:** | "Like I said, he's just a brat, so like his father, I can't believe it." |

## *Example of Therapy in Stage Two:*

| | |
|---|---|
| **Therapist:** | "How has this week been?" |
| **Nina:** | "I'm still feeling pretty down. I don't want the children around all the time. . . . They annoy me . . . but it's the emptiness when I'm alone. It's like I don't exist." |
| **Therapist:** | "Does that make you feel sad, scared?" |
| **Nina:** | "It's all of that, sometimes I feel . . . well weird. The other day it was like I felt like when I was little." |
| **Therapist:** | "Like when you were little?" |
| **Nina:** | "Like no one cared . . . when I was small and huddled. . . ." |
| **Therapist:** | "Under the bed?" |
| **Nina:** | "Yes, and I hate that feeling because I'm afraid . . . but angry too." |
| **Therapist:** | "Angry that no one really cared?" |
| **Nina:** | "No one does and the children just want, want, all the time. Sometimes I want to just sleep or run away but then I find a man." |
| **Therapist:** | "Finding a man helps." |
| **Nina:** | "Of course; it's good." |
| **Therapist:** | "I worry you'll get hurt. You need to be kept safe." |
| **Nina (angry):** | "Just tell me I'm no good and take the children." |
| **Therapist:** | "I know it's hard to believe anyone is interested in you and will be there for you." |
| **Nina:** | "No one ever is." |
| **Therapist:** | "No one?" |
| **Nina:** | "Well you're just doing it because it's your job. You're paid. All you care about is the children. I don't tell you what goes on. . . . You think it's okay." |
| **Therapist:** | "You think I would go if I really know the truth of who you are?" |
| **Nina:** | "Yes, I lie to you, you believe me . . . but you don't understand." |

**Therapist:** "I can't understand how you feel about yourself? How you feel so worthless?"

**Nina:** "That I am so bad."

**Therapist:** "You can tell me about it and I will come back."

**Nina:** "Meg cried so much yesterday. I think she was scared I might go away to drug treatment again, so she clung to me. I didn't know what to do. . . . It upsets me and I feel all vulnerable again, but I know I've got to help her. It all feels too much—but now at least I understand what she needs."

**Therapist:** "That makes it easier?"

**Nina:** "Yes, and I notice, like you said, if I pay attention to her and let her know I understand, she calms down more quickly."

**Therapist:** "That is so great that you can do that and see the difference. It must make Meg feel so good when you can be gentle and understanding with her . . . the way you are."

**Nina:** "Yes, it's the same with the boys, I let them know that I understand how it has been hard for them, too."

### Example of Therapy in Stage Three:

**Therapist:** "Did you have a good week?"

**Nina:** "Yes, I really did, I'm really enjoying AA, it's—months now. I actually am helping someone else now. Meg is so much better, not whining so much. We went out together shopping."

**Therapist:** "So you are enjoying other people in new ways?"

**Nina:** "Yes, people look up to me. . . . I seem to understand the children better now. . . . I don't freak out at Meg. You know Derrick is so bright, he's probably the brightest, and he seems happier and more self-confident . . . like he feels strong inside."

**Therapist:** "Did he do something special?"

**Nina:** "Well, he was at child care and he told everyone that he can read, and he knows a few words, and he organized this game in which everyone had to work hard . . . to go to . . . school. I realized he's playing out things about me, but it's not me going to jail but me learning things. That feels good and I realize how much what I am thinking and feeling affects them. Of course, what I'm doing does too, but they seem to be happier now that I feel better. Sometimes I feel so bad about what I did."

**Therapist:** "But what you're doing now is so great and makes all the difference. You see it and feel it too. Are you working hard at school?"

**Nina:** "Yes, I've been doing studying and the kids like that. . . . Sometimes it's hard and I can't concentrate. Then I get scared that I can't . . ."

**Therapist:** "That you can't make it?"

**Nina:** "Yes, it's not just the studying, it's the drinking and being with the kids right and men. . . . Sometimes I'm so tired and I want to go back."

**Therapist:** "What makes you keep going . . . and succeeding?"

**Nina:** "Well, all of the things I do at the center really help, but now I understand what drags me down. I relax. I write in my journal. But it's like I'm always an alcoholic. These things I do now aren't natural but it's all right."

**Therapist:** "Remember how we talked about being strong at the broken places?"

**Nina (quietly):** "Yes, that's what it is, isn't it?"

## CONCLUSION

This chapter presents a number of suggestions to enhance the capacity for self-reflectivity. Much of the work with the client who lacks self-reflectivity will, for some time, be supportive in nature, consisting of making regular home visits or clinic sessions, encouraging positive behaviors, and working from the parents' existing strengths. Supporting parents is usually necessary before parents can commit to other services and begin to gain an understanding of their child and an ability to think about or consider their own thinking. A number of additional interventions that concentrate on enhancing parents' interaction with their child partly by enhancing their self-reflectivity have been researched and are used in a number of early intervention programs. They are described in Chapter 10 and throughout other chapters in Section III.

## CHAPTER 8

# Enhancing Parents' Sense of Competence and Social Support

Before they become parents, men and women have established a sense of self-esteem that may be positive or more negative. The transition to parenthood brings a number of new challenges, however, which result in a new type of self-evaluation of personal competence. *Parental sense of competence* can, therefore, be defined as the beliefs that parents develop about their ability to understand, care for, and enhance the development of their child.

## Parental Sense of Competence and Related Characteristics

Many characteristics and practices are related to parents' sense of competence. The ramifications of these characteristics can be far reaching, both back into the past and in the future.

A sense of competence in parenting and in other types of functioning has been linked in some studies to positive parenting. Gross and Rocissano described it as the "necessary mediator between knowledge and action" (1988, p. 20) or between knowing what to do and actually doing it. Thus, it is clear how important it is to enhance parents' sense of competence in order to enable them to use newly acquired knowledge to enhance their interactions with their children.

A number of researchers have found a relationship between parental confidence about being a parent and self-esteem, as well (e.g., Brody, Stoneman, & McCoy, 1994b; Mercer & Ferketich, 1995). Parental competence has also been linked to other characteristics such as locus of control, coping style, and perceived self-efficacy.

A number of studies have considered self-esteem and/or parental competence as contributors to parenting skills and child outcomes. Many researchers who studied the effect of maternal self-confidence on parenting found that high self-confidence or sense of mastery is linked with provision of better home environments for children, positive parenting behaviors (Coleman & Karraker, 1998; Rogers, Parcel, & Meaghan, 1991), and greater maternal responsiveness (Hubbs-Tait, Osofsky, Hann, & McDonald, 1994). Conversely, low self-confidence is related to poor mother–infant interactions (Bohlin & Hagekull, 1987; Johnston, 1996; MacPhee, Fritz, & Miller-Heyl, 1996; Teti & Gelfand, 1991), and, in adolescent mothers, to low child acceptance (East, Malthaws, & Felice, 1994). In addition, as discussed in Chapter 12, Bugental and colleagues found that parents who attribute low control to themselves and high control to their child have caregiving problems, and often use punitive discipline and even abuse their child (Bugental, 1990; Bugental, Blue, & Lewis, 1990; Bugental & Shennum, 1984).

A relationship has also been found between a mother's locus of control and parenting style. A parent with a more internal locus of control feels that events are dependent on her own actions, whereas the person with an external locus of control believes that events are controlled by destiny or luck and are unrelated to her own behaviors. In one very interesting study, Galejs and Pease (1987) found that mothers who believed that fate had little influence over events in their lives (i.e., an internal locus of control) stressed the importance of personal and close involvement with their children and of showing affection, listening, and talking to them. Those who believed that external events controlled what happened stressed instead educational toys, including word and number games for their children. It appeared that those with an internal locus of control saw the use of self in interactions as critical, whereas those with a belief in external control relied instead on resources outside of themselves. Having an external locus of control has also been linked to maternal depression, which has been associated with poor child outcomes (Dunn, Burbine, Bowers, & Tantleff-Dunn, 2001).

Other research has considered how *learned helplessness,* a global and stable belief in one's inability to do things adequately, can affect one's ability to parent. One study simulated a mother's inability to terminate an infant's cry and demonstrated that the inability generated a sense of helplessness in the mothers watching the simulation (Donovan & Leavitt, 1985). The researchers found that intervention conducted to enable the mothers to terminate the cries could overcome the observing mothers' feelings of failure, however.

## Problem Solving and Ability to Deal with Stress

Feelings of control and competence have been linked to coping strategies that are used by parents to deal with stress and parenting problems, and to parenting practices and the use of social support. For example, parents with children with autism were less depressed and isolated if they reached out to others and adopted a problem-focused style of coping and confronted the problems with their children as opposed to avoiding them and withdrawing from interactions with others (Dunn et al., 2001). Cutrona and Troutman (1986b) used similar concepts to illustrate how some mothers coped with infants who were temperamentally difficult by being persistent in finding effective caregiving strategies. Those who persisted rather than giving up showed adaptive coping and had less anxiety and depression.

## Excessive Self-Confidence

Although having high self-esteem or sense of parenting competence and control has been linked with better adjustment to parenting and more sensitive interactions with young children, some researchers have cautioned that excessively high maternal self-confidence and illusory control may not allow for acknowledging the complexity of parenting choices or asking for advice. As with self-esteem, the relationship between maternal self-confidence and parenting ability may be complex and curvilinear, such that very high or very low levels may be deleterious. For example, a study of 50 mothers and toddlers found that the least knowledgeable and most confident mothers had fewer positive interactions with their children than mothers who were less confident and had some knowledge (Conrad, Gross, Fogg, & Ruchala, 1992). The researchers suggested that some very confident mothers have low parental knowledge and may be naïve about parenting but not open to the input of others, making intervention with these mothers very difficult. A related research study found that mothers who had a very high illusion of being able to control the audiotaped cries of an infant before the experiment seemed to pay very little attention to the task, and when they found they could not stop the cries, acted as if they had an increased sense of helplessness in relation to completing the task (Donovan, Leavitt, & Walsh, 1990).

## Early Experiences and Sense of Competence

A number of characteristics that affect parenting are described in Chapter 1, and some can significantly influence the development of a sense of parenting competence. Some of these risks include difficulty with emotion regulation, planning and problem solving, and unresolved loss and trauma. As described in Chapter 9, parents who have had difficult experiences in their early years that go unresolved, especially if these experiences included abuse, neglect, or loss of parenting figures, are likely to perceive themselves as weak, shameful, and unlovable and have problems trusting others. They may, for example, also perceive their children's normal push for independence as rejection of them. When the child says no or has a tantrum, this can lead the parent to engage in an angry outburst or very punitive discipline because the child's behavior reminds him of very early experiences of rejection, corporal punishment, or even abuse. Seemingly less traumatic experiences can also lead to a sense of learned helplessness if a child was repeatedly not responded to when she was hurt or upset. As a child, the parent may have had very little opportunity for learning experiences suitable for her developmental level and may not have been supported with interest and responsiveness by parents when they succeeded in doing a task (Deseiden, Teti, & Corns, 1995; Priel & Besser, 2000).

## Other Parent Characteristics and Parental Sense of Competence

As discussed in Chapter 1, being a teenage parent, experiencing depression, and having a cognitive delay can also influence parental sense of self-efficacy. Teenage parents, for example, may experience a drop in their self-esteem if they become more isolated from their peer group as a result of having a baby, and if their parents reject them and do not provide them with much-needed support. Having to drop out of school can also contribute to feelings of low self-confidence, especially if a teenager's self-esteem was low before she became pregnant (Hubbs-Tait, Osofsky, et al., 1994; Osofsky, Hann, & Peebles, 1993).

The link between depression and low self-confidence is clear, and mothers with postpartum depression are especially at risk. Specifically, mothers with postpartum depression often experience a sense of hopelessness, despair, and incompetence in their parenting role. It also appears that parents living in high-risk neighborhoods who have very low incomes and possibly meaningless jobs may suffer from a chronic low-grade depression that makes positive interaction with their children extremely difficult (Campbell, Cohn, & Meyers, 1995; Jacobsen, 1999). These circumstances are often accompanied by feelings of helplessness and passive coping styles (Donovan & Leavitt, 1985).

Parents who experience difficulty controlling their feelings and expressing them appropriately with their children, especially during discipline episodes, often feel out of control and ineffectual. Also, parents' failure to contain their own negative emotions may make it difficult for them to modulate their infants' emotions appropriately and can result in escalation of children's behavioral difficulties and symptoms of anxiety and depression, which in turn contribute further to the parents' feelings of being out-of-control (Belsky, Hsieh, & Crnic, 1998; Calkins, 2002; Crockenberg & Litman, 1990).

## The Effect of Child
## Characteristics on Parental Self-Confidence

A number of characteristics of children can negatively affect parents' sense of competence. For example, having a premature baby, a child with special needs, or a temperamentally difficult child can all lower parents' sense of self-efficacy (Crockenberg, 1981; Cutrona & Troutman, 1986b; Dunn et al., 2001; Gill & Harris, 1991; McGrath, Zachariah-Boukydis & Lester, 1993; McKinney & Peterson, 1987; Zarling, Hirsch, & Landry, 1988). In other words, in supporting interactions between parents and children, it is critical to consider the impact of the child's characteristics and provide extra support if necessary.

## The Importance of Social
## Supports on Parental Sense of Competence

Systems theory, outlined in Chapter 3, contends that the interactional style of parents is affected in part by determinants beyond the individual characteristics of the child and mother. These include marital status; family climate; and support from family, friends, neighbors, religious organizations, and service providers (Crnic, Greenberg, Ragozin, Robinson, & Basham, 1983; Crnic, Greenberg, & Slough, 1986; Dunst & Trivette, 1986; Pascoe, Loda, Jeffries, & Earp, 1981).

A number of studies have linked the social networks of parents to aspects of their parenting. Specifically, larger, supportive social networks have been associated with various aspects of more nurturing, sensitive, and responsive parenting, whereas lack of social supports have been linked with lower levels of warmth and more punitive discipline (Ceballo & McLoyd, 2002; Roberts, 1989).

Some researchers have found that social support was also related to secure attachment in the child (Crockenberg, 1981; Jacobson & Frye, 1991). Other studies have demonstrated a relationship between social support and child development and have conceptualized social support as a mediating factor between parenting variables and the child's developmental outcome (Crockenberg, 1981; Jacobson & Frye, 1991). However, these researchers emphasized that the support was only linked with child attachment for parents with poor coping capacities (Jacobson & Frye, 1991) and for mothers with temperamentally difficult infants (Crockenberg, 1981).

Families at multiple risk are often isolated from others, and helping these families find adequate supports is a very important role for service providers. Extreme cases of social isolation have been linked to child abuse and neglect (Berry, 1998; Gaudin, Polansky, Kilpatrick, & Shilton, 1993; Polansky, 1985; Polansky, Ammons, & Gaudin, 1985). Social support may be provided by a variety of people and organizations and the configuration of these various components of support can vary from parent to parent in terms of numbers and their significance, and Figure 8.1 could be used to describe the number of social supports and the importance of the different components in describing a parent's system of social support.

Other researchers have looked at the type and function of supports provided (Cochran & Niego, 2002; Crockenberg, 1988) (see Figure 8.2). These can be defined broadly as

- Concrete behaviors and support (e.g., providing childcare, perhaps doing some shopping occasionally for the parent)

- Emotional support in times of stress (e.g., someone who listens and understands).

- Informational support (e.g., giving parenting advice, helping complete forms, demonstrating toys)

- Role model (e.g., may model ways to interact sensitively with a child or talk about her own experience as a parent)

Recent research has indicated that it is not only the amount of social support but also how useful the parent finds the support that determines how effective it is in enhancing parenting. Social support can be a source of distress, for example, if those who provide it are perceived as intrusive and critical (Belle, 1982, 1990; Brodsky, 1999; Dressler, 1985; Longfellow, Zelkowitz, Saunders, & Belle, 1979). Support can cause stress if those providing it lack respect for the parents and assume incompetence. It can also be a source of frustration if it is perceived as withholding or irrelevant to the difficulties being encountered (Tucker & Johnson, 1989). Close and extended family members may be more problematic than other sources of support for some parents.

Other researchers have pointed out that although a great deal of research has identified an association between lots of social support, competent parenting, and positive child outcomes, little is known about how this occurs or how social support affects parents in terms of their interactions with their children. Some researchers have suggested that social support may buffer or protect parents from stressful situations and improve their sense of well-being and, as a result, enhance their parenting interactions (Crnic, Greenberg, et al., 1983; Melson, Hsu, & Ladd, 1993; Roberts, 1989). It is also possible that when parents engage in more positive relationships with others it has a direct effect on their children who are also involved in these engagements as opposed to being isolated from such opportunities.

**Figure 8.1.**    Aspects of social support that enhance parents' sense of competence.

In one prospective study, when measures indicated that a mother experienced a lack of social support during pregnancy, this predicted the presence of maternal depression after birth, indicating a possible causal relationship between lack of social support and the psychological functioning of new mothers. This suggests that social support affects the functioning of parents, which, in turn, influences their interactions with their infants and young children (Priel & Besser, 2002).

## Personal Characteristics of Parents and Social Support

Other researchers have suggested that psychological characteristics such as having a sense of personal self-confidence, locus of control, and personal initiative can influence the use of social support systems (Cochran, 1990). For example, Dunn and colleagues (2001) found that mothers who were more isolated tended to have an internal locus of control and a coping or defensive style of using escape–avoidance strategies. In a study of mothers in a particular neighborhood, in which one group was identified as neglectful and a control group, researchers found that the mothers in the neglectful group described the people in the neighborhood as less supportive and friendly than the control group mothers. However, parents in this neglectful group were found to be less helpful to others than were the control parents, and this difficulty or lack of motivation could have cut the former group off from the community network (Polansky, Gaudin, Ammons, & Davis, 1985).

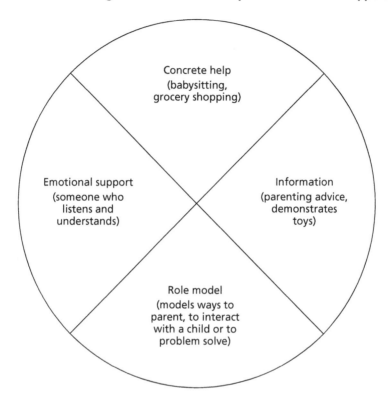

**Figure 8.2.**    Types of social support that enhance parents' sense of competence.

Consequently, both the direction and the mechanism by which social support influences parenting and child development are still unclear—primarily because of the dearth of longitudinal data needed to fully explain the nature and direction of its influence.

## THE IMPORTANCE OF SUPPORT DURING THE TRANSITION TO PARENTHOOD

Pregnancy and adjustment to new parenthood present major milestones and emotional upheavals that can lead to women having difficulties in adjusting to their infants. Some women quickly obtain a sense of competence in the maternal role and enjoy their identity as mothers. For other mothers, the transition is extremely difficult and they feel inadequate, anxious, resentful, or even out of control as they interact with their infants. These mothers may be experiencing lack of partner support or support from friends and extended family or the resurfacing of memories of difficult experiences of being parented themselves. They may also have given birth to a premature child with a disability or an infant with a difficult temperament. Also, early experiences of comforting their infants, getting their infants into a sleeping and feeding routine, managing the caretaking tasks of bathing, changing, and feeding and perceiving that they can "understand" their infants and read their cues can contribute to parents' sense of competence. A parent who feels out of control in these situations from very early in her baby's life may experience mounting feelings of helplessness and incompetence as a parent. Such a parent may also form negative views or attributions of her infant that can prove difficult to change later (Mercer & Ferketich, 1995; Walker, Crain, & Thompson, 1986; Williams et al., 1987). Given the significance of the early months after a baby is born for parental sense of competence, interventions provided at that time may be particularly helpful. Interventions can provide much-needed support during both the prenatal and postnatal periods. Both have been shown to be critical periods in which a sense of parental competence develops or can fail to develop, and may influence ongoing relationships between mother and baby.

## Prenatal Period

Although it is critically important to support parent to enhance their early interactions with infants, support provided in the prenatal period can also help to get the parent–infant relationship off to a good start. Traditionally, prenatal classes have primarily been about prenatal nutrition, obstetric care, and the birth process; however, recent evidence points to the fact that emotional challenges experienced by a mother during her pregnancy can affect a child's and family's outcomes, as well. For example, some of the child attributions that occur during this time can become powerful influences on later caregiving behavior (Aber, Belsky, Slade, & Crnic, 1999; Slade, Belsky, Aber, & Phelps, 1999). The tasks of pregnancy can be overwhelming and the mother may feel immense anxiety about the health of her baby, ambivalence about the new responsibility she faces, and anger over what she perceives as a lack of support and understanding from those around her. These feelings can be exacerbated if the mother has few supportive people in her life or if the baby was unplanned and unwanted (Cohen & Slade, 2000). During this period a woman must begin to see herself as a mother who will be able to care for and nurture her baby. For the mother with good experiences as a child, an identification with her own mother can occur without conflict; but for mothers with very negative experiences of rejection or maternal unavailability, this process may be difficult if not impossible and can result in rejection of the fetus and extreme emotional withdrawal from her baby before the baby's birth (Slade & Cohen, 1996).

Support groups provided during the prenatal period that encourage mothers to share their feelings and to discuss their impending roles can be extremely helpful in preparing mothers for having a more nurturing relationship with their infants and as a consequence having a greater sense of parenting competence.

Whenever possible, it is also important to provide opportunities for the baby's father to talk with other fathers about his experience of the pregnancy. Fathers may also have to deal with the triggering of memories of their early experiences of being parented. As well they may experience their partner as temporarily withdrawing from them as she focuses her thoughts and energy on the pregnancy and her baby's birth.

Such groups provide information if requested, but also focus on giving parents an opportunity and encouragement to share their emotional reactions to the pregnancy, and any ambivalence they may have about their new roles. Any negative attributions of the baby are reframed or phrased in a different way, and parents are encouraged to imagine their baby and his thoughts and feelings as he comes into the world. This can balance parents' anxiety, give them a sense of excited anticipation, and provide them with an early opportunity for developing self-reflectivity and the capacity to empathize with their infants. The support of other parents can be invaluable, especially for parents with few other supports who are feeling alone and isolated. During the groups, parents who seem particularly distressed or whose relationship appears to be significantly stressed or conflictual should be offered couple or individual counseling.

## Postnatal Period

As discussed previously, it is very important to provide parents with support during the postnatal period so that they can develop an early sense of understanding their baby and being capable of providing the care he needs. Parents will differ in terms of the ways they like to be offered this support. Many parents prefer to be visited in the home so that they do not have to take their baby out of the house and disturb the baby's routine. Other parents prefer to attend a parenting group where they can have the support of other parents and share experiences with them. Some parents want information and have many questions they want answered. They may be very ready for learning more about how to breast-feed or formula feed and when to introduce solids. They may want to learn about bathing their baby and establishing a routine for him. Other parents may want to talk about their concerns and feelings about becoming a parent and how it may be affecting their relationship with their partner or an older child in the family. Sharing these feelings may be critical to help individuals resolve issues around adjusting to their role as parents.

All parents will welcome discussing how to read their infants' cues and learning about how to help their infant fall asleep and to sleep during the night. Some parents with children with special needs or with infants who are very irritable or colicky will need information about how to interact with them. During these early days of an infant's life, public health nurses can be particularly helpful because of their knowledge and experience with breast-feeding and the physical needs of baby and mother.

In summary, what is most important is that parents receive early support and information so that they can feel successful as parents and begin to establish a sense of parenting competence. It is important to provide this information as early as possible to establish a foundation for a relaxed and secure relationship with their baby.

## INTERVENTIONS TO SUPPORT COMPETENCE

For parents who have low self-esteem from earlier experiences, it is important to point out and emphasize the positives in their caregiving as well as in their children's development. Some parents may feel helpless and out of control, and acknowledging things that are working well in their interactions with their children can be very encouraging.

## Emphasizing Parents' Strengths

If the intervention is being provided in an early intervention center, having participants suggest programs can be very useful in order to ensure that the programs will be well received. Also, groups that provide opportunities for a parent to show a special skill to other parents can be very helpful in order to enhance their sense of competence. Examples could be a community kitchen at which parents share recipes from their own culture and also cook and share a nourishing meal together. Another is the Mother Goose program during which parents are provided the support to share rhymes, finger plays, and interactive lap games with their infants and young children and with other parents in the group. This program can boost parents' sense of parenting competence by enhancing the feeling of connection a parent feels for her baby. (See Chapter 10 for further description of this program). Classes on toy making, bead or jewelry making, knitting, sewing, or crocheting, computer skills, ethnic dancing, and classes on child development and parenting skills can all be helpful, particularly when they are selected and organized by the parents themselves. Parents may also be interested in working in their community to develop a community garden, to improve community safety, or to volunteer in a child care room. These experiences can enhance feelings of self-esteem that can carry over into a sense of parenting competence. They may also provide parents with experiences that can be helpful if they are seeking employment at some time. Clearly, the way in which these programs are provided is essential and parents need to feel a sense of respect and understanding from all of the service providers with whom they come in contact, whether in the home or center, individually or in groups.

## Brief Solution-Focused Therapies

In brief solution-focused therapies, the parent brings a problem concerning their child and is helped to find a solution to it with the support of the service provider. Initially, the parent is encouraged to identify how she would like the situation to change, to identify any strategies that have worked in the past, to think about additional strategies, and then to choose a solution to try during the next week. Sometimes calming parents down and helping them to deliberate about the problem can be helpful in itself. The emphasis is on encouraging the parents to take control of their situation with their children so they can regain a sense of competence (Miller, Hubble, & Duncan, 1996). This approach can work for some parents but be rejected by others who want to be given information and a more expert type of approach.

For example, some parents may have been given suggestions by a number of professionals and relatives about what to do to overcome a parenting problem that continues to get worse. One woman who attended a parenting group conducted by the authors continued to complain in spite of a number of parenting strategies and approaches being suggested, so an individual session was offered. Using a brief solution approach, rather than giving more suggestions, the young mother was asked to remember things that she had found that did work and to think about how she would like her child to be. Surprisingly, with support she was able to remember that her child seemed to do better when she spent some time alone with him and if she provided more structure and routines for him. The process of talking about these strategies gave this mother a sense of the possibility of success and a belief that indeed she could "control" him by being firmer and more available to him.

## Parenting Classes

A variety of classes for parents that provide information about interactions with their infants and young children and enhance their sense of support from other parents can be provided. Some examples are outlined next.

*First-Time Fathers Class*     A class for first-time fathers can give them an opportunity to ask questions about caring for their baby and to express any concerns they may be experiencing in adjusting to their new baby and their new role as a parent. Although for a mother, the birth of a baby brings a number of physiological, psychological, and social changes, it can also present a number of challenges to fathers. Many parents express a drop in marital satisfaction after the birth of a baby and in extreme cases, relationships may actually break down in the early months after the baby's birth. Men may experience feelings of being displaced by the baby and may find it hard to find a new place in the family, especially if the mother is breast-feeding and does not encourage him to share in the baby care. Some men may feel too anxious or nervous to become involved in their baby's care. Group support to help new fathers to express these feelings and information on how to care for the new baby and deal with challenges can help considerably with fathers' transition to parenthood. A group may also identify fathers who need further counseling, either individually or with their partner.

*First-Time Mothers Class*     A group for new mothers in which they can ask questions about how to care for their baby and about settling into their role as mothers is very important. Topics that may arise include feeding issues, getting baby to sleep, reading the baby's cues and learning how to respond to her. Information about birth control and physical care for the mother may be provided. Mothers should be encouraged, as well, to discuss how they feel about being a mother with their new baby. Some first-time mothers may feel overwhelmed. Those with other children may find it challenging to cope with more than one child, especially if the older child or children are feeling confused or jealous and demanding extra attention. Some mothers may be suffering from postpartum depression, and such a group may be helpful in identifying them as needing extra counseling.

*Groups for Parents of Older Infants and Children*     Parents need help at every stage, not just the newborn period. Parents face challenges with young children at each new stage of development. Here is just one suggestion of how a group could be divided into three age groups: 1) infancy (3 months–14 months), 2) toddlers (15 months–30 months), and 3) preschoolers (30 months–5 years).

Each group can talk about the issues that occur at these ages and information can be provided about how to encourage expected developmental capacities. As concerns arise with the children's emerging individuation or difficulties occur within such areas as feeding, sleeping, toileting, separation, parents can be helped to deal with them before they get out of hand and more serious difficulties develop. Again, meeting parents with children of a similar age may help them find friends and strengthen their support systems.

***Groups Targeted at Specific Issues***    Groups of parents of children with identified difficulties such as aggression and behavior problems or developmental delays can be formed to give the parents support. For parents of children with either an identified biological risk; established disability; or social, emotional, or behavioral difficulties, the impact can be enormous and can result in deep feelings of guilt, lack of self-efficacy as a parent, and isolation. Isolation may occur because of the medical interventions that medically fragile infants and young children face, and because parents sometimes feel shame about having an acting-out or "damaged" child. Consequently parent groups can provide an opportunity to get information, express emotional issues, and help build a natural support system. Connecting parents with other families who have already been through many of the dilemmas and issues that they are facing can provide an invaluable perspective for parents who may be new to the issues.

A variety of other groups could also be developed on such topics as

- Encouraging self-esteem

- Encouraging language and communication

- Dealing with discipline

- Getting the preschooler ready for school

- Dealing with fears and separation anxiety

- Aggression and behavior problems in preschoolers

- Understanding temperament

- Helping your child play with other children

- Sibling rivalry

- Getting your baby to sleep through the night

- Feeding problems and ways to deal with them

These workshops could be provided if they are topics that seem to arise in general discussions with parents or that are asked for by parents. In these workshops and in other parenting groups, a combination of providing information; answering parents' questions; and encouraging parents to share their thoughts, feelings, and ideas with each other can enhance a sense of parenting competence and encourage parents to find a system of support amongst other parents.

In addition, some programs focusing on specific issues include The Family Matters Program and the Learning About Myself psychoeducational group. The Family Matters Program was a research-based program with five primary goals:

1.   To recognize the expertise of parents

2.   To exchange information about parenting

3.   To encourage and support parent–child activities

4. To exchange informal support such as baby sitting, advice, and emotional support

5. To support advocacy on the part of parents for their children

The program was provided to parents with 3-year-old children living in 10 different neighborhoods (Cochran, 1991). Home visiting was included. The families were compared with a comparison group of 128 families living in other neighborhoods. Social support networks were positively affected by the program and were associated with positive changes in parenting activities and attitudes. The results indicate that in agencies that provide parenting programs, efforts to organize various types of informal support between parents of infants and young children may be helpful in enhancing parenting behavior.

The Learning About Myself psychoeducational group meets for 12 weeks and has been used with parents who are at-risk for abusing their children (Rickard, 1998). Parents are taught to be more assertive, explore and make better choices, and improve their self-esteem. The emphasis on self-esteem, self-image, and social relationship skills is important. Group exercises and content include hands-on activities, games, and role play, and positive affirmations are provided each week. Parents are helped to explore their hopes and dreams, to have fun, and to learn about budgeting in a fun way. Parents have shown improved behaviors, and many parents made new friends.

## Interventions Focused on Enhancing the Social Supports of Parents

Because, as discussed earlier in this chapter, a strong relationship exists between parents' support systems, their sense of competence, and parenting behaviors, efforts made to enhance parents' supports can be helpful. One way, as discussed previously, can be to provide groups so parents can find supports and form friendships with other parents. In evaluating parenting groups, many parents identify meeting with other parents and their support as one of the most helpful aspects of their experience. Sometimes referrals can be made to drop-in centers or programs slightly outside of the neighborhood. If a mother seems hesitant about attending these programs, offering to accompany her the first few times may help her overcome her anxiety and to feel more comfortable. Agencies may be part of a network of other services and the network may share responsibility for providing a range of programs. For immigrant families, referral to various ethnic organizations and to English as a second language classes may also be helpful.

Sitting down with parents and drawing diagrams like the ones depicted in Figures 8.1 and 8.2 and discussing how helpful they find each component (i.e., type of support) to be may help them identify the amount and quality of the supports that they have and parts of the system where they need more support and can help the service provider understand how supported or isolated parents are. Also, the way parents talk about their support systems may give the service provider some ideas about how the parent feels about herself and others and can lead to a discussion of ways to increase support. Sometimes parents may identify that people in their "support" network stress them out. Perhaps they find people to be too intrusive, insistent on giving unsolicited advice, or instead are always wanting help themselves. Talking with parents about these issues and supporting them to find ways to deal with them can be very helpful and can potentially alleviate a great deal of stress. It may also help to identify people who can help with pragmatic issues, provide emotional support, and can be contacted when information on parenting or other types of support are needed. Sometimes it may become clear through this discussion that a mother is isolated because she cannot trust people, or perhaps because she feels it is too dangerous in her neighborhood to be involved outside her home. Information such as this can allow the service provider to understand the importance of factors outside of the parent–child interaction and the family circle that are affecting a particular parent.

Sometimes parents may feel isolated because they find it difficult to interact with others or lack communication and listening skills. In this case, sessions can provide a model of how to communicate and how to listen and engage in two-way conversations. Some of the skills that can be demonstrated and modeled include maintaining eye contact and paying attention to cues. Having these skills will increase the parents' capacity to make friends and enhance their feelings of self-efficacy.

## Family Counseling

Through the information-gathering process, it may become clear to service providers that a mother and her partner or the extended family are having difficulty coping with parenting issues and the care of the baby in a cooperative and helpful way. In such a case, a few sessions may help to clarify the problems and encourage the family members to find a solution together. Although family therapy is likely to be beyond the expertise of many of those working in early intervention programs, sessions in which parents' disagreements over discipline or other issues are discussed may give family members a chance to problem-solve together to find a common ground or solution. If there are two parents present, having them discuss their experiences of being parented and the kind of characteristics they want their child to have can open up discussion as to how best to parent their child in order for him to develop the qualities they both want to see develop. This can be challenging if parents remain very rigid about their ideas, but common ground can usually be found, especially if parents are informed about the most useful ways to develop the characteristics they would like to see in their child. Because positive family supports can enhance parents' interactions with their children, strategies to foster these relationships and to model problem-solving strategies can be very helpful. Having parents attend parenting groups together can be another way to encourage them to support one another in parenting their children.

## Crisis Intervention

Supporting a parent if a crisis arises can enhance his sense of competence and of having support. The very fact that someone is there to help and cares enough to be there may give the parent a new perspective on his sense of self worth. Because a crisis situation is so emotionally charged and relevant to the parent, discussing how to solve it will often make the discussion extremely meaningful to the parent. The details from the crisis situation and ways to avoid it happening again can be discussed later. As Linehan (1993) pointed out, the period immediately following a crisis or a time of great chaos is often a time that the client is able to gain insight in a different way. She suggested that the client is able to "grasp the whole picture instead of only parts . . . feeling the right choice in a dilemma, when the feeling comes from deep within rather than from a current emotional state" (p. 215). She also pointed out that the client may be in a state she called "wise mind," or one in which she has integrated the logical or rational mind with the emotional mind, similar to what has been called *intuition*. This kind of clarity of thinking helps parents understand that they can have an important influence on their situations and what happens to them.

## ENCOURAGING A SENSE OF COMPETENCE: CASE-STUDY FAMILIES

### Mark's Family

Joan and Michael's needs were somewhat different from those of many multi-risk families because they both experienced a great deal of success in their working situations and had adequate supports from friends and extended family. They also had sufficient income to be able to seek out and pay for services for their children.

When they referred themselves for services, however, they felt incompetent in their parenting roles. In fact, it was a time of great crisis for them because Mark had been expelled from school for being aggressive and unmanageable and they were obviously having extraordinary difficulty coping with what had happened. This sense of powerlessness in helping Mark prompted their referral of their son and allowed them to focus on the causes of his behavior and to problem-solve together about how to deal with it. Joan's realization of how she had been reacting to Mark's sadness and how this affected him was difficult but it did enable her to take control of her own behavior so she was able to provide the nurturance that he needed. Michael was supported to provide consistent structure and discipline, which empowered him to behave in a way that felt good for him. Providing information on Mark's difficulties and enabling his parents to find resources and supports in the community were all helpful in reestablishing a sense of parenting competence. Responding on a few occasions when a crisis arose for Mark in his school placement, and supporting the parents in a school meeting, while providing relevant developmental information about his needs encouraged his parents to continue their advocacy for him.

### Nina's Family

Because Nina had limited self-reflectivity at the beginning of the intervention period, she also had very little concept of her own contribution to her children's difficulties. She had very little trust in others or in herself that she could affect change in her situation. Initially, the most important intervention was to stabilize her situation and ensure safety for her and her children. Following that, efforts were made to help Nina begin to understand her children and her own influence on them. It was equally important throughout the interventions to provide Nina, whenever possible, with acknowledgement of improvements in interactions with her children, growth in her own competence, and understanding of how difficult her journey was.

As her efforts to improve her interactions with her children resulted in their enhanced behavior at home and school, Nina experienced pride and satisfaction in her achievements. She participated in a variety of parenting groups and took a leadership role in a group formed to advocate against abuse. She benefited from teaching beadwork to other parents. Perhaps she felt most accomplishment over her role of supporting other participants in AA and in her success when she returned to school. Reaching out in concrete ways when Nina was experiencing strong emotions of anger, anxiety, and despair made the interventions particularly powerful and relevant to her. These gains happened slowly over an extended period of time but gradually built in Nina a strong sense of personal efficacy.

Use of crisis intervention was also a powerful way to give Nina more control and a sense of competence. For example, when Nina was feeling extremely distraught and depressed and called her therapist, the therapist's ability to be present in that moment, acknowledge her feelings, and draw attention to events going on in the present helped bring a new insight and understanding for her. In one situation, Nina sat rocking and holding a doll after Paul had just started walking. Nina described how Paul "walked away from me and out of my life." Her therapist suggested that perhaps she felt more alone and abandoned by the baby she had held so close to her up to now. Immediately, Nina remembered that she had stopped taking her birth control pills and realized she was at risk for another pregnancy. It is probable that her baby's new mobility had triggered previous feelings and experiences of abandonment from her previously unconscious memories that were flooding her with emotions of despair and abandonment. The bonding with her therapist at a time of deep emotion, the clear picture of herself and her child that emerged as the scene was enacted, and the thoughtful discussion of her present reality gave Nina a sense of support as well as the opportunity to see her toddler in a new way and to take action about her more rational decision about not wanting more children.

## CONCLUSION

Interventionists can draw from a variety of ways to help parents have a greater sense of competence, both personally and in their parenting role. For some parents, just being listened to, visited on a regular basis, and having their strengths and positive behaviors noticed and acknowledged can go a long way toward helping them overcome a sense of helplessness and lack of control, and enable them to gain a greater sense of parenting competence. Other, more high-risk parents have few supports and have had difficult experiences of being parented themselves. These parents typically find it challenging to provide nurturance for their children; thus, more intensive individual and group interventions are necessary. Some of these approaches are discussed in this chapter, whereas more targeted and specialized interventions are provided in Section III.

## RESOURCES

For training in brief solution-focused approaches contact:

James Duvall
External Training
Hincks-Dellcrest Institute
114 Maitland Street
Toronto, Ontario M4Y 1E1
Canada
(416) 972-1935 ext. 3342
http://www.jduvall@hincksdellcrest.org

# PROVIDING INTERVENTIONS THAT MEET THE COMPLEX NEEDS OF MULTI-RISK FAMILIES

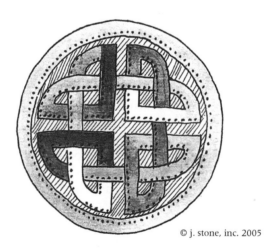

© j. stone, inc. 2005

*For every complex problem there is a solution that is simple, neat, and wrong.*

—H.L. Mencken

This section describes a number of intervention strategies that can be used to meet the needs of a variety of multi-risk parents, such as those who have unresolved loss and trauma, problems with emotion regulation, and difficulties with planning and problem-solving in all areas of their lives. These difficulties contribute to very complex situations and often chaotic home situations. In each chapter the case-study families from Chapter 4 are revisited to describe how these psychological characteristics were considered in tailoring interventions.

Chapter 9 describes the devastating effects of unresolved traumatic experiences and loss on individuals' physiological and psychological functioning. It details how trauma affects individuals at the time of the trauma and, for 10%–20% of individuals, long term. The particularly overwhelming effects when the trauma occurs in the early years are emphasized. Principles of treating parents with unresolved loss and trauma are provided and illustrated in the case-study examples. As well, evidence is given for the need for going through certain stages of intervention when treating various types of trauma.

Chapter 10 outlines the need for parents to provide responsive and sensitive interactions with children and suggests a number of interventions that have been shown to be effective in enhancing parent–child interactions. These are described as they pertain to various age groups of children, including infants, toddlers, and preschoolers; and for children who are typically developing and those whose development is compromised due to a variety of developmental delays or disorders.

Emotion regulation has been found to be crucial for an optimal developmental trajectory, and devastating effects can occur when it fails to develop. Lack of adequate emotion regulation can result in various types of psychopathology. Chapter 11 describes the importance of emotion regulation for parents and the major contributors to its development including genetic and biological influences, the caregiving environment, and the effects of attributions of self and others. The chapter then goes on to suggest ways in which these areas of influence could be used as targets of intervention, using a variety of strategies to enhance them.

Chapter 12 considers the important influence of parental attributions and parenting beliefs on parent–child interactions and on the development of children's self-images as a result. Attribution theory and attachment perspectives on the importance of these influences on parenting and more general parental functioning are discussed. Interventions for parents recommended from both perspectives are also described.

Because home visitors and other service providers so often find that parents do not follow through with recommendations and seem to have extraordinary difficulties with planning and problem solving in their lives, Chapter 13 considers the effect of these difficulties on overall functioning and on parenting. Using an approach that examines characteristics of coping strategies, the chapter describes a model that can be used to help parents to enhance their planning and problem solving and to overcome some of the difficulties that may be contributing to their problems with these abilities.

## CHAPTER 9

# Helping Parents Who Have Unresolved Loss and Trauma

Everyone experiences a certain level of stress. Stress can result from negative events as well as from positive experiences such as moving, getting a new job, or getting married. Stress is accompanied by physiological responses. Recovery usually occurs through a variety of modulating strategies that can lead to coping (Selye, 1956; Shalev, 1996). When people are exposed to traumatic stress or experiences, however, recovery and coping may not occur and the stress reactions, both physical and psychological, may continue beyond the event.

## DEFINITION AND INCIDENCE

Although trauma and its effects have been around since the dawn of humankind, the effects of trauma on individuals' lives were largely ignored or dismissed until the 1970s. At that time, a number of researchers identified posttraumatic stress disorder (PTSD) as a diagnostic classification and recognized that not only war veterans were affected but also children, women, and men who had been exposed to a variety of other traumas such as rape, abuse, and other types of violence (van der Kolk, McFarlane, & van der Hart, 1996). Since the 1980s there has been an explosion of research on the biological and psychological effects of trauma. Unfortunately, millions of children and adults are exposed to traumatic events that can lead to long-term consequences. According to Perry and colleagues, the number of children in the United States exposed to trauma each year exceeds 4 million (Perry, 1994; Perry, Pollard, Blakley, Baker, & Vigilante, 1995).

Events can be traumatic to an individual because of a number of characteristics. Trauma typically is related to an encounter with death, such as a near loss of one's own life or the actual death of someone close to a person. Traumatic events include a wide range of situations such as physical and sexual abuse or rape; exposure to or experience of violence in the home or community; car accidents; manmade disasters such as kidnapping, combat, terrorism, torture, or imprisonment in war or civil unrest and uprising; and natural disasters such as floods, hurricanes, and fires. Some of these traumas are single events, whereas others are ongoing over several years.

Another important element that makes an event traumatic is how threatened, overwhelmed, and helpless an individual feels at the time of its occurrence. In other words, although the reality of the event is significant, the meaning it holds for the person is more important in determining the level of trauma and how ongoing the effects will be (van der Kolk & McFarlane, 1996). The significance of the trauma can be related to a history of previous traumatic events, especially those experienced in childhood that may not even be remembered.

It is also important to point out that in childhood, although dramatic incidents such as abuse are most obviously traumatic, some situations that most people would not view as extreme can be traumatizing for young children, especially if their biological makeup makes them more susceptible. Some types of trauma falling into this category may include various levels of neglect and chronic failure to respond to and nurture a child when he is distressed or in pain. Gunnar (1998), for example, found that Romanian infants in orphanages, unlike children raised by nurturing parents, showed increased levels of the stress hormone cortisol throughout the day. As well, when a child has experienced the loss of an attachment figure and the overwhelming fear and feelings of helplessness that may accompany this loss, this can be extremely traumatic if the child is left unsupported. Even separation and divorce, hospitalization, or extended separations from parents or loved ones can be traumatic events for people, especially children (Gunnar & Barr, 1998; LeDoux, 1996; Terr, 1991, 1994). Other researchers have talked about the significance of the "loss of the assumptive world" as a result of trauma, which implies the shattering of the belief in the world as good, fair, and also predictable (Janoff-Bulman, 1992; Kauffman, 2002a, p. 2).

Most people who are exposed to trauma experience at least some posttraumatic stress or stress reactions, psychological and physical, which persist for some time following the event. These symptoms may include intrusive thoughts and nightmares about what has happened. For most people, these thoughts and experiences are gradually integrated and stored as accessible memories. For approximately 10%–20% of trauma victims, however, the symptoms persist for more than a month and they suffer from PTSD, with symptoms that include flashbacks, chronic hyperarousal, and impairment of function. These symptoms often lead to difficulties in a number of areas of functioning at work and home. For people with PTSD, integration of memories into a personal narrative of the past fails to occur, and the memories become dissociated and exist independent of previous memories. As a consequence, the sensations and emotions belonging to the event continue to be replayed, and stronger and stronger physiological and emotional reactions occur, resulting in constant retraumatization (van der Kolk & McFarlane, 1996). In other words, the event overwhelms people with PTSD, and the intrusive and persistent memories; psychiatric symptoms such as anxiety and panic disorders, dissociation, and psychological and behavior difficulties; and various somatic disorders that result, disable them and affect their lives. People with PTSD may develop various types of psychopathology including anxiety disorders, phobias, bipolar disorder, borderline personality disorder (BPD), depression, and a variety of physical illnesses such as fibromyalgia or chronic fatigue syndrome (Gunderson & Sabo, 1993; Scaer, 2001; van der Kolk & Fisler, 1994).

Exactly why some individuals suffer these lifelong sequelae following trauma whereas others do not is unclear, but it is hypothesized to be related to several factors: 1) the meaning of the event to the individual, 2) the severity and chronicity of the event, 3) predisposing characteristics of the individual such as level of emotion regulation and other genetic predispositions, 4) previous experiences of trauma or loss, 5) how young the child was at the time of the trauma, and 6) the support system available to the individual following the trauma.

When trauma occurs in young children, it affects the development and organization of the brain and can result in a chronic state of physiological hyperarousal and dissociative-related reactions such as anxiety, depression, withdrawal, helplessness, and dissociation (Perry, 2001). In early childhood, certain areas of the brain that store verbal memories are immature, such as the hippocampus and its connections to the neocortex, whereas the amygdala, which stores emotional and sensorimotor memories, develops much earlier. As a result of this immaturity of these areas of the brain in early childhood and the earlier development of the amygdala, rather than having verbal recall, an infant or very young child who has experienced trauma stores memories of the intense feelings, images, movements, reenactments, and sensory impressions of the smells, sounds, and sights present at the time of the trauma (Howe & Courage, 1993). This means it is difficult to integrate these memories into the other memory systems that are under the child's cortical control and that they can continue to be triggered under circumstances that are in some way reminiscent of the original trauma. Gaensbauer (2002) discussed examples of how early memories that were established in the preverbal stage of painful medical procedures, traffic accidents, and other traumas can be played out by the child dramatically in play therapy much later. This indicates that even these very early memories form internal representations of the traumatic events that can last over long periods of time. As a result of certain early experiences and memories, a child may act in an all-or-nothing fashion, displaying acts of aggression or extreme psychological withdrawal (Pynoos, Steinberg, & Goenjian, 1996).

## TRAUMA AND ITS EFFECTS ON THE INDIVIDUAL

Current research suggests that trauma affects people at multiple levels of functioning. In order to understand the sequelae of trauma, it is important to recognize that there are two types of effects: those that happen when the trauma occurs, and those that continue after the trauma.

### Effects at the Time of the Trauma

When trauma actually takes place, a reaction occurs in an individual's sympathetic nervous system similar to an alarm sounding, which results in increased heart rate, blood pressure, respiration, muscle tone, and hypervigilance. Trauma reactions also include the arousal of many neurotransmitter systems. Stress-responsive neurohormones such as epinephrine and norepinephrine from the adrenal medulla are also released, as are serotonin, endorphins, opioids, and stress hormones of the hypothalamic-pituitary-amygdala axis (HPA) such as cortisol (Scaer, 2001; van der Kolk, 2003). On the one hand, the secretion of endorphins and opioids may blunt an individual's emotional reaction to the trauma and also interfere with his capacity to store memories of it. On the other hand, the release of norepinephrine can cause excessive perceptual awareness and, as a result, memories of the specific event are excessively consolidated and reoccur later in panic attacks. These

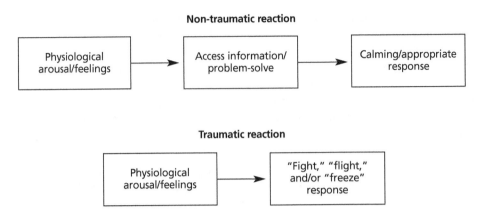

**Figure 9.1.** Steps related to actions taken during non-traumatic versus traumatic reactions.

physiological reactions can cause reactions termed *fight* (i.e., physiological over-arousal and ignoring of information), *flight* (i.e., dissociation if real running away is not possible) and/or *freeze* (i.e., problems with being able to move or do anything). In some cases the individual may be able to think about what is going on and devise strategies to deal with the situation or escape from it, in which case information-processing mechanisms will be activated (see Figure 9.1).

Adinah is lying alone in bed, trying to fall asleep while her husband is out of town. She suddenly hears a noise downstairs that sounds like footsteps. Her heart beats rapidly; her palms become sweaty; and she breathes heavily, feeling dizzy and paralyzed, unable to move. Gradually, she calms down a little, remembering that the phone is close. She decides to stay in bed, ready to telephone 911 if necessary. As this happens, her heart rate lessens and she feels somewhat calmer and more in control.

In this example, Adinah was able to move into a problem-solving mode, which helped calm some of the physiological reactions and gave her some sense of control. If the incident had resulted in an assault of some kind, however, the course of reactions could have been very different, resulting in a fight, flight, or freeze reaction without the transition into a problem-solving mode (Perry et al., 1995).

In order to understand the ongoing psychobiological effects of trauma, it is critical to understand how the brain and body process, remember, and in some instances, perpetuate traumatic reactions. Memory stores, records, and allows for recall of the information from the internal and external environment, and experiences are processed at an emotional, sensory, perceptual, and cognitive level. Memory involves three processes:

1. Encoding (like typing on a computer)

2. Storage (when the document is saved)

3. Retrieval (when the file is reopened)

Memory is categorized into two types that are stored in different parts of the brain: short-term memory, including items remembered briefly but lost quickly such as telephone numbers and shopping lists; and long-term memory, including material that has been permanently stored. Both short- and long- term memory can be explicit (sometimes called *declarative*) or implicit (sometimes called *procedural*). Explicit memory is conscious and depends on language and step-by-step narration (e.g., baking with a new recipe, learning a poem). It is stored in the frontal lobe and hippocampus, thus allowing the most important cognitive abilities of the brain to be involved, such as working memory and abstract reasoning. Implicit memory is unconscious. It bypasses language and stores learned procedures and behaviors (e.g., riding a bike or playing tennis). Implicit memory also contains the sensory and emotional imprints of certain events and is associated with particular areas of the central nervous system and the amygdala, which is part of the limbic system or the emotional center of the brain (Crittenden, Lang, Claussen, & Partridge, 2000; Squire, 1994). Because the amygdala is operating even in infancy and is responsible for the memory of movements, body experiences, and feelings, whereas the hippocampus that is responsible for explicit memories does not operate until later, the memory of the events that occurred during early childhood may be more implicit or procedural and unconscious. This explains infantile amnesia or the inability to remember events before the age of 3 (Perner & Ruffman, 1995; Perry, 1997; Schore, 2003; Siegel, 1999) (see Figure 9.2).

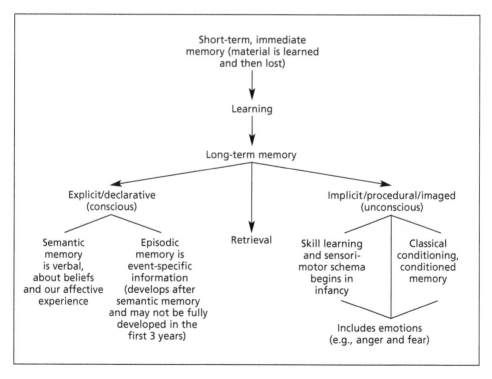

**Figure 9.2.** The tasks of short- and long-term memory systems.

Usually, stored memories are constantly reworked, and the mind reorganizes them and integrates them with new information. Memories are transformed into narratives or stories that we use to describe our lives to ourselves and to others to make our experiences of the world coherent (Schore, 2003; Siegel, 1999). In the recall of most events, the precise images of earlier experiences are not remembered. For individuals with PTSD, however, these thoughts or cognitions of the event are not available, and it is the emotions, images, sensations, and muscular reactions associated with the trauma that are imprinted on the mind and that continue to be re-experienced exactly as they were, without transformation, for months, years, or decades later (LeDoux, 1996; van der Kolk & van der Hart, 1991; van der Kolk & Fisler, 1995).

Because the frontal lobes responsible for cognitive functioning may not be operational at the time of the trauma, the memory may be implicit, or without words. It is now believed that subcortical regions of the brain such as the limbic system, the amygdala, and brain stem may produce emotions and sensations at the time of the trauma that contradict explicit or linguistic memory. In other words, the sensory, perceptual, and emotional experiences often override the cognitive in the registration of the trauma (van der Kolk, 1996b). In fact, certain areas of the brain responsible for storing explicit or declarative memory may cease to function or to put the experience into words. In some studies, Broca's area (responsible for language) and the hippocampus have been found to be smaller in clients with PTSD. However, it is not clear if this predated the trauma and contributed to the disorder or was caused by the bypassing of these parts of the brain during the constant re-experiencing of the original event (van der Kolk, 1994; Rauch, Shin, Wahlen, & Pitman, 1998). McEwen and colleagues have studied the biology of stress and have shown that marked degeneration of the dendrites in the hippocampus and a reduction in size and significant deficits in memory ability may occur as a result of excessive stress (McEwen & Sapolsky, 1995).

From the work of behaviorists such as Pavlov and Skinner, we also know that not only may the original stimulus get linked with the fear response and its physiological reactions but also related stimuli may cause the same physiological reactions. In other words, the traumatized person also becomes sensitized to a number of stimuli that in some way remind her of the traumatic event. In some individuals, the original traumatic memories are then retriggered by an increasing range of similar, conditioned sensory stimulations or stressful events in some way reminiscent of the original trauma. Consequently, if a rapist was wearing a red tie or running shoes when the rape occurred, these stimuli may retrigger memories in the victim later. Similarly, a young child who was constantly traumatized by being hit or yelled at when she spoke up may become panic stricken by being required to speak in public. According to LeDoux, this conditioned fear learning is "particularly resilient and may represent an indelible form of learning" (1996, p. 204). In addition, as a consequence of the initial reactions to the trauma, the person may experience frequent flashbacks and nightmares related to memories of the trauma that are not describable or consciously controllable. Through the use of various defense mechanisms, the person may not even realize that the feelings and actions are from the past and are not associated with what is currently occurring. In other words, the event cannot be put behind him or processed, modified, and integrated into a coherent whole with the rest of his life story. Instead, the memories of the event are dissociated and kept independent from other memories and current experiences.

## Ongoing Effects of Trauma

For individuals who suffer from the effects of chronic trauma or PTSD, stress can be chronic and the negative impact on the brain can be devastating. These effects can cause significant physical and mental health problems and a number of symptoms, which are described next.

*The Intrusion of Traumatic Memories*    Traumatic memories continue to intrude in the form of flashbacks, nightmares, sensorimotor reexperiencing, and intense emotions. These procedural or implicit memories over time become activated by a wider and wider range of cues and triggers. Consequently, someone who has been abused may have traumatic memories triggered by someone yelling, or a person who has been in an accident can experience reactivation of the memories of the accident by the screeching of brakes. This hyperalertness to certain perceptions leads to lack of attention to other stimulation that might be calming and pleasurable for the person.

Because of the re-experiencing of trauma, individuals may be *restless, hypervigilant, and easily scared.* Individuals may perceive the world as increasingly dangerous and frightening, and this can cause them to withdraw from activities and to overprotect their children. This can limit the opportunity for meaningful attachments to others.

*Out-of-Control Actions*    Sometimes actions will be triggered that are *totally out of rational control* that can result in abuse or violence. In other words, a parent may abuse a child without any thoughts about doing so before the trigger occurs.

*Chronic Stress*    The *chronic stress* that occurs from the continual retriggering of the event affects the immediate and ongoing adaptation of the nervous system, resulting in chronic changes in neurochemistry. On the one hand, increased concentration of glucocorticoids in the hippocampus results in a more sensitive and easily stimulated HPA axis and the secretion of endogenous opioids (Perry et al., 1995; Yehuda, 1998). Also, increased levels of catecholamines result in the sympathetic nervous system showing increased activity. Anxiety or panic attacks and obsessional preoccupations are common. These reactions all occur outside of rational control and, consequently, they cannot be contained. In addition, decreased levels of serotonin may occur as a result of trauma that can cause sleep disturbances, hyperirritability, arousal, and attention to irrelevant cues. When trauma is repeated over time, a condition called *hypocortisolism* (i.e., decreased levels of cortisol) may occur that blunts physiological stress reactivity to new stresses (Heim & Nemeroff, 2001; Teicher, 2002).

*Gradual Withdrawal from Everyday Activities*    Individuals with PTSD may *gradually withdraw and detach from everyday activities* in order to avoid further emotional arousal or feelings of irritability and distress. This withdrawal may in turn lead to changes in an individual's central nervous system, causing, for example, feelings of numbness and a lack of responsiveness to what is going on around her. This can lead to feelings of emptiness, abandonment, and betrayal, and may mean that the individual cannot enjoy ordinary events. Furthermore, the individual may lack the use of emotions as cues or thoughts to decide on when and how to take action (Fonagy, Steele, Steele, Moran, & Higgitt, 1991; Krystal, 1988). Some individuals may resort to the use of drugs and alcohol in order to overcome the painful memories. Others may avoid arousal through dissociation.

**Compulsive Exposure to Dangerous Situations**    Other trauma victims may *compulsively expose themselves to dangerous situations reminiscent of the trauma.* This may result in revictimization, self-cutting, eating disorders, risk taking and substance abuse, or the victimization of others. This tendency may appear to be paradoxical; however the repetition of previous traumas and the arousal that results may be a way to avoid some of the feelings of emptiness, abandonment, and betrayal that can follow trauma. The familiar experiences may create a sense of sameness and cohesiveness with the person's sense of self and thus, a feeling of security. Or the victim may become deeply attached to the abuser and identify with his behavior or believe she deserves the results of this dangerous behavior because she is only good enough for this kind of experience (Liotti, 2004). When an individual engages in self-abuse, such as cutting, the opioids that are released may provide the person with the pleasant feelings of numbness that may have protected her at the time of trauma and blunt the psychological pain she is currently experiencing (Rothschild, 2000; van der Kolk, 1996a).

**Altered Ability to Attend and Process Information**    Because the trauma affects the ability to attend to feelings and action patterns other than those related to the trauma, *the ability to attend to and process incoming information may be affected.* This is particularly significant if the person experiences multiple traumas and is constantly vigilant for certain signs of impending danger. It may also happen because a pattern of dissociating in the face of certain stimulation is occurring (van der Kolk & Fisler, 1994). *Dissociation* is believed to be a failure "in integrating memory, consciousness, and identity" (Liotti, 2004, p. 473). It can be seen as a sudden stopping of discussion, thought, or behavior when there is an intrusion of unintegrated memories and a lack of awareness of what is going on in the room or environment. Dissociation could also be shown as gazing into space and unresponsiveness to the interventionist or use of fragmented and incoherent comments that do not fit with what was being discussed. Sometimes a different voice may be used and the person sounds as if she is playing out another character.

**Loss of Trust in the World**    *The traumatized person will lose trust in the world as safe, and in her own and others' ability to protect her.* This biased view of the world often continues to influence how the world is perceived, what is remembered, and how the individual reacts. Because she has often experienced trauma at the hands of people in power, the traumatized person tends to cast subsequent encounters with people in terms of dominance, submission, and control. Consequently, intervention is often difficult and needs to address issues of trust, power, control, and safety.

**Alterations in Relationships**    Traumatized individuals typically have *problems with trusting others and in believing that they can be loved and respected.* Unfortunately, some people have a heightened or intensified trust in others and may deny any danger signs in them. Liotti (2004) has discussed the "drama triangle," which can be considered to be an internal working model formed in childhood out of early relationship experiences with parents and other caregivers, specifically of abuse, neglect, and/or hostile/helpless distortions in the caregiving interactions. He suggested that these unintegrated models of self and others, once formed, can continue to be played out in later relationships—including those developed with interventionists—and can create instability in how the person relates to others. He pointed out that sometimes a child feels like the victim of the caregiver who is seen as the persecutor; or he may perceive the caregiver as the persecutor and rescuer (when the caregiver does offer comforting) of the victim self. At other times, if the caregiver appears frightened or helpless, the child can feel like the persecutor or rescuer. In these ways the representations of both self and others remain unintegrated and can be played out, with the individual's perception of the interventionist changing rapidly from the victim who can become the target of hostility, the rescuer who can make everything better, or the persecutor who is responsible for the pain and symptoms.

*Poor Self-Perception*    A person who has been traumatized not only loses faith in the world but also in herself. Individuals who have been traumatized often *perceive themselves as weak, shameful, and unlovable.* An individual experiences a loss of a wholeness of self or a lack of integration of the parts of the self, so the person sometimes withdraws or exposes herself to crisis situations and at other times experiences intense rage or extreme despondence, often without any awareness of its origin. Sadly, their sense of competence may be shattered.

*Health Problems*    Trauma victims experience *a higher rate of illnesses,* probably because of actual pathophysiological changes that are associated with trauma. These may include fibromyalgia, endrocrinological abnormalities, hypertension, cardiovascular disease, and effects on the gastrointestinal system. Individuals who have experienced trauma often have an increased susceptibility to infection due to its impact on the immune system (Arnsten & Goldman-Rakic, 1998; Sapolsky, 1994). All of this results in a greater utilization of the health care system.

*Extreme Difficulties with Emotion Regulation*    Another significant result of trauma may be *extreme difficulties with emotion regulation.* Triggers may lead an individual to constantly re-experience the trauma and the flight, fight, or freeze reaction. Containing one's emotions—particularly intense rage, anxiety, or depression—may be extremely difficult. As mentioned before, the individual may withdraw in an effort to protect himself from constantly being overwhelmed by emotional reactions, or may act out in a way to avoid the sense of emptiness he experiences. Lack of ability to identify, name, and talk about emotions, called *alexithymia,* also makes emotional containment increasingly difficult (Fonagy, Steele, Steele, Moran, & Higgitt, 1991; Krystal, 1988).

## Types of Trauma Reactions

Although the symptoms that have been described are experienced by many trauma survivors, there are many differences in the number and severity of the symptoms depending on the person's history of trauma (Foa, Keane, & Friedman, 2000). Figure 9.3 illustrates the complexity of trauma categorizations and the influence these trauma categorizations have on intervention decisions. One of the major differences between trauma clients is whether they experienced a single traumatic event or repeated traumas. For those who have experienced repeated trauma, it is important to determine whether they had a stable upbringing and some resiliency was established or were never able to develop resilience. The Type 1 categorization (experiencing a single traumatic event) could apply to the person who was, for example, in a major accident, was raped, or was in a natural disaster such as a hurricane. Other people may have experienced repeated trauma (Type II). Even these experiences can vary significantly, from the person who can distinguish single traumas and address them separately (Type II-A) to others who may be so overwhelmed with multiple traumas that they cannot distinguish between them (Type II-B). As shown in Figure 9.3, differences exist even within this group of individuals. For example, some may seem to have had a "good enough" upbringing but then they experienced a trauma so intense and overwhelming that their previous resilience could not temporarily sustain them (Type II B-R) (e.g., Holocaust, 9/11, tsunami survivors). Still others may never have been able to develop resilience and continue to experience ongoing trauma (Type II-B [nR]) (Herman, 1992; Herman, Perry, & van der Kolk, 1989). Another category of clients is composed of those who have prolonged duress stress disorder (PDSD) symptoms, but no significant traumas can be identified (Rothschild, 2000). Their background, however, includes chronic, prolonged stress such as family violence or ongoing neglect. This "prolonged duress" takes its toll on the autonomic nervous system but does not reach the same level of trauma reaction as the others.

Clients from these different classifications may need different interventions. Usually for Type I and Type II-A, the therapeutic relationship is in the background

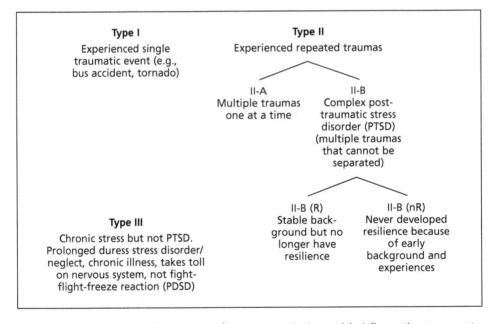

**Figure 9.3.** Schema illustrating the complexity of trauma categorizations and the influence these trauma categorizations have on intervention decisions. Adapted from THE BODY REMEMBERS: THE PSYCHOPHYSIOLOGY OF TRAUMA TREATMENT by Babette Rothschild. Copyright © 2000 by Babette Rothschild. Used by permission of W.W. Norton & Company, Inc.

and the need to work through the traumatic memories is most critical. With Type II-B, however, building resources will be crucial before directly addressing the trauma. With the client who has developed resilience, helping the client relink with their psychological resources that they had lost touch with may be most important. For those in the II-B (nR) and III (PDSD) or for parents with complex post-traumatic stress disorder, the therapeutic relationship and building the resources and resilience that were never there before will be crucial, and for these clients, the intervention often needs to be long term.

## An Example of a Type I Client

Mary had come from a family that she described as warm and loving. She fell in love with and married a man, Tom, who turned out to be abusive. Because they had a son together, Mary stayed with her husband, hoping he would change. Because of her own autonomous quality of attachment, her interactions with her child were sensitive and she was attuned to his cues. One terrifying night after an argument, Tom tried to stab Mary, inflicting some wounds, but she managed to run outside and escape to a shelter. After 3 months, Mary was still having flashbacks and nightmares about the event. She was concerned about her son, who was 2 years old at the time, and requested intervention. In this instance, the immediate need is for her to get necessary legal aid for the upcoming court case to gain custody of her son. After that, an emphasis on working through the memories is most important in order for her to be able to return to her previous level of functioning and her nurturing interactions with her son.

## An Example of a Type II-A Client

Mohammed had experienced a variety of traumas in his background. He had witnessed his father's sudden death from an accident. The family had also lost all of their possessions in a flood. He had been imprisoned and had fled as a political refugee, and most recently he had nearly lost his wife to a terrifying illness that had struck quickly. Mohammed had become depressed and reported nightmares about some of his previous trauma, especially being imprisoned. However, he did have warm memories of his early childhood, and had been successful in business before fleeing his native land. The most important emphasis of intervention for Mohammed needs to be on helping him to reestablish his high level of functioning and to support him in remembering and putting his repeated traumas into an integrated narrative of the past events.

## An Example of a Type II-B (R) Client

Kosta emigrated to Canada from the former Yugoslavia, where he experienced ongoing trauma, including the murder of family members, torture, and living in intolerable conditions. He reported that before the war he had been employed as a teacher, something he enjoyed very much. He also described a warm and supportive upbringing as a child. However, on arriving in Canada he found that his sleep was constantly interrupted with nightmares and flashbacks, and loud noises and people in uniform triggered his bad memories. Again, the intervention should center on retrieving memories, although establishing a trusting therapeutic relationship is also important because of Kosta's loss of trust in himself, his self-worth, and other people.

## An Example of a Type II-B (nR) Client

Nina, described first in Chapter 4, fits into the category II-B (nR), with multiple traumas and prolonged duress experienced during infancy and early childhood that prohibited her from developing early resilience. Multiple later traumatic experiences, such as her early marriage to a husband who kept her locked up and who totally controlled her, and attacks by her brother and later by a boyfriend, also contributed to the continual retriggering of her traumatic memories. Consequently, the therapeutic relationship and building of her resources and resilience is most critical in her intervention, although later in the therapy she should be helped to gain some insight into how her early experiences affected her in the present.

## An Example of a Type III Client (PDSD)

Joan, also discussed in Chapter 4, could not identify any significant abuse, loss, or other trauma during her childhood. During therapy, however, it became clear that her mother had been depressed, and Joan probably did not receive the calming, nurturing, and containment she had needed when she was upset. This contributed to her difficulty in containing her son, Mark's, sadness.

## Implications for Parenting

Given the wide-ranging effects of trauma and the particular vulnerability of children to these effects, efforts to prevent trauma in the early years and to treat it immediately if it does occur are crucial. It is also clear that when a parent experiences the symptoms of PTSD, it can make parenting extremely difficult, and the birth of an infant may trigger difficult emotional and physiological reactions. This is particularly true if the trauma was suffered during early childhood. Schechter (2004) studied mothers who reported histories of physical and sexual abuse and domestic violence and found that 59% met criteria for current PTSD and 90% met criteria for having had it at some time in their lives. These findings correlated with poor reflective functioning and negative attributions of their children. Also, when their infants cried, these mothers with PTSD were often triggered into re-experiencing their own helplessness during abuse because they were reminded of their own pain.

In considering the symptoms or personality changes that can result from trauma, it is clear how, without intervention, they can have a significant and ongoing effect on an individual's ability to parent. For example, the parent who is suffering from flashbacks or nightmares may have little energy left to provide the nurturing interactions an infant needs or the discipline, structure, and joint problem-solving experiences that a preschooler requires. Triggering may occur, causing the parent to exhibit frightening behavior such as yelling, threatening to leave, or hitting. The parent may be tired and irritable and lack patience to interact with the child, which may result in lack of affective involvement and little joy in interactions. Alternatively, she may be irritable, angry, anxious and hypervigilant. Because PTSD often promotes a tendency toward isolation and distrust of others, the parent may withdraw from people and the child may not have contact with other adults and children. The parent may have few support systems and may reject or fail to seek out services that could be helpful. If parents use substances, self-mutilate, or place themselves in dangerous situations in which they are revictimized, the child(ren) are adversely affected and can be placed at risk. Hypervigilance and lack of trust in the outside world may lead the parent to "overprotect" the child. If a parent has a toddler or preschooler, she may fail to allow the child to individuate, a necessary developmental step at that age. Parents who have depression or anxiety disorders may frequently appear frightened and will have difficulty regulating their own emotions, and they may find it intolerable to deal with their children's sadness, anger, anxiety, or fear. Also, the child's crying or yelling, disobedience, or even running off, can trigger excessive reactions that, in their extreme, can cause parental abuse or neglect and/or extreme withdrawal from the child. Without the ability to use problem solving or working memory at these times, a parent may also have little ability for self-reflectivity or empathy for others, including her child.

Moreover, as pointed out by Crittenden and colleagues (2000), parents tend to react without thinking and to rely on procedural memory in parenting interactions (Crittenden et al., 2000). When interactions during the parents' own early years included abuse and neglect, memories are likely to be triggered and thus, the parent then perpetuates the interactions, especially under stress. In some situations parents may fail to protect their children from various types of abuse by other people. As pointed out by Bugental and associates (1989, 2000), parents who have experienced trauma and abuse frequently cast their relationships and reactions to their children in terms of control issues. Consequently, they tend to see their children as controlling and themselves as powerless to do anything about their children's behavior, attributions that often result in abuse (Bugental, Blue, & Cruzcosa, 1989; Bugental et al., 2000).

Studies looking at parent–child interactions in terms of attachment used an experimental technique called the Strange Situation. The Strange Situation (SS) consists of eight 3-minute episodes in which a child is observed in a room with either a parent, a stranger, a stranger and parent, or totally alone. The episodes present the child with increasingly stressful situations that are intended to elicit attachment-related behaviors such as seeking proximity to the parent, crying, and wanting to be held and comforted (Ainsworth, Blehar, Waters, & Wall, 1978; Landy, 2002b). Three main categories were derived from the observations of these children: Secure, Insecure/Avoidant, and Insecure/Ambivalent/Resistant. Some researchers began to notice a group of infants with an established history of abuse and neglect whom they determined fitted none of these three categories of attachment and instead, exhibited unusual disorganized/disoriented behavior (Carlson, Cicchetti, Barnett, & Braunwald, 1989). Main and Solomon (1990) later identified these behaviors as falling into another pattern of attachment characterized by a breakdown of an organized strategy to deal with the stress elicited by the SS, called Disorganized/ Disoriented (D). During their reunion with their parents, these children often fell on the ground, appeared apprehensive, or covered their mouths. Some ran in circles, froze, or seemed to be in a trance-like state. A meta-analysis by van IJzendoorn, Schuengel and Bakermans-Kranenburg (1999) indicated that as many as 25% of infants may meet this classification in high-risk populations, and the percentage is much higher if the children have been abused. When mental representations of attachment relationships of parents whose children displayed these disorganized behaviors were explored with the Adult Attachment Interview (AAI), a meta-analysis found that approximately 53% were in a classification they identified as an Unresolved state of mind (van IJzendoorn et al., 1999). This classification was related to the adult's signs of disorientation and even dissociation in discussing traumatic events such as loss by death or physical or sexual abuse and to frightened and/or frightening parental behavior with their children (Main & Hesse, 1990).

Later, additional questions were added to the AAI in order to identify adults with unresolved trauma and loss. Parents with unresolved trauma and loss have been found to have signs of what have been called Hostile/Helpless states of mind. It has been found that these states explain a significant portion of the variance linking unresolved trauma in the parent to disorganization in the child and capture "indicators of a pervasively unintegrated state of mind" (Lyons-Ruth, Yellin, Melnick, & Atwood, 2005). These two states of mind have been found to relate to two types of "disrupted" interactions parents exhibit with their children.

Many believe that the unresolved classification, or Hostile/Helpless state of mind, results in parents displaying frightened or frightening (i.e., "fr") behavior with their infants (Lyons-Ruth, Melnick, Bronfman, Sherry, & Llanas, 2004; Lyons-Ruth, Repacholi, McLeod, & Silva, 1991; Schuengel, Bakermans-Kranenburg, van IJzendoorn, & Blom, 1999). Also, their behavior may be confusing, with parents alternating between being threatening, seducing, and looking helpless without any obvious or external reason (Crittenden, 1992a, 1995). Parents in this classification have also been shown to display the following parenting behaviors:

- Impaired ability for well-attuned affective communication (Hann, Castino, Jarosinki, & Britton, 1991)

- Impaired ability to problem solve and to negotiate conflict, including with their young children

- Less affection for their children and less emotional availability

- Increased risk for outbursts and abusive behavior toward their children

Bronfman, Parsons, and Lyons-Ruth (2000) developed a coding system for scoring parent–infant interactions that show atypical caregiving behaviors. Called the *Atypical Maternal Behavior Instrument for Assessment and Classification* (AMBIANCE), it incorporates some of the items from the Main and Hesse (1992) coding instrument entitled "Frightening, Frightened, Dissociated, or Disorganized Behavior on the Part of the Parent: A Coding System for Parent–Infant Interactions" and items from other coding instruments that have looked at similar behaviors.

Five dimensions of parent behaviors scored by the instrument include the following:

1. *Affective communication errors:* These include incongruence between voice tone and message, facial expression with voice tone or message, or incongruent physical behaviors and failure to respond to infant cues or signals (e.g., uses

friendly voice with threatening pose, does not comfort a crying or distressed infant, laughs when infant is crying or distressed).

2. *Role/boundary confusion:* This includes difficulty separating the infant's needs from one's own needs or treating a child as a sexual or spousal partner (e.g., speaks in hushed, intimate tone to the infant).

3. *Frightened/disoriented behavior:* This is demonstrated through frightened behavior and sudden, unexplainable changes in mood (e.g., holds the infant as if he were inanimate, coos at the baby and then flies into a rage when he won't stop crying)

4. *Intrusiveness/negativity:* This can be evident in physical or verbal communications or by exerting control over objects (e.g., uses loud, sharp, or angry voice; removes and withholds toy from interested child when he wants it).

5. *Withdrawal:* This is displayed when the parent creates physical distance or uses verbal communication to maintain distance (e.g., holds infant away from one's body with stiff arms).

On the basis of the scores obtained, a parent is evaluated according to her level of disrupted communication, with any scores over 4 considered as one of two subtypes of disrupted communication: Intrusive/Self-Referential (Hostile or Frightening) subtype or Helpless/Fearful (Frightened) subtype.

## INTERVENTIONS WITH PARENTS WITH POSTTRAUMATIC STRESS DISORDER OR UNRESOLVED LOSS OR TRAUMA

Because parents with PTSD or unresolved loss and trauma are likely to have difficulties parenting their children, early intervention may be particularly important, although very challenging. Techniques for providing interventions for people with PTSD are becoming increasingly more sophisticated. The first and most important goal for working with parents who are dealing with PTSD or issues of unresolved loss and trauma that are affecting their parenting is to ensure the safety of the children and parents. Another goal is to restore the parent's sense of self by validating the experience of the posttraumatic stress response through empathizing with the pain of it, acknowledging how common and universal are the responses they are experiencing, and explaining the meaning of and reason for the parents' reactions. A crucial goal of treating parents is to increase their ability to deal with stress and to help them to maintain normal levels of arousal rather than the hypervigilance or psychic numbing that is common. Included in this goal is the desire to increase the parent's ability to use realistic cognitive appraisal of a situation so as to reduce incidents of explosive anger, panic, or numbing and withdrawal. Similarly, it is important to enable the parent to return to a more normal engagement in daily life by teaching adaptive coping and helping them to determine future goals. The last goal of intervention, and one that will not usually be part of early intervention services, is to place the memories of trauma in perspective or to reintegrate them into the parent's life story. This helps the parent to avoid constantly reliving these memories through flashbacks and nightmares and other repercussions, and the traumatic event can be increasingly "understood" and given some meaning. As well, nurturing hope and emphasizing the person's strengths needs to be an all-encompassing goal throughout intervention.

When treating a parent with unresolved loss and trauma, it is crucial to be aware of the effects of trauma and how to treat them. It is also critical to consider a number of principles of providing intervention when working as a service provider in an early intervention program with traumatized parents:

- It is essential that the interventionist–parent relationship be collaborative, and that it leads to a sense of empowerment for the parent rather than a sense of being controlled or abused.

- As each person will have his own way to work on recovery, it is crucial to follow the parent's lead. In other words, the intervention must be titrated to each person's capacity and tolerance and should not be too challenging or allow the person to stagnate and make no improvements.

- Recent research suggests that in order to reduce the incidence of disorganization in infants and young children, interventions that focus on improving the parent–child interaction should not be provided during a time when any uncovering of traumatic memories is taking place. The parent is unlikely to be able to fully focus on enhancing the interaction with her child if memories are resurfacing (Bakermans-Kranenburg & Juffer, 2005) (see Chapter 1).

- In general, shorter term intervention is suitable for uncomplicated forms of PTSD, whereas intensive, longer term, multimodal intervention is needed for those with more complex histories of multiple traumas that may have begun in infancy or early childhood.

- Because accessing memories too early can retraumatize and overwhelm a person, any "uncovering" of memories needs to be carefully modulated and should only occur after the person has been given some strategies to deal with any intense feelings or sensory memories that may be experienced (Haskell, 2003). For example, in early sessions the parent may be taught deep breathing, which can bring physiological arousal under control.

- "Talking cures" may not be sufficient; work that focuses on dealing with the effects of the memories on the body (e.g., meditation, deep breathing, relaxation) may be necessary as well (Fosha, 2003; Rothschild, 2000).

- It may be necessary to refer parents and children for further intervention beyond the early intervention services. Consequently, service providers need to understand the interventions that could be helpful and be aware of where they are available in their community.

- In working with parents, it is important to teach them ways to deal with their negative emotions such as anger as early as possible in the intervention to help them to avoid losing control and hurting their child. For many people, a return to their previous level of functioning and understanding will be sufficient and the intervention can be concluded. Others may wish to continue with other services in order to find a new level of understanding and acceptance and a sense of greater purpose in life (Landsman, 2002). Sometimes, these efforts may occur concurrently with the process of the trauma intervention.

Although it is difficult to specify stages of intervention that need to apply to all clients, it is helpful in working with parents with unresolved loss and trauma to consider the following three stages (Chu, 1992; Courtois, 1999; Williams & Sommer, 1994). All of the stages may not be included because a step may not be necessary or the situation may already be stabilized. In each case, however, the necessity for going through each stage needs to be considered. Under the heading for each stage, some intervention approaches are included that may need to be provided by other agencies (e.g., EMDR).

## Stage One: Assessment, Stabilization, and Symptom Reduction

A very important first step for an interventionist is to gain a full understanding of a parent's history of trauma including the timing, type, severity, and duration of the trauma they experienced.

*Understanding the Parent's History*    Parents with different histories will have different pathways to recovery. A parent's experience of being parented herself is also helpful if she can talk about it. The history will influence the need for intervention and the length and intensity of intervention that will be required (Foa et al., 2000). (See Figure 9.3 for an explanation of the different types of trauma clients).

Assessment is critical in order to determine the category in which the client best fits. It is also crucial in order to decide what type of intervention would be most useful and if Stage I will be necessary for initial stabilization (Kluft, 1994). Some of the important aspects to consider include

- Whether the individual needs a mental status examination to be conducted by a mental health professional in order to identify any psychotic symptoms or suggestions of character disorder or depression and thoughts of suicide

- Whether the individual reports any history of sustained relationships and if he seems willing to develop a therapeutic relationship

- If there is any evidence of dissociation

- Whether the client has a great deal of difficulty speaking and articulating her thoughts, which suggests that there is a lack of integration of her thought processes and possible dissociation

- If the level of risk behavior the person discloses includes impulsivity, self-endangerment (e.g., cutting or eating disorders), or interpersonal violence including child abuse or substance abuse

- Whether the parent is showing signs of trauma in the body (e.g., flushing, rapid breathing) or reporting feeling symptoms in the body and whether she has any self-care methods to calm herself down

Other responsibilities associated with assessment include

- Identifying available support systems and other employment and financial re-sources as well as identifying between-session contacts

- Assessing the need for inpatient care and medication if the parent seems to be at risk

- Gaining an idea of how anxiety is dealt with and which defense mechanisms are used (e.g., projection, denial, splitting, acting-out)

Further assessments by a substance abuse counselor and other professionals may be necessary if certain issues are identified (e.g., client uses alcohol or drugs or self harms to regulate her emotional states).

### *Establishing the Therapeutic Relationship*    One of the common factors

that has been identified in research as crucial for therapy outcome for all kinds of interventions and with people with unresolved loss and trauma in particular has been the quality of the therapeutic relationship (Chu, 1992). Based on Figure 9.3 and the differentiation of clients, however, it is clear that the relationship is more central with some clients than with others. Although in some ways, having a meaningful therapeutic relationship can be healing and effective, in trauma inter-vention it is not sufficient for many clients. Perhaps it is less the relationship than the interventionist's attunement to the client's affects, needs, and anxieties that is essential to some clients. This sensitivity is what provides the client with assurance that the right level of empathy and understanding of her experience or situation is being provided and ensures that the intervention is correctly sequenced. As noted previously, with some clients the necessary level of trust can be established rela-tively quickly and the second stage can be reached quite rapidly. Nevertheless, it is also important to point out that because the very nature of trauma is to feel out of control, it is also likely that a core component of the intervention relationship for all people will be having a sense of control and input into the type of inter-vention being provided.

For some clients who have had ongoing trauma and little chance to develop resilience, memories of early experience will be likely to arise primarily around the transference or the clients' experience of the relationship with the therapist. In extreme situations, this can include the triggering of the original experience of abuse and, in less extreme examples, feelings of helplessness and of rejection (Chu, 1992). At times, the client may feel like leaving the therapy, as in the case of Nina in Chapter 4. If this can be worked through, the experience can gradually stabilize the relationship. These responses can also trigger intense feelings in the therapist as well—an experience called *countertransference*—especially if a parent is projecting certain aspects of himself onto the therapist (see Chapters 6 and 15).

For the II-B or III client who has experienced massive and/or multiple trau-mas, the therapeutic relationship may be the most important aspect of interven-tion. It can be an important mechanism to establish trust in an individual that she has never experienced with anyone or to reestablish trust that has been lost. With-out this preliminary building of trust in Stage One of therapy, traumatic memories should not be accessed. The therapist who develops trust with a client will be able, then, to be an ally and a support in order for the client to confront the trauma memories. For Nina, for example, it took a long time to reach Stage Two before any memories or issues from the past could be discussed. However, it was possible to work with the parent–child interaction before any memories were accessed.

***Concentrating on Strengths***     As has been discussed at length in this and other chapters, in the early sessions, many parents who have experienced unresolved trauma or loss will be quite mistrustful and may overreact to perceived criticism or be easily upset by simple suggestions about how to manage a situation, perceiving it as criticism. In order to make a parent feel more in control, commenting on strengths, especially parenting strengths, can be very helpful. Including the parent in the discussion and choice of goals for intervention sessions will be crucial.

***Setting Limits and Boundaries***     Establishing the client's safety for herself and her child(ren) is paramount. Sometimes it may be necessary to clearly lay out the boundaries of intervention, which may include letting her know, for example, that she will not be allowed to come in for her therapy or intervention if she comes under the influence of drugs or alcohol, that any suicidal gestures must stop, and that appointments cannot be missed except in exceptional circumstances. It will also be important to inform parents that if any abuse or neglect is suspected it will be necessary to report it to Child Protective Services. Usually, clients find that the structure and boundaries help to alleviate their anxiety and make them feel more in control. Because the parent may be overinvolved in a dangerous lifestyle and may go from one crisis to another at the beginning, however, crisis intervention may be crucial and efforts may be needed to help stabilize her life.

***Grounding in the Present***     During this initial phase of intervention, it will be important to avoid triggering memories of the trauma. The focus instead should be on stabilizing and helping the parent to contain her psychological distress and current situation. If discussion of the individual's trauma does come up, however, it is important to acknowledge the pain of what happened and the client's strength in managing it. It is also important to let her know that any current difficulties that she talks about are common occurrences following trauma or loss. This will both normalize the symptoms and possibly shift the client's beliefs and cognitions about herself as inadequate and powerless to a more positive understanding about herself. Any discussion of the trauma that does happen should be present oriented and cognitively focused, should not push for past memories, and should explore how it is affecting current functioning, particularly her parenting. Other ways to ground a client in the present include having her think about how the present is different from her past and getting her to focus on the present in her body and mind and to remind her that she now has choices that she did not have in the past. Have her refer to the present in positive terms (e.g., "It is now _____ and a new time for me"). Help her to stabilize her sensorimotor reactions by giving her grounding skills such as being aware of what is going on around her in the room and have her describe what she sees. Also, cognitive grounding skills can be taught by having her think about what the date and season is and what she can expect next. Have her list the resources she now has, such as some people and services she can call and some self-calming strategies she can employ, such as mindfulness activities and writing her feelings in a journal. This has been called *grounding in the present*, which helps an individual to increase contact with the here and now.

***Self-Soothing and Calming Down***    In early sessions it is very important to provide parents with strategies that can be used to help them avoid any acting out behaviors resulting from a reactivation of the intense reactions at the time of the trauma. These may include deep breathing, taking a short time out, or visualizing something more pleasant. Cognitive strategies such as beginning to identify the triggers for the reactions can be very helpful. As some of the intense reactions are likely to be in relation to a child's behavior strategies, ways to manage them can be discussed with a parent and support provided to help him put them into practice. Some calming strategies include self-monitoring for possible reactions and learning to use containing images and stopping of negative thoughts. Have the client visualize a container in which to keep all of the flashbacks, nightmares, and bad thoughts, such as a safe or a steel vault.

***Preventing Dissociation***    Dissociation can be dangerous because it can place an individual and her child at risk. For some people, however, it can be pleasurable, and may be used to escape from painful feelings. Therefore, the danger to the individual and the individual's children must be made clear. Some of the key strategies, therefore, include getting the parent to agree that dissociation is not helpful to her. Help her to recognize the triggers and practice using grounding techniques or self-soothing when they occur to avoid dissociation occurring. Drawing her attention to periods when she dissociates can make these discussions particularly meaningful.

***Identifying and Labeling Small Emotions***    Another important focus of early sessions is to help an individual to begin to experience normal emotions in everyday situations. Helping her to do this may be possible through sharing enthusiasm about a child's developmental gain or showing interest in an event she talks about. Noticing a mild fear reaction and mentioning it to the mother may also help her to begin to recognize mild emotions, and this observation can be part of the process of having her gradually identify triggers for when she gets very upset.

***Improving Parent–Child Interactions***    If a parent is willing and can tolerate interventions to increase her sensitivity and responsiveness in interactions with her child at this time, such interventions may discourage the development of disorganization in her child and reduce potentially frightening and frightened behaviors in the parenting.

These types of interventions should be considered during the first phase, and are described in the last part of this chapter or in Chapter 10 (see also Table 10.1 for a summary of some of these strategies).

***Pharmacotherapy***    Because of evidence that as a result of trauma, individuals experience a variety of chronic biological difficulties, pharmacotherapy is a likely option for the majority of individuals. Various biological systems may become dysregulated, resulting in changes in neurochemistry. Depression and anxiety disorders often accompany these changes. A number of types of drugs that have been used with people with PTSD including

- *Selective serotonin reuptake inhibitors (SSRIs)* have been found to help reduce the symptoms and to reduce depression.

- *Monoamine oxidase inhibitors (MAOIs)* have been moderately effective but are more likely to have side effects.

**Table 9.1.**   Summary of strategies to use with parents with unresolved loss and trauma in home visits and clinical intervention

| Approach | Reason for approach | Strategies |
|---|---|---|
| Concentrating on strengths | To enable the parent to overcome her sense of shame, weakness, and of being unlovable | Take every opportunity to notice gains and to normalize her reactions to past trauma. |
| | | Provide classes that she will enjoy and can do well in (e.g., cooking, computers). |
| | | Use strategies like videotape viewing and emphasize the positive interactions. |
| | | Have the parent as a collaborator in choosing her goals for intervention. |
| Grounding in the present | To avoid triggering memories and to deal with memories that do surface | If memories are brought up, acknowledge the pain and affirm the parent's strength in dealing with them. |
| | | Normalize the symptoms as much as possible. |
| | | Ask her how it affects her current parenting. |
| | | Have her think about her present situation compared with how it was for her during the trauma. |
| | | Point out that she now has choices about her life. |
| | | Review choices. |
| | | Talk about resources available to her. |
| | | Have her talk about her current feelings. |
| | | Use journaling about her current life. |
| | | Use cognitive grounding skills (e.g., What is the date? What is the year?). |
| | | Use sensory grounding skills (e.g., What can you see and hear? What are you feeling?). |
| Self-soothing, calming down, and reducing hypervigilance and hyperarousal | To avoid angry outbursts or panic attacks or withdrawal that can affect parenting | Point out that you noticed the parent getting upset, if this is the case. |
| | | Suggest she take a deep breath and think about something positive to calm her reactions. |
| | | Suggest that she visualize a container for all of her bad thoughts, nightmares, and flashbacks that will keep them locked up and safe. |
| | | Suggest cognitive behavior therapy (CBT) groups in the community. |

*(continued)*

**Table 9.1.**  *(continued)*

| Approach | Reason for approach | Strategies |
|---|---|---|
| Reducing acting-out behaviors | To reduce risk to the child and parent | Set boundaries for behaviors and parenting interactions that are not acceptable and that place the child or parent at risk. |
| | | Provide an assessment and referral for treatment for depression and anger management. |
| | | Help the parent identify when she is feeling like acting out and have her ask for help or notice what is happening, and offer strategies to help. |
| | | Help her be aware of body reactions such as hyperarousal and have her use calming strategies. |
| | | Have the parent rate her emotional reaction—either anger, anxiety, or sadness—on a scale of 1 to 10 and then help her talk about what is going on and come up with some ways to calm down. Have her rate herself again at the end of the session. |
| Preventing dissociation | To avoid the parent dissociating or going away in her head | Explain what dissociation is and why it occurs. |
| | | Help parent to agree that dissociating is not helpful for her or her child. |
| | | Teach her to recognize what triggers dissociation. |
| | | After a parent has dissociated, ask her if she "went someplace else" in her head and show an understanding and empathy for her need to do that at times. |
| | | Encourage her to use grounding and self-soothing to avoid dissociating. |
| Identifying and labeling small emotions | To enable the parent to recognize small emotional reactions before they escalate out of control | Have parent acknowledge small gains and share her enjoyment in them. |
| | | Point out a small fear reaction (e.g., backing away from the child) and discuss what she felt. |
| | | Give her strategies to use with her child to calm him down such as "Coaching the emotions" (see Chapter 11). |
| | | Use strategies to overcome splitting (see Chapter 6). |

**Table 9.1.**    *(continued)*

| Approach | Reason for approach | Strategies |
|---|---|---|
| Avoiding hyper-arousal and anxiety | To help direct attention that is too inwardly focused to the outside and current events | Discuss with the parent what is currently going on in her life.<br>Encourage her to relax and let go of bodily arousal.<br>Look at the room and talk to her about the colors and objects that she can see there. |

- *Tricyclic antidepressants (TCAs)* are mildly effective and do not have as many side effects as MAOIs.

In conclusion, the use of medication may add an important component of intervention for many people with PTSD and consequently, referral to a psychiatrist or physician will often be an important aspect of early sessions.

**Cognitive Behavior Therapy (CBT)**    In Cognitive behavior therapy (CBT), much of the intervention focuses not so much on the trauma itself but on reducing the maladaptive behavior and thoughts or feelings that developed following the trauma. These may include extreme anxiety, chronic depression, phobias, and retriggering of the event. CBT techniques are usually short-term, with an average of 3–12 sessions. The intervention may use a particular technique or a combination of several, including assertiveness training, relaxation training, biofeedback, and systematic desensitization to the situation that causes the anxiety. Another technique is cognitive processing therapy, in which strategies are used such as helping the person change negative thoughts about an event to more positive ones. Foa and Meadows (1997) reviewed the research on these approaches and found that the evidence for effectiveness was strongest for cognitive processing therapy and for exposure or desensitization, although some of the other approaches may be more successful with certain populations such as younger mothers.

**Body Work**    Because much of the trauma response that people experience is felt in the body, therapy needs to incorporate use of the body into intervention. This means that an individual is alerted to what is going on in her body and is asked to identify any body sensations and body processes. The parent is encouraged to become aware of such things as breathing, temperature, muscle tenseness, pulse rate, and body position (Levine, 1992). Parents who are accustomed to perceiving certain body sensations such as an increased heart rate or flushing as dangerous are "reintroduced" to them as signs and signals of what is going on inside them and in the world. This approach is used to help individuals to be able to monitor their arousal so that they can recognize when a particular technique needs to be discontinued if it becomes too rapid or intense for them to manage. The clinician also monitors the client's arousal by observing body signs, thus allowing him to drop the level of arousal and reestablish a sense of safety if the arousal seems to become too intense. The person is taught certain strategies to calm these reactions or to put the "brakes on" as they begin to be felt. These may include focusing on the breath, deep breathing, visualizing pleasant situations, and changing thoughts to more positive ones (Rothschild, 2000).

## Stage Two: Deconditioning, Mourning Losses, Resolution, and Integration of Trauma into Self-Narratives

The relevance of this phase will depend on the type of trauma and the client's capacity to tolerate accessing memories and the physical and emotional reactions that may occur. On the one hand, for clients in categories Type I, II-A, and II-B (R), it may be possible to move relatively quickly into this phase. On the other hand, for clients in categories II-B (nR) and III, this stage of accessing memories may not be used (Chu, 1992; Courtois, 1999; Haskell, 2003). After assessment, if the decision is made to proceed with accessing memories, this process must be carefully regulated so that the client does not become overwhelmed and flooded with the memories. A variety of strategies and approaches can be used depending on the findings from the assessment of the client and the type of intervention that can best help him. These strategies are used by specialists for treating trauma and are a way to bring the memories to the surface or into consciousness and to integrate them with other types of memories. Early intervention programs can refer parents to these interventions if they are available through community networks.

*Eye Movement Desensitization and Reprocessing (EMDR)*    Eye Movement Desensitization and Reprocessing (EMDR) was originated by Shapiro (2001) after she noticed that the back-and-forth movements of her eyes seemed to help to reduce troubling thoughts. Later, she used the technique with trauma victims, asking them to think of a troublesome thought or memory while visually tracking her finger as she moved it across their visual field. She later developed the method further as a way to foster emotional and cognitive changes in people suffering from trauma (Shapiro, 1998, 2001; Shapiro & Solomon, 1995). Shapiro noted that EMDR was developed as a method that would specifically "help integrate new desirable self-statements while allowing for rapidly desensitizing traumatic cues" (2001, p. 26). With this intervention, various stages are also recommended. These include

1.  *Assessment and Intervention Planning:* This stage primarily emphasizes the need to be sure that the person is ready and motivated for the intervention. A history is taken in this first phase and a determination made of whether the person has sufficient ego functioning to deal with the intense emotions that may be evoked. Traumatic memories are then identified that can be the foci of the intervention.

2–3.  *Preparation/Assessment:* An intervention relationship is developed initially and education provided about trauma. The EMDR process is explained and any concerns addressed. The person is taught relaxation techniques to deal with any intense emotions that are aroused. The person is then asked to access memories of the trauma and to remember distressing images and negative cognitions, such as "It was all my fault," "I didn't deserve to be the one that was saved." Then, a more positive cognition or rationale is identified. The client also learns how to rate the intensity of the emotion on a 10-point subjective unit-of-disturbance scale.

4. *Desensitization and Reprocessing:* During this most critical phase of the intervention, while the person holds in mind a disturbing memory and the thoughts and bodily sensations associated with it, the clinician moves her finger back and forth about 12 inches in front of the person's face while he tracks the finger with his eyes. Hand taps or other auditory tones can be used as alternatives. The client then provides feedback about any changes that take place in terms of self-image, bodily sensations, emotions, or thoughts about himself. After each of these experiences, the clinician facilitates linking the memory with other adaptive information in order to reach a stage where the individual experiences no discomfort.

5. *Installation of Positive Cognition:* Once the client reports that she has no or minimal discomfort with the memory following desensitization, further memories will be dealt with similarly. In addition, specific coping skills designed to deal with these past memories and emotions will be practiced and more positive cognitions about the event suggested.

6. *Body Scan:* The client is asked to check for any discomfort or tension in their body that is taken to be an indication of incomplete trauma processing.

7. *Closure:* The person is provided with strategies that can be used to overcome any residual body tension such as relaxation, visualization, and journaling. The person is returned to a state of emotional equilibrium at the end of the session.

8. *Reevaluation:* This step includes checking that the original goals of the intervention are being maintained and the person is doing well. The journal log will be reviewed to verify the intervention effects.

The research results using EMDR are good, although it is unclear how much the use of eye movements contributes to the overall effectiveness (Shapiro, 2002). It is essential that people who use EMDR are experienced clinicians and trained in the approach. If there is no one trained in EMDR, a referral will need to be made to an agency in the community that provides these services. It may be most effective with victims of a single traumatic event. When clients have histories of repeated traumas, intervention may need to be more intense and longer term than that provided in EMDR sessions (Shapiro, 2001). Information on obtaining training in EMDR is provided at the end of the chapter.

*Hypnosis*    Hypnotic procedures have been used since the 19th century to treat combat troops and others with neuroses, and more recently, PTSD. During hypnosis the clinician uses suggestion in order to induce changes in sensations, thoughts, perceptions, and behavior in the client. The hypnotist asks the client to forget other concerns and relax, focusing on something like a metronome ticking or deep breathing. These procedures are used with people with PTSD in order to overcome the dissociation of the memory of the trauma and to provide the client with specific techniques to modulate and contain any distressing phenomena that arise. Hypnosis is often used with psychodynamic and cognitive-behavioral approaches.

Although research indicates that hypnosis can be helpful for clients with PTSD, it must also be remembered that it may at times induce false memories, and thus needs to be used with caution (Courtois, 1999). It is also critical to accompany intervention with hypnosis with "re-integration" and "re-synthesis" and not to rely simply on releasing the distress that accompanies retrieval of the memories. In fact, increasing coping skills and a sense of competence may be the most crucial part of the intervention (Kirsch, Capafons, Cardéna-Buelna, & Amigó, 1999).

*Creative Therapies*    Like CBT, creative therapies include a variety of modalities such as art therapy, dance/movement therapy, music therapy, drama therapy, writing and journaling, poetry, and psychodrama. Originally, creative therapies were seen as an alternative for "talking" therapies. Now, creative therapies are used to overcome a variety of symptoms of PTSD and to improve associated conditions such as depression and hyperarousal and anxiety. Creative therapies may provide a safe place to explore feelings about trauma and to help access nonverbal memories. These therapies often overlap with CBT techniques and utilize relaxation, desensitization, and the changing of cognitive distortions.

In general, creative therapies are used instead of verbal discussion in order to work on the presenting problem. Sometimes a particular aspect of the trauma is worked on; at other times the client engages in drawing, dance, and music/singing, and the clinician deals with issues linked to the trauma as they arise. Again, the intervention is often brief, about 6–8 weeks, but can be longer term. Creative therapies may also be used as adjuncts to other "talking" therapies. Although there is little research to validate their efficiency, creative therapies are well accepted by clients. It is critical, however, that clinicians using them are cautious about accessing trauma memories too quickly or with too much intensity.

## Stage Three: The Development of Self and Relationships and the Reconsolidation of Strengths

This last phase may take months or even years to reach for some clients. The emphasis is on building or rebuilding what may have been damaged by the trauma. This includes establishing, perhaps for the first time, social contacts and participating in meaningful and recreational activities. It can also mean exploring the possibility of finding meaningful employment by beginning an educational program. Some of these types of activities may be available in two-generation early intervention programs or the parent may be able to be referred out to other services for them. Some clients may want to develop a new view of the world, and perhaps a new view of spirituality or religion. The final phase will also include termination of the therapy with an invitation to return if necessary to resolve new issues that arise or in times of new crises. Although some programs that are suitable for this phase may be available in early intervention programs, it is likely that most of this type of rebuilding and consolidation will occur after closing of the case and referral to other services.

## Other Interventions for Parents with Unresolved Loss and Trauma

The following are other interventions that have been used successfully with parents with unresolved loss and trauma.

*Modified Interaction Guidance*    Benoit (2001) and Benoit, Madigan, Lecce, Shea, and Goldberg (2001) have described a brief focused intervention that can be used in situations in which the parent has unresolved loss and trauma and the child either has or is at risk for developing a disorganized attachment. Modified Interaction Guidance builds on Interaction Guidance used to enhance positive interactions (McDonough, 2000), and has a similar goal to increase sensitive responsiveness in the parent. However, this modified approach focuses on reducing the atypical disrupted communication and behaviors identified on the AMBIANCE that have been associated with disorganized attachment (see an earlier section of this chapter). In a pilot project that compared the intervention with the use of behavior modification, the Modified Interaction Guidance (but not the other intervention) was found to significantly reduce the mother's number of atypical or "fr" behaviors shown in the interactions and to decrease the disrupted communication. What differentiates the Modified Interaction Guidance from other types of interaction guidance in terms of effectiveness is that, although it also builds on the strengths observed in the interactions, the disturbed or atypical behaviors in the interaction are also identified and strategies are introduced that focus on reducing them.

The intervention takes place over five to seven sessions, in the home or clinic setting. In the first session the parent identifies a problem she is having with her child or in interactions with her child, and then she decides on what interaction goal(s) she wants to work on. These are reviewed at the beginning of subsequent sessions. In each session, toys are provided and 10–15 minutes of interaction are videotaped and played back to the parent. Throughout the replaying of the videotaped interaction, the interventionist makes both positive and negative comments. The parent is told that she is to put herself in her child's shoes and think about what he is feeling and thinking. The tape is then played back, and two types of behaviors are pointed out to the parent:

1. Positive aspects of the interaction, including displaying affection, positioning herself at the child's level, using face-to-face interaction, making eye contact, responding to the child's initiative in a positive way, or displaying positive mood.

2. Atypical, or disrupted behaviors (see information on the AMBIANCE instrument) that occurs most frequently, such as ignoring the child or withdrawing when he gives a cue.

Two negative behaviors are usually identified in each session, and the mother is asked what she thinks the child is feeling at the time. Any frightening or frightened behaviors she engaged in are pointed out to the mother as well. At the end of the session, the parent is given "homework" such as setting aside 5 to 10 minutes, once a day or every other day, during which she looks at the child's face without initiating interactions (but responding warmly to the child's initiation of interactions) and wonders what the child is feeling and thinking. Or she may be given strategies to work on the parenting issue she has identified (Benoit, 2001). Information on obtaining training for conducting this intervention is given at the end of the chapter.

*Brief Videotaped Feedback Intervention*    Schechter (2004) described a videotaped feedback intervention that has been used with mothers identified with PTSD with children between 8 and 50 months old. The mother and child were videotaped using a split screen in an interaction that included a separation–reunion episode. The interventionist selected four excerpts of about 30 seconds each that showed an optimal moment of interaction and separation/reunion play moments. They were then played back to the mother 2–4 weeks later in a single session video feedback intervention, and the mother was asked after each 30-second clip, "What happened?" "What is going on in your/your child's/ or the interventionist's mind?" "Does it remind you of anything?" (Schechter, 2004, p. 47). Negativity in the interactions and the amount of distortions of child attributions were reduced; however, the positive changes were believed to be related to the mother's high level of reflective functioning and to her having fewer PTSD symptoms.

*Dyadic Developmental Psychotherapy (DDP)*    Daniel Hughes has developed an exciting approach to working with individuals who have experienced trauma or other extremely stressful situations. His approach, called Dyadic Developmental Psychotherapy (DDP) is useful for working with infants, children, and adults who have been exposed to trauma, neglect, loss, or an extreme lack of nurturing interactions, particularly in the early years. An individual who has experienced these things is likely to be displaying symptoms of trauma and to be having difficulty in accepting and responding appropriately to efforts on the part of the caregiver or partner to show affection and commitment to his ongoing welfare.

In a DDP session, an important attachment figure in the person's life is present to facilitate a sense of greater safety and containment for the client within the session. When the client is a child or adolescent, this attachment figure is typically the natural parent(s), foster or adoptive parent(s), or a staff member from the group home or other facility in which the child is living. When the client is an adult, it is usually the individual's partner. Prior to encouraging the client—whether that person is a child, adolescent, or adult—to address areas of trauma and shame, Hughes is careful to determine that the attachment figure has a sufficient degree of reflective and empathic capacity to contain whatever experiences are being expressed.

The therapist adopts an attitude described by Hughes (1997, 1998) as PACE, which stands for

**P**layfulness

**A**cceptance

**C**uriosity

**E**mpathy

Within the "holding" environment provided by the therapist and attachment figure, the therapist adopts a directive, client-centered stance in order to "explore, resolve and integrate a wide range of memories, emotions, and current experiences that are frightening, shameful, avoided or denied" (Hughes, 1997, p. 2). As described in this chapter, this process can allow previously unconscious or split-off, dissociated memories to be integrated into a coherent, personal narrative or a new autobiography. This new narrative is co-constructed with the client, therapist, and attachment figure in such a way that the child experiences understanding, empathy, affective matching, and containment, making the elicited memories tolerable, understandable, and validated (Hughes, 2004).

The therapist uses a number of strategies within the sessions by communicating to the child verbally and nonverbally and with affective matching or attunement in order to provide "moments of meeting," or of true understanding and acceptance (Fosha, 2000; Stern, 2004). At times during the sessions, psychodrama, illustrated stories, journaling, paradoxical interventions, and so forth are used to facilitate the attachment process between the client and her attachment figure and the reintegration of the traumatic memories. In addition, the approach has been used successfully to reduce severe symptoms of aggression, withdrawal, chronic arousal, and/or dissociation.

Although DDP was developed to address childhood trauma and attachment difficulties secondary to abuse, neglect, and loss within foster or adoptive homes, Hughes is also applying it in natural families in which a wide range of family dysfunction and distress is evident. This model of family therapy is attachment-focused in the principles and interventions that are utilized. Hughes provides training at a beginning and advanced level. See details in the Resources section of this chapter for information as to how to contact Hughes about the intervention approach and training.

***Psychological Debriefing***    Psychological debriefing can be an extremely important component of any trauma intervention and is provided immediately after a trauma has occurred. Counselors often provide such an intervention following an event such as the terrorist attacks of September 11, 2001; for troops when they return from combat; and in a school following a tragedy. If it is carried out shortly after the traumatic event it may help prevent psychological difficulties following the event. Other related approaches include crisis intervention (e.g., support following a disaster) and grief counseling (e.g., following the loss of a baby). Although individual counseling is used most frequently, group approaches have also been used following large-scale disasters.

The debriefing method is used as far as possible to avoid people developing PTSD. It is also used to assess the psychological condition of the individual and to determine whether a need exists to provide ongoing counseling. It is not seen as an intervention but as a way to promote emotional processing through the ventilation and normalization of reactions. As such, it does not explore earlier experiences that may shape people's individual reactions. Several authors have developed strategies and stages of psychological debriefing, outlining its essential components (Dyregrov, 1998; Mitchell & Everly, 1995; Rose, 1997):

1. *The introduction:* The person is told that the session(s) will be used to discuss his reactions to the event and to help him deal with it to prevent further problems.

2. *Expectations and facts:* Participants will discuss what happened and what they thought was going to happen.

3. *Thoughts and impressions:* The person is asked what he thought about and did. Sensory impressions (seeing, hearing, smelling, touching, tasting) are discussed in an effort to link these memories with thoughts and cognitions. The goal is to make the memory realistic and to help with its integration into long-term memory.

4. *Emotional reactions:* Attempts are made to have the person release some of the many emotions he has about the event, including anger, fear, guilt, depression, and self-reproach. This may take a long time.

5. *Normalization:* The person is assured that his reactions are normal and informed about other things he may experience later, such as startle reactions, depression, intrusive thoughts and images, and nightmares.

6. *Future planning/coping:* In this stage the person is given ways to deal with any symptoms and to maximize coping strategies and external supports.

7. *Closure:* The emphasis is on giving the client information as to what symptoms she may need to seek further help for and where it can be obtained.

In spite of its wide use, little research evidence shows that psychological debriefing is necessarily successful in preventing PTSD. Research findings suggest that it needs to be provided by well-trained professionals, may need to go beyond a single session, and should not be mandatory. It may be most useful as a way to identify people who need more long-term and intensive intervention and to inform them of where to seek further counseling if they need it (Foa & Meadows, 1997).

For young children who experience a significant trauma, play therapy can often be used effectively to help the child deal with the triggered memories and to make sense of what occurred. If possible, it is important for this to happen within 3 months of the occurrence of the event.

## PROVIDING INTERVENTIONS FOR
## UNRESOLVED LOSS AND TRAUMA: CASE-STUDY FAMILIES

### Joan

Referring back to our case studies, Joan did not identify any particular losses or traumas in her background. Michael, Mark's father, reported having a close, nurturing family who remained in close contact with him and his family. However, Joan's difficulty with dealing with Mark's sadness or pain was found to be connected to her own experience of being brought up by a depressed mother who could not provide containment for her own sadness as Joan was growing up. Although no obvious trauma was identified as underlying these reactions, her own lack of containment may have placed her in the category of prolonged duress stress disorder (PDSD). As such, the psychodynamic intervention she received was necessary to help her to identify the reasons for her difficulty in containing Mark when he became very upset and sad. With excellent ego functioning and the support of her husband, she was able to remember how she had felt about her mother's failure to be available when she was distressed and to see how she was repeating the same cycle. It was also necessary for her to acknowledge her grief over her multiple miscarriages and her feelings of incompetence caused by her failure to have a successful pregnancy.

## Nina

Nina had been found to have complex PTSD and, as a result, she experienced all of the symptoms and parenting difficulties described in this chapter. Her trauma experiences were frequent and intense throughout her life and could hardly be differentiated from each other. She had been physically, emotionally, and sexually abused, and often neglected. She had a need to repeat the trauma and engaged in impulsive and dangerous behavior including involvement in a number of violent relationships. She also used alcohol and drugs, seemingly to cover her sense of emptiness and aloneness. She did not react to small emotions, yet was frequently triggered and was known to dissociate or act out against her children. She had very little self-reflectivity at the beginning of the intervention and used primitive defenses instead. These included projection, splitting, acting-out, and extreme denial. Although Nina and her children were involved in a variety of interventions including parenting groups, interactional guidance, a mother's club, and educational activities, it was crucial that she received the following: 1) drug and alcohol counseling; 2) long-term therapy that incorporated a number of therapeutic strategies including cognitive behavioral strategies, empowerment, and containment; and 3) crisis intervention at times. The process of therapy is described in some detail in Chapter 4, and it also is incorporated in the strategies discussed in early sections of this chapter.

A summary of the course of Nina's intervention is described next. It illustrates both the need for staged intervention and for multidimensional strategies to be made available during the different stages.

### Stage One

- The interventionist helped to establish a level of functioning that kept Nina's risk-taking behaviors to a minimum. Set up expectations of acceptable behavior in the sessions and outside, such as letting her know what was unacceptable in the session (e.g., coming in drunk) and outlining the responsibility for reporting any signs of abuse or neglect of the children to Child Protective Services. This could be included with the goals of intervention and shared with the parent.

- The interventionist worked to establish regularity and consistency and a basic level of trust in the therapist. With Nina, it was not difficult to establish regular attendance, but she was easily triggered to perceive rejection or to feel that she would be abandoned.

- The interventionist worked on developing a trusting relationship in which Nina was comfortable sharing her feelings. At first, her comments about what had gone on during the previous week were simply about the events and were described without any emotion. Sometimes the interventionist noted how difficult it must have been for her and talked about what she might have felt. This strategy was successful in allowing Nina to think about her feelings and to identify and label them and to gradually use them to identify small triggers before she became too upset.

- The interventionist helped Nina to understand how her past trauma was affecting her present functioning. She let her know that her reactions were normal, and showed empathy for her suffering. This was done by describing some of the effects of trauma so that what Nina was experiencing could be normalized.

- The interventionist dealt with transference issues as they arose. These transference issues primarily related to her perception that the interventionist would not keep her safe and that she would abandon her like everyone else had done.

- The interventionist provided Nina with strategies to use to self-soothe and calm down if she felt herself getting upset such as deep breathing, visualization, and relaxation techniques. Grounding techniques were also demonstrated and encouraged.

- The interventionist frequently provided crisis intervention by letting her come for an extra session to talk about a concern that had arisen and occasional home visits when she was particularly upset.

- As Nina was able to tolerate it, she was introduced to interaction coaching, developmental guidance, and parenting classes in order to focus on the interactional and parenting issues that were so difficult for her to change. These interventions were provided by a child and youth worker experienced in parenting approaches.

## Stage Two

- The interventionist and Nina worked through issues of Nina's past at several levels, including physiological, practical, emotional, and cognitive. Efforts were primarily made to reintegrate Nina's memories and to work with her to construct a new understanding of her past so that she could reflect on what happened with sadness rather than feel shame for the little child she was at the time of the traumas.

- The intervention modalities available to Nina were increased, including having her attend a mother's group, a dance and movement class, and an anger-management group at appropriate times during the intervention.

- As Nina opened up to reveal her true feelings and actions, continued support and confrontation was provided as necessary. Sometimes it was necessary to set boundaries around her behavior, after which the interventionist would let Nina know that she was still accepted and that the interventionist understood the reasons for her behavior. In this way, her interventionist could demonstrate that any disruption could be repaired.

- Nina's case worker insisted that Nina accept treatment for alcoholism because it was believed that it was necessary for her to deal with her drug and alcohol addiction before she could be a reliable parent.

- An additional social work student was added to Nina's intervention team who was able to provide home visiting and intervention for the children.

- Expressive therapies that appealed to Nina such as art, bead making, and journaling were used as ways to help her access memories and to provide her with further ways to discuss them.

## *Stage Three*

- The interventionist and Nina began to bring various aspects of her history into a coherent narrative so she could talk and think about it and reinterpret it.

- Therapy focused on consolidating gains and increasing understanding of her past and its effect on her current functioning.

- Intervention looked at enriching Nina's interactions with her children and helping her to have some fun times with them and to show empathy for them.

- The interventionist helped her to engage in empowerment activities and to attend university classes. During these activities she learned how to research and write papers and to teach bead making and to be president of a parent organization at the center.

- Nina continued to be taught coping strategies: anger management, budgeting, relaxation, and meditation. She continued working through issues of her past at several levels.

- The final task was termination of the intervention, with an understanding that Nina could come back at any time and an invitation to stay in touch.

Certainly, the interventions described here, especially for Nina and her family, were long, arduous, and costly. When we consider the possible costs without long-term intervention, however, possibly including incarceration and intergenerational transmission of difficulties with the children, the costs are minor.

## CONCLUSION

Intervention with individuals who have experienced trauma is complex and may need to be longer term than intervention of parents who have not experienced trauma. Because of this it may be crucial that children who are involved receive interventions such as child care and a therapeutic pre-school. Also, if possible, parents should have interactional interventions with their children to help prevent the development of child disorganization because children often cannot and should not wait for long periods of time before receiving direct interventions.

Some clients who have experienced trauma may need inpatient intervention in a hospital for some established period, especially if they are depressed or suicidal, using extreme self-mutilation, or are triggered frequently and experience rage reactions that could endanger their children. They may also need to receive drug and alcohol intervention. While parents receive intervention, or if interactions with their parents are neglectful or abusive, children may need to be in foster care until the situation has been stabilized.

## RESOURCES

### *Modified Interactional Guidance*

Diane Benoit, M.D.
Hospital for Sick Children
555 University Avenue
Toronto, Ontario M5GIX8
Canada
416-813-7528
e-mail: dianebenoit@sickkids.com

### *Eye Movement Desensitization and Reprocessing (EMDR)*

EMDR Institute
Post Office Box 51010
Pacific Grove, CA 93950
831-373-3900
web site: http://www.EMDR.com
e-mail: inst@EMDR.com

### *Dyadic Developmental Psychotherapy*

Dan Hughes, Ph.D.
571 Vassalboro Road
South China, Maine 04358
207-445-3120
e-mail: dhughes1060@adelphia.net

## CHAPTER 10

# Enhancing Parents' Interactions with Infants and Young Children

A significant part of the early intervention literature that has discussed parents' interactional behavior with infants and young children has considered how the behaviors are linked to the child's attachment classification. Attachment refers to the emotional tie between an infant or child and a caregiver (Landy 2002b), and has been the focus of a growing field of study since the 1950s (e.g., Bowlby, 1958, 1965). Attachment has been categorized into various types, with the main types being secure and insecure (which is also broken down into several types). Attachment has been discussed elsewhere in this book; however, here it will be looked at in more detail.

In the late 1970s, Mary Ainsworth and several other researchers followed 26 mother–infant pairs in Baltimore at 3-week intervals from 3 to 54 weeks after each baby's birth and compared maternal interactional behaviors with the baby's attachment classification at 1 year. Four maternal behaviors were identified as characteristic of secure attachment in the child (Ainsworth, Bell, & Stayton, 1979). These were

1. Sensitivity to the child's cues

2. Acceptance, or degree to which parent has positive feelings toward her child

3. Accessibility, or how much the parent focuses her attention on the child

4. Cooperation or how much the parent takes the child's needs into account and respects his need to be separate and autonomous

The scoring of these dimensions included analyzing a large number of measures of behavior on 9-point rating scales in various situations such as when an infant was crying, during face-to-face encounters and holding time, while feeding, giving infant directives, leaving the room, and having physical contact. Other researchers have since emphasized the importance of the caregiver's attunement to a full range of a child's affective display and acceptance and containment of the child's emotions as central to the development of attachment (Cassidy & Shaver, 1999; Cummings & Davies, 1996; Goldberg, Mackay-Soroka, & Rochester, 1994; Haft & Slade, 1989).

A number of research studies have suggested that a child who develops a *secure* attachment has a caregiver who is accessible when the child is ill, hurt, upset, frustrated, or lonely. The caregiver of a securely attached child is accepting of the child, sensitive to her cues, and allows the child to be separate and autonomous in exploring, as long as it is safe. Children with secure attachment seek contact and interactions with their parents when they are upset. They are easily soothed and explore the environment readily (Bretherton, Biringen, & Ridgeway, 1991; Cummings & Cummings, 2002).

The child who develops an *insecure/avoidant* attachment typically has a caregiver who ignores her when she is expressing unhappiness (i.e., negative affect) and who consistently fails to respond when the child is upset. In other words, the caregiver may be accessible to the infant for teaching activities but is insensitive and does not read the infant's cues, especially as they relate to neediness. The parent may also be hostile and rejecting, tense and irritable, and may not allow close body contact. They may at times be intrusive and overstimulating. Children with this kind of attachment classification show little distress when separated from their primary caregiver and avoid her on her return (Belsky, Rovine, & Taylor, 1984; Sroufe, 1988).

The child who develops an *insecure ambivalent/resistant* attachment has a caregiver who is very anxious about the child and can be overprotective and interfering at times. The caregiver tends to be inconsistently responsive and available, sometimes responding to the child and sometimes not. Infants with ambivalent/resistant attachment are extremely distressed during separation, and at reunion they may seek contact and yet resist it, showing a great deal of ambivalence toward their caregivers (Erickson, Sroufe, & Egeland, 1985).

The child who is *disorganized/disoriented* in respect to attachment generally receives unpredictable caregiving within a chaotic environment. At times, the caregiver presents as frightened and unable to manage the situation, including the child, while at other times the caregiver can be frightening, presenting with extreme hostility and anger. Many of these children may experience abuse and neglect, family violence, and other trauma, whereas others experience more subtle negative parenting behaviors. Disorganized/disoriented children often lack observable goals in their behavior, which tends to be contradictory or incomplete, reflects confusion and/or fear, and often involves episodes of freezing or stilling (Main & Solomon, 1987, 1990).

## ATTACHMENT AND CHILD OUTCOMES

Attachment theorists such as Sroufe hypothesized that the different patterns of behavioral organization described by Ainsworth represent qualitatively different patterns of adaptation. Assuming that the quality of caregiving remains stable, Sroufe proposed that these patterns remain consistent across development, affecting the child's subsequent adaptation in significant ways (Sroufe, 1983). Secure attachment in infancy has been empirically related to a toddler's capacity for problem solving (Fagot, Gauvain, & Kavanagh, 1996), negotiating her environment (Cassidy, 1986), socializing with peers in toddlerhood (Booth, Rose-Krasnor, & Rubin, 1991; Fagot, 1997; Pastor, 1981; Suess, 1987), coping with challenges in preschool (Waters, Wippman, & Sroufe, 1979), and ego control and resilience in early childhood (Arend, Grove, & Sroufe, 1979). A number of other studies have examined the relationship between an insecure attachment and problematic outcomes, such as behavior problems in school and emotional difficulties (DeKlyen, 1996; Erickson, Sroufe, & Egeland, 1985; Lewis, Feiring, McGuffog, & Jaskir, 1984; Moss, Parent, Gosselin, Rousseau, & St. Laurent, 1996; Speltz, Greenberg, & De-Klyen, 1990). This relationship is particularly strong in very high-risk samples. In two longitudinal studies of high-risk families, insecurely attached preschoolers (particularly those who had also been rated as disorganized) were more likely to be hostile to peers and to have parental ratings of behavior problems (Lyons-Ruth, Alpern, & Repacholi, 1993; Shaw, Owens, Vondra, Keenan, & Winslow, 1996). Longitudinal research has also found a relationship between disorganization in infancy and later child psychopathology (Green & Goldwyn, 2002; Lyons-Ruth & Jacobvitz, 1999; van IJzendoorn & Bakermans-Kranenburg, 2003).

## Contribution of Caregiver Sensitivity to Child Outcomes

One would expect that the representations of self and other that are formed as a result of early interactions would show continuity across ages, even into adulthood. However, research has shown that, especially in multi-risk populations in which situations frequently change, stability is quite low and change from one attachment classification to another is common (Belsky, Campbell, Cohn, & Moore, 1996; Lewis, Feiring & Rosenthal, 2000; Waters, Merrick, Treboux, Crowell, & Albersheim, 2000; Waters, Weinfield, & Hamilton, 2000). Instability may be a result of such changes as family structure, divorce or separation, death of a family member, birth of a sibling, mother's return to the workforce, or a move away from support systems. Other changes may occur because as children get older, parents may find their parenting role easier or more difficult to cope with. Parents are often more comfortable with children at one age or another. Some parents may be more comfortable as a nurturer of an infant, whereas others are more comfortable as a teacher, limit setter, or playmate of an older child. Teenage parents and parents with borderline personality disorder (BPD), for example, often find the demands of parenting a toddler or preschooler far more challenging than parenting an infant (Lawson, 2002; Masterson, 1988; Osofsky, Hann, & Peebles, 1993).

As mentioned previously, an infant needs a caregiver who responds promptly and contingently to their cues and provides an appropriate level of nurturance and comfort when the child is hurt, upset, or tired. Parental warmth and responsivity also provide the infant with a sense of security, control, and trust in the environment (Lamb, Ketterlinus, & Fracasso, 1992). Although the constructs of maternal sensitivity and responsiveness are central to attachment theory, however, less attention has been paid to what constitutes these characteristics after infancy. Important goals of the parent–child relationship during the toddler and preschool years are the promotion of autonomy and the joint regulation of the relationship (Greenberg & Speltz, 1988; Kochanska, 1997a). Children's increasing autonomy at this time is supported by helping them gain awareness of themselves and others, and by increasing communication strategies that can allow them to develop joint plans and goals with other people. According to Greenberg and Speltz (1988), if parents adjust their goals and plans to include the child's desires and feelings in decision making, the child will be aided in developing security and trust during the preschool years. Similarly, a number of writers have defined important components of mother's responsiveness as 1) talking about internal states, 2) willingness to allow the child some degree of control in the interaction, 3) using the child's state of involvement as a guide to adjust her suggestions and requests, 4) warmth and supportive presence, and 5) maintaining dialogue with the child (Gardner, 1994; Kochanska, 1997a; Landy & Menna, 1997; Westerman, 1990).

As the child matures, parental behavior should change from a mainly protective function to one in which the emphasis is on the teaching of skills and the encouragement of self-regulation (Solomon, George, & Ivins, 1987). In a study that looked at mother–child interaction and security of attachment at age 6, it was found that, on the one hand, mothers of secure children were accepting and supportive, but on the other hand they also emphasized self-regulation and the learning of skills. Insecure patterns of attachment were associated with maternal rejection, infantilization of the growing child, or role reversal. George and Solomon (1989) suggested that parental support of competence is important to the development of security in middle childhood because autonomy is based on feeling confident about one's own competence as well as having an internalized, secure base. Many new skills are needed by the caregiver: carefully scaffolding and assisting during challenging tasks while allowing the child to solve the task himself; solving conflicting desires between the caregiver and the child; and adopting a directive role, also called a *goal-directed partnership*, with the child in which the child and caregiver negotiate with each other while managing a task or difficult situation (Kochanska, 1997b; Lamb et al., 1992; Thompson, 2000; van Aken & Ricksen-Walraven, 1992).

## Other Parenting Theories and Child Outcomes

In a series of important studies, Baumrind and associates followed preschoolers into adolescence and found that certain components of family interactions and, particularly, discipline style were associated with various developmental outcomes (Baumrind, 1971, 1973). Three primary types of discipline were defined: 1) *authoritarian* (in which the parent is very demanding and does not show responsiveness to the child's emotional needs); 2) *authoritative* (in which the parent is nurturing and loving but also provides clear enforcement of rules and standards, encourages the child's individuality, and allows open discussion between parent and child); and 3) *permissive* (in which the parent makes few demands, and has few expectations of the child and expects the child to discipline and regulate himself). When permissive parenting is extreme it can amount to neglect or disengagement from the needs of the child—especially his emotional needs.

Children who received these different types of discipline showed very different response styles by 8 or 9 years of age. Children in the authoritative families were more competent, socially responsive, and cooperative than the other two types, who had lower social and cognitive competence. Authoritative parenting was also more likely to be associated with high grades than the other styles of parenting (Dornbusch, Ritter, Leiderman, Roberts, & Fraleigh, 1987). The neglected children did worse than any other group in terms of their sense of competence and were more likely to engage in high levels of antisocial and impulsive behavior and delinquency. Alcohol and drug use was also high for these children.

Steinberg and colleagues concluded that a number of parenting behaviors appeared to contribute to the positive outcomes of authoritative parenting, including parental warmth and acceptance, behavioral control, and parental involvement (Steinberg, Lamborn, Darling, Mounts, & Dornbusch, 1994; Steinberg, Lamborn, Dornbusch, & Darling, 1992; Steinberg, Mounts, Lamborn, & Dornbusch, 1991). Simply put, when both warmth and appropriate limit setting are present, internalization of control and willingness to cooperate with parents are more likely (Maccoby & Martin, 1983). Conversely, inconsistently responding to children's behavior or noncontingent, unpredictable maternal behavior have been found to result in higher levels of parent–child conflict and aversive child behavior (Dumas & Wahler, 1985; Wahler, Williams, & Cerezo, 1990). Also, frequent assertion of power and harsh physical punishment and spousal abuse by parents have been associated with increased child aggression and behavior problems (Brody & Schaffer, 1982; Campbell, 1995; Crockenberg & Litman, 1990; George & Main, 1979; Kuczynski & Kochanska, 1990; Maccoby & Martin, 1983; Olwens, 1980; Patterson, 1980, 1995). Rothbaum and Weisz (1994), who conducted a meta-analysis of 47 studies on the association between parental caregiving and behavior problems in children, concluded that parents' rejection and unresponsiveness were related to child externalizing behavior and behavior problems.

Patterson (1980, 1995) developed a theory that has shown that inconsistent discipline and coercive parent–child interactions are related to behavior problems and conduct disorders in children. The model has been supported by empirical testing and describes how parents who are hostile, inconsistent, and permissive create a family environment in which aggressive cycles are learned. Patterson described sequences of behaviors between parents and their child that reinforce the child's demanding and oppositional behavior and allow the child to escape the parent's demands. As a consequence, the child learns that this behavior pays off, and may escalate it when confronted with obstacles or threats of punishment. This happens at the cost of the relationship, however, which becomes highly negative. The more demanding the child, the more frustrated the parent becomes, and this interferes with the development of more constructive discipline (Dishion, French, & Patterson, 1995). Gardner (1987, 1992) also found that mothers of boys with conduct disorder are more likely than mothers in a control group, whose children did not have behavior problems to back off from a directive they have given if the child refuses to comply and responds with conflict behavior. Bugental (1992), whose theory is described in Chapter 12, has a model that differs but is not inconsistent with Patterson's framework and describes how the parent's view of a child as uncontrollable leads to the parent's high emotional arousal level that results in her reacting automatically rather than with more constructive problem-solving approaches. Bugental referred to these patterns as "threat-oriented family systems."

Although enhancing the sensitivity and responsivity of parents toward their infants' cues in the early months is important, it should not be the only focus of early intervention. For instance, a new mother's concerns and need for support may not only be about her baby but also about behavioral issues related to an older child who is having difficulty adjusting to the new baby. It may also be important to be available during periods of developmental change within the child in order to support the parent and to inform her about the new developmental needs of her child.

## ENHANCING THE INTERACTION

Much of parenting or caring for infants and young children takes place at a preconscious level of procedural memory. In other words, parenting is intuitive and based on sensorimotor and emotional schemata that are not dependent on memory systems based on language (Crittenden, Lang, Claussen, & Partridge, 2000). (See Chapter 9 for a discussion of various memory systems and how they influence behavior.) Procedural memory is found in such tasks as riding a bike, swimming, or playing tennis that, once learned, tend to be put into action without thinking or talking about them (Crittenden et al., 2000). When parents' early experiences of being parented are of sensitive, gentle, and responsive interactions, the parenting they provide tends to be the same. If abuse was experienced, however, parents may have to make a conscious effort and to concentrate intensely in order to avoid repeating the same behavioral patterns. Nevertheless, it has been found that under stress, old patterns may be repeated and buried feelings and sensorimotor reactions can be reactivated. Consequently, it can be very helpful to provide new learning experiences for parents on how to provide sensitive and responsive behaviors with their children so new and more adaptive memories of parenting can be laid down (Crittenden et al., 2000).

As well, as Figure 1.5 in Chapter 1 points out, shifts in the behaviors of the parent may very well change the child's behavior and, ultimately, the parent's view of the child. In other words, the system may be able to shift in a more positive direction. Rather than coercive cycles, more adaptive interactions may occur so that reciprocal and synchronous behaviors between parent and child can be established. Although the first few months of the child's life should not be the only focus of early intervention and prevention programs, when early synchronous interactions are encouraged and a secure attachment is established, this can provide an excellent foundation in the child for a sense of trust and security leading to more resilience and competence in later development.

In the interventions described next, *how* the intervention is carried out is important. For example, parents should be encouraged to discuss the experience and the feelings that are aroused in them during interactions with their children. As well, every opportunity should be given to enhance parents' sense of competence and to build on positive aspects of the interaction.

Finally, as pointed out in Chapter 2, parents may be more comfortable with certain intervention approaches than with others. As the research of Bakermans-Kranenburg, Juffer, and van IJzendoorn (1998) demonstrated, parents who were classified as insecure-dismissive (i.e., who are not as interested or comfortable talking about relationships and emotions) tended to profit more from written information and videotaped feedback only. Parents who were classified as preoccupied (who are very interested in talking about their emotions and relationships with others) preferred and profited more from an intervention that provided printed information and videotaped feedback as well as encouraged them to talk about their childhood attachment experiences. Certainly, for many parents, an approach that emphasizes learning and practicing parenting techniques or strategies can be very meaningful, especially if the parent has identified concerns about her relationship with her infant or child, problems with the child's responsiveness or behavior, or anxiety about how to be a "good" parent. Other parents may benefit more from approaches to enhancing the interaction that focus on enhancing self-reflectivity and empathy for the child. As well, it is critical to listen closely to the concerns about the child and parenting that a parent raises and to follow her lead in discussing her anxieties about her child's development or her dilemmas as to how best to respond to him.

Parents, particularly those described in Chapter 9 who have unresolved loss and trauma, may respond to their children at times at an automatic or unconscious level when preoccupied with other thoughts or under stress. In other words, they may be responding negatively for much of the time with hostility or anger or by withdrawal or fear with little consideration about what they are doing. In other words, when they are stressed, the poor parenting is happening at an unconscious level without thought or consideration of what they are doing as they are interacting with their children. This is considered to be Level 1 (unconscious–poor parenting), and at this level it is important, along with intervention for complex posttraumatic stress disorder, to provide strategies to self-regulate and to help ground the individual in the present. Also helpful are approaches described in this chapter that can enhance self-reflectivity and empathy for her child such as Watch, Wait, and Wonder and Interactional Guidance. At Level 2 (conscious–poor parenting) the parent is now aware of some of the parenting practices she uses that are not helpful for her child and that she would like to change, and as a consequence, she is more open to new information. Strategies such as developmental guidance at a teachable moment and the Circle of Security parenting program may be helpful. At Level 3 (conscious–good parenting) the parent is now working hard to change her interactions and needs support, modeling, and affirmation of improvements in the interaction. Sometimes actual coaching of the interaction can be effective, as well as helping her to understand the unique needs of her child according to his age and temperament. At level 4 (unconscious–good parenting) the parent is able to parent positively in a more intuitive way and may only need some continuing support and affirmation that she is doing this. After closing the case it is important to allow the parents to recontact the agency if they have questions about a new developmental stage or their situation changes (see Table 10.1).

The next sections describe a number of approaches to enhancing the interaction that have been shown to be effective.

## Enhancing Parent–Infant and Parent–Child Interactions

The following strategies have been shown to be helpful in enhancing parent–infant and parent–child interactions. Most are relatively inexpensive and easy to implement, although some require special training.

*Use of Soft Baby Carriers*     Using a soft baby carrier (e.g., Snugli) instead of a hard infant seat in which the baby is placed away from the mother has been

**Table 10.1.*** Levels of parent–child interactions and interventions

| Level | Thought processes and parenting responses | Approaches to intervention |
|---|---|---|
| **Level 1:** Unconscious–poor parenting | Parent responds at an automatic or unconscious level in a way that she was parented, which may have included abuse, neglect, and/or non-responsive patterns of parenting<br><br>Parent lacks self-reflectivity and empathy for her child<br><br>Interactions are insensitive, unresponsive, and hostile or helpless | Provide intervention for complex posttraumatic stress disorder.<br><br>Use setting limits approach with abusive or neglecting behavior with involvement of Child Protective Services.<br><br>Use approaches to enhance self-reflectivity and empathy for the child.<br><br>Encourage self-regulation strategies to ground the parent in the present (see Chapter 9).<br><br>Provide modified interactional guidance (see Chapter 9) or interactional guidance (see Chapter 10).<br><br>Use Mother Goose program to encourage warm interactions.<br><br>Use Watch-Wait-and Wonder program.<br><br>Use infant massage.<br><br>Notice aspects of interaction that are positive and give encouragement and praise for them.<br><br>Use Minding the Baby program.<br><br>Use Parents First program.<br><br>Use Pathways to Competence groups.<br><br>Use cognitive and attributionally based approaches. |
| **Level 2:** Conscious–poor parenting | Parent still responds at times at an automatic or unconscious level but is now more conscious of what she would like to change and more open to new information | Provide parenting information at teachable moments or when parent is asking about how to respond to or discipline her child.<br><br>Help her to see that how she was parented is influencing how she parents.<br><br>Provide developmental guidance.<br><br>Using videotapes such as "A Simple Gift."<br><br>Teach toy making.<br><br>Modify the environment and play space.<br><br>Use NCAST approach to enhancing parent–child interaction.<br><br>Use Circle of Security parenting program. |

| Level | Thought processes and parenting responses | Approaches to intervention |
|---|---|---|
| **Level 3:** Conscious–good parenting | Parent is working hard to interact sensitively to her child and to provide consistent and effective limits. She is capable of higher self-reflectivity and empathy for her child | Support and continually affirm her efforts to enhance interactions. Respond to parenting questions and provide information. Use a community home visitor to demonstrate ways to play with his child and to model sensitive interaction. Give information to deal with common developmental issues. Help her to get to know her child's unique temperament. |
| **Level 4:** Unconscious–good parenting | Parenting is more intuitive and natural and parent does not have to think or work so hard to "get it right" | Use infant-previewing. Encourage touch and holding. Maintain and continue support until parent is confident about her parenting. Describe Touchpoints approach so parent is encouraged to contact agency if she has questions or is having difficulty with certain parenting issues and developmental stage of her child. |

*Interventions provided will vary according to parents' willingness to be involved and the availability of services.

shown to successfully encourage secure attachment in babies in multi-risk situations (Anisfeld, Casper, Nozyce, & Cunningham, 1990). In addition, maternal interactions were found to be more sensitive and contingently responsive to the infant's cues when a soft baby carrier was used. This simple way of encouraging physical contact between mothers and infants helps to enhance the relationship between parent and child and the infant's regulation, and makes the infant less irritable and easier to soothe.

This brief, inexpensive intervention has great potential for prevention programs, especially when parents perceive the carrier as a gift rather than as a criticism of their parenting behavior. Before introducing this approach, however, it is important to include a brief explanation of the importance of using the carrier as well as some follow-up and discussion to improve the potential of the carriers to be used successfully and to improve the parent–child relationship. This is also the kind of concrete, evidence-based intervention that could be funded by a foundation or service club.

***Use of Infant Massage***    As discussed in Chapter 2, the use of infant massage has been shown in several studies to have benefits for infant development, and it can also be used to enhance interactions between parents and their infants (Field, 2000). Infant massage is used in a number of cultures to calm infants and to enhance their eating and sleeping and is therefore often an intervention that is acceptable for parents from a variety of cultures. Also it can be helpful to encourage nonthreatening touch for parents who would otherwise be uncomfortable holding and touching their babies. Infant massage has been used successfully with teenage mothers, mothers with depression, and other high-risk parent groups. It has been used in home visits, in early intervention centers, individually, and in groups. Using deep pressure, parents are shown how to massage various parts of their infants' bodies and to avoid other parts. (It is important to point out that for some very hypersensitive infants, infant massage may not be appropriate.)

***Use of a Videotape on the Importance of Affectionate Interaction for Infants***     In one intervention, new mothers were shown one of two videotapes at the hospital. One group watched a videotape of the Brazelton Neonatal Behavior Scale being administered to an infant and affectionate handling of the infant was stressed. This videotape was far more effective in improving the interaction of mothers with their infants than a video showing basic caregiving skills (Wendland-Carro, Piccinini, & Millar, 1999). The Brazelton Scale is an assessment of the infant that focuses on the newborn's capacities for early interaction, particularly habituation, responsiveness, and cuddliness. Many parents are powerfully affected when they see clearly on a video a newborn infant's capacity for focused attention, responsiveness to the human voice and face, and positive reaction to calming. Parents also appear to respond well to an immediate discussion of their own baby's need for similar touch and interaction after they watch such a video. The time after birth is a particularly important window of opportunity for encouraging bonding with the baby and for building on parents' strong desire and openness to maximize their capacity to parent.

***Coaching the Interaction***     For some parents simple, concrete, coaching of their interactions with their infant can be very meaningful. Coaching can be particularly helpful for parents of infants who are temperamentally difficult (van den Boom, 1994, 1995), and for parents of infants with physical or developmental disabilities.

In the coaching intervention, parents can be helped to sensitively respond to their infant's unique cues. The intervention can take place in play sessions between parents and infants during home visits or in groups. Strategies can include verbal instructions, modeling, and use of positive reinforcement of the parents' interactional strengths. The intervention may begin with videotaping of a brief parent–infant interaction, which is used to reinforce positive interactional behaviors and to introduce a few changes if necessary (Clark & Seifer, 1983). However, use of videotaping is not necessary. The following is a list of suggestions for enhancing the parent–child interaction.

1.  Encourage the parent to carry and touch her baby and to make eye contact in the face-to-face position.

2.  Teach the parent to perceive the infant's signals. One way to do this is to encourage the parent to delay responding immediately and intrusively with the baby and to watch, wait, and wonder instead. This is not suggested here as the quite complex intervention discussed later in this chapter, but rather as an easy way to encourage parents to take a little time to become aware of and understand their infant's cues and to learn about their infant through them.

The parent can also be shown that sometimes her baby may signal her desire for engagement and at other times she may show a need for momentary disengagement or for the caregiver to pull back. Teaching the parent about her baby's cues allows her to learn more about what the infant is trying to tell her. Some of the cues that can be pointed out are the meaning of the babies' various cries; signs of disengagement (e.g., yawning, looking away, gaze aversion, fidgeting, and jerky movements, stilling, fussing, pulling away); and signs of engagement (e.g., smiling, alerting with eyes bright, head raising, sustained eye-to-eye contact). Also see the Resources list at the end of the chapter for where to purchase pictures and lists of cues that can be used as well.

3. Teach parents appropriate responses to their baby's cues. Some of the responses include

- Imitating their infant's behavior

- Repeating their infants' verbal expressions such as babbling back or talking gently to the baby, with comments such as "Oh really," "You don't say," "Is that so?"

- Quieting and waiting when their baby shows signs of disengagement

- Playing simple infant games when the baby show signs of desiring interaction, including Pat-a-Cake, Itsy Bitsy Spider, Peekaboo, and I'm Gonna Get You

- Settling a crying baby and recognizing the meaning of different cries as feeling overloaded, tired, hungry, or in need of a diaper change

4. Show parents how to respond to the special needs of their infant. Some infants may need gentler interactions if they become easily overloaded or seem to be hypersensitive to particular sensory modalities such as sound, visual stimulation, or touch. The child with hypersensitivities may need the environment to be less noisy, more calming, and less cluttered with visual stimulation such as toys. He may also require less touching than other infants. The infant with low muscle tone, poor postural control, and very passive behavior may need to have a great deal of visual and auditory stimulation in order to increase his interest in motor activities. Other infants who are hyposensitive and less responsive may need exaggerated gestures and very focused stimulation to get them engaged in interactions.

**Infant Previewing**    Trad (1989, 1992) has described an approach called *infant previewing* in which parents are coached to interact with their baby or toddler using specific behavioral exercises. The exercises chosen represent the developmental skill the infant is either already working on or is expected to master soon. Parents are encouraged to support their child to practice the new skill while letting him return to his present developmental level when he seems tired of the previewing exercise. Some examples might be learning to grasp an object, build with blocks, crawl, or walk. The approach informs parents about behaviors that are likely to appear soon and encourages them to interact with their infants in ways that will encourage their development. As well, the tasks are in the *zone of* *proximal development*; that is, they are not too easy or too difficult for the infant to try and, as a consequence, they provide excellent motivation. Trad has used the approach with parents individually and in groups.

Many of the strategies already described can also be used with older children. As the infant becomes a toddler and then a preschooler, however, parents may be presented with new challenges and dilemmas. Some of these include disciplining the child, dealing with the child's difficult emotions, helping a child whose language is delayed, and encouraging a child to concentrate and play alone. For many parents, the dilemma becomes how to continue to nurture their child but also to provide the limits and encouragement for his growing independence. Some parents may find it hard to provide the comforting and nurturing the child continues to need, whereas others may have more difficulty in letting the child explore the environment and have the opportunity to individuate.

**The "Greenspan" Floor Time Model**    *Floor time* is an approach that encourages parents to provide sensitive and responsive interactions with their infants, toddlers, and preschoolers. This approach has been used successfully with children with challenges such as autism spectrum disorders to extend their play in ways that can enhance their ability for pretend play, encourage two-way interaction, and encourage them to socialize more (Greenspan & Wieder, 1998). Floor time encourages children to communicate and to take more initiative. In addition, the program helps parents to understand their children's interactional styles better and has been shown to help parents who have irritable toddlers (DeGangi & Greenspan, 1997). The model identifies five steps that are taught to parents:

*Step One:* Observation

Parents are supported to listen and to watch their child and to be good observers of facial expressions, tone of voice, gestures, body posture, and words or lack of words.

*Step Two:* Approach—Opening Circles of Communication

Parents are encouraged to build on the play themes that the child introduces. Parents are also coached to approach the child and to acknowledge any emotional displays or communication attempts the child makes.

*Step Three:* Following the Child's Lead

Parents are shown how to be "assistants" to the child while allowing the child to choose the toys or play theme. This supportive and nonintrusive approach encourages self-esteem and a sense of warmth and connectedness for both the parent and child.

*Step Four:* Extend and Expand the Play

Parents are asked to remain nonintrusive but to make supportive comments and to ask questions to stimulate creative thinking and to keep the drama going. Parents may talk to the child about what is going on.

*Step Five:* Child Closes the Circle of Communication

One of the goals of the intervention is to help the child to communicate. During this step the child is encouraged to build on the parents' communication with comments or gestures of her own. By having these back-and-forth interactions or circles of communication, the child begins to understand and participate in two-way communication.

***Developmental Guidance***    Developmental guidance (i.e., providing relevant developmental information), can be used in order to enhance parent–child interactions in a variety of ways. These include

- Answering questions about development or children's behavior and giving information on helpful, related parenting techniques in printed form or using videotapes. The approach can be used in home visits, counseling sessions, and parenting groups.

- Having parents complete a developmental screen such as the Ages & Stages Questionnaires® (ASQ; Bricker & Squires, 1999). The ASQ monitors five areas of development: 1) communication, 2) gross motor, 3) fine motor, 4) problem-solving, and 5) personal–social and social-emotional skills. During and after the assessment, the parents can be given some suggestions on how to interact with their infant to enhance development in any areas in which difficulties are identified or about which they have questions. Many parents perceive the focus on the baby as very nonthreatening, and strengths can be noted and their contribution to the development of their baby acknowledged.

- Sharing brief stories about the service provider's own or other parents' similar experiences. Perhaps most useful and encouraging is talking about approaches that other parents have found to work. This kind of discussion can help to normalize the parents' struggles and also to provide them with some approaches to try with their children that other parents have found practical and helpful.

***Teaching Parents Toy Making***    Many parents find it difficult to play with their infants and young children, sometimes because they see it as a waste of time, or because they were never played with themselves. Having parents involved in making toys can give them a sense of mastery and often reveals their hidden strengths and talents. In addition, homemade toys can provide children with play materials for very little cost. Playing with the baby or child with the completed toy can be a very satisfying experience for the parent and can enhance the interaction between parent and child. If this activity is incorporated into a workshop, the toys can be chosen for a particular age group or for children with a particular developmental challenge. Toys can be used to focus discussion on the interactional needs of the children; for example, toys can be made to encourage exploration, pretend play (e.g., puppets), or motor development (e.g., swings from tires and "houses" from large boxes).

***Mother Goose Intervention***    The Parent–Child Mother Goose Program approach is a group intervention for mothers of children between the ages of birth and 2½ that has been developed using rhymes and songs focusing on enhancing the parent–child relationship and the development of language and cognition. Parents are encouraged to sing songs, rhymes, and games from their own culture. In the groups, parents are encouraged to hold their children on their laps and to sing to them and with them. They are also encouraged to use the rhymes and songs they learn with their children at home. The group finishes with a story or folktale provided by the facilitator.

Singing songs from their own childhoods can often encourage parents to feel close to their children and may bring back memories of happy times spent with their own parents or other caregivers. The holding and rhythm of the songs can be very positive and nonthreatening ways to enhance parent–child interactions and relationships and the development of the child (Canadian Institute of Child Health, 2001; Parent–Child Mother Goose Program, 2002).

## Modifying the Environment and Play Space to Meet the Needs of the Growing Child

Essential to all aspects of children's development is the opportunity to explore their world and feel some control over the environment, and to feel safe and comfortable doing it. Parents and service providers can engage in collaborative problem solving to find ways to adapt the environment to enable the child to do this. Some examples are

- Encouraging parents to create and use routines for bedtime and mealtimes

- Encouraging parents to play with their child and to follow their child's lead in the play

- Teaching parents that even a brief period a day of playing with their child may actually improve the child's ability and interest in playing alone at other times

- Helping parents to childproof the environment and redesigning the play space for a toddler to provide more space for safe exploring and freedom of movement

- Providing information on appropriate discipline and limits and, with the parent's permission, modeling some useful approaches

Some parents may want to focus on preparing their children for school so they will be able to succeed in the classroom setting. Interventionists can help parents do this by suggesting age-appropriate activities and encouraging them to support children in these activities by being available to help them when they become frustrated. It can also be helpful to suggest that children need to be able to concentrate for increasing periods of time and that parental support during these activities can reinforce the importance of focusing and concentrating on a task.

## Dealing with Common Developmental Issues

Some of the parenting issues that parents of young children are most likely to confront are in the following areas or topics:

- Eating and sleeping

- Toilet training

- Difficult behavior and discipline

- Tantrums and aggressive outbursts

- Separation anxiety or more generalized anxiety, particularly if the child has started to attend child care

- Fears of certain objects, living creatures, people, or situations

- Difficulty concentrating and playing alone

When these problems are within typical limits and appear to be age appropriate, parents can be given information in printed form, topics can be discussed, and appropriate ways to deal with the issues modeled and encouraged. Some parents may need support to be firm, whereas others may need to be encouraged to allow some flexibility without continually setting limits on every behavior. Sometimes parents go to the opposite extreme of the parenting they received themselves. For example, the parent who was raised with rules she found to be too strict may set no limits, or the parent who was constantly pushed to succeed may not encourage his child to try to do well. Discussions about these tendencies and information about the importance of limits or encouragement can help parents to better understand their motivations so that they can make positive changes in their interactions. Another approach can be to have a parent keep a record of when the challenging behavior occurs and what the circumstances are. For example, a record of eating and meals or sleeping patterns can be helpful if these are issues of concern. This helps the parent to focus on what is really happening and may help her to begin to identify some reasons for the difficulty the child is having. The parent may also find that the issue is not as big as she had believed, and this may allow her to relax and alleviate the problem.

Parenting groups can be an excellent way to provide parents with information to enhance their interactions with young children. Some groups can be somewhat nondirective and respond primarily to parents' questions, whereas others are more structured and make use of program manuals, specially produced videos, and workbooks. Nobody's Perfect (Health Canada, 2000) and Right from the Start (Niccols & Mohamed, 2000) are two groups that use a structured program. Although the information provided is important, the support provided by other parents and the experience of finding that other parents share similar challenges can be invaluable.

In some cases when the child is not developing typically it will be necessary for the parent and/or child to receive appropriate intervention or more in-depth intervention. Some examples of such interventions are described next. When children have language delays, for example, it is important that parents are encouraged to provide appropriate interactions with them that can enhance their language, including following their child's lead and acknowledging and repeating any words that the child is trying to say. Parents can be given information about how to do this and can be supported to carry the strategies out. These include speaking clearly and often to their children to label things for them. Questions can sometimes keep the child talking. Sometimes, encouraging children to use language to get the thing they want can be helpful as long as it is not too frustrating for a child who does not have a word for something. Of course, reading books and singing songs are extremely important. These kinds of strategies can be taught in groups. Videotaping parents' interactions with their children and playing them back can help parents to be more supportive and less intrusive when trying to enhance their children's language. An excellent program of this type is It Takes Two to Talk or the Hanen Program, which has been developed for children with language delays as well as those with language delays who fall in the autism spectrum (Manolson, Ward, & Dodington, 1995).

## More Focused Interventions to Enhance Especially Challenging Interactions

Other, more focused approaches may be necessary when parents are already having significant difficulties interacting with their children. They may also be needed when other approaches are not successful in helping them to be more sensitive to their child's needs. Approaches that also focus on enhancing parents' views of themselves and their children and that enable them to be more self-reflective may be necessary. Interventions that have been successful in improving attachment and/or enhancing the parent–child relationship are described in this section.

*The Use of Videotape Viewing*    In addition to using videotaped interactions such as the Brazelton videotape mentioned previously, other videotape interventions have proven useful in helping to improve parent–child interactions. An intervention in which a 10- to 20-minute play or feeding interaction between a mother and her infant or child is videotaped and then played back for discussion between the parent and interventionist has been used in a number of programs. These include the STEEP (Steps Toward Effective and Enjoyable Parenting) Program at the University of Minnesota; an intervention for mothers who are experiencing depression at the University of Wisconsin (Clark, 2000); and the Center Home Visiting Comparison Study with teenage mothers with preterm infants at the University of Florida (Field, Widmayer, Stringer, & Ignatoff, 1980). The method has been outlined in detail in a number of articles (Bernstein, 1997; McDonough, 1993a, 1995, 2000).

Different approaches to interaction guidance using videotape viewing have been used. In one method an interaction is videotaped, reviewed by the interventionist after the session to select appropriate moments to comment on, and played back and discussed with the parent at the next appointment. In another approach an interaction is videotaped and played back immediately and discussed in the same session. Usually parts of the interaction that are positive are identified and the parent is encouraged to continue to provide them. When interactions are more negative, the interventionist may stop at these times and ask the parent to comment on them, and then make suggestions of other strategies to try.

In carrying out this intervention, a number of questions are used that can help elicit ideas from a parent about what she was thinking about during the interaction, what she thinks about a piece of the videotape, and how she felt at a particular time in the interaction. Posing these questions, as well as encouraging the mother to think about how her baby may be thinking, can encourage self-reflectivity. Standing back and viewing the interaction can be very helpful in enabling her to think in a different way about her own thoughts and feelings about her baby and how they interact together. Examples of questions that can be used are listed here:

- "You seemed to know just what she wanted you to do there. How could you tell what to do?"

- "Your baby really seemed to enjoy doing that with you. Do you often do that together?"

- "That is a really great way to get her attention. See how she started to try to talk back to you."

- "You really seemed to have fun with her today; she certainly loved the way you played with her."

- "I wonder how it feels to. . . when you. . . ?" (pointing out some positive behavior such as touching, and noticing the child's cues).

- "What did you think your child was feeling then?"

- "What do you think he was trying to tell you then?"

The following are a few more techniques:

- Talk to the parent before the videotape is played back and ask her to comment on the session. Ask about whether she enjoyed the play session and whether it is the same or different from what she has experienced with her child before. Also see if there was anything that surprised her about the session.

- Stop the tape if the mother is not responding to the child's cues and ask her what she was thinking about.

- Stop the tape when the child is on screen and the mother seems upset, angry, frightened, or sad, and ask her what the child is reminding her of.

- Talk for the baby. For example, say "Mom, I really like it when you play with me and talk to me."

The method has been evaluated in two studies that showed positive outcomes that are described in Chapter 2 (Bakermans-Kranenburg et al., 1998; Robert-Tissot et al., 1996).

***Using the Watch, Wait, and Wonder Program to Enhance Self-Reflectivity and the Interaction***    Wesner, Dowling, and Johnson introduced the Watch, Wait, and Wonder (WWW) approach in 1982. Later expanded on and researched, it has stimulated interest as an exciting short-term intervention for parents and young children with attachment difficulties (Cohen et al., 1999; Muir, 1992; Muir, Lojkasek, & Cohen, 1999).

Theoretically, the WWW program is based on attachment theory; consequently, the emphasis is on enhancing the mother–child relationship. It has also been shown to help mothers understand and begin to deal with the intense and difficult emotions that may be elicited by the interactions that occur in the first part of the session. Containing the parent's feelings and helping the parent to reflect on their meaning can also contribute to her ability to self-reflect, especially as it relates to her experience with her infant.

Evaluation of the effectiveness of the WWW program compared it with another intervention used at the Children's Mental Health Center of a short-term psychodynamic family approach. The WWW approach was successful in reducing disorganization in the child, reducing child problems such as difficulties with eating and sleeping, and enhancing the interactional behaviors of the mother. Parents' sense of competence was improved and parenting stress was reduced. WWW was more successful than the psychodynamic approach in enhancing interactions and promoting secure attachment and reducing disorganized attachment. See Chapter 2 for a description of the evaluation (Cohen et al., 1999).

The WWW technique has two components: 1) an infant-led interaction and 2) a discussion between the mother and the therapist in which she can discuss her observations about what occurred in the session and her experience of it. Each is described next.

*Infant-Led Interaction*    Infant-led interaction is carried out in a room with toys suitable to the child's developmental level. The same toys are used each week. During the interaction, the parent is asked to get down on the floor, to remain in contact with her child, and to follow his lead. She is encouraged to respond to her child's cues but not to teach or direct the intervention in any way. She is asked not to initiate the play or take over the activity and play out her own scenarios. She is told that whatever the child does in the room she is just to Watch, Wait, and Wonder. The play sequence usually takes about 20–30 minutes but may be stopped earlier if an infant becomes too upset or if a parent is becoming stressed by the situation.

*Parent-Led Discussion*    When the play is finished, a discussion takes place for the remainder of the 50-minute session while the child continues to play in the room. In this part of the intervention, the parent is encouraged to lead. The idea is to facilitate discussion of the parent's view and observations of what occurred, including what the infant did and how it made the parent think and feel. It has been found that at first, responses are only about observations, but over time the observations begin to increase in understanding and depth, and the parent will begin to explore her thoughts and feelings about what she saw and experienced.

Some parents may comment on something that made it difficult to continue to Watch, Wait, and Wonder. It may become possible to explore with the mother what was difficult about it. Other observations may lead into a discussion about a mother's experiences with her own mother. These moments may allow for exploration of how these experiences of relational difficulties could be repeated and could affect her current relationships, particularly the one with her infant. These memories should not be pushed for and, in fact, discussion of them has not been found to be crucial for the success of the intervention in improving the relationship between mother and infant (Muir et al., 1999).

It has been suggested that WWW works best when the problem is primarily with the parent–child relationship in the form of eating and sleeping problems, angry and aggressive behavior, or separation anxiety. The mother may not feel bonded with her infant, and it usually is clear from the initial assessment that the parent is having difficulty being sensitive and playing responsively with her child.

The following situations are usually not suitable for parents contemplating WWW:

- A significant marital problem
- The father openly opposes the idea of his wife and baby coming for the intervention
- Mother is very depressed or preoccupied with significant external stressors

- A recent or impending loss or illness of a close family member, or impending or recent marital breakup

- Psychiatric disorder in the mother

Although the WWW intervention is primarily focused on enhancing the interaction, relationship, and attachment between parents and their children, it can have a significant impact on enhancing the self-reflectivity of parents, and consequently contributes in this way to a more responsive and sensitive interaction and secure attachment.

The intervention as described may seem deceptively simple; however, the issues that are brought to the surface may be very disturbing for the mother, and it is important that those carrying it out have access to supervision when necessary. Training is available in using WWW and details of it are listed at the end of the Chapter.

*The Minding the Baby Project*    The Minding the Baby project is a home visiting program developed by Slade and colleagues to encourage the development of self-reflectivity (Slade et al., 2004). The program begins during the mother's second trimester of her pregnancy and continues until the child's second birthday. The emphasis is on helping the mother "keep her baby in mind," and a clinical social worker and pediatric nurse provide the program together in order to integrate a nursing and mental health model. Home visitors are trained to help the mother to keep her baby's mental and physical state foremost in her mind and to model this way of thinking and feeling about the baby and young child. Outcome data is not yet available on the approach; however, preliminary clinical impressions suggest that it can enhance parents' interactions with their infants. See Resources at the end of the chapter on where to obtain further information on the program.

*The Nursing Child Assessment Satellite Training (NCAST) Approach*    Barnard and associates have developed an approach to enhancing the parent–child interaction based on the use of the NCATS Teaching and Feeding Scales (Barnard, Eyres, Lobo, & Snyder, 1983; Barnard & Kelly, 1990; Sumner & Spietz, 1994a,b). The scales are used from birth to 3 years to identify any areas of concern with the parents' sensitivity to the infant's cues, response to distress, social-emotional growth fostering, and cognitive growth fostering. Any specific difficulties are identified and the mother is informed about them and coached to overcome them. This could include encouraging the mother to talk to her infant. She is also helped to read her child's cues and to learn ways to enhance his responsiveness. The NCATS scales are repeated every few months and changes and improvements are identified and commented on by the home visitor in order to encourage the parent. Useful handouts and picture cards are also provided for parents on understanding cues for engagement and disengagement and state behaviors.

## Group Interventions

The following interventions have been shown to be successful with groups.

*The Parents First Program*    The Parents First Program was developed by Goyette-Ewing, Slade, Knoebber, Gilliam, Truman, and Mayes (2002), and is a group program for parents of children in child care centers and preschools. The groups are for parents of children from 1 to 5 years of age and meet for 12 weeks. Parents are encouraged to think about the meaning behind their child's behavior rather than being given strategies or discipline solutions. As a result of the group, parents report improvement in problems with sleeping or transitions and are more able to understand their children (Goyette-Ewing et al., 2002). The group intervention curriculum includes handouts for parents, suggestions for group activities, and journaling exercises. A curriculum is being developed for mothers and fathers during the pregnancy and perinatal periods. See Resources at the end of the chapter for information on how to learn more about the program.

### The Circle of Security: An Attachment-Based Intervention

The Circle of Security intervention is a 20-week group program designed to increase parents' sensitivity and responsivity to their children's cues and increase parent self-reflectivity and ability to reflect on their own experience of being parented (Marvin, Cooper, Hoffman, & Powell, 2002). Videotaped vignettes of each parent's interaction with his or her child are shown to the group and parents learn from the group discussion. One positive aspect of the interaction is shown as well as a piece of the tape that illustrates a less-used capacity or a point of struggle between the child and parent. Also, individualized intervention goals are developed for each parent and their attachment pattern with their child is assessed before the group begins. These are then reviewed at the end of the group. The authors are currently analyzing the data on 75 dyads, with preliminary results suggesting that children with Disordered patterns of attachment are moving to more Ordered classifications, the number of children classified as Secure is increasing, and the number of caregivers classified as Disordered is decreasing. Further information is available on the website: see Resources at the end of the chapter.

### Pathways to Competence Parenting Groups

The Pathways to Competence Parenting Program groups (Landy & Thompson, 2006) can be provided for 10–20 weeks, during which parents learn about important developmental capacities that their children need to thrive and how they can assist their children to develop them. These include secure attachment, language and communication, body self, play, self-esteem, behavioral control, emotion regulation, concentration and problem-solving, social competence, and empathy. When each developmental achievement is discussed, parents think about their experiences growing up and explore how it is for their child. The emphasis throughout is on how their child is affected by their parenting and how the child thinks and feels about it. Parents also discuss child behavioral issues and how to cope with them. As they begin to understand the importance of their relationship with their child, as well as of playing, communicating, containing their emotions, and showing empathy to their children, the information enables them to understand their children differently and to adapt to their children's developmental needs. A variety of approaches are used including role playing, group exercises and discussions family of origin (i.e., encouraging parents to see how the way they were parented is affecting them), and self-care.

The program was effective with parents of preschoolers ages 3–6 years in reducing aggressive behavior problems, enhancing parents' sense of competence in their parenting role, reducing maternal depression, and increasing parenting knowledge. Parents' acceptance and richness of perceptions of and caregiving sensitivity to the child, as measured by the Working Model of the Child Interview, were also improved (Landy & Menna, 1998; Landy & Menna, 2006; Menna & Landy, 2001). The program has also been effective with parents receiving Child Protective Services and with mothers who have been exposed to spousal abuse and whose children witnessed the violence. The program is based on the book *Pathways to Competence* (Landy, 2002b). A manual is available to use in the parenting groups that outlines each component or step, provides charts for group exercises, and outlines the principles of parenting that are used to encourage each developmental component. Discussion of group process and the use of the group for training professionals are also provided (Landy & Thompson, 2006). See Resources at the end of the chapter for more information on the groups.

## USING ENHANCEMENT OF PARENT INTERACTIONS: CASE-STUDY FAMILIES

Although coaching the interactions with their children was not the only focus of the intervention for either of the case-study families, nevertheless, every opportunity for intervening at a behavioral level was optimized in order to enhance their interactions and thus their relationships with their children.

### Mark's Family

Approaches to improve interactions were an important component of this intervention. Because Mark was in preschool, the emphasis was on helping his parents to provide appropriate structure and discipline for him and assisting them to overcome his barriers to learning certain tasks and information. In order to do this, Mark's parents were given information on how to provide consistent discipline for him and to respond to his emotional needs. Although information was helpful to enhance their interactions, developmental guidance that was provided around concrete situations as they were occurring or right after they occurred was also very helpful in changing interactions. For example, the fact that Mark's parents allowed him to wave a stick around repeatedly after having it removed several times could be used to illustrate the need for more structure and control of Mark's behavior. When Joan was concerned about Mark not sleeping, she was asked to keep a record of how long he slept and encouraged to be extremely firm about putting him to bed and getting him to fall asleep on his own.

Because Mark was having difficulty learning to write his letters and yet often refused to practice, his parents were encouraged to insist that he spend at least 10 minutes a day doing "homework" with his numbers and letters. During this time they were shown how to encourage Mark's efforts, to insist that he stayed focused, and to teach him how to talk himself through the task by saying, for example, "I can do it, just one more letter to do" or, "It goes down here and around, now I can do it." They were also shown how to notice his efforts toward completion and not to wait to only praise the finished product.

Michael already played a great deal with Mark and his younger brother, but Joan was less comfortable playing with her children. She was, therefore, asked to spend some time each week playing with Mark, following his lead, and encouraging him to play out and discuss any concerns about home or school.

Development guidance was also used to help Mark's parents understand the need to help him move beyond his present developmental stage of grandiosity and ego-centricity to one in which he was more aware of other people's needs and was able to be more thoughtful and empathetic of others. If he was aggressive toward other children, his parents were instructed to talk about the feelings and thoughts of the children he hurt. They were also told to encourage him to share and to take turns.

Joan was involved in psychodynamic psychotherapy, which was primarily focused on her tendency to ignore or punish Mark's sad reactions and emotions. As she began to understand the reasons behind these reactions, she was coached to acknowledge Mark's feelings when he was upset, to empathize with him and to calm him down, and then to support him to find a solution to deal with the problem. This was very different for Mark, who had previously had his sad reactions dismissed and even punished.

## Nina's Family

For Nina, some interactional coaching was carried out with her and baby Paul during occasional mother–infant sessions. When encouraged, Nina became better able to read Paul's cues and to play with him and respond sensitively by talking to him and imitating his verbalizations.

In order to learn to deal with Derrick's acting out, Nina attended a parenting group in the community on positive parenting that she found very helpful. However, providing information as she requested it on what to do as difficulties arose was also very helpful.

Nina's individual sessions in which she gradually began to see how Meg reminded her of herself as a defenseless little girl were the most useful for improving her interactions with Meg so that they were more responsive and nurturing. In the joint family sessions, as Nina made comments to the children or ignored their requests for help, coaching and encouraging her to be more responsive was helpful.

## CONCLUSION

In conclusion, although the suggestions made in this chapter to help parents change their behaviors with their children can, at times, be helpful, the importance of a much more broadly focused and intensive approach with many multi-risk and complex families cannot be forgotten. Short-term, focused clinical approaches to improve parent–child interaction within a framework of frequent and sometimes long-term support may be necessary. Also, the approaches described here may be introduced at the beginning of an intervention with a parent who is requesting help with her relationship with her child or for a parent who seems most comfortable with an approach that provides information about topics she is concerned about or is interested in.

Parents' interactions with their children are influenced by their feelings and beliefs about their child and the behavior that they have seen modeled by other parents, including their own. They are also affected by the children's temperament and other characteristics. Approaches that only focus on improving parents' behavior and ignore thoughts and feelings may not be effective with some parents, but typically should be used in combination with encouragement to talk about and express the beliefs and emotions that are contributing to their interactional behavior.

## RESOURCES

### Pictures and Lists of Cues to Use to Coach the Parent–Child Interaction

Thoman, E., & Browder, S. (1987). *Born dancing: How intuitive parents understand their baby's unspoken language and natural rhythms.* New York: Harper & Row.

Erickson, M., & Kurz-Riemer, K. (1999). *Infants, toddlers, and families* (pp. 64–65 Table 3.2. Definitions of infant cues) New York: Guilford Press.

Lynch-Fraser, D., & Tiegerman, E. (1987). *Baby signals: The breakthrough parenting guide for the 90s.* New York: St. Martins Paperbacks.

### Watch, Wait, and Wonder

Muir, E., Lojkasek, M., & Cohen, N.J. (1999). *Watch, Wait and Wonder: A manual describing a dyadic infant-led approach to problems in infancy and early childhood.* Toronto: Hincks-Dellcrest Institute.

Manual and training available from

Mirek Lojkasek, M.D.
Hincks-Dellcrest Institute
114 Maitland Street
Toronto, Ontario M4Y 1E1
Canada
416-924-1164 Ext. 3313

### The Minding the Baby Program

Slade, A., Sadler, L., Mayes, L., Ezepchick, J., Webb, D., De Dios-Kenn, C., Klein, K. Mitcheom, K., & Shader, Z. (2004). *Minding the baby: A working manual.* Unpublished manuscript, Yale Child Study Center.

e-mail: arietta.slade@yale.edu

### Parents First Program

Goyette-Ewing, M., Slade, A., Knoebber, K., Gilliam, W., Truman, S., & Mayes, L. (2002). *Parents First: A developmental parenting program.* Unpublished manuscript, Yale Child Study Center.

e-mail: arietta.slade@yale.edu

### Pathways to Competence Parenting Program

Landy, S., & Thompson, E. (2006). *Pathways to competence for young children: A Parenting Program.* Baltimore: Paul H. Brookes Publishing Co.

Sarah Landy, Ph.D.
Hincks-Dellcrest Institute
114 Maitland St.
Toronto, Ontario M4Y 1E1
Canada

Based on the book Landy, S. (2002). *Pathways to competence: Encouraging healthy social and emotional development in young children.* Baltimore: Paul H. Brookes Publishing Co.

### The Parent–Child Mother Goose Program

Lottridge, C.B. (1999). *Favorite interactive rhymes and how to use them in your Parent–
Child Mother Goose Program.* Toronto: Parent–Child Mother Goose Program.

Book and training available from

Parent–Child Mother Goose Program
National Office
720 Bathurst St., Suite 500A
Toronto, Ontario M5S 2R4
Canada
website: http://www.nald.ca/mothergooseprogram
e-mail: mgoose@web.net

### The Circle of Security Parenting Program

Information on the program available on the web site:
    http://www.security@attbi.com

### Floor Time

Hanna, S., & Wilford, S. (1990). *Floor time: Tuning in to each child.* New York:
    Scholastic.

### NCATS Resources

*Keys to Caregiving: Study guide*

Sumner, G., & Spietz, A. (1994). *Caregiver/Parent–child interaction: Teaching manual.*
    Seattle, Washington: NCATS Publications, University of Washington.

Sumner, G., & Spietz, A. (1994). *Caregiver/Parent–child interaction: Feeding manual.*
    Seattle, Washington: NCATS Publications, University of Washington.

NCATS Programs
University of Washington
Box 357920
Seattle, Washington
web site: http://www.ncast@u.washington.edu

## *Videos*

Infant Mental Health Project (IMP). *A simple gift: Helping your young child cope with feelings.* Videotape and manual. Toronto: Infant Mental Health Promotion Project, the Hospital for Sick Children.

Infant Mental Health Promotion (IMP) Project. *A simple gift: Comforting your baby.* Videotape and manual. Toronto: Infant Mental Health Promotion Project, The Hospital for Sick Children.

Infant Mental Health Project (IMP). *A simple gift: Ending the cycle of hurt.* Videotape and manual, Toronto: Infant Mental Health Promotion Project, the Hospital for Sick Children.

## *Parenting Programs*

### Nobody's Perfect

Nobody's Perfect is a parenting education and support program for parents of children between birth and 5 years. It was developed and is available for parents who are young, single, or socially or geographically isolated and who have low income or limited formal education. It can be offered over 6–8 weekly group sessions or on a one-to-one basis.

Health Canada (2000). *Working with Nobody's Perfect: A facilitator's guide.* Ottawa, ON: Health Canada.

### Right from the Start

The program is for parents of children from birth to 2 years and is attachment based. It uses an active learning approach and videotaped examples of parent–child interactions that are used for parents to identify common parenting errors. The eight sessions use large and small discussion groups and homework practice. A pilot evaluation showed that the group produced lower levels of parent–child dysfunctional interaction, parental distress, and depression in a group of parents with children with developmental delays (Niccols & Mohamed, 2000).

Niccols, A. (2001). *Right from the Start: An attachment-based course for parents of infants under 2 years. Leaders Manual.* Hamilton, Ontario: Infant–Parent Program, Hamilton Health Sciences and McMaster University.

Available from

Infant–Parent Program
Dr. Alison Niccols
Chedoke Child and Family Centre
Children's Hospital
Hamilton Health Centre
Hamilton, Ontario L8W 3Z5
Canada
email: niccols@hhsc.ca

## *Hanen Groups*

Manolson, A., Ward, B., & Dodington, N. (1995). *You make the difference in helping your child learn.* Toronto: The Hanen Centre.

Available from

The Hanen Centre
252 Bloor St. West, Room 390
Toronto ON M5S 1V5
Canada

# Encouraging Emotion Regulation in Parents

Many researchers and other writers have acknowledged emotion regulation to be key to an individual's mental and physical health and to contribute to psychopathology when failure to regulate emotions is extreme; however, it has been very difficult to define (Bradley, 2000; Bridges, Denham, & Ganiban, 2004; Gross, 2002; Thompson & Calkins, 1996). Historically, researchers have tended to focus on different aspects of emotion, rendering consensus difficult. For example, much of the early research on emotions, especially of infants and young children, emphasized examining the facial displays of various types of discrete emotions when they are first displayed in children (Ekman, 1984, 1992; Izard, 1992; Tomkins, 1984). More recently, many theorists have concentrated instead on differences between the two affective states of positive (pleasant) and negative (unpleasant) feelings and the importance of negative affective states in understanding the development of psychopathology (Bradley, 2000; Feldman, 1995; LeDoux, 1996). Some researchers have begun to look at what occurs during the experience of negative emotions in order to be able to suggest various targets for intervention when these negative emotions become overwhelming (Gross, 1998).

This chapter looks at various approaches to defining emotions and their regulation. Most definitions of emotion have acknowledged their complexity and that the state of the emotional system is dynamic and changes continuously (Hoeksma, Oosterlaan, & Schipper, 2004). For the purposes of this chapter, *emotion* (or *affect*) *regulation* "refers to the process by which people control or self-regulate internal reactions to emotions as well as their outward expression" (Landy, 2002a, p. 421).

Various systems and responses that are activated when emotions are intense have been identified (Bradley, 2000; Gross, 1998; Kagan, 1994a). These include the following:

- *Physiological reactions* that include activation of the autonomic nervous system (i.e., changes in the function of the heart, blood vessels, muscles, and stomach and intestines); the hypothalamic-pituitary-adrenal (HPA) axis; and the frontal lobes of the brain. As well, neurotransmitters are released that may facilitate or modulate the transmission of information across neural synapses and networks (Fox, 1994; Fox, Schmidt, Calkins, Rubin, & Coplan, 1996; LeDoux, 1996; Panksepp, 1993; Porges, 1996; Rogeness & McClure, 1996).

- *Cognitions and subjective interpretations and experiences of the emotional response,* including how relevant, positive or negative, controllable, and compatible the emotion is with self-perceptions (Caspi & Bern, 1990; Ellsworth, 1994; Gross, 1999)

- *Action responses* that would probably include facial expressions, subtle body movements, and sometimes motor responses such as moving away from or toward the elicitor of the emotion

Longer lasting emotional responses that are built up over time and become enduring states are created by hundreds of different emotional experiences. These prolonged emotional experiences can result in a chronic state of arousal and are thought to underlie the development of various types of psychopathology including depression, anxiety, and conduct disorders (Bradley, 2000; Landy, 2002a). Therefore, it is clear that the capacity to regulate emotions in an adaptive way is crucial for a sense of emotional well-being and the development of coping and resilience.

## WHAT CONTRIBUTES TO THE DEVELOPMENT OF EMOTION REGULATION?

Failures of emotion regulation are evident in media stories covering such incidents as school shootings and acts of road rage and abuse, and depression and suicide are on the rise nationwide and particularly in some groups (e.g., members of some native reservations in North America and inner-city youth involved in gangs). Understanding what contributes to the development of adaptive coping strategies and to the failure in containment and regulation of emotions is crucial for service providers who work with multi-risk families. This is true whether the professionals are seeking to eliminate factors leading to difficulties in emotion regulation and intervene when disorders do occur or to teach parents how to avoid developing serious difficulties. The next sections briefly review some of these contributors to difficulties with emotion regulation.

### Genetic and Temperament Characteristics

In recent years, researchers have been exploring how genetic factors contribute to a variety of disorders attributed in part to emotion regulation failure. Although relative contributions of genetic factors vary for different disorders, they are generally in the range of 30%–50% (Bradley, 2000). Other factors in the individual's past and present environment contribute to the other portion. When children have genetic or biological disorders such as autism or Down syndrome, their emotion regulation may be significantly affected.

Individuals with a genetic vulnerability to various disorders of emotion regulation such as anxiety, mood disorders, and—to a lesser extent—problems managing anger and aggression, usually have higher levels of arousal to stressful situations or an increased sensitivity to various aspects of life events and situations. For these individuals, not only do they experience more intense arousal but also—once their nervous systems are activated—the effect is more prolonged than for individuals who are less affected.

The concept of *temperament* refers to inborn individual differences in infants. Various temperament characteristics have also been linked to difficulties in emotion regulation in children. These are reactivity (i.e., the speed or intensity of the initial reaction) and self-regulation (i.e., the capacity to modify the emotion by adopting various behavioral strategies). Various studies using physiological measures have provided evidence that infants of different temperaments regulate emotions differently and use different strategies when distressed (Stifter & Braungart, 1995).

Behavioral inhibition is another area that has been studied in relation to the effects of temperament. For example, Kagan and associates found that fearful and inhibited children have a number of physiological reactions that appear to contribute to their temperament traits (Kagan, 1989, 1997, 1999; Kagan & Snidman, 1991). These have included high and stable heart rate and higher cortisol readings, implying a lower threshold or increased reactivity in the sympathetic nervous system. As well, increased cortical asymmetry in the right frontal cortex has been identified (Calkins & Fox, 1992; Dawson, Panagiotides, Klinger, & Hill, 1992). Other temperament characteristics and temperament "clusters" that have been linked to difficulties with emotion regulation in children include hyperactivity (often correlated with distractibility) (Carlson, Jacobvitz, & Sroufe, 1995) and the "difficult" child cluster. This cluster, composed of the traits of low regularity, withdrawal, slow adaptability, high intensity, and negative mood, originated with Thomas, Chess and Birch in 1968 and since then has been generally accepted in the clinical and temperament literature (e.g., Brody, Stoneman, & McCoy, 1994a; DeGangi, DiPietro, Greenspan, & Porges, 1991). The temperament traits that they considered were activity level, regularity/rhythmicity, approach/withdrawal, adaptability, sensitivity, intensity of reactions, mood, distractibility, and persistence/attention span. Kochanska and colleagues have also found that fearlessness in children can lead to difficulty in regulating behavior and in internalizing standards and rules (Kochanska, Murray, & Coy, 1997). Although studies of the continuity of various temperament traits have produced mixed results, the highest stabilities have been found for measures that assess dimensions of affectivity (e.g., mood, intensity, rhythmicity), activity, and clusters or more global concepts of temperament such as the "difficult child" construct (Guerin, & Gottfried, 1994; Sanson, Pedlow, Cann, Prior, & Oberklaid, 1996).

## Intrauterine Environment and the Immediate Postnatal Experiences

The intrauterine environment, birth, and the immediate postnatal experiences clearly affect an infant's brain function and subsequent development. Some of the intrauterine influences include infections such as rubella, metabolic changes caused by external agents such as alcohol and drug use, and phenylketonuria (PKU) in the mother (Rogeness & McClure, 1996). Animal studies have also suggested that psychosocial stress during pregnancy (e.g., severe loss, spousal conflict or abuse) can affect brain function of the fetus (Schneider, 1992). The evidence for the effects of stress during pregnancy for humans has been primarily correlational; however, it does suggest that maternal anxiety and tension can affect various developmental factors in the infant and contribute to an increase in irritability, difficulty settling, hyperactivity, and inattention, all relevant for the development of affect regulation difficulties (Enkin, Keirese, Renfrew, & Neilson, 2000; Teixeira & Fisk, 1999; Weinstock, 1997). In addition, infants who experience delivery complications such as anoxia and/or prematurity or low birth weight (LBW) often experience difficulties with the early self-regulatory tasks of settling and achieving physiological homeostasis, which include maintaining temperature and establishing a feeding routine (Porges, 1996). Many of these high-risk infants continue to have later developmental difficulties with emotion regulation and attention (Allen, Lewinsohn, & Seeley, 1998; Breslau, 1995; Downie, Jacobsen, Frisk, & Ushycky, 2003; Graham, Heim, Goodman, Miller, & Nemeroff, 1999; Schothorst & van Engeland, 1996).

## Neurobiological Factors

Summarizing all of the neurobiological problems that can contribute to difficulties in emotion regulation is beyond the scope of this chapter, so only a few will be highlighted. The brain is a complex system that can be conceptualized at various levels, with the neuron as the most basic component. Neurons are organized into systems designed to sense, process, store, perceive, and act on information from the external and internal world. The interconnecting parts of the brain beginning with the lower structures include the following:

- The *brainstem* is responsible for states of arousal and alertness and physiological activities such as temperature control, respiration, and heart rate.

- The *thalamus* is at the top of the brainstem and is considered the gateway for sensory information because it connects to other regions of the brain.

- Above the thalamus is the *limbic system*, which includes the hippocampus, amygdala, orbitofrontal cortex, and the anterior angulate. This area plays an important role in coordinating lower and higher brain structures and is significant for emotion, motivation, and goal-directed behavior. It also plays a critical role in regulating emotion.

- On the highest level is the *cerebral cortex* with the frontal lobes and the prefrontal cortex. Parts of the frontal cortex are believed to play a critical role in focusing attention, working memory, and other executive functions. The orbitofrontal area lying just behind the eyes and in the upper part of the limbic system is close to a number of areas that carry information from other parts of the brain.

All parts of the brain are highly interconnected; however, some circuits of the brain may function as distinct subsystems and create their own states of processing. For example, the left and right sides of the brain have distinct subsystems and have different neurotransmitters, with the right hemisphere being activated during emotions associated with "withdrawal" such as anxiety and sadness and the left hemisphere activated with "approach" emotions such as anger and happiness. On the one hand, Fox and associates have found unique patterns of right frontal EEG assymetry in behaviorally inhibited toddlers (Fox, Calkins, & Schmidt, 1995; Fox et al., 1996). On the other hand, highly reactive infants who show a great deal of positive affect and sociability, and in some instances anger and impulsivity, have greater reactivity of the left hemisphere.

Various neurotransmitters play a significant role in passing information across certain neural synapses and are believed to play a role in emotion regulation. They include the monamines (e.g., dopamine, norepinephrine, serotonin, acetylcholine); amino acids (including gamma-aminobutyric acid (GABA); and neuropeptides (e.g., oxytocin, vasopressin) (Bradley, 2000). In addition, a number of hormones are secreted during stressful experiences, such as cortisol and the adrenocorticotropic hormone (ACTH), and have negative physiological effects when stress becomes chronic. A number of key areas of the brain and its pathways have been linked to issues with emotion regulation and various kinds of psychopathologies. These include the hypothalamic-pituitary-adrenal (HPA) axis and the connections between the thalamus and the amygdala and the cortex and the amygdala. The connections between the thalamus and the amygdala and the HPA axis have been implicated in difficulty in calming down and emotion regulation, hypersensitivity to various stimuli, and the storing of unconscious emotional memories following trauma. Memories that pass through the cortex and are stored in the hippocampus are under more conscious control, however. For some individuals who have experienced significant trauma, emotional responses occur without the processing of the frontal cortex that are involved in thinking, reasoning, and consciousness (LeDoux, 1996). In other words, information may bypass the cortex and go directly from the sensory thalamus to the amygdala and may account for many responses that are inappropriate for the situation or the social context. For further discussion of the effects of trauma, see Chapter 9. Other individuals, particularly those with attention-deficit/hyperactivity disorder (ADHD) appear to have difficulty with executive functions such as working memory, effortful and attentional control, inhibition of responses, and focusing (Barkley, 1998; Sergeant, 1995). These difficulties, which are believed to be located in the lateral prefrontal cortex and its connections to the various sensory systems, contribute not only to learning and academic problems but also to difficulties with the regulation of behavior and emotions. For instance, an individual with these difficulties, when faced with a stressful situation, is not able to maintain focus in order to calm down or to conceptualize a possible solution to overcome the situation confronting him.

## The Caregiving Environment

Although genetic and biological influences contribute significantly to the development of emotion regulation, the brain is sensitive to experience, especially in the early years (Cole, Martin, & Dennis, 2004). As explained by Perry and colleagues, "Experience can change the mature brain—but experience during the critical periods of early childhood *organizes* brain development" (Perry, Pollard, Blakley, Baker, & Vigilante, 1995, p. 290). It is widely recognized that infants' experiences with primary caregivers or attachment figures are most significant in developing their brains and influencing particular aspects of personality and behaviors.

Four different attachment categories have been identified in children that parallel those found in adults with respect to their relationships with their own parents: 1) secure–autonomous, 2) avoidant–dismissing, 3) ambivalent/resistant–preoccupied, and 4) disorganized–unresolved with respect to loss or trauma. A rich and compelling literature on the effects of early parent–infant interactions and the attachment relationships that develop as a result have demonstrated that a secure–autonomous attachment generally results in adequate emotion regulation.

Conversely, an avoidant-dismissing style of attachment is related to repression of negative emotions and an insecure–ambivalent/resistant–preoccupied style results in escalation of negative emotional displays in an attempt to get attention. The disorganized–unresolved pattern has been related to psychopathology of various kinds (Lyons-Ruth & Spielman, 2004).

Caregivers of children with secure attachments are generally consistently sensitive and responsive to their infants' cues and, in particular, nurturing and calming when their children are upset, hurt, frustrated, ill, or lonely. They are also accepting of their children's positive and negative feelings and cooperate with them in a way that can encourage their children's later self-regulation. Caregivers of securely attached children also regulate their children's emotional states by reading and understanding their emotional signals and providing stimulation or modulation of their arousal state.

Parental discussion of emotion with children has been linked to the children's understanding of emotion and emotional competence, as well (Eisenberg, Cumberland, & Spinrad, 1998). In contrast, when mothers have difficulty providing reciprocity, mirroring, and attunement to their children's emotions, the children usually have an insecure or disorganized attachment and may develop symptoms of aggression and noncompliance (Tsuk & Landy, 2000).

Cummings and Davies (1996) introduced the concept of *emotional security*, or a sense of felt security, as crucial for the development of emotion regulation. They described emotional security as a regulatory system that is influenced by biological factors in the child and multiple aspects of family functioning (particularly ways of dealing with conflict), extended family, siblings, peers, and other caregivers such as child care providers. They placed a particular emphasis on the effects of family violence (i.e., child abuse and spousal abuse) on emotional security and pointed out how these experiences can increase the child's reactivity to stress and the risk for internalizing or externalizing disorders. Other researchers have also emphasized the influence of the school context and culture in the socialization of emotions (Bugental & Goodnow, 1998; Greenberg & Kusche, 1997). This approach does not ignore the importance of the quality of parent–child attachment but expands it to include the contribution to the child's security beyond this narrower realm of influence (Gottman, 1997).

Some researchers have considered the influence of coercive or punitive styles of discipline on the development of emotion regulation. Baumrind (1989) referred to "affectionless control," Bugental (1992) to "threat-oriented discipline," and Patterson (1980) to "coercive cycles." In each of these parent–child models, the child is perceived by the parent as difficult and uncontrollable, whereas the child perceives the parent as hostile and critical. Sometimes these interactions can terminate in physical abuse or criticism and hostility, and feelings of rejection and lack of warmth on the part of the child. In addition, exposure to such interactions may result in prolonged states of hyperarousal in an individual and a tendency toward greater arousal when exposed to similar situations later (Ballard, Cummings, & Larkin, 1993). These patterns of interaction may result in either externalizing or internalizing disorders in children and may also contribute to an internal working model or attributions of self and others as "bad" or ineffectual.

# The Effects of Trauma

Chapter 9 describes in detail the dramatic and devastating effects that can occur as a result of traumas of various kinds. If these traumas or significant losses occur in infancy or early childhood, the effects can last a lifetime (LeDoux, 1996; Perry et al., 1995), this is because not only are the effects psychosocial and experiential but also the neurobiological system is affected (van der Kolk, McFarlane, & Weisaeth, 1996). Sometimes the psychological symptoms that result are so intense and numerous that they become psychopathological and may contribute to a variety of disorders in adults including character disorders (e.g., borderline personality disorder [BPD]), addictions, eating disorders, chronic depression, and aggressive conduct disorder (van der Kolk, 1994). In children, unresolved loss and trauma seem to contribute significantly to behavioral and acting-out disorders, anxiety, phobias, and depression (Schwartz & Perry, 1994). As described in more detail in Chapter 9, another group of symptoms characterized by constant retriggering of the traumatizing event through nightmares and flashbacks is called *posttraumatic stress syndrome* (PTSD), which occurs in about 10%–20% of children and adults who experience various kinds of trauma.

Although the effects of trauma in adults are becoming better understood from such massive traumas as the terrorist attacks of September 11, 2001; the Tsunami in Southeast Asia; the devastation in the U.S. Gulf of Mexico after Hurricane Katrina; and warfare occurring across the world, far less attention had been paid to the effects of trauma on infants and young children (Perry, 1994, 1996). This gap is due in part to the belief that if the event is not discussed, children will have no memory of it, so the effects, if any, will be negligible. Perry (1994) has estimated that in the United States at least 4 million children experience trauma that is pervasive and chronic (abuse of various kinds and family violence) or time limited such as natural disasters, community violence, and the loss of significant others (Kauffman & Henrich, 2000; Osofsky, 1999; Shonkoff & Phillips, 2000). Neglect (physical and emotional) can be just as devastating, however, and for a child with genetic or temperamental sensitivities, it can cause chronic and devastating malfunctioning in the developing brain and destruction of trust in the safety of the world (Bloom, 2002; Crittenden, 1997a, 1999; Kauffman, 2002b).

As described in detail in Chapter 9, there are two main memory systems: 1) *explicit* (i.e., conscious), which can be talked about and are event specific, and 2) *implicit* (i.e., unconscious), which are conditioned to be retriggered in an increasing range of similar sensory stimulations or stressful events in some way reminiscent of the original trauma. The triggering of these memories is also accompanied by the arousal of many neurotransmitter systems that, if chronic, can have devastating effects on the brain and cause significant physical and mental health risks. Parents who have unresolved loss and trauma may react excessively when their child expresses certain behaviors or emotional reactions. These excessive reactions are often caused by a failure of emotion regulation and may include screaming at the child and, in extreme cases, abuse or extreme withdrawal from the child. On an ongoing basis the parent may be unable to provide the nurturing containment and calming of excessive emotions that the child needs, thus perpetuating difficulties with emotion regulation across generations (Crittenden, Lang, Claussen, & Partridge, 2000). As well, parents who have experienced trauma and loss may have difficulty with labeling and talking about their own emotions and those of their children (called *alexithymia*) and this can result in difficulties with emotion regulation (both on the part of children and parents) (Taylor, Bagby, & Parker, 1997).

## Attributions, Cognitions, and Attentional Systems

A variety of cognitive biases or negative views of self and the world have been found to relate to difficulties with emotion and behavioral regulation. For example, Dodge and associates have demonstrated how children identified as aggressive and as having behavior disorders who are shown pictures involving children in ambiguous situations are more likely than children in normal control groups to misattribute negative intent to others and to talk about aggressive or other negative acts as responses (Dodge, 1993; Dodge, Murphy, & Buchsbaum, 1984). Other research has shown that anxious individuals pay more attention to threatening as opposed to neutral information and this tendency can affect learning (MacLeod, Matthews, & Tata, 1986; Mathews, 1990; McNally, Kaspi, Riemann, & Zeitlin, 1990). They also have difficulty shifting attention from cues in negative locations. It is assumed that these cues are relevant to or fit with the subject's self-concept (Reed & Derryberry, 1995). These same attentional biases have been found in children (Rothbart & Derryberry, 1981) and can limit a child's ability to pay attention to and remember events that are more positive. As a consequence, the child may miss multiple sources of information that could help him cope with stressful situations, and negative representations are increasingly more accessible, a process called *kindling* (Cortez & Bugental, 1995; Post, 1992). Also, such individuals constantly bypass coping strategies such as problem solving that are needed to deal with the difficult situation (Segal, Williams, Teasdale, & Gemar, 1996).

Attributions also relate to self-representations, which are primarily formed in early maternal–child interactions and are positive for securely attached infants and more negative for insecure and disorganized infants. These "internal working models" are also thought to guide a child's view of others and affect her interpersonal relationships (Bretherton, 1991). Some children may develop self-reliant avoidant behavior, whereas others may show a helpless dependency (Manassis & Bradley, 1994). Cicchetti (1991) has found that abused children demonstrate negative emotional reactions to their image when they see themselves in a mirror, suggesting very negative self-representation.

Other cognitive capacities have also been related to poor emotion regulation. For example, children with language delays or disorders have a higher prevalence of emotional and behavioral difficulties than children with typically developing speech and language capacities (Cohen, 1996). This is assumed to be because most coping strategies are language-based and require certain kinds of attentional strategies that may also be affected.

A number of researchers have explored the need for effortful control or management of attention by shifting attention and focusing and concentration in emotion regulation (Lewis & Stieben, 2004). For example, in their definition of emotion regulation, Eisenberg, Fabes, Guthrie and Reiser stated, "We suggest that emotion regulation is often achieved through effortful management of attention (attention shifting and focusing, distraction) and cognitions that affect the interpretation of the situations (e.g., positive cognitive restructuring)" (2000, p. 137). Gross (2002) talked about the need for attentional deployment, which can be used to select which aspect of a situation will be the main focus. An individual uses this type of focusing of attention not only to disengage from a threatening situation but also to make attention more flexible in relation to multiple information sources. On the one hand, this may enable the individual to develop positive representations of self and other and may help the individual to modulate ongoing stress responses of the endocrine, autonomic, and neural systems (Derryberry & Reed, 1996). On the other hand, difficulties with effortful control can result in frequent impulsive reactions that can impede the development of more adaptive coping strategies.

## CHARACTERISTICS OF PARENTS THAT MAKE EMOTION REGULATION CHALLENGING

For many parents, regulating their children's emotions and behavior can be very challenging. Parents in parenting groups frequently identify the most difficult tasks they face as stopping themselves from becoming angry with their children and trying to keep their "cool." Parents are particularly challenged when they face the crying of a colicky baby, deal with the tantrums of a toddler, cope with a whiny 3-year-old who cannot get his way, or try to reassure a fearful child who is protesting because he has to go to child care or go to bed at night. Parents with unresolved loss and trauma also have great difficulty with parenting and often have particular difficulty with managing angry or noncompliant behavior in their children (Lyons-Ruth & Jacobvitz, 1999). As previously mentioned, these reactions may sometimes trigger in a parent painful memories and related physiological reactions that are very hard to contain. Some parents may find a certain emotion such as sadness that their child is expressing too difficult to deal with and may refuse to comfort the child. A parent may deny any sign of unhappiness in a child, or may be unable to discipline or contain a child who is acting out. Sometimes, when a parent denies her child's emotions, this results in the opposite of the desired effect— the emotion can escalate. Or, the child may learn to suppress the emotion and his behavioral response, but the effects may still be experienced in the child's body. Studies have shown, in fact, that helping infants and young children contain rather than suppress their reactions to stress is critical to reduce stress reactions in their bodies (Gunnar, 1998; Gunnar & Barr, 1998).

A parent may have a mental illness that makes emotion regulation very challenging. The literature on the effects of maternal depression, for instance, has demonstrated that infants and children of parents who are depressed are at increased risk for behavior problems and emotional difficulties (Dawson et al., 2003; Field et al., 1996). The children are also more likely to exhibit poorer motor and mental development (Abrams, Field, Scafidi, & Prodromides, 1995; Murray & Cooper, 1997).

Studies have shown that the children of depressed mothers, including infants and toddlers as well as 3- to 6-year-old children, have been found to have reduced left frontal lobe activity (usually activated during the expression of approach emotions such as joy, anger, and interest) and increased right frontal lobe activity (usually activated by withdrawal emotions such as sadness and anxiety) (Dawson, Frey, Panagiotides, et al., 1999; Jones, Field, & Davalos, 2000). Dawson and colleagues (2003) found that 3-year-old children whose mothers' depression had remitted still exhibited lingering effects, and many of the children continued to have higher levels of externalizing and internalizing disorders. In addition, by age 3 the children of mothers with chronic depression showed a generalized pattern of reduction in cortical left frontal activation found earlier in their interactions with their depressed mothers. They suggest that this occurs because of children's reduced attentiveness and engagement with the environment. These patterns are believed to reflect individual differences in emotion and behavior regulation.

Researchers do not believe that genetic factors account fully for these findings and instead, think that interactions of depressed mothers and their infants and toddlers contribute significantly to these outcomes. Some depressed mothers have been shown to interact with a sad, withdrawn style, whereas others have been observed to have a more angry, intrusive style. Sometimes family conflict and lack of social support may also contribute to a mother's difficulty (Cohn, Matias, Tronick, Connell, & Lyons-Ruth, 1986; Hart, Field, del Valle, & Palaez Nogueras, 1998). As discussed in Chapter 1, the children of parents with severe anxiety disorders, character disorders, and criminality have also been found to have difficulty with emotion regulation. These effects are also likely to be caused by genetic influences and the effects of interactions with their parents on the functioning of the brain. Many children living with parents with BPD have disorganized attachment due to the inconsistent parenting that they receive. By 5 to 7 years of age, the disorganized behavior is gradually replaced by controlling and oppositional, noncompliant behavior or inappropriate role reversal and caregiving behavior. Many children of parents with BPD also develop the disorder (Fonagy, Leigh, et al., 1995).

The children of parents who have schizophrenia have been found to have significant difficulties including problems attending and externalizing and internalizing behaviors. They often also have learning difficulties and many have insecure attachments to their parents (Gamer, Gallant, & Grunebaum, 1976; Jacobsen & Miller, 1999; Walker & Emory, 1983).

Thus, it is clear that parents with various types of psychopathology have severe difficulties regulating their own emotions and as a consequence they experience difficulty in dealing with their children's emotional displays. Because these failures can result in significant behavioral, emotional, cognitive, and neurobiological problems for their children, it is crucial that intervention strategies that can help parents provide more containing interactions for their children are provided in early intervention programs or in other community programs.

## Contributors to Poor Emotion Regulation

In this section we return to the contributors to poor emotion regulation that were discussed previously and show how working on reducing their impact can enhance the emotion regulation capacities of parents and as a consequence those of their children (see Figure 11.1). In these sections, some of the strategies are suggested in order to improve parents' own emotion regulation, whereas others are intended to help parents to interact with their children so that their children can

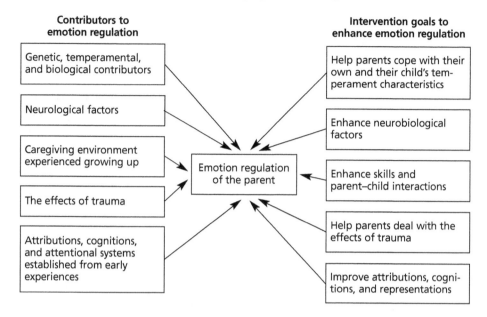

**Contributors to emotion regulation**

- Genetic, temperamental, and biological contributors
- Neurological factors
- Caregiving environment experienced growing up
- The effects of trauma
- Attributions, cognitions, and attentional systems established from early experiences

Emotion regulation of the parent

**Intervention goals to enhance emotion regulation**

- Help parents cope with their own and their child's temperament characteristics
- Enhance neurobiological factors
- Enhance skills and parent–child interactions
- Help parents deal with the effects of trauma
- Improve attributions, cognitions, and representations

**Figure 11.1.** Various factors contribute to emotion regulation, as do interventions to reduce their impact. Reducing the impact of these contributors can enhance emotion regulation capacities.

learn optimal emotion regulation strategies. Using both types of approaches will enhance parent–child relationships and enable the parents to develop emotion regulation strategies that they will be able to use in other areas of their lives.

## Helping Parents Deal with Their Own and Their Child's Temperament Characteristics

During home visits and in parenting groups, it is very important to help parents understand that children have very different temperaments and personalities just as adults do. It is crucial to assure parents that with support and encouragement, their children can be encouraged to use their more difficult temperament traits adaptively. Empathizing with difficulties parents may be having adapting to their child is an important first step. Service providers can point out that improving one's awareness of the "goodness of fit" between the child's temperament traits and how the parent reacts to them can make a dramatic difference. In other words, changing their negative reactions to be more understanding that a child's more challenging characteristics might be the result of the child being a different temperament type than the parent, can change the child's sense of who she is and her self-esteem (Kristal, 2005). Some of the other points most important to get across include the following:

- Sometimes, extreme temperament characteristics, including hypersensitivities in certain sensory modalities such as touch, sight (e.g., bright lights), sounds (e.g., loud noises), smells, and tastes can lead to regulatory disorders in infants that can be manifested in extreme crying, sleeping, and eating problems. In other situations the infant may have difficulty with sensory integration, or integrating stimulation from sights, sounds, and so forth that can result in the child becoming overwhelmed in places and situations in which there is a lot of stimulation such as in a shopping mall or at a large gathering. Adapting the environment to a baby by providing a lot of quiet calming, soothing interactions and not overwhelming her with too much stimulation can be helpful to avoid sensitizing or overloading the child's various physiological systems.

- If a child is very shy or slow-to-warm-up and finds it difficult to adjust to new situations (i.e., withdrawing and/or low in adaptability), it is very important to encourage her to try new things (Aron, 2002; Kagan, 1994b). At first, the child will need to be supported until she feels more comfortable. However, if a child does not get an opportunity to try out and succeed in new situations, she will never learn that she can manage them and eventually begin to enjoy them. It is important to keep in mind, however, that if the child is forced to do things too quickly it could increase her anxiety and cause her to be even less willing to try new things.

- If a child is more "difficult" and has a tendency to be quite irritable, intense, and impulsive, inform the parents that research shows that these children are more likely to follow the rules and structures at home if their relationship with their parents is as accepting and loving as possible (Kochanska, 1995, 1997a). The more critical and rejecting these children perceive their parents to be, the more likely they are to become oppositional and angry. This is something the service provider may need to work on with both parents over time, especially if negative patterns between parent and child have already been established. See Landy (2002c, pp. 50–53), for further suggestions for working with temperament characteristics. Some other books that parents may find useful for understanding their child's temperament are listed in the Resources at the end of this chapter.

During intervention, it can also be very helpful for parents to think about their own personalities or temperaments and to compare them with a particular child's. This will help them determine how similarities and/or differences affect how comfortable they feel with the child. Parents should also keep in mind that they may have different similarities and differences with each child if they have more than one child. In thinking about themselves and the child, here are some questions that can help parents to explore their own characteristics and differences with their child.

- Am I an extrovert who enjoys being around people most of the time, or an introvert who likes people but needs quiet reflective time alone as well? What about my child?

- What are my main interests and things that I enjoy doing? What are my child's?

- Think about each of your children and describe his or her temperament. Identify which traits you enjoy and find more challenging for each.

- Make a list of ways that you know are helpful with each child and their more difficult characteristics.

- Are there any characteristics in myself that I have wanted to change or have managed to change over the years?

- Do I have any temperament characteristics that I am still working on improving? If so, what is working and what is proving to be challenging?

- How did my parents deal with their temperament characteristics, and which parent did I feel I had the best fit with?

- Did my parents use any adjectives about me that made me uncomfortable, such as the "difficult one," the "shy one," or the "challenging one"? Do I use any of these types of adjectives with my child?

After this last question, have parents think about descriptions they would rather have heard used.

## Enhancing the Neurobiology of Parent and Child

Although prenatal classes that focus on health aspects of pregnancy and the birth are very important, it is also crucial to prepare both parents emotionally to "receive" their baby.

*Prenatal Interventions to Reduce Anxiety*    Research now suggests that anxiety or depression during pregnancy can affect the neurobiology of the fetus, so interventions in the prenatal period are particularly relevant (Teixeira & Fisk, 1999; Weinstock, 1997). These interventions should focus on changing any negative attributions or fears the mother may have about her baby, for example, that he is so active that it will be difficult to manage his behavior. Also helping her feel confident about caring for her baby and discussing how she feels about her changing role can be supportive, especially if other parents express their own fears as well. It is also important that the baby's father is involved in at least some of the sessions so that he can feel like an important part of the experience. Interventions should also look at particular aspects of a family's situation. If a mother is facing a stressful life situation, such as unemployment or living in a dangerous neighborhood, for example, the interventionist may try to help her in a more pragmatic way according to what she needs in order to alleviate this stress as much as possible. Also, helping parents to build a support system and, if they are interested, involving them in parenting groups or attending a drop-in center may help reduce anxiety for some parents-to-be.

*Avoiding Neurological Rekindling*    Since the mid 1990s, a handful of studies have been able to demonstrate that therapeutic approaches that focus on changing thoughts and beliefs about dreadful things that might happen or feelings of worthlessness can eliminate various symptoms associated with depression and anxiety and improve behavioral patterns. Even more significantly, these strategies have been shown to be as effective as medication in changing metabolism in the affected area of the brain and in preventing relapse in cases of depression (Schwartz & Begley, 2002; Schwartz, Stoessel, Baxter, Martin, & Phelps, 1996). The interventions have been used to treat people with depression, anxiety disorders, obsessive-compulsive disorder, and Tourette syndrome (i.e., tic disorder) (Teasdale, 1999; Teasdale, Segal, & Williams, 1995, 2000). Also, helping people calm down can often avoid angry outbursts and rages occurring. In other words, evidence is beginning to mount that changing the way people think about their situations can improve behavior and reduce symptoms and, in turn, improve brain functioning. In order to better cope with problems with emotion regulation, including anxiety, depression, and excessive anger, then, a parent can learn ways of thinking to activate the cerebral cortex and hippocampal system and bring actions and memories under conscious control instead of having the intense emotions triggered without conscious control through the amygdala system.

Many communities have clinics that provide individual and group cognitive-behavioral therapy and/or mindfulness-based cognitive therapy to teach these new ways of thinking and to bring emotional reactions under conscious control (Linehan, 1993; Segal, Williams, & Teasdale, 2002). Meditation groups may also be available. It is useful to integrate some of the approaches and strategies used in these groups into home visitation sessions, and in individual and group sessions with parents who have difficulties with emotion regulation. Some of these strategies are outlined next.

- Parents learn to interrupt automatic negative thoughts and feelings and the bodily sensations of the sympathetic nervous system that contribute to depression, anxiety, or rage reactions. Parents, without denying their feelings, can be taught to attend to more positive thoughts and avoid getting caught up in negative thought patterns that have been perpetuated in the past.

- Mindfulness-based approaches use a mental body scan that participants perform on themselves in order to learn to be aware of physical sensations in their bodies. Participants are encouraged to be aware of their breath and to allow other intrusive thoughts, feelings, and sensations to pass as they focus on their breathing (Kabat-Zinn, 1990).

- Parents record thoughts, feelings and bodily sensations that accompany situations. Talking about these feelings and thoughts and discussing what it may have been that made them feel good or upset at the time can help parents see how and why they perceive events as pleasant or unpleasant. It may also be possible to encourage parents to avoid negative situations if possible, or to be able to see them in a more positive light. Some parents may enjoy putting these thoughts and feelings in a journal.

- Parents learn to use visualization of pleasant places or situations, which can also be helpful in times of stress. Some parents may like to use drawing of a special place in individual or group sessions.

## Enhancing Parent–Child Interactions through Improving Emotion Regulation

A number of approaches to helping parents improve their interactions with their infants and young children are described in Chapter 10, so the strategies outlined here emphasize helping parents and children improve emotion regulation.

***An Emotion Coaching Approach to Emotion Regulation***    Gottman (1997) has developed a five-step "emotion coaching" process that parents can use with their children to help them to understand, cope with, and regulate their emotional world. Children whose parents use the approach have been found to have better cognitive and emotional and social outcomes in adolescence. The steps of emotion coaching include the following:

1. *Noticing and being aware of children's emotions, even if the emotions are subtle.* Parents are advised to think about what the emotions may be about and to observe make-believe play and behaviors that may also indicate emotional upset.

2. *Recognizing that an emotion can be an opportunity for intimacy and teaching rather than backing away from them or punishing them.* Comforting an upset child or acknowledging the difficult feelings a child has can really enrich the parent–child bond.

3. *Listening empathetically and then letting the child know his feelings are valid.* At this time it is essential to acknowledge and show understanding of the child's feelings about the situation. This process of empathizing gives the child an opportunity to feel understood at a deep level.

4. *Helping the child label the emotions she is feeling.* This can make a scary, uncomfortable feeling seem more understandable and manageable and encourages the child to be able to do this herself later. This can also increase attentional focusing and can calm the child down.

5a. *Setting limits while helping the child problem solve.* Some parents think that this method accepts bad behavior but, in fact, the child is told that acting out or running away is not acceptable and is taught to problem solve instead. This again brings in the cognition of the child, and the steps of problem solving (identifying goals and solutions) will provide a tool that the child can use in other situations. The child is then helped to choose a strategy and supported to try it out.

5b. *Helping the child choose a solution and supporting her to use it so she can see if it is workable.* If it is not successful, encourage her to try another possibility.

For young children, role playing and pretend play can be a useful way to show some alternative solutions or things to try. Using puppets that illustrate two different ways to solve the problem through pretend play can be fun. Gottman (1997) acknowledged that use of these strategies may be limited with peers in middle childhood, but that children who have had emotion coaching earlier fare better than their peers with emotion regulation at later ages. The process also encourages effortful control or focusing on a problem and the building of positive attributions of self and other.

## Programs Focusing on Changing the Caregiving Environment When Children are Having Emotional or Behavioral Difficulties

This section focuses on a few parenting programs featuring groups that are particularly helpful for coping with children who are displaying various symptoms of emotion dysregulation.

**The Incredible Years**  The first program, the Incredible Years, was developed by Webster-Stratton and associates and is primarily for parents of children with externalizing behavior problems such as aggressiveness, extreme noncompliance, and impulsivity. Parents are given strategies to work on with their children and ways to discipline their children to encourage consistency. Videotapes are shown that illustrate positive parenting techniques and are discussed by participants in the groups. In some situations, groups for the children are also provided that focus on learning skills to solve conflicts and other ways to enhance their socialization capacities. Additional groups are provided for parents that help them deal with other stressful aspects of their lives and that can provide them with problem-solving approaches to use with these other stresses that may also be affecting their children. The program has been able to demonstrate positive outcomes in terms of reducing symptoms in children, and improving parent child interactions in the home. Children were also shown to have significant improvements in problem-solving skills (Webster-Stratton & Hammond, 1997; Webster-Stratton & Hooven, 1998). In the research, adding the child component enhanced the improvements in the child, whereas adding strategies for the parents to decrease social isolation and learn effective ways to get support significantly improved the program's success in engaging low-income, resistant, and unmotivated parents. Incentives such as holding the groups in community centers at flexible times with an interpreter if parents are non–English speaking, and providing snacks, child care, and money for transportation were also found to be very helpful in getting parents to attend.

***Errorless Compliance Training***    Errorless Compliance is a method originally developed by Ducharme and others (e.g., Ducharme, Atkinson, & Poulton, 2000; Ducharme & Popynick, 1993) for working with children with severe oppositional behavior. The treatment approach is designed to provide both the parent and child with a sense of success in their daily interactions. The program is focused on enhancing parent–child cooperation and as a consequence, reducing negative child behaviors. Parents are initially asked to come up with a list of requests that range from those the child will cooperate with readily (e.g., "Throw me the ball," "Eat your cookie") to those that the child typically ignores (e.g., "Turn off the television," "Pick up your toys"). The parent begins the intervention by providing many of the requests that are likely to lead to child cooperation. These typically lead to frequent episodes of child compliance, which offer the parent many opportunities to provide the child with praise and attention for cooperation. After a few weeks, the parent introduces requests that are a little more challenging for the child. The parent is encouraged to continue praising the child for following through with the requested tasks. This process is continued for several weeks until the most difficult requests, those that presented serious compliance difficulties before intervention, are introduced by the parent. With this gradual and positive approach, parents typically find that their children are considerably more cooperative to the demanding requests after intervention. This approach has been used with a broad range of children with conduct difficulties, including children with developmental disabilities (e.g., Ducharme & Crain, 2004), children who have experienced family violence (e.g., Ducharme, Atkinson, et al., 2000), and children of parents with cognitive and emotional difficulties (e.g., Ducharme, Spencer, Davidson, & Rushford, 2002). The parent participants of this program report high levels of satisfaction with the immediate success they have in getting the child to cooperate and the improvement they experience in their relationship with their child. Parents' sense of success is enhanced and daily conflicts are significantly reduced.

If used as intended, all of these gains are possible without the use of punishment or coercion on the parents' part.

*Emotion Regulation Components of Parenting Groups*    Many parenting groups only focus on ways to discipline children. However, these programs need to be expanded to include strategies that also encourage emotion regulation strategies. Here are some examples:

• Have parents think about what it is that gets in the way of their effective parenting. Encourage them to alter some of the irrational beliefs that they have about their child. For example, changing "My child is completely uncontrollable" to "My child is very strong and has characteristics of independence that will be very helpful later on."

• Teach parents how to use nonviolent approaches to discipline such as using time-outs and logical and natural consequences.

• Encourage parents to join their child in child-directed play and show them how to follow their child's lead, extend play themes, and learn about their child's emotional concerns and preoccupations by watching the play.

• Teach parents how to tell their child to do something using a positive approach (e.g., using "do" rather than "don't" all the time, and "I" messages instead of "you" and blaming the child), and how to attend to the child's positive behaviors, notice them, and give praise and encouragement.

• Emphasize support from other group participants, mutual problem solving, and collaborative partnership with the group leaders.

• Teach parents the steps of emotion coaching parenting (Gottman, 1997) outlined previously. Before describing the approach, it is very helpful to ask parents what they like to receive from a friend or partner when they are upset. Most will say that they want to be listened to and to know that they are understood. They also typically indicate that if they are in a particularly difficult situation, they would like to be shown some caring. They will usually also agree that at that moment they do not want to be criticized, laughed at, or told what to do, although discussing solutions may be helpful a little later. Introducing, teaching, or modeling the strategies will then be likely go more smoothly and to be much more acceptable than they might be without this discussion.

Although the approaches that are included in these groups are focused on the parents' behavior with their children, the cognitive approach suggested can also assist parents to avoid going into very negative reactions immediately without considering other ways to respond, and these skills can readily be used in other situations in their lives.

## Groups to Help Parents Deal with the Effects of Trauma

It is clear that parents with unresolved loss and trauma often have significant difficulties with parenting, particularly in dealing with their own emotion regulation and helping their children with theirs. Some groups that can help traumatized parents with their emotion regulation are discussed below.

*Anger Management Groups*    Anger management groups have been provided for a long time for men who abuse their partners, but less attention has been given to providing groups for women who have experienced trauma, in order to help them to enhance their emotion regulation and to improve their parenting. Schooling the Emotions is a 10-week group intervention that has been offered in communities for parents who have been identified as having difficulty with emotion regulation to the extent that it has affected their parenting (Martyn & Dundas, 1997).

In a pilot study, the group was effective in decreasing anger states and increasing feelings of control. Mothers reported increased self-esteem and a perception of having greater social support available to them. More than three quarters (77%) of the participants planned to seek out other parenting groups and community services. Perhaps most important, before the group began, this high-risk group of mothers had indicated on a questionnaire that they had significant difficulty processing emotional states, with 74% showing the symptoms of alexithymia. Post-tests, however, showed a significant increase in the mothers' abilities to identify, express, and process emotional states, with the number of parents showing alexithymic symptoms reduced to 47%. The intervention focuses on the following:

- Identifying and exploring emotions and the regulation of negative states using a combination of cognitive-behavioral, expressive, and supportive techniques

- Using experiential exercises and discussions designed to increase recognition of personal triggers and characteristic responses

- Discussing and practicing alternative behaviors and relaxation techniques to curb escalating negative emotional states

- Role playing of effective communication techniques to use in specific circumstances

- Using humor to mitigate against overwhelming states of fear, rage, and humiliation and encouraging both expression and reflectivity

- Providing a positive and supportive group environment

*Mindfulness-Based Trauma Counseling (MBTC)*    Mindfulness-Based Trauma Counseling (MBTC) integrates mindfulness philosophy and practice with well-informed trauma counseling. Harris and Laskin (2004) have developed the approach and have applied it to adult women who have experienced childhood sexual abuse and other trauma. Many of the participants are parents who are having difficulty with various aspects of parenting.

Jon Kabat-Zinn defined mindfulness as "paying attention in a particular way: on purpose in the present moment, and nonjudgmentally" (1994, p. 4). In his Stress Reduction Clinic, Kabat-Zinn teaches participants mindfulness meditation to relieve a variety of chronic physical illnesses. He also provides them with ways to reduce mental reactions and thoughts that can worsen stress and interfere with effective problem solving. Participants in mindfulness-based training are taught to take a wider perspective and to observe their own thinking as it is occurring. By becoming aware of their breathing, feelings, bodily sensations, and thoughts, people can eliminate negative thoughts and even avoid becoming depressed or triggered under stress.

The MBTC groups teach mindfulness practices to strengthen women's ability to be aware of what is happening when memories of trauma resurface. Participants also learn how to approach their trauma story and its impact using specially designed exercises for focusing on the breath and increasing body awareness. As a result, women are supported to approach the trauma and its impact "with skills and a framework that enables them to meet and relate to their suffering in a different way" (Harris & Laskin, 2004, p. 3). Women who attend the groups report feeling more equipped to overcome their trauma experiences and deal with traumatic memories.

## THE STEPS OF EMOTION REGULATION

Gross (1998, 2002) developed and researched a model that distinguishes between emotion regulation that is used to adjust situations to avoid negative emotions occurring (antecedent-focused) and strategies that are used to suppress the emotions once they have been triggered (response-focused) (Butler, Egloff, Wilhelm, Smith, Erickson, & Gross, 2003; Gross & Levenson, 1993; Harris, 2001; House, Landis, & Umberson, 1988). In his research he has been able to demonstrate that antecedent-focused approaches that include cognitive appraisal are able to interrupt the triggering of negative affect in individuals and reduce negative behavioral responses and the neurobiological consequences of negative emotions. This cognitive consideration of ways to adjust situations also keeps memory of an event intact.

Gross (2002) pointed out that trying to suppress emotions and not expressing them (response-focused) can impair intimate and genuine communication with others. Also, because the emotions are still experienced in the body, they can have significant cumulative physiological costs that can be devastating to health outcomes.

The difference between the effects of the use of antecedent-focused strategies and suppression of emotions has been examined under experimental conditions, with some participants being told to watch slides without any particular instructions while others were instructed to inhibit their expression of emotions. This inhibiting of expression suppression was found to significantly affect their verbal memory of the slides, and they were less able to describe what they saw than were parents who did not inhibit their emotional response (Richards & Gross, 2000).

Gross and John (2002) proposed the following steps of antecedent-focused emotion regulation:

1.  *Situation selection* involves approaching or avoiding certain situations (e.g., Mary, who often becomes anxious and has difficulty sleeping as a result of watching certain television programs, avoids watching them in the evening before going to bed).

2.  *Situation modification* entails changing a situation that is causing uncomfortable feelings (e.g., Whenever possible, Mary changes a discussion that is causing her anxiety).

3.  *Attentional deployment* involves concentrating on aspects of a situation that are more positive (e.g., Mary makes an effort to focus on some positive aspects of her life such as success she is having at work).

4.  *Cognitive change* is selecting a positive meaning for a situation (e.g., Mary looks for events in her life that were initially difficult but that have worked out for the best over time).

This type of approach could be adapted to a parenting program by having parents choose some situations with their children that arouse anger and other negative emotions. Helping the parent to problem solve to determine ways to prevent the child's behavior from happening and/or helping the parent see the meaning of the behavior in a more positive light may prevent the parent from being constantly triggered by her child's behavior.

## Learned Optimism

In a book called *Learned Optimism: How to Change Your Mind and Life,* Martin Seligman (1998) outlined a number of strategies that can be used to help parents who are depressed or chronically pessimistic or who believe that they can do nothing to improve their situation. In the 1970s, Seligman introduced the concept of *learned helplessness,* and gradually evolved it into an understanding that it was not so much what happens to people but how they viewed the event that influenced how they acted over time. Out of his research and clinical work, Seligman developed a variety of cognitive strategies that can be taught to parents to significantly enhance their sense of self-efficacy or competence in dealing with their lives. Some of the strategies he suggested include the following:

- Ceasing to generalize everything in a negative way and instead, looking at what happened in a specific situation (e.g., "All men are terrible" to "My brother was very mean to me.")

- Determining what is usually causing a child's misbehavior and not believing that what happened or is happening will be permanent (e.g., "My child never behaves and there is nothing I can do to make him stop," to "My child seems to misbehave when he's tired or upset, so I can try to help him at those times by giving him more attention.")

- Looking for hope in situations (e.g., "I have no chance of finding a job," to "If I get some more skills and keep looking, I will find a job.")

- Ceasing to externalize and blame everyone for what happens (e.g., "The other team's win was an absolute fluke, and they cheated," to "We worked hard to win but it wasn't good enough.")

Seligman also introduces a number of cognitive strategies that can be used to overcome anxiety and depression and to stop obsessive and negative thoughts that have become self-defeating.

As discussed in Chapter 3, successful interventions share several common factors. These include a number of therapist characteristics such as the ability to convey a warm, caring, concern for the person's pain as well as a sense of support. Bradley suggested that "all effective interventions influence affect regulation, albeit in different ways" (2000, p. 139). She went on to note that these qualities of concern and warmth in the therapist "are necessary for the patient to feel safe enough to express feelings and to risk exploring painful aspects of his or her life" (p. 141). Through the therapeutic relationship, a "corrective emotional experience" is provided within which the person is able to learn to develop different strategies to contain responses to negative affect, to rework negative beliefs, and to experience a sense of mastery of these feelings within the supportive presence of the interventionist (Fosha, 2000).

This chapter has focused on a number of short-term strategies to enhancing emotion regulation. By exploring the process of change in the case-study families, however, the importance of the experiential and psychodynamic longer term approach will also be demonstrated.

## ENHANCING EMOTION REGULATION WITH THE CASE-STUDY FAMILIES

### Mark's Family

The interventionist working with Mark and his family found it difficult at first to determine the extent of his mother Joan's traumatization as a young child. Joan's mother had been depressed, and initially rejected Joan as a result. Joan had learned to adopt defensive approaches to avoid sadness and denied these feelings both in herself and in Mark. This made her appear at times to have very little empathy or sympathy for Mark, when in fact, his pain and lack of self-esteem were devastating for Joan at an unconscious level, and occasionally her deep feelings and concern for him would break through. Although Joan's use of humor may have helped Mark to see a situation in a more positive light, on the whole he experienced the strategy as dismissive and frequently felt rejected and misunderstood.

Joan found it helpful to learn how to respond to Mark's emotional responses using Gottman's emotion-coaching approach; however, these strategies did not appear to transfer readily to all of her interactions with Mark; his siblings; or her husband, Michael. This difficulty with transferring techniques across situations is not unusual but was exacerbated for Joan because of her high-pressure work life, in which she used very different techniques and characteristics than those she needed to use to interact with Mark.

In Joan's therapy, then, the interventionist believed that a more psychodynamic approach was needed in order for her to explore the pain of her relationship with her mother. She needed to experience some of the painful memories of the past and to understand how she was playing out the same type of relationship she had had with her mother with Mark. Efforts were made to follow up any hint of real feelings when she described her upbringing—not by forcing her to discuss it further—but by acknowledging how painful it must have been for her. This allowed her to explore more procedural memories and to begin to make sense of them. As therapy was progressing, Joan was gradually able to respond more empathetically to Mark's emotions. This gradually began to enrich their relationship and to reduce some of the symptoms that brought Mark to therapy. It was also important to be available to Joan if she became upset between sessions. This seldom happened, but when it did, this availability provided her with the "holding" environment she needed in order for her to progress.

During sessions it was also important to acknowledge any attempts that Joan made to spontaneously discuss or begin to change her defensive representations of being able to be in control and not to touch her hurt and sad feelings. She was helped to understand that her approach to emotions had been very adaptive for her as a little girl and had worked in many areas of her life but that it did not work with her as a parent. It was also helpful for her to understand that although it was difficult for her to tap into conscious memories before age 5, the unconscious memories were probably being triggered automatically because Mark was almost the same age she had been when her mother was so depressed. She learned to understand and identify the bodily signs of anxiety that she often experienced when Mark cried or was anxious. This convinced her of the presence of these buried but very real feelings and her denial of them. The interventionist also explained to Joan that just as her defensiveness was destructive for Mark, it was also likely to be causing some of the physical problems that she was experiencing with high blood pressure and difficulty calming down in order to fall asleep.

The interventionist, then, was able to use an integrated approach with Joan that blended the following approaches together:

- Experiential (e.g., helping her recognize her bodily reactions and experience them in a new way)

- Attachment based (e.g., exploring her own attachment history and how it influenced how she related to Mark)

- Relational (e.g., helping her to relate to Mark in a new way as she was enabled to relate to him and her husband in a new way)

- Supportive (e.g., providing her support especially during times when Mark was having his most difficult problems)

- Cognitive-behavioral (e.g., using mindfulness-based strategies and helping her problem solve about some of her parenting issues enabled Joan to confront her painful, yet previously unconscious feelings and to learn new ways to cope when her own or Mark's emotional responses began to overwhelm her).

## Nina's Family

For Nina, her difficulties were far more generalized because she had suffered from years of significant trauma and abuse. Nina used drugs and alcohol as a crutch to help her to cope with her painful memories, but this did not stop her from being triggered into extreme fear and rage reactions and occasional dissociative states. At the beginning of the intervention, Nina was alexithymic and was unable to describe her emotions. She also appeared unable to enjoy small pleasures in simple things or to identify early signs of fear or anger that could enable her to start to use calming techniques or change her attributions of a situation to something more positive. This meant that in the early stages of her therapy she never talked about feelings, but instead talked primarily about events that had happened. This made efforts to get her to explore her emotions around them unsuccessful.

As has been described in Chapter 4, the approach with Nina had to be very different from the one adopted with Joan because any premature move to gaining access to memories would have been too traumatic. It would have been likely to result in more acting out and possibly dissociative episodes, and it would almost certainly have raised so much anxiety and resistance in Nina that she would have left the intervention prematurely. In the first stage of the intervention, the therapist let Nina know that she understood how difficult the circumstances that she had experienced must have been and that it was unacceptable for anyone to have experienced them. However, it took almost 18 months before Nina was really able to discuss any feelings at all, which finally occurred only after the therapist had seen her in situations that had caused her extreme fear or sadness. It was in those moments, when her therapist was able to point them out to Nina and to contain and mirror them, that her emotions became real to her. For example, when Nina was feeling an intense sense of abandonment and sadness when her baby began to walk, she was able to become aware of how she was feeling when her body language and the comments she was making were pointed out to her. Then she could acknowledge what she was feeling emotionally and in her body in the moment and to discuss that the feelings may have been triggered because of similar experiences when other people had "walked out on her." Similarly, when she experienced intense fear when her psychotic brother became violent toward her and the children, she was able to relate the intense feeling to the way it had felt to her night after night as a child, when she had huddled under the bed looking after her siblings while her father abused her brother and attacked her mother. These were feelings that she could now feel some control over because the events could be included in her conscious memory and talked about in a way that gave her some freedom from their continual retriggering.

Nina also attended a number of groups and learned meditation, relaxation, and anger management techniques that enabled her to get some control of her feelings. She also enjoyed writing in a journal and drawing pictures that began to help her explore her situation and experiences and brought understanding of the triggers for her depressive feelings, fear, and anger. These strategies were only one small part of Nina's intervention, and getting addiction treatment and making significant gains in her sense of competence were critical for her to be able to regulate her painful emotions.

In some sense, both of these case studies present a number of approaches to the treatment of emotion regulation difficulties in parents, but they also illustrate the deleterious effects that dysregulation in parents can have on their children's development. These effects in each of the case-study situations had led to the development of symptoms in the children that indicated that psychopathology would develop in late childhood, adolescence, and adulthood without the intervention that was provided.

## RESOURCES

### Books

Books that parents may find helpful for parenting children with more difficult temperaments:

Greene, R.W. (1998). *The explosive child: A new approach to understanding and parenting easily frustrated, "chronically inflexible" children.* New York: Harper Collins.

Knanowitz, C.S. (1998). *The out-of-sync child: Recognizing and coping with sensory integration dysfunction.*New York: Perigree Books.

Kristal, J. (2005). *The temperament perspective: Working with children's behavioral styles.* Baltimore: H. Paul Brookes Publishing Co.

Kurscinka, M.S. (1991). *Raising your spirited child.* New York: Harper Perennial.

Yack, E., Sutton, S., & Aquilla, P. (1998). *Building bridges through sensory integration.* Available from: 132 Queen's Drive, Weston, ON., M9N 2H6, Canada (416) 785-7899

### Errorless Compliance Training

Joseph Ducharme, Ph.D.
Department of Human Development and Applied Psychology
University of Toronto (OISE)
252 Bloor Street West
Toronto, Ontario M5S 1V6
Canada

### Encouraging Learned Optimism

Seligman, M.E.P. (1998). *Learned optimism: How to change your mind and life* (2nd ed.). New York: Simon and Schuster.

### Webster-Stratton Groups

http://www.incredibleyears.com

### "Schooling the Emotions"

For a manual on conducting "Schooling the Emotions" group, contact

Denise Martyn
Hincks-Dellcrest Centre
114 Maitland Street
Toronto, Ontario M4Y 1E1
Canada
416-924-1164 ext. 3304
e-mail: dmartyn6954@rogers.com

### Mindfulness-Based Trauma Counseling

For training in conducting Mindfulness-Based Trauma Counseling (MBTC) contact

Susan Harris
Catholic Family Services of Peel-Dufferin
Suite 201
10 Gillingham Drive
Brampton, Ontario LGX 5A5
Canada
e-mail: sharris@cfspd.com

# Enhancing Parenting Knowledge and Encouraging Positive Attributions of the Child

Parents have a variety of types of cognitions about child development and child rearing that can affect their parenting behavior and every aspect of their children's developmental outcomes. Some of these cognitions include parenting knowledge, beliefs, attitudes, and attributions about the reasons children do things. Parents may respond to identical behavior in infants in very different ways based on their interpretation of it. For example, one parent may respond to her crying baby with comforting and sympathy because she believes her infant is tired. Another parent may respond to her baby's crying behavior with irritation or anger because she believes that once the baby has been fed and changed, crying behavior means the baby is spoiled. The same parent may even respond to the same behavior differently some days later if her baby is sick or if she had received new information about how to get a baby to sleep at night. In spite of researchers' acknowledgment of the importance of these cognitions, causal links to child outcomes have been difficult to prove due to the paucity of prospective longitudinal data (Benasich & Brooks-Gunn, 1996). As well, finding ways to intervene with and change cognitions has also been challenging. Although there are large and separate literatures about the various types of cognitions, a number of common themes cut across each of them. In this chapter these similar themes will be discussed first. After that some studies unique to each of the types of cognitions are presented and any appropriate strategies to enhance them are described. The literature and approaches to enhancing parent attributions of their children are discussed in somewhat more depth because of their links to attachment theory and some successful approaches to early intervention with multi-risk families that have been developed to encourage more positive attributions of children.

## COMMON THEMES ABOUT PARENTING COGNITIONS

Some of the common themes about parents' cognitions are summarized here.

### What Do Parents Think About in Relation to Their Children?

Although professionals in the field of early childhood differ in their definitions of various types of parental cognitions, common interest exists across researchers in each of their areas of expertise in exploring some of the things that parents think about in relation to their children and their own parenting. For example, parents all think about their child's development and how well their child is doing either compared with other children they know or according to various schedules of development with which they are familiar. In relation to development, parents may also wonder and be concerned about any delays or emotional, social, or behavioral difficulties that they believe their child is experiencing (Russell, 2003). When parents think about child rearing, they mainly consider areas such as child management, how to help their child learn or solve problems, and how best to foster their child's self-esteem. Ideas about how they see their roles as parents and their goals for their child's development are also very influential.

Some researchers have examined the accuracy of parenting knowledge and beliefs about child development and child rearing. For example, it is possible to judge some statements such as "Newborns cannot see and hear" as inaccurate. Because of the complexity of some issues, however, and because each child is unique, answers will differ depending on the child, and determining a "correct" or incorrect answer is not possible (e.g., "What is the major influence on child development?"). The level of the parents' knowledge can best be evaluated according to how it fits with current research and in terms of how sophisticated their reasoning is when absolute answers are difficult.

## Where Do Parents' Cognitions Come From?

Although researchers vary in terms of their emphasis on cognitions, what they research, and even how they study them, common threads are woven throughout the discussions of how parents' cognitions develop and what maintains them.

*The Way Parents Are Parented*    One of the most important sources of parenting cognitions is the *way parents were parented themselves*. It is clear that during pregnancy and at the time of their child's birth, parents' attributions and attitudes toward the child have already been somewhat formed. Parents often parent as they were parented, especially under stress or when they have competing demands on their attention, and they are influenced by procedural or implicit memories that are not conscious (Bugental & Happaney, 2000; Reznick, 1999). These memory-based knowledge structures are activated automatically, do not involve effort, and have sometimes been called *intuitive*. (Greenwald, McGhee, & Schwartz, 1998). Some of these implicit reactions may at times be in conflict with explicit attitudes that are more likely to be activated in situations that require more intentional efforts or thinking the situation through to be retrieved (Wilson, Lindsey, & Schooler, 2000). For example, a father may know from what he has read and from how he felt as a child that yelling at his son is not helpful, and he can stop himself yelling in most situations. When he is under stress, however, such as when his son is defiant and oppositional, the father may not use this cognitive monitoring and could be triggered by implicit or unconscious memories of when he was yelled at by his parents when he was young. As a consequence, without cognitive appraisal of what is happening in the moment, he could act at an automatic level and respond to his son in a way that he had been parented. Further information on the effect of implicit memories on parenting is discussed in more detail in Chapters 9 and 10.

***The Effect of Having Children of One's Own***    Parents' cognitions about child rearing are also affected by *having children of their own*. For example, parents often report that their attitudes change toward such topics as corporal punishment after they have their children. In one survey some parents moved to being less in favor of corporal punishment (36%) compared with others (30%) who became more in favor of it (Holden, Thompson, Zambarano, & Marshall, 1997). Parents can also be affected by child characteristics such as having a child with special needs or a chronic illness (McPhee, 1983; Meadow-Orlans, 2002; Noll, McKellop, Vannatta, & Kalinyak, 1998).

***Cultural Values***    Another major contributor that has been discussed is the *rules and values of a parent's cultural group*. Systematic research has been conducted across cultures or in different countries about parents' beliefs and attitudes toward child development (Bornstein et al., 1996; Reznick, 1999). For example, children with physical or cognitive disabilities are viewed in different ways in different cultures. Using traditional folk beliefs as opposed to finding out about new and researched information is found to be more common in some cultures than in others. In the United States and Canada, the greatest concerns that are usually identified by parents of children with disabilities are the risks that are posed for the child's later development. In other cultures, however, spiritual implications play an important role in perceptions about disability; for example, they may contribute to the child being seen in a positive light or they may foster the attitude that having a child with a disability brings great shame to the family (Kalyanpur & Harry, 1999; Kisanji, 1995; Lynch & Hanson, 2004). Some researchers have demonstrated that within-culture differences such as levels of education and geographic environment (i.e., whether rural or urban) are also powerful influences, and the effects of these within-culture variances may be even stronger than across-cultural differences (Palacio & Moreno, 1996).

***Level of Education and Socioeconomic Status***    In general *level of education* (Reich, 2005; Richman, Miller, & LeVine, 1992) and *socioeconomic status* (Tamis-Lemonda, Chen, & Bornstein, 1998) have been found to have a strong influence on parenting knowledge and beliefs. In general, parents with the highest socioeconomic backgrounds expect child development milestones to occur at an earlier age (Sameroff & Feil, 1985). These parents are also more likely to seek out and remember information about parenting (Seginer, 1983). Palacio and Moreno (1996) found that parents with higher education are more likely to believe that positive caregiving and effort is important, whereas parents from lower educational backgrounds tend to fall back on strict discipline if they are having problems with their child.

***Religious Beliefs***    *Religious beliefs*, similar to cultural values, can also be significant influences on parenting, particularly on approaches to child management. In a national survey, parents with more conservative scriptural beliefs reported that they engaged in more physical punishment than parents with less conservative theological views (Ellison, Bartowski, & Segal, 1996). Similarly, Gershoff, Miller, and Holden (1999) found that conservative Protestants reported spanking their 3-year-old children more and had more positive attitudes about corporal punishment than parents whose religious beliefs were less conservative.

*Influence of Other Family Members*    Parents often rate *partners and members of the extended family* as important sources of information and knowledge, with parents who are surveyed usually rating them high as sources. As discussed in Chapter 8, however, these sources of support within the immediate and extended family vary significantly in terms of how helpful parents perceive them to be (Belle, 1990; Brodsky, 1999).

## The Relationship Between Cognitions and Emotions

Researchers have also considered the relationship between cognitions and emotions and how cognitions are influenced by the person's mood (e.g., depressed, optimistic). This is particularly true of attitudes and attributions that are considered to be more likely to be related to the affective content of parent–child interactions and the emotional climate of the family.

Researchers have also discovered that mood affects the extent to which people look for knowledge and information about parenting; namely, interest is growing in how thinking, feeling, and acting are continually interwoven. As Hoffman pointed out, "Affect may initiate, terminate, accelerate, or disrupt information processing" (1986, p. 260). Certainly, positive affect facilitates the recall of information and problem solving, whereas low and moderate levels of negative affect and stress usually result in an inability to consider many alternatives (Isen, Means, Patrick, & Nowicki, 1982). Just as affects influence cognition, ideas can change emotions. Attributions are seen as having *affective tags,* and the affect related to that attribution will be aroused when the attribution is brought to mind (e.g., thinking "my child is difficult compared with other children" can result in frustration and anger). Also studies of depressed mothers have demonstrated how their attributions of their situations and children are often negative and they frequently evaluate their competence as parents very negatively (Goodnow, 1984).

## Parent Cognitions and Parenting Behaviors

All researchers who examine the effects of parent cognitions acknowledge that a relationship exists between how parents think about their children and how they act with them (Holden & Buck, 2002; Milner & Foody, 1994). The number of research studies that support this statement is relatively small and the relationships tend to be modest, however (Benasich & Brooks-Gunn, 1996). As Goodnow (1988) pointed out, not only are overt behaviors affected by cognitions but also nonverbal signs can be affected and can be important indicators of the parents' cognitions. These nonverbal signals are seldom assessed in studies, however; so as a consequence, some important indicators of the cognitions of the parents are not studied (Goodnow, 1988). These behaviors are important influences on how children develop, but also important is how children interpret them (e.g., "My father is strict because he loves me and wants to keep me safe" compared with "My father doesn't like me as much as my brother and that's why he is so strict with me"). For example, knowledge of child development has been linked to parental behavior in the home environment and to provision of a stimulating physical and verbal environment (Benasich & Brooks-Gunn, 1996). Strong evidence also points to a link between attitudes about spanking and spanking behavior (Holden, Coleman, & Schmidt, 1995) and attitudes about punishment and abuse (Corral-Verdugo, Frias-Armento, Romero, & Munoz, 1995). Miller (1988) suggested that even if parental beliefs are not always reflected in discrete behaviors with their children, they may affect the interactions more subtly and cumulatively, and these differences may contribute to the quality of the parent–child relationship.

## Parent Cognitions and Child Outcomes

Other studies have considered parent cognitions as mediators of parenting behaviors that are then associated with child outcomes. In the child outcome literature about cognitions, parents' concepts of child development have been linked to a child's cognitive functioning (McGillicuddy-DeLisi, 1985; Seifer & Sameroff, 1987). On the one hand, mothers' accuracy of knowledge of child development has been linked to positive child development outcomes. On the other hand, overestimations of ability have been found to be detrimental for child development outcomes (Hunt & Paraskevopoulos, 1980). A number of researchers have found that parents' cognitions are also related to their children's academic achievement in science, math, and English (also known as language arts). Musun-Miller and Blevins-Knabe (1998) found that adults' understanding of how preschool children learn math was related to their math skills later. A link has been found between parent-centered goals and child- or relationship-focused goals and child outcomes. Parents whose goals were more parent-focused were more punitive and angry and their children had poorer social outcomes, whereas the children of parents with child- or relationship-focused goals had better social development. Other cognitions that have been linked to positive child outcomes include nurturing attitudes (Andersson, Sommerfelt, Sonnander, & Ahlsten, 1996) and goals for having respectful and well-behaved children (Brody, Flor, & Gibson, 1999). Conversely, parents' negative attributional biases have been linked to aggressive behavior in children (Hastings & Coplan, 1999; Hastings & Grusec, 1998).

Parents have been found to maintain some beliefs and attitudes about child development and parenting for long periods of time. In one study mothers showed stability for maternal investment in the motherhood role (Hock & Demeis, 1990), and in another they showed stability toward corporal punishment for almost 4 years (Buck, Holden, & Stickels, 2000). Nevertheless, parents do change their child-rearing cognitions, and the circumstances under which they change and some strategies that can support positive change are discussed later in this chapter.

## PARENTAL KNOWLEDGE AND EXPECTATIONS

A number of surveys of parents have been conducted to assess their knowledge of child development and their attitudes toward being a parent. Yankelovich and DYG, Inc. (2000) conducted a national survey of knowledge about aspects of child development from birth up to 3 years of age. Participants in this survey, who were primarily White, married, well-educated, and affluent parents, scored between

60% and 77% correct. Reich (2005) sampled 203 low-income mothers with babies and examined their level of knowledge in various content areas. Overall, 65% of questions were answered correctly—a number similar to the Yankelovich and DYG, Inc., national survey. Parents had high levels of knowledge related to routines and maternal health following childbirth, but lacked knowledge about sleep patterns and the developmental ability of 6-month-old infants.

In a Canadian survey conducted with single and married parents and with mothers and fathers from various socioeconomic backgrounds, it was found that 92% of parents surveyed thought that being a parent was their most important role and 84% believed that the way children are parented is critical for a successful transition into adulthood. Interestingly, when asked which area of development they had the most knowledge about, the majority of parents identified physical development, yet when they were asked about the areas in which they believed they had the most influence, 44% chose emotional development and 32% selected social development compared with 69% who chose physical development. It was found that parents had the least knowledge and the lowest confidence in parenting in these developmental domains. When asked who they would turn to for advice and information, they listed the following most frequently: child's physician (61%), spouse/partner (58%), friends (58%), own mother (57%), books (56%), and magazines (45%). Parents tend to seek out information at certain points in their children's lives and may make less use of unsolicited information. Many parents, especially during pregnancy and after their baby is born, welcome information and having their questions answered about such topics as childbirth, breast feeding their new baby, and getting the baby to sleep (Oldershaw, 2002). They may also seek out information at other developmental stages if they have concerns about how their child is developing or about any emotional, social, or behavior difficulties their child is experiencing. Parents are far less likely to seek out information when things are going well.

## Where Does Parenting Knowledge Come From?

Parents have many sources from which to obtain information and experience in child rearing, including prenatal classes, community-based parenting programs, television programs, and the Internet. There are a myriad of parenting websites and most receive thousands of "hits" every year for advice or parenting tips (Russell, 2003). Little is known about how accurate this knowledge is or how effective these sources of information are in changing parenting practices and child outcomes (Miller, 1988).

Knowledge has often been provided through large, formal campaigns such as ones to change parenting behavior to put infants to sleep on their backs rather than their stomachs to reduce SIDS, to increase breast feeding, to encourage parents not to smoke during pregnancy and around the child later, and to enforce car seat usage for infants and children. In general these have proved to be somewhat successful but are less likely to change the behavior of the most at-risk parents without other intervention strategies being used (Powles, 2000).

In general, research has shown that interventions designed to increase parenting knowledge have resulted in positive outcomes for children (Culp, Culp,

Blankemeyer, & Passmark, 1988). Research indicates that when and how information about child development and parenting is provided affects whether it is seen as relevant by parents and influences if it will be used or ignored (Goodnow, 2002).

## What Influences Parents' Receptivity to Information?

Interventionists who are providing parenting information in prevention and early intervention programs should consider the following factors influencing parent receptivity to information (see Table 12.1 for a summary).

*Timing*    The *timing* of when information is provided is crucial. In general parents are most open to new information when old explanations about how to parent are not working. For example, a parent who thinks that toilet training can be done before 12 months may seek out information about toilet training methods if their child is not trained by that time. The work of Prochaska (1999) also indicates that the timing is critical, especially in terms of how open the parent is to make any necessary changes to her child-rearing practices or how ready she is to begin to make those changes.

*Fit with Self-Image or Self-Concept*    Another important component is whether the *new information fits with the parents' image of who they are and their self concepts.* Parents would be more likely to accept information on disciplining their child if it fits to some degree with how they are already parenting (Cashmore & Goodnow, 1985). Similarly, information is more acceptable when it is not too dissonant with ideas and information they already have about a topic of parenting or child development. For example, parents of a child with disabilities may take a long time to be able to accept information about their child's development being delayed until it becomes more obvious to them or a final diagnosis shifts their perception of the child into a more realistic one. Also, a parent with a child with ADHD who does not believe in medication may search the Internet to find an entry that says that the side effects of using Ritalin are very negative. Parents are more likely to seek out parenting knowledge when it is easily accessible, as has been demonstrated with the wide use of parenting web sites. In other words, if parents want advice or information, they want it immediately rather than waiting for a referral to an agency.

**Table 12.1**    Influences on acceptance of parenting information

- Whether the timing is correct
- Whether it fits with self-image
- Whether it fits with or builds on other beliefs (e.g., cultural) or background (e.g., socioeconomic, geographical location) and is not too dissonant
- Relationship with interventionist or service provider
- Whether it is accessible
- Whether it is solicited or not
- Mood (e.g., anxiety or frustration) may add a sense of emergency
- Experiences growing up
- Whether it is related to parents' goals for their children
- The medium from which it is derived (e.g., print, Internet, group)

***Sense of Belonging to a Cultural Group***    Culture affects parents' receptivity to information as well as their cognitions about children and child rearing. In other words, parents are affected by their sense of belonging to a *cultural or religious group* and how the information fits with the beliefs and values of the groups. For example, a parent brought up in the United States may be more open to new information and knowledge if she thinks it will help her child than would a parent in a culture such as Mexico, with a stronger respect for tradition where doing something different may alienate her from others in her culture or religion (Sameroff & Feil, 1985). In fact, for many parents these values may be the most important influence on their parenting knowledge and may be very difficult to adjust; thus, information that is given, as far as possible, should be adapted to fit with these cultural beliefs. For example, in an intervention that provides a group on parenting toddlers, it will be very important to understand at least some of the cultural beliefs of the participants about individuality versus collectivism. As stated by Lynch and Hanson,

> Individuality, the explicit expression of self, is a value that some families prize highly. Children are encouraged to "be who they are" and stand out from the crowd. . . . In other families, however, interdependence is the primary value. Contributing to the functioning of the family as a whole is far more important than expressing one's individuality. In fact, to become fully independent is viewed as selfish and as a rejection of the family. (2004, p. 51)

To work in a culturally sensitive way, it is necessary to understand that cultural groups vary in their knowledge and ideas about child development and what influences it, in their definitions of maltreatment and methods of controlling their children, family relationships, and their aspirations for their child (Greenfield & Suzuki, 1998; Harkness & Super, 1996; Schweder, Goodnow, Hatano, LeVine, Markus, & Miller, 1998). Not only do group differences exist between cultures, much within-group variability exists between, for example, middle-income and blue-collar levels within national groups (Tudge, Hogan, Snezhjova, Kulakova, & Etz, 2000). Other within-group variables that are important are place of residence, such as living in a rural or urban setting, and the level of acculturation of the family into the new culture.

***Relationship Between Interventionist and Parent***    The *relationship between interventionist and parent* and the *way the information is provided* are very important. In Chapter 1, studies showed that parents with depression who were socially isolated did better when the nurse functioned more as a listener and was responsive to their needs than if they were given information alone. The first approach had a stronger effect on the mothers' depression and their parenting expectations (Booth, Mitchell, Barnard, & Spieker, 1989). Similarly, mothers who were identified as having preoccupied attachment did better when given an opportunity to talk about their experiences growing up after watching a video on infant care, whereas more dismissive parents did better when the video was followed with information on care of the infant (Bakermans-Kranenburg, Juffer, & van IJzendoorn, 1998). Parents who are in what Prochaska (1999) has called *precontemplation* or *contemplation* stages and are not ready to commit to changing or to taking action toward improvement of their parenting skills might be open to being given information about where to go if they need information at a later time. At these times, unsolicited advice that is not requested by a parent may feel intrusive and imply to her that she is being judged as incompetent and needing help.

Prevention and early intervention programs typically provide parenting information through parenting groups, during home visits, or in counseling sessions by professionals and paraprofessionals. As noted in Chapter 2, some of these approaches have been shown to increase parenting knowledge that in turn has been linked to improvements in parenting behavior and child outcomes. Increase in parenting knowledge has also been linked to improvement in behavior for children with behavior problems (Barlow, 1997) and reduced maternal anxiety and depression (Barlow & Coren, 2000). Research on parenting groups is generally positive and parents improve their level of parenting knowledge, reduce child symptoms, and improve parenting behavior and interactions. It is often hard to determine what aspect of the experience had the most influence or contributed to the changes, for example, meeting with other parents or the strategies used to provide the information or qualities of the group leaders. Stirtzinger and colleagues (2002) developed a 10-week parenting group with high-risk adolescent parents and found that the teenagers' depression was decreased and that parents were less likely to use coercive discipline tactics and made fewer attributions typically linked with child abuse. The researchers believed that when interventionists went beyond just providing information and also emphasized the enhancement of self-reflectivity through group discussions and having parents reflect on how they were parented and how this parenting influenced them, it contributed to positive outcomes for parents. A review of parenting programs found that maternal knowledge and parenting ability increased and were related to reduction in child abuse 3 to 5 years later (Britner & Reppucci, 1997). Similarly, Landy and Menna (in press) found that parenting knowledge of parents of aggressive young children increased following the Pathways to Competence for Young Children parenting group. This group intervention focused on improving parents' knowledge of child development and enhancing the parent–child relationships using a variety of strategies including role plays, group discussion, exploration of the parents' experience of being parented, and other techniques to enhance self-reflectivity. The group resulted in improvements in the participants' parent–child relationships, reduction in child symptoms, and improvement in parenting confidence.

## PARENT BELIEFS

Research on parent beliefs as contributors to parenting practices and the course of children's development has increased since the 1990s, primarily because of a growing interest in the effect of cognition on different aspects of family life (Bugental & Johnston, 2000; Sigel & McGillicuddy-DeLisi, 2002). Just how these beliefs are effective in improving or influencing the development of children is unclear, however; and because the concept of *belief* is often difficult to distinguish from attitudes, perceptions, and even opinions, it is difficult to distinguish what concept is operating when parents talk about their "beliefs" (McGillicuddy-DeLisi & Sigel, 1995). Although beliefs operate at a cognitive, conscious level, Sigel and

McGillicuddy-DeLisi pointed out that they may also operate "on an unconscious or tacit level" (2002, p. 487).

Studies of parents' beliefs in early Head Start programs showed a relationship between parents' early beliefs when their children were infants and child outcomes across cultural groups (Galper, Wigfield, & Seefeldt, 1997; Mantzicopoulos, 1997). For example, a relationship was found between early parental beliefs about the importance of academic achievement and children's achievement when they were in elementary school. A similar link has been found between parent beliefs about the value of reading when their children were 4 or 5 years of age and their children's later reading ability in school (Sonnenschein, Baker, Serpell, Scher, Trout, & Munsterman, 1997). Associations were also found between parents' beliefs about how preschoolers acquire math skills and their behavior around math activities with them. When parents valued math and believed that they had a role in their children's development of mathematics ability, they engaged in more math activities with their children (Musun-Miller & Blevins-Knabe, 1998). These prospective studies indicate that parental beliefs affect child outcomes by influencing parents' behavior with their children.

Research on parent beliefs about their children's social development is sparse, particularly as it relates to younger children. In one study, however, Hastings and Rubin (1999) found that parental beliefs about aggressive and withdrawn behavior in their 2-year-olds (e.g., if they believed the aggression was biologically based and intentional) were related to the same beliefs at a later age. Beliefs about pretend play with toddlers were examined and it was found that they were related to how both mothers and fathers played with their children (Haight, Parke, & Black, 1997).

Parents' beliefs about punishment often influence how they discipline. In one study, reliance on corporal punishment was found to be influenced by parents' own history of being disciplined as well as by cultural norms (Davis, 1999). It is important to note, however, that much of discipline and other interactions with children are believed to be nonreflective or not thought about and are influenced by implicit or procedural memories (Mills, 1999) (see Chapters 9 and 10 for a further discussion of parenting reactions and memory systems). As discussed previously, Hastings and Grusec (1998) and Hastings and Coplan (1999) showed that the goals that parents have for their parenting behaviors made a difference in terms of their discipline. Specifically, discipline was likely to be more punitive if the goals were more self-focused than if the goals were more child- or relationship-centered. This suggests that goals for behavior, or what the parent says she wants to achieve, may be important for determining how parents behave and should be addressed by interventionists.

McGillicuddy-DeLisi and Sigel (1995) cautioned that although most of the research has considered the effect of parent beliefs on their parenting behavior, which is then linked to child outcomes, it is likely that the relationship between child outcomes and parent beliefs is bidirectional, with the mother and child influencing each other. In spite of this confusion, it is clear that beliefs and other cognitions of parents do influence parenting behavior and as such, need to be considered in any intervention that is undertaken to enhance parenting behaviors or interactions.

## PARENT ATTITUDES

Parent attitudes are cognitions that are biases or evaluations that are made about various entities including child rearing. They are related to knowledge, beliefs, and attributions and are formed about, for example, "spoiling" an infant, discipline and punishment, and the importance of education. Attitudes go beyond knowledge and beliefs, however, and include opinions and an emotional component that can make them hard to change. Up until about the 1960s they were believed to be a major determinant of parenting behaviors and child outcomes. Later it was realized that the causative relationship was not simple and parental attitudes were not always reflected in how parents behaved with their children. Researchers also realized that parents often gave biased answers to attitude questionnaires, reporting what they thought they should say and not what their attitudes actually were (Holden & Buck, 2002). For example, a parent may report that he uses positive discipline methods even when he is usually quite punitive. From 1990–2000 the most researched topics on child-rearing attitudes have been cross-cultural issues and attitudes of special populations, such as parents with special-needs children and teenage parents, with other topics far behind (Holden & Buck, 2002).

Evidence increasingly shows that—just like parental beliefs—attitudes are multi-determined or are developed from a number of sources of influence including gender, level of education, culture, number of children, experience of being parented, geographical location, and children's characteristics (Bornstein et al., 1996, 1998; Bugental & Goodnow, 1998). All parents have attitudes about the centrality of children in their lives, the need for discipline, and child maltreatment, however.

Some attitudes have been linked to outcomes in children. For example, Brody, Flor, and Gibson (1999) found that when single mothers' child-rearing attitudes or goals for their children included being polite and respectful of others, this was related to the children's ability to regulate their behavior. As would be expected, in groups of mothers who endorsed the idea that punishment was beneficial, physical abuse occurred at higher rates than in a control group (Corral-Verdugo et al., 1995).

## PARENT ATTRIBUTIONS OF THEIR CHILD

*Parent attributions* are causal inferences and usually center on the reasons that a child develops in a certain way and the way she behaves (e.g., is disobedient or anxious and shy). They are considered to be learned beliefs from one's own experiences and observing the experience of others. A number of theories have described how parents' perceptions of their child and their views about child rearing influence their interactions with their child and the child's developmental outcomes.

### Attachment Theory and Attributions

Despite the growing evidence linking parental representations to children's behavior and development, the influence of parental representations of their child has not been given as much attention in attachment theory as interactional behaviors

(Benoit, Parker, & Zeanah, 1997). However, clinicians and researchers have, for some time, recognized the importance of understanding the subjective experience of the mother and child. For example, how the mother views her child; what her experience is with him; who she listens to; and her belief systems regarding infants, children, and being a parent are all significant influences on how she interacts with her child. As Lieberman (1999) pointed out, parental attributions can "help determine whether or how infant behaviors are responded to, misinterpreted, or ignored" (1999, p. 739). When these attributions are negative, the interactions and discourse with the child that result can be extremely damaging to the child's sense of self, as well as her emotional and behavioral manifestations of these internalized views of self and other. Some evidence indicates that parents have already constructed a generalized model of infants and of being a parent even before the pregnancy. Certainly, most parents construct an idea of their baby during the pregnancy and before the birth (Mebert, 1989, 1991; Zeanah, Keener, & Anders, 1986; Zeanah, Keener, Stewart, & Anders, 1985). It is also important to point out that mothers and fathers may have very different views of who the baby is and their expected relationship with her.

In order to understand parents' views of their child, some attachment researchers have developed ways to investigate this subjectivity more systematically and objectively. Two interviews have been developed in order to assess parents' attachment experiences with their children: The Parent Attachment Interview (Biringen & Bretherton, 1988) and the Working Model of the Child Interview (WMCI) (Zeanah, Benoit, & Barton, 1993), both described in Chapter 1. They are structured interviews to elicit and classify parents' perceptions of and thoughts and feelings about their child and their relationship with him. Stern developed an interview that has been used to study the effects of psychotherapy on maternal representations of their infant (Cramer et al., 1990).

## Other Approaches Focusing on Attributions

Another approach has been to assess parents' views of themselves as parents, the emotional aspects of their relationship with the child, and how they managed separations such as when their child first started in child care. The interview, called the Experiences of Mothering Interview, is based on the Parent Development Interview (Aber, Slade, Berger, Bresgi, & Kaplan, 1985). It is scored on the basis of how much a parent views the child as an individual and understands the needs of her child (George & Solomon, 1989).

In addition, some research on parental representations has been carried out using temperament questionnaires to understand parents' perceptions of infant characteristics from pregnancy through the first few months of life (e.g., Fava-Vizziello, Antonioli, Cocci, & Invernizzi, 1993; Mebert, 1989; Mebert & Kalinowski, 1986; Zeanah et al., 1985; Zeanah, Keener, & Anders, 1996). In general, it would appear that parents' perceptions of temperament may be both subjective (i.e., related to her own experience) and objective (i.e., related to the actual characteristics of the child) (Biringen, 1990; Wolk, Zeanah, Garcia-Coll, & Carr, 1992).

Interesting work by Zeanah and associates using the WMCI has found strong concordance between WMCI classifications from pregnancy through the first months of life and infant attachment classifications assessed concurrently (69%-73%) (Benoit et al., 1997; Zeanah, Benoit, Hirshberg, Barton, & Regan, 1994). In addition, George and Solomon (1989) found strong associations between working models of parenting (using the Experiences of Mothering Interview) and child attachment classifications or representations. Similarly, using the Parent Attachment Interview, Bretherton and colleagues (1989) found that scores on the interview were significantly correlated with child attachment measures. Specifically, they found that scores on the sensitivity/insight scale were found to have the strongest relationship (Bretherton, Biringen, Ridgeway, Maslin, & Sherman, 1989). Researchers have also been looking for relationships between these parental representations or attitudes and parenting behaviors and interactions with their children. In general, positive parental attitudes toward infants were significantly correlated with a positive interaction variable for both mothers and fathers. The positive interaction variable was made up of behaviors such as sensitivity, positive affect, animation, attitude toward play, activity, encouragement of achievement, amount of vocalizing to the child, and amount of reciprocal play (George & Solomon, 1996, 1999).

In conclusion, parents' positive representations of a child and representations that reflect the individuality and reality of the child's characteristics can be strong protective factors that correlate with positive child developmental outcomes.

## Attribution Theory

Attribution theory is a social learning and cognitive theory that emphasizes the importance of parents' attributions and expectations of their child on their parenting behavior and child development. Parents form attributions from their beliefs about typical development (Dix & Grusec, 1985). As parents seek out and establish ideas about or explanations of their child's behavior, these cognitions, stable knowledge systems, or schemas arouse emotions that are then linked to behavioral responses. Originally, attribution theory considered the effect of these ideas on children's self-esteem. In a study by Compas, Friedland-Bandes, Bastien, and Adelman (1981) of parents of children with behavior and emotional problems and learning disorders, the parents all believed the problems were due to dispositional factors. These attributions may be internalized by the child, which may influence the child's self-esteem and motivational systems. The use of attributions in understanding parenting and clinical problems was a later development.

Parents tend to ask questions about why their children do certain things and how they should respond. In other words, they engage in cognitive appraisal of situations, particularly if situations are ambiguous or hard to understand, novel, undesired, or potentially threatening. When parents engage in this consideration, they can come up with very different reasons for what is occurring. Nix, Pinderhughes, Dodge, Bates, and Pettit (1999) identified a hostile attributional style that was held by some parents that predicted later aggressive behavior in their children. Other parents may react more automatically without cognitive appraisal of the situation, which can lead to acting out and negative responses as well (Bugental & Happaney, 2000).

Some of the important theorists who have advanced the field of attributions include Heider, Kelley, and Weiner. Heider (1958) introduced the idea that people perceive causes as primarily external (i.e., due to situational or environmental factors) or internal (i.e., due to individual factors such as personality traits or wishes and desires). He also introduced the concept of attributional biases. He described the self-serving bias in which individuals see themselves in a way that protects their self-esteem and validates their belief systems, thus perpetuating their attributional bias (Heider, 1958). Heider's work provided more of a conceptual framework than a theory based on empirical studies, however. Kelley (1967) wrote about the process by which the individual formulates the reasons for behaviors. He proposed that these "causal attributions" are made on the basis of consensus (or information coming from several different people), distinctiveness (or information coming from the situation or context), and consistency (or information gathered over time). Weiner (1979, 1986) developed his model of attributions in the area of the causes of academic success or failure, using it to develop a theory of achievement motivation. He considered three dimensions: locus of causality (internal/external), stability (how much the attribution is constant or fluctuates), and controllability (whether a factor can be controlled either by the person or someone else). Weiner also proposed that there is a causative relationship between cognition (or attributions) and emotions, with cognitions influencing emotions that, in turn, can lead to certain behaviors. Weiner's model inspired much of the research on parental attributions and was used in the development of the Parent Attribution Test (PAT) (Bugental & Shennum, 1984). (See Chapter 1 for more information on this measure.)

Attributions, including parents' attributions and beliefs about their children and parenting, are subject to biases or distortions that when negative, can be extremely damaging for the development of infants and young children. In a meta-analysis of eight studies, Joiner and Wagner (1996) found support for the importance of a number of dimensions of attributions. The dimensions of their stability over time and the fact that they were broadly applied had the most support, and intent, selfish motivation, and blame were also found to have enough support to be researched further.

One of the biases that parents may have, especially when parent–child relationships are conflictual, is to view misbehaviors as due to internal, stable, and controllable causes inherent in a child. The child is blamed for negative behaviors, but no credit is given for positive behaviors, which are instead attributed to uncontrollable or situational causes. The parent then believes that because the child could control his behavior he must intend it. This influences the parent's emotional reaction as well as how she tries to socialize the child. These attributions allow the parent's self-esteem to be preserved because the parent does not consider her own contribution to the child's difficult behaviors (Dix & Grusec, 1985). These types of attributions are often turned into criticism of the child and failure on the part of parents in trying to find ways to overcome the child's difficulties.

Another bias mentioned previously in this chapter, which falls on the extreme end of the attribution continuum, is that of "overattribution," in which situational constraints are minimized as causes of child behaviors or the parent believes the child's behavior is directed at the parent or is motivated by malicious intention on the child's part. This leads to negative affective states and can result, in turn, to automatic or implicit processes or responses that are extremely punitive, even abusive (Dix & Grusec, 1985).

The reasons for these rigid, stereotypic attributions are unclear. Because they are often present during pregnancy and predict problematic relationships post-natally, they seem to predate actual experiences with the child and are likely to be based on the parents' internal representations of relationships that were formed in interactions in early childhood with primary caregivers. It is likely that they are ingrained during disciplinary exchanges with parents that are then repeated, as Bugental and colleagues suggested, at the level of implicit or procedural memory (Bugental et al., 2000).

In one study of parents identified as maltreating their children, which had a large number of dismissive and preoccupied parents in the sample, the researchers found that parental attributions were different for parents with different attachment styles (Grusec et al., 1993). Dismissive parents rated their children's control over events as being higher than did secure parents, who rated children's control higher than did preoccupied parents (Grusec, Adam, & Mommone, 1993). Consequently, preoccupied parents saw themselves as having the most control and dismissive parents saw themselves as having the least control in a difficult child-rearing situation. Preoccupied parents expressed the most negative thoughts about the child and situation.

***Levels of Parent Understanding of the Child***    Another related concept has been to consider levels of parental understanding of their child (Newberger & White, 1989). The levels chosen were

1. *Egoistic orientation:* The parent role is organized around his own wants and needs and not the child's.

2. *Conventional orientation:* The parent role is organized around cultural beliefs or traditional views of child rearing.

3. *Subjective-individualistic orientation:* The parent role is organized around the needs of a particular child.

4. *Systems orientation:* The parent role is conceived as part of an ever-changing system in which the child's needs are met.

A relationship has been found between parent awareness levels and parental behavior, with parents with high levels of awareness more responsive to their child's needs (Cook, 1979; Newberger, 1980; Newberger & Cook, 1983). This adds support to the idea that levels of parental understanding and awareness contribute to parental function and dysfunction.

Studies linking attributional biases to parental behaviors and child outcomes have been conducted with parents identified as depressed and abusive. Just as cognitions produce particular emotions, affective states can modify cognitions. Research has linked maternal depression to a more negative perception of the child (Bendell, Field, Yando, Lange, Martinez, & Pickens, 1994; Cummings & Davies, 1994b; Dix, 1993; Webster-Stratton & Hammond, 1988). A link between maternal depression and perception of behavior problems in children has also been found. Parents who report higher levels of depression and anxiety tend to rate their infants' temperament more negatively (Vaughn, Bradley, Joffe, Seifer, & Barglow, 1987; Ventura & Stevenson, 1986; Zeanah et al., 1986; Zeanah, Keener, Anders, & Vieira-Baker, 1987). In one study, when children with perceived behavior problems were brought to a clinic and found to have no deviant behavior, the mothers were found to be more depressed than mothers of children who did have behavior problems or mothers in the control group (Rickard, Forehand, Wells, Grist, & McMahon, 1981). Findings of a link between postpartum depression and more difficult infant temperament have also been found (Cutrona & Troutman, 1986a; Mebert, 1991). The reasons for these links have been somewhat controversial, with some proposing that maternal depression results in distortion of the child's behavior, whereas others believe that depressed mothers report more child behavior problems because the children are actually more difficult.

Research has also been conducted regarding abusive parents' perceptions, expectations, and attributions of their children. Abusive parents have been found to report more behavior problems in their children, which are not confirmed by independent observers (Bradley & DeV Peters, 1991; Crittenden, 1985; Mash, Johnston, & Kovitz, 1983; Reid, Kavanagh, & Baldwin, 1987; Susman, Trickett, Iannotti, Hollenbeck, & Zahn-Waxler, 1985). In turn, child abuse can lead to increased rates of child problems (Lorber, Felton, & Reid, 1984; Reid, Patterson, & Lorber, 1982). Twentyman and colleagues have emphasized that abusive parents tend to set unrealistic expectations for their children, which, when not met by the child, lead to excessive punishment. They also suggest that abusive parents attribute hostile intent to their children (Bauer & Twentyman, 1985; Larrance & Twentyman, 1983; Twentyman & Plotkin, 1982).

Bugental and colleagues also conducted another group of studies about the role of parental attributions in the etiology of child abuse. In her model, Bugental (1992) has found that abusive parents attribute high control to their child and low control to themselves in situations involving difficult child behavior (Bugental, Blue, & Cruzcosa, 1989). Bugental sees these attributions—which she described as "threat-oriented schema"—as placing parents in a power disadvantage. These schema place the child as the problem source and the parents as helpless victims and eventually operate automatically, especially in stressful situations. Research has demonstrated that when parents who attribute high power to their children and low power to themselves as caregivers are asked child management questions and are stressed by also being asked to carry out another learning task, they are more likely to answer without monitoring their response and to react in a way that gives them low power. If they are not stressed by the additional task, however, they are able to correct this attribution and rate themselves as more dominant than their child (Bugental, Lyon, Krantz, & Cortez, 1997).

Feeling out of control can also lead to feelings of depression and negatively focused thoughts. The messages given by threat-oriented adults toward the child are, therefore, primarily negative and often confusing, raising, in turn, anger and anxiety in the child. In an attempt to cope with these feelings the child may withdraw and become avoidant or difficult to control, confirming the parents' attributions of the child. As emotions and negative behavioral tendencies are increased, there is a greater risk of abuse (Bugental & Shennum, 1984). Bugental has used this model to develop an intervention that works with parents to redefine their attributions of their children to be less threat-based and blaming and to help parents to use problem solving to find new ways to interact with and to discipline their children (Bugental et al., 2000). She was able to show that adding the strategy to a home visiting program significantly reduced the incidence of abuse. (See a later section of this chapter for more details of the research.)

Parental attributions have also been linked to children with emotional and behavior problems. A number of studies have found that parents of children with these types of problems were more likely to attribute the causes of the misbehavior to characteristics of the child (Dix & Lochman, 1990; Rubin & Mills, 1990). Other studies have also confirmed the importance of perceived intentionality in the child for maintaining coercive cycles in parent–child interactions. These included a study of 4- to 11-year olds with oppositional defiant behaviors (Johnston & Patenaude, 1994), aggressive children of mother–son dyads (MacKinnon-Lewis, Lamb, Arbuckle, Baradaran, & Volling, 1992), and adolescents with conduct disorder (Davidson-Baden & Howe, 1992). They also found that parents of boys with conduct disorder not only attributed their children's misbehavior to intent but also described the behavior as stable and global and outside their control, which the researchers pointed out caught them in a stance of helplessness, leading to ineffectual discipline and withdrawal.

Before closing this discussion of the effects of parent attributions on parenting behavior, it is important to mention that the process is, of course, bidirectional, with the behavior and emotions of the child and parent continually influencing the other and escalating across time. An important consideration is that not only do parents have cognitive-affective biases with their children but also, as a result of continually hostile and critical interactions, the children develop their own hostile and biased attributions or working models of their parents, peers, and other adults that can perpetuate their problematic behavior (Dodge, 1986; Dodge, Murphy & Buchsbaum, 1984; MacKinnon, Lamb, Belsky, & Baum, 1990).

Given the clear relationship between various types of parent cognitions, parental behaviors, and child development, the importance of intervening at the cognitive and representational level of the parent is clear. The next sections describe various intervention strategies that can affect parent cognitions.

## INTERVENTIONS TO ENHANCE PARENTS' KNOWLEDGE, BELIEFS, ATTITUDES, AND ATTRIBUTIONS OF THE CHILD

Although parental cognitions are deep-seated and affect children every day, interventions can be employed to improve parental cognitions, beliefs, attitudes, and attributions, and thus, child outcomes.

### Interventions During Pregnancy

Pregnancy is often a time during which parents are interested in learning about many aspects of pregnancy and also about the birth process. It appears that some parents construct negative attributions during pregnancy. These may occur because of difficult circumstances or because the baby is not wanted. A single or teenage mother may be concerned about her ability to provide or care for her infant. Sometimes the infant's birth order in the family may trigger a parent's unconscious feelings about his own position in the family. How the mother feels physically during her pregnancy can also influence her view of her baby. Perhaps she is unable to keep nourishment down or the baby is very active and the kicking is painful. In other instances, the parent may have difficulty imagining the fetus as a person at all, and in extreme cases the mother may deny she is pregnant until the birth of the baby.

With high-risk populations such as teenage parents, parents who have abused a previous child, or parents who are substance abusers, it is especially important to try to begin the intervention during pregnancy and to provide parents with as much information as they request. Sometimes parents may not identify a particular piece of information that they require but describe feeling a more generalized type of anxiety and want to talk about some of the concerns they have.

Melish, who knows she is carrying a boy, had heard her mother speak frequently about how difficult her labor was with Melish's brother, and how she knew he was going to be difficult because he moved too much inside her. As it turned out, her brother *was* a difficult child, and is still having problems holding down a job and with his relationships within the family and outside it. Consequently, Melish worries about the baby she is carrying because he is a boy and seems to be very active, even though she knows he is healthy. Allowing her to talk freely about her concerns and giving her support and understanding about them will allow her to be more open to seeing her baby as he is and getting to know his individuality.

Sometimes a father may express concern that his wife is pushing him away because she is so focused on the baby and the impending birth. Although assuring him that this is a very normal feeling that fathers often have may be helpful for him, he will also need an opportunity to talk about his fears and to explore the reasons for them. It might also be appropriate to meet with the couple so that they can share their anticipation of the baby coming with each other and any concerns that they have. If significant issues arise, they could be given encouragement to have more sessions to further discuss and hopefully resolve them. Sometimes a parent in a very high-risk situation is not able to verbalize his concerns, such as when the family is being followed by Child Protective Services (CPS) and he is worried the child will be taken away, or he may not be aware of any issues that could place the child at risk. Sometimes it may be necessary to gently insist that the parent think about why CPS is involved.

**Interventionist:** "How has the pregnancy been going for the two of you?"

**Pierre:** "It's going well, although Maria is very tired and she's worried that they will take the baby away."

**Interventionist:** "What have you been told about what will happen after the baby is born?"

**Pierre:** "They say they have to check us out because they had to take our other baby away, and we didn't do anything to her."

**Interventionist:** "Can you tell me more about what happened?"

| Pierre: | "She kept losing weight and she wouldn't feed and people told us it was our fault she didn't feed well and lost weight—but we tried so hard." |
| --- | --- |
| Interventionist: | "So you worry that could happen again. Do you have any ideas of why Alexandra didn't gain weight and had to be placed in the care of Child Protective Services?" |
| Pierre: | "She cried all the time and Maria tried to hold her and the baby pushed her away and then they put her in the hospital and she gained weight and so they said it was us and put her in a foster home. We're hoping we can get her back; she cries for us." |
| Interventionist: | "Maybe we can talk some more about what happened with your Child Protection worker and try to make sure it doesn't happen again. What are you planning to do so it won't happen again?' |
| Pierre: | "Well, Maria's hoping to breast-feed this time, the nurse will visit, and I have a great pediatrician to check him out." |
| Interventionist: | "They sound like terrific plans. If you do have any problems with breast feeding we have an emergency number so you could use that as well and call me if you have any concerns." |

Some of the strategies to encourage parents to be able to reflect on what is going on during a pregnancy and to elicit information on the attributions that are being formed include the following:

- Having the mother and father talk about their thoughts and feelings about the baby and helping them correct any misconceptions that may already be in place

- Wondering about what they might name their baby and why the name might be chosen

- Discussing the gender of the baby, specifically if it is already known, and what either gender would mean to the couple if it is not known

- Discussing any anxieties and answering any questions the parents might have

- Discussing the fetus's movements and giving parents information about what the baby can see and hear in the womb. For example, explaining that in the third trimester, the baby can already hear the parents' voices and how the tone of voice may affect him or her

In addition, it is very important to check about prenatal care and to make sure that the mother will have support during labor and that it will be someone she would like to have with her. These kinds of discussions give parents the opportunity to talk about any anxieties and can focus their thoughts on the baby and who he or she might be. As well, they give the service provider an opportunity to subtly correct any misconceptions and confirm parents' interest in and concern for their baby. They may also help identify any attributions that would indicate that the infant might be at risk for abuse and neglect and allow for careful monitoring after the birth.

## Interventions During the Neonatal Period

Once the birth has taken place, interventionists can learn more about parents' attributions of their infant and provide information about the newborn's remarkable capacities for responsiveness, perceptual awareness, and readiness to attach to parents. As described in Chapter 2, administration of the Brazelton Neonatal Behavioral Assessment Scale (BNBAS) has been used in many hospitals to provide parents with a demonstration of the newborn's capacities and the child's individual characteristics. Nurses could use these items on home visits; for example, they could show parents how their baby can hold his head up and is calmed by being held. Demonstrating to parents how their baby can alert to sights and sounds, particularly to parents' voices as opposed to the nurse's, can often help parents form attributions of pride in their baby's capacities and a realization of how important they are to their baby. Sometimes if an infant is identified as having a hypersensitivity to touch, for example, parents can be helped to find ways to feel close to their baby without holding him all the time. Perhaps they could look at him and talk to him or hold him in a way that is not so close. If parents help to administer some of the more easily administered items, the effects on parental confidence and sensitivity of interactions is enhanced (Nugent & Brazelton, 2000; Gomes-Pedro, Patricio, Carvalho, Goldschmidt, Torgal-Garcia, & Monteiro, 1995). Sometimes a videotape of the BNBAS being administered to another baby can be substituted for the actual administration. In either case, discussing parents' observations of their newborn and answering any questions about their behaviors and their capabilities even at birth can be invaluable. Again, any misattributions of behaviors can be corrected. For example, a parent who perceives her infant's crying to mean "I don't like you" can be shown that the baby is trying to communicate "I really need you to hold me" by having the parent hold the crying baby in order to comfort him.

## Reframing

As noted by Fraiberg (1980) and Lieberman, Silverman, and Pawl (2000), some parents have negative or very distorted views of their infants and young children, often due to their own unresolved traumatic experiences during childhood. *Reframing* has been used for several years in family therapy in order to give a different meaning to the behavior of family members. It is a technique that has also been used to redefine descriptions of, for example, difficult temperament characteristics or behaviors. For instance, the child who is hyperactive can be described as "busy," the child who tends to get into everything could be considered "curious," and the child who is seen as irritable could be described as "expressive" or "emotional." Negative attributions can also be changed by talking from the child's point of view and explaining behaviors from a developmental perspective. When a child cries because the parent leaves the room, a parent may define the behavior as being spoiled. A positive reframing would explain to the parent that the child trusts her because she looks after him so well and he feels sad and uncertain when she leaves. The developmental significance of having a secure attachment can also be explained. This can be an especially important approach when an infant is becoming a toddler and is having tantrums and pushing to do things her way. Helping the parents to reframe this as an important developmental phase in which their child is becoming his own person with a mind of his own can be helpful. This kind of reframing may also provide an opportunity for a discussion of how the parents feel about a new developmental phase and how they can support their child to negotiate it.

## Speaking for the Child

*Speaking for the child* is very similar to reframing, except the interventionist actually talks for the baby in order to correct any misattributions. This will be particularly important when parents are beginning to see their child's behavior as directed at them with the intent of controlling them. For example, a parent may say, "He's getting so bad; he never listens to us, and he does it to get us annoyed. Nothing we try ever works." Because child development experts know that a child's negative behavior can be activated as a result of being ignored, speaking for the child might be "I know it doesn't seem like it, but I would really like you to play with me and talk gently to me. I don't know how else to ask you."

This strategy can be used at a teachable moment during a home visit or a clinic session. It can be used when a parent ignores or misinterprets the action of a child. It does not judge the parent's attribution but points out the child's love and caring for the parent. Osofsky and colleagues have used the technique with teenage parents in a different way by having them speak in the first person to describe what they believe their child is thinking and feeling at a particular moment or in a certain developmental phase (Carter, Osofsky, & Hann, 1990).

## Pediatric Guidance

*Pediatric guidance* involves the interventionist and sometimes a physician, nurse, or other clinician or home visitor, who provide information or suggestions about a particular child or developmental stage the child is going through. Information about the infant or young child is gathered through the medical and developmental history, questions or concerns parents have, and observations of the parents interacting with their child. If the child has delays the clinician may demonstrate to the parents by interacting with the child aspects of the child's development and their capabilities and any delays or limitations. The aim is to adjust their attitude or beliefs about the child to be realistic but to make sure to let the parents keep their hopes alive for the child to make gains and to continue to progress, even if the progression is at a slower pace than that of a child who is typically developing. New representations of the child to fit the current reality of his capabilities and to correct any misconceptions will need to be formed gradually. Suggestions are made to parents about how best to adapt their interactions to their child and how they can help encourage his development.

The work of Brazelton and colleagues is an example of pediatric guidance. In his book *Touchpoints: Your Child's Emotional and Behavioral Development*, Brazelton (1992) suggested that this kind of approach could be used at critical points in a child's development by a pediatrician or home visitor in order to support parents and to update their perceptions of their child. Some of the developmental "touchpoints" that he suggested occur at the following stages: pregnancy, birth, 6–8 weeks, 9 months, 1 year, 18 months, 2 years, 3 years, 4 years, 5 years, and 6 years.

## Focusing on Causal and Problem-Solving Appraisal

Bugental and colleagues (2000) developed a cognitive appraisal approach to enhance parents' attributions and behavior with their child that could be used in a prevention program with parents at risk for abuse. It was added to the Healthy Families home visiting program in which community home visitors supported parents and showed them how to use toys to play with their baby. In the cognitive appraisal approach at the beginning of each visit, parents report any problems that they are having with their child. They are asked what they think causes the problems. The interventionist continues to ask for suggestions until the parents come up with one that does not blame the child and does not suggest intent on the part of the child to threaten or to be hostile toward the parent. Some questions that can be asked to facilitate the process include, "Did he intend to do it?", "Do you think he knew what the effect of his behavior would be?", "Was there anything else that led to what your child did?" Then parents are asked to come up with some ways to solve the problem and to try them out before the next visit. On the following visit, discussion takes place about how successful their strategy was. If the strategy was successful, parents will be asked about another problem and the same sequence is followed. If the strategy was not considered to be successful, it is refined if necessary or a new one is suggested for use before the next visit.

In this approach, misattributions are not pointed out. For example, if a parent discusses a child who is refusing to eat certain foods, she will be asked to come up with a reason. It might be that the child finds the food hard to swallow or does not like having to sit still to eat. Interventionists can make suggestions to the parents such as having the child sit at the table for a shorter time and including a food the child does like.

Individuals who participated in the home visiting program and who participated in this cognitive appraisal approach were compared with a group who only received the home visiting program and a control group that received only services routinely available in the community. The effects on the incidence of child abuse were highly significant, with the enriched home visiting program having only a 4% incidence; home visiting only program, 20%; and the control group, 36%. The intervention was believed to be successful because it encouraged the parents to engage in cognitive appraisal of the situation, opened up the possibility of changing attributions, and stopped automatic responding that did not consider the child and reasons for the child's behavior. Bugental pointed out that if abuse has actually already occurred, it may be necessary to be more directive and to correct misattributions and to insist on parents making behavioral changes in the interaction.

## Improving Parenting Awareness and Understanding of the Child

When parents show low levels of awareness of the needs of their child, and particularly when parents are focused instead on their own needs or have very rigid or inaccurate ideas about parenting, parent education programs that provide information on child development and parenting can be useful interventions. In these groups, combining discussion of child-rearing problems, role playing of parenting strategies, and discussions about how their parents handled these issues with di-dactic presentation on child development can be very effective in helping parents better understand their children. The combination of strategies can also help parents to change attributions to more positive ones and improve parent–child inter-actions. When parents have particularly hostile attributions, changing attributions within short-term parenting groups can be very challenging. For these parents who are likely to have experienced very early traumas, longer term approaches designed for parents with complex trauma may be necessary. During this inter-vention, using opportunities to empathize with the parents' own feelings while using some of the other strategies discussed in this chapter may enable them to gradually shift attributions to more positive ones. A number of parenting groups are described in other chapters in this section of the book.

## Parent–Infant Psychotherapy

When distortions are extreme and damaging to the child, parent–child psycho-therapy will often be needed to correct the projections that have been assigned to the child. This approach is based on psychodynamic theory and is described by Fraiberg (1980), Lieberman (1991), and Lieberman and Pawl (1993). The ap-proach is used to "free the baby from the engulfment of the parents" (Lieberman et al., 2000, p. 746). During the intervention the child is in the room with the par-ent, and distortions that arise as a result of the parents' conflicts or past experiences are identified and addressed as they occur. During the intervention the therapist will provide emotional support for the baby and interpretations of the meaning of the parents' thoughts and behaviors. The approach remains nondirective and is not didactic, and may involve crisis intervention as necessary. In the intervention, the therapist moves back and forth describing and clarifying the behaviors and ex-periences of the mother and child. During the therapy strategies such as reframing and speaking for the child may be used. If the mother talks about her past experi-ences, her behavior and experience may be explained by linking it with her be-haviors with her child. It may be necessary to define the boundaries of the par-ents' behavior toward the child, or to explain what is not acceptable by linking it to the developmental needs of the child and explaining how some behaviors are damaging for the child.

Throughout the intervention, the clinician has to be able to contain her own feelings about the parents' treatment of the child as well as to modulate the par-ents' intense feelings. It is also crucial to support the parent and to make sure that disapproval and judgmental comments are avoided so that the parent does not feel criticized in her handling of the child. Intervention may be long, and it will be im-portant to periodically assess various intervention strategies for their suitability and, if necessary, revise them and try new approaches.

## Cognitive Approaches to Supporting Parents with Posttraumatic Stress Disorder (PTSD)

Increasingly cognitive approaches or cognitive behavior therapy (CBT) are being used in groups or individually with people with depression and anxiety disorders to help them develop strategies to change their negative attributions, to stop negative thoughts, and to develop more optimistic views of the world. These approaches generally result is less relapse and provide participants with strategies they can use after the intervention is over. Such approaches are also being used with people who are ill, have other stresses in their lives, or have experienced trauma. These mindfulness approaches are described in more detail in Chapters 9 and 11.

## USING INTERVENTIONS TO ENCOURAGE POSITIVE ATTRIBUTIONS OF THE CHILDREN: CASE-STUDY FAMILIES

### Mark and His Family

Although Mark's parents, Joan and Michael, did not use negative and blaming attributions with him, they tended to see him as having problems that were stable, global, and outside their control. They seemed to feel powerless in being able to discipline him and bring his behavior under control. This situation arose for a number of reasons, primarily because his parents felt sorry for him and did not want to "break his spirit," but also because they had few strategies to discipline him and to deal with the rudeness and oppositional behavior that occurred at home and at school. They seemed to feel that there was something in Mark that meant that he could not be disciplined. Partly this seemed to be because Mark had been adopted and his early medical history was unclear, and also because he was under the care of a neurologist because of an abnormal electroencephalogram (EEG) and for the possibility of Tourette syndrome. After an intellectual assessment was completed and the information that Mark's intellectual capacity was in the normal range was shared, it helped to change Joan and Michael's perceptions that Mark could not understand consequences or be disciplined. Also helpful were clear instructions on how to discipline him and help in coming up with ways to work on his behavioral issues; for example, the interventionist encouraged them to be firmer with Mark and to take control of his behavior and to stop any aggression and rudeness immediately. Also it was important that the parents worked together to support one another to enforce any rules that they decided on.

### Nina and Her Family

Because Nina had very negative attributions of Derrick and Meg, efforts were made to change them to more positive views. Every opportunity was used to talk for Meg and to reframe her whining and crying into a desire for her mother's attention and affection. This would take place in meetings at the center, on home visits, and in family sessions. The interventionist also tried to point out how much Meg loved and cared for her mother. Providing information on her developmental needs for nurturing was also somewhat helpful.

In order to address her negative attributions of Derrick, Nina was asked to describe a parenting problem that she was experiencing with Derrick—the one that she wanted to work on the most. She chose Derrick's tendency to be aggressive with Meg and baby Paul. The interventionist pressed her into giving a reason for the aggression. It took many questions to get her to go from blaming statements such as "He hates us all," "He has the devil inside him," and "He's like his father," to a more positive framing in which she could express understanding that he felt jealous and left out and was hurt and angry because he had missed her so much during his foster placements out of the house. After this, the interventionist helped Nina to come up with a way to deal with Derrick's aggression. She was encouraged to tell him that hitting was not acceptable and to send him to his room for a brief period so that they could both calm down, and then to talk to him about finding a better way to express his frustration. It was also suggested that she spend some special time with him. Over time, this strategy was effective in reducing Derrick's aggressive acting-out behavior.

From the work of changing the attributions of the parents in these two families, it was clear how important an aspect of the parent–child relationship these attributions were. Changes made to the parents' attributions significantly improved their interactional behavior with their children and their children's outcomes in terms of reducing symptoms and problematic behaviors and improving the children's sense of security or attachment with their parents. These changes were very gratifying for both the children and their parents.

## CHAPTER 13

# Enhancing Parents' Problem Solving and Planning

Not a day passes when parents do not have to make decisions and solve problems. In order to maintain adequate structure in day-to-day life and to successfully carry out the tasks of parenting, it is essential to have good problem-solving and planning abilities. Of course, problem solving is not something that begins in adulthood; rather, it begins from the first few months of an individual's life—such as when an infant hits a mobile to make it move—and becomes more complicated with age.

## DEFINING PROBLEM SOLVING

All problem solving has certain elements in common. It involves having a goal in mind that cannot be attained immediately because of the presence of one or more obstacles, recognizing the obstacles to that goal, having strategies for overcoming the obstacles, and being able to evaluate the results of the strategies (DeLoache, Miller, & Pierroutsakos, 1998). Sometimes a problem takes several attempts before it is solved, and one must be able to evaluate progress toward the goal so as to know when the problem has been solved. The competent person typically develops some rules for problem solving and some ways to proceed. For example, if a parent finds out that her usual child care provider is sick and cannot take her baby for the day, she may go through a list of possible substitute sitters or explore the possibility of staying home for the day.

Planning is an important part of problem solving that should occur before any action toward solving the problem is taken. Scholnick and Friedman defined planning as "the use of knowledge for a purpose, and the construction of an effective way to meet a goal" (1993, p. 145). Planning involves thinking about a desired outcome before acting and deciding on the actions that need to be taken before actually taking them (Bjorklund, 2000). Planning also includes the ability to use past knowledge to provide relevant information about the actions to be taken, and the ability to monitor a plan's execution, revising it along the way as feedback for the performance of the plan occurs. It is the opposite of impulsive responding, which happens without thinking ahead or considering a plan of action and its possible consequences.

### Problem Solving and Coping

The capacity to problem solve is also linked to coping. Research examining the relations between stress and adjustment among adults indicates that successful adjustment is mediated by coping (Lazarus, 1991; Lazarus & Folkman, 1983). The term *coping* refers broadly to efforts to manage environmental and internal conflicts and demands. Coping efforts are actions taken in specific situations that are intended to reduce stress. Coping may include using strategies for problem solving such as cognitively reframing the stressor (e.g., thinking about what is upsetting and difficult to manage about the stressor), selectively attending to positive aspects of the self or the situation, and asking for help. Studies have shown that individuals with an overall sense of well-being are better able to think of ways to address interpersonal problems, to construct coherent strategies for resolving them, and to generate more problem-solving strategies. They also are more likely to consider possible consequences of their actions for themselves and for others.

## Problem Solving and Personal Characteristics

Studies have found that the ability to solve problems is linked to an individual's personal resources, which include attitudes about the self (i.e., self-esteem), attitudes about the world (i.e., belief in mastery), intellectual capacity, and interpersonal skills (Hobfoll & Leiberman, 1987; Lazarus, 1991; Pearlin & Schooler, 1978).

People who find it difficult to problem solve are often constantly fearful about the future and what may happen. They become overwhelmed and unable to think frequently. Those whose experiences have led to an attitude of learned helplessness (i.e., a feeling or belief that they have no control over their lives or have an external locus of control) often fail to prevent problems because they have difficulty planning ahead and do not try to solve problems when they arise (Barkley, 2002). Planning can also be difficult for individuals with poor executive functioning—the ability to inhibit other activities or thoughts in order to focus on problem solving or task-planning. A tendency to respond impulsively, particularly during crises, also can be a problem (Barkley, 2002).

## Problem Solving and Parenting Tasks

Parental sense of competence in various areas of parental responsibility is related to style of problem solving (Mondell & Tyler, 1981). Some of the specific areas of parenting that are influenced by problem-solving ability include discipline; monitoring, supervising, and keeping children safe; and encouraging social interactions. Perhaps just as important is the problem solving that parents engage in when they plan activities such as getting their children into child care; getting up in the morning and picking them up at night; and providing a consistent, regular structure that ensures that things run smoothly and that each child experiences a sense of containment, predictability, and safety. For parents, providing adequate structure can be extremely demanding and requires a great deal of pre-planning and monitoring on a regular basis, and parents who are successful in finding solutions to parenting challenges in general feel more competent in their parenting roles.

In order to maintain adequate structure and routine for their children and to carry out other parenting tasks, parents need to plan and problem solve. This can be especially important when both parents are working. It is necessary to plan ahead and set up structures so that morning routines, for example, getting up, getting dressed, and eating breakfast, can run reasonably smoothly. Setting limits and providing discipline are also parenting practices that need more than impulsive responding on the parents' part. Deciding on reasonable rules and limits and enforcing them consistently requires adequate planning and problem solving, especially if a child is more difficult to manage.

Parents also need to be able to problem solve and plan around problems and stresses in their lives. Research suggests that parents who are overwhelmed by continual daily hassles or who are in constant crisis have more difficulty nurturing and attending to their children (Dohrenwend, Dohrenwend, Dodson, & Shrout, 1984; Kagan & Schlosberg, 1989). Certainly the ability to problem solve can be compromised when difficulties are intense, ongoing, and uncontrollable. If a parent is in constant crisis without satisfactory resolution, however, it may be an indication of difficulty with problem solving and planning.

## GROUPS WHO TEND TO HAVE DIFFICULTY WITH PLANNING AND PROBLEM SOLVING

A number of multi-risk parent populations have significant difficulty with problem solving for a variety of reasons. This section looks at some of these groups and their particular challenges when it comes to planning and problem solving.

### Parents Who Have Experienced Trauma

As described in Chapter 9, some parents continue to deal with the effects of a history of abuse, neglect, or more recent traumas. These parents can easily be triggered by their children's behavior and may act out with anger against their children. The re-experiencing of the trauma may leave parents tired, irritable, and unable to interact in a containing or purposeful way with their children or in other important situations in their lives. They also may be unable to negotiate conflict and may act out against their children if they behave in any way that is reminiscent of the original trauma.

### Teenage Parents

Teenage parents may also have difficulty with planning and problem solving. Teenagers are typically very present-oriented and seldom think about the future. They may act impulsively and place themselves at risk. Their behavior may be unpredictable because of hormonal changes that can result in dramatic mood swings. This is particularly true for young parents who also have experienced trauma and loss. Teenage parents have often been shown to lack developmental information and realistic expectations for their children's behavior, making it difficult to problem solve around appropriate parenting strategies (Benasich & Brooks-Gunn, 1996; Miller, Miceli, Whitman, & Borkowski, 1996). It is essential that this population learn to use planning strategies in order to manage their lives and the lives of their infants and young children (Field, 1998a).

## Parents with Depression

Parental depression has been shown to interfere with problem-solving abilities. Beck's (1987) cognitive theory of depression states that negative self-schemas or attributions bias how a person processes information. These errors in thinking include overgeneralization, magnification, minimization, and personalization (Holmes, 1997). Beck's theory is developmental in that it indicates that negative self-schemas arise from a person's early interactions with the environment, such as relationships with a caregiver. Parents with depression tend to view their children as more difficult and themselves as incompetent and helpless (Christensen, Phillips, Glasgow, & Johnson, 1983). Because of these cognitions, engaging in realistic problem solving—particularly regarding child discipline—is difficult for parents who are depressed. Research has shown that maternal mood disorders, particularly if they are severe or bipolar in nature, are related to poor outcomes in children, particularly in terms of mood disturbances and difficulties with self-regulation (Cummings, Davies, & Campbell, 2000; Goodman & Gotlib, 1999). Depressed parents who are under stress give up and are lax and ineffective at times, or become angry and upset and use power-assertion methods, often alternating between the two and consequently providing little predictability for their children (Cummings & Davies, 1994a; Fendrich, Warner, & Weissman, 1990; Kochanska, 1991).

## Parents with Intellectual Disabilities

Parents with intellectual disabilities often have significant difficulties with planning and problem solving in all areas of their lives. Their level of cognitive functioning, the presence of other pathologies, and their own experience of being parented all influence how they parent their children. Those who have difficulties in these areas will probably find the complexity of meeting the needs of children overwhelming and will struggle particularly with transferring what they learn in one situation to another. Planning ahead or remembering how and what to do about even routine tasks such as getting children dressed in the morning, doing the shopping, and cooking a meal may prove very challenging. Strategies to support parents who have intellectual disabilities with parenting tasks are discussed in a later section of this chapter.

## Parents with Mental Illness and Substance Abuse Problems

Parents with mental illness and substance abuse problems may vary dramatically from day to day in their ability to meet their responsibilities and manage the tasks of daily living. When they have a relapse, it may be impossible for them to parent adequately, and children may need to be placed in care because of the possibility of abuse or neglect—especially if other family supports are not available.

Parents who have little self-reflectivity and empathy for their child(ren) often have significant difficulty with planning and problem solving to find ways to overcome any challenging problems they may have with parenting their children. These parents cannot see the contribution that their behavior makes toward their children's development and behavior and cannot understand the perspective of their children.

## INTERVENTIONS THAT ENCOURAGE PLANNING AND PROBLEM SOLVING

When parents go from one crisis to another, it can be extremely stressful for service providers. Typically in these situations, parents have forgotten or failed to do something that could have prevented the crisis, such as purchasing enough food or formula; instead, they have spent their money on something else because of lack of planning. These parents tend to respond primarily at an emotional rather than a cognitive level, which hinders their ability to plan in order to avoid crises (Crittenden, 1999). Similarly, when parents are chronically depressed or overwhelmed, an interventionist may find helping them to problem solve very difficult. It can be frustrating when parents are provided with information to help them overcome a parenting problem, yet they continually fail to follow through. For instance, a parent may not follow up on an important referral to a medical appointment, or she may fail to try out a play activity with her infant. Thus, knowing how to intervene in these situations can be challenging.

As explained in Chapter 3, it is important to adapt intervention strategies to a particular parent by beginning "where the parent is" and with the kind of intervention approach that may be most acceptable and helpful for that parent. For example, with the family whose situations are often chaotic, it will be important to first engage the family at an *affective* level—the level at which they are more comfortable—before proceeding to help them with problem solving and planning. In other words, the interventionist needs to connect at a feeling level first and to show empathy for the family's problems, and this emphasis needs to remain a basis for the intervention even when things begin to stabilize. Similarly, for traumatized and depressed parents, although helping them with problem solving may be useful, establishing an empathetic, caring, and understanding relationship will be key, and providing some pragmatic assistance will also be crucial at the beginning of the intervention. In other words, the timing of when service providers suggest problem solving and planning strategies will be of great importance.

Service providers also benefit from having a good sense of when to shift from telling the parent what to do to helping the parent come up with a solution himself, and to giving the parent a model with which to solve problems. In other words, an effective interventionist knows when to move away from directing or controlling the content of home visits or sessions to establishing a sense of partnership and jointly solving problems. First, it is important to help the parent to choose an area in which she would like to make changes by following her lead in identifying a problem that is causing her stress or one that she feels unable to cope with. The service provider can then work through a series of steps with the parent in order to help her to conceptualize a strategy to use to deal with the situation. Each of the steps is interrelated. (See Figure 13.1.)

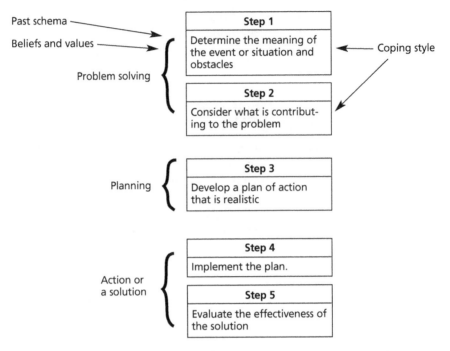

**Figure 13.1.**   Steps of planning and problem solving.

## Step 1: Determine the Meaning of the Event

Determining the *meaning of the event* or problem for the parent is crucial. Some events, such as a marital breakup, serious illness, or death are stressful for everyone; other events can have very different meanings for different people. These different meanings come from schemas or memories that are established in early childhood and are emotional and cognitive patterns that lead to repeating behaviors that can elicit certain kinds of reactions. Bringing the past into the present can be very helpful in determining what may be hindering a parent's ability to cope with problems (Purkey & Schmidt, 1987; Young, Klosko, & Weishaar, 2003). For example, a parent may find it almost impossible to problem solve about getting a job, which could have resulted from the individual having seen no limits, structures, or follow-through on plans in the home as a child. Alternatively, the parent could have had parents who were chronically unemployed and on welfare. During this step it also is important to talk about and deal with feelings of anger, distress, withdrawal, or fear that may be accompanying the issue.

## Step 2: Consider What Is Getting in the Way

The next step is helping the parent *identify what is getting in the way of solving the problem,* changing the situation, or doing something he would like to accomplish. It is critical at this time to identify and to help the parent deal with certain beliefs that block progress, such as "There's nothing to be concerned about" or "I've tried everything and nothing will work."

Values can also be helpful, but can get in the way, too. For example, if a person feels that she is ruled by fate, she may have no interest in trying to change what is difficult in her life.

## Step 3: Develop a Plan of Action

The parent is then helped to come up with a *plan of action* that may include deciding on a career possibility and considering what education would be required or how to go about looking for a job. As far as possible, the service provider should encourage the parent to come up with the plan (while making sure that the ideas are realistic—see next paragraph). In some home visiting programs, the home visitor or other professional may accompany the parent to some job interviews for support.

It is crucial at this point that the *strategies that are chosen are realistic* because if the parent is set up for failure, it can result in the parent being unwilling to try to manage similar situations and will add to the parents' feelings of inadequacy. Conversely, effective problem solving and successful strategies based on realistic expectations can give the parent a sense of competence and encourage the parent to try future planning and problem-solving strategies.

## Step 4: Implement the Plan

During Step 4, *the plan is tried out or put into practice* while the approach is monitored from week to week by the interventionist. During the period in which the plan is put into practice, the parent may need a lot of support—particularly if the change does not bring any immediate results. This could apply to trying to get a job, cleaning up the house, or using a new discipline strategy.

## Step 5: Evaluate the Effectiveness of the Solution

The interventionist can then help the parent to *evaluate the success of the plan* by discussing how it is working and problem solving again for a different plan if the first one did not work.

This whole process can then be repeated as different problems arise, or during more informal exchanges, so that it becomes a valuable tool that the parent can use by going through the steps automatically as problems arise. When the steps are clearly followed, they enable parents to

- Determine what is contributing to the event or problem, taking into consideration beliefs, values, and any cognitive patterns built on past experiences

- Think about their own behaviors that may be part of the problem and allow them to identify areas in which they can make changes

- Change from an impulsive style of responding to a more cognitive or reflective way of dealing with events and problems

The problem-solving strategies that are adopted are not good or bad in themselves. Rather, their value depends on how a particular parent perceives them and how successful they are for her. For example, if the problem is a behavior problem, it is possible that a parent could read an appropriate book, attend a parenting group, consult a specialist, or work with a home visitor to brainstorm about a way to interact with her child by using a new type of response.

## Correcting Cognitive Patterns that Can Interfere with Problem Solving and Planning

Some parents facing multiple risks have difficulty problem solving and planning because of distortions in their thinking or negative schema about themselves or their children. These distortions and negative ways of thinking contribute to defeating behavioral patterns and a tendency to avoid making decisions or problem solving to find solutions to life's challenges. Some parents may have attentional difficulties, in which case it may be necessary to help them develop effortful control. *Effortful control* is the ability to focus in on a problem and to not be distracted while one thinks about appropriate strategies to use to solve the problem. In both instances, helping parents to go through the steps of problem solving in individual home visits sessions or in groups can be very effective. Some of these areas of difficulties and strategies to overcome them are described next.

*Identifying the Source of the Stress*    Many parents focus on their *reactions* to stress instead of the *sources* of the stress. They may concentrate on the feelings of anger, sadness, or fatigue rather than trying to deal with the events that precipitate them. Similarly, they may not try to identify reasons for their child's behavior. Various steps can be used to help parents to focus on the source of the problem:

- Ask a parent to remember times in the last week that she has experienced stress reactions such as anger, sadness, or irritability.

- Help the parent review these occasions and reflect on how she coped with the situations and how she was able to mitigate the feelings.

- Generate different ways of coping with the situations and choose useful strategies. For example, if the situation involves a child or other family member with a disability, the interventionist could help the parent to go through different approaches to finding a support group and help him to choose the suggested strategy that the parent may feel most comfortable with, such as looking in the local newspaper's community section or calling local service agencies.

- If necessary, add an additional step of reviewing any negative reactions that were used in these situations.

*Using Self-Talk*    When parents think negative and self-critical thoughts, they experience negative emotions. Hurtful thoughts such as "My child hates me" interfere with a parent's problem-solving abilities and lead to responses that may not be helpful and in the best interest of other family members such as another child or spouse. An interventionist who helps parents identify these thoughts and change them to constructive, positive, and self-empowering ones can help eliminate the negative emotional reactions. Strategies can be used to improve a parent's self-talk. The parent can learn to transform thoughts from hurtful (e.g., "I'm an awful mother") to helpful (e.g., "She is happy most of the time; she's just a little tired today"). When the parent is able to identify, challenge, and stop hurtful thoughts, she can act on the helpful thoughts that she has generated as alternatives (e.g., "Let her fuss until she falls asleep") (Christopherson & Mortweet, 2003).

The effective countering of hurtful thoughts requires practice because such statements tend to be automatic and subconscious. The interventionist can encourage the parent to exercise these cognitive coping skills in less-emotional situations. This will help the parent to begin to identify when he is engaging in hurtful thoughts so that he can challenge them. The interventionist can generate helpful thoughts with the parent and then list them on a note card for the parent to carry. The parent can then read the helpful thoughts when hurtful thoughts occur in order to challenge them (Christopherson & Mortweet, 2003).

Worksheets can be used to help a parent identify hurtful self-thoughts and to learn more helpful ones (Barrish & Barrish, 1989) (see Figure 13.2). The interventionist can assign the sheets for homework and discuss the responses with the parent, or the interventionist can fill out the worksheets with the parent. On these sheets, parents may be asked to list answers to statements and questions designed to illuminate them about negative thoughts.

---

### Worksheet to Identify Negative Thoughts

1. Choose a difficult situation that occurred recently and describe what happened.

2. What did you think to yourself when the situation occurred that did not help you come up with a strategy to deal with it? For example, "Everything happens to me and there is nothing I can do about it."

3. What did you actually do at the time? For example, did you get very angry and end up arguing with everyone, or did you withdraw and avoid dealing with it?

4. What could you have thought to yourself that would have helped you come up with a plan?

5. What could your behavior have looked like or what could you have done differently?

---

**Figure 13.2.** Blank worksheet to help parents identify negative thoughts getting in the way of planning and problem solving.

Parents can also use self-talk or private speech to talk themselves through a task or a situation that is frustrating. This can be done by using statements such as "I can do it," "Try this," or "Don't give up." For many parents, these kinds of thoughts are new and may need to be rehearsed several times.

***Imagining Alternatives***    A barrier to choosing alternative problem-solving strategies is that serious consequences seem too distant to matter. Asking the parent to imagine the problem and future consequences helps the parent to bring the future into the present and arouses the parent's emotions to the point where she is ready to make a firm commitment to take action and try different problem-solving approaches (Prochaska, Norcross, & Diclemente, 1994). To encourage alternative problem-solving strategies, ask the parent to imagine distressing scenarios and to concentrate on the negative aspects of the problems. Then, ask the individual to think about what she might do in this negative state of mind and what feelings arise as a result. This will sensitize the parent to the drawbacks of negative thoughts and how they lead to problem behavior (e.g., how feeling angry at a child might lead a parent to saying hurtful, deprecating things). Ask the parent to visualize the consequences of her behavior (e.g., the child stops communicating with the parent as she grows into adolescence).

***Using Flashcards***    As part of their intervention approach, Young and colleagues (2003) suggested that the interventionist and the parent compose flash cards about problematic behavior. These flash cards can be used to describe the situation, the views or cognitions triggered, the reality of the problem, and healthy responses. In using such flashcards in interventions, they can be kept together and read when preparing for a situation to remind the parent not to revert to their old behavioral patterns, thoughts, and feelings.

A number of similar strategies can be used to improve parents' problem-solving skills and as a consequence, their behavior. These include using self-instruction techniques to go through the five steps of problem solving, acquiring assertiveness skills, and decreasing irrational beliefs (Forman, 1993; Kendall & Braswell, 1985).

## Teaching Parents to Problem Solve About Difficult Parenting Issues

In addition to devising problem-solving strategies, it is very important to provide parents with opportunities to practice them. One way is to have parents use problem-solving approaches in conflict situations with their children. Later, the interventionist and the parent can discuss these conflict situations and problem solve about how to deal with the situations in the future in order to help the parent see that she can have more control and power over what happens. Encouraging a parent to use these strategies with his child will support the child's problem-solving ability and cognitive development as she sees a model that will help her learn how to cope with conflict (Davies, 1999; Hammen, 1992; Hammen, Burge, & Adrian, 1999).

***Dealing with Conflicts with Children***    Problem solving involves several skills (e.g., sharing and cooperation, communication). The interventionist can assess the parents' and child's problem-solving skills used in times of conflict and encourage the development of skills that are lacking. When a problem arises, the service provider can provide instruction in the particular skill to be learned, model the behavior, provide opportunities for the child and parent to practice, and provide verbal reinforcement and corrective feedback after observing the practice (Henggeler, Schoenwald, Rowland, & Cunningham, 2002). Henggeler and colleagues (2002) noted that the following steps are central to problem solving:

- Identifying the problem in dispassionate terms (e.g., "We both want to play with the computer," not "John is a lazy pig for not letting me play with the computer")

- Understanding that there are multiple perspectives of the problem

- Generating all possible solutions

- Evaluating the positive and negative consequences of the solutions

- Selecting solutions that capitalize on positive consequences and minimize negative consequences

- Practicing the implementation of the solution

***Identifying Obstacles***    Parents make certain assumptions that can become obstacles to encouraging children's problem-solving abilities. In their research, Brooks and Goldstein (2001) have identified the following as three of the most common assumptions falling in this category:

1. Believing that young children do not have the ability to make decisions, so parents must do it for them

2. Expecting more than children can deliver

3. Allowing children to make decisions only as long as what they decide agrees with what the parent feels is best

The interventionist can ask the parent to reflect on how these three obstacles relate to her parenting and can help the parent find opportunities to offer choices that are within a child's emotional and cognitive abilities. The choices should be ones about which the parent feels comfortable. Point out that parents need to encourage these abilities in their young children so that they will be able to manage alone in situations at school and when they face moral dilemmas as adolescents. Removing these obstacles and encouraging decision making will help children to learn problem-solving skills from an early age (Brooks & Goldstein, 2001).

Parents can also join a number of groups that can help them to problem solve around various parenting dilemmas. Some of the best known and researched are the following:

- The Incredible Years ADVANCE program (Webster-Stratton & Hammond, 1997)

- The Early Childhood Systematic Training of Effective Parenting (STEP) (Dinkmeyer, McKay, & Dinkmeyer, 1989)

- Pathways to Competence for Young Children: A Parenting Program (Landy & Thompson, 2006) (described in Chapter 7).

***Conducting a Group that Teaches Coping***    Some parents who have difficulties with problem solving and planning may enjoy and benefit from group approaches. These include teenage parents who particularly enjoy interactions with peers, parents with cognitive delays, and parents with children with developmental challenges or behavioral difficulties who benefit from the support of other parents with children with the same difficulties. These groups can help parents identify their own coping styles and any strengths and vulnerabilities associated with it (Zeitlin & Williamson, 1994).

Ideally, the group should take place over six to eight sessions, depending on parent availability, and can be most effective if participants share similar goals. Parents also learn strategies that other parents have used successfully with their children. A suggested structure is as follows:

1. *Introduction* to other participants and to the concept of coping or problem solving

2. *Analysis* of parents' own coping style. The *Coping Inventory* questionnaire can be used for parents to do this (Zeitlin, 1985). Parents share examples of times they believed they were able to cope well and identify patterns that may not be useful or may be self-defeating (e.g., ignoring the problem, withdrawing, getting angry in a way that becomes overwhelming, retreating from friends and supports).

3. *Discussion* of parenting beliefs about coping and problem solving

4. *Presentation of the model* of problem solving outlined earlier. Parents may volunteer to have the group problem solve around a challenge, situation, or problem they are dealing with. Some of the parents will contribute ways they managed a similar problem. During this process, the group leader can have group members identify any self-defeating patterns or inappropriate strategies or beliefs that they use at times. To encourage this sharing, the group leader could share an example from his own history. It is intended that all group members will take a turn with problem solving their issue.

5. *Identification of resources* that can be used when problems arise or when parents feel overwhelmed or stressed. These may include

   - Immediate family members
   - Extended family members
   - Best friends, neighbors
   - Early intervention resources or support systems
   - Other professionals such as family doctors
   - Community programs such as drop-in centers, libraries, free groups, adult education programs

Parents are asked to think about the quantity and quality of their supports in talking about them. For example, some family members and friends may actually be detrimental if parents are trying to make changes. Also, parents with children with disabilities may feel overwhelmed by the number of professionals who are coming into the house or the appointments they have to attend.

In this case, parents should be helped to establish some control over their relationships or encounters with these people.

6. Identifying other resources and supports that could be useful. During the process of discussing the supports they have, parents may identify additional supports that could be useful and could make plans to meet again as a support group.

## Strategies for Working with Parents Who Have Intellectual or Cognitive Disabilities

Parents with intellectual/cognitive disabilities are another multi-risk group that struggles with problem solving. The types of cognitive difficulties or disabilities that parents have can vary greatly from genetic to birth-related to adult onset from an injury. The way in which these parents approach the intervention process may have profound implications for interventionists seeking to engage them. Sometimes, parents with cognitive delays may not initiate the process of looking for help because they are unable to understand some of the more complex issues of parenting and their need for support to manage them, making them a difficult population to reach. Or, they may have been referred by Child Protective Services or another agency or even mandated to attend intervention as a condition for keeping their children, which means that they might not be as receptive as the interventionist would like because they didn't come of their own accord. Sometimes, from the point of view of the service providers, parents may lack parenting skills, but the parents themselves believe that they are not lacking these skills. Yet parents with intellectual disabilities often need to learn parenting skills several times in different settings to be able to transfer these skills across situations (Case & Gang, 1999; McGaha, 2002). Parents with intellectual/cognitive disabilities often think very concretely, as well, and may not understand the complexities of the parent–child relationships.

The following are strategies that can be used to encourage the problem solving of parents with cognitive delays as well as with other parents who seem very concrete in their thinking.

• Outline expectations for child safety and security clearly to parents at the outset, particularly if there are child protection concerns.

• In order not to overwhelm parents who are already very stressed with their situation, begin helping the parents acquire just one or two of the most important skills related to the child's well-being or safety.

• Break down even simple skills, such as heating a bottle for the baby, into very small steps and explain them over and over again. This will help the parent to identify and then learn the steps she has to go through.

• Provide instruction in the home or where the parent will actually be applying the skill. The home visitor can then demonstrate the skill and observe the parent performing it several times. Of course, if the skill involves taking public transportation or taking a child shopping, for example, the instruction should take place outside of the home where it will be applied.

- Because parents with cognitive difficulties may have problems transferring the skills learned in one situation to another, provide numerous examples of the same skill being applied across various contexts.

- Identify the parents' strengths in learning and incorporate these into teaching. For example, some parents may learn better using visual modalities, whereas others benefit more from verbal instructions that they can repeat to themselves.

- Incorporate a variety of instructional methods including modeling of the skill or parenting method, role-playing during which the parent practices the skill, videotaping the task being done, leaving the tape to be played again later, and using instructional pictures that can be put in different rooms of the house such as the bathroom, kitchen, and laundry room. It is important to consider challenges that the parent might have in choosing these strategies, such as specific difficulties with auditory processing or limited reading skills.

- Have a service provider available who can ensure that practical resources such as income, housing, and social support are in place.

- Consider whether the parent can meet the cognitive needs of an older child and if not, try to obtain some outside care or tutoring for the child.

- Consider the challenge of facilitating parenting skills that require more abstract and complex reasoning. The availability of ongoing, supportive consultation is essential to help parents who have cognitive difficulties make more complex judgments about the appropriateness of child behaviors. For example, a parent may perceive her child's early curiosity about sexual differences as an interest in sex and punish her severely as a result. It is necessary to show her that the child's curiosity is a normal developmental stage.

- Determine through frequent, ongoing reviews what changes in supportive services are needed as the child grows and develops, as the parents' circumstances change, and as the demands of parenting change. It is important to try to keep as many of the services as possible in place on an ongoing basis because frequent changes make it more difficult for the parents to generalize what is learned from one context to another.

- Give positive feedback to help parents to develop a sense of self-efficacy and competence. If a parent makes an error, then it should be pointed out directly and supportively with adequate acknowledgment of the things that she is doing right. Also, it is important to try to help the parent become successful in at least one area of her life (Paris, 1998).

# ENCOURAGING PROBLEM SOLVING
# AND PLANNING: CASE-STUDY FAMILIES

## Mark's Family

Mark, introduced in Chapter 4, came from a middle-income family. Both of his parents, Michael and Joan, had demanding jobs and juggled the roles of work and parenting. Their organizational, problem-solving, and planning skills were excellent in almost all areas of their life except when it came to parenting Mark, who had a number of behavioral challenges.

Joan's unresolved trauma from childhood interactions with her depressed mother significantly affected her ability to respond in a nurturing way to Mark. Her immediate reactions to his sadness were outside of her cognitive control. Her typical response of dismissing his sadness and laughing at him was totally unplanned, and she was unaware of its consequence on Mark's sense of self, attachment security, and development. Like Joan, Michael had a great deal of difficulty problem solving around parenting issues, although in other areas he did well.

Joan and Michael were extremely enthusiastic about learning ways to discipline Mark. They were also open to using a problem-solving approach in which both parents chose a parenting dilemma or one of Mark's behavioral issues and went through the stages of problem solving in order to identify a strategy agreeable to both. After that, both parents were able to cooperate in order to use the strategy consistently over the period of time needed to make it work. Having an increased understanding of the need for consistency across time and between themselves, especially when it brought needed changes, was very useful. As these approaches gradually brought improvements in Mark's behavior, their confidence as parents improved. Thus their ability to work together in this more-difficult area for them, that of parenting, soon matched their capacity to problem solve in other areas of their lives.

## Nina's Family

During the early part of the intervention with Nina, it was very difficult for her to plan or problem solve. She was overwhelmed by a multitude of problems and saw any suggestions that planning and problem solving could be helpful as a criticism and rejection. What was most concerning, however, was her impulsive acting out, which placed her children and herself at risk.

A variety of approaches were used in order to get Nina to a stage in which she was able to talk about her plans and begin to problem solve in different parts of her life. Initially it was critical to develop a therapeutic relationship in which the interventionist was able to show empathy for her past pain and current difficult situation.

In the initial stages of therapy, perhaps the most important strategies were having exchanges during or immediately following crises. In such instances, Nina could not deny how her impulsivity and failure to consider possible consequences for her actions had resulted in very serious situations for herself and her family. These therapeutic "gold mine" incidents included the altercation with her brother who had schizophrenia, the time she had stopped taking her birth control pills, the abuse from her new partner, and the time when she drove intoxicated and had an accident. All of these brought insight into how Nina's behavior had placed her and her children in danger and provided an opportunity to begin some planning and problem solving with her.

Throughout counseling sessions, whenever Nina showed a tendency for splitting or black-and-white thinking (i.e., she was seeing something as totally good or bad) she was gently reminded about some of the other aspects of the person or the situation that she had not been considering. Nina sometimes rejected this approach but gradually, it became more acceptable to her and eventually she was able to do this herself.

Because having constant crises can prevent problem solving and planning, helping Nina to set boundaries about safety issues for herself and the children and around abuse was critical to begin to bring some structure to her life. This was a first stage in helping Nina to begin to plan things in the future and to be less impulsive in making decisions about many situations in her life.

The strategies in Stage 3 of Nina's intervention enabled her to use her new planning and problem solving strategies the most. Her therapist often went through the steps of problem solving and planning with her as she acted as president of her Mother's Club and in her efforts toward furthering her education and career by helping her make telephone calls and write application letters. During this time, she also learned to problem solve about her children's behaviors and how to discipline and re-establish appropriate control with them. In counseling sessions, Nina was given support to develop these approaches. Perhaps most important, Nina began to be able to consider other options if one did not work out rather than to immediately give up and blame herself or the children. As a result, she developed a sense of ownership, empowerment, and control in her life and was not as overwhelmed by everyday problems because she could see that she now had the skills to manage and learn from them. Gradually, she developed the confidence and the inner resources to meet challenges that arose in her life and in the lives of her children.

# PUTTING IT ALL TOGETHER

© j. stone, inc. 2005

*We do not remember days; we remember moments.*
—Cesare Pavese

This final section of the book outlines how the intervention strategies described in previous sections can be conceptualized into a cohesive model. Ways to support the model within the service system are also described. The need for multisystem approaches has been discussed throughout the book. These approaches obviously require that the various family interventions that are provided are well integrated within coordinated community systems.

Chapter 14 expands on the meaning of an integrative approach and illustrates its importance for the case-study families. It also considers how the process of change took place in the families and some of the principles of facilitating positive change in multi-risk families.

Chapter 15 describes the importance of supporting the difficult work with multi-risk families within agencies. The chapter cites evidence of the effects of vicarious trauma on service providers, especially when situations place children and parents at risk. A variety of other stresses on service providers are discussed and the organizational policies and procedures described that need to be in place to overcome these stressors as much as possible. The need for and the necessary components of reflective supervision are also discussed. The chapter closes with the description of optimal services systems that can support the provision of services for multi-risk families. It also suggests the optimal strategies for service coordination for families who may be involved with several organizations such as Child Protective Services, mental health services for children and parents, child care, and the health care system.

Chapter 16 describes the theoretical context in which services for children at multiple risk and their families occur, including brain research and the contributions of nature and nurture. The chapter ends with a consideration of the importance of work with multi-risk families and how it needs to be fitted into the total prevention and early intervention service system in every community for early intervention to be effective in enhancing the development of children and reducing the incidence of psychopathology in adults.

## CHAPTER 14

# Putting the Pieces Together and Facilitating the Process of Change

Because this book is about an integrative approach to early intervention with mult-risk families, this section of the book discusses how the intervention strategies can be conceptualized into a more cohesive model that can, in turn, be supported within the service system.

For the integrative model of intervention provided in this book, a formulation or assessment of the types of risks a family faces is of central importance so that strategies can be matched, prescribed, and then offered to infants, young children, and their families. However, the choice of strategies depends on four main considerations. They are summarized here briefly but are outlined in more detail in Chapter 3:

1. The *theoretical approach* is considered that can best inform the choice of a type of intervention. Once the interventionist(s) has an understanding of various theories of development and of how change can occur, this will form a natural part of the discussion and choice of intervention and will ensure that consideration is given by the service providers to a variety of causes and possible ways to intervene. For example, without some basic understanding of developmental milestones, attachment theory, and the effects of trauma, it is very difficult to have a broad consideration of how some of the interventions related to them may or may not be appropriate. Different agencies may select some of the possible theories as a basis for their understanding of development and choice of intervention strategies.

2. It is also crucial to consider the characteristics of the parents that may significantly influence their *willingness to be involved* and their satisfaction with the services offered. Some of this will depend on the family's time and availability, where they would like the services to be provided (in the home or at a center), the kind of services they would like to receive, their readiness for change, and the style or type of approach they would be most comfortable with. When possible, a choice of approaches to begin with should be offered, either group, individual, or interactional. Remember that multi-risk families may need a great deal of outreach before a relationship can be established between the parent and interventionist. Also, giving parents an opportunity to have their choice of services considered and having a chance to discuss them is likely to result in a high degree of acceptance of the intervention recommendations (Robert-Tissot & Cramer, 1998).

3. A full *assessment of the risks and strengths of the child and family* should take place that considers the development of the child, the characteristics of the parents,

the parent–child interactions, the family situation, and the environment in which the family lives. On the basis of the determination of these risks and strengths, various types of intervention or strategies will be considered.

4.   A final choice will, of course, depend on the *availability of staff* trained and willing to do certain kinds of interventions within an agency or the possibility of referring children and parents to other services within the wider system. The approaches will need to be matched to the policies and procedures of the agencies that may dictate the number of sessions that can be provided and where the services can be offered.

In one sense then, the appropriate services for a family are chosen from a menu of strategies that is available in a service system, that is appealing to the parents, and that fits with the beliefs and the philosophy of the agency. Although this process of choosing strategies may be time-consuming, the prescriptive matching it allows is most likely to be successful. This is especially true of families who, at first, may be resistant and may find it difficult to believe in the credibility of the service providers (Crittenden, 1997b; Garfield, 2003).

## PROVIDING MULTILEVEL INTERVENTION

The strategies discussed in this book are described in a linear way by necessity, as if following each other, when in fact intervention with a child and family typically occurs in a nonlinear fashion and simultaneously at a variety of levels of change. For example, the following are characteristic of early childhood intervention:

• Different parts of the parent–child interaction may at times be the focus of efforts to change the system using a variety of short-term interventions and longer term strategies.

• Sometimes, the interventionist may be using more cognitive approaches and at other times, be working at a more emotional level, with the intent that a parent will eventually be able to integrate the two and use them in interactions with her child and others. For example, a parent who has problems containing her emotional reactions, who goes from crisis to crisis, and who engages in excessive acting-out behavior may be engaged at an emotional level initially and then be taught some cognitive strategies to bring her reactions under control so that she learns to plan and problem solve to avoid crises. A parent who is more dismissive of emotions, however, may be engaged initially at a cognitive level, with the interventionist providing information and answering her questions about child development and parenting, and then moving her to a more reflective mode and deeper emotional understanding by the introduction of more discussion of the emotional content of conversations and the parent–child interactions.

• At times, interventionists may be dealing with different levels of consciousness or memory systems by talking about how the past can affect present functioning and particularly, a parent's interactions with his child. Eventually, it is hoped that the parent will be able to integrate past memories with understanding of how they affect the present into a coherent system of meaning that can be used to understand his own reactions and those of others.

- Shifts in the "dance" can be expected during interventions, too. Sometimes the interventionist will be following the parents' lead while at other times she will need to create a "misstep in the dance" or some tension by suggesting that the parent's automatic reactions or old defenses are not working for her child and that some new ways of interacting will be necessary.

Interventions can also be shared across service providers. At times, service providers from more than one organization may be providing interventions simultaneously focused on particular problems that the child or family have. In other words, the various intervention strategies are woven together to encourage positive change in a number of parts of the parent–child system, enabling the people in it to function well both individually and as a well-functioning family system that supports each of its members. For example, for Mark and his family, it was necessary to work at different parts of the system including with Mark directly, with Joan individually, and with Joan and Michael together. With these different strategies it was possible to assist them to agree on approaches to use for disciplining Mark, supporting him to learn, and playing with him. Occasionally, intervention was provided to the whole family. Crisis intervention was seldom necessary, although on the occasions that it was, it allowed the therapist to connect with both parents at a deeper emotional level in order to bring about change. Joan had new insights during interventions at an unconscious or implicit level that she was previously unable to access, which enabled her to gradually connect her childhood experiences to her current functioning and interactions with Mark (see Figure 14.1). For both parents, strategies were introduced to increase their understanding of child development and parenting approaches and to change their attributions of Mark. For example, they were helped to change their negative perception that Mark had a great deal of power and that they were being ineffective in supporting him to gain back his self-esteem and to overcome his behavioral issues. Joan learned new ways to regulate her own and Mark's emotions. This was criti-

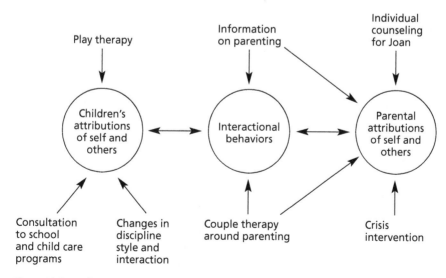

**Figure 14.1.** A diagram depicting intervention designed to change the system for the case-study family of Joan, Michael, and Mark.

cal in supporting her to be able to be more sensitive or empathetic of Mark when he was sad and upset, and opened the way for her to respond to him with empathy and caring. This, in turn, reduced Mark's acting-out behavior and increased both parents' sense of competence in their parenting roles.

Because of the complexity of Nina's difficulties and the significant risk they presented to her children, a variety of types of interventions—provided by a number of interventionists from different disciplines in various agencies—were necessary. These included long-term counseling, parenting groups, drug and alcohol treatment, interactional guidance, and groups to encourage a sense of competence. Various cognitive–behavioral strategies were also used, including changing negative attributions and teaching relaxation and visualization, and helping her learn to problem solve. The complexity of this intervention, although not characteristic of all very high-risk families, clearly illustrates how necessary it is to work at a variety of levels and in a nonlinear fashion within the parent–child interactional system. Also, the intervention called for an integrated approach, not only in terms of using several strategies but also by facilitating coordination between service providers from various disciplines and agencies that were involved with the family (see Figure 14.2). Intervention for Nina and her children was linear in the sense that it occurred over time and included three stages, but the focus of intervention and the process of change was very much nonlinear and multidimensional and was designed to influence various parts and levels of the parent–child system. In this way, efforts were made to improve various aspects of Nina's psychological functioning and her parenting of her children and to enhance the children's development and their sense of themselves and the world. From the beginning of the intervention, Nina's service providers tried to encourage more adaptive defensive functioning, enhance her capacity for self-reflectivity, encourage her sense of parental and personal competence, strengthen her social net-

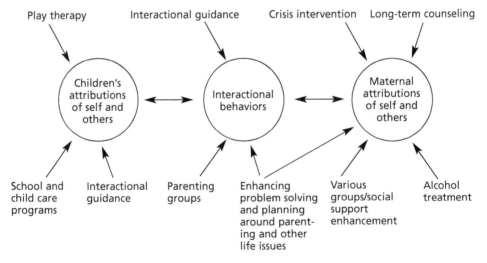

**Figure 14.2.**   A diagram depicting intervention designed to change the system for the case-study family of Nina and her family.

work, encourage emotion regulation, increase her knowledge of child development, and change her negative attributions of her children to more positive ones. They also helped to enhance her planning and problem-solving strategies and to improve her sensitivity and responsiveness to her children. Throughout, the intervention efforts were made to encourage Nina to continue involvement in the program even when she regressed and wanted to leave. It was important to understand and respect that many of her issues were a result of her traumatic early upbringing and unresolved loss and trauma, and this often determined the way in which intervention was provided and the choice of intervention strategies.

For Nina and her family, change occurred in response to a variety of these intervention strategies. However, moments of change also occurred due to more intangible factors, when Nina felt truly understood and connected with her therapist and certain of her emotional needs were met, such as being listened to and given information that met her particular situation. In addition, during counseling sessions or crisis intervention in her home, when she gained new insight into how experiences from the past continued to affect her current functioning and parenting, it shifted her to a deeper level of understanding of the impact of her past on her interactions and relationships with her children and enabled her to make changes.

Both of these families were similar in that they went through three stages: 1) stabilizing the situation 2) accessing and reintegration of memories, and 3) moving to termination, when the family was able to return to a more stable level of functioning and any necessary supports and services were in place to do that.

## The Process of Change

Although knowing the necessary ingredients for successful intervention is helpful, it does not explain how change can take place. This question is being pursued by a number of researchers and clinicians including the Process of Change Study Group, which includes a number of infant specialists who have contributed significantly to developmental theory and/or work with infants and families (e.g., Bruschweiler-Stern et al., 1998; Stern et al., 1998; Tronick et al., 1998). More recently, Stern has emphasized the importance of the "actual experience, a subjectively lived happening" for understanding how change can occur (2004, p. xiii). Some of the insights about the process of change have come out of recent writings. For example, according to Bruschweiler-Stern and colleagues (1998), change typically occurs not as a result of interpretation but in *now moments* or *moments of meeting*. These are characterized as times when the most meaningful contacts between the therapist and client occur and the client feels that her intentions and feelings are most understood and accepted and a sense of caring is communicated. These moments can occur in different settings such as a clinic or medical setting, in a home visit, during a crisis intervention, or when concrete help is provided (Lyons-Ruth et al., 1998). They are not just about communicating through words but through what is seen in facial expressions and body language, what is heard in the tone of voice, and what may be experienced in the body if the autonomic nervous system is activated; also—and perhaps most important—they are communicated through what is felt emotionally (Tronick et al., 1998).

As explained by Fosha, "Through affective resonance, sharing, and empathy, the therapist's affective response to the patient's experience amplifies their affective experience" (2000, p. 29). It is through this kind of attunement to and acceptance of the person's scary, painful, and previously unrevealed feelings that the person can overcome her experience of aloneness and isolation, overcome resistance, and set the stage for a deeper self-understanding. The change is at an implicit or procedural memory level, where sensorimotor and affective memories are stored. Because the earliest memories are procedural, a shift may occur in the memories and internal representations that were laid down at a very early stage of development (Stern, 2004). As a result of this meaningful contact, a shift occurs in the client and the relationship between the client and interventionist, and a deeper level of understanding grows. This can contribute to a new sense of intersubjectivity, or melding of the minds, between the client and the therapist that can be transferred to relationships with other people and her child as well (Stern, 2004; Stern et al., 1998).

Some of these moments of change occurred for the case-study families in times of crisis and despair when the parents were most open to change. This was also true when certain sensorimotor experiences or feelings of pain were being played out while the client and interventionist experienced them together; for example, when Nina was depressed and suicidal because she was experiencing her newly walking toddler as abandoning her. The understanding occurred at a procedural level when the interventionist was able to point out what was going on in the moment as Nina sat rocking and crying. This was something that could not have happened if the interventionist had ignored her emotional state and only provided information on birth control or told her how to avoid another pregnancy. Similarly, when the interventionist attended a school meeting about Mark and was able to support his staying in his school, the emotional support that Joan felt enabled her to cry for the first time and share her pain for Mark. This allowed her to connect at a more authentic level about her struggle to protect him from having to deal with the sadness she found so difficult to tolerate.

Interventionists should be aware of this caveat regarding emotional support, however: Although attunement to the parent is critical, when a parent is not conscious of issues she is having in interactions with her children it may be necessary to create some tension or to be directive about changing certain interactional behaviors and to move beyond where the mother appears to be stuck. For example, a parent who is consistently unresponsive to her baby's cries needs to have this pointed out and to be given a directive about the importance of responding at those times, rather than complete empathy for what she is dealing with.

## Direct Intervention with Children

In general, this book has not discussed direct intervention with children. It is clear that many multi-risk families may also have children born at biological risk and with a number of special needs. These include extreme prematurity, cerebral palsy, Down syndrome, hearing and vision loss, and difficult temperamental or behavioral difficulties. As has been mentioned previously, for many of these children, direct intervention in specialized child cares may be very important, and as well, most center-based programs also provide programs for the parents, often in the home. For those children with special needs who are integrated into child care programs within the community, consultation with child care staff may be crucial so that they can learn how to best interact with the children to help enhance various areas of their development. From recent brain research it is clear that some children can be helped significantly at a neurological and behavioral level by intense interventions focused on their difficulties. Consequenly, assessment and specialized treatments provided by various disciplines such as speech and language pathologists, occupational therapists and physiotherapists, developmental pediatricians, geneticists, neurologists, and other specialists is essential. Other interventions that are less specialized can be provided by community home visitors, nurses, and other interventionists, such as helping to set up a routine for a child who is not sleeping, finding equipment such as adaptive devices or medical equipment for children with ongoing medical conditions, and training parents how to use them. These service providers can help to identify ways within the environment to modify it to meet the specific needs of children with special needs, such as reducing stimulation so as to help calm a hypersensitive child, or ensuring ways to stimulate and interest a very passive or withdrawn child.

Other ways in which children can receive intervention include the following (also discussed elsewhere in the book):

- *Home visitation:* Home visitors can demonstrate to parents how to play with their children and support the development of a secure attachment relationship.

- *Floor time:* Parents can be coached to play with their children in a way that can encourage symbolization and speech and enhance intersubjectivity and empathy in the child.

- *Play therapy:* For children who may have experienced loss or trauma or other emotional or behavioral issues, play therapy can help them to overcome their anxiety, integrate the memory of the trauma, and develop strategies to cope with the resultant stress.

- *Teaching parents some ways to interact with a child* with a disorder such as autism that can enhance the more intense treatments the child may be receiving from various professionals who are working with the child (e.g., speech-language pathologists, behaviorists, those enhancing the child's capacity for relatedness).

## CONSIDERING THE STRATEGIES FOR INTERVENTION

In Sections II and III of this book, a number of strategies are suggested that can be used to improve parents' interactional behavior with their children and to enhance their attributions of self and others. In Table 14.1, the strategies are listed in an integrated way under headings that resemble the format of the system outlined in Figures 14.1 and 14.2.

In conclusion, although the strategies are presented in different chapters in this book, in order for them to be effective it is critical that they are integrated into intervention plans that meet the needs of a specific child and family. In this way, the intervention plan will be able to meet the family's needs appropriately and best facilitate change in order to enhance the child's outcome in all developmental areas. Chapter 15 looks at the importance of supporting service providers and case coordination.

**Table 14.1.** Interventions goals and strategies based on child and parent attributions and interactional behavior

| | Intervention goals and strategies based on | | | |
|---|---|---|---|---|
| Child attributions/ development | Child interactional behavior | Parent interactional behavior | Parent attributions | Parents' view of self and others |
| Intervening to help with unresolved loss and trauma<br>• Play therapy<br>Enhancing self-reflectivity<br>• Play therapy<br>• Floor time with parent and child involved<br>Enhancing interactions and attachment<br>• Floor time with parent and child involved<br>• Dyadic Development Psychotherapy<br>• Enhancing development in various areas<br>• Speech therapy<br>• Therapeutic nurseries and specialized programs in child cares<br>• Teaching and supporting parents to interact in ways to enhance the development of children with special needs<br>• Direct intervention by specialists such as speech language pathologists, physiotherapists, and occupational therapists<br>• Infant massage | Enhancing interactions and attachment<br>• Use of soft baby carriers<br>• Floor time with parent and child involved<br>• Mother Goose program<br>• Modifying environment and play space to meet needs of child<br>• Speech therapy<br>• Intervention by specialists such as occupational therapy<br>• Applied behavior analysis (ABA) for children with autism<br>Encouraging emotion regulation<br>• Errorless Compliance Training<br>• The Incredible Years groups<br>• Enhancement of positive temperament characteristics of children and support for parents around challenging characteristics | Intervening to help with unresolved loss and trauma<br>• Modified interactional guidance<br>• Cognitive behavior strategies<br>• Grounding in the present<br>Enhancing parents' sense of competence and social support<br>• Errorless compliance training<br>• Parenting groups<br>Enhancing self-reflectivity and empathy for the child<br>• Teach way to contain their emotions<br>• Videotape viewing<br>• Watch-Wait-Wonder<br>• Pathways to Competence groups<br>Encouraging emotion regulation<br>• Adapting to the temperament of the child<br>• Emotion-coaching approach | Intervening to help with unresolved loss and trauma<br>• Staged intervention<br>• Psychological debriefing<br>• Creative therapies<br>• Various approaches to retrieving memories and reintegrating them into narratives (e.g., EMDR)<br>• Mindfulness-based approaches<br>Enhancing parents' sense of competence and social support<br>• Enhancing a positive sense of self (learned optimism)<br>• Brief solution focused therapy<br>• Emphasizing strengths<br>• Support prenatally and postnatally<br>• Enhancing social support<br>• Family counseling<br>• Parenting classes for first-time mothers and fathers<br>• Family Matters program | Parents' defensive functioning<br>• Positive and supportive therapeutic relationship<br>• Encouraging identification and tolerance of different feelings<br>• Using gentle interpretation<br>• Strategies to deal with splitting, denial and withdrawal, devaluation and projection, and dissociation<br>Intervening to help with unresolved loss and trauma<br>• Therapeutic relationship that can enhance a sense of empowerment<br>• Staged intervention<br>Enhancing parents' sense of competence and social support<br>• Groups to enhance sense of parenting competence<br>• Family counseling<br>• Brief solution focused therapy |

Enhancing problem-solving and adaptive functioning
- Referral to drop-in centers, parent groups
- Setting clear goals and boundaries *with* the client

Enhancing attributions of the child
- Enhancing attributions of child in pregnancy and neonatal period
- Reframing
- Speaking for the child
- Pediatric guidance

Enhancing self-reflectivity
- Psychodynamic supportive counseling to enhance understanding of self and other
- Minding the Baby program
- Parents First Group Program
- Developmental approach to enhancing self-reflectivity and empathy for the child
- Identifying feelings of self and child

Enhancing interactions and attachment
- Showing videotapes on importance of attachment
- Developmental guidance
- Toymaking
- Dealing with common developmental issues

- Prenatal approaches to reduce anxiety
- Anger management groups
- Mindfulness-based trauma counseling
- Incredible Years groups
- Steps of emotion coaching
- Using the stages of problem-solving
- Learned optimism
- The Incredible Years groups
- Errorless Compliance Training

Enhancing interactions and attachment
- Use of soft baby carriers
- Coaching the interaction
- Floor time with parent and child involved
- Mother Goose
- Infant previewing
- Using videotapes and discussion
- Minding the Baby program
- Parents' first program
- Developmental guidance
- Teaching toy making

*(continued)*

**Table 14.1.** *(continued)*

| | Intervention goals and strategies based on | | |
|---|---|---|---|
| Child attributions/ development | Child interactional behavior | Parent interactional behavior | Parent attributions | Parents' view of self and others |
| | | • Providing the parent with developmental information | • Using items from Brazelton Neonatal Behavior Scale (NBAS) | |
| | | • Modifying space to meet child's needs | • Infant massage | |
| | | • Using videotape viewing | • Circle of Security parenting groups | |
| | | • Watch-Wait-Wonder approach | | |
| | | • NCAST approach | | |
| | | • Pathways to Competence groups | | |
| | | Enhancing problem solving | | |
| | | • Coping groups | | |
| | | • Using self-talk | | |
| | | • Imagining alternatives and learning ways to deal with negative thoughts | | |
| | | • Using flashcards | | |
| | | • Problem solving around parenting issues | | |

## CHAPTER 15

# Supporting Work with Multi-Risk Families within Programs, Organizations, and Service Systems

A number of unique characteristics of early intervention with multi-risk families have to be considered in planning and setting up service delivery systems. Work with multi-risk families can be extremely stressful and can result in vicarious traumatization for the staff involved. Because of the number and complexity of the risks that many families contend with, a variety of strategies need to be in place to support the work. Staff training and supervision may be essential to increase the types of interventions and to enhance the quality of the available strategies that can be provided in a program. One program does not usually have service providers with the expertise needed to meet all of the needs of families, so referral between programs is critical. A system needs to be in place that encourages cooperation and coordination between several service systems.

These issues or considerations are discussed in subsequent sections of this chapter.

## THE STRESSES OF WORKING WITH MULTI-RISK FAMILIES

Because of the bi-directional nature and intensity of the relationships interventionists have with multi-risk families, interventionists face several different types of stresses in working with multi-risk families.

### Vicarious Trauma

Chapter 9 described the possible effects of unresolved loss and trauma and how these effects can result in a number of ongoing changes in functioning. People who frequently witness traumatic events as part of their work, such as men and women serving in the armed forces during a war, police, emergency personnel, and firefighters, can develop posttruamatic stress disorder (PTSD) unless they have adequate training and debriefing following the events. Researchers have also defined a reaction of *secondary traumatic stress* (STS), a term coined by Stamm in 1996. A similar condition is *vicarious traumatization,* which can occur as a result of hearing frequent descriptions of violent events, continually being exposed to the cruel realities of the lives of many multi-risk individuals, and being a helpless bystander to tragedies (Figley, 1995; Pearlman & Saakvitne, 1995; Wilson & Lindy, 1994). Figley (1995) has referred to the issue as *compassion fatigue*.

People who develop STS experience some of the same symptoms as people who have been directly exposed to the trauma, including intrusive memories, nightmares, severe anxiety, irritability, emotional numbing, and withdrawal from certain situations that are similar to those discussed by families. Compassion fatigue can develop and, if left unchecked, it can result in burnout, with a drop in performance on the job and difficulties in interpersonal relationships.

In a recent study, Regehr (2003) surveyed fire fighters, paramedics, and child protection workers for traumatic stress arousal symptoms. Unexpectedly, it was found that the child protection staff, particularly managers, had the highest number of symptoms and degree of traumatic stress. Although the exact reasons for this are not totally understood, it appears that it may be due to a variety of factors. Child protection workers do not have specific training or support for dealing with traumatic stress, and although emergency workers see horrifying events, they do not have to keep encountering the people concerned on an ongoing basis or have to deal with their extreme anger, grief, and despair over a period of time following the event.

For early intervention professionals who deal with parents with unresolved loss and trauma and whose lives may continue to be affected by traumatic crises and violence, the results can be the anxiety, irritability, numbing, and other STS symptoms just described. Mental health workers who think and feel empathetically toward parents and children and who use their own affective self to engage the family and bring about change can be deeply affected. At the very least, their view of the world and people can be permanently changed as they come to the realization of how unjust circumstances can be for many. These shifts in understanding and feelings can result in an emotional numbness and a sense that nothing can affect or upset them anymore. Service providers can also become pessimistic, believing that they cannot make a difference and that helping a few clients is not important given that more and more families will continue to be referred with the same horrific stories of trauma. Unfortunately, this can ultimately result in withdrawal from emotional involvement or intense anger at multi-risk clients (McCann & Pearlman, 1990).

***Transference and Countertransference***   *Transference* occurs when an individual repeats with an interventionist unconscious patterns of experiences, thoughts, feelings, and behaviors originating from important early relationships. These repeated patterns may have previously been repressed. Parents often experience transference during sessions with a service provider. For psychoanalytically trained therapists, much of the work of therapy involves working with and interpreting these reactions to the person.

Conversely, *countertransference,* using a more traditional definition, refers to an interventionist's reactions that are unconscious and reflect the transference onto the parent of significant relationships from the past (Pearlman & Saakvitne, 1995).

A broader definition of countertransference is that it is any response the service provider has to a parent, positive or negative, conscious or unconscious. Obviously, countertransference is a part of every intervention relationship, but it can be a problem if it leads an interventionist to have a distorted understanding of clients. This can occur if memories are triggered by the family's situation of their own background and experience and, as a consequence, intense feelings are aroused.

If an interventionist does not have an awareness and understanding of these feelings, she may fail to empathize, may draw away from families, or may idealize some families and dislike others. These reactions can be influenced by parental transference; for example, a parent may have a desire to see an interventionist positively as someone who will make her situation better, or negatively as someone who will neglect and abandon her. As a result, the interventionist may misinterpret what is going on and transfer the views and feelings evoked by these interpretations onto the family. This can prevent the interventionist from seeing what is actually going on and result in continual distortion of the reality of the family's situation.

*Job Responsibility and Workload*    In a study conducted by Regehr and associates (2003), one of the most significant factors that correlated with a high level of vicarious trauma was an interventionist's workload and her level of responsibility for the welfare of others (Regehr, 2003; Regehr & Cadell, 1999; Regehr, Hill, Goldberg, & Hughes, 2003). For child protective services workers with very large caseloads of families considered extremely high-risk, the consequences can be very significant.

For service providers with caseloads of almost exclusively multi-risk families, a sense of being overwhelmed can build when situations are difficult and chaotic, when changes are slow, and when crises are frequent. If parents are difficult to engage and resistant to many of the suggestions for changing their interactions with their child and for trying out various short-term interventions, a sense of powerlessness and failure can result.

The issue that most concerns early intervention service providers and causes the greatest ongoing anxiety is often the possibility that one of the family members with whom they work could be seriously injured or even die as a result of child abuse or family violence (Regehr et al., 2003). Although cases of this happening are, fortunately, relatively rare, the public media coverage and scrutiny that can accompany such situations is often dramatic. When these service providers see the media treating professionals like themselves as scapegoats who lose their jobs and careers, it can produce significant anxiety and a generalized fear that the same could happen to them (Regehr, Chau, Leslie, & Howe, 2002).

Reduced funding has increased workloads in many agencies while opportunities for adequate training, support, and supervision have often decreased. Policies and procedures in some early intervention agencies do not allow workers to provide either the variety, length, or type of services needed by multi-risk families. Consequently, this lack of adequate supports in the work environment coupled with increased public expectations of accountability places practitioners more at risk for vicarious trauma and burnout.

## Burnout from Pressures Related to Service Provision

The ultimate result of these various pressures on service providers may be burnout that is characterized by increasing anger and a sense of futility and withdrawal. Sometimes the feelings are temporary and fleeting, and the service provider can take a break or get enough support to enable her to return to the work with renewed enthusiasm. Unfortunately, however, an individual who does not get a break or the proper support may no longer want to be involved in the work and may then leave the agency. This may result in significant staff turnover and loss of experienced staff, which becomes stressful for the remaining workers and disastrous for the service system.

## SOLUTIONS FOR COPING WITH INTERVENTION-RELATED STRESSORS

A variety of solutions have been suggested in order to support workers who are involved with very multi-risk families. Some of these are discussed below.

### Supportive Program Policies

Program goals, objectives, and policies need to be in place that can provide a "holding" and supportive structure for staff while allowing some flexibility in work with families. For example, brief interventions alone do not meet the needs of many families. Policies must support the need for longer term, innovative approaches adapted to the specific characteristics of each family. They need to allow parents to discontinue involvement in a program at times, with the understanding that they will find encouragement and acceptance to return if new issues arise with their child or their life circumstances change (e.g., if a marriage or relationship breaks up, if the child begins to act up after he begins child care).

Program policies need to be based on a theoretical framework as well as on research on effective practices. Requirements set out by funders of a program also need to be incorporated into guidelines when applicable. Clear guidelines must be in place delineating how referrals come into a program and what the criteria is for entry into the program. The specifics about how initial screening assessment and formulation of cases needs to be clear and should be made available. Having an assessment tool to use to carry out this formulation can be very helpful (Landy, 2004). Having clear goals and objectives for the program is also helpful to guide the direction of intervention for individual families and to suggest outcomes that could be measured if a process or outcome evaluation of the program is carried out. Some possible measures that could be used for evaluation are described in Chapter 1.

Policies around caseloads and supervision are also essential. Because early intervention often takes place in homes or in community settings such as hospitals or in informal community settings such as coffee shops and libraries, the necessary boundaries of the interventionists' role can become blurred—particularly for paraprofessionals who are not educated in professional colleges such as those for nurses, psychologists, and social workers that delineate expectations about clinical roles and practice. Thus, for these paraprofessionals, role definitions and job descriptions need to be in place. Boundaries can help distinguish the differences between the role of an interventionist and a friend, particularly if the interventionist lives and works in the same community as the parents. Policies about boundaries assist the service provider to establish a relationship that is supportive and open but not equal so there is an understanding that the parent is there in order to gain knowledge and to learn parenting strategies from the interventionist that can enhance her child's development. These strategies are based on knowledge and research and not on the opinions of the service provider, although it may be useful at times to share appropriate strategies that worked with one's own or others' children. Although the parents have a right and need to know about the interventionist's training and experience, her past history, present circumstances, or family situation should not be discussed. Policies regarding confidentiality, crisis responses, safety issues, giving and acceptance of gifts, attendance at occasions such as a christening or a funeral, and inappropriate responsibilities such as babysitting children and lending money need to be in place. In some situations flexibility instead of rigid adherence to a rule is needed, and in situations in which there are no clear procedures in place, it is important that a provider check with a supervisor.

Other important policies include a code of conduct that defines team behavior and explains what is and is not acceptable. Because of the nature of the work, programs need to have procedures to be followed when a critical incident occurs, including immediate debriefing and ongoing counseling if necessary. Agencies need to provide health benefits and disability coverage if workers need to take time off to recover from a serious event related to their work or from burnout. Programs should also develop forms for recording services and various characteristics of the child, parent, and parent–child relationship, which could sometimes be used as pretests and outcome variables.

## Effective Supervision

Effective supervision must include case management, which considers the type and number of cases a worker has, and ongoing review of files to make sure policies and procedures of the agency are followed. Annual evaluations and identification of training needs is also important. Research has also shown that supervision that is reflective and is within the context of a supportive supervisory relationship and allows staff an opportunity and time to stand back from their day-to-day work with families in order to consider certain cases can help some service providers to overcome some of the symptoms of vicarious trauma and to avoid burnout (Bernstein, 2002; Fenichel, 1992; Gilkerson, 2004; Gilkerson & Shahmoon-Shanok, 2000; Landy, 2003; Parlakian, 2001, 2002). It is also helpful in order to enhance the quality of interventions that are provided.

Four main components of supervision need to be made available to staff:

1. Supervision is available *regularly,* relatively *frequently,* and without interruption.

2. It is *collaborative and supportive* and occurs in a *respectful* interpersonal climate that encourages open discussion of difficult feelings and frustrations.

3. It has a *sound theoretical base* that is accepted and understood within the agency.

4. It is *reflective* and allows staff members supportive opportunities to think about their cases and the ways they are working and to consider other possible approaches.

***Regular***    First, supervision needs to be available regularly, on a weekly or at least semi-weekly basis—and it should occur as much as possible without the interruption of a telephone ringing or someone knocking on the door. In addition, the supervisor needs to be available for support, advice, or debriefing when an interventionist has a real concern about a family that cannot wait until the next regular session.

***Collaborative and Supportive***    The relationship between supervisor and direct care provider must be collaborative and include a sharing of expertise, knowledge, and experience. The provider will understand things about the child and family that the supervisor does not, and she can often bring important information to the supervision session about the cultural and religious beliefs and customs of the family. The experienced supervisor will be able to suggest possible new approaches to intervention on the basis of her experience of working with challenging families. Trust between the supervisor and service provider must be established so that the interventionist can share difficult feelings and uncertainty about what to do comfortably, and with the support and reassurance of the supervisor as they problem solve together about strategies to try. In other words, a safe space must be provided that supports the staff member to be able to provide that same supportive experience to the family. The relationship focus of the supervision is enhanced by awareness of this parallel process of supervisor to worker and worker to the parent and child.

***Based on a Sound Theoretical Basis***    Theory can make what may seem to be random, disconnected, or incoherent behavior on the part of the family into something that is understandable and more coherent and can provide a common understanding of what is occurring during intervention. This sense of context and meaning can increase the interventionist's genuine connection with the family. Some of the theoretical underpinnings that are critical for both the supervisor and staff include an understanding of developmental theory, an understanding of the importance of the parent–child relationship and attachment; the effects of trauma on parental functioning, parenting, and psychological make-up; and the most effective intervention strategies to use with multi-risk, complex families. Perhaps most important for the success of reflective supervision is an understanding and acceptance of the importance of both conscious and unconscious aspects of the parents' responses with their children in the therapeutic relationship and of the intervention process on the interventionist. Understanding the inevitability and importance of certain feelings and thoughts can open the door to the process of true reflective supervision.

***Reflective***    A good supervisor teaches providers to consider intervention objectives and to question the approaches they are using to achieve them. Reflective supervision provides an opportunity to step back from the work and to sort out thoughts and feelings about what is going on over the course of the intervention. Providers should be encouraged to share feelings about what is happening in a particular situation or with a particular child or parent. With reflective supervision the service provider can begin to understand not only what is actually happening in the family and why but also her reaction to it. Most of all, providers learn about issues and biases that may be clouding their judgment, including intense feelings that may be out of proportion to the situation and resurfacing of feelings about similar situations in their past.

A supervisor may point out countertransference on the part of a service provider if, for example, the provider seems to be reflecting the same sense of helplessness that the parent shows by refusing to try any suggestions that are made by the home visitor. At times, the provider may need help understanding whether something is not right and she might need a place to discuss and explore the reality of the situation, to talk about frustrations and disappointments when a parent falls back, or to discuss options when a child stops improving. Of course, it is also important to acknowledge success when a parent and/or child make valuable gains (Landy, 2004). Some service providers may need support in setting limits or boundaries with a family without feeling guilty. Others may need support in not giving up on a family too soon before various strategies have been explored, or in understanding the parent's pain. The supervisor needs to make sure that the needs of the child are not lost when parents consume time and energy from the home visitor and conversely, support may need to be provided so that parents' needs are not ignored as the particular needs of the child are met. In other words, maintaining a balance between the needs of the parent and child is crucial. Finally, supervision can mean supporting staff in developing new skills or knowledge so that they can learn to work in new ways.

Gilkerson and colleagues have described the process of a reflective supervisory session in seven stages:

1. Preparing (getting into a state of mind for the supervision)

2. Greeting and reconnecting

3. Opening the session and finding out what the supervisee would like to talk about

4. Discussing the details of the case and what is happening

5. Making hypotheses

6. Thinking about what could be tried next

7. Closing with showing acknowledgment for the good work being done with the family

As with the parent–interventionist sessions, much of the time of the supervision will be spent listening to how the intervention is proceeding, but at times it will be important to push the supervisee to consider another point of view regarding the client and to create an opportunity for her to consider another hypothesis and think about what is happening in a different way (Gilkerson, 2004; Gilkerson & Shahmoon-Shanok, 2000). For example, the interventionist and client may look for different reasons for why the client may be responding to her children in a certain way. Is it because she is following cultural beliefs about child development? Is her husband pushing her to mother in a certain way, or could it be related to her fears or dreams about the future of her child? Encouraging the interventionist to explore with the parent why she acts in certain ways may provide the service provider with new information and help. The parent, in turn, may be able to reconsider her responses to her child and adapt them if they are not helpful for her child's development.

Optimally reflective supervision is provided individually and by someone other than the supervisor who is responsible for case management and evaluation. Because of time constraints and budget considerations, some agencies cannot manage to provide individual reflective supervision for all staff. In that case, peer or group supervision can be provided with staff members from a variety of disciplines and viewpoints providing input about a family and child. It is also possible for agencies to use consultants who—on a biweekly or monthly basis—join the team and provide clinical input on some of the more challenging cases (Levkoe, 2003; Manio-Dimayuga, 2003; Moher, 2003). Sometimes time could be built into the beginning of administrative meetings for staff to check in and discuss what is on their minds—positive and/or negative—or what is particularly pressing about their work with families. This can demonstrate to staff that the agency is supportive of this kind of reflection.

## A Collaborative Team

Service providers in the field of early childhood mental health come from multiple service systems and a diverse range of professional disciplines including nursing, social work, medicine, psychology, early childhood education, occupational therapy, and speech-language pathology. In many programs paraprofessionals or lay home visitors trained on the job also provide support to families. In 2002, a committee from the Infant Mental Health Promotion Program (IMP) in Toronto, Ontario, Canada, developed a document outlining the knowledge and skills needed to provide "competent care specific to each infant and family." The committee acknowledged that the level of knowledge and skills would be different for different disciplines and various service systems. Also, although no individual service provider was expected to have all of the competencies, it was believed that each needed to be available on the team as practitioners, through supervision, other team members, or collaboration with other agencies (Infant Mental Health Promotion Program, 2004).

This document noted that practitioners in infant mental health need to be able to demonstrate the following:

- Understanding of
    Child development
    Influences on child development
    Intervention principles
    Discipline specific interventions

- Ability to
    Relate to families
    Intervene with families
    Collaborate with other service providers
    Provide assessment and formulation of families

- Characteristics of
    Empathy
    Flexibility
    Ability to communicate

This document is available from the Infant Mental Health Promotion Program and can be very useful for supervisors in hiring staff for an early intervention team and in identifying areas for training and consultation. Individual practitioners may also find it useful to identify areas in which they may need further training.

*The Work of Paraprofessionals*    Many early intervention programs with a significant number of families who come from different cultural backgrounds rely on paraprofessionals to carry out much of the work. Paraprofessionals bring special abilities that professionals may not have and can often understand the language and behavioral cues of families from their culture and interpret program objectives to families in ways that will be non-threatening and acceptable. Often, they can make a program acceptable to a community, as well. Nevertheless, for paraprofessionals the challenges of countertransference may be particularly powerful and they may become triggered if parents remind them of their own struggles growing up or of parenting their children. This may lead to overidentification with parents or blaming them because they were able to overcome the challenges of their situation whereas the families they are working with seem unable to do the same. Training and supervision can overcome some of these dilemmas, but it is unrealistic to expect paraprofessionals to undertake counseling roles or to conduct therapy (Halpern, 1990; Musick & Stott, 2000; Olds & Kitzman, 1993).

Hiring paraprofessionals should include some evaluation of their capacity for self-reflection, complexity of thinking about parenting, and ability to problem solve. Hiring interviews could include posing some parenting dilemmas, such as how to help a parent who has run out of money before the end of the month or how to work with a single parent who says that her child always has an intense tantrum at the grocery store. Answers to these kinds of questions can often be just as helpful when hiring new staff as collecting information on their educational background and previous experience in other types of work. Contrary to what might be assumed, hiring paraprofessionals may not be very cost effective due to the training and supervisory efforts required. Shortages of trained workers and the special insight paraprofessionals can bring to teams working with families from other cultures can make them important members of early intervention programs, however.

*Team Structure*    Access to various professional disciplines is essential. Teams that work with multi-risk families, prenatally, in the early postnatal period, and throughout the preschool years need mental health workers (e.g., psychologists, social workers), nurses, and staff such as early childhood educators with expertise in early development and parenting or child interactional needs.

Some teams may have specialists who work with all of the very multi-risk families. Other team models have all staff carrying some multi-risk cases, with the specialists carrying some of the cases and providing supervision and mentoring to other team members as well. Those who assume the position of multi-risk specialist *must* have extensive training and expertise with this population and have a love and passion for the work.

Although they have not been specifically evaluated, blended approaches in which paraprofessionals and professionals work together seem to be excellent models. An example of such a model used in a public health department with access to birth notices and referrals from hospital obstetric departments and other agencies is given in Figure 15.1. In blended models, paraprofessionals may provide the direct services to a family with supervision from a professional, both a para-

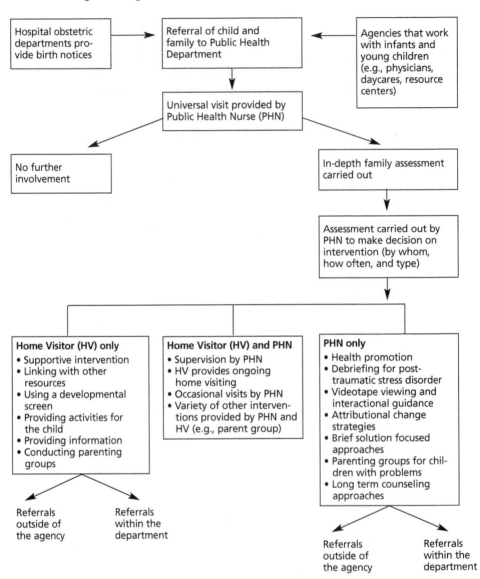

**Figure 15.1.** An example of a blended model of early intervention services provided by public health nurses and paraprofessional home visitors.

professional and a professional may be involved with certain families, or a professional may carry out all of the work with a family.

## Training

All early intervention professisonals sometimes feel that they lack the skills and knowledge to work with a particular parent or family. Although knowledge alone cannot overcome all challenges, training in a variety of areas to help staff understand and apply new intervention strategies can build morale and enhance interventions. Sometimes staff can receive training from a staff member with specialized expertise or from an outside consultant. A team discussion of complex cases with various disciplines present can also be excellent training opportunities for staff. It is important that all staff members receive information and training related to important legislation that applies to their work, including child abuse and neglect reporting protocols, so that they are clearly informed about how to proceed if abuse is suspected. At other times, a staff member may be given the opportunity to receive training in an area of particular interest, especially if the expertise obtained would be valuable for the team.

## KEEPING HOPE ALIVE

Because of the complexity of issues faced by many multi-risk families, interventionists need various tools and support to help them maintain a realistic but hopeful view of positive changes that can occur. Consequently, it is important for interventionists to establish small and obtainable objectives for the work and to use some qualitative measures of the process of change (see Appendix in Chapter 1 for a list of some of these measures). An evaluation from parents who have progressed enough to terminate about what they found most useful can be very helpful. Many clients in previous research studies have assessed the therapist's attitudes and caring towards them as most helpful (e.g., Norcross & Arkowitz, 1992). This kind of information can be useful and encouraging for the workers involved.

Service providers should also be encouraged to understand the significance of very small gains for some parents and children. For example, for a parent who was initially very resistant to being involved with a program, helping him get to the point when regularity of attendance at sessions is established can be extremely important. Even very small signs of increasing self-reflectivity such as when an individual moves beyond mere reporting of concrete events to talking about thoughts and feelings can be significant signs of the potential for change. Also, the ability to link current behavior to past experiences can be indicators of positive change.

Table 15.1 describes a measure developed by Greenspan and Wieder (1984) that considers steps in the therapeutic process in the areas of regularity and stability, attachment, and process. Parents may progress through each of the areas simultaneously, but often regularity and stability of session attendance is established first, which forms the basis for further work. The areas of attachment and process may develop together (Greenspan & Wieder, 1987).

The framework presented in this book recognizes the multiplicity of influences on child and family development and proposes that a number of comprehensive interventions need to be provided for many families. These interventions can be offered over a period of time—as they were for the two case study families—as briefer interventions provided during times of stress, or when a child is at a challenging developmental period. It can be helpful, therefore, to evaluate the success of small pieces of work such as a parenting group or interactional guidance sessions. Sometimes, it is difficult to see changes in parents, although the progress of their children may be significant. Evaluation or assessment of children should include cognitive areas but also consider socioemotional development and whether difficult behaviors or other symptoms have been reduced or even eliminated.

**Table 15.1.** Dimensions of the therapeutic relationship

| Steps in the therapeutic process | | |
| --- | --- | --- |
| Regularity and stability | Attachment | Process |
| 1. Willingness to meet with an interventionist or therapist to convey concrete concerns or hear about services<br>2. Willingness to schedule meetings again<br>3. Meeting according to some predictable pattern<br>4. Meeting regularly with occasional disruptions<br>5. Meeting regularly with no disruptions | 1. Interest in having concrete needs met that can be provided by anyone (e.g., food, transportation)<br>2. Emotional interest in the person of the therapist (e.g., conveys pleasure or anger when they meet)<br>3. Communicates purposefully in attempts to deal with problems<br>4. Tolerates discomfort or scary emotions<br>5. Feels "known" or accepted in positive and negative aspects | 1. Preliminary communication, including verbal support and information gathering<br>2. Ability to observe and report single behaviors or action patterns<br>3. Focuses on relationships involved in the behavior-action pattern<br>4. Self-observing function in relationship to feelings<br>5. Self-observing function in relationship to complex and interactive feeling states<br>6. Self-observing function for thematic affective elaboration<br>7. Makes connections between the key relationships in life including the therapeutic relationship<br>8. Identification of patterns in current, therapeutic, and historical relationships to work through problems and facilitate new growth<br>9. Consolidation of new patterns and levels of satisfaction and preparing to separate from the therapeutic relationship |

From Greenspan, S.I. & Wieder, S. (1984). Dimensions and levels of the therapeutic process. *Psychotherapy: Theory, research, and practice, 21,* 5–23. Copyright © 1984 by Division of Psychotherapy (29), American Psychological Association, reprinted by permission.

## Maintaining a Realistic Perspective

Practitioners who have experience in early intervention know that it is not always possible to reach, let alone to be successful with, every family. As in medicine, parents and children may have certain problems that cannot be fixed or cured, and the best that can be accomplished may be to try to ensure the safety of family members and to work on very small goals. In a study that Patricia Crittenden

(1992b) carried out in Florida with child protection services, she identified a number of levels of family functioning. These levels ranged from families she termed "independent and adequate," to families she termed "inadequate." Specifically, Crittenden (1992b) described five levels of family functioning:

1. *Independent and adequate:* These families are able to meet their children's needs and solve their own problems through a combination of supports from friends and relatives, their own skills, and services that they seek.

2. *Vulnerable to crisis:* These families typically function independently but need help in dealing with unusual and/or unexpected crises (e.g., the birth of a child with disabilities, divorce). The "vulnerable" classification results not from the event but from the family's response to it. These families typically need services for a short time ranging from 6–12 months.

3. *Restorable:* These families face multiple problems and need training and services to learn specific skills or to have therapy to deal with particular issues. It is believed that these families can return to independent functioning, but intervention is usually longer term, between 1–4 years in duration. Active case management may be needed to organize services.

4. *Supportable:* These families are not expected to become independent and to achieve adequate functioning because the problems are chronic or of a severity that cannot be solved (e.g., parent has mental retardation or is chronic drug abuser). Ongoing services can be provided, however, to help the family meet the basic needs of their children until they are grown.

5. *Inadequate:* It is believed that for these families, no services will be enough to enable them to meet to meet their children's basic needs, and therefore, the children should be removed from the home.

She recommended that in these inadequate families, children should be removed because the parents were uncaring, abusive, or extremely neglectful. (Crittenden, 1992b). Consequently, in assessing parents and families it is important, as pointed out in Chapter 3 (see Figure 3.1), to consider the characteristics of the parents and the availability of services in determining how possible it will be for changes to occur.

## Support for Self-Care

Most service providers working in early intervention acknowledge the need to have a balanced lifestyle and to care for themselves; however, it is often very difficult for them to find the time or to be willing to take steps to deal with their own stress. To help in this process, some organizations take time for staff retreats that include strategies for self-care in an atmosphere that can encourage relaxation, self-reflection, and self-nurturing. Staff can be encouraged to consider their own well-being and how they can nurture themselves and connect with others in each of four areas using a well-being wheel (see Figure 15.2). The four areas include the following:

1. Mental energy (e.g., learning something that is exciting, new, or different, exploring a new intellectual interest, engaging in mindful meditation)

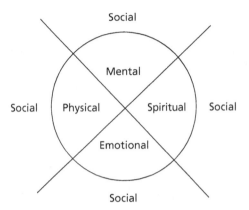

**Figure 15.2.** A well-being wheel illustrating the four areas in which staff members can consider their personal well-being and the well-being of their relationships with others.

2. Spiritual energy (e.g., enjoyment of art, nature, an organized religion, or something that the person feels gives life a purpose)

3. Emotional energy (e.g., enjoyment of connection with family and friends, pursuing a hobby or a way to nurture themselves such as a break away)

4. Physical energy (e.g., nutrition, exercise, and rest)

For each area, activities can be done individually or alone or with other people with whom the person has a meaningful, supportive relationship. Discussion of these strategies at a retreat or team meeting and follow-up to see how people are implementing ideas can be a fun group activity and encourage meaningful encounters between staff.

## COORDINATING SERVICES

Most of the time, one service provider or program cannot provide all of the types of services needed to meet the multiplicity of needs of multi-risk families. For this reason, programs need to be part of a coordinated system of agencies or have well-established arrangements for cooperation with other service providers.

Organizing a system for early intervention may be difficult because it requires the availability of parts of the larger service system, including Child Protective Services, early childhood mental health services, clinical infant programs, health care programs for children with established disabilities and those at risk due to biological or environmental factors, and child care systems.

Many children and parents in multi-risk families could be involved in one or all of these service systems at any time. Each of these systems may also be providing services to families at varying levels of risk and will have different philosophies, goals, and mandates. Consequently, some of the work done by each system (less so by Child Protective Services) may be more preventative (and less intense), whereas others will use interventions to meet the needs of multi-risk families that are based on the family's risks and protective factors and will be more specialized and often intense.

The complexities of working with a number of other agencies and organizations can be extremely challenging. Two of the primary difficulties are the enormous amount of time required for collaboration and the great diversities of goals, theoretical beliefs, and expertise across the agencies. Another issue seldom discussed is that coordination meetings can become a way to "pass on a problem." Interagency rivalry may surface, particularly if funding is involved. As well, taking on the role of case manager when a number of agencies are involved with a family can be complex at best and overwhelming at worst. Harbin, McWilliam, and Gallagher (2000) have identified a number of models for organizing networks of programs ranging from a single program that provides most services and only coordinates with other programs as necessary in an informal way to much more complex coordination models. In their model, described as a "comprehensive system for all children," a universal system of services for young children in a community is developed, allowing for prevention, early identification, and early intervention services to be provided (Harbin et al., 2000, p. 395). The model has a broad local coordinating body with representatives from service agencies and government, business, and community agencies such as churches and libraries. This encourages a normalizing of the programs that are offered to families. When grant proposals are submitted, they are developed cooperatively, although one agency might take the lead. In this way the multiple systems mentioned above can be coordinated and links made with other supports.

Less comprehensive systems can be successful when one of the agencies takes the lead or a group of agencies work closely together as if they are from one agency. Having a single contact phone number for parents to use can avoid them having to phone multiple places about obtaining services for their child and the family.

Setting up a coordinating body requires clear guidelines, preferably from state or local governments. Service boundaries need to be delineated and discussed so that a clear system of services can be set up covering all areas and communities. Training may also be necessary in order to assist coordinating agencies with very different mandates to integrate them into a coherent whole that supports every agency to provide the very best services for young children and families.

Figure 15.3 presents a checklist of organizational policies and procedures that are needed to support interventionists in order for them to provide high-quality services to multi-risk families. The document was developed by a committee of supervisors and practitioners working in early intervention programs as a means of informing agency directors, funding agencies, and government policy makers about what needs to be in place in organizations to support service providers working with very high-risk families. It is a useful document that helps organizations to evaluate the quality of their support to staff and to identify areas that are lacking and need to be developed in the future (Infant Mental Health Promotion Program, 2004).

**Checklist of Organizational
Policies and Practices
Needed for Quality Service**

Organizations responsible for services to young children and their families must develop policies and procedures that ensure

**Capacity to meet the individual needs of infants and their families**

___ Reasonable workloads based on the complexity of cases (e.g., no more than 10 cases when a child is at high risk for compromised development and a family's complex needs require frequent, intensive intervention in the home; more cases when the needs of a child and family are less complex)

___ Adequate time to allow appropriate culturally sensitive observations and in-depth assessments with each family

___ Based on individual family needs, flexibility in the number of hours of service that families may receive and the length of time over which they may receive service

___ Flexibility in when and where families may be seen appropriate to their individual needs (e.g., conducting evening or weekend home visits and in-center programs, meeting families in the community, accompanying families to other services)

___ Recognition of the importance of realistic expectations and of helping families to appreciate their strengths and develop a sense of hope for the future

___ After ending a period of intervention, flexible follow-up for further short-term interventions should problems arise at different stages

___ Clarity regarding practitioner roles and boundaries with families

**Flexibility in work arrangements**

___ Flexibility in work hours and time off to accommodate family responsibilities of practitioners and to relieve some of their home stress (e.g., child care, eldercare, medical appointments)

___ Varied responsibilities and opportunities related to worker interests and strengths (e.g., service delivery, research, education, community meetings, rotations among teams)

**Adequate staff remuneration**

___ Salaries and benefits that adequately recognize the contribution of workers

**Clear staff hiring and retention practices**

___ Staff selection criteria and procedures that ensure adequate personal and interpersonal skills and responsiveness to language and culture

___ Involvement of team members in the selection process and ensuring a "fit" with organizational values and beliefs

___ A plan for staff recognition and retention strategies (*see Staff Support & Supervision*)

**Solid staff training and supervision**

___ Staff:supervisor ratios appropriate to the support and supervision needed by front-line practitioners so that they can reflect on the needs of families and adapt interventions accordingly (i.e., no more than 10 staff per supervisor in most settings)

___ Adequate practitioner training and resources for the work

___ Adequate supervisor training for reflective supervision

**Figure 15.3.** Checklist of organizational policies and practices needed for quality service. (Adapted by permission of Rhona Wolpert, Director of the Infant Mental Health Promotion Program [IMP], Hospital for Sick Children, Toronto, Canada, http://www.sickkids.ca/imp)

**Safe working environments**

___ Guidelines for preventing, identifying, and responding to unsafe situations both inside and outside the immediate work environment (i.e., office building, agencies, homes)

___ Safety plans for working after hours, working in homes, managing client crisis (e.g., mental illness, suicide), travel, animals in homes, drug/alcohol concerns, domestic violence, criminal activity

___ Directions for reporting incidents that have an impact on staff physical and psychological health and well being

**Staff training**

Organizations responsible for services to young children and their families must provide or support participation of both frontline practitioners and supervisors in **specialized initial training and ongoing continuing education** to achieve the broad range of knowledge and skills needed in this field. Training is needed in the following areas:

___ Child development and parenting practices

___ Atypical child development and the supports needed by young children with special needs and their families

___ Recognition and reporting of child maltreatment

___ Parent mental health including unresolved loss and trauma

___ A variety of theoretically and clinically sound and evidence-based screening, assessment, and intervention approaches designed for work with young children and their families

___ Cultural competence when working with families

___ Peer support and reflective practice

___ Recognizing of signs and symptoms of vicarious trauma and ways to manage it

___ Self-care to deal with stress and find a balance of mental, physical, spiritual, and emotional well-being in self and clients

___ Networking, collaboration, and service coordination

___ Personal safety

**Staff support and supervision**

Organizations responsible for services to young children and their families must provide adequate support to increase staff satisfaction and ability to adapt practices appropriate to each child and family. Such support involves

*Valuing staff*

___ Creating an atmosphere of appreciation (e.g., recognition for accomplishments and hard work, incentives)

___ Recognizing that self care is necessary and offering health promotion practices (e.g., time off for family responsibilities, workshops dealing with stress, Employee Assistance Programs)

___ Ensuring staff input into the day-to-day organization of their own work arrangements as well as organizational policies and procedures

*Reflective practice*

___ Regularly scheduled reflective supervision appropriate to the needs of individual staff members (i.e., at least bi-weekly for most practitioners)

___ Clear separation between the supervision needed for administration requirements of service and the supervision needed to nurture and encourage practitioner reflection on their work (e.g., at separate times or by separate supervisors)

___ Opportunities for reflective peer support (e.g., regular team meetings, mentoring)

___ Identifying primary support persons for challenging situations (e.g., a peer mentor, team leader, or supervisor)

___ Regular clinical consultation from experts to support the work with individual cases

*(continued)*

**Figure 15.3.**   *(continued)*

*Supporting staff members during organizational change, conflict, and case crises*

___ All levels of staff are kept informed of proposed changes

___ Steps are provided so that all levels of staff are encouraged to take ownership and invest in all staff in organizational plans

___ A process for managing conflict between workers, between a worker and manager, and with other agencies

___ A defined debriefing and/or peer support process for dealing with traumatic incidents involving work with clients

**Relationships with families**

Organizations responsible for services to young children and their families must ensure appropriate practitioner–family relationships. This involves

___ Clear recognition and support for the critical importance of establishing therapeutic relationships with families that are responsive, respectful, and family-centered. Such trusting relationships open family receptivity to the services that help them establish the responsive relationships needed by young children.

___ Clearly defined procedures for specifying goals and contracts with families, both on initial contact and again later in the intervention process when families are more able to hear and integrate information

___ Support to establish and manage empathic boundaries with families

___ Support for the time needed for practitioners to build relationships with families

___ An atmosphere of warmth and welcome within the agency that encourages families to feel safe and allows for continuity when there are staff changes

**Collaboration, coordination, and consultation**

Organizations responsible for services to young children and their families must ensure capacity for effective networking and collaboration with a broad range of services. This involves

___ Recognition that no one agency can meet all family needs and that multiple interventions may be needed

___ Appropriate training in the process of smooth and effective service coordination

___ Adequate staff time for effective collaboration with other agencies

___ An organized system of readily available specialized consultation and assessments regarding infant and child mental health, adult mental health services for parents, and parenting capacity

## CHAPTER 16

# Putting Intervention with Multi-Risk Families into Perspective

T hroughout this book, the imperative need for integrated, comprehensive, and appropriately focused services for children and families facing multiple risks has been established. The purpose of this chapter is to touch on information in earlier chapters in order to provide evidence for and emphasize the critical importance of early intervention for multi-risk families, review the model for providing services to multi-risk families described in this book, and describe the place of services for multi-risk families in the larger prevention and early intervention service system.

## THE CRITICAL IMPORTANCE OF EARLY INTERVENTION SERVICES FOR MULTI-RISK FAMILIES

As discussed in the Introduction, significant and increasing numbers of infants and young children are showing early symptoms and signs of disorders or of developing psychopathology (Knitzer, 2000).

### The Increasing Number of Disorders and Psychopathology in Infants and Young Children

Some of the problems that appear to be increasing in young children are attention-deficit/hyperactivity disorder, oppositional defiant disorder (including excessive aggression and acting-out behaviors), regulatory disorder (including extreme separation anxiety and sleeping and eating disorders), and autism spectrum disorders (Björkquist, Öesterman, & Kaukiainen, 1992; Campbell, 1990, 1995, 1996; Campbell & Ewing, 1990; Campbell, Shaw, & Gilliom, 2000; Duncan, Forness, & Hartsough, 1995; Fonagy, Target, Cottrell, Phillips, & Kurtz, 2002; Forness & Finn, 1993; Lavigne, Gibbons, Christoffel, Arend, Rosenbaum, Binn, et al., 1996). Underlying most of these disorders are failures to develop a number of developmental capacities and functioning abilities. Although some of these difficulties, even without intervention, will remit with increasing maturity, a significant percentage will not. In fact, some individuals will experience increasing difficulties as they mature and face life tasks such as completing school; finding employment; managing finances; and establishing long-term, meaningful relationships (Campbell & Ewing, 1990; Fonagy et al., 2002; Verhulst, Achenbach, Ferdinand, & Kasius, 1993).

Various capacities need to be developed in the first 6 years of life in order to lay a foundation for optimal functioning later. These are so critical that failing to develop them can contribute to some of the disorders mentioned previously (Landy, 2002b). These capacities or competencies include

- Establishing a secure attachment and a sense of trust in caregivers

- Communicating and, particularly, *sharing* thoughts, feelings, and beliefs with others

- Establishing a strong sense of self and self-efficacy

- Building the capacity to regulate behavior

- Managing the intensity of negative emotions

- Maintaining focus and shifting attention

- Developing social competence including perspective taking and empathy

A number of child characteristics can significantly affect the development of these capacities, including biological and genetic factors and temperamental characteristics such as emotional lability, hypersensitivities to sensory input from certain or all sensory modalities, and neurobiological vulnerabilities in various learning areas such as language and motor/perceptual, visual, or auditory processing. However, the environment and particularly parent–child interactions have been clearly identified as major contributors to a child's cognitive, social, and emotional developmental outcomes (Atkinson, Vetere, & Grayson, 1995; Caspi, Henry, McGee, Moffitt, & Silva, 1995; Greenspan & Wieder, 1993, 1998; Landy, 2002b; Pennington, 2002; Shonkoff & Phillips, 2000).

## Early Brain Development

Excitement mounted in the early 1990s about the significance of early experiences for later development. In the late 1990s, information about sensitive periods for brain development and the importance of relationships and parenting interactions appeared in a variety of newspaper articles, in magazines, and on radio and television. Much of this discussion focused on the child's ability to enter school ready to learn. Little attention was given to the need to reduce deleterious parenting practices such as abuse and neglect and harsh and punitive discipline, to alleviate the effects of parental depression and isolation and other mental health issues of parents, or to provide support and services to enhance the parenting interactions of the most at-risk parents. Thus, although the renewed attention on infants and young children was exciting and at times exhilarating, the focus on how to provide stimulation to them was sometimes questionable, and suggestions for reaching and influencing the most challenging parents were less common.

Still, we have come to a number of conclusions about the early development of the brain and how it and a child's development can be affected by experiences in the environment that can inform the practice of early intervention. Some of these conclusions have been discussed in various other chapters, but are reviewed here in more detail.

Research has shown that in the prenatal period, the development and migration of cortical neurons (i.e., nerve cells) occurs. This migration can be adversely affected by poor maternal nutrition, drug and alcohol consumption, and—it is increasingly believed—maternal stress (Elman et al., 1996; Huttenlocher, 1994). At birth, the human infant has about a billion neurons. For these neurons to be functional or for information to be conveyed between them, connections or synapses need to be made at which axons "output" and dendrites receive information from the neurons. In the first year of life, the number of synapses between the cells increases twenty-fold, from 50 trillion to 1,000 trillion (Kolb, 1989).

A process of sculpting, pruning, and eliminating excessive neurons and synapses also occurs in the first year of life. While some of the random connections made at birth are pruned, significant restructuring and reorganization of synapses occurs as the neural system becomes more complex and functional. Although much of the restructuring is preprogrammed or genetic, some appears to be experience-dependent and results from children's unique interactions with their environments, particularly their primary caregivers (Huttenlocher & Dabholkar, 1997; Shatz, 1992).

Different parts of the brain become functional at different times and are responsible for various aspects of our development. Starting from the base of the brain, these parts are the 1) brainstem, 2) diencephalon, 3) limbic system, and 4) cortical area. The lower areas are responsible for more basic and primitive functions such as breathing, sleeping, and hunger. The higher areas are responsible for emotional responses, thought, and modification of intense emotional responses (Greenfield, 1997). Within each of these larger areas, further localization of brain functions is possible. For example, dysfunction in various areas of the brain, particularly parts of the limbic system and cortical areas, has been found to be linked to psychopathology (Pennington, 2002).

Although the structure and organization of the neural system is critical, development and functioning depends on communication between brain cells as well as communication between brain cells and the rest of the body. Neurotransmitters and neuromodulators are released by one cell and then they facilitate the transmission of the message to the next cell. These neurochemicals include dopamine, serotonin, endorphins, and hormones such as glucocorticoids, which are increased during stress. Again, evidence exists that certain extreme environmental factors such as trauma, abuse, and neglect can affect the amount and location of depletion or excess of these biochemical influences, and certain distinct and varying patterns have been identified with various types of disorders (Bradley, 2000; Pennington, 2002).

Although the presence of sensitive periods in a child's first 5 years (i.e., when the child's brain is highly vulnerable to permanent dysfunction if certain experiences are absent) has been demonstrated for certain aspects of the sensory system, it has been more difficult to demonstrate in other aspects of development. Research has proven, for example, that acquisition of language primarily occurs up until age 10, mental development continues to be influenced by growth in the frontal cortex through age 16, and the emotional limbic system is not fully developed until puberty (Bruer, 1999; Nelson, 2000). It is difficult for neuroscience to delineate optimal parental strategies for enhancing brain development, partly because ethical issues make experimentation with humans difficult except in naturally occurring situations and partly because "optimal" parenting may vary significantly depending on children's biological or genetic predispositions and early experiences. However, many brain researchers have identified the importance of sensitive and attuned interactions with caregivers for optimal brain development and the deleterious effect of neglect and abuse on the developing brain (Perry, 1994, 1996, 1997; Siegel, 1999). For example, studies have found that abuse and neglect can destroy synapses. In one study that imaged the brains of abused children, it was found that compared with nonabused children, children who had been abused had smaller brain volumes, larger fluid-filled cavities of the brain, and smaller areas of connections between the left and right brain (De Bellis, Keshavan, Clark, Casey, Giedd, Borina, et al., 1999). As pointed out in Chapter 1, maternal depression can have a significant impact on infants' brains, and infants of depressed mothers show reduction in serotonin levels and increases in stress hormones such as cortisol and norepinephrine (Kennedy, Javanmard, & Vaccarino, 1997). In interactions with their depressed mothers, infants mirror the same activation of the right frontal hemisphere compared with the left frontal hemisphere, a pattern that appears to be permanent by 3 years of age. In other words, the dysynchrony of the hemispheric response does not change even when these infants are interacting with a very containing, animated, and responsive person (Field et al., 1988). These examples dramatically illustrate the effects of deleterious patterns of interaction on early brain development and biochemistry that can continue to have dramatic effects on functioning for a lifetime.

## Nature and Nurture

As discussed in Chapter 1, although most early intervention practitioners would acknowledge the importance of both nature (biology) and nurture (experience), it is still common to find individuals who adhere to a particular theoretical perspective that stresses the importance of one over the other in spite of a convincing literature that dramatically illustrates the contribution of both and the role of environment on eventual developmental outcome.

At conception the genes of the male and female mix and replicate to produce a unique human infant. These genes regulate the biochemistry of every cell in the body, guide other genetic activity, and affect the physical and behavioral characteristics of every individual, including the creation and modification of various brain structures. To make their influence more complicated, genes work in complex interactions with each other, with some acting continuously while some turn on and off and others are never expressed. The process of activating and expressing genes turns the genotype into a phenotype, or the DNA is transformed into actual tissue, with the environment or experience affecting the physiological mechanisms by which this happens (Pennington, 2002).

Many methods for evaluating genetic influences on development did not directly examine DNA sequences until the late 1990s. Instead, a number of areas of research have provided information on the importance of both genetic and environmental influences on development. These include twin studies and adoption studies and animal or comparative research. The findings from this research are briefly described in this section.

**_Twin and Adoption Studies_**     Twin and adoption studies have been used to study the relative contribution of the genotype and environment (Plomin, DeFries, McClearn, & Rutter, 1997). Identical or monozygotic (MZ) twins are genetically identical, whereas nonidentical, fraternal, or dyzygotic (DZ) twins share only about half their genes. It is therefore possible to compare the genetic influence of any behavioral trait or disorder by comparing the similarity of the trait for MZ versus DZ pairs. If MZ similarity is significantly greater than DZ similarity, a genetic influence is supported and its size estimated. When twins are brought up by adoptive parents, the characteristics of the adopted child are compared with both their natural and adoptive mothers. In other words, the adoptive parent is unrelated genetically but provides the rearing environment, whereas the biological parents contribute the genes but not the rearing environment. These methods have been useful in analyzing the occurrence of disorders and how severe they are. However, even if an estimate of heritability for a disorder is obtained, it does not indicate anything about how it will be displayed at later ages and does not take into account the possible influence of the environment. On the one hand, evidence indicates that characteristics—even when their heritability is high, such as with height and weight— can be influenced by the environment with improved nutrition and medical care. On the other hand, evidence exists that genetic influence on brain structure for disorders such as dyslexia and schizophrenia is likely to affect neuronal migration and connectivity at an early stage, and thus contribute to major ongoing negative effects on brain organization resulting in poorer coping ability (Shonkoff & Phillips, 2000).

Family studies have also been used to determine the occurrence of a trait or disorder among relatives. Many disorders, such as schizophrenia, bipolar disorder, dyslexia, ADHD, and autism spectrum disorders show familial links. Consequently, evidence supports the position that genetic influences underlie the familial liability of some disorders (Bradley, 2000). This does not prove that genetics totally cause a disorder, however, because it may still be mediated by parenting and other aspects of the environment.

The effects of severe deprivation have been studied in children who were raised in institutions and later adopted. There have been a number of studies of these adoptees, including early- and late-placed Romanian adoptees in the United Kingdom and Canada (Ames, 1997; Chisholm, 1998; Marcovitch, Cesaroni, Roberts, & Swanson, 1995; Marcovitch, Goldberg, Gold, Washington, Wasson, Krekewich, et al., 1997; O'Connor, Bredenkamp, Rutter, English, & Romanian Adoptees (ERA) Study Team, 1999; O'Connor, Rutter, Beckett, Keaveney, Kreppner, English, et al., 2000).

Early studies of children in institutions found that few of the children seemed to form attachments to caregivers in the institutions. This was due, in part, to the low caregiver-to-child ratio and also to the policies of many institutions in which caregivers were not allowed to develop close relationships with particular children. Although some of the children seemed clingy, many appeared to be emotionally detached (Tizard & Hodges, 1978; Tizard & Rees, 1975). Early studies of the development of children after placement in adoptive homes or foster homes demonstrated mixed findings. Goldfarb (1945 a, b) found that children who were moved from the orphanages into foster homes before 6 months of age did well, whereas those who were moved after 3 years of age had poor social relationships. For the latter group, about half the children had lived in three to four foster homes. In a study conducted at a similar time by Tizard (1977), however, it was found that 83% of mothers felt that their children were deeply attached to them by the time these children were 4½ years old.

Analysis of more recent studies has shown that children who are adopted from institutions in which they have little opportunity to attach do have the capacity to attach to their adoptive parents. The age of the child at adoption and the length of institutionalization does not relate to the ability to eventually attach. Characteristics of the child (e.g., IQ score, temperament, behavior problems) and of the family (e.g., family stress, low socioeconomic status, parents' availability to the child) relate to whether the child becomes attached, however (Chisholm, 1998; O'Connor et al., 1999, 2000; Marcovitz et al., 1995, 1997). Although these children did become attached, the process was often slower than typical, and a larger percentage than in the general population had disorganized attachments that could lead to psychological problems later.

***Animal Studies***    Because it is not possible to manipulate the rearing environments of children, researchers have carried out research instead with primates, rats, and other animals. Some of this research has explored the attachment relationships of mothers and infant monkeys and how experimental manipulation of them produced certain development effects. Removing the infant from the mother in the infant's first 6 months of life produced dramatic social and emotional impairments later, including social incompetence, stereotypic movements, and aggression. If the isolation occurred later, the impairments did not happen (Hofer, 1995). Even when the infant monkeys were reared with peers, similar effects were found. Other manipulations to the environment improved outcomes but did not prevent the difficulties totally (Suomi, 1995). For example, animals provided with vestibular stimulation did not develop rocking behaviors, and those reared by dogs were capable of social relationships, although not as complex as those developed by monkeys reared with their mothers. Alterations in brain chemistry have been found to contribute to these behavioral difficulties (Suomi, 1995).

In another manipulation study, infant monkeys were raised with their mothers and the social group for 3–6 months. The mother was then removed while the infant monkeys remained in the social groups. The infant monkeys showed extreme agitation that gave way to depression. They showed dramatic changes in numerous physiological measures including neurotransmitters, such as decreases in serotonin and dopamine and increases in norephinephrine (Reite & Boccia, 1994). These neurotransmitters are important for regulating a number of behavioral systems such as motor activity, sleep, aggression, attachment, anxiety, and memory. These systems have also been implicated in the development of a number of types of psychopathology such as affective disorders and schizophrenia (Bradley, 2000).

These findings, of course, cannot be directly applied to humans; however, they do suggest that infants from various species are particularly susceptible to disruption in the formation of social experiences during early development, and the disruptions may cause changes in various neurotransmitters that regulate the behavioral systems and may result in behavioral and emotional problems (Boccia & Pederson, 2001).

Clearly, then, both nature (i.e., genetics) and nurture (i.e., environment) play important roles in the development of children. Research on early brain development also suggests the importance of early experience on the structure and the functioning of the brain and evidence from adoption and animal studies shows how changes in the environment can enhance brain development and the ability of the child to develop the capacities described earlier in this chapter.

## THE MODEL FOR PROVIDING SERVICES FOR MULTI-RISK FAMILIES DESCRIBED IN THIS BOOK

Section I, Chapter 1, points out that research has clearly shown that the number and type of risk factors to which a child is exposed significantly affect his developmental outcome. Some of the effects of multiple risk factors on development include lowering of IQ score, reducing the incidence of secure attachment, and increasing behavioral, emotional, and social problems (Fergusson, Horwood, & Lynskey, 1995; Rutter, 1990, 2000 b; Sameroff & Fiese, 2000 b). Although the number of risk factors is important, it is clear that certain types of parent problems and challenges significantly affect the developmental outcomes of children and, in some cases, have been found to affect the neurochemistry of the brain.

Some of the categories of parental risks that are discussed in Chapter 1 include teenage parenthood; parental psychopathology, including depression and character disorders; parents with unresolved loss and trauma; substance abuse; abusive parents; and family dysfunction, particularly family violence. A number of parent characteristics including self-reflectivity and empathy for the child, planning and problem solving, emotion regulation, and beliefs about child rearing and attributions of the child—if compromised—can contribute to negative parenting interactions.

Throughout the book, two case studies are presented to illustrate the strategies described in each of the chapters. Although the children and families who are introduced in Chapter 4 face very different challenges, the children described in the two families are significantly at risk for long-term developmental difficulties. In Mark's case, his neurological difficulties, some issues related to his adoption, and difficulties his parents had with containing his behavior and emotions contributed to considerable behavior, academic, and social and emotional problems that affected his success in child care, school, and home environments. A variety of coordinated interventions were provided to help him to develop on a more positive developmental trajectory.

Nina and her children faced a significant number of risks that contributed to the need for longer term, comprehensive treatment of a number of aspects of the parent, child, and parent–child and family interactions. Although intervention was difficult and regressions frequently occurred, it was possible to return all four children to a more positive developmental course, the family was able to stay together, and the children were likely to avoid severe pathology in later years.

Although the intervention described in these case studies was complex and multidimensional, it did reduce the negative effects on the children and their parents and the enormous cost of social services that would likely to have been needed by the children in later years.

## THE IMPORTANCE OF INTERVENTION WITH MULTI-RISK FAMILIES AND ITS PLACE IN THE PREVENTION AND EARLY INTERVENTION SERVICE SYSTEM

Although the number of infants and young children exposed to high-risk conditions of parenting is only a small percentage of all infants and young children, research suggests that without support and intervention with their families, the percentage of mental health problems, psychiatric disorders, criminality, school dropout, and alcoholism that result will be a significant proportion of the disorders within the total population. As outlined in Chapter 9, in very high-risk situations, particularly if abuse and neglect are involved, as many as 80% of children may have disorganized attachment, a style of attachment that results in the development of various forms of psychopathology and a variety of behavioral and emotional problems at later ages (Greenberg, 1999; Lyons-Ruth & Jacobvitz, 1999). These problems are multigenerational. When parents have low self-reflectivity and empathy for their child, negative attributions and deleterious beliefs about child rearing as well as more severe psychological difficulties, particularly of more extreme forms such as clinical depression, psychosis, severe anxiety disorders, and character disorders, the parents are more likely to have children with disorganized attachments (Lyons-Ruth, Connell, Grunebaum, & Botein, 1990; Teti, Gelfand, Messinger, & Isabella, 1995). It has also been found that the results of parents' unresolved loss and trauma may contribute significantly to a display of helpless and frightened or hostile and frightening caregiver behavior leading to these attachment classifications (Lyons-Ruth, Melnick, Bronfman, Sherry, & Llanas, 2004).

Various community and societal characteristics make rearing children more difficult, such as the increasing level of poverty for many families, the need for both parents to be in the workforce, violent neighborhoods, unemployment, welfare cuts, and poor medical coverage. Also the incidents of abuse and neglect continue to rise. When children must be removed from their families and placed in foster care, outcomes for those children are often bleak. There are not enough foster homes available to meet the needs of these children, and child protective systems are already under enormous strain.

As outlined in Chapter 15, a study conducted by Patricia Crittenden (1992b) carried out in Florida with Child Protective Services identified a number of levels of family functioning. She indicated that for families that she identified as "inadequate," the children should be removed and that for families with more intense needs, extensive and long-term services are necessary. She also pointed out, however, that regardless of the level of risk, parents were typically only offered one parenting class that for many was totally ineffective and was unable to reduce the risks or to return the family to a level of functioning that would result in positive outcomes for the children. Consequently, the intergenerational repetition of nega-

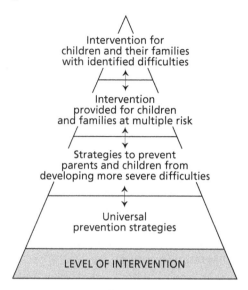

**Figure 16.1.** Services for multi-risk families within the service system.

tive parenting and, in its extreme, abuse and neglect continued with the majority of families. As shown in Figure 16.1, the interventions suggested in this book are designed for a relatively small group of families in any community at the highest levels of the triangle when children and families have already been identified as having multiple risks and intervention is required. It is critical, therefore, to consider the level of risk in each family and to provide the most appropriate services that are required to move them to a level of functioning that can prevent the development of psychopathology in the children and the repetition of deleterious parenting from one generation to the next. Clear evidence exists that approaches that are not focused on an identified difficulty, that are provided by untrained and unsupported staff, or are not comprehensive enough, are often insufficient to affect the functioning of most high-risk parents with their children or to improve the development of their children. These multi-risk families and their children cannot be ignored, however, for without effective interventions for this group, the promise of early intervention can never be fulfilled. Without intervention for very high-risk families with multiple risks, the costs to society can be enormous, both in terms of human suffering and in the financial costs of incarceration, welfare payments, policing in violent communities, and the intergenerational repetition of similar parenting problems.

## A RAY OF HOPE

Not all of the information on the outcomes of children at high risk is negative, however. For instance, evidence exists that children brought up in some of the most deprived situations of institutional care can become healthy and well-functioning when placed with warm and caring parents (Ames, 1997). As pointed out in Chapter 2, a variety of evidence points out that well conceptualized and operated early intervention programs and approaches to intervention can have significant effects on outcomes for parents and children including reducing child abuse and neglect, maternal depression, enhancing parents' interactions with their children, reducing disorganized attachment in children, and enhancing child development into adulthood.

Also, there is some evidence that certain interventions can affect brain functioning and structure and eliminate behavioral symptoms and psychopathology. For example, in one study, cognitive behavior therapy produced metabolic changes in brain structures and brain activation. Such changes can significantly affect the behavior and parenting of those who received the intervention (Schwartz, Stoessel, Baxter, Martin, & Phelps, 1996).

Many of the approaches suggested in this book have been demonstrated to enhance parenting interaction with their children and to bring about symptom reduction and improvement in the developmental outcomes of children. Various early intervention programs have also demonstrated that interventions provided by well-trained and supported interventionists that are intensive and prescriptive can enhance parenting interactions in high-risk families and improve the outcomes for their children (Brooks-Gunn, Klebanov, Liaw, & Spiker, 1993; Halpern, 2000; Kitzman, Olds, & Henderson, 1997). Some of the programs must be adapted to the needs of families in order to be seen as useful and acceptable by them. They need to be offered at appropriate hours in locations that are convenient, and respect the cultural beliefs of parents. Parents must be encouraged to contribute to the choice of goals and objectives and format, such as whether it uses an individual, family, or group format. Interventionists must also adjust the approach whenever possible to the style of information provision that the parents would find most helpful.

The work of service providers is difficult, and if properly funded and supported, it can be costly. The costs to society of not funding and supporting integrated, comprehensive services to children are beyond measure, however. These integrated interventions must become a vital part of the entire service system in order for all children and families to be served for the greater good of all society.

# REFERENCES

# REFERENCES

Aber, J.L., Belsky, J., Slade, A., & Crnic, K. (1999). Stability and change in mothers' representations of their relationship with their toddlers. *Developmental Psychology, 35,* 1038–1047.

Aber, J.L., Slade, A., Berger, B., Bresgi, I., & Kaplan, M. (1985). *The Parent Development Interview.* Unpublished manuscript, City University of New York.

Abrams, S.M., Field, T., Scafidi, F., & Prodromides, M. (1995). Newborns of depressed mothers. *Infant Mental Health Journal, 16,* 233–239.

Achenbach, T.M., Phares, V., Howell, C., Rauh, V., & Nurcombe, B. (1990). Seven-year outcome of the Vermont Intervention Program for low-birthweight infants. *Child Development, 61,* 1672–1681.

Ainsworth, M.D.S., Bell, S., & Stayton, D. (1979). Attachment as related to mother–infant interaction. In J.S. Rosenblatt, R.A. Hinde, C. Beer, & M. Busnel (Eds.), *Advances in the study of behavior* (Vol. 9, pp. 1–51). New York: Academic Press.

Ainsworth, M.D.S., Blehar, M.C., Waters, E., & Wall, S. (1978). *Patterns of attachment: A psychological study of the Strange Situation.* Mahwah, NJ: Lawrence Erlbaum Associates.

Alexander, J.F., Waldron, H.B., Barton, C., & Mas, C.H. (1989). The minimizing of blaming attributions and behaviors in delinquent families. *Journal of Consulting and Clinical Psychology, 57,* 19–24.

Allen, J.G. (2001). *Traumatic relationships and serious mental disorders.* New York: John Wiley & Sons.

Allen, M.C., Bruin, P., & Finlay, B. (1992). *Helping children by strengthening families: A look at family support programs.* Washington, DC: Children's Defense Fund.

Allen, M.C., Donohue, P.K., & Dusman, K. (1993). The limit of viability: Neonatal outcome of infants born at 22 to 25 weeks gestation. *New England Journal of Medicine, 329,* 1597–1601.

Allen, N.B., Lewinsohn, P.M., & Seeley, J.R. (1998). Prenatal and perinatal influences on risk for psychopathology in childhood and adolescence. *Development and Psychopathology, 10,* 513–529.

American Psychiatric Association. (2000). *Diagnostic and Statistical Manual of Mental Disorders* (4th ed., text revision). Washington, DC: Author.

Ames, E.W. (1997). *Development of Romanian orphanage children adopted in Canada.* Final Report to Human Resources Development Canada.

Andersson, H.W., Sommerfelt, K., Sonnander, K., & Ahlsten, G. (1996). Maternal child-rearing attitudes, IQ, and socioeconomic status as related to cognitive abilities of five-year-old children. *Psychological Reports, 79,* 3–14.

Andrews, S.R., Blumenthal, J.B., Johnson, D.L., Malone, P.E., & Wallace, D.B. (1982). The skills of mothering: A study of parent–child development centers. *Monographs of the Society for Research in Child Development, 47* (Serial No. 198).

Anisfeld, E., Casper, V., Nozyce, M., & Cunningham, N. (1990). Does infant carrying promote attachment? An experimental study of the effects of increased physical contact on the development of attachment. *Child Development, 61,* 1617–1627.

Anthony, E.J. (1982). The preventive approach to children at high risk for psychopathology and psychosis. *Journal of Children of Contemporary Society, 15,* 67–72.

Appleby, D.R., & Faragher, B. (1999). Mother–infant interaction in post-partum women with schizophrenia and affective disorders. *Psychological Medicine, 29,* 991–995.

Appleyard, K., Egeland, B., van Dulmen, M.H.M., & Sroufe, L.A. (2005). When more is not better: The role of cumulative risk in child behavior outcomes. *Journal of Child Psychology and Psychiatry, 46,* 235–245.

Arcia, E., Keyes, L. Gallagher, J.J., & Herrick, H. (1993). National portrait of sociodemographic factors associated with underutilization of services: Relevance to early intervention. *Journal of Early Intervention, 17,* 283–297.

Arend, R., Grove, F., & Sroufe, L.A. (1979). Continuity of individual adaptation from infancy to kindergarten: A predictive study of ego-resiliency and curiosity in preschoolers. *Child Development, 50,* 950–959.

Arnsten, A.F.T., & Goldman-Rakic, R.S. (1998). Noise stress impairs prefrontal cortical cognitive functioning in monkeys: Evidence for a hyperdopaminergic mechanism. *Archives of General Psychiatry, 55,* 362–368.

Aron, E.N. (2002). *The highly sensitive child: Helping our children thrive when the world overwhelms them.* New York: Broadway Books.

Astington, J.W., Harris, P.L., & Olson, D.R. (Eds.). (1988). *Developing theories of mind.* Cambridge: Cambridge University Press.

Astley, S.J., & Clarren, S.K. (1997). *Diagnostic guide for FAS and related conditions.* Seattle: University of Washington.

Atkinson, E., Vetere, A., & Grayson, K. (1995). Sleep disruptions in young children: The influence of temperament on the sleep patterns of preschool children. *Child Care, Health and Development, 21,* 233–246.

Ayoub, C., & Jacewitz, M.M. (1982). Families at risk of poor parenting: A model of service delivery, assessment, and intervention. *Child Abuse and Neglect, 6,* 351–358.

Badger, E. (1977). The infant stimulation/mother training project. In B.M. Caldwell & D.J. Stedman (Eds.), *Infant education: A guide for helping handicapped children in the first three years* (pp. 45–62). New York: Walker & Co.

Badger, E. (1979). Effects of a parent education program on teenage mothers and their children. In K.G. Scott, T. Field, & E. Robertson (Eds.), *Teenage mothers and their offspring* (pp. 15–28). New York: Grune & Stratton.

Baker, A.J.L. (1996). The HIPPY program in Yonkers, New York. In A.J.L. Baker, D.W. Britt, R. Halpern, & M. Westheimer (Eds.), *Family-oriented childhood programs: An in-depth case study of the Home Instruction Program for Preschool Youngsters.* New York: National Council of Jewish Women.

Baker, A.J.L., & Piotrkowski, C.S. (1995). *The Home Instruction Program for Preschool Youngsters: An innovative program to prevent academic underachievement: Final report.* New York: National Council of Jewish Women.

Baker, A.J.L. Piotrkowski, C.S., & Brooks-Gunn, J. (1998). Home visiting recent program evaluations: The Home Instruction Program for Preschool Youngsters (HIPPY). *The Future of Children, 9,* 116–133.

Bakermans-Kranenburg, M.J., & Juffer, F. (2005). Disorganized infant attachment and preventive interventions: A review and meta-analysis. *Infant Mental Health Journal, 26,* 191–216.

Bakermans-Kranenburg, M.J., Juffer, F., & van IJzendoorn, M.H. (1998). Interventions with video feedback and attachment discussions: Does type of maternal insecurity make a difference? *Infant Mental Health Journal, 19,* 202–219.

Bakermans-Kranenburg, M.J., van IJzendoorn, M.H., & Juffer, F. (2003). Less is more: Meta-analysis of sensitivity and attachment interventions in early childhood. *Psychological Bulletin, 129,* 195–215.

Ballard, M.E., Cummings, E.M., & Larkin, K. (1993). Emotional and cardiovascular responses to adults' angry behavior and to challenging tasks in children of hypertensive and normotensive parents. *Child Development, 64,* 500–515.

Barkley, R.A. (1998). A theory of ADHD: Inhibition, executive functions, self-control, and time. In R.A. Barkley, *Attention Deficit Hyperactivity Disorder: A handbook for diagnosis and treatment* (2nd ed., pp. 225–260). New York: Guilford Press.

Barkley, R.A. (2002). Major life activity and health outcomes associated with attention-deficit/hyperactivity disorder. *Journal of Clinical Psychiatry, 63 (Supp112),* 10–15.

Barkley, R.A., Fischer, M., Edelbrock, C.S., & Smallish, L. (1990). The adolescent outcome of hyperactive children diagnosed by research criteria: I. An 8-year prospective follow-up study. *Journal of the American Academy of Child and Adolescent Psychiatry, 29,* 546–557.

Barlow, J. (1997). *Systematic review of the effectiveness of parent training programmes in improving the behavior of 3- to 7-year-old children.* Oxford, England: Health Services Research Unit.

Barlow, J., & Coren, E. (2000). *Parenting programs for improving maternal psychosocial health (3).* Oxford, England: Cochrane Library.

Barnard, K.E. (1979). *Instructor's Learning Resource Manual.* Seattle, NCAST. University of Washington.

Barnard, K.E. (1998). Developing, implementing, and documenting interventions with parents and young children. In J.L. Berlin (Ed.), Opening the black box: Understanding how early intervention programs work (Special issue). *Zero to Three, 18,* 23–39.

Barnard, K.E., Bee, H.L., Booth, C.L., Mitchell, C.K., & Sumner, G.A. (1981). *Clinical nursing model for infants and their families.* Washington, DC: National Institute of Mental Health.

Barnard, K.E., Eyres, S., Lobo, M., & Snyder, C. (1983). An ecological paradigm for assessment and intervention. In T.B. Brazelton & B.M. Lester (Eds.), *New approaches to developmental screening of infants* (pp. 199–218). New York: Elsevier/North Holland.

Barnard, K.E., & Kelly, J.F. (1990). Assessment of parent–child interaction. In S.J. Meisels & J.P. Shonkoff (Eds.), *Handbook of early childhood intervention* (pp. 278–302). Cambridge: Cambridge University Press.

Barnard, K.E., Magyary, D., Sumner, G.A., Booth, C.L., Mitchell, S.K., & Spieker, S.J. (1988). Prevention of parenting altercations for women with low social support. *Psychiatry, 51,* 248–253.

Barquest, A., & Martin, H. (1984). Use of lay home visitors: A primary prevention strategy for families with a newborn. *The Personnel and Guidance Journal, 62,* 558–560.

Barrera, I., & Corso, R.M. (2003). *Skilled dialogue: Strategies for responding to cultural diversity in early childhood.* Baltimore: Paul H. Brookes Publishing Co.

Barrera, M.E., Doucet, D.A., & Kitching, K.J. (1990). Early home intervention and socio-emotional development of preterm infants. *Infant Mental Health Journal, 11,* 142–157.

Barrera, M.E., Rosenbaum, P.L., & Cunningham, C.E. (1986). Early home intervention with low birth-weight infants and their parents. *Child Development, 57,* 20–23.

Barrish, I.J., & Barrish, H.H. (1989). *Managing and understanding parental anger.* Kansas City, MO: Westport.

Barth, R.P., Hacking, S., & Ash, J. (1988). Preventing child abuse: An experimental evaluation of the Child Parent Enrichment Program. *Journal of Primary Prevention, 8,* 201–217.

Bauer, W.D., & Twentyman, C.T. (1985). Abusing, neglecting, and comparison mothers' responses to child-related and non-child-related stressors. *Journal of Consulting and Clinical Psychology, 53,* 335–343.

Baumrind, D. (1971). Current patterns of parental authority. *Developmental Psychology, 4,* 1–103.

Baumrind, D. (1973). The development of instrumental competence through socialization. In A.D. Pick (Ed.), *Minnesota Symposium on Child Psychology* (Vol. 7, pp. 3–46). Minneapolis: University of Minnesota Press.

Baumrind, D. (1989). Rearing competent children. In W. Damon (Ed.), *Child development today and tomorrow* (pp. 349–378). San Francisco: Jossey-Bass.

Bayley, N. (1933). *The California First-Year Mental Scale.* Berkeley: University of California Press.

Bayley, N. (1969). *Bayley Scales of Infant Development: Birth to two years.* New York: Harcourt Assessment.

Bayley, N. (1993). *Bayley Scales of Infant Development—Second Edition manual.* San Antonio, TX: Harcourt Assessment.

Beardslee, W.R., Bemporad, J., Keller, M.B., & Klerman, G.L. (1983). Children of parents with major affective disorder: A review. *American Journal of Psychiatry, 140,* 825–832.

Beck, A.T. (1973). *Depression, causes and treatment.* Philadelphia: University of Pennsylvania Press.

Beck, A.T. (1976). *Cognitive therapy and emotional disorders.* New York: International Universities Press.

Beck, A.T. (1987). Cognitive models of depression. *Journal of Cognitive Psychotherapy, 1,* 5–37.

Beckwith, L. (1988). Intervention with disadvantaged parents of sick preterm infants. *Psychiatry, 51,* 242–247.

Beckwith, L., Howard, J., Espinosa, M., & Tyler, R. (1999). Psychopathology, mother–child interaction, and infant development: Substance-abusing mothers and their offspring. *Development and Psychopathology, 11,* 715–726.

Beeghly, M., Brazelton, T.B., Flannery, K.A., Nugent, J.K., Barrett, D.E., & Tronick, E.Z. (1995). Specificity of preventative pediatric intervention effects in early infancy. *Developmental and Behavioural Pediatrics, 16,* 158–166.

Beiser, M. (1998). An update on the epidemiology of schizophrenia. *Canadian Journal of Psychiatry, 35,* 657–668.

Bell, R.Q., & Pearl, D. (1982). Psychosocial changes in risk groups: Implications for early interventions. *Prevention in Human Services, 1,* 45–59.

Bellak, L. (1989). *Ego Function Assessment (EFA).* Larchmont, NY: CPS, Inc.

Bellak, L., & Bellak, S. (1974). *Children's Apperception Test* (CAT).

Bellak, L., Hurvich, M., & Gediman, H. (1973). *Ego functions in schizophrenics, neurotics, and normals.* New York: John Wiley & Sons.

Belle, D. (1982). Social ties and social support. In D. Belle (Ed.), *Lives in stress: Women and depression* (pp. 133–144). Beverley Hills, CA: Sage Publications.

Belle, D. (1990). Poverty and women's mental health. *American Psychologist, 45,* 385–389.

Beller, E.K. (1983). The Philadelphia study: The impact of preschool on intellectual and socioemotional development. In consortium for longitudinal studies. *As the twig is bent: Lasting effects of preschool programs* (pp. 333–376). Mahwah, NJ: Lawrence Erlbaum Associates.

Belsky, J., Campbell, S.B., Cohn, J.F., & Moore, G. (1996). Instability of infant–parent attachment security. *Developmental Psychology, 32,* 921–924.

Belsky, J., Hsieh, K., & Crnic, K. (1998). Mothering, fathering, and infant negativity as antecedents of boys' externalizing problems and inhibition at 3 years: Differential susceptibility to rearing experience. *Development and Psychopathology, 10,* 301–319.

Belsky, J., & Isabella, R.A. (1988). Maternal, infant, and sociocontextual determinants of attachment security. In J. Belsky & Nezworski (Eds.), *Clinical implications of attachment* (pp. 41–94). Mahwah, NJ: Lawrence Erlbaum Associates.

Belsky, J., Rovine, M., Taylor, D.G. (1984). The Pennsylvania Infant and Family Development Project: III. The origins of individual differences in infant–mother attachment: Maternal and infant contributions. *Child Development, 55,* 718–728.

Benasich, A.A., & Brooks-Gunn, J. (1996). Maternal attitudes and knowledge of child rearing: Associations with family and child outcomes. *Child Development, 67,* 1186–1205.

Benasich, A.A., Brooks-Gunn, J., & Clewell, J.J. (1992). How do mothers benefit from early intervention programs? *Journal of Applied Developmental Psychology, 13,* 311–362.

Bendell, D., Field, T.M., Yando, R., Lange, C., Martinez, A., & Pickens, J. (1994). "Depressed" mothers' perception of their preschool children's vulnerability. *Child Psychiatry and Human Development, 24,* 183–190.

Benoit, D. (2001). Modified interaction guidance. *IMPrint, 32,* 6–10.

Benoit, D., Madigan, S., Lecce, S., Shea, B., & Goldberg, S. (2001). Atypical maternal behavior toward feeding-disordered infants before and after intervention. *Infant Mental Health Journal, 22,* 611–626.

Benoit, D., & Parker, K.C.H. (1994). Stability and transmission of attachment across three generations. *Child Development, 65,* 1444–1456.

Benoit, D., Parker, K.C.H., & Zeanah, C.H. (1997). Mothers' representations of their infants assessed prenatally: Stability and associations with infants' attachment classifications. *Journal of Child Psychology and Psychiatry, 38,* 307–314.

Berlin, L.J., O'Neal, C.R., & Brooks-Gunn, J. (1998). What makes early intervention programs work? *Zero to Three, 18,* 4–15.

Bernstein, D.P., & Fink, L. (1998). *Childhood Trauma Questionnaire Manual.* San Antonio, TX: The Psychological Corporation.

Bernstein, V.J. (1997). Using home videos to strengthen the parent–child relationship. *IMPrint, 20,* 2–5.

Bernstein, V.J. (2002). Standing firm against the forces of risk: Supporting home visiting and early intervention workers through reflective supervision. *IMPrint, 35,* 7–12.

Berrueta-Clement, J.R., Schweinhart, J., Barnett, W.S., Epstein, A., & Weikart, D.P. (1984). *Changed lives: The effects of the Perry Preschool Program on youths through age 19.* Ypsilanti, MI: High/Scope Press.

Berry, M. (1998). Getting to know you: Psychoeducational groups to counter social isolation of neglectful mothers. *Family Preservation Journal, 3,* 1–20.

Beutler, L.E., & Clarkin, J.F. (1990). *Systematic treatment selection: Towards targeted therapeutic interventions.* New York: Brunner/Mazel.

Bird, H.R., Canino, G., Rubio-Stipec, M., Gould, M.S., Ribera, J., Sesman, M., Woodberry, M., Huertas-Goldman, S., Pagan, A., Sanchez-Lacy, A., & Moscoso, M. (1988). Estimates of the prevalence of childhood maladjustment in a community survey in Puerto Rico: The use of combined measures. *Archives of General Psychiatry, 45,* 1120–1126.

Biringen, Z. (1990). Direct observation of maternal sensitivity and dyadic interactions in the home: Relations to maternal thinking. *Developmental Psychology, 26,* 278–284.

Biringen, Z., & Bretherton, I. (1988). *The insight/sensitivity scale for evaluating parent attachment interviews.* Unpublished manuscript, University of Colorado Health Sciences Center, Denver.

Biringen, Z., Robinson, J.L., & Emde, R.N. (1988/93). *Manual for scoring the Emotional Availability Scales.* Unpublished document, University of Colorado Health Sciences Center, Denver.

Bjöerkquist, K., Öesterman, K., & Kaukiainen, A. (1992). The development of direct and indirect aggressive strategies in males and females. In K. Bjöerkquist & P. Niemelae (Eds.), *Of mice and women: Aspects of female aggression* (pp. 51–64). San Diego: Academic Press.

Bjorklund, D.F. (2000). *Children's thinking: Developmental function and individual differences.* Scarborough, ON: Wadsworth.

Black, M.M., Dubowitz, H., Hutcheson, J., Berenson-Howard, J., & Starr, R.H. (1995). A randomized trial of home intervention for failure to thrive. *Pediatrics, 95,* 807–814.

Blackman, J.S. (2004). *101 defenses: How the mind shields itself.* New York: Brunner-Routledge.

Blair, C., & Ramey, C.T. (1997). Early intervention for low-birth-weight and premature infants and the path to second-generation research. In M. Guralnick (Ed.), *The effectiveness of early intervention* (pp. 77–98). Baltimore: Paul H. Brookes Publishing Co.

Bloom, S.L. (2002). Beyond the bevelled mirror: Mourning and recovery from childhood maltreatment. In J. Kauffman (Ed.), *Loss of the assumptive world: A theory of traumatic loss* (pp. 139–170). New York: Brunner-Routledge.

Bloomquist, M.L., & Schnell, S.V. (2002). *Helping children with aggression and conduct problems: Best practices for intervention.* New York: Guilford Press.

Boccia, M.L., & Pedersen, C. (2001). Animal models of critical and sensitive periods in social and emotional development. In D.B. Bailey Jr., J.T. Bruer, F.J. Symons, & J.W. Lichtman (Eds.), *Critical thinking about critical periods* (pp. 107–127). Baltimore: Paul H. Brookes Publishing Co.

Bohlin, G., & Hagekull, B. (1987). "Good mothering": Maternal attitudes and mother–infant interaction. *Infant Mental Health Journal, 8,* 352–363.

Bond, M.L., Gardner, S.T., Christian, J., & Sigal, J.J. (1983). Empirical study of self–rated defense styles. *Archives of General Psychiatry, 40,* 333–338.

Booth, C.L., Mitchell, S.K., Barnard, K.E., & Spieker, S.J. (1989). Development of maternal social skills in multiproblem families: Effects on the mother–child relationship. *Developmental Psychology, 25,* 403–412.

Booth, C.L., Rose-Krasnor, L., & Rubin, K.H. (1991). Relating preschoolers' social competence and their mothers' parenting behaviors to early attachment security and high-risk status. *Journal of Social and Personal Relationships, 8,* 363–382.

Bornstein, M.H., Mayes, L.C., & Park, J. (1998). Language, play, emotional availability, and acceptance in cocaine-exposed and non-cocaine-exposed children and their mothers. *Parole, 1,* 7–8.

Bornstein, M.H., Tamis-LeMonda, C.S., Pascual, L., Haynes, O.M., Painter, K.M., Galperin, C.Z., & Pêcheux, M. (1996). Ideas about parenting in Argentina, France, and the United States. *International Journal of Behavioral Development, 19,* 347–367.

Bowker, L.H., Arbitell, M., & McFerron, J.R. (1988). On the relationship between wife beating and child abuse. In K. Ylloe & M. Bograd (Eds.), *Feminist perspectives on wife abuse* (pp. 158–174). Beverly Hills, CA: Sage Publications.

Bowlby, J. (1958). The nature of the child's tie to the mother. *International Journal of Psychoanalysis, 39,* 350–373.

Bowlby, J. (1965). *Child care and the growth of love* (2nd ed.). New York: Penguin Books.

Boyce, W.T. (2001). *Biology and context: Symphonic causation and origins of childhood psychopathology*. Paper presented at the Millennium Dialogue on Early Child Development, University of Toronto.

Boyce, W.T., & Ellis, B.J. (2005). Biological sensitivity to context: 1. An evolutionary-developmental theory of the origins and functions of stress reactivity. *Development and Psychopathology, 17*, 271–301.

Boyle, M.H., Offord, D.R., Hofmann, H.G., Catlin, G.P., Byles, J.A., Cadman, D.T., Crawford, J.W., Links, P.S., Rae-Grant, N.I., & Szatmari, P. (1987). Ontario Child Health Study. *Archives of General Psychiatry, 44*, 826–831.

Bradley, E.J., & DeV. Peters, R. (1991). Physically abusive and nonabusive mothers' perceptions of parenting and child behavior. *American Journal of Orthopsychiatry, 61*, 455–460.

Bradley, S.J. (2000). *Affect regulation and the development of psychopathology*. New York: Guilford Press.

Brandenberg, H.A., Friedman, R.M., & Silver, S.E. (1990). The epidemiology of childhood psychiatric disorders: Prevalence findings from different studies. *Journal of the American Academy of Child and Adolescent Psychiatry, 29*, 76–83.

Brazelton, T.B. (1992). *Touchpoints: Your child's emotional and behavioural development*. Reading, MA: Addison–Wesley.

Breslau, N. (1995). Psychiatric sequelae of low birth weight. *Epidemiologic Reviews, 17*, 96–106.

Bretherton, I. (1991). Pouring new wine into old bottles: The social self as internal working model. In M.R. Gunnar & L.A. Sroufe (Eds.), *Self processes and development: The Minnesota Symposium on Child Development* (pp. 1–42). Mahwah, NJ: Lawrence Erlbaum Associates.

Bretherton, I., Biringen, Z., & Ridgeway, D. (1991). The parental side of attachment. In K.A. Pillemer & K. McCartney (Eds.), *Parent–child relations throughout life* (pp. 1–24). Mahwah, NJ: Lawrence Erlbaum Associates.

Bretherton, I., Biringen, Z., Ridgeway, D., Maslin, C., & Sherman, M. (1989). Attachment: The parental perspective. *Infant Mental Health Journal, 1*, 203–221.

Bricker, D., & Squires, J. (with assistance from Mounts, L., Potter, L., Nickel, R., Twombly, E., & Farrell, J.) (1999). *Ages and Stages Questionnaires® (ASQ): A parent completed, child-monitoring system* (2nd ed.). Baltimore: Paul H. Brookes Publishing Co.

Bridges, L.J., Denham, S.A., & Ganiban, J.M. (2004). Definitional issues in emotion regulation research. *Child Development, 75*, 340–345.

Briere, J., & Conte, J. (1993). Self-reported amnesia in adults molested as children. *Journal of Traumatic Stress, 6*, 21–31.

Brinich, E., Drotar, D., & Brinich, P. (1989). Security of attachment and outcome of preschoolers with histories of nonorganic failure to thrive. *Journal of Clinical Child Psychology, 18*, 142–152.

Brinker, R.P. (1992). Family involvement in early intervention: Accepting the unchangeable, changing the changeable, and knowing the difference. *Topics in Early Childhood Special Education,12*, 307–332.

Britner, P., & Reppucci, N.D. (1997). Prevention of child maltreatment: Evaluation of a parent education program for teen mothers. *Journal of Child and Family Studies, 6*, 165–175.

Brodsky, A.E. (1999). Making it: The components and process of resilience among urban, African-American, single mothers. *American Journal of Orthopsychiatry, 69*, 148–160.

Brody, G.H., Flor, D.L., & Gibson, N.M. (1999). Linking maternal efficacy beliefs, developmental goals, parenting practices, and child competence in rural single-parent African American families. *Child Development, 70*, 1197–1208.

Brody, G.H., & Schaffer, D.R. (1982). Contributions of parents and peers to children's moral socialization. *Developmental Review, 2*, 31–75.

Brody, G.H., Stoneman, Z., & McCoy, J.K. (1994a). Contributions of family relationships and child temperaments to longitudinal variations in sibling relationship quality and sibling relationship styles. *Journal of Family Psychology, 8*, 274–286.

Brody, G.H., Stoneman, Z., & McCoy, J.K. (1994b). Contributions of protective and risk factors to literacy and socioemotional competency in former Head Start children attending kindergarten. *Early Childhood Research Quarterly, 9*, 407–425.

Bronfenbrenner, U. (1979). *The ecology of human development.* Cambridge, MA: Harvard University Press.

Bronfman, E.T., Parsons, E., & Lyons-Ruth, K. (2000). *Atypical Maternal Behavior Instrument for Assessment and Classification (AMBIANCE)–Manual for coding disrupted affective communication.* Unpublished manuscript, Harvard Medical School, Boston, MA.

Brooks, C.S., Zuckerman, B., Bamforth, A., Cole, J., & Kaplan-Sanoff, M. (1994). Clinical issues related to substance-involved mothers and their infants. *Infant Mental Health Journal, 15,* 202–217.

Brooks, R., & Goldstein, S. (2001). *Raising resilient children.* New York: Contemporary Books.

Brooks-Gunn, J., Berlin, L.J., & Fuligni, A.S. (2000). Early childhood intervention programs: What about the family? In J.P. Shonkoff & S.J. Meisels (Eds.), *Handbook of early childhood intervention* (2nd ed., pp. 549–588). Cambridge: Cambridge University Press.

Brooks-Gunn, J., Klebanov, P.K., Liaw, F., & Spiker, D. (1993). Enhancing the development of low-birthweight, premature infants: Changes in cognition and behavior over the first three years. *Child Development, 64,* 736–753.

Brooks-Gunn, J., McCormack, M.C., Shapiro, S., Benasich, A.A., & Black, G.W. (1994). The effects of early-education intervention on maternal employment, public assistance, and health insurance: The Infant Health and Development Program. *American Journal of Public Health, 84,* 924–930.

Bruer, J.T. (1999). *The myth of the first three years: A new understanding of early brain development and lifelong learning.* New York: Free Press.

Bruschweiler-Stern, N., Harrison, A.M., Lyons-Ruth, K.C., Morgan, A.C., Nahum, J.P., Sander, L., Stern, D.N., & Tronick, E.Z. (1998). Reflections on the process of psychotherapeutic change as applied to medical settings. *Infant Mental Health Journal, 19,* 320–323.

Buck, M.J., Holden, G.W., & Stickels, A.C. (2000). *A longitudinal study of the onset and stability of disciplinary practices.* Austin: University of Texas.

Buell, B. (1952). *Community planning for human services.* New York: Columbia University Press.

Bugental, D.B. (1992). Affective and cognitive processes within threat-oriented family systems. In I.E. Sigel, A.V. McGillicuddy-DeLisi, & J.J. Goodnow (Eds.), *Parental belief systems: The psychological consequences for children* (2nd ed., pp. 219–248). Mahwah, NJ: Lawrence Erlbaum Associates.

Bugental, D.B. (1999, October). *Power-oriented cognitions as predictors of family violence.* Paper presented at the meeting of the Society for Experimental Social Psychology, St. Louis, MO.

Bugental, D.B., Blue, J., & Cruzcosa, M. (1989). Perceived control over caregiving outcomes: Implications for child abuse. *Developmental Psychology, 25,* 532–539.

Bugental, D.B., Blue, J., & Lewis, J. (1990). Caregiver beliefs and dysphoric affect directed to difficult children. *Developmental Psychology, 26,* 631–638.

Bugental, D.B., Ellerson, P.C., Lin, E.K., Rainey, B., Kokotovic, A., & O'Hara, N. (2002). A cognitive approach to child abuse prevention. *Journal of Family Psychology, 16,* 243–258.

Bugental, D.B., & Goodnow, J.J. (1998). Socialization processes. In W. Damon (Series Ed.) & N. Eisenberg (Vol. Ed.), *Handbook of child psychology: Vol. 3. Social, emotional, and personality development* (5th ed., pp. 389–462). New York: John Wiley & Sons.

Bugental, D.B., & Happaney, K. (2000). Parent–child interaction as a power contest. *Journal of Applied Developmental Psychology, 21,* 267–282.

Bugental, D.B., & Johnston, C. (2000). Parental and child cognition in the context of the family. *Annual Review of Psychology, 51,* 315–344.

Bugental, D.B., Kokotovic, A., O'Hara, N., Holmes, D., Ellerson, P.C., Lin, E.K., & Rainey, B. (2000). *A cognitive approach to child abuse prevention.* Unpublished manuscript, University of California, Santa Barbara.

Bugental, D.B., Lyon, J.E., Krantz, J., & Cortez, V. (1997). Who's the boss? Differential accessibility of dominance ideation in parent–child relationships. *Journal of Personality and Social Psychology, 72,* 1297–1369.

Bugental, D.B., Matyla, S.M., & Lewis, J. (1989). Parental attributions as moderators of affective communications. In D. Cicchetti & V. Carlson (Eds.), *Child maltreatment: Theory and research on the causes and consequences of child abuse and neglect* (pp. 254–279). Cambridge: Cambridge University Press.

Bugental, D.B., & Shennum, W.A. (1984). "Difficult" children as elicitors and targets of adult communication patterns: An attributional-behavioral transactional analysis. *Monographs of the Society for Research in Child Development, 49* (1, Serial No. 205). Chicago: University of Chicago Press.

Butler, E.A., Egloff, B., Wilhelm, F.H., Smith, N.C., Erickson, E.A., & Gross, J.J. (2003). The social consequences of expressive suppression. *Emotion, 3,* 48–67.

Byrd, M.E. (1997). Child–focused single home visiting. *Public Health Nursing, 14,* 313–322.

Bzoch, K.R., & League, R. (1971). *Receptive-Expressive Emergent Language (REEL) Scale.* Austin, TX: PRO-ED.

Caldwell, B.M., & Bradley, R.H. (1984). *Manual for the Home Observation for Measurement of the Environment.* Little Rock: University of Arkansas.

Calkins, S.D. (2002). Does aversive behavior during toddlerhood matter? The effects of difficult temperament on maternal perceptions and behavior. *Infant Mental Health Journal, 23,* 381–402.

Calkins, S.D., & Fox, N.A. (1992). The relations among infant temperament, security of attachment, and behavioral inhibition at twenty-four months. *Child Development, 63,* 1456–1472.

Campbell, F.A., & Ramey, E.F. (1994). Effects of early intervention on intellectual and academic achievement: A follow-up study of children from low-income families. *Child Development, 65,* 684–698.

Campbell, S.B. (1990). Longitudinal studies of active and aggressive preschoolers: Individual differences in early behavior and outcome. In D. Cicchetti & S.L. Toth (Eds.), *Internalizing and externalizing expressions of dysfunction* (pp. 57–90). Mahwah, NJ: Lawrence Erlbaum Associates.

Campbell, S.B. (1995). Behavioral problems in preschool children: A review of recent research. *Journal of Child Psychology and Psychiatric and Allied Disciplines, 36,* 113–149.

Campbell, S.B. (Ed.). (1996). *Journal of Clinical Child Psychology: Special Section on the Development of Psychopathology in Young Children, 25.*

Campbell, S.B., & Ewing, L.J. (1990). Follow-up of hard-to-manage preschoolers: Adjustment at age 9 and predictors of continuing symptoms. *Journal of Child Psychology and Psychiatry, 31,* 871–889.

Campbell, S.B., Cohn, J.F., & Meyers, T. (1995). Depression in first-time mothers: Mother-infant interaction and depression chronicity. *Developmental Psychopathology, 31,* 349–357.

Campbell, F.A., Helms, R., Sparling, J.J., & Ramey, E.F. (1998). Early-childhood programs and success in school: The Abecedarian Study. In W.S. Barnett & S.S. Boocock (Eds), *Early care and education for children in poverty: Promises, programs, and long-term results* (pp. 145–166). Albany, NY: State University of New York Press.

Campbell, S.B., Shaw, D.S., & Gilliom, M. (2000). Early externalizing behaviour problems: Toddlers and preschoolers at risk for later maladjustment. *Development and Psychopathology, 12,* 467–488.

Campos, J., & Stenberg, C.R. (1981). Perception, appraisal and emotion: The onset of social referencing. In M.E. Lamb & L.R. Sherrod (Eds.), *Infant social cognition* (pp. 273–314). Mahwah, NJ: Lawrence Erlbaum Associates.

Canadian Institute of Child Health (2001). *A preliminary evaluation of the Parent–Child Mother Goose Program as a family literacy program.* Ottawa: Canadian Institute of Child Health.

Carlson, B.E. (1984). Children's observations of interpersonal violence. In A.R. Roberts (Ed.), *Battered women and their families: Intervention strategies and treatment programs* (pp. 147–167). New York: Springer-Verlag.

Carlson, E.A., Jacobvitz, D., & Sroufe, L.A. (1995). A developmental investigation of inattentiveness and hyperactivity. *Child Development, 66,* 37–54.

Carlson, V., Cicchetti, D., Barnett, D., & Braunwald, K. (1989). Disorganized/disoriented attachment relationships in maltreated infants. *Developmental Psychology, 25,* 525–531.

Carpenter, M., Nagell, K., & Tomasello, M. (1998). Social cognition, joint attention, and communicative competence from 9 to 15 months of age. *Monographs of the Society for Research in Child Development, 63,* 176.

Carro, M.G., Grant, K.E., Gotlib, I.H., & Compas, B.E. (1993). Postpartum depression and child development: An investigation of mothers and fathers as sources of risk and resilience. *Development and Psychopathology, 5,* 567–579.

Carter, S., Osofsky, J.D., & Hann, D.M. (1990). *Maternal depression and affect in adolescent mothers and their infants.* Paper presented at the biennial meeting of the Society for Research in Child Development, Seattle.

Caruso, G.H. (1989). Optimum growth project: Support for families with young children. *Prevention in Human Services, 6,* 123–139.

Case, L., & Gang, B.C. (1999). *People with developmental disabilities as parents.* Toronto: Front Porch Publications.

Cashmore, J.A., & Goodnow, J.J. (1985). Agreement between generations: A two-way process approach. *Child Development, 56,* 493–501.

Caspi, A., & Bern, D.J. (1990). Personality continuity and change across the life course. In L.A. Pervin (Ed.), *Handbook of personality: Theory and research* (pp. 549–575). New York: Guilford Press.

Caspi, A., Henry, B., McGee, R.O., Moffitt, T.E., & Silva, P.A. (1995). Temperamental origins of child and adolescent behavior problems: From age three to age fifteen. *Child Development, 66,* 55–68.

Cassidy, B., Zoccolillo, M., & Hughes, S. (1996). Psychopathology in adolescent mothers and its effects on mother–infant interactions: A pilot study. *Canadian Journal of Psychiatry, 41,* 379–384.

Cassidy, J. (1986). The ability to negotiate the environment: An aspect of infant competence as related to quality of attachment. *Child Development, 57,* 331–337.

Cassidy, J., & Mahr, J.J. (2001). Unsolvable fear, trauma, and psychopathology: Theory, research and clinical considerations related to disorganized attachment across the lifespan. *Clinical Psychology: Science and Practice, 8,* 275–298.

Cassidy, J., & Shaver, P.H. (Eds.). (1999). *Handbook of attachment: Theory, research, and clinical applications.* New York: Guilford Press.

Ceballo, R., & McLoyd, V.C. (2002). Social support and parenting in poor, dangerous neighbourhoods. *Child Development, 73,* 1310–1321.

Chalmers, K.I. (1992). Giving and receiving: An empirically derived theory on health visiting practice. *Journal of Advanced Nursing, 17,* 1317–1325.

Chalmers, K.I. (1993). Searching for health needs: The work of health visiting. *Journal of Advanced Nursing, 18,* 900–911.

Chalmers, K.I. (1994). Difficult work: Health visitors' work with clients in the community. *International Journal of Nursing Studies, 31,* 168–182.

Chalmers, K.I., & Luker, K.A. (1991). The development of the health visitor–client relationship. *Scandinavian Journal of Caring Science, 5,* 33–41.

Chisholm, K. (1998). A three year follow-up of attachment and indiscriminate friendliness in children adopted from Romanian orphanages. *Child Development, 69,* 1092–1106.

Christensen, A., Phillips, S., Glasgow, R.E., & Johnson, S.M. (1983). Parental characteristics and interactional dysfunction in families with child behavior problems: A preliminary investigation. *Journal of Abnormal Child Psychology, 11,* 153–166.

Christopherson, E., & Mortweet, S.L. (2003). *Parenting that works: Building skills that last a lifetime.* Washington, DC: American Psychological Association.

Chu, J.A. (1992). The therapeutic roller coaster: Dilemmas in the treatment of childhood abuse survivors. *Journal of Psychotherapy Practice and Research, 1,* 351–370.

Cicchetti, D. (1991). Fractures in the crystal: Developmental psychopathology and the emergence of self. *Developmental Review, 11,* 271–287.

Cicchetti, D., & Barnett, D. (1991). Attachment disorganization in maltreated preschoolers. *Development and Psychopathology, 3,* 397–411.

Cicchetti, D., & Beeghly, M. (1987). Symbolic development in maltreated toddlers: An organizational perspective. In D. Cicchetti & M. Beeghly (Eds.), *New directions in child development: Vol. 36. Symbolic development in atypical children* (pp. 5–29). San Francisco: Jossey–Bass.

Cicchetti, D., & Olsen, K. (1990). The developmental psychopathology of child maltreatment. In M. Lewis & S.M. Miller (Eds.), *Handbook of developmental psychopathology* (pp. 261–280). New York: Plenum Press.

Cicchetti, D., & Rogosch, F.A. (1996). Equifinality and multifinality in developmental psychopathology. *Development and Psychopathology, 8,* 597–600.

Clark, G.N., & Seifer, R. (1983). Facilitating mother–infant communication: A treatment model for high-risk and developmentally delayed infants. *Infant Mental Health Journal, 4,* 67–81.

Clark, R. (1986). *The Parent Child Early Relational Assessment Manual.* University of Wisconsin Medical School, Madison, WI.

Clark, R. (2000). Maternal depression and the mother–infant relationship. *IMPrint, 27,* 100–103.

Cochran, M. (1990). Factors influencing social initiative. In M. Cochran, M. Larner, D. Riley, L. Gunnarsson, & C. Henderson, Jr. (Eds.), *Extending families: The social networks of parents and their children* (pp. 297–306). Cambridge: Cambridge University Press.

Cochran, M. (1991). Personal social networks as a focus of support. In D. Unger & D. Powell (Eds.), *Families as nurturing systems* (pp. 45–68). New York: Haworth Press.

Cochran, M., & Niego, S. (2002). Parenting and social networks. In M.H. Bornstein (Ed.), *Handbook of parenting* (2nd ed., Vol. 4). *Social conditions and applied parenting* (pp. 123–148). Mahwah, NJ: Lawrence Erlbaum Associates.

Cohen, L.J., & Slade, A. (2000). The psychology and psychopathology of pregnancy: Reorganization and transformation. In C.H. Zeanah Jr. (Ed.), *Handbook of infant mental health* (2nd ed., pp. 20–37). New York: Guilford Press.

Cohen, N.,& Radford, C. (1999). *The impact of early childhood intervention on early life.* Ottawa: NHRDP, Health Canada.

Cohen, N. J. (1996). Unsuspected language impairments in psychiatrically disturbed children: Developmental issues and associated conditions. In J.H. Beitchman, N.J. Cohen, M.M. Konstantareas, & R. Tannock (Eds.), *Language, learning, and behavior disorders* (pp. 105–127). Cambridge: Cambridge University Press.

Cohen, N.J., Lojkasek, M., Muir, E., Muir, R., & Parker, C.J. (2002). Six-month follow-up of two mother–infant psychotherapies: Convergence of therapeutic outcomes. *Infant Mental Health Journal, 23,* 361–380.

Cohen, N.J., Muir, E., Lojkasek, M., Muir, R., Parker, C.J., Barwick, M.B., & Brown, M. (1999). Watch, Wait, and Wonder: Testing the effectiveness of a new approach to mother–infant psychotherapy. *Infant Mental Health Journal, 20,* 429–451.

Cohler, B.J., & Paul, S. (2002). Psychoanalysis and parenthood. In M.H. Bernstein (Ed.), *Handbook of parenting (2nd Ed.): Vol. 3. Being and becoming a parent* (pp. 563–599). Mahwah, NJ: Lawrence Erlbaum Associates.

Cohler, B.J., Gallant, D.H., Grunebaum, H.U., Weiss, J.L., & Gamer, E. (1980). Child-care attitudes and development of young children of mentally ill and well mothers. *Psychological Reports, 46,* 31–46.

Cohler, B.J., Stott, F., & Musick, J. (1987, May). *From infancy to middle childhood.* Paper presented at Schizophrenic Consortium Conference on risk in infancy, Newport, RI.

Cohn, J.F., Matias, R., Tronick, E.Z., Connell, D., & Lyons-Ruth, K. (1986). Face-to-face interactions of depressed mothers and their infants. In E.Z. Tronick & T. Field (Eds.), *Maternal depression and infant disturbance* (pp. 31–45). San Francisco: Jossey-Bass.

Coie, J., Watt, N., West, P., Hawkins, K., Asarnow, J., Markham, H., Ramey, S., Shure, M., & Long, B. (1993). The science of prevention: A conceptual framework and some directions for a national research program. *American Psychologist, 48,* 1013–1022.

Cole, P.M., Martin, S.L., & Dennis, T.A. (2004). Emotion regulation as a scientific construct: Methodological challenges and directions for child development research. *Child Development, 75,* 317–333.

Coleman, P.K., & Karraker, K.H. (1998). Self-efficacy and parenting quality: Findings and future applications. *Developmental Review, 18,* 47–85.

Coll, G.C., Kagan, J., & Resnick, J.S. (1984). Behavioral inhibition in young children. *Child Development, 55,* 597–600.

Compas, B.E., Friedland-Bandes, R. Bastien, R., & Adelman, H.S. (1981). Parent and child causal attribution related to the child's clinical program. *Journal of Abnormal Child Psychology, 9,* 389–397.

Conduct Problems Prevention Research Group (1992). A developmental and clinical model for the prevention of conduct disorder: The FAST Track Program. *Development and Psychopathology, 4,* 509–527.

Conrad, B., Gross, D., Fogg, L., & Ruchala, P. (1992). Maternal confidence, knowledge, and quality of mother–toddler interactions: A preliminary study. *Infant Mental Health Journal,* *13,* 353–362.

Cook, S. (1979). *Parental conceptions of children and childrearing: A study of rural Maine parents.* Unpublished master's thesis, Tufts University, Medford, MA.

Cooper, P.J., & Murray, L. (1997). The impact of psychological treatments of postpartum depression on maternal mood and infant development. In L. Murray & P.J. Cooper (Eds.), *Postpartum depression and child development* (pp. 201–261). New York: Guilford Press.

Cooper, P.J., Murray, L., Wilson, A., Romaniuk, H. (2003a). Controlled trial of the short- and long-term effect of psychological treatment of post-partum depression. 1. Impact on maternal mood. *British Journal of Psychiatry, 182,* 412–419.

Cooper, P.J., Murray, L., Wilson, A., & Romaniuk, H. (2003b). Controlled trial of the short- and long-term effect of psychological treatment of post-partum depression. 2. Impact on the mother–child relationship and child outcome. *British Journal of Psychiatry, 182,* 420–427.

Cordero, J.F., Floyd, R.L., Martin, M.L., Davis, M., & Hymbaugh, K. (1994). Tracking the prevalence of FAS. *Alcohol and Research World, 18,* 82–85.

Corral-Verdugo, V., Frias-Armenta, M., Romero, M., & Munoz, A. (1995). Validity of a scale measuring beliefs regarding the "positive" effects of punishing children: A study of Mexican mothers. *Child Abuse and Neglect, 19,* 669–679.

Cortez, V.L., & Bugental, D.B. (1995). Priming of perceived control in young children as a buffer against fear-inducing events. *Child Development, 66,* 687–696.

Costello, E.J. (1989). Developments in child psychiatric epidemiology. *Journal of the American Academy of Child and Adolescent Psychiatry, 28,* 851–888.

Courtois, C.A. (1999). *Recollections of sexual abuse: Treatment principles and guidelines.* New York: W.W. Norton.

Cox, J.L., Holden, M.J., & Sagovsky, R. (1987). Detection of postnatal depression: Development of the 10-item Edinburgh Postnatal Depression Scale. *British Journal of Psychiatry, 150,* 782–786.

Cramer, B., Robert-Tissot, C., Stern, D.N., Serpa-Rusconi, S., De Muratt, M., Besson, G., Palacio-Espasa, F., Bachmann, J.P., Knauer, D., Berney, C., & D'Arcis, U. (1990). Outcome evaluation in a brief mother–infant psychotherpay: A preliminary report. *Infant Mental Health Journal, 11,* 278–300.

Crittenden, P.M. (1981). Abusing, neglecting, problematic, and adequate dyads: Differentiating by patterns of interaction. *Merrill-Palmer Quarterly, 27,* 201–218.

Crittenden, P.M. (1985). Maltreated infants: Vulnerability and resilience. *Journal of Child Psychology and Psychiatry, 26,* 85–96.

Crittenden, P.M. (1992a). Quality of attachment in the preschool years. *Development and Psychopathology, 4,* 209–241.

Crittenden, P.M. (1992b). The social ecology of treatment: Case study of a service system for maltreated children. *American Journal of Orthopsychiatry, 62,* 22–34.

Crittenden, P.M. (1995). *Coding manual: Classification of quality for preschool-aged children.* Miami, FL: Family Relations Institute.

Crittenden, P.M. (1997a). Toward an integrative theory of trauma: A dynamic–motivational approach. In D. Cicchetti & S. Toth (Eds.), *The Rochester Symposium in Developmental Psychopathology: Vol. 10. Risk, trauma, and mental process* (pp. 34–84). Rochester, NY: University of Rochester Press.

Crittenden, P.M. (1997b). Truth, error, and deception: The application of attachment theory to the assessment and treatment of psychological disorder. In S.M. Clancy Dollinger & L.F. DiLalla (Eds.), *Assessment and intervention across the life span* (pp. 35–76). Mahwah, NJ: Lawrence Erlbaum Associates.

Crittenden, P.M. (1999). Child neglect: Causes and contributors. In H. Dubowitz (Ed.), *Neglected children: Research, practice, and policy* (pp. 47–68). Thousand Oaks, CA: Sage Publications.

Crittenden, P.M., Lang, C., Claussen, A.H., & Partridge, M.F. (2000). Relations among mothers' dispositional representations of parenting. In P.M. Crittenden & A.H. Claussen (Eds.), *The organization of attachment relationships: Maturation, culture, and context* (pp. 214–233). Cambridge: Cambridge University Press.

Crnic, K., Greenberg, M., Ragozin, A., Robinson, N., & Basham, R. (1983). Effects of stress and social support on mothers of premature and full-term infants. *Child Development, 54,* 209–217.

Crnic, K., Greenberg, M., & Slough, T. (1986). Early stress and social support influences on mothers' and high-risk infants' functioning in late infancy. *Infant Mental Health Journal, 7,* 19–33.

Crockenberg, S.B. (1981). Infant irritability, mother responsiveness, and social support influences on security of infant–mother attachment. *Child Development, 52,* 857–865.

Crockenberg, S.B. (1987). Predictors and correlates of anger toward and punitive control of toddlers by adolescent mothers. *Child Development, 58,* 964–975.

Crockenberg, S. (1988). Social support and parenting. In W. Fitzgerald, B. Lester, & M. Yogmans (Eds.), *Research on support for parents and infants in the postnatal period* (pp. 67–92). New York: Ablex.

Crockenberg, S., & Litman, C. (1990). Autonomy as competence in 2-year-olds: Maternal correlates of child defiance, compliance, and self-assertion. *Developmental Psychology, 26,* 961–971.

Culp, A.M., Culp, R.E., Blankemeyer, M., & Passmark, L. (1998). Parent Education Home Visitation Program: Adolescent and nonadolescent mother comparison after six months of intervention. *Infant Mental Health Journal, 19,* 111–123.

Cummings, E.M., & Cichetti, D. (1990). Towards a transactional model of relations between attachment and depression. In M.T. Greenberg, D. Cicchetti, & E.M. Cummings (Eds.), *Attachment and the preschool years: Theory, research and intervention* (pp. 339–372). Chicago: University of Chicago Press.

Cummings, E.M., & Cummings, J.S. (2002), Parenting and attachment. In M.H. Bernstein (Ed.), *Handbook of Parenting,* (Vol. 5, pp. 35–38), Mahwah, N.J.: Lawrence Erlbaum Associates.

Cummings, E.M., & Davies, P. (1994a). *Children and marital conflict: The impact of family dispute and resolution.* New York: Guilford Press.

Cummings, E.M., & Davies, P. (1994b). Maternal depression and child development. *Journal of Child Psychology and Psychiatry, 35,* 73–112.

Cummings, E.M., & Davies, P. (1996). Emotional security as a regulatory process in normal development and the development of psychopathology. *Development and Psychopathology, 8,* 123–140.

Cummings, E.M., Davies, P.T., & Campbell, S.B. (2000). *Developmental psychopathology and family process: Theory research, and clinical implications.* New York: Guilford Press.

Cummings, E.M., & O'Reilly, A. (1997). Fathers in family context: Effects of marital quality on child adjustment. In M.E. Lamb (Ed.), *The role of the father in child development* (3rd ed., pp. 49–65). New York: John Wiley & Sons.

Cummings, E.M., & Zahn-Waxler, C. (1992). Emotions and the socialization of aggression: Adults' angry behavior and children's arousal and aggression. In A. Fraczek & H. Zumley (Eds.), *Socialization and aggression* (pp. 61–82). New York: Springer-Verlag.

Cutrona, C., & Russell, D. (1989). The provision of social relationships and adaptation to stress. *Advances in Personal Relationships, 1,* 37–67.

Cutrona, C.E., & Troutman, B.R. (1986a). Causal attributions and perinatal depression. *Journal of Abnormal Psychology, 92,* 161–172.

Cutrona, C.E., & Troutman, B.R. (1986b). Social support, infant temperament, and parenting self-efficacy: A mediational model of postpartum depression. *Child Development, 57,* 1507–1518.

D'Angelo, E.J. (1986). Security of attachment in infants with schizophrenic, depressed, and unaffected mothers. *Journal of Genetic Psychology, 147,* 421–424.

Dail, P.W. (1990). The psychosocial context of homeless mothers with young children: Program and policy implications. *Child Welfare, 69,* 291–308.

Dale, P.S., Crain-Thoreson, C., Notari-Syverson, A., & Cole, K. (1996). Parent–child book reading as an intervention technique for young children with language delays. *Topics in Early Childhood Special Education, 16,* 213–235.

Daro, D. (1993). Child maltreatment research: Implications for program design. In D. Cicchetti & S. Toth (Eds.), *Child abuse, child development, and social policy* (pp. 331–367). Norwood, NJ: Ablex.

Davidson, R.J., & Fox, N.A. (1989). Frontal brain asymmetry predicts infants' response to maternal separation. *Journal of Abnormal Psychology, 98,* 127–131.

Davidson-Baden, A.D., & Howe, G.W. (1992). Mothers' attributions and expectancies regarding their conduct-disordered children. *Journal of Abnormal Child Psychology, 20,* 467–485.

Davies, D. (1999). *Child development: A practitioner's guide.* New York: Guilford Press.

Davis, P.W. (1999). Corporal punishment cessation: Social context and parents' experiences. *Journal of Interpersonal Violence, 14,* 492–510.

Dawson, G., & Osterling, J. (1997). Early intervention in autism. In M.J. Guralnick (Ed.), *The effectiveness of early intervention* (pp. 307–326). Baltimore: Paul H. Brookes Publishing Co.

Dawson, G., Ashman, S.B., Panagiotides, H., Hessl, D., Self, J., Yamada, E., & Embry, L. (2003). Preschool outcomes of children of depressed mothers: Role of maternal behavior, contextual risk, and children's brain activity. *Child Development, 74,* 1158–1175.

Dawson, G., Frey, K., Panagiotides, H., Yamada, E., Hessl, D., & Osterling, J. (1999). Infants of depressed mothers exhibit atypical frontal electrical activity during interactions with mother and with a familiar, non-depressed adult. *Child Development, 70,* 1058–1066.

Dawson, G., Frey, K., Self, J., Panagiotides, H., Hessl, D., Yamada, E., & Rinaldi, J. (1999). Frontal brain electrical activity in infants of depressed and nondepressed mothers: Relations to variations in infant behavior. *Development and Psychopathology, 11,* 589–605.

Dawson, G., Grofer Klinger, L., Panagiotides, H., Hill, D., & Spieker, S. (1992). Frontal lobe activity and affective behaviour of infants of mothers with depressive symptoms. *Child Development, 63,* 725–737.

Dawson, G., Panagiotides, H., Klinger, L.G., & Hill, D. (1992). The role of frontal lobe functioning in the development of infant self-regulatory behavior. *Brain and Cognition, 20,* 152–175.

De Bellis, M.D. (2001). Developmental traumatology: The psychobiological development of maltreated children and its implications for research, treatment, and policy. *Development and Psychopathology, 3,* 539–564.

De Bellis, M.D., Keshavan, M.S., Clark, D.B., Casey, B.J., Giedd, J.N., Boring, A.M., Frustaci, K., & Ryan, N.D. (1999). Developmental traumatology: II. Brain development. *Biological Psychiatry, 45,* 1271–1284.

De Wolff, M., & van IJzendoorn, M.H. (1997). Sensitivity and attachment: A meta-analysis on parental antecedents of infant attachment. *Child Development, 68,* 571–591.

DeGangi, G.A., & Greenspan, S.I. (1997). The effectiveness of short-term interventions in the treatment of inattention and irritability in toddlers. *Journal of Developmental and Learning Disabilities, 1,* 277–298.

DeGangi, G.A., DiPietro, J.A., Greenspan, S.A., & Porges, S.W. (1991). Psychophysiological characteristics of the regulatory disordered infant. *Infant Behavior and Development, 14,* 37–50.

DeKlyen, M. (1996). Disruptive behavior disorders and intergenerational attachment patterns. A comparison of clinic-referred and normally functioning preschoolers and their mothers. *Journal of Consulting and Clinical Psychology, 64,* 357–365.

de la Cuesta, C. (1994a). Marketing: A process in health visiting. *Journal of Advanced Nursing, 19,* 347–353.

de la Cuesta, C. (1994b). Relationships in healthy visiting: Enabling and mediating. *International Journal of Nursing Studies, 31,* 451–459.

DeLoache, J.S., Miller, K.F., & Pierroutsakos, S.L. (1998). Reasoning and problem solving. In W. Damon (Series Ed.), D. Kuhn & R.S. Siegler (Vol. Eds.), *Handbook of child psychology: Vol 2. Cognitive, language and perceptual development* (pp. 801–850). New York: John Wiley & Sons.

DeMulder, E.K., & Radke-Yarrow, M. (1991). Attachment with affectively ill and well mothers: Concurrent behavioral correlates. *Development and Psychopathology, 3,* 227–242.

Derryberry, D., & Reed, M.A. (1996). Regulatory processes and the development of cognitive representations. *Development and Psychopathology, 8,* 215–234.

Deseiden, D., Teti, D.M., & Corns, K.M. (1995). Maternal working models of attachment, marital adjustment and parent–child relationships. *Child Development, 66,* 1504–1518.

Dimigen, G., Del Priore, C., Butler, S., Evans, S., Ferguson, L., & Swan, M. (1999). Psychiatric disorder among children at the time of entering local authority care: A questionnaire survey. *British Medical Journal, 319,* 675–676.

Dinkmeyer, D., McKay, G.D., & Dinkmeyer, J.S. (1989). *Early childhood STEP.* New York: American Guidance Service.

Dishbrow, M.A., Doerr, H., & Caulfield, C. (1977). Measuring the components of parents' potential for child abuse and neglect. *International Journal of Child Abuse and Neglect, 1,* 279–296.

Dishion, T.J., French, D.C., & Patterson, G.R. (1995). The development and ecology of antisocial behavior. In D. Cicchetti & D.J. Cohen (Eds.), *Developmental psychopathology: Vol. 2. Risk, disorder, and adaptation* (pp. 421–471). New York: John Wiley & Sons.

Dix, T.H., & Grusec, J.A. (1985). Parent attribution processes in the socialization of children. In I.E. Sigel (Ed.), *Parental belief systems: The psychological consequences for children* (pp. 201–233). Mahwah, NJ: Lawrence Erlbaum Associates.

Dix, T.H., & Lochman, J.E. (1990). Social cognition and negative reactions to children: A comparison of mothers of aggressive and nonaggressive boys. *Journal of Social and Clinical Psychology, 36,* 418–438.

Dockett, S., & Smith, I. (1995, March). *Children's theories of mind and their involvement in complex shared pretense.* Poster presented at the biennial meeting at the Society for Research in Child Development, Indianapolis.

Dodge, K.A. (1986). A social information processing model of social competence in children. In M. Perlmutter (Ed.), *Minnesota symposium on child psychology* (Vol. 18, pp. 77–125). Mahwah, NJ: Lawrence Erlbaum Associates.

Dodge, K.A. (1993). Social-cognitive mechanisms in the development of conduct disorder and depression. *Annual Review of Psychology, 44,* 559–584.

Dodge, K.A., Murphy, R.R., & Buchsbaum, K. (1984). The assessment of intention-cue detection skills in children: Implications for developmental psychopathology. *Child Development, 55,* 163–173.

Dohrenwend, B.S., Dohrenwend, B.P., Dodson, M., & Shrout, P.E. (1984). Symptoms, hassles, social supports, and life events: Problem of confounded measures. *Journal of Abnormal Psychology, 93,* 222–230.

Doll, E.A. (1965). *Vineland Social Maturity Scale: Condensed manual of directions.* Circle Pines, MN: American Guidance Service.

Donovan, W.L., & Leavitt, L.A. (1985). Stimulating conditions of learned helplessness: The effects of interventions and attributions. *Child Development, 56,* 594–603.

Donovan, W.L., Leavitt, L.A., & Walsh, R.O. (1990). Maternal self-efficacy: Illusory control and its effects on susceptibility to learned helplessness. *Child Development, 61,* 1638–1647.

Dornbusch, S.M., Ritter, P.L., Leiderman, P.H., Roberts, D.F., & Fraleigh, M.J. (1987). The relation of parenting style to adolescent school performance. *Child Development, 58,* 1244–1257.

Downie, A.L.S., Jakobson, L.S., Frisk, V., & Ushycky, I. (2003). Periventricular brain injury, visual motion processing, and reading and spelling abilities in children who were extremely low birthweight. *Journal of the International Neuropsychological Society, 9,* 440–449.

Dressler, W. (1985). Extended family relationships, social support, and mental health in a southern black community. *Journal of Health and Social Behavior, 26,* 39–48.

Dryden, W. (Ed.). (1992). *Integrative and eclectic therapy: A handbook.* Buckingham: Open University Press.

Dubow, E.F., Edwards, S., & Ippolito, M.F. (1997). Life stressors, neighbourhood disadvantage, and resources: A focus on inner-city children's adjustment. *Journal of Clinical Child Psychology, 26,* 130–144.

Dubrow, N.F., & Garbarino, J. (1989). Living in the war zone: Mothers and young children in a public housing development. *Child Welfare, 68,* 3–20.

Ducharme, J.M., Atkinson, L., & Poulton, L. (2000). Success-based, noncoercive treatment of oppositional behavior in children from violent homes. *Journal of the American Academy of Child & Adolescent Psychiatry, 39,* 995–1004

Ducharme, J.M, & Drain, T. (2004). Treatment and generalization effects of errorless academic compliance training for children with autism. *Journal of the American Academy of Child and Adolescent Psychiatry, 43,*163–171.

Ducharme, J.M, & Popynick, M. (1993). Errorless compliance to parental requests: Treatment effects and generalization. *Behavior Therapy, 24,* 209–226.

Ducharme, J.M., Spencer, T., Davidson, A., & Rushford, N. (2002). Errorless compliance training: Building a cooperative relationship between brain-injured parents at risk for maltreatment and their oppositional children. *American Journal of Orthopsychiatry, 72,* 585–595.

Dumas, J., & Wahler, F.G. (1985). Indiscriminate mothering as a contextual factor in aggressive-oppositional child behavior: "Damned if you do and damned if you don't." *Journal of Abnormal Child Psychology, 13,* 1–18.

Duncan, B.B., Forness, S.R., & Hartsough, C. (1995). Students identified as seriously emotionally disturbed in school-based day treatment: Cognitive, psychiatric, and special education characteristics. *Behavioral Disorders, 20,* 238–252.

Dunn, M.E., Burbine, T., Bowers, C.A., & Tantleff-Dunn, S. (2001). Moderators of stress in parents of children with autism. *Community Mental Health Journal, 37,* 39–52.

Dunn, L.M., & Markwardt, F.C. (1970). *Peabody Individual Achievement Test.* Circle Pines, MN: American Guidance Service.

Dunst, C.J., & Trivette, C.M. (1986). Looking beyond the parent–child dyad for the determinants of maternal styles of interaction. *Infant Mental Health Journal, 7,* 69–80.

Dunst, C., Trivette, C., & Thompson, R. (1991). Supporting and strengthening family functioning: Toward a congruence between principles and practice. *Prevention in Human Services, 9,* 19–43.

Dyregrov, A. (1998). Psychological debriefing—an effective method? *Traumatology, 4,* 3–12.

East, P.L., Malthaws, K.L., & Felice, M.E. (1994). Qualities of adolescent mothers' parenting. *Journal of Adolescent Health, 15,* 163–168.

Egeland, B., & Erickson, M.F. (2004). Lessons from STEEP: Linking theory, research, and practice for the well-being of infants and parents. In A.J. Sameroff, S.C. McDonough, & K.L. Rosenbaum (Eds.), *Treating parent–infant relationship problems: Strategies for intervention* (pp. 213–242). New York: Guilford Press.

Egeland, B., Weinfield, N.C., Bosquet, M., & Cgebg, V.K. (2000). Remembering, repeating, and working through: Lessons from attachment-based interventions. In J.D. Osofsky & H.E. Fitzgerald (Eds.), *WAIM handbook of infant mental health: Vol. 4. Infant mental health in groups at high risk* (pp. 35–89). New York: John Wiley & Sons.

Eisenberg, N., Cumberland, A., & Spinrad, T.L. (1998). Parental socialization of emotions. *Psychological Inquiry, 9,* 241–273.

Eisenberg, N., & Fabes, R.A. (1994). Mothers' reactions to children's negative emotions: Relations to children's temperament and anger behaviour. *Merrill-Palmer Quarterly. Special Issue: Children's emotions and social competence, 40,* 138–156.

Eisenberg, N., Fabes, R.A., Guthrie, I.K., & Reiser, M. (2000). Dispositional emotionality and regulation: Their role in predicting quality of social functioning. *Journal of Personality Child Social Psychology, 78,* 136–157.

Ekman, P. (1984). Expression and the nature of emotion. In K.R. Scherer & P. Ekman (Eds.), *Approaches to emotion* (pp. 319–343). Mahwah, NJ: Lawrence Erlbaum & Associates.

Ekman, P. (1992). Facial expression of emotion: New findings, new questions. *Psychological Science, 3,* 34–38.

Ellison, C.G., Bartowski, J.P., & Segal, M.L. (1996). Conservative Protestantism and the parental use of corporal punishment. *Social Forces, 74,* 1003–1028.

Ellsworth, P.C. (1994). Some reasons to expect universal antecedents of emotions. In P. Ekman & R.J. Davidson (Eds.), *The nature of emotion: Fundamental questions* (pp. 150–184). New York: Oxford University Press.

Elman, J.L., Bates, E.A., Johnson, M.H., Karmiloff-Smith, A., Parisi, D., & Phinkett, K. (1996). *Rethinking innateness: A connectionist perspective on development.* Cambridge, MA: MIT Press.

Enkin, M., Keirese, M., Renfrew, M., & Neilson, J. (2000). *A guide to effective care in pregnancy and childbirth* (2nd ed.). Toronto, ON: Oxford University Press.

Epstein, A.S. (1979, March). *Pregnant teenagers' knowledge of infant development.* Paper presented at the meeting of the Society for Research in Child Development, San Francisco.

Epstein, A.S. (1980a). *Assessing the child development information needed by adolescent parents with very young children* (Final report, Grant No. 90-C-1341, U.S. Dept. HHS). Washington, DC: Department of Health, Education, and Welfare.

Epstein, A.S. (1980b). New insights into problems of adolescent parenthood. *Bulletin of High/Scope Educational Research Foundation, 5,* 6–8.

Erel, O., & Burman, B. (1995). Interrelatedness of marital relations and parent–child relations: A meta-analytic review. *Psychological Bulletin, 118,* 108–132.

Erickson, M. (1991). *Evaluating early intervention services: A cost-effectiveness analysis.* Unpublished doctorial dissertation, Brandeis University, Waltheim, MA.

Erickson, M., & Kurz-Riemer, K. (1999). *Infants, toddlers, and families.* New York: Guilford Press.

Erickson, M.F., Sroufe, L.A., & Egeland, B. (1985). The relationship between quality of attachment and behavior problems in preschool in a high-risk sample. *Monographs of the Society for Research in Child Development, 50* (1–2, Serial No. 209), 147–166.

Esser, G., Schmidt, M.H., & Woerner, W. (1990). Epidemiology and course of psychiatric disorders in school-age children: Results of a longitudinal study. *Journal of Child Psychology and Psychiatry, 31,* 243–263.

Fabes, R.A., Eisenberg, N., Karbon, M., & Bernzweig, J. (1994). Socialization of children's vicarious emotional responding and prosocial behaviour: Relations with mothers' perceptions of children's emotional reactivity. *Developmental Psychology, 30,* 44–55.

Fagot, B.I. (1997). Attachment, parenting, and peer interactions of toddler children. *Developmental Psychology, 33,* 489–499.

Fagot, B.I., Gauvain, M., & Kavanagh, K. (1996). Infant attachment and mother–child problem-solving: A replication. *Journal of Social and Personal Relationships, 13,* 295–302.

Fairbairn, W. (1954). *An object relations theory of the personality.* New York: Basic Books.

Farran, D. (2000). Another decade of intervention for children who are low income or disabled: What do we know now? In J.P. Shonkoff & S.J. Meisels (Eds.) *Handbook of early childhood intervention* (2nd ed.) (pp. 510–548). Cambridge, MA: Cambridge University Press.

Farran, D., Kasari, C., Comfort, M., & Jay, S. (1986). *Parent/Caregiver Interaction Scale.* Chapel Hill: University of North Carolina Press.

Fava-Vizzielo, G., Antonioli, M.E., Cocci, V., & Invernizzi, R. (1993). From pregnancy to motherhood: The structure of representative and narrative change. *Infant Mental Health Journal, 14,* 4–16.

Feldman, L.A. (1995). Valence focus and arousal focus: Individual differences in the structure of affective experience. *Journal of Personality and Social Psychology, 69,* 153–166.

Feldman, R., & Guttman, H.A. (1984). Families of borderline patients: Literal minded parents, borderline parents, and parental protectiveness. *American Journal of Psychiatry, 141,* 1392–1396.

Fendrich, M., Warner, V., & Weissman, M.M. (1990). Family risk factors, parental depression, and psychopathology in offspring. *Developmental Psychology, 26,* 40–50.

Fenichel, E. (Ed.). (1992). *Learning through supervision and mentorship to support the development of infants, toddlers and their families: A sourcebook.* Baltimore: Zero to Three.

Fergusson, D.M., Horwood, L.J., & Lynskey, M.T. (1992). Family change, parental discord and early offending: Neuropsychological deficits. *Journal of Child Psychology and Psychiatry and Allied Disciplines, 33,* 1059–1075.

Fergusson, D.M., Horwood, L.J., & Lynskey, M.T. (1995). The stability of disruptive childhood behavior. *Journal of Abnormal Child Psychology, 23,* 379–396.

Fergusson, D.M., Horwood, L.J., Shannon, F.T., & Lawton, J.M. (1989). The Christchurch Child Development Study: A review of epidemiological findings. *Paediatric and Perinatal Epidemiology, 3,* 302–325.

Fey, M.E., Cleave, P.L., Long, S.H., & Hughes, D.L. (1993). Two approaches to the facilitation of grammar in children with language impairment: An experimental evaluation. *Journal of Speech and Hearing Research, 36,* 141–151.

Field, T.M. (1984). Early interactions between infants and their postpartum depressed mothers. *Infant Behavior and Development, 7,* 527–532.

Field, T.M. (1995). *Touch in early development.* Mahwah, NJ: Lawrence Erlbaum Associates.

Field, T.M. (1998a). Maternal depression effects on infants and early interventions. *Preventive Medicine, 27,* 200–203.

Field, T.M. (1998b). Touch therapies. In R.R. Hoffman, M.F. Sherrick, & J.J. Warm (Eds.), *Viewing psychology as a whole: The integrative science of William N. Dember* (pp. 603–624). Washington, DC: American Psychological Association.

Field, T.M. (2000). Infant massage therapy. In C.H. Zeanah, Jr. (Ed.), *Handbook of infant mental health* (2nd ed., pp. 494–500). New York: Guilford Press.

Field, T.M., Fox, N.M., Pickens, J., & Nawrocki, T. (1995). Right frontal EEG activation in 3- to 6-month old infants of depressed mothers. *Development and Psychopathology, 31,* 358–363.

Field, T.M., Healy, B., Goldstein, S., Perry, S., Bendall, D., Schanberg, S., Zimmerman, E., & Kuhn, C. (1988). Infants of depressed mothers show "depressed" behavior even with nondepressed adults. *Child Development, 59,* 1569–1579.

Field, T.M., & Hernandez-Reif, M. (2001). Sleep problems in infants decrease following massage therapy. *Early Child Development & Care, 168,* 95–104.

Field, T.M., Hernandez-Reif, M., Diego, M., Feijo, L., Vera, Y., & Gil, K. (2004). Massage therapy by parents improves early growth and development. *Infant Behavior and Development, 27,* 435–442.

Field, T.M., Lang, C., Martinez, A., Yando, R., Pickens, J., & Bendell, D. (1996). Preschool follow-up of infants of dysphoric mothers. *Journal of Clinical Child Psychology, 25,* 272–279.

Field, T.M., Widmayer, S.M., Greenberg, R., & Stoller, W. (1982). Effects of parent training on teenage mothers and their infants. *Pediatrics, 69,* 703–707.

Field, T.M., Widmayer, S.M., Stringer, S., & Ignatoff, E. (1980). Teenage, lower-class, black mothers and their preterm infants: An intervention and developmental follow-up. *Child Development, 51,* 426–436.

Figley, C.R. (Ed.). (1995). *Compassion fatigue: Coping with secondary traumatic stress disorder in those who treat the traumatized.* New York: Brunner/Mazel.

Fisher, D.G. (1995). *Family relationship variables and programs influencing juvenile delinquency.* Ottawa: Solicitor General of Canada.

Fitts, W.H. & Warren, W.L. (1996). *Tennessee Self-Concept Scale: 2nd Edition.* Los Angeles, CA: Western Psychological Services.

Fitzpatrick, K.M. (1997). Aggression and environmental risk among low-income African-American youth. *Journal of Adolescent Health, 21,* 172–178.

Fivaz-Depeursinger, E., & Corboz-Warnery, A. (1999). *The primary triangle: A development, systems view of fathers, mothers, and infants.* New York: Basic Books.

Foa, E., & Meadows, E.A. (1997). Psychosocial treatments for post-traumatic stress disorder: A critical review. In J. Spence, J.M. Darley, & D.J. Foss (Eds.), *Annual review of psychology* (Vol. 48, pp. 449–480). Palo Alto, CA: Annual Reviews.

Foa, E., Keane, T., & Friedman, M. (Eds.). (2000). *Treatment guidelines for Post Traumatic Stress Disorder.* New York: Guilford Press.

Fodi, A., Grolnick, W., Bridges, L., & Berko, J. (1990). Infants of adolescent and adult mothers: Two indices of socioemotional development. *Adolescence, 25,* 363–374.

Fonagy, P. (1994). Mental representations from an intergenerational cognitive science perspective. *Infant Mental Health Journal, 15,* 57–68.

Fonagy, P., Gergely, G., Jurist, E.L., & Target, M. (2002). *Affect regulation, mentalization, and the development of the self.* New York: Other Press.

Fonagy, P., Leigh, T., Kennedy, R., Matteon, G., Steele, H., Target, M., Steele, M., & Higgitt, A. (1995). Attachment, borderline states and the representation of emotions and cognitions of self and other. In D. Cicchetti & S.S. Toth (Eds.), *Rochester symposium on developmental psychopathology: Cognition and emotion* (Vol. 6, pp. 371–414). Rochester, NY: University of Rochester Press.

Fonagy, P., Steele, H., & Steele, M. (1991). Maternal representations of attachment during pregnancy predict the organization of infant-mother attachment at one year. *Child Development, 62,* 891–905.

Fonagy, P., Steele, M., Steele, H., Higgitt, A., & Target, M. (1994). Theory and practice of resilience. *Journal of Child Psychology and Psychiatry and Allied Disciplines, 35,* 231–357.

Fonagy, P., Steele, M., Steele, H., Moran, G.S., & Higgitt, A.C. (1991). The capacity for understanding mental states: The reflective self in parent and child and its significance for security of attachment. *Infant Mental Health Journal, 12,* 201–218.

Fonagy, P., & Target, M. (1997). Attachment and reflective function: Their role in self-organization. *Development and Psychopathology, 9,* 679–700.

Fonagy, P., & Target, M. (1998). Mentalization and the changing aims of child psychoanalysis. *Psychoanalytic Dialogues, 8,* 87–114.

Fonagy, P., Target, M., Cottrell, D., Phillips, J., & Kurtz, Z. (2000). *A review of the outcomes of psychiatric disorder in childhood: MCH 17–33. Final report to the National Health Service Executive.*

Fonagy, P., Target, M., Cottrell, D., Phillips, J., & Kurtz, Z. (2002). *What works for whom?: A critical review of treatments for children and adolescents.* New York: Guilford Press.

Fonagy, P., Target, M., Steele, H., & Steele, M. (1998). *The Reflective-Functioning Manual.* Unpublished manuscript.

Forman, S.G. (1993). *Coping skills interventions for children and adolescents.* San Francisco: Jossey-Bass.

Forness, S.R., & Finn, D. (1993). Screening children in Head Start for emotional or behavioral disorders. *Severe Behavioral Disorders Monographs, 16,* 6–14.

Fosha, D. (2000). *The transforming power of affect: A model for accelerated change.* New York: Basic Books.

Fosha, D. (2003). Dyadic regulation and experiential work with emotions and relatedness in trauma and disorganized attachment. In M.F. Solomon & D.J. Siegel (Eds.), *Healing trauma: Attachment, body, and brain* (pp. 221– 281). New York: W.W. Norton.

Fox, N.A. (1994). Dynamic cerebral processes underlying emotion regulation. In N.A. Fox (Ed.), The development of emotion regulation: Biological and behavioral considerations. *Monographs of the Society for Research in Child Development, 59* (2–3, Serial No. 240), 152–166.

Fox, N.A., Calkins, S.D., & Schmidt, L.A. (1995, March). Putting humpty dumpty back together: Or in search of a unified field theory to explain temperament. In M.R. Gunnar (Chair), *Physiological stress reactivity and behavioral inhibition: Are we talking about the same thing.* Symposium conducted at the biennial meeting of the Society for Research in Child Development, Indianapolis, IN.

Fox, N.A., Schmidt, L.A., Calkins, S.D., Rubin, K.H., & Coplan, R.J. (1996). The role of frontal activation in the regulation and dysregulation of social behavior during the preschool years. *Development and Psychopathology, 8,* 89–102.

Fraiberg, S. (1980). *Clinical studies in infant mental health.* New York: Basic Books.

Freir, K. (1994). In utero drug exposure and maternal–infant interaction: The complexities of the dyad and their environment. *Infant Mental Health Journal, 15,* 176–188.

Freud, A. (1936–1946). *The ego and the mechanisms of defense.* New York: International Universities Press.

Freud, S. (1894). The neuro-psychoses of defence. *Standard Edition, 3,* 45–61. London: Hogarth Press.

Freud, S. (1906). My views on the part played by sexuality in the aetiology of the neuroses. *Collected Papers, Vol. 1,* pp. 272–280. London: Hogarth Press.

Freud, S. (1949). *The origins of psychoanalysis.* New York: Basic Books.

Freud, S. (1955). Beyond the pleasure principle. In J. Strachey (Ed.), *The standard edition of the complete psychological works of Sigmund Freud* (pp. 1–64). London: Hogarth.

Frodi, A. (1983). Attachment behavior and sociability with strangers in premature and full-term infants. *Infant Mental Health Journal, 4,* 13–22.

Frodi, M.A., & Lamb, M.E. (1980). Child abusers' responses to infant smiles and cries. *Child Development, 51,* 238–241.

Fuerst, J.S., & Fuerst, D. (1993). The Chicago experience with an early childhood program: The special case of the child parent center program. *Urban Education, 38,* 69–96.

Furstenberg, F.F., Jr., Cook, T., Eccles, J., Elder, G.H., & Sameroff, A.J. (1999). *Urban families and adolescent success.* Chicago: University of Chicago Press.

Gaensbauer, T. (2002). Representations of trauma in infancy: Clinical and theoretical implications for the understanding of early memories. *Infant Mental Health Journal, 23,* 259–277.

Galejs, I., & Pease, D. (1987). Parenting beliefs and locus of control orientation. *The Journal of Psychology, 120,* 501–509.

Galper, A., Wigfield, A., & Seefeldt, C. (1997). Head Start parents' beliefs about their children's abilities, task values, and performance on different activities. *Child Development, 68,* 897–907.

Gamer, E., Gallant, D., & Grunebaum, H. (1976). Children of psychotic mothers: An evaluation of 1-year-olds on a test of object permanence. *Archives of General Psychiatry, 33,* 311–317.

Garbarino, J. (2002). Foreward: Pathways from childhood trauma to adolescent violence and delinquency. In R. Greenwald (Ed.), *Trauma and juvenile delinquency: Theory, research, and interventions* (pp. xix–xxv). New York: Haworth Press.

Gardner, F.E.M. (1992). Parent–child interactions of conduct disorder. *Educational Psychology Review, 4,* 135–163.

Gardner, F.E.M. (1994). The quality of joint activity between mothers and their children with behavior problems. *Journal of Child Psychology and Psychiatry, 35,* 935–948.

Garfield, S.L. (2003). Eclectic psychotherapy: A common factors approach. In J.C. Norcross & M.R. Goldfried (Eds.), *Handbook of psychotherapy integration* (pp. 169–201). New York: Oxford University Press.

Garmezy, N. (1985). Stress-resistant children: The search for protective factors. In J. Stevenson (Ed.), *Recent research in developmental psychopathology* (pp. 213–233). Oxford: Pergamon Press.

Garmezy, N. (1987). Stress competence and development. *American Journal of Orthopsychiatry, 57,* 159–174.

Garmezy, N., Masten, A., & Tellegen, A. (1984). The study of stress and competence in children: A building block for developmental psychopathology. *Child Development, 55,* 97–111.

Gaudin, J.M., Polansky, N.A., Kilpatrick, A.C., & Shilton, P. (1993). Loneliness, depression, stress, and social supports in neglectful families. *American Journal of Orthopsychiatry, 63,* 597–605.

Gelfand, D.T., Teti, D.M., Seiner, S.A., & Jameson, P.B. (1996). Helping mothers fight depression: Evaluation of a home-based intervention program for depressed mothers and their infants. *Journal of Clinical Child Psychology, 25,* 406–422.

George, C., Kaplan, N., & Main, M. (1985). *The Adult Attachment Interview.* Unpublished manuscript, University of California at Berkeley.

George, C., & Main, M. (1979). Social interactions of young abused children: Approach, avoidance, and aggression. *Child Development, 50,* 306–318.

George, C., & Solomon, J. (1989). Internal working models of caregiving and security of attachment at age six. *Infant Mental Health Journal, 10,* 222–237.

George, C., & Solomon, J. (1996). Representational models of relationships: Links between caregiving and attachment. *Infant Mental Health Journal, 17,* 198–216.

George, C., & Solomon, J. (1999). Attachment and caregiving: The caregiving behavioral system. In J. Cassidy & P.R. Shaver (Eds.), *Handbook of attachment: Theory, research, and clinical applications* (pp. 649–670). New York: Guilford Press.

Gerard, A.B. (1994). *Parent–Child Relationship Inventory (PCRI) Manual.* Los Angeles, CA: Western Psychological Services.

Gergely, G. (2000). Reapproaching Mahler: New perspectives on normal autism, symbiosis, splitting and libidinal object constancy from cognitive developmental theory. *Journal of the American Psychoanalytic Association, 48,* 1197–1228.

Gershoff, E.T., Miller, P.D., & Holden, G.W. (1999). Parenting influences from the pulpit: Religious affiliation as a determinant of parental corporal punishment. *Journal of Family Psychology, 13,* 307–320.

Gil, D.G. (1970). *Violence against children: Physical child abuse in the United States.* Cambridge, MA: Harvard University Press.

Gilkerson, L. (2004). Reflective supervision in infant–family programs: Adding clinical process to nonclinical settings. *Infant Mental Health Journal, 25,* 424–439.

Gilkerson, L., & Shahmoon-Shanok, R. (2000). Relationships for growth: Cultivating reflective practice in infant, toddler, and preschool program. In J.D. Osofsky & H.E. Fitzgerald (Eds.), *WAIM handbook of infant mental health: Vol. 2. Early intervention, evaluation, and assessment* (pp. 34–79). New York: John Wiley & Sons.

Gill, M.J., & Harris, S.L. (1991). Hardiness and social support as predictors of psychological discomfort in mothers of children with autism. *Journal of Autism and Developmental Disorders, 21,* 407–416.

Glaser, D. (2000). Child abuse and neglect and the brain: A review. *Journal of Child Psychology and Psychiatry and Allied Disciplines, 41,* 97–116.

Gobel, S., & Shindledecker, R. (1993). Characteristics of children whose parents have been incarcerated. *Hospital and Community Psychology, 44,* 656–660.

Gold, J.R. (1996). *Key concepts in psychotherapy integration.* New York: Plenum Press.

Goldberg, S., Mackay-Soroka, S., & Rochester, M. (1994). Affect, attachment, and maternal responsiveness. *Infant Behavior and Development, 17,* 335–339.

Goldfarb, W. (1945a). Effects of psychological deprivation in infancy and subsequent stimulation. *American Journal of Orthopsychiatry, 102,* 18–33.

Goldfarb, W. (1945b). Psychological privation in infancy and subsequent adjustment. *American Journal of Orthopsychiatry, 14,* 247–255.

Gomby, D.S., Larson, C.S, Lewit, E.M., & Behrman, R.E. (1993). Home visiting: Analysis and recommendations. *The Future of Children, 3,* 6–22.

Gomes-Pedro, J., Patricio, M., Carvalho, A., Goldschmidt, T., Torgal-Garcia, F., & Monteiro, M.B. (1995). Early intervention with Portuguese mothers: A two-year follow-up. *Developmental and Behavioral Pediatrics, 16,* 21–28.

Goodman, S.H. & Brumley, H.E. (1990). Schizophrenic and depressed mothers: Relational deficits in parenting. *Developmental Psychology, 26,* 31–39.

Goodman, S.H., & Gotlib, I.H. (1999). Schizophrenic and depressed mothers: A developmental model for understanding mechanisms of transition. *Psychological Review, 106,* 458–490.

Goodnow, J.J. (1984). Parents' ideas about parenting and development: A review of issues and recent work. In M.E. Lamb, A.L. Brown, & B. Rogoff (Eds.), *Advances in developmental psychology* (Vol. 3, pp. 193–242). Mahwah, NJ: Lawrence Erlbaum Associates.

Goodnow, J.J. (1988). Parents' ideas, actions, and feelings: Models and methods from developmental and social psychology. *Child Developmental, 59,* 286–320.

Goodnow, J.J. (2002). Parents' knowledge and expectations: Using what we know. In M.H. Bornstein (Ed.), *Handbook of parenting (2nd Ed.): Vol. 3. Being and becoming a parent* (pp. 439–460). Mahwah, NJ: Lawrence Erlbaum Associates.

Goodson, B.D., Layzer, J.I., St. Pierre, R.G., Bernstein, R.S., & Lopez, M. (2000). Effectiveness of a comprehensive, five-year family support program for low-income children and their families: Findings from the Comprehensive Child Development Program. *Early Childhood Research Quarterly, 15,* 5–39.

Göpfert, M., Webster, J., & Seeman, M.V. (1996). *Parental psychiatric disorder: Distressed parents and their families.* Cambridge: Cambridge University Press.

Gordon, I.J., & Jester, R.E. (1977). The Florida parent education infant and toddler programs. In M.C. Day & R.K. Parker (Eds.), *The preschool in action* (pp. 95–127). Needham Heights, MA: Allyn & Bacon.

Gottman, J. (1997). *Raising an emotionally intelligent child: The heart of parenting.* New York: Simon & Schuster.

Goyette-Ewing, M., Slade, A., Knoebber, K., Gilliam, W., Truman, S., & Mayes, L. (2002). *Parents First: A developmental parenting program.* Unpublished manuscript, Yale Child Study Center.

Graham, Y.P., Heim, C., Goodman, S.H., Miller, A.H., & Nemeroff, C.B. (1999). The effects of neonatal stress on brain development: Implications for psychopathology. *Development and Psychopathology, 11,* 545–565.

Gray, P. (1973). Psychoanalytic technique: The ego's capacity to view intrapsychic activity. *Journal of the American Psychoanalytic Association, 21,* 474–494.

Gray, S.W., Ramsey, B., & Klaus, R. (1983). The early training project, 1962–80. In Consortium for Longitudinal Studies (Ed.), *As the twig is bent: Lasting effects of preschool programs* (pp. 33–70). Mahwah, NJ: Lawrence Erlbaum Associates.

Green, J., & Goldwyn, R. (2002). Annotation: Attachment disorganization and psychopathology: New findings in attachment research and their potential implications for developmental psychopathology in childhood. *Journal of Child Psychology and Psychiatry, 43,* 835–846.

Greenberg, M.T. (1999). Attachment and psychopathology in childhood. In J. Cassidy & P.R. Shaver (Eds.), *Handbook of attachment: Theory, research, and clinical application* (pp. 469–496). New York: Guilford Press.

Greenberg, M.T., & Kusche, C.A. (1997, April). *Improving children's emotion regulation and social competence: The effects of the PATHS curriculum.* Paper presented at the Society for Research in Child Development, Washington, DC.

Greenberg, M.T., & Speltz, M. (1988). Attachment and the ontogeny of conduct problems. In J. Belsky & T. Nezworski (Eds.), *Clinical implications of attachment* (pp. 177–218). Mahwah, NJ: Lawrence Erlbaum Associates.

Greene, R.W. (1998). *The explosive child: A new approach to understanding and parenting easily frustrated, "chronically inflexible" children.* New York: Harper Collins.

Greenfield, P.M. (1997). Culture as process: Empirical methods for cultural psychology. In J.W. Berry & Y.H. Poortinga (Eds.), *Handbook of cross-cultural psychology: Vol. 1. Theory and method* (2nd ed., pp. 301–346). Needham Heights, MA: Allyn & Bacon.

Greenfield, P.M., & Suzuki, L.K. (1998). Culture and human development: Implications for parenting, education, pediatrics, and mental health. In W. Damon (Ed.), *Handbook of child psychology* (Vol. 4, pp. 1059–1109). New York: John Wiley & Sons.

Greenspan, S.I. (1986). Developmental morbidity in infants in multirisk families: Clinical perspectives. *Public Health Reports, 97,* 18–23.

Greenspan, S.I. (1997). *Developmentally based psychotherapy.* Madison, CT: International Universities Press.

Greenspan, S.I., & Wieder, S. (1984). Dimensions and levels of the therapeutic process. *Psychotherapy: Theory, research, and practice, 21,* 5–23.

Greenspan, S.I., & Wieder, S. (1987). Dimensions and levels of the therapeutic process. In S.I. Greenspan, S. Wieder, R.A. Nover, A.F. Lieberman, R.S. Lourie, & M.E. Robinson (Eds.), *Infants in multirisk families: Case studies in preventive intervention. Clinical infant reports series of the National Center for Clinical Infant Programs, No. 3* (pp. 391–430). Madison, CT: International Universities Press.

Greenspan, S.I., & Wieder, S. (1993). Regulatory disorders. In C.H. Zeanah (Ed.), *Handbook of infant mental health* (pp. 280–290). New York: Guilford Press.

Greenspan, S.I., & Wieder, S. (1998). *The child with special needs: Encouraging intellectual and emotional growth.* Reading, MA: Addison-Wesley.

Greenspan, S.I., Wieder, S., Nover, R.A., Lieberman, A.F., Lourie, R.S., & Robinson, M.E. (Eds.) (1987). Infants in multirisk families: Case studies in preventive intervention. *Clinical infant reports series of the National Center for Clinical Infant Programs, No. 3.* Madison, CT: International Universities Press.

Greenwald, A.G., McGhee, D.E., & Schwartz, J.L.K. (1998). Measuring individual differences in implicit cognition. *Journal of Personality and Social Psychology, 74,* 1464–1480.

Gresham, F.M., & Elliott, S.W., (1990). *Social skills rating system manual.* Circle Pines, MN: American Guidance Service.

Grienenberger, J., Kelly, K., & Slade, A. (April, 2001). *Maternal reflective functioning and the caregiving relationship: The link between mental states and mother–infant affective communication.* Paper presented at the biennial meeting of the Society for Research in Child Development, Minneapolis, MN.

Gross, D., Conrad, B., Fogg, L., & Wothke, W. (1994). A longitudinal model of maternal self-efficacy, depression, and difficult temperament during toddlerhood. *Research in Nursing and Health, 17,* 207–215.

Gross, D., Fogg, L. Webster-Stratton, C., Garvey, C., Julion, W., & Grady, J. (2003). Parent training with families of toddlers in day care in low-income urban communities. *Journal of Consulting and Clinical Psychology, 71,* 261–278.

Gross, D., & Rocissano, L. (1988). Maternal confidence in toddlerhood: Its measurement for clinical practice and research. *Nurse Practitioner, 13,* 19–22, 25, 28–29.

Gross, J.J. (1998). Antecedent- and response-focused emotion regulation: Divergent consequences for experience, expression, and physiology. *Journal of Personality and Social Psychology, 74,* 224–237.

Gross, J.J. (1999). Emotion and emotion regulation. In L.A. Pervin & O.P. John (Eds.), *Handbook of personality: Theory and research* (pp. 525–552). New York: Guilford Press.

Gross, J.J. (2002). Emotion regulation: Affective, cognitive, and social consequences. *Psychophysiology, 39,* 281–291.

Gross, J.J., & John, O.P. (2002). Wise emotion regulation. In L.F. Barrett & P. Salovey (Eds.), *The wisdom in feeling: Psychological processes in emotional intelligence. Emotions and social behavior* (pp. 297–319). New York: Guilford Press.

Gross, J.J., & Levenson, R.W. (1993). Emotional suppression: Physiology, self-report, and expressive behavior. *Journal of Personality and Social Psychology, 64,* 970–986.

Grusec, J.E., Adam, E., & Mammone, N. (April, 1993). *Mental representations of relationships, parent belief systems, and parent behavior.* Paper presented at the biennial meeting of the Society for Research in Child Development, New Orleans.

Grych, J.H., Jouriles, E.N., Swank, P.R., McDonald, R., & Norwood, W.D. (2000). Patterns of adjustment among children of battered women. *Journal of Consulting and Clinical Psychology, 68,* 84–94.

Guerin, D.W., & Gottfried, A.W. (1994). Temperamental consequences of infant difficultness. *Infant Behavior and Development, 17,* 413–421.

Gunderson, J.G., & Sabo, A.N. (1993). The phenomenological and conceptual interface between borderline personality disorder and PTSD. *American Journal of Psychiatry, 150,* 19–27.

Gunnar, M.R. (1998). Quality of care and the buffering of stress physiology: Its potential role in protecting the developing human brain. *IMPrint, 21,* 4–7.

Gunnar, M.R., & Barr, R.G. (1998). Stress, early brain development, and behavior. *Infants and Young Children, 11,* 1–14.

Gunnar, M.R., Brodersen, L., Nachmias, M., Buss, K., & Rigatuso, J. (1996). Stress reactivity and attachment security. *Developmental Psychobiology, 29,* 192–204.

Guralnick, M.J. (1997). Second-generation research in the field of early intervention. In M.J. Guralnick (Ed.), *The effectiveness of early intervention* (pp. 3–20). Baltimore: Paul H. Brookes Publishing Co.

Gutelius, M.F., Kirsch, A.D., MacDonald, S., Brooks, M.R., & McErlean, T. (1977). Controlled study of child health supervision: Behavioural results. *Pediatrics, 60,* 294–304.

Haan, N. (1977). *Coping and defending.* San Diego: Academic Press.

Haan, N. (1993). The assessment of coping, defense, and stress. In L. Golberger & S. Breznitz (Eds.), *Handbook of stress: Theoretical and clinical aspects* (2nd ed., pp. 258–273). New York: Free Press.

Hack, M., Taylor, G., & Klein, N. (1994). School outcomes in children with birth weight under 750 g. *New England Journal of Medicine, 331,* 753–159.

Haft, W.L., & Slade, A. (1989). Affect attunement and maternal attachment: A pilot study. *Infant Mental Health Journal, 10,* 157–172.

Haight, W.L., Parke, R.D., & Black, J.E. (1997). Mothers' and fathers' beliefs about and spontaneous participation in their toddlers' pretend play. *Merrill-Palmer Quarterly, 43,* 271–290.

Halpern, R. (1990). Community-based early intervention. In J.P. Shonkoff & S.J. Meisels (Eds.), *Handbook of early childhood education* (pp. 469–498). Cambridge: Cambridge University Press.

Halpern, R. (2000). Early childhood intervention for low-income children and families. In S.P. Shonkoff & S.J. Meisels (Eds.), *Handbook of early childhood intervention* (2nd ed., pp. 361–415). Cambridge: Cambridge University Press.

Hammen, C. (1992). Cognitive, life stress, and interpersonal approaches to a developmental psychopathology model of depression. *Development and Psychopathology, 4,* 189–206.

Hammen, C., Burge, D., & Adrian, C. (1991). The timing of mother and child depression in a longitudinal study of children at risk. *Journal of Consulting and Clinical Psychology, 59,* 341–345.

Hann, D.M., Castino, R.J., Jarosinki, J., & Britton, H. (April, 1991). *Consequences of teenage parenting predicting problems in toddlers and preschoolers.* Symposium conducted at the biennial meeting of the Society of Research in Child Development, Seattle, Washington.

Hanna, S., & Wilford, S. (1990). *Floor time: Tuning in to each child.* New York: Scholastic.

Hanson, M.J., & Lynch, E.W. (2003). *Understanding families: Approaches to diversity, disability, and risk.* Baltimore: Paul H. Brookes Publishing Co.

Harbin, G.L., McWilliam, R.A., & Gallagher, J.J. (2000). Services for families with young children with disabilities and their families. In J.P. Shonkoff & S.J. Meisels (Eds.), *Handbook of early childhood intervention* (2nd ed., pp. 387–415). Cambridge: Cambridge University Press.

Hardy, J.B., Shapiro, S., Astone, N.M., Brooks-Gunn, J., Miller, T.L., & Hilton, S.C. (1997). Adolescent childbearing revisited: The age of mothers at delivery as a determinant of children's self-sufficiency at age 27–33. *Pediatrics, 100,* 802–809.

Harkness, S., & Super, C.M. (Eds.). (1996). *Parents' cultural belief systems: Their origins, expressions, and consequences.* New York: Guilford Press.

Harris, C.R. (2001). Cardiovascular responses of embarrassment and effects of emotional suppression in a social setting. *Journal of Personality and Social Psychology, 81,* 886–897.

Harris, S., & Laskin, B. (2004, Jan/Feb). Bringing mindfulness awareness practice to the experience of childhood sexual abuse and trauma. *Peel Committee on Sexual Assault Newsletter,* pp. 3–4.

Hart, S., Field, T., del Valle, C., & Pelaez Nogueras, M. (1998). Depressed mothers' interactions with their one-year-old infants. *Infant Behavior and Development, 21,* 519–525.

Hartmann, H. (1956). Notes on the reality principle. In H. Hartmann, *Essays on ego psychology* (pp. 268–290). New York: International Universities Press.

Hartmann, H. (1958). *Ego psychology and the problem of adaptation.* New York: International Universities Press.

Harwood, R.L., Miller, J.G., & Irizarry, N.L. (1995). *Culture and attachment: Perceptions of the child in context.* New York: Guilford Press.

Haskell, L. (2003). *First stage trauma treatment: A guide for mental health professionals working with women.* Toronto: Centre for Addiction and Mental Health.

Hastings, P.D., & Coplan, R. (1999). Conceptual and empirical links between children's social spheres: Relating maternal beliefs and preschoolers' behaviors with peers. In C.C. Piotrowski & P.D. Hastings (Eds.), *New directions for child and adolescent development: Vol. 86. Conflict as a context for understanding maternal beliefs about child rearing and children's misbehavior* (pp. 43–59). San Francisco: Jossey-Bass.

Hastings, P., & Grusec, J.E. (1998). Parenting goals as organizers of responses to parent–child disagreements. *Developmental Psychology, 34,* 465–479.

Hastings, P.D., & Rubin, K.H. (1999). Predicting mothers' beliefs about preschool-aged children's social behavior: Evidence for maternal attitudes moderating child effects. *Child Development, 70,* 722–741.

Hatcher, R., Hatcher, S., Berlin, M., Okla, K., & Richards, J. (1990). Psychological mindedness and abstract reasoning in late childhood and adolescence: An exploration using new instruments. *Journal of Youth and Adolescence, 19,* 307–326.

Hauser-Cram, P., Warfield, M.E., Upshur, C.C., & Weiser, T.S. (2000). An expanded view of program evaluation in early childhood intervention. In J.P. Shonkoff & S.J. Meisels (Eds.) *Handbook of early childhood intervention* (2nd ed.) (pp. 487–509). Cambridge: Cambridge University Press.

Hayes, S.C., Follette, W.C., & Follette, V.M. (1995). Behavior therapy: A contextual approach. In A.S. Gurman & S.B. Messer (Eds.), *Essential psychotherapies: Theory and practice* (pp. 128–181). New York: Guilford Press.

Health Canada (2000). *Working with Nobody's Perfect: A facilitator's guide.* Ottawa, Ontario: Health Canada.

Hechtman, L. (1989). Teenage mothers and their children: Risks and problems: A review. *Canadian Journal of Psychiatry, 34,* 569–575.

Heider, F. (1958). *The psychology of interpersonal relations.* New York: John Wiley & Sons.

Heim, C., & Nemeroff, C.B. (2001). The role of childhood trauma in the neurobiology of mood and anxiety disorders: Preclinical and clinical studies. *Biological Psychiatry, 49,* 1023–1039.

Heinicke, C.M., Fineman, N.R., Ruth, G., Recchia, S.L., Guthrie, D., & Rodning, C. (1999). Relationship based intervention with at-risk mothers: Outcome in the first year of life. *Infant Mental Health Journal, 20,* 349–374.

Henggeler, S.W., & Lee, T. (2003). Multi-systemic treatment of serious clinical problems. In A. Kazdin & J.R. Weisz (Eds), *Evidence-based psychotherapies for children and adolescents* (pp. 301–322). New York: Guilford Press.

Henggeler, S.W., Schoenwald, S.K., Rowland, M.D., & Cunningham, P.C. (2002). *Serious emotional disturbance in children and adolescents: Multisystemic therapy.* New York: Guilford Press.

Herman, J.L. (1981). *Father and daughter incest.* Cambridge, MA: Harvard University Press.

Herman, J.L. (1992). *Trauma and recovery.* New York: Basic Books.

Herman, J.L., Perry, J.C., & van der Kolk, B.A. (1989). Childhood trauma in borderline personality disorder. *American Journal of Psychology, 146,* 490–496.

Herman, J.L., & Shatzow, E. (1987). Recovery and verification of memories of childhood sexual trauma. *Psychoanalytic Psychology, 4,* 1–14.

Hewstone, M. (1989). *Causal attribution: From cognitive processes to collective beliefs.* Oxford: Blackwell.

Hobfoll, S.E., & Leiberman, J.R. (1987). Personality and social resources in immediate and continued stress resistance among women. *Journal of Personality and Social and Psychology, 52,* 18–26.

Hock, E., & Demeis, D.K. (1990). Depression in mothers of infants: The role of maternal employment. *Developmental Psychology, 26,* 285–291.

Hoeksma, J.B., Oosterlaan, J., & Schipper, E.M. (2004). Emotion regulation and the dynamics of feelings: A conceptual and methodological framework. *Child Development, 75,* 354–360.

Hofer, M. (1995). Hidden regulators: Implications for a new understanding of attachment, separation, and loss. In S. Goldberg, R. Muir, & J. Kerr (Eds.), *Attachment theory: Social, developmental, and clinical perspectives* (pp. 203–231). Mahwah, NJ: Analytic Press.

Hoffman, M. (1986). Affect, cognition, and motivation. In R.M. Sorrentino & E.T. Higgins (Eds.), *Handbook of motivation and cognition* (pp. 244–280). New York: Guilford Press.

Hoffman, M.L. (2000). *Empathy and moral development: Implications for caring and justice.* Cambridge: Cambridge University Press.

Holden, G.W., & Buck, M.J. (2002). Parental attitudes towards childrearing. In M.H. Bornstein (Ed.), *Handbook of parenting (2nd ed.): Vol. 3. Being and becoming a parent* (pp. 537–562). Mahwah, NJ: Lawrence Erlbaum Associates.

Holden, G.W., Coleman, S.M., & Schmidt, K.L. (1995). Why 3-year-old children get spanked: Parent and child determinants as reported by college-educated mothers. *Merrill-Palmer Quarterly, 41,* 431–452.

Holden, G.W., Thompson, E.E., Zambarano, R.J., & Marshall, L.A. (1997). Child effects as a source of change in maternal attitudes toward corporal punishment. *Journal of Social and Personal Relationships, 14,* 481–490.

Holden, J.M., Sagovsky, R., & Cox, J.L. (1989). Counselling in a general practice setting: Controlled study of health visitor intervention in treatment of postnatal depression. *British Medical Journal, 298,* 223–226.

Hollender, M.H., & Ford, C.V. (1990). *Dynamic psychotherapy: An introductory approach.* Washington, DC: American Psychiatric Press.

Holmes, D.S. (1997). *Abnormal psychology.* New York: Longman.

Hoover, H.D., Dunbar, S.B., Frisbie, D.A., et al. (2001). *Iowa Tests of Basic Skills, Complete Battery, Form A, Levels 5 & 6.* Chicago: Riverside.

Horejsi, C., Craig, B.H.R., & Pablo, J. (1992). Reactions by Native American parents to child protection agencies: Cultural and community factors. *Child Welfare League of America, LXXI,* 329–342.

Horowitz, M.J. (1986). *Stress response syndromes* (2nd ed.). Northvale, NJ: Jason Aronson.

Horowitz, M.J. (1988). *Introduction to psychodynamics: A new synthesis.* New York: Basic Books.

Horowitz, M.J., Znoj, H.J., & Stinson, C.H. (1996). Defensive control processes: Use of theory in research, formulation, and therapy of stress response syndromes. In M. Zeidner & N.S. Endler (Eds.), *Handbook of coping: Theory, research and applications* (pp. 532–553). New York: John Wiley & Sons.

House, J.S., Landis, K.R., & Umberson, D. (1988). Social relationships and health. *Science, 241,* 540–545.

Howe, M.L., & Courage, M.L. (1993). On resolving the enigma of infantile amnesia. *Psychological Bulletin, 113,* 305–326.

Hubbs-Tait, L., Osofsky, J.D., Hann, D.M., & McDonald, C.A. (1994). Predicting behavior problems and social competence in children of adolescent mothers. *Family Relations: Interdisciplinary Journal of Applied Family Studies, 43,* 439–446.

Hughes, C., & Dunn, J. (1998). Understanding mind and emotion: Longitudinal associations with mental-state talk between friends. *Developmental Psychology, 34,* 1026–1037.

Hughes, D.A. (1997). *Facilitating developmental attachment: The road to emotional recovery and behavioural change in foster and adopted children.* Lanham, MD: Jason Aronson.

Hughes, D.A. (1998). *Building the bonds of attachment: Awakening love in deeply troubled children.* Lanham, MD: Jason Aronson.

Hughes, D.A. (2004). An attachment-based treatment for maltreated children and young people. *Attachment and Human Development, 6,* 263–278.

Hunt, J., & Paraskevopoulous, J. (1980). Children's psychological development as a function of the inaccuracy of their mother's knowledge of their abilities. *Journal of Genetic Psychology, 136,* 285–298.

Huttenlocher, P.R. (1994). Synaptogenesis in human cerebral cortex. In G. Dawson & K.W. Fischer (Eds.), *Human behavior and the developing brain* (pp. 137–152). New York: Guilford Press.

Huttenlocher, P.R., & Dabholkar, A.S. (1997). Regional differences in synaptogenesis in human cerebral cortex. *The Journal of Comparative Neurology, 387,* 167–178.

Infant Health and Development Program (1990). Enhancing the outcomes of low-birthweight, premature infants. *Journal of the American Medical Association, 263,* 3035–3042.

Infant Mental Health Promotion Program (IMP) (2004). *Organizational policies and practices needed for high quality services.* Toronto: Author.

Isen, A.M., Means, B., Patrick, R., & Nowicki, G. (1982). Some factors influencing decision-making strategy and risk-taking. In M.S. Clark & S.T. Fiske (Eds.), *The 17th Annual Carnegie Symposium on Cognition: Affect and cognition* (pp. 243–262). Mahwah, NJ: Lawrence Erlbaum Associates.

Izard, C.E. (1992). Basic emotions, relations among emotions, and emotion-cognitive relations. *Psychological Review, 99,* 561–565.

Jack, S.M. (1999). *Factors which influence the establishment of a working relationship between lay home visitors and at-risk families.* Unpublished doctoral dissertation, McMaster University, Hamilton, ON.

Jacobsen, T. (1999). Effects of postpartum disorders on parenting and on offspring. In L.J. Miller (Ed.), *Postpartum mood disorders* (pp. 119–139). Washington, DC: American Psychiatric Press.

Jacobsen, T., & Miller, L.J. (1999). Attachment quality in young children of mentally ill mothers: Contribution of maternal caregiving abilities and foster care context. In J. Solomon & C. George (Eds.), *Attachment disorganization* (pp. 347–378). New York: Guilford Press.

Jacobson, S.W., & Frye, K.F. (1991). Effect of maternal social support on attachment: Experimental evidence. *Child Development, 62,* 572–582.

Jaffe, P.G., Sudermann, M., & Reitzel, D. (1992). Child witnesses of marital violence. In R.T. Amemerman & M. Hersen (Eds.), *Assessment of family violence* (pp. 313–331). New York: John Wiley & Sons.

Jameson, P.B., Gelfand, D.M., Kulcsar, E., & Teti, D.M. (1997). Mother–toddler interaction patterns associated with maternal depression. *Development and Psychopathology, 9,* 537–550.

Janoff-Bulman, R. (1992). *Shattered assumptions: Towards a new psychology of trauma.* New York: The Free Press.

Jenkins, J.M., & Smith, M.A. (1991). Marital disharmony and children's behaviour problems: Aspects of a poor marriage that affect children adversely. *Journal of Child Psychology and Psychiatry and Allied disciplines, 32,* 793–810.

Jester, R.E., & Guinagh, B.J. (1983). The Gordon Parent Education Infant and Toddler Program. In Consortium for Longitudinal Studies (Ed.), *As the twig is bent: Lasting effects of preschool programs* (pp. 103–132). Mahwah, NJ: Lawrence Erlbaum Associates.

Johnson, D.L. (1988). Primary prevention of behaviour problems in young children: The Houston Parent–Child Development Centre. In R.H. Price, E.L. Cowen, R. Lomen & J. Ramos-McKay (Eds.), *Fourteen ounces of prevention: A casebook for practitioners* (pp. 44–52). Washington, DC: American Psychological Association.

Johnson, D.L. & Walker, T. (1991). *Final report of an evaluation of the Avance parent education and family support program.* Report submitted to the Carnegie Corporation. San Antonio, TX: Avance.

Johnston, C. (1996). Parent characteristics and parent–child interactions in families of non-problem children and ADHD children with higher and lower levels of oppositional-defiant behavior. *Journal of Abnormal Child Psychology, 24,* 85–104.

Johnston, C., & Mash, E.J. (1989). A measure of parenting satisfaction and efficacy. *Journal of Clinical Child Psychology, 18,* 167–175.

Johnston, C., & Patenaude, R. (1994). Parent attribution for inattentive-overactive and oppositional-defiant child behaviors. *Cognitive Therapy and Research, 18,* 261–275.

Joiner, T.E., & Wagner, K.D. (1996). Parental, child-centred attributions and outcome: A meta-analytic review with conceptual and methodological implications. *Journal of Abnormal Child Psychology, 24,* 37–82.

Jones, N.A., Field, T., & Davalos, M. (2000). Right frontal EEG asymmetry and lack of empathy in preschool children of depressed mothers. *Child Psychiatry and Human Development, 30,* 189–204.

Joseph, J.G., Joshi, S.V., Lewin, A.B., & Abrams, M. (1999). Characteristics and perceived needs of mothers with serious mental illness. *Psychiatric Services, 50,* 1357–1359.

Jouriles, E., Murphy, C., Farris, A.M., Smith, B.A., Richters, J.E., & Waters, E. (1991). Marital adjustment, parental disagreements about child rearing, and behavior problems in boys: Increasing the specificity of marital assessments. *Child Development, 62,* 1424–1333.

Jouriles, E., Pfiffner, L.J., & O'Leary, S.G. (1988). Marital conflict, parenting, and toddler conduct problems. *Journal of Abnormal Child Psychology, 16,* 197–206.

Juffer, F., Bakermans-Kranenburg, M.J., & van IJzendoorn, M.H. (2005). The importance of parenting in the development of disorganized attachment: Evidence from a preventive intervention study in adoptive families. *Journal of Child Psychology and Psychiatry, 46,* 263–274.

Juffer, F., Hoksbergen, R.A.C., Riksen-Walraven, J.M., & Kohnstamm, G.A. (1997). Early intervention in adoptive families. Supporting maternal sensitive responsiveness, infant–mother attachment and infant competence. *Journal of Child Psychology and Psychiatry, 38,* 1039–1050.

Kabat-Zinn, J. (1990). *Full catastrophe living: Using the wisdom of your body and mind to face stress, pain, and illness.* New York: Dell Publishing.

Kabat-Zinn, J. (1994). *Wherever you go, there you are: Mindfulness meditation in everyday life.* New York: Hyperion.

Kagan, J. (1989). Temperamental contributions to social behavior. *American Psychologist, 44,* 668–674.

Kagan, J. (1994a). Distinctions among emotions, moods, and temperamental qualities. In P. Ekman & R.J. Davidson (Eds.), *The nature of emotions: Fundamental questions* (pp. 74–78). New York: Oxford University Press.

Kagan, J. (1994b). *Galen's prophecy: Temperament in human nature.* New York: Basic Books.

Kagan, J. (1997). Temperament and the reactions to infamiliarity. *Child Development, 68,* 139–143.

Kagan, J. (1999). The concept of behavioral inhibition. In L.A. Schmidt & J. Schulkin (Eds.), *Extreme fear, shyness, and social phobia: Origins, biological mechanisms, and clinical outcomes. Series in affective science* (pp. 3–13). New York: Oxford University Press.

Kagan, J., & Snidman, N. (1991). Temperamental factors in human development. *American Psychologist, 46,* 856–862.

Kagan, R., & Schlosberg, S. (1989). *Families in perpetual crisis.* New York: W.W. Norton.

Kalyanpur, M., & Harry, B. (1999). *Culture in special education: Building Reciprocal Family–Professional Relationships.* Baltimore: Paul H. Brookes Publishing Co.

Karnes, M.B., Schwedel, A.M., & Williams, M.B. (1983). A comparison of five approaches for educating young children from low income homes. In Consortium for Longitudinal Studies (Ed.), *As the twig is bent: Lasting effects of preschool programs* (pp. 133–170). Mahwah, NJ: Lawrence Erlbaum Associates.

Karoly, L., Greenwood, P., Everingham, S., Hoube, J., Kilburn, R., Rydell, P., Sanders, M., & Chiesa, J. (1998). *Investing in our children: What we know and don't know about the cost and benefits of early childhood intervention.* Palo Alto, CA: The Rand Corporation.

Kauffman, J. (2002a). Introduction. In J. Kauffman (Ed.), *Loss of the assumptive world: A theory of traumatic loss* (pp. 1–9). New York: Brunner-Routledge.

Kauffman, J. (2002b). Safety and the assumptive world: A theory of traumatic loss. In J. Kauffman (Ed.), *Loss of the assumptive world: A theory of traumatic loss* (pp. 205–212). New York: Brunner-Routledge.

Kauffman, J., & Henrich, C. (2000). Exposure to violence and early childhood trauma. In C.H. Zeanah Jr. (Ed.), *Handbook of infant mental health* (pp. 195–210). New York: Guilford Press.

Kazdin, A.E. (1995). *Conduct disorders in childhood and adolescence* (2nd Ed.). Beverly Hills, CA: Sage Publications.

Kazdin, A.E. (1997). Parent management training: Evidence, outcomes and issues. *Journal of the American Academy of Child and Adolescent Psychiatry, 36,* 1349–1356.

Kazdin, A.E. (2000a). *Psychotherapy for children and adolescents: Directions for research and practice.* Oxford: Oxford University Press.

Kazdin, A.E. (2000b). Treatments for aggressive and anti-social children. *Child and Adolescent Psychiatric Clinics of North America, 9,* 841–858.

Kazdin, A.E. & Weisz, J.R. (Eds) (2003). *Evidence-based psychotherapies for children and adolescents.* New York: Guilford Press.

Keating, D.P., & Hertzman, C. (Eds.)(1999). *Developmental health and the health of nations: Social, biological and educational dynamics.* New York: Guilford Press.

Kelley, H.H. (1967). Attribution theory in social psychology. In D. Levine (Ed.), *Nebraska symposium on motivation* (Vol. 15, pp. 192–240). Lincoln: University of Nebraska Press.

Kendall, P.C., & Braswell, L. (1985). *Cognitive-behavioral therapy for impulsive children.* New York: Guilford Press.

Kendall, P.C., & Panichelli-Mindel, S.M. (1995). Cognitive-behavioral treatments. *Journal of Abnormal Child Psychology, 23,* 107–124.

Kendler, K.S., Kessler, R.C., Walters, E.E., MacLean, C., Neale, M.C., Heath, A.C., & Eaves, L. (1995). Stressful life events, genetic liability, and onset of an episode of major depression in women. *American Journal of Psychiatry, 152,* 833–842.

Kennedy, S.H., Javanmard, M., & Vaccarino, F.J. (1997). A review of functional neuroimaging in mood disorders: Positron emission tomography and depression. *Canadian Journal of Psychiatry, 42,* 467–475.

Kernberg, O.F. (1975). *Borderline conditions and pathological narcissism.* New York: Jason Aronson.

Kernberg, O.F. (1976). *Object relations theory and clinical psychoanalysis.* New York: Jason Aronson.

Kernberg, O.F. (1984). *Severe personality disorders.* New Haven: Yale University Press.

Kirsch, I., Capafons, A., Cardéna-Buelna, E., & Amigó, S. (1999). Clinical hypnosis and self-regulation: An introduction. In I. Kirsch, A. Capafons, E. Cardéna, & S. Amigó (Eds.), *Clinical hypnosis and self-regulation therapy: A cognitive-behavioral perspective* (pp. 3–18). Washington, DC: American Psychological Association.

Kisanji, J. (1995). Interface between culture and disability in the Tanzanian context: I. *International Journal of Disability, Development and Education, 42,* 93–108.

Kitzman, H., Olds, D.L., & Henderson, C.R. (1997). Effect of prenatal and infancy home visitation by nurses on pregnancy outcomes, childhood injuries, and repeated child-bearing: A randomised control trial. *Journal of the American Medical Association, 278,* 644–652.

Klehr, K.B., Cohler, B.J., & Musick, J.S. (1983). Character and behavior in the mentally ill and well mothers. *Infant Mental Health Journal, 4,* 250–271.

Klein, M. (1975). Some theoretical conclusions regarding the emotional life of the infant. In M. Klein (Ed.), *Envy and gratitude and other works, 1946–1963* (pp. 61–93). New York: Delacorte Press.

Klein, M.D., & Briggs, M. (1987). Facilitating mother–infant communicative interaction in mothers of high-risk infants. *Journal of Childhood Communication Disorders, 10,* 91–106.

Klinnert, M.D., Campos, J.J., Sorce, J., Emde, R.N., & Svejda, M. (1983). Social referencing: Emotional expressions as behavior regulators. In R. Plutchnik & H. Kellerman (Eds.), *Emotion: Theory, research, and experience* (Vol. 2, pp. 57–86). New York: Academic Press.

Kluft, R.P. (1994). Treatment trajectories in multiple personality disorder. *Dissociation, 7,* 63–76.

Knanowitz, C.S. (1998). *The out-of-sync child: Recognizing and coping with sensory integration dysfunction.* New York: Perigree Books.

Knitzer, J. (2000). *Promoting resilience: Helping young children and parents affected by substance abuse, domestic violence, and depression in the context of welfare reform.* New York: Columbia University, National Center for Children in Poverty.

Kochanska, G. (1991). Patterns of inhibition to the unfamiliar in children of normal and affectively ill mothers. *Child Development, 62,* 250–263.

Kochanska, G. (1995). Children's temperament, mothers' discipline, and security of attachment: Multiple pathways to emerging internalization. *Child Development, 66,* 597–615.

Kochanska, G. (1997a). Multiple pathways to conscience for children with different temperaments: From toddlerhood to age 5. *Developmental Psychology, 64,* 325–347.

Kochanska, G. (1997b). Mutually responsive orientation between mothers and their young children: Implications for early socialization. *Child Development, 68,* 94–112.

Kochanska, G., Murray, K., & Coy, K.C. (1997). Inhibitory control as a contributor to conscience in childhood: From toddler to early school age. *Child Development, 68,* 263–277.

Kohut, H. (1971). *The analysis of the self.* New York: International Universities Press.

Kohut, H. (1977). *The restoration of the self.* New York: International Universities Press.

Kolb, L.C. (1989). Brain development, plasticity, and behavior. *American Psychologist, 44,* 1203–1212.

Korfmacher, J. (1998). Examining the service provider in early intervention. *Zero to Three, 18,* 17–22.

Korfmacher, J., O'Brien, R., Hiatt, S., & Olds, D. (2000). *Differences in program implementation between nurses and paraprofessionals in prenatal and infancy home visitation: A randomised trial.* Unpublished manuscript available from the author.

Kris, A.O. (1982). *Free association: Method and practice.* New Haven, CT: Yale University Press.

Kristal, J. (2005). *The temperament perspective: Working with children's behavioral styles.* Baltimore: Paul H. Brookes Publishing Co.

Krupnick, J.L., Sotsky, S.M., Simmens, S., Moyer, J., Elkin, K., Watkins, P., & Pilkoris, S. (1996). The role of the therapeutic alliance in psychotherapy and pharmacotherapy outcome: Findings in the National Institute of Mental Health Treatment of Depression Collaborative Research Program. *Journal of Consulting & Clinical Psychology, 64,* 532–539.

Krystal, H. (1988). *Integration and self-healing: Affect, trauma, and alexithymia.* Mahwah, NJ: Analytic Press.

Kuczynski, L., & Kochanska, G. (1990). Development of children's noncompliance strategies from toddlerhood to age 5. *Developmental Psychology, 26,* 398–408.

Kurscinka, M.S. (1991). *Raising your spirited child.* New York: Harper Perennial.

Kurtz, Z. (2004). *What works in promoting children's mental health.* Nottingham: Sure Start.

Lahey, B.B., Conger, R.D., Atkinson, B.M., & Treiber, F.A. (1984). Parenting behavior and emotional status of physically abusive mothers. *Journal of Consulting and Clinical Psychology, 52,* 1062–1071.

Lally, J.R., Mangione, P.L., & Honig, A.S. (1988). The Syracuse University Family Development Research Program: Long-range impact on an early intervention with low-income children and their families. In D.R. Powell (Ed.), *Parent education as early childhood intervention: Emerging directions in theory, research and practice* (Vol. 3, pp. 79–104). Norwood, NJ: Ablex.

Lamb, M.E., & Elster, A.B. (1986). Parental behavior of adolescent mothers and fathers. In A.B. Elster & M.E. Lamb (Eds.), *Adolescent fatherhood* (pp. 89–106). Mahwah, NJ: Lawrence Erlbaum Associates.

Lamb, M.E., Ketterlinus, R.D., & Fracasso, M.P. (1992). Parent–child relationships. In M.H. Bornstein & M.E. Lamb (Eds.), *Developmental psychology: An advanced textbook* (pp. 465–517). Mahwah, NJ: Lawrence Erlbaum Associates.

Lamborn, S.D., Mounts, N.S., Steinberg, L., & Dornbusch, S.M. (1991). Patterns of competence and adjustment among adolescents of authoritative, authoritarian, indulgent, and neglectful families. *Child Development, 62,* 1049–1065.

Landsman, I.S. (2002). Crises of meaning on trauma and loss. In J. Kauffman (Ed.), *Loss of the assumptive world: A theory of traumatic loss* (pp. 14–30). New York: Brunner-Routledge.

Landy, S. (2002a). Encouraging emotion regulation. In S. Landy, *Pathways to competence: Encouraging healthy social and emotional development in young children* (pp. 419–472). Baltimore: Paul H. Brookes Publishing Co.

Landy, S. (2002b). *Pathways to competence: Encouraging healthy social and emotional development in young children.* Baltimore: Paul H. Brookes Publishing Co.

Landy, S. (2002c). Understanding early child development and temperament. In S. Landy, *Pathways to competence: Encouraging healthy social and emotional development in young children* (pp. 1–84). Baltimore: Paul H. Brookes Publishing Co.

Landy, S. (2003). Reflective supervision. *IMPrint, 36,* 6–8.

Landy, S. (2004). *Tool for determining type and frequency of home visiting intervention.* Toronto: Toronto Public Health.

Landy, S., Clark, C., Schubert, J., & Jillings, C. (1983). Mother–infant interactions of teenage mothers as measured at 6 months in a natural setting. *The Journal of Psychology, 115,* 245–258.

Landy, S., & Menna, R. (1997). Mothers' reactions to the aggressive play of their aggressive and non-aggressive young children: Implications for caregivers. *Early Development and Care, 138,* 1–20.

Landy, S., & Menna, R. (1998). *An outcome study of the effects of the Helping Encourage Affect Regulation (HEAR) parenting program for parents of aggressive children.* Unpublished manuscript, Toronto, ON: Hincks-Dellcrest Institute.

Landy, S. & Menna, R. (in press). An evaluation of a group intervention for parents with aggressive young children: Improvements in child functioning, maternal confidence, knowledge and attitudes toward parenting. *Early Child Development and Care.*

Landy, S., Montgomery, J., Schubert, J., Cleland, J., & Clark, C. (1983). Mother–infant interaction of teenage mothers and the effect of experience of the observational sessions on the development of their infants. *Early Child Development and Care, 10,* 165–186.

Landy, S., Peters, R. DeV., Arnold, R., Allen, A.B., Brookes, F., & Jewell, S. (1998). Evaluation of "Staying on Track": An early identification, tracking, and referral system. *Infant Mental Health Journal, 19,* 34–58.

Landy, S., & Tam, K.K. (1997). Yes, parenting can make a difference in the development of Canadian children. In Statistics Canada, *Growing up in Canada: National longitudinal study of children and youth.* Ottawa: HRDC, Statistics Canada, 103–118.

Landy, S., & Thompson, E. (2006). *Pathways to Competence for Young Children: A Parenting Program.* Baltimore: Paul H. Brookes Publishing Co.

Laplanche, J., & Pontalis, J.B. (1973). *The language of psychoanalysis.* Oxford, England: Reprinted London: Karnac, 1988.

Larrance, D.T., & Twentyman, C.T. (1983). Maternal attributions and child abuse. *Journal of Abnormal Psychology, 92*, 449–457.

Larson, C. (1980). Efficacy of prenatal and postpartum visits on child health and development. *Pediatrics, 66*, 191–196.

Lavigne, J.V., Gibbons, R.D., Christoffel, K.K., Arend, R., Rosenblum, D., Binns, H., Dawson, N., Sobol, H., & Isaacs, C. (1996). Prevalence rates and correlates of psychiatric disorders among preschool children. *Journal of the American Academy of Child and Adolescent Psychiatry, 35*, 204–214.

Lawson, C.A. (2002). *Understanding the borderline mother: Helping her children transcend the intense, unpredictable, and volatile relationship.* Northvale, NJ: Jason Aronson.

Lazarus, A.A. (1997). *Brief but comprehensive psychotherapy: The multimodal way.* New York: Springer.

Lazarus, R.S. (1991). *Emotion and adaptation.* Oxford: Oxford University Press.

Lazarus, R.S., & Folkman, S. (1983). *Stress, appraisal and coping.* New York: Springer-Verlag.

Leadbeater, B., Bishop, S., & Raver, C.C. (1996). Quality of mother–child interaction, maternal depressive symptoms, and behaviour problems in preschoolers of adolescent mothers. *Developmental Psychology, 32*, 280–288.

Leadbeater, B.J., & Linares, O. (1992). Depressive symptoms in black and Puerto Rican adolescent mothers in the first three years post partum. *Development and Psychopathology, 4*, 451–468.

LeDoux, J.E. (1996). *The emotional brain: The mysterious underpinnings of emotional life.* New York: Simon & Schuster.

Lee, C.L., & Bates, J.E. (1985). Mother–child interaction at age two years and perceived difficult temperament. *Child Development, 56*, 1314–1325.

Lerner, R.M., Walsh, M.E., & Howard, K.A. (1998). Developmental contextual considerations: Person-context relations as the bases for risk and resiliency in child and adolescent development. In A.S. Bellack & M. Hersen (Eds.), *Comprehensive clinical psychology: Vol. 5. Child and adolescence* (pp. 1–24). New York: Elsevier/North Holland.

Lester, B.M. (1992). Infants and their families at risk: Assessment and intervention. *Infant Mental Health Journal, 13*, 54–66.

Lester, B.M., Boukydis, C.F.Z., & Twomey, J.E. (2000). Maternal substance abuse and child outcome. In C.H. Zeanah, Jr. (Ed.), *Handbook of infant mental health* (2nd ed., pp. 161–175). New York: Guilford Press.

Levenstein, P., Levenstein, S., Shiminski, J.A., & Stolzberg, J.E. (1998). Long-term impact of a verbal interaction program for at-risk toddlers: An exploratory study of high school outcomes in a replication of the mother–child home program. *Journal of Applied Developmental Psychology, 19*, 267–286.

Levenstein, P., O'Hara, J., & Madden, J. (1983). The mother–child home program of the Verbal Interaction Project. In Consortium for Longitudinal Studies (Ed.), *As the twig is bent: Lasting effects of preschool programs* (pp. 237–263). Mahwah, NJ: Lawrence Erlbaum Associates.

Leventhal, T., Brooks-Gunn, J., & Kanerman, S. (1997). Communities as place, face, and space: Provision of services to poor, urban children and their families. In J. Brooks-Gunn, G.J. Duncan & J. L. Aber (Eds.). *Neighborhood poverty: Context and consequences for children. Conceptual, methodological, and policy approaches to studying in neighborhoods* (Vol. 2) (pp. 181–205). New York: Russell Sage Foundation Press.

Levine, P. (1992). *The body as healer: Transforming trauma and anxiety.* Lyons, CO: Author.

Levkoe, J. (2003). A practical approach to reflective practice in early childhood education. *IMPrint, 35*, 12–14.

Lewis, M., & Brooks-Gunn, J. (1979). *Social cognition and the acquisition of self.* New York: Plenum Press.

Lewis, M., Feiring, C., McGuffog, C., & Jaskir, J. (1984). Predicting psychopathology in six-year-olds from early social relations. *Child Development, 55*, 123–136.

Lewis, M., Feiring, C., & Rosenthal, S. (2000). Attachment over time. *Child Development, 71*, 707–720.

Lewis, M.D., & Stieben, J. (2004). Emotion regulation in the brain: Conceptual issues and directions for developmental research. *Child Development, 75*, 371–376.

Lieberman, A.F. (1985). Infant mental health: A model for service delivery. *Journal of Clinical Child Psychology, 14*, 196–201.

Lieberman, A.F. (1989). What is culturally sensitive intervention? *Early Child Development and Care, 50,* 197–204.

Lieberman, A.F. (1990). Culturally sensitive intervention with children and families. *Child and Adolescent Social Work, 7,* 101–120.

Lieberman, A.F. (1991). Attachment theory and infant–parent psychotherapy: Some conceptual, clinical and research considerations. In D. Cicchetti & S.L. Toth (Eds.), *Rochester symposium on developmental psychopathology: Vol. 3. Models and integrations* (pp. 261–287). Rochester, NY: University of Rochester Press.

Lieberman, A.F. (1999). Negative maternal attributions: Effects on toddlers' sense of self. *Psychoanalytic Inquiry, 19,* 737–750.

Lieberman, A.F., & Pawl, J. H. (1993). Infant–parent psychotherapy. In C.H. Zeanah Jr. (Ed.), *Handbook of infant mental health* (pp. 427–442). New York: Guilford Press.

Lieberman, A.F., Silverman, R., & Pawl, J.H. (2000). Infant–parent psychotherapy: Core concepts and current approaches. In C.H. Zeanah Jr. (Ed.), *Handbook of infant mental health* (2nd ed., pp. 472–484). New York: Guilford Press.

Lieberman, A.F., Weston, D., & Pawl, J. (1991). Preventive intervention and outcome with anxiously attached dyads. *Child Development, 62,* 199–209.

Lieberman, A.F., & Zeanah, C.H. (2000). Infant–parent psychotherapy: Core concepts and current approaches. In C.H. Zeanah (Ed.), *Handbook of infant mental health* (pp. 472–484). New York: Guilford Press.

Linehan, M.M. (1993). *Cognitive behavioral treatment of borderline personality disorder.* New York: Guilford Press.

Liotti, G. (1999). Disorganization of attachment as a model for understanding dissociative psychopathology. In J. Solomon & C. George (Eds.), *Attachment disorganization* (pp. 291–317). New York: Guilford Press.

Liotti, G. (2004). Trauma, dissociation, and disorganized attachment: Three strands of a single braid. *Psychotherapy: Theory, Research, Practice, Training, 41,* 472–486.

Loevinger, J. (1985). Revision of the Sentence Completion Test for ego development. *Journal of Personality and Social Psychology, 48,* 420–427.

Longfellow, C., Zelkowitz, P., Saunders, E., & Belle, D. (1979, March). *The role of support in moderating the effects of stress and depression.* Paper presented at the biennial meeting of the Society for Research in Child Development, San Francisco.

Lorber, R., Felton, D.K., & Reid, J. (1984). A social learning approach to the reduction of coercive processes in child abusive families: A molecular analysis. *Advances in Behavior Research and Therapy, 6,* 29–45.

Luker, K.A., & Chalmers, K.I. (1990). Gaining access to clients: The case of health visiting. *Journal of Advanced Nursing, 15,* 74–82.

Luthar, S.S., & Zigler, E. (1992). Intelligence and social competence among high-risk adolescents. *Development and Psychopathology, 4,* 287–299.

Luthar, S.S., Cicchetti, D., Becker, B. (2000). The construct of resilience: A critical evaluation and guidelines for future work. *Child Development, 71,* 543–562.

Lynch, E.W., & Hanson, M.J. (2004). *Developing cross-cultural competence: A guide for working with children and their families (3rd ed.).* Baltimore: Paul H. Brookes Publishing Co.

Lynch-Fraser, D., & Tiegerman, E. (1987). *Baby signals: The breakthrough parenting guide for the 90s.* New York: St. Martin's Paperbacks.

Lyons-Ruth, K., Alpern, L., & Repacholi, B. (1993). Disorganized infant attachment classifications and maternal psychosocial problems as predictors of hostile-aggressive behavior in the preschool classroom. *Child Development, 64,* 572–585.

Lyons-Ruth, K., Bronfman, E., & Atwood, G. (1999). A relational diathesis model of hostile-helpless states of mind: Expressions in mother-infant interactions. In J. Solomon & C. George (Eds.), *Attachment disorganization* (pp. 33–07). New York: Guilford Press.

Lyons-Ruth, K., Connell, D.B., Grunebaum, H.U., & Botein, S. (1990). Infants at social risk: Maternal depression and family support services as mediators of infant development and security of attachment. *Child Development, 61,* 85–98.

Lyons-Ruth, K., & Jacobvitz, D. (1999). Attachment disorganization: Unresolved loss, relational violence, and lapses in behavioral and attentional strategies. In J. Cassidy & P.R. Shaver (Eds.), *Handbook of attachment: Theory, research, and clinical application* (pp. 520–554). New York: Guilford Press.

Lyons-Ruth, K., Melnick, S., Bronfman, E., Sherry, S, & Llanas, L. (2004). Hostile-helpless relational models and disorganized attachment patterns between parents and their young children: Review of research and implications for clinical work. In L. Atkinson & S. Goldberg (Eds.), *Attachment issues in psychopathology and intervention* (pp. 65–94). Mahwah, NJ: Lawrence Erlbaum Associates.

Lyons-Ruth, K., Repacholi, B. McLeod, S. & Silva, E. (1991). Disorganized attachment behavior in infancy: Short-term stability, maternal and infant correlates, and risk-related subtypes. *Development and Psychopathology, 3,* 377–396.

Lyons-Ruth, K., & Spielman, E. (2004). Disorganized infant attachment strategies and helpless-fearful profiles of parenting: Integrating attachment research with clinical interventions. *Infant Mental Health Journal, 25,* 318–335.

Lyons-Ruth, K., Yellin, C., Melnick, S., & Atwood, G. (2005). Expanding the concept of unresolved mental states: Hostile/Helpless states of mind on Adult Attachment Interview are associated with disruptive mother–infant communication and infant disorganization. *Development and Psychopathology, 17,* 271–301.

Lyons-Ruth, K.C., Bruschweiler-Stern, N., Harrison, A.M., Morgan, A.C., Nahum, J.P., Sander, L., Stern, D.N., & Tronick, E.Z. (1998). Implicit relational knowing: Its role in development and psychoanalytic treatment. *Infant Mental Health Journal, 19,* 282–289.

Maccoby, E., & Martin, J. (1983). Socialization in the context of the family: Parent–child interaction. In P.H. Mussen (Series Ed.) & E.M. Hetherington (Vol. Ed.), *Handbook of child psychology: Vol. 4. Socialization, personality, and social development* (pp. 1–101). New York: John Wiley & Sons.

MacKinnon, C.E., Lamb, M.E., Belsky, J., & Baum, C. (1990). An affective-cognitive model of mother–child aggression. *Development and Psychopathology, 2,* 1–13.

MacKinnon-Lewis, C., Lamb, M.E., Arbuckle, B., Baradaran, L.P., & Volling, B.L. (1992). The relationship between biased maternal and filial attributions and the aggressiveness of their interactions. *Development and Psychopathology, 4,* 403–415.

MacLeod, C., Mathews, A., & Tata, P. (1986). Attentional bias in emotional disorders. *Journal of Abnormal Psychology, 95,* 15–20.

MacLeod, J., & Wilson, G. (2000). Programs for the promotion of family wellness and the prevention of child maltreatment: A meta-analytic review. *Child Abuse and Neglect, 24,* 1127–1149.

MacMillan, H. (2000). Child maltreatment: What do we know in the year 2000. *Canadian Journal of Psychiatry, 45,* 702–709.

MacPhee, D. (1981). *Knowledge of infant development inventory.* Unpublished manual and questionnaire. University of North Carolina, Chapel Hill.

MacPhee, D. (1983, April). *The nature of parents' experience with and knowledge about infant development.* Paper presented at the meeting of the Society for Research in Child Development, Detroit.

MacPhee, D., Fritz, J., & Miller-Heyl, J. (1996). Ethnic variations in personal social networks and parenting. *Child Development, 67,* 3278–3295.

Madden, J., O'Hara, J., & Levenstein, S. (1984). Home again: Effects of the Mother–Child Home Program on mother and child. *Child Development, 55,* 636–647.

Madigan, S., Hawkins, E., Goldberg, S., & Benoit, D. (in press). Reduction of disrupted caregiver behaviour using Modified Interaction Guidance. *Infant Mental Health Journal.*

Mahler, M.S. (1968). *On human symbiosis and the vicissitudes of individuation.* New York: International Universities Press.

Mahler, M.S., Pine, F., & Bergman, A. (1975). *The psychological birth of the human infant.* New York: Basic Books.

Main, M. (1991). Metacognitive knowledge, metacognitive monitoring, and singular (coherent) vs. multiple (coherent) models of attachment: Findings and direction for further research. In P. Hams, J. Stevens, & C. Parkes (Eds.), *Attachment across the life cycle* (pp. 127–159). New York: Rutledge.

Main, M., & Goldwyn, R. (1984). Predicting rejection of her infant from mother's representation of her own experiences: Implications for the abused-abusing intergenerational cycle. *Child Abuse and Neglect, 8,* 203–217.

Main, M., & Goldwyn, R. (1994). *Adult attachment scoring and classification system.* Berkeley, CA: University of California.

Main, M., & Hesse, E. (1990). Parents' unresolved traumatic experiences are related to infant disorganized attachment status: Is frightened and/or frightening parental behavior the linking mechanism? In M.T. Greenberg, D. Cicchetti, & E.M. Cummings (Eds.), *Attachment in the preschool years: Theory, research, and intervention* (pp. 161–184). Chicago, IL: University of Chicago Press.

Main, M., & Hesse, E. (1992). *Frightening, frightened, dissociated, or disorganized behavior on the part of the parent: A coding system for parent–infant interaction.* Unpublished manuscript, University of California at Berkeley.

Main, M., & Solomon, J. (1987). Discovery of an insecure disorganized/disoriented attachment pattern: Patterns, findings, and implications for the classification of behavior. In M. Yogman & T.B. Brazelton (Eds.), *Affective development in infancy* (pp. 95–124). Norwood, NJ: Ablex.

Main, M., & Solomon, J. (1990). Procedures for identifying infants as disorganized/disoriented during the Ainsworth Strange Situation. In M.T. Greenberg, D. Cicchetti, & E.M. Cummings (Eds.), *Attachment in the preschool years: Theory, research and intervention* (pp. 121–160). IL: University of Chicago.

Manassis, K., & Bradley, S.J. (1994). The development of childhood anxiety disorders: Toward an integrated model. *Journal of Applied Developmental Psychology, 15*, 345–366.

Manio-Dimayuga, R. (2003). Reflective practice in a family support program. *IMPrint, 35,* 14–15.

Manolson, A., Ward, B., & Dodington, N. (1995). *You make the difference in helping your child learn.* Toronto: The Hanen Centre.

Mantini-Atkinson, T. (1993). *Competence and adaptation in developmentally handicapped children and their families.* Unpublished doctoral dissertation, University of Toronto.

Mantzicopoulos, P.Y. (1997). The relationship of family variables to Head Start children's preacademic competence. *Early Education and Development, 8*, 357–375.

Marcovitch, S., Cesaroni, L., Roberts, W., & Swanson, C. (1995). Romanian adoption: Parents' dreams, nightmares, and realities. *Child Welfare, 74*, 993–1017.

Marcovitch, S., Goldberg, S., Gold, A., Washington, J., Wasson, C., Krekewich, K., & Handley-Derry, M. (1997). Determinants of behavioral problems in Romanian children adopted in Ontario. *International Journal of Behavioral Development, 20*, 17–31.

Marcovitch, S., Goldberg, S., & MacGregor, D. (1992). *Risk factors in the functioning of school age developmentally handicapped children and their families.* Final Report to the Ministry of Community and Social Services, Toronto, ON.

Martyn, D., & Dundas, S. (April, 1997). *Schooling the emotions: Results of an experimental emotion regulation group in a sample of high risk parents.* Poster presented at the Society for Research in Child Development, Albuquerque, New Mexico.

Marvin, R., Cooper, G., Hoffman, K., & Powell, B. (2002). The Circle of Security project: Attachment-based intervention with caregiver-pre-school child dyads. *Attachment and Human Development, 4*, 107–124.

Mash, E.J., Johnston, C., & Kovitz, K. (1983). A comparison of the mother–child interactions of physically abused and non-abused children during play and task situations. *Journal of Child Clinical Psychology, 12*, 337–346.

Masten, A., & Coatsworth, J.D. (1998). The development of competence in favorable and unfavorable environments: Lessons from successful children. *American Psychologist, 53*, 205–220.

Masten, A., Morrison, P., Pellegrini, D., & Tellegen, A. (1990). Competence under stress: Risk and protective factors. In J. Rolf, A. Masten, D. Cicchetti, K. Nuechterlein, & S. Weintraub (Eds.), *Risk and protective factors in the development of psychopathology* (pp. 236–256). Cambridge: Cambridge University Press.

Masterson, J.F. (1988). *The search for the real self: Unmasking the personality disorder of our age.* New York: The Free Press.

Mathews, A. (1990). Why worry? The cognitive function of anxiety. *Behavior Research and Therapy, 28*, 455–468.

McCallum, M., & Piper, W.E. (1997). *Psychological mindedness: A contemporary understanding.* Mahwah, NJ.: Lawrence Erlbaum Associates.

McCann, J.B., James, A., Wilson, S., & Dunn, G. (1996). Prevalence of psychiatric disorders in young people in the care system. *British Medical Journal, 313*, 1529–1530.

McCann, L., & Pearlman, L. (1990). Vicarious traumatization: A framework for understanding the psychological effects of working with victims. *Journal of Traumatic Stress, 3*, 131–149.

McCarton, C.M., Brooks-Gunn, J., Wallace, I.F., Bauer, C.R., Bennett, F.C., Bernbaum, J.C., Broyles, R.S., Casey, P.H., McCormick, M.C., Scott, D.T., Tyson, J., Tonascia, J., & Meinert, C.L. (1997). Results at age 8 years of early intervention for low-birth-weight premature infants: The Infant Health and Development Program. *JAMA: Journal of the American Medical Association, 277,* 126–132.

McDonough, S.C. (1993a). *Interaction guidance treatment* (Rev. ed.). Ann Arbor, MI: University of Michigan.

McDonough, S.C. (1993b). Interaction guidance: Understanding and treating early infant–caregiver relationship disturbances. In C.H. Zeanah Jr. (Ed.), *Handbook of infant mental health* (pp. 414–426). New York: Guilford Press.

McDonough, S.C. (1995). Promoting positive early parent–infant relationships through interaction guidance. *Child and Adolescent Psychiatric Clinics of North America, 4,* 661–672.

McDonough, S.C. (2000). Interaction guidance: An approach for difficult-to-engage families. In C.H. Zeanah Jr. (Ed.), *Handbook of infant mental health* (2nd ed., pp. 485–493). New York: Guilford Press.

McEachin, J.J., Smith, T., & Lovass, O.I. (1993). Long-term outcomes for children with autism who received early intensive behavioural treatment. *American Journal of Mental Retardation, 97,* 359–372.

McEwen, B., & Sapolsky, R. (1995). Stress and cognitive functioning. *Current Opinions in Neurobiology, 5,* 205–216.

McGaha, C.G. (2002). Development of parenting skills in individuals with an intellectual impairment: An epigenetic explanation. *Disability and Society, 17,* 81–91.

McGillicuddy-DeLisi, A.V. (1985). The relationship between parental beliefs and children's cognitive levels. In I.E. Sigel (Ed.), *Parental belief systems* (pp. 7–24). Mahwah, NJ: Lawrence Erlbaum Associates.

McGillicuddy-DeLisi, A.V., & Sigel, I.E. (1995). Parental beliefs. In M.H. Bornstein (Ed.), *Handbook of parenting: Vol. 3. Status and social conditions of parenting* (pp. 333–358). Mahwah, NJ: Lawrence Erlbaum Associates.

McGrath, M.I., Zachariah-Boukydis, C.F., & Lester, B.M. (1993). Determinants of maternal self-esteem in the neonatal period. *Infant Mental Health Journal, 14,* 35–48.

McHale, J.P. (2003). Thinking three: Coparenting and family-level considerations for infant mental health professionals. *The Signal, 11,* 1–10.

McHale, J.P., & Fivaz-Depeursinger, E. (1999). Understanding triadic and family group process during infancy and early childhood. *Clinical Child and Family Psychology Review, 2,* 107–127.

McKinney, B., & Peterson, R.A. (1987). Predictors of stress in parents of developmentally disabled children. *Journal of Pediatric Medicine, 12,* 133–150.

McLoyd, V.C., & Wilson, L. (1991). The strain of living poor: Parenting, social support, and child mental health. In A.C. Huston (Ed.), *Children in poverty* (pp. 105–135). Cambridge: Cambridge University Press.

McNally, R.J., Kaspi, S.P., Riemann, P.C., & Zeitlin, S.B. (1990). Selective processing of threat cues in posttraumatic stress disorder. *Journal of Abnormal Psychology, 99,* 398–402.

McWilliams, N. (1994). *Psychoanalytic diagnosis: Understanding personality structure in the clinical process.* New York: Guilford Press

Meadow-Orlans, K.P. (2002). Parenting with a sensory or physical disability. In M.H. Bornstein, *Handbook of parenting: Vol. 2. Applied issues in parenting* (pp. 259–294). Mahwah, NJ: Lawrence Erlbaum Associates.

Mebert, C.J. (1989). Stability and change in parents' perceptions of infant temperament: Early pregnancy to 13.5 months postpartum. *Infant Behavior and Development, 12,* 237–244.

Mebert, C.J. (1991). Dimensions of subjectivity in parents' ratings of infant temperament. *Child Development, 62,* 352–361.

Mebert, C.J., & Kalinowski, M.F. (1986). Parents' expectations and perceptions of infant temperament: Pregnancy status differences. *Infant Behaviour and Development, 9,* 321–334.

Meij, J.T. (1992). *Social support, attachment, and early competence.* Unpublished doctoral dissertation, Catholic University, Nijmegen, the Netherlands.

Meins, E., Ferneyhough, C., Fradley, E., & Tuckey, M. (2001). Rethinking maternal sensitivity: Mothers' comments on infants' mental processes predict security of attachment at 12 months. *Journal of Child Psychology and Psychiatry, 42,* 637–648.

Meins, E., Ferneyhough, C., Wainwright, R., Clark-Carter, D., Gupta, M.D., Fradley, E., & Tuckey, M. (2003). Pathways to understanding mind: Construct validity and predictive validity of maternal mind-mindedness. *Child Development, 74,* 1194–1211.

Melson, G.F., Hsu, C.-H., & Ladd, G.W. (1993). The parental support networks of mothers and fathers: A multidimensional approach. *Early Development and Parenting, 2,* 169–182.

Meltzer, H., Gatward, R., Corbin, T., Goodman, R., & Ford, T. (2003). *Persistence, onset, risk factors, and outcome of childhood mental health disorders.* London: TSO.

Meltzer, H., Gatward, R., Goodman, R., & Ford, T. (2000). *Mental health of children and adolescents in Great Britain.* London: Social Survey Division of ONS, TSO.

Menna, R., & Landy, S. (2001). Working with parents of aggressive preschoolers: An integrative approach to treatment. *Journal of Clinical Psychology, 57,* 257–269.

Mercer, R.T., & Ferketich, S.L. (1995). Experienced and inexperienced mothers' maternal competence during infancy. *Research in Nursing and Health, 18,* 333–343.

Miller, C.L., Miceli, P.J., Whitman, T.L., & Borkowski, J.G. (1996). Cognitive readiness to parent and intellectual–emotional development in children of adolescent mothers. *Developmental Psychology, 32,* 533–541.

Miller, L.B., & Bizzell, R.P. (1983). The Louisville experiment: A comparison of four programs. In Consortium for Longitudinal Studies (Ed.), *As the twig is bent: Lasting effects of preschool programs* (pp. 171–200). Mahwah, NJ: Lawrence Erlbaum Associates.

Miller, L.B., & Bizzell, R.P. (1984). Long-term effects of four preschool programs: Ninth- and tenth-grade results. *Child Development, 55,* 1570–1587.

Miller, L.J., & Finnerty, M. (1996). Sexuality, pregnancy, and childrearing among women with schizophrenia-spectrum disorders. *Psychiatric Services, 47,* 502–506.

Miller, L.S., Wasserman, G.A., Neugebauer, R., Gorman-Smith, D., & Kamboukos, D. (1999). Witnessed community violence and anti-social behavior in high-risk urban boys. *Journal of Clinical Child Psychology, 28,* 2–11.

Miller, S., Hubble, M., & Duncan, B. (Eds.). (1996). *Handbook of solution focused brief therapy.* San Francisco: Jossey-Boss.

Miller, S.A. (1988). Parents' beliefs about children's cognitive development. *Child Development, 59,* 259–285.

Mills, R.S.L. (1999). Exploring effects of low power schema in mothers. In C.C. Piotrowski & P.D. Hastings (Eds.), *New directions for child and adolescent development: Vol. 86. Conflict as a context for understanding maternal beliefs about child rearing and children's misbehavior* (pp. 43–59). San Francisco: Jossey-Bass.

Milner, J.S. (1993). Social information processing and physical child abuse. *Clinical Psychology Review, 13,* 275–294.

Milner, J.S., & Foody, R. (1994). The impact of mitigating information on attributions for positive and negative child behavior by adults at low- and high-risk for child-abusive behavior. *Journal of Social and Clinical Psychology, 13,* 335–351.

Mitchell, J.T., & Everly, G.S. (1995). *Critical incident stress debriefing: An operations manual for the prevention of traumatic stress among emergency services and disaster workers.* Ellicott City, MD: Chevron Publishing.

Moher, C. (2003). Putting reflective practice into practice: One program's experience. *IMPrint, 35,* 15–16.

Mohr, W.K., & Fantuzzo, J.W. (2000). The neglected variable of physiology in domestic violence. *Journal of Aggression, Maltreatment & Trauma. Special Issue: Children exposed to domestic violence: Current issues in research, intervention, prevention, and policy development, 3,* 69–84.

Mondell, S., & Tyler, F.B. (1981). Parental competence and styles of problem-solving/play behavior with children. *Developmental Psychology, 17,* 73–78.

Moore, K.A., Morrison, D.R., & Greene, A.D. (1997). Effects on the children born to adolescent mothers. In R.A. Maynard (Ed.), *Kids having kids: Economic costs and social consequences of teen pregnancy.* Washington, DC: Urban Institute.

Moroney, R.M. (1992). Social support systems: Families and social policies. In S.L. Kagan, B., Weissbord, & E. Zigler (Eds.), *America's family support programs: Perspective and prospectives* (pp. 31–37). New Haven, CT: Yale University Press.

Moss, E., Parent, S., Gosselin, C., Rousseau, D., & St. Laurent, D. (1996). Attachment and teacher-reported behaviour-problems during the preschool and early school-age period. *Development and Psychopathology, 8,* 511–525.

Muir, E. (1992). Watching, Waiting, and Wondering: Applying psychoanalytic principles to mother–infant interventions. *Infant Mental Health Journal, 13,* 319–328.

Muir, E., Lojkasek, M., & Cohen, N.J. (1999). *Watch, Wait, and Wonder: A manual describing a dyadic infant-led approach to problems in infancy and early childhood.* Toronto: Hincks-Dellcrest Institute.

Murray, L., & Cooper, P.J. (1992). The impact of postnatal depression on infant development. *Journal of Child Psychology and Psychiatry, 33,* 543–561.

Murray, L., & Cooper, P.J. (1997). Post-partum depression and child development. *Psychological Medicine, 27,* 253–260.

Musick, J., & Stott, F. (2000). Paraprofessionals revisited and reconsidered. In J.P. Shonkoff & S.J. Meisels (Eds.), *Handbook of early childhood intervention* (2nd ed., pp. 439–453). Cambridge: Cambridge University Press.

Musun-Miller, L., & Blevins-Knabe, B. (1998). Adults' beliefs about children and mathematics: How important is it and how do children learn about it? *Early Development and Parenting, 7,* 191–202.

Myers, J.K., & Weissman, M.M. (1980). Use of a self-report symptom scale to detect depression in a community sample. *American Journal of Psychiatry, 37,* 1081–1084.

Naslund, B., Persson-Blennow, J., McNeil, T., McNeil, T.F., Kaij, L., & Malmquist-Larsson. A. (1984) Offspring of women with non-organic psychosis: Infant attachment to the mother at one year of age. Acta Psychiatrica Scandinavica, 69, 231–341.

Nellen, M., Mack, K., & Traver, T. (1999). Schizophrenia, mental state and mother–infant interaction: Examining the relationship. *Australian and New Zealand Journal of Psychiatry, 33,* 902–911.

Nelson, C.A. (2000). The neurological bases of early intervention. In J.P. Shonkoff & S.J. Meisels (Eds.), *Handbook of early childhood intervention* (pp. 204–227). Cambridge: Cambridge University Press.

Newberger, C.M. (1980). The cognitive structure of parenthood: The development of a descriptive measure. In R. Selman & R. Yando (Eds.), *New directions in child development: Vol. 7. Clinical developmental research* (pp. 45–67). San Francisco, CA: Jossey-Bass.

Newberger, C.M., & Cook, S.J. (1983). Parental awareness and child abuse: A cognitive-developmental analysis of urban and rural samples. *American Journal of Orthopsychiatry, 53,* 512–524.

Newberger, C.M., & White, K.M. (1989). Cognitive foundations for parental care. In D. Cicchetti & V. Carlson (Eds.), *Child maltreatment: Theory and research on the causes and consequences of child abuse and neglect* (pp. 302–316). Cambridge: Cambridge University Press.

Niccols, A. (2001). *Right from the Start: An attachment-based course for parents of infants under 2 years: Leader Manual.* Hamilton, ON: Infant–Parent Program, Hamilton Health Sciences and McMaster University.

Niccols, A., & Mohamed, S. (2000). Parent–child interaction skills training in groups: Pilot study with parents of infants with developmental delays. *Journal of Consulting and Clinical Psychology, 53,* 846–851.

Nix, R.L., Pinderhughes, E.E., Dodge, K.A., Bates, J.E., & Pettit, G.S. (1999). The relation between mothers' hostile attribution tendencies and children's externalizing behavior problems: The mediating role of mothers' harsh discipline. *Child Development, 70,* 896–909.

Noll, R., McKellop, J.M., Vannatta, K., & Kalinyak, K. (1998). Child-rearing practices of primary care-givers of children with sickle cell disease: The perspective of professionals and caregivers. *Journal of Pediatric Psychology, 23,* 131–140.

Norcross, J.C., & Arkowitz, H. (1992). The evolution and current status of psychotherapy integration. In W. Dryden (Ed.), *Integrative and eclectic therapy* (pp. 1–40). Buckingham: Open University Press.

Norcross, J.C., Glass, C.R., Arnkoff, D.B., Lambert, M.J., Shoham, V., Stiles, W.B., Shapiro, D.A., Barkham, M., & Strupp, H.H. (1993). Research directions for psychotherapy integration: A roundtable. *Journal of Psychotherapy Integration, 3,* 91–131.

Norcross, J.C., & Goldfried, M.R. (Eds.). (1992). *Handbook of psychotherapy integration.* New York: Basic Books.

Norcross, J.C., & Newman, C.E. (1992). Psychotherapy integration: Setting the context. In J.C. Norcross and M.R. Goldfried (Eds.), *Handbook of psychotherapy integration* (pp. 3–45). New York: Basic Books.

Nugent, J.K., & Brazelton, T.B. (2000). Preventive infant mental health: Uses of the Brazelton Scale. In J.D. Osofsky & J.E. Fitzgerld (Eds.), *WAIM handbook of infant mental health* (Vol. 2, pp. 159–301). New York: John Wiley & Sons.

Nurcombe, B., Howell, D., Rauh, V., Teti, D., Ruoff, P., & Brennan, J. (1984). An intervention program for mothers of low-birthweight infants: Preliminary results. *Journal of the American Academy of Child Psychiatry, 23,* 319–325.

O'Connor, T., & Rutter, M. (1996). Risk mechanisms in development: Some conceptual and methodological considerations. *Developmental Psychology, 32,* 787–795.

O'Connor, T.G., Bredenkamp, D., Rutter, M., & English and Romanian Adoptees (ERA) Study Team (1999). Attachment disturbances and disorders in children exposed to early severe deprivation. *Infant Mental Health Journal, 20,* 10–29.

O'Connor, T.G., Rutter, M., Beckett, C., Keaveney, L., Kreppner, J.M., & English and Romanian Adoptees Study Team (2000). The effects of global severe privation on cognitive competence: Extension and longitudinal follow-up. *Child Development, 71,* 376–390.

Offord, D.R., & Lipman, F.L. (1996). Emotional and behavioral problems. National Longitudinal Study of Children and Youth. In Statistics Canada, *Growing up in Canada,* Ottawa: Statistics Canada.

Offord, D.R., Boyle, M.H., Fleming, J.E., & Blum, H.M. (1989). The Ontario Child Health Study: Summary of selected results. *Canadian Journal of Psychiatry, 34,* 483–491.

Offord, D.R., Boyle, M.H., Racine, Y.A., Fleming, J.E., Cadman, D.T., Blum, H.M., Byrne, C., Links, P.S., Lipman, E.L., Macmillan, H.L., Rae Grant, N.L., Sanford, M.N., Szatmari, P., Thomas, H., & Woodward, C.A. (1992). Outcome, prognosis, and risk in a longitudinal follow-up study. *Journal of the American Academy of Child and Adolescent Psychiatry, 31,* 916–923.

Oldershaw, L. (2002). *A national survey of parents of young children.* Toronto, ON: Invest in Kids Foundation.

Olds, D. (1997). The Prenatal Early Infancy Project: Preventing child abuse in the context of promoting maternal and child health. In D.A. Wolfe, A.J. McMahon, R. DeV. Peters (Eds.), *Child abuse: New directions in prevention and treatment across the lifespan* (pp. 130–156). Thousand Oaks, CA: Sage Publications.

Olds, D., Chamberlain, R., & Tatelbaum, R. (1986). Preventing child abuse and neglect. *Pediatrics, 78,* 65–78.

Olds, D.L., Eckenrode, J., Henderson, C.R., Jr., Kitzman, H., Powers, J., Cole, R., Sidora, K., Morris, P., Pettitt, L.M., & Luckey, D. (1997). Long-term effects of home visitation on maternal life course and child abuse and neglect: Fifteen-year follow-up of a randomized trial. *The Journal of the American Medical Association, 278,* 637–643.

Olds, D.L., Henderson, C.R., Kitzman, H., Eckenrode, J., Cole, R., & Tatelbaum, R. (1998). The promise of home visitation: Results of two randomized trials. *Journal of Community Psychology, 26,* 5–21.

Olds, D., Hill, P., Robinson, J., Song, N., & Little, C. (2000). Update on home visiting for pregnant women and parents of young children. *Current Problems in Pediatrics, 30,* 107–141.

Olds, D.L., & Kitzman, H. (1993). Review of research on home visiting for pregnant women and parents of young children. *The Future of Children, 3,* 53–92.

Olds, D., Robinson, J., Luckey, D., O'Brien, R., Korfmacher, J., Hiatt, S., Pettitt, L., & Henderson, C. (1999). *Comparison of pregnancy and infancy home visitation by nurses versus paraprofessionals: A randomized controlled trial. Final report to the Colorado Trust on Home Visitation, 2000.*

Olds, D.L., Robinson, J., O'Brien, R., Luckey, D.W., Pettitt, L.M., Henderson, C.R., Ng, R.K., Sheff, K.L., Korfmacher, J., Hiatt, S., & Talmi, A. (2002). Home visiting by paraprofessionals and by nurses: A randomized controlled trial. *Pediatrics, 110,* 486–496.

Olwens, D. (1980). Familial and temperamental determinants of aggressive behavior in adolescent boys: A causal analysis. *Developmental Psychology, 16,* 644–660.

Osofsky, J.D. (1999). The impact of violence on young children. *The Future of Children: Domestic Violence and Children, 9,* 33–49.

Osofsky, J.D., Culp, A.W., Eberhart-Wright, A., Ware, L.M., & Hann, D.M. (1988). *Final report to the Kenworthy Foundation.* University Medical Center, New Orleans.

Osofsky, J.D. & Eberhart-Wright, A. (1988). Affective exchanges between high risk mothers and infants. *International Journal of Psychoanalysis, 69,* 221–231.

Osofsky, J.D. & Eberhart-Wright, A. (1992). Risk and protective factors for parents and infants. In G. Suci & S. Robertson (Eds.), *Human development: Future directions in infant development research* (pp. 25–39). New York: Springer-Verlag.

Osofsky, J.D., Hann, D.M., & Peebles, C. (1993). Adolescent parenthood: Risks and opportunities for mothers and infants. In C.H. Zeanah Jr. (Ed.), *Handbook of infant mental health* (pp. 106–119). New York: Guilford Press.

Ottenbacher, K.J., Muller, L., Brandt, D., Heintzelman, A., Hojem, P., & Sharpe, P. (1987). The effectiveness of tactile stimulation as a form of early intervention: A quantitative evaluation. *Journal of Developmental and Behavioral Pediatrics, 14,* 68–76.

Palacio, J., & Moreno, M.C. (1996). Parents' and adolescents' ideas on children, origins, and transmission of intracultural diversity. In S. Harkness & C.M. Super (Eds.), *Parents' cultural belief systems: Their origins, expressions, and consequences* (pp. 215–253). New York: Guilford Press.

Panksepp, J. (1993). Neurochemical control of moods and emotions: Amino acids to neuropeptides. In M. Lewis & J.M. Haviland (Eds.), *Handbook of emotions* (pp. 87–107). New York: Guilford Press.

Pape, B., Byrne, C., & Ivask, A. (1996). *Analysis of the impact of affective disorders on families and children.* Submitted to the Strategic Fund for Children's Mental Health, Health Canada, Ottawa.

Parent-Child Mother Goose Program (2002). *The Parent-Child Mother Goose Program: Program policy handbook.* Toronto: Author.

Paris, J. (1990). Empirical investigation of the role of development in the etiology and outcome of borderline personality disorder. In P.S. Links (Ed.), *Family environment and borderline personality disorder* (pp. 123–130). Washington, DC: American Psychiatric Press.

Paris, J. (1996). *Social factors in the personality disorder.* Cambridge: Cambridge University Press.

Paris, J., Zweig-Frank, H., & Guzder, H. (1993). The role of psychological risk factors in recovery from borderline personality disorder. *Comprehensive Psychiatry, 34,* 410–413.

Park, R.D., Power, T.G., & Fisher, T. (1980). The adolescent father's impact on the mother and child. *Journal of Social Issues, 36,* 88–106.

Parker-Loewen, D., & Lytton, H. (1987). Effects of short-term interaction coaching with mothers of pre-term infants. *Infant Mental Health Journal, 8,* 277–287.

Parlakian, R. (2001). *Look, listen, and learn: Reflective supervision and relationhsip-based work.* Baltimore: Zero to Three.

Parlakian, R. (2002). *Reflective supervision in practice: Stories from the field.* Baltimore: Zero to Three.

Pascoe, J.M., Loda, F.A., Jeffries, V., & Earp, J.A. (1981). The association between mothers' social support and provision of stimulation to their children. *Journal of Developmental and Behavioral Pediatrics, 2,* 15–19.

Pastor, D.L. (1981). The quality of mother–infant attachment and its relationship to toddler's initial sociability with peers. *Developmental Psychology, 17,* 326–337.

Patterson, G.R. (1980). Mothers: The unacknowledged victims. *Monographs of the Society for Research in Child Development, 45.* New York: Blackwell.

Patterson, G.R. (1995). Coercion as a basis for early age of onset for arrest. In J. McCord (Ed.), *Coercion and punishment in long-term perspectives* (pp. 81–105). Cambridge: Cambridge University Press.

Paul, G.L. (1969). Behavior modification research: Design and tactics. In C.M. Franks (Eds.), *Behavior therapy: Appraisal and status* (pp. 29–62). New York: McGraw-Hill.

Pawl, J.H. (1993). A stitch in time: Using emotional support, developmental guidance, and infant–parent psychotherapy in a brief preventive intervention. In E. Fenichel & S. Provence (Eds.), *Development in jeopardy: Clinical responses to infants and families* (pp. 203–229). Madison, CT: International Universities Press.

Pearlin, L., & Schooler, C. (1978). The structure of coping. *Journal of Health and Social Behavior, 19,* 1–21.

Pearlman, L.A., & Saakvitne, K.W. (1995). *Trauma and the therapist: Counter transference and vicarious traumatization in psychotherapy with incest survivors.* New York: W.W. Norton.

Pedersen, W. (1994). Parental relations, mental health, and delinquency in adolescence. *Adolescence, 29,* 975–990.

Pennington, B.F. (2002). *The development of psychopathology: Nature and nurture.* New York: Guilford Press.

Perner, J., & Ruffman, T. (1995). Episodic memory and autonoetic consciousness: Developmental evidence and a theory of childhood amnesia. *Journal of Experimental Child Psychology, 59,* 516–548.

Perry, B.D. (1994). Neurobiological sequelae of childhood trauma: Post-traumatic stress disorders in children. In M. Murberg (Ed.), *Catecholamine function in posttraumatic stress disorder: Emerging concepts* (pp. 253–276). Washington, DC: American Psychiatric Press.

Perry, B.D. (1996). *Maltreated children: Experience, brain development and the next generation.* New York: W.W. Norton.

Perry, B.D. (1997). Incubated in terror: Neurodevelopmental factors in the "cycle of violence." In J.D. Osofsky (Ed.), *Children in a violent society* (pp. 124–149). New York: Guilford Press.

Perry, B.D. (1999). The memory of states: How the brain stores and retrieves traumatic experience. In J. Goodwin, & R. Attias (Eds.), *Splintered reflections: Images of the body in treatment* (pp. 9–38). New York: Basic Books.

Perry, B.D. (2001). Violence and childhood: How persisting fear can alter the child's developing brain. In D. Schetky & E. Benedek (Eds.), *Textbook of child and adolescent forensic psychiatry* (pp. 221–238). Washington, DC: American Psychiatric Press.

Perry, B.D., Pollard, R.A., Blakley, T.L., Baker, W.L., & Vigilante, D. (1995). Childhood trauma, the neurobiology of adaptation, and "use-dependent" development of the brain: How "states" become "traits." *Infant Mental Health Journal, 16,* 271–292.

Perry, J.C., & Cooper, S.H. (1986). A preliminary report on defenses and conflicts associated with borderline personality disorder. *Journal of the American Psychoanalytic Association, 34,* 863–894.

Peters, R. DeV., Arnold, R., Petrunka, K., Angus, D., Bélanger, J.-M., Boyce, W., Brophy, K., Burke, S.O., Cameron, G., Craig, W., Evers, S., Herry, Y., Mamatis, D., Nelson, G., Pancer, S.M., Roberts-Fiati, G., Russell, C.C., & Towson, S. (2004). *Better Beginnings, Better Futures: A comprehensive, community-based project for early childhood development. Highlights of lessons learned.* Kingston, ON: Better Beginnings, Better Futures Research Coordination Unit Technical Report.

Peters, R. DeV., Arnold, R., Petrunka, K., Angus, D., Brophy, K., Burke, S.O., Cameron, G., Evers, S., Herry, Y., Levesque, D., Pancer, S., Roberts-Fiati, G., Towson, S., & Warren, W.K. (2000). *Developing capacity and competence in Better Beginnings, Better Futures communities: Short-term findings report.* Kingston, ON: Queen's University.

Phares, V., & Compas, B.E. (1993). The role of fathers in child and adolescent psychopathology: Make way for Daddies. In M.E. Hertzig & E.A. Faber (Eds.), *Annual progress in child psychiatry and child development* (pp. 344–401). New York: Brunner-Mazel.

Pharis, M.E., & Levin, V.S. (1991). "A person to talk to who really cares" High-risk mothers' evaluations of services in an intensive intervention research program. *Child Welfare, 70,* 307–320.

Phillips, L.H.C. & O'Hara, M.W. (1991). Prospective study of postpartum depression: 4½ year follow-up of women and children. *Journal of Abnormal Psychology, 100,* 151–155.

Pickrel, S. (1997). *Multisystemic therapy for infants, young children, and their families.* Presented at Zero to Three 12th National Training Institute, Nashville, TN.

Pine, F. (1985). *Developmental theory and clinical process.* New Haven, CT: Yale University Press.

Piper, W.E., McCallum, M, & Hassan, F.A.A. (1992). Psychological mindedness and psychodynamic work. In W.E. Piper, M. McCallum, & F.A.A. Hassan (Eds.), *Adaptation to loss through short-term group psychotherapy* (pp. 169–190). New York: Guilford Press.

Plomin, R., DeFries, J. C., McClearn, G. E., & Rutter, M. (1997). *Behavioral genetics* (3rd. ed.). New York: Freeman.

Polansky, N., Gaudin, J., Ammons, A., & Davis, K. (1985). The psychological ecology of the neglectful mother. *Child Abuse and Neglect, 9,* 265–275.

Polansky, N.A. (1985). Determinants of loneliness among neglectful and other low income mothers. *Journal of Social Service Research, 8,* 1–15.

Polansky, N.A., Ammons, P.N., & Gaudin, J.M. (1985). Loneliness and isolation in child neglect. *Social Casework, 66,* 34–47.

Porges, S.W. (1996). Physiological regulation in high-risk infants: A model for assessment and potential intervention. *Development and Psychopathology, 8,* 43–58.

Post, R.M. (1992). Transduction of psychosocial stress into the neurobiology of recurrent affective disorder. *American Journal of Psychiatry, 149,* 999–1010.

Powell, C., & Grantham-McGregor, S. (1989). Home visiting of varying frequency and child development. *Pediatrics, 84,* 157–164.

Powles, W. (2000, July). *Healthier progress: Historical perspectives on social determinants of health.* Canberra, Australia.

Priel, B., & Besser, A. (2000). Adult attachment styles, early relationships, antenatal attachment, and perceptions of infant temperament: A study of first-time mothers. *Personal Relationships, 7,* 291–310.

Priel, B., & Besser, A. (2002). Perceptions of early relationships during the transition to motherhood: The mediating role of social support. *Infant Mental Health Journal, 9,* 343–360.

Prior, S. (1996). *Object relations in severe trauma.* Northvale, NJ: Jason Aronson.

Process of Change Study Group (1998). Non-interpretative mechanisms in psychoanalytic therapy. *International Journal of Psychoanalysis, 79,* 903–921.

Prochaska, J.O. (1995). Common problems: Common solutions. *Clinical Psychology: Science and Practice, 1,* 101–105.

Prochaska, J.O. (1999). How do people change, and how can we change to help many more people? In M.A. Hubble, B.L. Duncan, & S.D. Miller (Eds.), *The heart and soul of change: What works in therapy?* (pp. 227–255). Washington, DC: American Psychological Association.

Prochaska, J.O., & DiClemente, C.C. (1984). *The transtheoretical approach: Crossing the boundaries of therapy.* Homewood, IL: Dow Jones-Irwin.

Prochaska, J.O., DiClemente, C.C., & Norcross, J.C. (1992). In search of how people change: Application to addictive behaviors. *American Psychologist, 47,* 1102–1114.

Prochaska, J.O., Norcross, J.C., & Diclemente, C.C. (1994). *Changing for good: A revolutionary six-stage program for overcoming bad habits and moving your life positively forward.* New York: Avon Books.

Procidano, M.E., & Heller, K. (1983). Measures of perceived social support from friends and family: Three validation studies. *American Journal of Community Psychology, 11,* 1–24.

Purkey, W.W., & Schmidt, J.J. (1987). *The inviting relationship: An expanded perspective for professional counseling.* Englewood Cliffs, NJ: Prentice-Hall.

Pynoos, R.S., Steinberg, A.M., & Goenjian, A. (1996). Traumatic stress in childhood and adolescence: Recent developments and current controversies. In B. van der Kolk, A.C. McFarlane, & L. Weisaeth (Eds.), *Traumatic stress: The effects of overwhelming experience on mind, body, and society* (pp. 331–358). New York: Guilford Press.

Quint, J.C., Bos, I.M., & Polit, D.F. (1997). *New Chance: Final report of a comprehensive program for disadvantaged young mothers and their children.* New York: Manpower Demonstration Research Corporation.

Radke-Yarrow, M., McCann, K., DeMulder, E., Belmont, B., Martinez, P., & Richardson, D. (1995). Attachment in the context of high-risk conditions. *Development and Psychopathology, 7,* 247–266.

Radke-Yarrow, M., & Sherman, T. (1990). Hard growing: Children who survive. In J. Rolf, A. Masten, D. Cicchetti, K. Nuechterlein, & S. Weintraub (Eds.), *Risk and protective factors in the development of psychopathology* (pp. 97–119). Cambridge: Cambridge University Press.

Rae-Grant, N., Thomas, H., Offord, D., & Boyle, M. (1989). Risk, protective factors and the presence of behavioral and emotional disorders in children and adolescents. *Journal of the American Academy of Child and Adolescent Psychiatry, 28,* 262–268.

Ramey, C.T., Bryant, D.M., Wasik, B.H. , Sparling, P., Fendt, S., & LaVange, P. (1992). The Infant Health and Development Program for low birth weight, premature infants: Program elements, family participation, and child intelligence. *Pediatrics, 89,* 454–465.

Rauch, S.L., Shin, L.M., Wahlen, P.J.H., & Pitman, R.K. (1998). Neuroimaging and the neuroanatomy of post traumatic stress disorder. *CNS Spectrums, 3* (Suppl. 2), 31–41.

Reed, M.A., & Derryberry, D. (1995). Temperament and attention to positive and negative trait information. *Personality and Individual Differences, 18,* 135–147.

Regehr, C. (2003). Vicarious trauma in working with high risk children. *IMPrint, 36,* 4–5.

Regehr, C., & Cadell, S. (1999). Secondary trauma in sexual assault crisis work: Implications for therapy and therapists. *Canadian Social Work, 1,* 56–63.

Regehr, C., Chau, S., Leslie, B., & Howe, P. (2002). Inquiries into the death of children: Impacts on child welfare workers and their organizations. *Child and Youth Services Review, 24,* 885–902.

Regehr, C., Hill, J., Goldberg, G., & Hughes, J. (2003). Postmortem inquiries and truama responses in firefighters and paramedics. *Journal of Interpersonal Violence, 18,* 607–622.

Reich, S. (2005). What do mothers know? Maternal knowledge of child development. *Infant Mental Health Journal, 26*, 143–156.

Reich, W., Earls, F., Frankel, O., & Shayka, J.J. (1993). Psychopathology in children of alcoholics. *Journal of the American Academy of Child and Adolescent Psychiatry, 32*, 995–1002.

Reid, J.B. (1993). Prevention of conduct disorders before and after school entry: Relating interventions to developmental findings. *Development Psychopathology, 5*, 243–262.

Reid, J.B., Kavanagh, K., & Baldwin, D.V. (1987). Abusive parents' perceptions of child problem behaviors: An example of parental bias. *Journal of Abnormal Child Psychology, 15*, 457–466.

Reid, J.B., Patterson, G.P., & Lorber, R. (1982). The abused child: Victim, instigator, or innocent bystander? In D.J. Bernstein (Ed.), *Response structure and organization* (pp. 47–68). Lincoln: University of Nebraska Press.

Reid, J.B., Taplin, P.S., & Lorber, R. (1981). A social interactional approach to the treatment of abusive families. In R. Stuart (Ed.), *Violent behavior: Social learning approaches to prediction, management, treatment* (pp. 83–101). New York: Brunner/Mazel.

Reite, M., & Boccia, M.L. (1994). Physiological aspects of adult attachment. In M.B. Sperling & W.H. Berman (Eds.), *Attachment in adults: Clinical and developmental perspectives* (pp. 98–127). New York: Guilford Press.

Repachol, B.M., & Gopnik, A. (1997). Early reasoning about desires. Evidence from 14- and 18-month-olds. *Developmental Psychology, 33*, 12–21.

Reynolds, A.J. (1994). Effects of a preschool plus follow-up intervention for children at risk. *Developmental Psychology, 30*, 787–804.

Reynolds, A.J. (1997). *The Chicago Child Parent Centers: A longitudinal study of extended early childhood intervention* (Discussion paper #1126–1197). Madison, WI: Institute for Research on Poverty.

Reynolds, A.J., Temple, J.A., Robertson, D.L., & Mann, E.A. (2001). Long-term effects of an early childhood intervention on educational achievement and juvenile arrest: A 15-year follow-up of low-income children in public schools. *JAMA, 285*, 2339-2346.

Reznick, J.S. (1999). Influences on maternal attribution of infant intentionality. In P.D. Zelazo, J.W. Astington, & D.R. Olson (Eds.), *Developing theories of intention: Social understanding and self-control* (pp. 243–367). Mahwah, NJ: Lawrence Erlbaum Associates.

Riblatt, S.N. (April, 1995). *Theory of mind in preschoolers: False beliefs, deception and pretense.* Paper presented at the biennial meeting of the Society for Research in Child Development: Indianapolis.

Richards, J.M., & Gross, J.J. (2000). Emotion regulation and memory: The cognitive costs of keeping one's cool. *Journal of Personality and Social Psychology, 79*, 410–424.

Richman, A., Miller, P., & LeVine, R. (1992). Cultural and educational variations in maternal responsiveness. *Developmental Psychology, 28*, 614–621.

Rickard, K.M., Forehand, R., Wells, K.C., Grist, D.L., & McMahon, J.J. (1981). Factors in the referral of children for behavioral treatment: A comparison of mothers for clinic-referred deviant, clinic-referred non-deviant and non-clinic children. *Behavior Research and Therapy, 19*, 201–205.

Rickard, V. (1998). *The Learning About Myself Program* for at-risk parents. Binghampton, New York: Haworth Press.

Riordan, D., Appleby, L., & Faragher, B. (1999). Mother–infant interaction in post-partum women with schizophrenia and affective disorders. *Psychological Medicine, 29*, 991–995.

Ritsher, J.E.B., Coursey, R.D., & Farrell, E.W. (1997). A survey on issues in the lives of women with severe mental illness. *Psychiatric Services, 48*, 1273–1282.

Roberts, W.L. (1989). Parents' stressful life events and social networks: Relations with parenting and children's competence. *Canadian Journal of Behavioural Science, 21*, 132–146.

Robert-Tissot, C., & Cramer, B. (1998). When patients contribute to the choice of treatment. *Journal of Infant Mental Health, 19*, 245–259.

Robert-Tissot, C., Cramer, B., Stern, D.N., Serpa, S.R., Bachmann, J.P., Palacio-Espasa, F., Knauer, D., de Muralt, M., Berney, C., & Mendiguren, G. (1996). Outcome evaluation in brief mother–infant psychotherapies: Report on 75 cases. *Infant Mental Health Journal, 17*, 97–114.

Rogeness, G.A., & McClure, E.B. (1996). Development and neurotransmitter-environmental interactions. *Development and Psychopathology, 8*, 183–200.

Rogers, S.J., Parcel, T.L., & Meaghan, E.G. (1991). The effects of maternal working conditions and mastery on child behavior problems: Studying the intergenerational transmission of social control. *Journal of Health and Social Behavior, 32,* 145–164.

Rogler, L.H., Malgady, R.G., Costantino, G., & Blumenthal, R. (1987). What do culturally sensitive mental health services mean? The case of Hispanics. *American Psychologist, 42,* 565–570.

Rose, S. (1997). Psychological debriefing: History and methods of counselling. *Journal of the British Association of Counselling, 8,* 48–51.

Rose, S.L., Rose, S.A., & Feldman, J.F. (1989). Stability of behavior problems in young children. *Development and Psychopathology, 1,* 5–19.

Rosenberg, M. (1965). *Society and the adolescent self-image.* Princeton, NJ: Princeton University Press.

Rosenberg, M. (1979). *Conceiving the self.* New York: Basic Books.

Rossman, B.B.R., & Ho, J. (2000). Posttraumatic response and children exposed to parental violence. *Journal of Aggression, Maltreatment and Trauma, 3,* 85–106.

Rothbart, M.K., & Derryberry, D. (1981). Development of individual differences in temperament. In M.E. Lamb & A.L. Brown (Eds.), *Advances in developmental psychology* (Vol. 1, pp. 37–86). Mahwah, NJ: Lawrence Erlbaum Associates.

Rothbaum, F., & Weisz. J.R. (1994). Parental caregiving and child externalizing behavior in nonclinical samples: A meta-analysis. *Psychological Bulletin, 116,* 55–74.

Rothschild, B. (2000). *The body remembers: The psychophysiology of trauma and trauma treatment.* New York: W.W. Norton.

Rotter, J.B. (1966). Generalized expectancies for internal versus external control. *Psychological Monographs, 80,* 1–28.

Rubin, K.H., & Mills, R.S. (1990). Maternal beliefs about adaptive and maladaptive social behaviors in normal, aggressive, and withdrawn preschoolers. *Journal of Abnormal Child Psychology, 18,* 419–435.

Russell, C.R. (2003). *Parenting in the beginning years: Priorities for investment.* Toronto, ON: Invest in Kids Foundation.

Rutter, M. (1987). Psychosocial resilience and protective mechanisms. *American Journal of Orthopsychiatry, 57,* 316–331.

Rutter, M. (1989). Pathways from childhood to adult life. *Journal of Child Psychology and Psychiatry, 36,* 23–51.

Rutter, M. (1990). Psychosocial resilience and protective mechanisms. In J. Rolf, A. Masten, D. Cicchetti, K. Nuechterlein, & S. Weintraub (Eds.), *Risk and protective factors in the development of psychopathology* (pp. 181–214). Cambridge: Cambridge University Press.

Rutter, M. (1996). Connections between child and adult psychopathology. *European Child and Adolescent Psychiatry, 5,* 4–7.

Rutter, M. (2000a). *Biological and experiential influences on psychological development.* Paper presented for WebForum 2001: A Millenium Dialogue on Early Child Development, Toronto, ON: University of Toronto.

Rutter, M. (2000b). Resilience reconsidered: Conceptual considerations, empirical findings, and policy implications. In J.P. Shonkoff & S.J. Meisels (Eds.), *Handbook of early childhood intervention* (pp. 651–682). Cambridge: Cambridge University Press.

Rutter, M., & Smith, D.J. (Eds.). (1995). *Psychosocial disorders in young people. Time trends and their causes.* New York: John Wiley & Sons.

Rutter, M., Tizard, J., & Yule, W. (1976). Isle of Wight studies, 1964–1974. *Psychological Medicine, 6,* 313–332.

Sabo, A.N. (1997). Etiological significance associations between childhood trauma and borderline personality disorder: Conceptual and clinical implications. *Journal of Personality Disorders, 1,* 50–70.

Sagatum, I.J. (1991). Attributions of delinquency by delinquent minors, their families, and probation officers. *Journal of Offender Rehabilitation, 16,* 43–56.

Sajaniemi, N., Mäkelä, J., Salokorpi, T., von Wendt, L., Hämälämen, T., & Hakamies-Blomqvist, L. (2001). Cognitive performance and attachment patterns at four years of age in extremely low birth weight infants after early intervention. *European Child & Adolescent Psychiatry, 10,* 122–129.

Sameroff, A.J. (1983). Developmental systems: Contexts and evolution. In W. Leessen (Ed.), *Handbook of child psychology: Vol. 1. History, theories and methods* (pp. 238–294). New York: John Wiley & Sons.

Sameroff, A.J. (1993). Models of development and developmental risk. In C.H. Zeanah, Jr. (Ed.), *Handbook of infant mental health* (pp. 3–13). New York: Guilford Press.

Sameroff, A.J., & Chandler, M.J. (1975). Reproductive risk and the continuum of caretaking casualty. In F.D. Horowitz, M. Hetherington, S. Scarr-Salapatek, & G. Siegel (Eds.), *Review of child development research* (Vol. 4, pp. 187–244). Chicago: University of Chicago Press.

Sameroff, A.J., & Feil, L.A. (1985). Parental concepts of development. In I.E. Sigel (Ed.), *Parental belief symptoms* (pp. 83–105). Mahwah, NJ: Erlbaum.

Sameroff, A.J., & Fiese, B.H. (2000a). Models of development and developmental risk. In C.H. Zeanah Jr. (Ed.), *Handbook of infant mental health* (2nd ed., pp. 3–19). New York: Guilford Press.

Sameroff, A.J., & Fiese, B.H. (2000b). Transactional regulation: The developmental ecology of early intervention. In J.P. Shonkoff & S.J. Meisels (Eds.), *Handbook of early childhood intervention* (2nd ed., pp. 135–159). Cambridge: Cambridge University Press.

Sameroff, A.J., Seifer, R., Baldwin, A., & Baldwin, C. (1993). Stability of intelligence from preschool to adolescence: The influence of social and family risk factors. *Child Development, 64,* 80–97.

Sameroff, A.J., Seifer, R., Barocas, R., Zax, M., & Greenspan, S. (1987). Intelligence quotient scores of 4-year-old-children: Social environmental risk factors. *Pediatrics, 79,* 343–350.

Sanson, A., Pedlow, R., Cann, W., Prior, M., & Oberklaid, F. (1996). Shyness ratings: Stability and correlates in early childhood. *International Journal of Behavioral Development, 19,* 705–724.

Sapolsky, R.M. (1994). *Why zebras don't get ulcers: A guide to stress, stress-related diseases, and coping.* New York: Freeman.

Scaer, R.C. (2001). *The body bears the burden: Trauma, dissociation, and disease.* New York: The Haworth Medical Press.

Schechter, D.S. (2004). How post-traumatic stress affects mothers' perceptions of their babies: A brief video feedback intervention makes a difference. *Zero to Three, 24,* 43–49.

Schneider, M.L. (1992). Prenatal stress exposure alters postnatal behavioral expression under conditions of novelty challenge in rhesus monkey infants. *Developmental Psychobiology, 25,* 529–540.

Schneider, W., Buchheim, P., Cierpka, M., Dahlbender, R.W., Freyberger, H.J., Grande, T., Hoffmann, S.O., Heuft, G., Janssen, P.L., Kuchenhoff, J., Muhs, A., Rudolf, G., Ruger, U., & Schussler, G. (2002). Operationalized psychodynamic diagnostics: A new diagnostic approach in psychodynamic psychotherapy. In L.E. Beutler & M.L. Malik (Eds.), *Rethinking the DSM: A psychological perspective.* Washington, DC: American Psychological Association.

Scholnick, E.K., & Friedman, S.L. (1993). Planning in context: Developmental and situational considerations. *International Journal of Behavioral Development, 16,* 145–167.

Scholz, K., & Samuels, C. (1992). Neonatal bathing and massage intervention with fathers, behavioral effects 12 weeks after birth of the first baby: The Sunraysia Australia Intervention Project. *International Journal of Behavioral Development, 15,* 67–81.

Schore, A.N. (1994). Affect regulation and the origin of the self. Mahwah, NJ: Lawrence Erlbaum Associates.

Schore, A.N. (2003). *Affect dysregulation and disorders of the self.* New York: W.W. Norton.

Schothorst, P., & van Engeland, H. (1996). Long-term behavioral sequelae of prematurity. *Journal of the American Academy of Child and Adolescent Psychiatry, 35,* 175–183.

Schteingart, J.S., Molnar, J., Klein, T.P., & Lowe, C.B. (1995). Homeless and child functioning in the context of risk and protective factors moderating child outcome. *Journal of Clinical Child Psychology, 24,* 320–331.

Schuengel, C., Bakermans-Kranenburg, M.J., van IJzendoorn, M.H., & Blom, M. (1999). Unresolved loss and infant disorganization: Links to frightening maternal behavior. In J. Solomon & C. George (Eds.), *Attachment disorganization* (pp. 71–94). New York: Guilford Press.

Schultz-Jøgensen, P., Kyng, B., Maar, V., Rasmussen, L., & Højlund, L. (1987). Is prevention possible in the preschool years? A longitudinal study of a group of preschool children in a local community. *Nordic Psychology, 39,* 255–267.

Schwartz, E.D., & Perry, B.D. (1994). The post-traumatic response in children and adolescents. *Psychiatric Clinics of North America, 17,* 311–326.

Schwartz, J.M., & Begley, S. (2002). *The mind and the brain: Neuroplasticity and the power of mental force.* New York: Harper Collins.

Schwartz, J.M., Stoessel, P.W., Baxter, L.R., Jr., Martin, K.M., & Phelps, M.E. (1996). Systematic changes in cerebral glucose metabolic rate after successful behavioral modification treatment of obsessive-compulsive disorder. *Archives of General Psychiatry, 53,* 109–113.

Schweinhart, L.J., Montie, J., Xiang, Z., Barnett, W.S., Belfield, C.R., & Nores, M. (2005). *Lifetime effects: The High/Scope Perry Preschool study through age 40* (Monographs of the High/Scope Educational Research Foundation, 14). Ypsilanti, MI: High/Scope Press.

Schweinhart, L.J., & Weikart, D.P. (1997). The High Scope Preschool Curriculum Comparison Study through age 23. *Early Childhood Research Quarterly, 12,* 117–143.

Schweinhart, L.J., Weikart, D.P., & Larner, M.B. (1986). Child initiated activities in early childhood programs may help prevent delinquency. *Early Childhood Research Quarterly, 1,* 303–312.

Scott, S., Knapp, M., Henderson, J., & Maughan, B. (2001). Financial cost of social exclusion: Follow up study of antisocial children into adulthood. *British Medical Journal, 323,* 1–5.

Segal, Z.V., Williams, J.M.G., & Teasdale, J.D. (2002). *Mindfulness-based cognitive therapy for depression.* New York: Guilford Press.

Segal, Z.V., Williams, J.M., Teasdale, J.D., & Gemar, M. (1996). A cognitive science perspective on kindling and episode sensitization in recurrent affective disorder. *Psychological Medicine, 26,* 371–380.

Seginer, R. (1983). Parents' educational expectations and children's academic achievements: A literature review. *Merrill-Palmer Quarterly, 29,* 1–23.

Seifer, R., & Sameroff, A.J. (1987). Multiple determinants of risk and invulnerability. In E.J. Anthony & B.J. Cohler (Eds.), *The invulnerable child* (pp. 51–69). New York: Guilford Press.

Seifer, R., Sameroff, A., Baldwin, C., & Baldwin, A. (1992). Child and family factors that ameliorate risk between 4 and 13 years of age. *American Academy of Child and Adolescent Psychiatry, 31,* 893–903.

Seitz, V., & Apfel, N.H. (1994). Parent–focused interventions: Diffusion effects on siblings. *Child Development, 65,* 677–683.

Seitz, V., Rosenbaum, L.K., & Apfel, N.H. (1985). Effects of family support intervention: A ten-year follow-up. *Child Development, 56,* 376–391.

Seligman, M.E.P. (1998). *Learned optimism: How to change your mind and life.* (2nd ed.) New York: Simon and Schuster.

Seligman, S. (2000). Clinical interviews with families of infants. In C.H. Zeanah Jr. (Ed.), *Handbook of infant mental health* (2nd ed., pp. 211–221). New York: Guilford Press.

Seligman, S.P., & Pawl, J.H. (1984). Impediments to the formation of the working alliance in infant–parent psychotherapy. In J.D. Call, E. Galenson, & R.L. Tyson (Eds.), *Frontiers of infant psychiatry* (Vol. 2, pp. 232–237). New York: Basic Books.

Selye, H. (1956). *The stress of life.* New York: McGraw-Hill.

Sergeant, J.A. (1995). A theory of attention: An information processing perspective. In G.R. Lyon & N.A. Krasnegor (Eds.), *Attention, memory, and executive function* (pp. 57–69). Baltimore: Paul H. Brookes Publishing Co.

Shalev, A.Y. (1996). Stress versus traumatic stress: From acute homeostatic reactions to chronic psychopathology. In B.A. van der Kolk, A.C. McFarlane, & L. Weisaeth (Eds.), *Traumatic stress: The effects of overwhelming experience on mind, body, and society* (pp. 77–101). New York: Guilford Press.

Shapiro, F. (1998). Eye movement desensitization and reprocessing (EMDR): Historical context, recent research, and future directions. In L. VanderCreek & T. Jackson (Eds.), *Innovations in clinical practice: A source book* (Vol. 16, pp. 143–162). Sarasota, FL: Professional Resources Press.

Shapiro, F. (2001). *Eye movement desensitization and reprocessing: Basic principles, protocols, and procedures* (2nd ed.). New York: Guilford Press.

Shapiro, F. (2002). EMDR twelve years after its introduction: Past and present research. *Journal of Clinical Psychology, 58,* 1–22.

Shapiro, F., & Maxfield, L. (2003). EMDR and information processing in psychotherapy treatment: Personal development and global implications. In M.F. Solomon & D.J. Siegel (Eds.), *Healing trauma: Attachment, body, and brain* (pp. 196–220). New York: W.W. Norton.

Shapiro, F., & Solomon, R. (1995). Eye movement desensitization and reproducing: Neuro-cognitive information processing. In G. Everley & J. Mitchell (Eds), *Critical incident stress management*. Ellicott City, MD: Chevron.

Shatz, C.J. (1992, September). The developing brain. *Scientific American, 267,* 60–67.

Shaw, D.S., Owens, E.B., Vondra, J.I., Keenan, K., & Winslow, E.B. (1996). Early risk factors and pathways in the development of early disruptive behavior problems. *Development and Psychopathology, 8,* 679–699.

Shaw, D., & Vondra, J. (1993). Chronic family adversity and infant security. *Journal of Child Psychology and Psychiatry, 34,* 1205–1217.

Shea, E., & Tronick, E.Z. (1988). The Maternal Self-Report Inventory. In H.E. Fitzgerald, B.M. Lester, & M.W. Yogman (Eds.), *Theory and research in behavioral pediatrics* (Vol. 4, pp. 100–139). New York: Plenum Press.

Shonkoff, J.P., Meisels S.J., (Eds.) (2000). *Handbook of early childhood intervention* (2nd ed). New York: Cambridge University Press.

Shonkoff, J.P., & Phillips, D.A. (2000). Promoting healthy development through intervention. In J.P. Shonkoff & D.A. Phillips, *From neurons to neighborhoods: The science of early childhood development* (pp. 337–380). Washington, DC: National Academy Press.

Shweder, R.A., Goodnow, J.J., Hatano, G., LeVine, R.A., Markus, H.R., & Miller, P.J. (1998). The cultural psychology of development: One mind, many mentalities. In W. Damon (Ed.), *Handbook of Child Development* (Vol. 1, pp. 865–938). New York: John Wiley & Sons.

Siegel, D.J. (1999). *The developing mind: Towards a psychobiology of interpersonal experience*. New York: Guilford Press.

Sigel, I.E., & McGillicuddy-DeLisi, A.V. (2002). Parent beliefs are cognitions: The dynamic belief systems model. In M.H. Bornstein (Ed.), *Handbook of parenting (2nd Ed.): Vol. 3. Being and becoming a parent* (pp. 485–508). Mahwah, NJ: Lawrence Erlbaum Associates.

Sivik, T. (1993). Alexithymia and hypersensitivity to touch and palpation. *Integrative Physiological and Behavioral Science, 28,* 130–136.

Slade, A. (2002). Keeping the baby in mind: A critical factor in perinatal mental health. *Zero to Three, 22,* 11–16.

Slade, A., Belsky, J., Aber, J.L., & Phelps, J.L. (1999). Mothers' representations of their relationships with their toddlers: Links to adult attachment and observed mothering. *Developmental Psychology, 35,* 611–619.

Slade, A., Bernbach, E., Grienenberger, J., Wohlgemuth Levy, D., & Locker, A. (2001). *Addendum to Reflective Functioning Scoring Manual: For Use with the Parent Development Interview*. Unpublished manuscript, The City College and Graduate Center of the City University of New York.

Slade, A., & Cohen, L.J. (1996). The process of parenting and the remembrance of things past. *Infant Mental Health Journal, 17,* 217–238.

Slade, A., Grienenberger, J., Bernbach, E., Levy, D., & Locker, A. (April, 2001). *Maternal reflective functioning and attachment: Considering the transmission gap*. Paper presented at the biennial meeting of the Society of Research on Child Development, Minneapolis, MN.

Slade, A., Sadler, L., Mayes, L., Ezepchick, J., Webb, D., De Dios-Kenn, C., Klein, K., Mitcheom, K., & Shader, Z. (2004). *Minding the baby: A working manual*. Unpublished manuscript. New Haven, CT: Yale Child Study Centre.

Snellen, M., Mack, K., & Trauer, T. (1999). Schizophrenia, mental state, and mother–infant interaction: Examining the relationship. *Australian and New Zealand Journal of Psychiatry, 33,* 902–911.

Solomon, J., George, C., & Ivins, B. (April, 1987). *Mother–child interaction in the home and security of attachment at age six*. Paper presented at the biennial meeting of the Society for Research in Child Development, Baltimore, MD.

Sonnenschein, S., Baker, J., Serpell, R., Scher, D., Trout, V.G., & Munsterman, K. (1997). Parental beliefs about ways to help children read: The impact of an entertainment or a skills perspective. *Early Child Development and Care, 111–118,* 127–128.

Sontag, J.C., & Shacht, R. (1993). Family diversity and patterns of service untilization in early intervention. *Journal of Early Intervention, 17,* 431–444.

Spangler, G. & Schieche, M. (1998). Emotional and adrenocortical responses of infants to the Strange Situation: The differential function of emotional expression. *International Journal of Behavioral Development, 22,* 681–706.

Sparrow, S., Balla, D., & Cicchetti, D. (1984). *Vineland Adaptive Behavior Scales (VABS).* Circle Pines, MN: American Guidance Service.

Speltz, M.L., Greenberg, M.T., & DeKlyen, M. (1990). Attachment in preschoolers with disruptive behavior: A comparison of clinic-referred and nonproblem children. *Development and Psychopathology, 2,* 31–46.

Spillius, E.B. (1992). Clinical experiences of projective identification. In R.Anderson (Eds.), *Clinical lectures on Klein and Bion* (pp. 59–73). London: Routledge.

Squire, L.R. (1994). Declarative and non-declarative memory: Multiple brain systems supporting memory. In D.L. Schacter & E. Tulving (Eds.), *Memory systems.* Cambridge, MA: MIT Press.

Sroufe, L.A. (1983). Infant–caregiver attachment and patterns of adaptation in preschool. In M. Perlmutter (Ed.), *Minnesota symposium on child psychology: Vol. 16. The roots of maladaptation and competence* (pp. 41–83). Mahwah, NJ: Lawrence Erlbaum Associates.

Sroufe, L.A. (1988). The role of infant–caregiver attachment in development. In J. Belsky & T. Nezworski (Eds.), *Clinical implications of attachment* (pp. 18–38). Mahwah, NJ: Lawrence Erlbaum Associates.

Sroufe, L.A. (1990). Considering normal and abnormal together: The essence of developmental psychology. *Development and Psychopathology, 2,* 345–357.

Sroufe, L.A. (1997). Psychopathology as an outcome of development. *Development and Psychopathology, 9,* 251–268.

St. Pierre, R.G., & Layzer, J.I. (1998). Using home visits for multiple purposes: The Comprehensive Child Development Program. *The Future of Children, 8,* 134–151.

St. Pierre, R.G., Layzer, J.I., Goodson, B.D., & Bernstein, L.S. (1997). *National impact evaluation of the Comprehensive Child Development Program: Final report.* Cambridge, MA: Abt Associates

St. Pierre, R.G., Swartz, J.P., Gamse, B., Murray, S., Ceck, D., & Nickel, P. (1995). *National evaluation of Even Start Family Literacy Program: Final report.* Cambridge, MA: Abt Associates.

Stamm, B.H. (1996). *Measurement of stress, trauma, and adaptation.* Lutherville, MD: The Sidran Press.

Steinberg, L., Lamborn, S.D., Darling, N., Mounts, N., & Dornbusch, S.M. (1994). Impact of parenting on adolescent achievement: Authoritative parenting, school involvement, and encouragement to succeed. *Child Development, 65,* 754–770.

Steinberg, L., Lamborn, S.D., Dornbusch, S.M., & Darling, N. (1992). Impact of parenting, school involvement, and encouragement to succeed. *Child Development, 63,* 1266–1281.

Steinberg, L., Mounts, N.S., Lamborn, S.D., & Dornbusch, S.M. (1991). Authoritative parenting and adolescent adjustment across varied ecological niches. *Journal of Research on Adolescence, 1,* 19–36.

Stern, D.N. (1995). *The motherhood constellation: A unified view of parent–infant psychotherapy.* New York: Basic Books

Stern, D.N. (2004). *The present moment in psychotherapy and everyday life.* New York: W.W. Norton.

Stern, D.N., Bruschweiler-Stern, N., Harrison, A.M., Lyons-Ruth, K.C., Morgan, A.C., Nahum, J.P., Sander, L., & Tronick, E.Z. (1998). The process of therapeutic change involving implicit knowledge: Some implications of developmental observations for adult psychotherapy. *Infant Mental Health Journal, 19,* 300–308.

Stiffman, A., Jung, K., & Feldman, R. (1986). A multivariate risk model for child behaviour problems. *American Journal of Orthopsychiatry, 56,* 204–211.

Stifter, C.A., & Braungart, J.M. (1995). The regulation of negative reactivity in infancy: Function and development. *Developmental Psychology, 31,* 448–455.

Stirtzinger, R., McDermid, S., Grusec, J., Bernardine, S., Quinlan, K., & Marshall, M. (2002). Interrupting the inter-generational cycle in high risk adolescent pregnancy. *The Journal of Primary Prevention, 23,* 7–22.

Stratton, K., Howe, C., & Battaglia, F. (Eds.) (1996). *Fetal alcohol syndrome: Diagnosis, epidemiology, prevention, and treatment.* Washington, DC: National Academy Press.

Straus, M.A., & Gelles, R.J. (1990). Societal change and change in family violence from 1975–1985 as revealed in two national surveys. In M.A. Straus & R.J. Gelles (Eds.), *Phys-*

*ical violence in American families: Risk factors and adaptation to violence in 8,145 families* (pp. 113–132). New Brunswick, NJ: Transaction Publishers.

Strayhorn, J.M., & Weidman, C.S. (1988). A parent practices scale and its relation to parent and child health. *Journal of the Academy of Child and Adolescent Psychiatry, 27,* 613–618.

Sudermann, M. & Jaffe, P. (1999). *A handbook for health and social service providers and educators on children exposed to woman abuse/family violence.* The Family Violence Prevention Unit, Health Canada. Ottawa: Minister of Public Works and Government Services Canada.

Suess, G.K. (1987). *Consequences of early attachment experiences on children's competence in kindergarten.* Unpublished doctoral dissertation, University of Regensberg, Germany.

Suh, E., & Abel, E.M. (1990). The impact of spousal violence on the children of the abused. *Journal of Independent Social Work, 4,* 27–34.

Sumner, G., & Spietz, A. (1994a). *Caregiver/Parent–child interaction: Teaching manual.* Seattle, Washington: NCATS Publications, University of Washington.

Sumner, G., & Spietz, A. (1994b). *Caregiver/Parent–child interaction: Feeding manual.* Seattle, Washington: NCATS Publications, University of Washington.

Suomi, S.J. (1995). Influence of attachment theory on ethological studies of biobehavioral development in nonhuman primates. In S. Goldberg, R. Muir, & J. Kerr (Eds.), *Attachment theory: Social, developmental, and clinical perspectives* (pp. 185–201). Mahwah, NJ: Analytic Press.

Susman, E.J., Trickett, P.K., Iannotti, R.J., Hollenbeck, B.E., & Zahn-Waxler, C. (1985). Childrearing patterns in depressed, abusive, and normal mothers. *American Journal of Orthopsychiatry, 55,* 237–251.

Swartz, J., Bernstein, L., & Levin, M. (2000). *Evaluation of the Head Start Family Service Center Demonstration Projects. Volume I: Final Report from the National Evaluation.* Commissioner's Office of Research and Evaluation (CORE) and the Head Start Bureau, Administration on Children, Youth and Families, U.S. Department of Health and Human Services.

Swartz, J., Smith, C., Berghauer, G., Bernstein, L., & Gardine, J. (1994). *Evaluation of Head Start Family Service Center Demonstration Projects: First-year evaluation results.* Cambridge, MA: Abt.

Szapocnik, J., Kurtines, W., & Santisteban, D.A. (1994). The interplay of advances among theory, research, and application in family interventions for Hispanic behavior-problem youth. In R.G. Malgady & O. Rodriguez (Eds.), *Theoretical and conceptual issues in Hispanic mental health* (pp. 156–179). Malabar, Florida: Krieger Publications.

Tamis-LeMonda, C.S., Chen, L., & Bornstein, M.H. (1998). Mothers' knowledge about children's play and language development: Short-term stability and interrelations. *Developmental Psychology, 34,* 115–124.

Target, M. & Fonagy, P. (1994a). The efficacy of psychoanalysis for children with emotional disorders. *Journal of the American Academy of Child and Adolescent Psychiatry, 33,* 361–371.

Target, M. & Fonagy, P. (1994b). The efficacy of psychoanalysis for children: Developmental considerations. *Journal of the American Academy of Child and Adolescent Psychiatry, 33,* 1134–1144.

Taylor, G.J., Bagby, R.M., & Parker, J.D.A. (1991). The Alexithymia Construct: A potential paradigm for psychosomatic medicine. *Psychosomatics, 32,* 153–164.

Taylor, G.J., Bagby, R.M., & Parker, J.D.A. (1997). *Disorders of affect regulation: Alexithymia in medical and psychiatric illness.* Cambridge: Cambridge University Press.

Teasdale, J.D. (1999). Metacognition, mindfulness, and the modification of mood disorders. *Clinical Psychology and Psychotherapy, 6,* 146–155.

Teasdale, J.D., Segal, Z.V., & Williams, J.M.G. (1995). How does cognitive therapy prevent depressive relapse, and why should attentional control (mindfulness) training help? *Behavior Research and Therapy, 33,* 25–39.

Teasdale, J.D., Segal, Z.V., & Williams, J.M.G. (2000). Prevention of relapse/recurrence in major depression by mindfulness-based cognitive therapy. *Journal of Consulting and Clinical Psychology, 68,* 615–673.

Teicher, M.H. (2002). Scars that won't heal: The neurobiology of child abuse. *Scientific American, 286,* 68–75.

Teixeira, J.M., & Fisk, M.N. (1999). Association between maternal anxiety in pregnancy and increased uterine artery resistance index: Cohort based study. *British Medical Journal, 318,* 153–157.

Terr, L. (1991). Childhood traumas: An outline and overview. *American Journal of Psychiatry, 148,* 10–20.

Terr, L. (1994). *Unchained memories: True stories of traumatic memories, lost and found.* New York: Basic Books.

Teti, D.M., & Gelfand, D.M. (1991). Behavioral competence among mothers of infants in the first year: The mediational role of maternal self-efficacy. *Child Development, 62,* 918–929.

Teti, D.M., Gelfand, D.M., Messinger, D.S., & Isabella, R. (1995). Maternal depression and the quality of early attachment: An examination of infants, preschoolers, and their mothers. *Developmental Psychology, 31,* 364–376.

Thapar, A., & McGuffin, P. (1996). The genetic etiology of childhood depressive symptoms: A developmental perspective. *Development and Psychopathology, 8,* 751–760.

The Commonwealth Fund. (1993, July). *The commonwealth fund's survey on women's health.* New York: Author.

Thoman, E., & Browder, S. (1987). *Born dancing: How intuitive parents understand their baby's unspoken language and natural rhythms.* New York: Harper & Row.

Thomas, A., & Chess, S. (1985). Genesis and evolution of behavioral disorders: From infancy to early adult life. In S. Chess & A. Thomas (Eds.), *Annual Progress in Child Psychiatry and Child Development,* 140–158.

Thomas, A., Chess, S., & Birch, H.G. (1968). *Temperament and behavior disorders in children.* NewYork: New York University Press.

Thompson, R.A. (2000). The legacy of early attachments. *Child Development, 71,* 145–152.

Thompson, R.A., & Calkins, S.D. (1996). The double-edged sword: Emotional regulation for children at risk. *Development and Psychopathology, 8,* 163–182.

Thorndike, R.L., Hagen, E.P., & Sattler, J.M. (1986). *Stanford-Binet Intelligence Scale* (4th ed.). Chicago: Riverside.

Tizard, B. (1977). *Adoption: A second chance.* London: Open Books.

Tizard, B., & Hodges, J. (1978). The effect of early institutional rearing on the development of eight year old children. *Journal of Child Psychology and Psychiatry and Allied Disciplines, 19,* 99–118.

Tizard, B., & Rees, J. (1975). The effect of early institutional rearing on the development of eight-year old children. *Journal of Child Psychology and Psychiatry, 19,* 99–118.

Tomasello, M. (1995). Joint attention as social cognition. In C. Moore & P. Dunham (Eds.), *Joint attention: Its origins and role in development* (pp. 103–130). Mahwah, NJ: Lawrence Erlbaum Associates.

Tomasello, M. (1999). *The cultural origins of human cognition.* Cambridge, MA: Harvard University Press.

Tomkins, S.S. (1984). Affect theory. In K.R. Scherer & P. Ekman (Eds.), *Approaches to emotion* (pp. 163–196). Mahwah, NJ: Lawrence Erlbaum Associates.

Trad, P.V. (1989). *Infant previewing.* New York: Springer-Verlag.

Trad, P.V. (1992). Providing adaptive development in caregiver–infant dyads. *Families in Society: The Journal of Contemporary Family Services, 73,* 282–291.

Travers, J., Nauta, M., & Irwin, N. (1982). *The effects of a social program: Final report of the Child and Family Resource Program's infant–toddler component.* Cambridge, MA: Abt Associates.

Trickett, P.K., & Kuczynski, L. (1986). Children's misbehaviors and parental discipline strategies in abusive and non-abusive families. *Developmental Psychology, 22,* 115–123.

Trocmé, N., & Caunce, C. (1995). The educational needs of abused and neglected children: A review of the literature. *Early Child Development and Care, 106,* 101–135.

Trocmé, N., & Wolfe, D. (2001). *Child maltreatment in Canada: Selected results from the Canadian incidence study of reported child abuse and neglect.* Ottawa, Ontario: Minister of Public Works and Government Services, Canada.

Tronick, E.Z., Bruschweiler-Stern, Harrison, A.M., Lyons-Ruth, K.C., Morgan, A.C., Nahum, J.P., Sander, L., & Stern, D.N. (1998). Dyadically expanded states of consciousness and the process of therapeutic change. *Infant Mental Health Journal, 19,* 290–299.

Tsuk, K., & Landy, S. (2000). *The emotional relationship between mothers and their aggressive young children. An observation of mother–child interaction.* Poster presented at the International Conference on Infant Studies, Toronto, Canada.

Tucker, M.B., & Johnson, O. (1989). Competence promoting vs. competence inhibiting social support for mentally retarded mothers. *Human Organization, 48,* 95–107.

Tudge, J., Hogan, D.M., Snezhkova, I.A., Kulakova, N.N., & Etz, K.E. (2000). Parents' child rearing values and beliefs in the United States and Russia: The impact of culture and social class. *Infant and Child Development, 9,* 105–122.

Tutek, D.A., & Linehan, M.M. (1993). Comparative treatments for borderline personality disorder: Theory and research. In T.R. Giles (Ed.), *Handbook of effective psychotherapy* (pp. 355–378). New York: Plenum Press.

Twentyman, C.T., & Plotkin, R.C. (1982). Unrealistic expectations of parents who maltreat their children: An educational deficit pertaining to child development. *Journal of Clinical Psychology, 38,* 497–503.

U.S. Bureau of Investigation (1997). *1996 Uniform Crime Report.* Washington, DC: U.S. Department of Justice.

Vaillant, G.E. (1977). *Adaptation to life.* Boston: Little, Brown.

Vaillant, G.E. (1986). *Empirical studies of ego mechanisms of defense.* Washington, DC: American Psychiatric Association.

Vaillant, G.E. (1992). *Ego mechanisms of defense.* Washington, DC: American Psychiatric Press.

Vaillant, G.E., & Drake, R. (1985). Maturity of ego defenses in relation to DSM III Axis II personality disorder. *Archives of General Psychiatry, 42,* 597–601.

Vaillant, G.E., & McCullough, L. (1998). The role of ego mechanisms of defense in the diagnosis of personality disorders. In J.W. Barron (Eds.), *Making diagnosis meaningful: Enhancing evaluation and treatment* (pp. 139–157). Washington, DC: American Psychological Association.

van Aken, M.A.G., & Ricksen-Walraven, J.M. (1992). Parental support and the development of competence in children. *International Journal of Behavioral Development, 15,* 101–123.

van den Boom, D.C. (1994). The influence of temperament and mothering on attachment and exploration: An experimental manipulation of sensitive responsiveness among lower-class mothers with irritable infants. *Child Development, 65,* 1457–1477.

van den Boom, D.C. (1995). Do first-year intervention effects endure? Follow-up during toddlerhood of a sample of Dutch irritable infants. *Child Development, 66,* 1798–1816.

van der Kolk, B.A. (1994). The body keeps the score: Memory and the evolving psychobiology of posttraumatic stress. *Harvard Review of Psychiatry, 1,* 253–265.

van der Kolk, B.A. (1996a). The complexity of adaptation to trauma: Self-regulation, stimulus discrimination, and characterological development. In van der Kolk, B.A., McFarlane, A.C., & Weisaeth, L. (Eds.), *Traumatic stress: The effects of overwhelming experience on mind, body, and society* (pp.182–213). New York: Guilford Press.

van der Kolk, B.A. (1996b). Trauma and memory. In van der Kolk, B.A., McFarlane, A.C., & Weisaeth, L. (Eds.), *Traumatic stress: The effects of overwhelming experience on mind, body, and society* (pp. 279–302). New York: Guilford Press.

van der Kolk, B.A. (2003). Posttraumatic stress disorder and the nature of trauma. In M.F. Solomon & D.J. Siegel (Eds.), *Healing trauma: Attachment, mind, body and brain* (pp. 168–195). New York: W.W. Norton.

van der Kolk, B.A., Dreyfuss, D., Michaels, M., Shera, D., Berkowitz, R., Fisler, R., & Saxe, G. (1994). Fluoxetine in posttraumatic stress disorder. *Journal of Clinical Psychiatry, 55,* 517–522.

van der Kolk, B.A., & Fisler, R.E. (1994). Childhood abuse and neglect and loss of self-regulation. *Bulletin of the Menninger Clinic, 58,* 145–168.

van der Kolk, B.A., & Fisler, R.E. (1995). Dissociation and the fragmentary nature of traumatic memories: Overview and exploratory study. *Journal of Traumatic Stress, 8,* 505–525.

van der Kolk, B.A., & McFarlane, A.C. (1996). The black hole of trauma. In B.A. van der Kolk, A.C. McFarlane & L. Weisaeth (Eds.), *Traumatic stress: The effects of overwhelming experience on mind, body, and society* (pp. 3–23). New York: Guilford Press.

van der Kolk, B.A., McFarlane, A.C., & van der Hart, O. (1996). A general approach to treatment of posttraumatic stress disorder. In B.A. van der Kolk, A.C. McFarlane, & Weisaeth, L. (Eds.), *Traumatic stress: The effects of overwhelming experience on mind, body, and society* (pp. 417–440). New York: Guilford Press.

van der Kolk, B.A., & van der Hart, O. (1991). The intrusive past: The flexibility of memory and the engraving of trauma. *American Imago, 48,* 425–454.

van IJzendoorn, M.H., & Bakermans-Kranenburg, M.J. (2003). Attachment disorders and disorganized attachment: Similar and different. *Attachment and Human Development, 5,* 313–320.

van IJzendoorn, M.H., Schuengel, C., & Bakermans-Kranenburg, M.J. (1999). Disorganized attachment in early childhood: Meta-analysis of precursors, concomitants and sequelae. *Development & Psychopathology, 11*, 225–249.

Vaughn, B.E., Bradley, C.F., Joffe, L.S., Seifer, F., & Barglow, P. (1987). Maternal characteristics measured prenatally predict ratings of temperamental difficulty on the Carey Infant Temperament Questionnaire. *Developmental Psychology, 23*, 152–161.

Ventura, J.N., & Stevenson, M.B. (1986). Relation of mothers' and fathers' reports of infant temperament, parents' psychological functioning and family characteristics. *Merrill-Palmer Quarterly, 32*, 275–289.

Verhulst, F.C., Achenbach, T.M., Ferdinand, R.F., & Kasius, M.C. (1993). Epidemiological comparisons of American and Dutch adolescents' self-reports. *Journal of the American Academy of Child and Adolescent Psychiatry, 32*, 1135–1144.

Vernon-Feagans, L. (1996). *Children's talk in communities and classrooms.* Cambridge, MA: Blackwell.

von Bertalanffy, L. (1968). *General systems theory.* New York: George Braziller.

Wachs, T.D. (2000). *Necessary but not sufficient: The respective roles of single and multiple influences on individual development.* Washington, DC: The American Psychological Association.

Wachtel, P.L. (1993). *Therapeutic communication: Knowing what to say when.* New York: Guilford Press.

Wachtel, P.L. (1997). *Psychoanalysis, behavior therapy, and the relational world.* Washington, DC: American Psychological Association.

Wagner, M., & McElroy, M. (1992). *Home the first classroom: A pilot evaluation of the Northern California Parents as Teachers project.* Mento Park, CA: SRI International.

Wagner, M.M., & Clayton, S.L. (1999). The Parents as Teachers Program: Results from two demonstrations. *The Future of Children, 9*, 91–115.

Wahler, R.G., Williams, A.J., & Cerezo, A. (1990). The compliance and predictability hypotheses: Sequential and correlational analyses of coercive mother–child interactions. *Behavioral Assessment, 12*, 391–407.

Walker, E., & Emory, E. (1983). Infants at risk for psychopathology: Offspring of schizophrenic parents. *Child Development, 54*, 1269–1285.

Walker, L.O., Crain, H., & Thompson, E. (1986). Maternal behavior and maternal role attainment during the postpartum period. *Nursing Research, 35*, 352–355.

Walsh, J., Wilson, G., & McLellarn, R. (1989). A confirmatory analysis of the Tennessee Self-Concept Scale. *Criminal Justice and Behavior, 16*, 465–472.

Wasik, B., Bryant, D., & Fishbein, J. (1980). *Assessing parent problem solving skills.* Paper presented at the 15th Annual Conference on Advancement of Behaviour Therapy, Toronto, Canada.

Wasik, B.H., & Roberts, R.N. (1994). Home visitors: Characteristics, training and supervision: Results of a national survey. *Family Relations, 43*, 336–341.

Wasik, B.H., Ramey, C.T., Bryant, D.M., & Sparling, J.J. (1990). A longitudinal study of two early intervention strategies: Project CARE. *Child Development, 61*, 1682–1696.

Waters, E., Merrick, S., Treboux, D., Crowell, J., & Albersheim, L. (2000). Attachment security in infancy and early adulthood: A twenty-year longitudinal study. *Child Development, 71*, 684–689.

Waters, E., Weinfield, N.S., & Hamilton, C.E. (2000). The stability of attachment security from infancy to adolescence and early adulthood. *Child Development, 71*, 703–706.

Waters, E., Wippman, J., & Sroufe, L.A. (1979). Attachment, positive affect, and competence in the peer group: Two studies in construct validation. *Child Development, 50*, 821–829.

Webster-Stratton, C., & Hammond, M. (1988). Maternal depression and its relationship to life stress, perceptions of child behavior problems. *Journal of Abnormal Child Psychology, 16*, 299–315.

Webster-Stratton, C., & Hammond, M. (1997). Treating children with early-onset conduct problems: A comparison of child and parent training interventions. *Journal of Consulting and Clinical Psychology, 65*, 93–109.

Webster-Stratton, C., & Hammond, M. (1999). Marital conflict management skills, parenting style, and early onset conduct problems: Processes and pathways. *Journal of Child Psychology and Psychiatry, 40*, 917–927.

Webster-Stratton, C., & Hooven, C. (1998). Parent training for child conduct problems. In A.S. Bellak & M. Hersen (Eds.), *Comprehensive child psychology: Vol. 5. Children and adolescents: Clinical formulation and treatment* (pp. 185–219). New York: Elsevier Science.

Webster-Stratton, C., Kolpacoff, M., & Hollinsworth, T. (1988). Self-administered videotape therapy for families with conduct problem children: Comparison with two cost-effective treatments and a control group. *Journal of Consulting and Clinical Psychology, 56,* 558–566.

Wechsler, D. (1974). *Wechsler Intelligence Scale for Children–Revised.* New York: Harcourt Assessment.

Wechsler, D. (1989). *Wechsler Preschool and Primary Scale of Intelligence–Revised.* New York: The Psychological Corporation.

Weinberger, J. (1993). Common factors in psychotherapy. In G. Stricker & J.R. Gold (Eds.), *Comprehensive handbook of psychotherapy integration* (pp. 45–56). New York: Plenum Press.

Weiner, B. (1979). A theory of motivation for some classroom experiences. *Journal of Educational Psychology, 71,* 3–25.

Weiner, B. (1986). *An attributional theory of motivation and emotion.* New York: Springer-Verlag.

Weinman, M., Robinson, M., Simmons, J., Schreiber, N., & Stafford, B. (1989). Pregnant teens: Differential pregnancy resolution and treatment implications. *Child Welfare, 68,* 45–55.

Weinstock, M. (1997). Does prenatal stress impair coping and regulation of the hypothalamic-pituitary-adrenal axis? *Neuroscience and Biobehavioral Reviews, 21,* 1–10.

Weisglas-Kuperus, N., Baerts, W., Smirkovsky, M., & Sauer, P.J. (1993). Effects of biological and social factors on the cognitive development of very low birth weight infants. *Pediatrics, 92,* 658–665.

Weiss, C.H. (1995). Nothing as practical as a good theory: Exploring theory-based evaluation for comprehensive community initiatives for children and families. In J. P. Connell, A.C. Kubisch, L.B.Schorr, & C. H. Weiss (Eds.) *New approaches to evaluating community initiatives: Concepts, methods, and contexts.* Washington, DC: The Aspen Institute.

Weiss, G., & Hechtman, L.T. (1993). *Hyeractive children grown up* (2nd Ed.). New York: Guilford Press.

Weissbourd, B. (1993). Family support programs. In C.H. Zeanah Jr. (Ed.), *Handbook of infant mental health* (pp. 402–413). New York: Guilford Press.

Wells, H. (2000). *Emotional disorders and metacognition: Innovative cognitive therapy.* Chichester, West Sussex: John Wiley & Sons.

Wendland-Carro, J., Piccinini, C.A., & Millar, W.S. (1999). The role of an early intervention on enhancing the quality of mother–infant interaction. *Child Development, 70,* 713–721.

Werman, D.S. (1984). *The practice of supportive psychotherapy.* New York: Brunner/Mazel.

Werner, E.E. (1989). High-risk children in young adulthood: A longitudinal study from birth to 32 years. *American Journal of Orthopsychiatry, 59,* 72–81.

Werner, E.E. (1995). Resilience in development. *Current Directions in Psychological Science, 4,* 81–85.

Werner, E.E., & Smith, R. (1977). *Kauai's children come of age.* Honolulu: University of Hawaii Press.

Werner, E.E., & Smith, R. (1982). *Vulnerable but invincible: A study of resilient children.* New York: McGraw-Hill.

Werner, E.E., & Smith, R. (1992). *Overcoming the odds: High risk children from birth to adulthood.* Ithaca: Cornell University Press.

Wesner, D.O., Dowling, J., & Johnson, F.K. (1982). What is maternal–infant intervention? The role of infant psychotherapy. *Psychiatry: Journal for the Study of Interpersonal Processes, 45,* 307–315.

Westen, D., Novotny, C.M., & Thompson–Brenner, H. (2004). The empirical status of empirically supported psychotherapies: Assumptions, findings, and reporting in controlled clinical trials. *Psychological Bulletin, 130,* 631–663.

Westerman, M.A. (1990). Coordination in maternal directives with preschoolers' behavior in compliance-problems and healthy dyads. *Developmental Psychology, 26,* 621–630.

Weston, D.R., Ivins, B., Zuckerman, B., Jones, C., & Lopez, R. (1989). Drug exposed babies: Research and clinical issues. *Zero to Three, 9,* 1–7.

Whitehurst, G.J., Falco, F., Lonigan, C.J., Fischel, J.E., Valdez-Menchaca, M.C., & Caulfield, M. (1988). Accelerating language development through picture-book reading. *Developmental Psychology, 24,* 552–558.

Wieder, S., & Greenspan, S.J. (1987). Staffing, process, and structure of the clinical infant development program. In S.I. Greenspan, S. Wieder, R.A. Nover, A. F. Lieberman, R.S. Lourie, & M.E. Robinson (Eds.), *Infants in multirisk families: Case studies in preventive intervention* (pp. 9–21). Madison, CT: International Universities Press.

Wieder, S., Jasnow, M., Greenspan, S.I., & Strauss, M. (1983). Identifying the multirisk family prenatally: Antecedent psychosocial factors and infant development trends. *Infant Mental Health Journal, 4,* 165–201.

Wierzbicki, M., & Pekarik, G. (1993). A meta-analysis of psychotherapy dropout. *Professional Psychology: Research and Practice, 24,* 190–195.

Williams, M.B., & Sommer, J.F. (Eds.). (1994). *Handbook of post-traumatic therapy.* Westport, CT: Greenwood Press.

Williams, T.M., Joy, L.A., Travis, L., Gotowiec, A., Blum-Steele, M., Aiken, L.S., Painter, S.L., & Davidson, S.M. (1987). Transition to motherhood: A longitudinal study. *Infant Mental Health Journal, 8,* 251–265.

Wilson, J.P., & Lindy, J.D. (1994). Empathetic strain and countertransfer. In J.P. Wilson & J.D. Lindy (Eds.), *Countertransference in the treatment of PTSD* (pp. 5–30). New York: Guilford Press.

Wilson, T.D., Lindsey, S., & Schooler, T.Y. (2000). A model of dual attitudes. *Psychological Review, 107,* 101–126.

Witwer, M.B., & Crawford, C.A. (1995). *A coordinated approach to reducing family violence: Conference highlights* (National Institute of Justice Publication, No. NCJ155184). Washington, DC: National Institute of Justice.

Wolfe, D.A., Fairbank, J.A., Kelly, J.A., & Bradlyn, A.S. (1983). Child abusive parents' physiological responses to stressful and non-stressful behavior in children. *Behavioral Assessment, 3,* 363–371.

Wolk, S., Zeanah, C., Garcia-Coll, C., & Carr, S. (1992). Factors influencing parents' perceptions of temperament in early infancy. *American Journal of Orthopsychiatry, 62,* 17–82.

Wolpe, J. (1969). *The process of behavior therapy.* Oxford, UK: Pergamon Press.

Woodcock, R.W., & Johnson, M.B. (1989a). *Woodcock–Johnson Psychoeducational Battery–Revised.* Allen, TX: DLM.

Woodcock, R.W., & Johnson, M.B. (1989b). *The Woodcock–Johnson–Revised Tests of Achievement.* Chicago: Riverside.

World Health Organization (2002). *Reducing risks, promoting healthy life.* Geneva: World Health Organization.

Worobey, J., & Belsky, J. (1986). Employing the Brazelton Scale to influence mothering: An experimental comparison of three strategies. *Developmental Psychology, 18,* 736–743.

Wright, B.M. (1992). Treatment of infants and their families. In J.R. Brandell (Ed.), *Countertransference in psychotherapy with children and adolescents* (pp. 127–139). Northvale, NJ: Jason Aronson.

Yankelovich, D., & DYG, Inc. (2000). *What grown-ups know about child development: A national benchmark study.* Washington, DC: Civitas Corporation, Zero to Three, and Brio Connection.

Yehuda, R. (Ed.). (1998). *Psychological trauma. Review of Psychiatry Series.* Washington, DC: American Psychiatric Association.

Yoshikawa, H. (1994). Prevention as cumulative protection: Effects of early family support and education on chronic delinquency and its risks. *Psychological Bulletin, 115,* 28–54.

Yoshikawa, H. (1995). Long-term effects of early childhood programs on social outcomes and delinquency. *The Future of Children, 5,* 51–75.

Young, J.E., Klosko, J.S., & Weishaar, M.E. (2003). *Schema therapy: A practioner's guide.* New York: Guilford Press.

Zahn-Waxler, C., & Radke-Yarrow, M. (1990). The origins of empathetic concern. *Motivation and Emotion, 14,* 107–130.

Zahn-Waxler, C., Duggal, S., & Gruber, R. (2002). Parental psychopathology. In M.H. Bornstein (Ed.), *Handbook of parenting: Vol. 4. Social conditions and applied parenting* (2nd ed., pp. 295–327). Mahwah, NJ: Lawrence Erlbaum Associates.

Zarling, C.L., Hirsch, B.J., & Landry, S. (1988). Maternal social networks and mother–infant interactions in full-term and very low birth weight, pre-term infants. *Child Development, 59,* 178–185.

Zeanah, C.H., & Barton, M. (1989). Introduction: Internal representations and parent-infant relationships. *Infant Mental Health Journal, 10,* 135-141.

Zeanah, C.H., & Benoit, D. (1995). Clinical applications of a parent perception interview. *Child Psychiatry Clinics of North America, 4*, 539–554.

Zeanah, C.H., Benoit, D., & Barton, M. (1993). *Working Model of the Child Interview.* Unpublished document, Brown University, RI.

Zeanah, C.H., Benoit, D., Hirshberg, L., Barton, M.L., & Regan, C. (1994). Mothers' representations of their infant are concordant with infant attachment classifications. *Developmental Issues in Psychiatry and Psychology, 1*, 9–18.

Zeanah, C.H., Boris, N.W., & Larrieau, J.A. (1997). Infant development and developmental risk: A review of the past 10 years. *Journal of the American Academy of Child and Adolescent Psychiatry, 36*, 165–178.

Zeanah, C.H., Keener, M.A., & Anders, T.F. (1986). Developing perceptions of temperament and their relation to mother and infant behavior. *Journal of Child Psychology & Psychiatry & Allied Disciplines, 27*, 499–512.

Zeanah, C.H., Keener, M.A., & Anders, T.F. (1996). Adolescent mothers' prenatal fantasies and working models of their infants. *Psychiatry, 49*, 193–203.

Zeanah, C.H., Keener, M.A., Anders, T.F., & Vieira-Baker, C.C. (1987). Adolescent mothers' perceptions of their infants before and after birth. *American Journal of Orthopsychiatry, 57*, 351–360.

Zeanah, C.H., Keener, M.A., Stewart, L., & Anders, T.F. (1985). Prenatal perceptions of infant personality: A preliminary investigation. *Journal of the American Academy of Child Psychiatry, 24*, 204–210.

Zeitlin, S. (1985). *Coping Inventory.* Bensonville, IL: Scholastic Testing service.

Zeitlin, S., & Williamson, G.G. (1994). *Coping in young children: Early intervention practices to enhance adaptive behavior and resilience.* Baltimore: Paul H. Brookes Publishing Co..

Zyblock, M. (1996). *Child poverty trends in Canada: Exploring depth and incidence from a total money perspective, 1979–1992.* Ottawa: Human Resources Development Canada.

# INDEX

Page numbers followed by *f* indicate figures; those followed by *t* indicate tables.